Europe against Revolution

Europe against Revolution

Conservatism, Enlightenment, and the Making of the Past

MATTHIJS LOK

Great Clarendon Street, Oxford, OX2 6DP,
United Kingdom

Oxford University Press is a department of the University of Oxford.
It furthers the University's objective of excellence in research, scholarship,
and education by publishing worldwide. Oxford is a registered trade mark of
Oxford University Press in the UK and in certain other countries

© Matthijs Lok 2023

The moral rights of the author have been asserted

First Edition published in 2023

All rights reserved. No part of this publication may be reproduced, stored in
a retrieval system, or transmitted, in any form or by any means, without the
prior permission in writing of Oxford University Press, or as expressly permitted
by law, by licence or under terms agreed with the appropriate reprographics
rights organization. Enquiries concerning reproduction outside the scope of the
above should be sent to the Rights Department, Oxford University Press, at the
address above

You must not circulate this work in any other form
and you must impose this same condition on any acquirer

Published in the United States of America by Oxford University Press
198 Madison Avenue, New York, NY 10016, United States of America

British Library Cataloguing in Publication Data
Data available

Library of Congress Control Number: 2022947763

ISBN 978–0–19–887213–9

DOI: 10.1093/oso/9780198872139.001.0001

Printed and bound by
CPI Group (UK) Ltd, Croydon, CR0 4YY

Links to third party websites are provided by Oxford in good faith and
for information only. Oxford disclaims any responsibility for the materials
contained in any third party website referenced in this work.

For Martine, Neelie, and Wisse

Acknowledgements

Like the writings studied in this work, this book is a cosmopolitan endeavour, firmly rooted in a local context. Most of the research over the past decade has been done in the research time allotted to me by my employer, the University of Amsterdam. I have been supported financially in various ways by the Amsterdam Institute for Humanities Research (AIHR), the Amsterdam School for Regional, Transnational and European Studies (ARTES), and the Amsterdam Centre for Contemporary European Studies (ACES). The cosmopolitan atmosphere of the Amsterdam European Studies department provided the institutional context. This interdisciplinary and multilingual department, populated by historians, literary specialists, lawyers, political geographers, political scientists, and economists, forms a twenty-first-century embodiment of the late eighteenth-century enlightened ideal of integrally studying Europe in its entirety rather than from one perspective.

I have been able to write chapters during sabbaticals accorded me by the Faculty of Humanities. Particularly useful was a research stay at the Netherlands Institute for Advanced Studies (NIAS) in the spring of 2020, which was unfortunately cut short by the COVID-19 pandemic. Notwithstanding, I would like to thank the fellows of the year group 2019–20, in particular Marijn Kruk, Mirjam Künkler, Anouk de Koning, Nadim Rouhana, Jean-Marc Dreyfus, and Luigi Corrias, and the excellent hosts Jan Willem Duyvendak and Fenneke Wekker, for their encouragement of slow science, as such was this book project.

Even in times of COVID, I benefitted from a research fellowship at the Lichtenberg Kolleg and Moritz Stern Institute in Göttingen (Autumn 2021, as guest of Martin van Gelderen), followed by an ETEE exchange in Leuven (Autumn 2022, hosted by Patrick Pasture and Gustavo Müller). Research trips have been made to London (British Library and the National Archives), Brussels (Koninklijke Bibliotheek), Rome (KNIR Royal Netherlands Institute and Vatican Library), Oxford (Bodleian Library), Vienna (Österreichische Nationalbibliothek), Berlin (Staatsbibliothek zu Berlin), Paris (Bibliothèque nationale de France and Archives nationales), Groningen (University Library), Den Haag (Koninklijke Bibliotheek), and Amsterdam (University Library) and I am grateful for the assistance of the staff of these institutions.

The book is as much the result of social interaction as it is an individual achievement. First of all, I am grateful to the co-conveners of the Amsterdam-Utrecht(-Groningen) Global Intellectual Seminar for providing the best possible, enjoyable, academic environment for conducting intellectual history: Annelien de

Dijn, Boyd van Dijk, René Koekkoek, Camille Creyghton, Lucia Admiraal, Arnab Dutta, and Lissa Kattenberg. I have discussed my research with the many renowned scholars from around the world who have accepted our invitation to speak at the seminar, among them David Armitage, Jennifer Pitts, Georgios Varouxakis, Richard Whatmore, Isaac Nakhimovsky, Shruti Kapila, Andrew Fitzmaurice, Dominic Sachsenmaier, and Stella Ghervas. Special thanks go to Darrin McMahon who has supported my writings and projects over many years and in many ways, and whose *Enemies of the Enlightenment* (OUP, 2001) formed an important inspiration for this book project.

The book has been shaped by the various conferences I organized in the preceding years and the collaborative research projects I was involved in, which covered various aspects related to the theme of this book. In 2018, Juliette Reboul and I organized the conference on 'cosmopolitan conservatism' in the monastic Ravenstein conference centre of the Radboud University, attended by many leading scholars in the field. This conference resulted in the Brill volume (2021), co-edited with Friedemann Pestel, which can be regarded as a companion to the present book. In 2016, Ido de Haan and I organized a workshop on the politics of moderation, attended by the main authority on the subject, Aurelian Craiutu, who has continued to provide intellectual encouragement. This workshop also culminated in an edited volume (published by Palgrave in 2019). Collaboration with Lotte Jensen resulted in a workshop on Early Modern Europeanisms in 2014 in Amsterdam.

Furthermore, panels were held at the conferences of the Council for European Studies (Amsterdam 2013, Washington 2014) and the Consortium of the Revolutionary Era (Atlanta 2019 and online 2021). I thank the participants. With European Studies colleagues Robin de Bruin and Marjet Brolsma, moreover, I edited a volume on *Eurocentrism in History and Memory* (AUP 2019), in honour of Michael Wintle, which includes many contributions that deal with topics in this study. I particularly thank Stefan Berger for his chapter on European historiography. With Joris van Eijnatten, I edited a special issue on the global Counter-Enlightenment, with contributors from all over the globe. With Iason Zarikos and Carolina Armenteros, I am currently editing volumes on conservatism and the making of Atlantic monarchism, to be published by Bloomsbury Publishing. Lectures on the separate chapters have been given all over Europe and the Americas. I thank all participants for their invitations, comments, and suggestions.

My special thanks also to Annelien de Dijn, for organizing a manuscript workshop in the Autumn of 2020, a truly intensive experience that greatly improved the manuscript and clarified the argument. Chapters in various stages have been critically read and commented upon by Annelien de Dijn, René Koekkoek, Camille Creyghton, Floris Solleveld, Beatrice de Graaf, Annie Jourdan, Ido de Haan, Wyger Velema, Eleá de la Porte, Morgan Golf-French, Martin Gierl, Michael Wintle, Robin de Bruin, Marleen Rensen, Marjet Brolsma, Joep Leerssen, Friedemann Pestel, Tom Verschaffel, Robbert-Jan Adriaansen,

Michiel van Dam, Lien Verpoest, Alicia Montoya, Carolina Armenteros, and Jan Drentje. Of course, I am solely responsible for the result. Useful comments have, moreover, been made on various occasions by Emily Jones, Brian Vick, Quentin Skinner, Erik de Lange, Ozan Ozavci, Theo Jung, Jörn Leonhard, Remieg Aerts, Glauco Schettini, Amerigo Caruso, Wessel Krul, Hanco Jürgens, Niek van Sas, Ambrogio Caiani, Iason Zarikos, Till van Rahden, Pauline Kleingeld, Laurent Nagy, Emmanuel Fureix, Birgit Aschmann, Martina Steber, Matthew d'Auria, Jan Vermeiren, Olivier Tort, and Monika Baár. No doubt other names should be added to this list.

The book has very much profited from the intellectual exchange and friendship over many years with Carolina Armenteros, Beatrice de Graaf, Natalie Scholz, Neeraja Sankaran, Martijn van der Burg, Daniel Gutiérrez Ardila, Joris Oddens, Earle Havens, Jeroen van Zanten, Sebastiaan Tijsterman, Margriet van der Waal, and Stefan Couperus. In particular, I would like to thank Gijs Kruijtzer, my unique Amsterdam roommate and global historian, for his hospitability at the Oudezijds Voorburgwal, lively conversations over dinner, and animated talks about reference systems and book titles. Moreover, I had the privilege of discussing my research with the nicest and brightest students from all the world during my various courses over the past decade. In particular, I would like to thank Oliver Callaghan, Corentin Lécine, David Reuter, Dieks van Gogh, Max Lokin, and Puck van Limburg for reading chapters and providing assistance in various ways.

I am proud that this book is published with Oxford University Press. I would like to thank the two anonymous peer reviewers for their thorough and in-depth comments on my manuscript, which were very helpful in the preparation of the final manuscript. Moreover, I would like to thank my editor Cathryn Steele for providing enthusiastic support for this project from the start, and Vasuki Ravichandran for efficiently managing the production of this book. Jennifer Hinchliffe, furthermore, copy-edited the manuscript in a thorough manner. Kate Delaney, finally, has provided indispensable corrections of my English wording and grammar.

Most of the writing has been done at home in the Helpman quarter of the lively city of Groningen in the North of the Netherlands. Over the past decade, my solitary studies have alternated with the enjoyable duties of family life, such as bike journeys to primary school, sporting events, music lessons and, in the summer, to the local outdoor swimming pool with my daughter Neelie and my son Wisse. I am also grateful to my family and friends in Groningen, Den Haag, Leiden, Amsterdam, and elsewhere, for their interest, patience, and support over the past years. Finally, I would like to thank my partner, architect Martine Drijftholt, a proud northerner with an open view of the world, for keeping a healthy balance between academic life and the world outside it.

Groningen & Amsterdam, 1 August 2022

Contents

Prologue: Politics of the Past	1
1. The Ancient Edifice	7
2. An Unfinished History	37
3. The Philosopher's Apprentice	67
4. Crusaders for Moderation	99
5. Equilibrium against Empire	137
6. The Pluralist Republic	165
7. Ancient and Modern State Systems	195
8. Vienna as a Missed Opportunity	229
9. Revivals of Historical Europeanism	260
Bibliography	303
Index	351

Prologue
Politics of the Past

On 3 and 4 February 2020, an international conference of European 'national conservatives' was held in Rome, organized—ironically—by the American 'Edmund Burke Foundation'. Among the two hundred participants were the Hungarian prime minister Viktor Orban and the then hope of the French far right, Marion Maréchal-Le Pen, as well as the controversial right-wing Dutch politician and publicist Thierry Baudet.[1] These self-proclaimed 'conservatives', despite their different outlooks and backgrounds, all shared a view of 'European civilization' as essentially consisting of homogeneous and primordial national states currently under threat from a deadly cocktail of mass migration of non-Europeans supported by a liberal political international order and rootless capitalism. They mostly defended a certain Christian-inspired and anti-modern nationalism as the true European historical heritage, which was in need of protection against its mortal enemies.[2]

A further common element uniting these nationalists was hostility towards the European Union and the post-war process of European integration. The self-appointed 'conservatives' objected to the representation of the European past as exhibited in the Brussels Museum's 'House of European History'. This House was the result of an initiative of the European parliament from 2007 to explain the European past to its citizens. The curators of this museum underscored 'the shared European experience' throughout history.[3] Underlying the exhibition was a narrative of an inevitable successful, peaceful integration after centuries of internal conflict and war, in particular the horrors of twentieth-century totalitarianism, genocide, and fascism.[4] In this story, the project of integration brought

---

[1] I will not go into the extensive debate on the terminology of the right in contemporary Europe, which has been labelled 'far right', 'radical right', 'new right', 'hard right', 'neo-nationalist', 'authoritarian', 'anti-liberal', 'nativist', and 'populist': recent studies include: Caiani, 'Radical Right', 394–411; Lagenbacher and Schellenberg, *Europe on the Right Path?*; Zielonka, *Counter-Revolution*; Mudde, *Populist Radical Right Parties*. On the divided character of early twenty-first-century conservatism and the right in the West: Fawcett, *Conservatism*, 328–414.

[2] See https://nationalconservatism.org/natcon-rome-2020 (accessed 6 November 2020); Lievisse Adriaanse, 'Een culturele wapenstilstand'; Applebaum, *Twilight*, 138–41. On the populist uses of European heritage: de Cesari and Kaya, *European Memory*. On the 'crisis' of the idea of the 'West' in the twenty-first century: Boutellier, *Westen*.

[3] Vovk van Gaal, 'Comment forger un récit européen?', 57–68.

[4] Bialasiewicz, 'Spectres', 98–119; Dinan, *Ever Closer Union*.

prosperity and peace as well as democracy and human rights to the inhabitants of the European continent.[5] Rather than forcing all European countries into one centralized and homogeneous 'empire', the Brussels presentation underlined, the EU allegedly protected its political and cultural 'diversity'.[6] This was in line with the EU's official motto of 'Unity in Diversity' (*In varietate concordia* in Latin), which had been adopted by the European parliament in 2000.[7]

Radically disagreeing with this finalist and somewhat triumphalist 'post-war' history of Europe, the 'national conservatives' meeting in Rome in 2020 emphasized, by contrast, the recent history of Europe as one of decline and betrayal by its cosmopolitan liberal elites.[8] The German *Alternative für Deutschland* (AfD) party has once again started to invoke the concept of a (secular) Christian *Abendland* under threat from an invasion of Islamic migrants.[9] Baudet, after winning the Dutch provincial elections on 20 March 2019, gave an infamous speech in which he invoked the ruins of a once proud European civilization. The political and intellectual elites had caused the downfall of this exceptional civilization through their 'oikophobia', or a loathing of one's native culture, a pathology allegedly unique to Western elites.[10] However, Baudet also brought a message of hope and redemption. Like Hegel's owl of Minerva, spreading its wings only at the falling of dusk, the Dutch electorate had realized at the eleventh hour that radical change was necessary and put their trust in a new messiah, Baudet himself.[11] Other European self-proclaimed anti-liberal politicians also urged a regeneration of Europe by returning to its primordial, national, and—in many but not all cases—its Christian roots.

The present study seeks to uncover the roots of these historically informed ideas of Europe and of European history, while at the same time underlining the fundamental differences between the writings of the older counter-revolutionary

---

[5] Judt, 'The Past Is Another Country'; Judt, *Postwar*. On European post-war historiography: Ifversen, 'Myth and History'; Woolf, 'Europe and Its Historians'.

[6] 'The House of European History is dedicated to the understanding of the shared past and diverse experiences of European people. It's a place where you can discover different points of view and common ground in European history.' See https://historia-europa.ep.eu/en/mission-vision (accessed 27 August 2018). See also: Building a House of European History. A Project of the European Parliament (Brochure European Parliament 2013; doi: 10.2861/67140).

[7] Sassatelli, *Becoming Europeans*, 36.

[8] Zielonka, *Counter-Revolution*; Krastev and Holmes, *Light That Failed*; Ziblatt and Levitsky, *How Democracies Die*, 238–40. The idea of decline has many precedents in anti-liberal thought. See for instance: Holmes, *Anatomy of Antiliberalism*.

[9] Weiß, *autoritäre Revolte*. On the concept of '*Abendland*': Rößner, *Geschichte Europas*.

[10] Baudet, *Oikofobie*.

[11] Speech by Thierry Baudet, 20 March 2019 (https://www.trouw.nl/nieuws/spreektekst-thierry-baudet-verkiezingsavond-20-maart-2019~be2a1539/). Baudet is a good example of a radical nationalist politician who situates himself in a venerable European 'conservative' tradition, publishing edited volumes on 'conservative authors' in the eighteenth, nineteenth, and twentieth centuries. According to Baudet, these thinkers taught important lessons, which are still relevant today, on the dangers of abstract utopia and the perilous hubris of modernism. Baudet and Visser, *Revolutionair Verval*; Baudet and Visser, *Conservatieve Vooruitgang*. On the ideological development of the 'new' Dutch conservatism since the 1990s: Oudenampsen, *conservatieve revolte*.

Europeanists and their self-appointed successors in the twenty-first century. This book examines ideas of Europe in the decades around 1800 when the European past also was the topic of fierce discussion, contestation, and political (ab)use.[12] These years were dominated by, in the eyes of many contemporaries, the shocking events of the French Revolution and its violent aftermath in Europe and beyond. The European order, as well as Europe's place in the world, was destroyed, rebuilt, and redefined at this moment. Perhaps comparable to the memory of the Second World War and the Holocaust in the twentieth century, the French Revolution, and in particular the Terror, acted as a 'foundational past' for inhabitants of the long nineteenth century until the First World War.[13]

Parallels have been drawn between the decades around 1800 and the reconfiguration of Europe during and in the aftermath of the twentieth-century world wars.[14] After 1918 and 1945, as well as after the final collapse of the Napoleonic Empire in 1815, Europe's past was seen as a source of inspiration and orientation at a time when all political authority and beliefs seemed to have disappeared. Institutions and customs lost their self-evident form, and everything seemed possible, or so the contemporaries believed.[15] Also in these decades, a flood of ideas and blueprints for a new international order and cultural renewal were published, as happened during and immediately after the world wars.[16] The twentieth-century European 'Civil War', like the Napoleonic and revolutionary wars, was as much about ideas as it was about arms.[17] Intellectuals of the right and the left yearned for a cultural and political regeneration of a corrupt and rotten European civilization. Ideas of past and future were invoked in the imagining of Europe and its place in the world.[18] After 1815, 1919, and 1945 the ideas of 'stability', 'forgetting', and 'moderation', often in combination with a strong state and a renewed emphasis on morality, were key concepts in a post-war order.[19]

In the age of eighteenth-century revolutions, just as after the world wars of the twentieth century, contemporaries turned to history, that of their own lives as well as that of society, to make sense of a confusing and troubling world, where previously unimaginable possibilities as well as horrors had opened up. The

---

[12] As Keith Baker wrote: 'Political Contestation takes the form of competing efforts to mobilise and control the possibilities of political and social discourse, efforts through which that discourse is extended, recast and—on occasion—even radically transformed.' Baker, *Inventing the French Revolution*, 32.

[13] Confino, *Foundational Pasts*; Steinberg, *Afterlives*.

[14] Stråth, *Utopias of Peace*; Ikenberry, *After Victory*; Macmillan, *Peacemakers*. The temporal aspect, in particular the expectations of the future, of European peace agreements since the eighteenth century was also underlined by Stella Ghervas in her *Conquering Peace*. Of course, a historical comparison of this kind does not imply that the two periods in history are also comparable in a moral way. Cf. de Haan, *Politieke reconstructie*.

[15] De Haan, *Politieke Reconstructie*.   [16] Rosenboim, *Emergence of Globalism*.

[17] Mazower, *Dark Continent*.   [18] See Chapter 9.

[19] Stråth, *Utopias of Peace*; de Graaf, *Fighting Terror*; de Graaf, *Tegen de terreur*; de Haan and Lok, *Politics of Moderation*.

main thesis of this book is that the European past and the idea of Europe as an essentially 'historical continent' was (re)invented by the critics of the French Revolution as part of their ideological struggle against the Revolution. For these 'counter-revolutionaries', the Revolution stood for a false idea of freedom and democratic sovereignty, which led to anarchy and despotism at the same time. In opposition to the new revolutionary world of universal principles, the counter-revolutionary publicists proclaimed the concept of a gradually developing European society and political order, founded on a set of historical and—ultimately divine—institutions that had guaranteed Europe's unique freedom, moderation, diversity, and progress since the fall of the Roman Empire.[20]

These counter-revolutionaries (ab)used and transformed an older historical narrative that had been developed in the preceding century by enlightened historians. Both the 'Enlightenment' and what is conventionally called the 'Counter-Enlightenment', or more historically accurate 'anti-philosophy', were sources of this counter-revolutionary construction of the European past.[21] The importance of the decades around 1800 lay in the fact that these older Enlightenment histories became politicized in response to the perceived threat of Revolution to this European society. In these years of ideological conflict and war, the idea of European history, and Europe as an essentially 'historical continent', was rethought and (re)constructed. Although the world of the eighteenth- and early nineteenth-century Counter-Revolution was radically different from our own, this counter-revolutionary 'historical Europeanism' has had a long afterlife and enjoyed revivals, still influencing the debate on the European past in the nineteenth, twentieth, and twenty-first centuries.[22]

This study will make clear that the counter-revolutionary Europeanists of the revolutionary age also differed markedly from their self-appointed successors in later centuries. To begin with, counter-revolutionaries around the turn of the century were certainly not ardent nationalists, who were as horrified by 'cosmopolitanism' as the new 'national conservatives' of the twenty-first century. On the contrary, they regarded unqualified expressions of 'nationalism' and 'patriotism' as excessive, immoderate, and fanatical. A concept such as 'national conservatism' would thus be incomprehensible for them.[23] Also, they primarily associated the glorification of the nation state and state power with their ideological enemies, the revolutionaries. The counter-revolutionary authors cited in this study in general strove for a new synthesis of 'enlightened cosmopolitanism' with loyalty to the *patria*, whether this was a country, a city, or an entity like the Holy Roman Empire.

---

[20] See for the elasticity of the concept of 'counter-revolutionary': Chapters 1 and 4.
[21] Lok, 'La construction de l'Europe moderne'.   [22] See Chapter 9.
[23] The protagonists of this study clearly do not fit in the twenty-first-century division of the political positions in Western societies between 'cosmopolitans' and 'conservatives', as they can be considered both. See https://www.bbc.com/news/uk-politics-32021853 (accessed 22 June 2021).

Counter-revolutionary Europeanists, perhaps counter-intuitively moreover, overall did not aim for a return to a primordial order of European civilization, as twenty-first-century 'conservatives' often do. They regarded the Revolution instead as a threat to a gradual development and improvement of European institutions, whose reform they generally applauded. Being often migrants, refugees, and exiles themselves, they did not entertain an anti-immigration discourse. Also, the populist criticism of a 'treacherous elite' cannot be found in their works: these counter-revolutionaries blamed, by contrast, the revolutionaries for giving 'uncultured' common people, who were unable to control their emotions, a say in political debate, leading to anarchy and despotism.[24] Instead they aimed for the legitimation of the traditional elites and their property, as well as the historical institutions, against the onslaught of mass politics.

Furthermore, although anti-philosophical elements can be found in their works, overall the protagonists studied in this book did not reject the legacy of Enlightenment but instead redefined it for their own purposes. Only in their fear of cultural decadence, and striving for moral and spiritual renewal, can we find some similarities with their self-appointed homologues in the twenty-first century, but these ideas can also be found among the revolutionaries as well. Finally, this moral regeneration was firmly understood from the framework of the Church, the institute of the papacy and the Christian religion. The counter-revolutionaries would probably have been horrified by the 'secular Christianity' of many twenty-first-century West European conservatives, regarding it as the ultimate triumph of revolutionary ideology.[25]

The conclusions of this book can be interpreted in various ways. To begin with, critical readers can understand this study as an attempt to uncover the hidden conservative and counter-revolutionary agenda's underlying mainstream ideas of Europe and narratives of European history, and thus undermining their legitimacy and self-evidence.[26] In a different vein, readers sympathetic to conservative ideas, can read this study as evidence that conservatism is not inherently inimical to cosmopolitanism and internationalism. Moreover, Europeanism can be recovered as a right-wing tradition rather than a dominantly progressive and liberal one as it is the beginning of the twenty-first century. A third way of looking at this study is to learn more about the unexpected and counter-intuitive aspects of familiar and topical historical themes and as proof of the insight that the past is

---

[24] Müller, *What is Populism?* [25] Roy, *Is Europe Christian?*
[26] In 2021, David Graeber and David Wengrow, for instance, published their influential 'new history of humanity', in which they extensively criticized the enlightened histories of mankind and their successors as the products of a conservative backlash. While, in my view, their book is as much a political statement as the Enlightenment histories the authors criticize, this study agrees with Graeber and Wengrow in emphasizing the uses made of enlightened historiography by political conservatives and counter-revolutionaries. Graeber and Wengrow, *Dawn of Everything*, 494–9.

always more complicated and ambivalent than later interpretations have made it out to be. It is this last perspective which I personally most identify with.

In this book, we shall travel to the violent and tumultuous years around 1800, the critical juncture at which ideas of Europe and European history were being forged anew on older fundaments. It is my conviction that by studying earlier moments of politicization of European history, as well as excavating the history of the idea European history, twenty-first-century people can become more aware of their own historical understanding and, hopefully, take a more critical look at those attempts to use and abuse the European past for their own political gain. The past is always an integral part of the political ordering of Europe, not as a passive echo but as an active force driving, as well as resisting, political change.

1
The Ancient Edifice

1. Historical Europeanism

In 1809, when the Napoleonic Empire reached its zenith, the Göttingen historian Arnold Hermann Ludwig Heeren (1760-1842) published his *Manual of the Political System of Europe and its Colonies*.[1] In this book, Heeren gave an account of the development of Europe as a state system over the centuries. He did not merely provide a summary of different national histories, as historians of Europe had done before him. His ambition was, in his own words, to connect the historical facts to underlying 'ideas', as well as to the general 'spirit of the age'. The European state system was unique in world history, according to the Göttingen history professor, due to the liberty and independence of the individual states which jointly formed the political balance within a pluriform common cultural, religious, and moral framework. The concept underlying the European system was, for Heeren, 'equilibrium' (*Gleichgewicht*).

When Heeren published the first edition of his *Manual* in 1809, he somewhat melancholically described a world that, in his view, no longer existed. On the title page he placed a citation from a pessimistic poem by Friedrich Schiller on the start of a new—nineteenth—century, that captured his uncertainty and sense of loss: 'the bond of the nations was broken, and the ancient edifice overthrown!'[2] The European commonwealth analysed in his book had been destroyed as a result of the phenomenal rise of Napoleon and his Empire, created a few years earlier in 1804, ending the Revolutionary Republic born in 1792. Heeren contrasted this new 'despotic' hegemon with the traditional monarchical European regimes, which were, again in his view, characterized by a moderate and bounded exercise of power.

The purpose of his book was to make readers understand why this free system had fallen into decline and had finally collapsed.[3] The earlier rise of an allegedly

---

[1] Heeren, *Handbuch Europäischen Staatensystems*. I have used the version in the collected works: Heeren, *Historische Werke*, vol VIII-IX. The *Historische Werke* will be abbreviated henceforth as *HW*. In 1834 and 1846, English translations appeared. Earlier, in 1821, a French edition was published: *Manuel Historique du système des états de l'Europe* (...), and a Dutch version appeared in 1822: *Handboek der geschiedenis van de staatsgesteldheid van Europa*.
[2] 'Und das Band der Staten ward gehoben, und die alten Formen stürzen ein!' See for the complete text of the poem: Schiller, 'Der Antritt des neuen Jahrhunderts', 497. The English translation of Schiller's citation was taken from the English edition of 1846. On Schiller: Albrecht, *Kosmopolitismus*, 106-50.
[3] Heeren, *Handbuch Europäischen Staatensystems*, 'Vorrede', x.

atheistic enlightened philosophy in the eighteenth century had undermined the foundations of the European institutional traditions in the decades before 1789, despite their outward appearance of opulence and the splendour of the eighteenth-century princely palaces. The institutions of the monarchy and the state had, furthermore, been hollowed out in the preceding century by the introduction of dangerous concepts such as 'popular sovereignty'. Secret societies had plotted the downfall of the existing order for many years. Except for a handful of visionaries, however, few contemporaries foresaw the dangers of the revolution that unfolded in France from 1789 onwards, termed the 'great catastrophe' by Heeren. This revolution, according to him without precedent in European history, resulted in a continent-wide 'war of ideas and men' that had destroyed the last vestiges of the commonwealth.[4]

The foreword of the third edition of 1819 was written in an entirely different tone from that of the first edition of 1809. The mighty Napoleonic Empire had suddenly collapsed in 1814–15, due to military defeats at the hands of the allied coalition, and was replaced by a new 'Restoration' order of monarchical regimes. Heeren's *Manual* was no longer a melancholy story about a lost world. It instead became a forward-looking statement on how to organize a new international system. His historical account of the European state system became a source of inspiration and historical legitimation for the participants of the Vienna Congress of 1814–15. The fortunes of Heeren's *Manual* formed thus a telling example of the close intertwining of European history writing and international politics.

Although Heeren's fame soon evaporated after his death in 1842, and his works are now almost exclusively read by academic specialists in historiography, his influence is not to be underestimated. His books were translated into several European languages. Many of his students at Göttingen would later hold important positions. His works were built upon by none other than the influential historian Leopold von Ranke in his manifold publications on European history. Heeren has even been credited with, or blamed for, the invention of the modern idea of the state system through his alleged influence on the 'English school of international relations'.[5]

Rather than being merely reactionary, Heeren and his works were characterized by an ambivalent attitude towards the past. His ideas were shaped by the heritage of the enlightened historians, classicists, and lawyers, particularly those working at the university of Göttingen. Heeren opposed the French Revolution because, in his eyes, these radical revolutionaries had destroyed Europe's freedom, ushering in an era of dark terror, anarchy, and above all despotism. He did not advocate an

---

[4] On Heeren and his works, see more extensively Chapter VII.
[5] International historians, since the turn of the twenty-first century, have underscored the 'reactionary' and 'Eurocentric' origins of idea of the international system and law, giving Heeren centre stage in this analysis. Keene, *Anarchical Society*, 14–26; Armitage, *Foundations*, 40–1. Cf. Chapter VII.

unequivocal return to the *ancien régime* but explicitly argued instead that the order that was to replace the Napoleonic Empire should be an improved version of the pre-revolutionary system, and 'old abuses' and injustices were to be reformed. At the same time, he also believed that this new order must be built on Europe's age-old constitutional and legal traditions and institutions, the 'ancient edifice'.

Heeren's ambivalent view on the role of European history in the shaping of the international order was not unique. In this study, I examine how self-appointed counter-revolutionaries made use of European history for their own specific political purposes, and in doing so, created their own version of the political European past. Through the writing of history, the authors studied in this book imagined their idea of the present and future state of Europe. These counter-revolutionary authors have been termed here 'historical Europeanists', although they did not use this term themselves.[6] According to the Merriam Webster Dictionary, the word 'Europeanism' can have two meanings. The first definition, 'the ideal or advocacy of the political and economic integration of Europe', is clearly not relevant in this context.[7] The second definition, 'attachment or allegiance to the traditions, interests, or ideals of Europeans', first articulated in 1824, is used here.[8]

'Historical Europeanism' is understood here as the articulation of ideas of Europe through history writing and the definition of 'Europe' predominantly in historical and temporal terms. As this study will show, at least four variations of historical Europeanism can be discerned. In the neutral variation, historical Europeanists regard Europe merely as the outcome of a long historical development and use historical writings to express their views. A more conservative variation positively values this alleged historical character, and fervently defends this valuable and supposedly free civilization with its gradually evolving institutions against perceived threats such as those posed by the French Revolution and its adherents, who radically wished to break with this tradition, or so these conservatives feared.[9] A third, and potentially more radical, form proposes the existence of a lost 'Golden Age' in the European past, and the need for regeneration and renewal to recover and restore this idealized moment. A fourth, 'eurocentrist', variation manifests itself by underscoring the alleged unique and superior historical nature of the European continent that sets it apart from the other continents that either lack a proper history or have become stagnant and arrested in their development. The four variations did not appear separately from each other, but coexisted in the writings of the various protagonists in this study.

---

[6] For my definition of 'conservatism', see the end of this chapter.
[7] See for this contemporary interpretation: McCormick, *Europeanism*.
[8] 'Europeanism'. *Merriam-Webster Dictionary*. See https://www.merriam-webster.com/dictionary/Europeanism (accessed 14 June 2021).
[9] See for the concept of 'historical Europeanism' in relation to the work of Maistre: Armenteros, *French Idea*, 115–55.

Historical Europeanism can be found among adherents of various ideologies and persuasions, but in this study mainly counter-revolutionary specimens have been dissected.[10] The reason for this choice is the key role played by counter-revolutionary publicists in the period around 1800 in the (re)making and transmission of this tradition, as well as their relative neglect by later historians. The uses of the European past by counter-revolutionary authors in a broad sense, however, have so far not yet been examined in a systematic manner beyond a national or biographical perspective. The ideas of these counter-revolutionary 'historical Europeanists' were generally forgotten and discarded by a nineteenth-century posterity that undervalued their work as being insufficiently national or liberal, or both at the same time. In the twentieth century, these authors were often understood anachronistically through the prism of the contemporary rise of continental fascism, anti-liberalism, and authoritarianism.

The purpose of this first chapter is to situate this study in the wider scholarly debates, as well as to clarify the concepts I am using and explain my overall approach. This book for the first time combines the examination of three key historical problems: the construction of a European pluralist past, the political legacies of the Enlightenment, and the transnational history of counter-revolutionary thought and the conservative tradition. While usually these topics are analysed in isolation from each other, these themes were in fact closely related and should therefore be studied jointly.

2. Constructing European History

In the 1980s and 1990s, under the influence of the dynamic of European integration in these decades, scholarly interest surged in the history of the idea of Europe.[11] Following Gerard Delanty's *Inventing Europe* (1995), most of these histories have rightfully taken a de-constructivist approach, overall providing a critical and non-essentialist account of European identity.[12] European identity was seen by these critical scholars as 'invented' by politicians and social groups for their own purposes, usually excluding other, disadvantaged, groups in the process. However, these long-term histories of the idea of Europe tend to place more emphasis on 'progressive', 'Enlightened', and 'liberal' versions of the European ideal, neglecting important conservative, anti-liberal, reactionary, and 'anti-

---

[10] For nineteenth-century liberal and even socialist forms of historical Europeanisms, see Chapter IX.

[11] For example: Duroselle, *Europe*. Cf. Verga, *Storie d'Europa*, 166–79.

[12] Delanty, *Inventing Europe*; on the history of the idea of Europe: van der Dussen and Wilson, *History of the Idea*; Pagden, *Idea of Europe*; Pagden, *Pursuit of Europe*; Wintle, *Image of Europe*; Pasture, *Imagining European Unity*. An excellent older work is: Hay, *Europe*. 'Constructive' accounts continue to be published. An example is: Arjakovsky, *Histoire de la conscience européenne*.

Enlightened' forms of Europeanism, which are just as much part of the European legacy.[13] This study's ambition is to fill part of this lacuna.

This study will, furthermore, demonstrate that, far from replacing Christianity as a common denominator, ideas of an enlightened Europe were often fused with concepts of a Christian commonwealth. Post-revolutionary European historical narratives usually carried strong religious and even esoteric overtones. Progress and providence were not regarded as antagonistic, but found each other in the development of European history, the protagonists of this study argued. Moreover, despite the appearance of so many publications on the history of the idea and identity of Europe, we still lack a comprehensive and critical 'history of the idea of European history'.[14] It is still often overlooked that European history— and European memory—has a history too.[15]

The years around 1800 formed a crucial historical juncture in this construction of the idea of a European past. This is, in itself, not a new insight. The German post-war historian Reinhard Koselleck (1923–2006) already famously drew attention to what he called the 'temporalization' (*Verzeitlichung*) and changing expectations of the past, present, and future in—what he termed—the '*Sattelzeit*', the years around 1800 (*c*.1750–1850).[16] Koselleck has argued that the semantic struggle for the definition of a political position belongs to all times of crisis; however, 'since the French revolution, this struggle has become more acute and has undergone structural shifts: concepts no longer serve merely to define given states of affairs but reach into the future (...)'.[17] Koselleck also observed a shift from a traditional cyclical to a modern linear idea of time in the revolutionary age.[18] Moreover, a new philosophy of history developed, according to him, as a response to the crisis created by the tension between eighteenth-century enlightened criticism and an unresponsive absolutist political system.[19]

---

[13] An exception is Gosewinkel, *Anti-liberal Europe*. In this edited volume, unfortunately, only twentieth-century examples are discussed.

[14] On the 'history of European history': d'Auria and Vermeiren, 'Narrating Europe'; Duchhardt and Kunz, *Europäische Geschichte*; Duchhardt et al., *Europa-Historiker*, 3 vol.

[15] By historicizing the idea of European history, this study also ties in with attempts of memory scholars to criticize the construction of a new European 'memory' on the model of the nineteenth-century national historical narratives, which, since the 1970s, have accompanied European political and administrative institution building. For criticism of attempts to create a 'European memory': Rigney, 'Transforming Memory'; Pakier and Stråth, *European Memory?*; Berger, 'The Past and Present'; Feindt, Krawatzek, Pestel, and Trimçev, 'European Memory: Universalising the Past?'; Müller, *Memory and Power*.

[16] Koselleck, *Vergangene Zukunft*; Koselleck, 'Einleitung', 13–27. Cf. Fritzsche, *Stranded in the Present*; Ankersmit, *Sublime Historical Experience*; Schiffmann, *Birth of the Past*; Salber Phillips, *Historical Distance*.

[17] Koselleck, 'Begriffsgeschichte and Social History', 80.

[18] For a criticism of the uniqueness of the revolutionary experience and a plea for the coexistence of forms of historical thinking: Kuijpers and Pollmann, 'Introduction', 1–24.

[19] Koselleck, *Critique and Crisis*, 127–87. See Chapter IX for an analysis of Koselleck as a historical Europeanist himself.

Koselleck's argument that, in this period, perceptions of time and the past changed and were foregrounded is still widely accepted. Political turning points such as 1789, 1792, 1799, 1804, and 1815 resulted not only in new political systems, but also in new 'historical regimes'.[20] What was to be remembered, and also what was to be forgotten, was redefined in these short periods of unstable and fluid politics, when the ancient institutional edifice was destroyed, but a new order had not yet appeared.[21] To a certain extent, this book, by pointing to the years around 1800 as a crucial moment in the reconstruction of a European history, fits the *Sattelzeit* thesis. As the German historian Heinz Gollwitzer (1917–99) already observed in the 1950s, in this era, Europe evolved from a geographical into a temporal idea: a geopolitical concept determined by time rather than space only.[22] However, this study will also show that older providential and cyclical narratives coexisted in this period with linear historical narratives, calling into question the notion of a radical shift in expectations of time in this era.

Since the 1980s, moreover, the 'construction' of national history in various European countries has been studied in depth by a great many researchers.[23] It is now generally accepted that the development of national identities was, above all, a pan-European and transnational, perhaps even global, development, in which the development of one national tradition influenced another without a clear hierarchy of centre and periphery.[24] As Stefan Berger, furthermore, has pointed out for national history: historiography did not merely reflect political circumstances, but also shaped politics in its own terms.[25] However, the focus of researchers of historiography is still almost exclusively on the nation as the subject and modus of nineteenth-century narratives. Alternative forms of nineteenth-century history writing beyond the national framework have received far less attention, although global history increasingly is in the academic spotlight.[26] History writing, however, formed a crucial source for the study of the history of European ideas and identities, too.

'European history' is usually regarded by researchers of the history of historiography as a variation of 'national' history, hardly worthy of study on its own.[27] In many ways, this contention is true. The national dimension was no doubt an essential element in the historiography of Europe: often the country or the region

---

[20] Fureix and Lyon-Caen, '1814–1815: Expérience de discontinuités'; Pestel and Rausch, 'Post-Revolutionary Experience'.

[21] Lok '"Un oubli total du passé"'. Cf. Hartog, *Régimes d'historicité*; de Haan, *Politieke reconstructie*.

[22] Gollwitzer, *Europabild*, 64–7.   [23] Berger, *Past as History*.

[24] Berger, *Past as History*; Thiesse, *Création des identités nationales*; Leerssen, *Nationaal denken*; for his online *Encyclopedia of Romantic Nationalism in Europe*, see https://ernie.uva.nl/viewer.p/21 (accessed 20 January 2020). Berger and Storm, *History of Nationalism*.

[25] 'The relationship between history and politics has not been a one-way street.' Berger, *Past as History*, 1. Cf. Berger, *History and Identity*. See also: Creyghton, *Résurrections*.

[26] Middell and Roura Aulinas, *Transnational Challenges*.

[27] '(...) Europe as a spatial entity different from the nation state was effectively nationalised.' Berger, *Past as History*, 365.

the author considers 'home' was regarded as the 'essence' of European history. A good example of this scaling mechanism can be found in the work of Niklas Vogt (1756–1836), professor of history at Mainz and the teacher of the Austrian statesman Clemens von Metternich.[28] Vogt considered the city of Mainz to be the heart of the Rhineland, the Rhineland the kernel of the Holy Roman Empire, the Empire in its turn to be the centrepiece of Europe, and, finally, Europe to be the centre stage of world history. Leading historians of Europe usually also published on local, regional, national, colonial, and universal (world) history. Their works of European history cannot therefore be interpreted in isolation from their other historical publications.

This study contends, nonetheless, that national, universal, and European histories do not entirely overlap. 'European history' became, from the eighteenth century onwards, a separate, relatively autonomous historiographical genre. This genre possessed its own 'canon' of eminent historians, as we shall see in the next chapter, and excluded those who were denied authority as historians of, and experts on, Europe. Stuart Woolf defined 'European histories' as 'histories of Europe viewed as a unitary whole and understood to signify far more than the aggregate of its states'.[29] Here I will not provide an anachronistic definition of 'European historiography', but instead will let the sources themselves speak and answer the question of what constituted, or should constitute, European history. Countries and regions were included or expelled from the European past depending on political circumstances. In this study, the historical protagonists themselves define the 'boundaries' of European history, as well as what constituted the 'core' and the 'periphery' of this continent and its past.[30]

3. The Fragmented Continent

The accounts of European history written by the counter-revolutionary protagonists of this book clearly show a great diversity in their choices of topics, actors, and events as well as interpretations. Nonetheless, four key elements keep reappearing in their historical narratives of Europe in some form or another. Firstly, most authors studied here described Europe often as a 'fragmented' and dynamic continent, uniquely shaped by pluriformity and diversity, and by contrasts and antagonisms. This European pluriformity was usually contrasted with the homogeneous centralism and despotic unity found in Antiquity or in Asia. A second key element was the crucial role of 'freedom' in the European past. Freedom had been present in European history from its beginnings, all authors seemed to agree, but it was also constantly threatened. Obviously, the counter-

---

[28] See Chapter VI.   [29] Woolf, 'Europe and Its Historians', 325.
[30] Lok and Montoya, 'Centre and Periphery'. See also Chapter IX.

revolutionary understanding of what this freedom entailed differed widely from the view of their revolutionary opponents, but they often used the same vocabulary.

A third overall characteristic of European civilization, according to its chroniclers, was the 'moderate' and bounded exercise of power and the moderation of manners and behaviour. Uniquely from a global perspective, European monarchs, nobles, priests, and fathers did not strive for a despotic rule over their subjects, faithful, and children, or when they did, they were hindered in this ambition and encountered obstacles. A final and fourth general narrative element was the idea of a gradual progress of European civilization towards a more evolved and complex society and culture. This progress was not understood in terms of a rupture with the past, but as a slow process, building on the foundation of ancient European institutions and traditions.

Although most authors studied here agreed on these four salient and enduring elements, they differed on the question of when European history had begun or which periods and centuries played a crucial role in the making of European civilization. Most historians pointed to the fall of the (Western) Roman Empire and the sixteenth century, but different and contrasting views were formulated on the contribution of the Greeks, Romans, and Hebrews. Varied interpretations were also put forward regarding the importance of, subsequently, the age of Charlemagne, the High and Late Middle Ages, the seventeenth century, and, finally, the eighteenth century and the revolutionary and Napoleonic contemporary age, as potential seminal epochs in the European past.

'Europe' was thus predominantly viewed by counter-revolutionary Europeanists, such as Heeren, as a civilization uniquely determined throughout the centuries by political and cultural diversity within a common Christian and legal framework. European civilization and the political system consisted essentially of a careful and continuously evolving balance of different elements. This particular version of Europe and the European past is termed here the 'pluralist narrative', although this word evidently was not used by contemporaries themselves. 'Pluralism' or 'diversity' is understood here thus as the idea that European history was shaped from its earliest beginnings onwards by political, economic, and cultural decentralization and division.[31] This fragmentation was, for Heeren and other historical Europeanists, valued positively and considered the main factor explaining the development of Europe's unique 'civilization', 'moderation', and 'freedom'.

---

[31] I have used the words 'pluralism' and 'diversity' here interchangeably. On the different interpretation of 'pluralism' and 'diversity' in the European context, see: Delanty, 'Europe and the Idea of "Unity in Diversity"'. Delanty only focusses on the contemporary political discourse and does not trace the long-term genealogy of the idea.

This transnational eighteenth-century narrative of European historical pluralism was articulated in different and overlapping ways. First, the idea of the European system as a political 'balance' or equilibrium can be discerned. The absence of one, single, European imperial centre of power provided Europe with a unique liberty. Political pluralism was sometimes seen as the legacy of the ancient Germanic constitution, but also as the result of the religious and political struggles of the sixteenth-century Reformation and Renaissance. A second variation is the notion that 'Europe' was not defined by a single (political or ideological) principle but consisted of several competing principles, such as democracy and monarchy, as, for instance, Vogt argued. This competition of principles gave Europe its unique character.

A third cultural variation on this theme was the notion that competition and struggle, caused by the lack of a centralized power or dominant cultural centre, resulted in the dynamic development of the European arts. Europe, fourthly, was also regarded not as one single homogeneous culture but as the result of the mingling of cultures: classical antiquity, Near Eastern Christianity, and the legacies of the Germanic peoples. Fifthly, Europe's pluralism was also described in economic terms by the enlightened historians as the result of free trade and economic competition. For counter-revolutionary Europeanists, economic factors were of crucial importance for defining European civilization, although their views on free trade and the benefits of the market differed in fundamental ways. Criticism of trade and markets, as well as support and calls for balance can be found among the counter-revolutionary Europeanists studied here.[32]

In this book, I study the notion of 'European pluralism' thus not as a given, as many historians and political scientists have done—and still do, but as a historical, and especially historiographical, construction. It was a prescriptive and not a descriptive or neutral view on Europe's past and future. The question as to what extent this pluralist discourse reflected a historical reality is not the main concern of this study.[33] My main interest as a historian lies in how Europeans have described themselves and their history in terms of a unique and rare diversity and lack of centralism and homogeneity. This malleable historical narrative was used for different political agendas, as will be shown in this study.[34] It should be pointed out that the pluralist interpretation of Europe's past was evidently not the

---

[32] Following the pioneering work of István Hont, many publications have appeared on enlightened views on 'political economy' and the social and political effects of trade. Hont, *Jealousy of Trade*; Kapossy and Sonenscher, *Politics in Commercial Society*; Rothschild, *Economic Sentiments*; Nakhimovsky, *Closed Commercial State*; Robertson, *Case for the Enlightenment*, 325–76. A systematic overview of the various and contrasting economic views of counter-revolutionary and anti-Enlightened authors, which is beyond the scope of this study, is regrettably still missing.

[33] This is the approach taken by Patrick Pasture in his *Imagining European Unity*. His conclusion is that the discourse of pluralism did not reflect reality and that Europe has, from its Christian beginnings, struggled with coming to terms with difference.

[34] Lok, 'Fragmented Continent', 43–64. Cf. Wintle, 'Cultural Diversity', 1–8; Wintle, *Image of Europe*.

only possible interpretation of European history articulated in this period. Often this pluralist narrative coexisted—or contrasted—with other 'counter-narratives', such as the notion of Europe as an enlightened commercial civilization, or as an imperial or Christian and Catholic unity.

In the eighteenth century, enlightened historians first crafted this comprehensive pluralist narrative of European history. More than the earlier humanist histories, they focussed on institutional and social change rather than a narrative of events.[35] These enlightened or 'cosmopolitan' historians, as they have been termed, exhibited both a 'detachment towards national prejudice' and an 'intellectual investment in the idea of a common European civilisation'.[36] It has traditionally been argued that, following the Napoleonic wars, this enlightened European history was supplanted by a new historiography that viewed history exclusively from a romantic-national perspective, driving alternative historical perspective to the historiographical periphery.[37] It is the hypothesis of this study, building on research by other scholars of historiography, that this enlightened 'historical Europeanism' did not disappear after 1800, but was instead appropriated by self-proclaimed counter-revolutionaries, such as Heeren, as part of their struggle with the revolutionary legacy. The idea of Europe as a historically fragmented continent subsequently continued to be discussed in the nineteenth century by a variety of authors from different political persuasions, even resurfacing after the cataclysmic events of the twentieth century, and are, even today, determining the way Europeans understand themselves and their past.[38]

4. The Politics of the (Counter-)Enlightenment

The counter-revolutionary Europeanists drew heavily upon the ideas developed by enlightened historians in the eighteenth century. This appropriation and reconfiguration of Enlightenment concepts and narratives by counter-revolutionary authors challenges the still prevailing 'progressive' and 'democratic' interpretation of the Enlightenment. As the protagonists of this study demonstrate, enlightened ideas did not only lead to the 'democratic' revolutions of the late eighteenth century, but also formed the ideological foundations of their fiercest ideological opponents.[39]

---

[35] Pocock, *Barbarism and Religion*, vol. II. See further Chapter II. [36] O'Brien, *Narratives*, 2.
[37] Berger, 'Past and Present', 26. On the rise of romantic nationalism: Leerssen, *Encyclopedia*; Leerssen, *National Thought*.
[38] Lok, 'Fragmented Continent'; for the continuity between the eighteenth-century narratives and the twentieth century: Verga, *Storie d'Europa*. Verga, however, omits the counter-revolutionary authors in his overview. See further Chapter IX.
[39] For the 'revolutionary' view of Enlightenment, see: Gay, *Enlightenment*. More recently: Israel, *Democratic Enlightenment*; Jacob, *Radical Enlightenment*; Jacob, *Secular Enlightenment*. For a more 'conservative' interpretation of the Enlightenment and its legacies, see: de Dijn, 'Politics of Enlightenment'; Blanning, *Pursuit of Glory*; Clarke, *English Society 1660–1832*; Lilti, *World of the*

The political legacy of the Enlightenment was both revolutionary and counter-revolutionary.

Since the late 1960s, the concepts of 'the conservative Enlightenment' and 'enlightened conservatism' have been pioneered by J.G.A. Pocock, among others, and for the Netherlands by Ernst Kossmann and Wyger Velema.[40] These concepts question the persisting view that conservatism as a political tradition found its origins in the resistance against the combined horrors of Enlightenment and revolution. The realization that there was no necessary or inevitable clash between the many varieties of political thought and the established political order during the eighteenth century has made it impossible to continue to regard the concept of enlightened conservatism as a contradiction in terms. As Jerry Muller put it: 'conservatism arose not *against* the Enlightenment but *within* it'.[41]

Furthermore, by studying the appropriation of eighteenth-century ideas by counter-revolutionaries, a fresh and unexpected perspective is provided on the study of the transmission and the reconfiguration of the Enlightenment legacy in the nineteenth century.[42] The focus on the Counter-Revolution also contributes to current debates over the questions of when the Enlightenment 'ended' and whether the Enlightenment 'failed'.[43] It will be argued here that the Enlightenment legacy survived, and was transformed, through the intermediary role of counter-revolutionaries, among others. By reflecting so explicitly on what they regarded as the eighteenth-century 'Enlightenment' (*Siècle des Lumières*) and its political impact, counter-revolutionary historians in this study also greatly influenced the understanding of this historical period and phenomenon by later generations.

Salons; Robertson, *Enlightenment: Pursuit of Happiness*, xx. Dorinda Outram gave a balanced view in her commanding textbook: 'it would thus seem that the dossier on the relationship between Enlightenment and Revolution is still open'. Outram, *Enlightenment*, 142.

[40] See for an overview of the debate on 'enlightened conservatism': Velema, 'Enlightenment against Revolution', 108–30. Cf. Pocock, 'Clergy and Commerce', 524–62; Pocock, 'Conservative Enlightenment and Democratic Revolutions', 81–105; Pocock, 'Josiah Tucker on Burke, Locke, and Price', 157–91. Cf. Porter, *Enlightenment*, 22–8. On the Dutch case, see: Kossmann, *Verlicht conservatisme*; Velema, *Enlightenment and Conservatism*.

[41] Muller, 'Introduction: What Is Conservative Social and Political Thought?', 24; according to Muller, conservatism is different from 'orthodoxy' because of its emphasis on history as well as utility. Cf. Muller, 'Conservatism: The Utility of History', 232–54.

[42] In the first volume of *The Cambridge History of Modern European Thought*, edited by Warren Breckmann and Peter Gordon, nineteenth-century thought is studied from the perspective of the legacy of the Enlightenment. A chapter on the evolution of the nineteenth-century concept of Europe itself is missing from this otherwise excellent volume.

[43] The 'ending' of the Enlightenment is currently studied by Richard Whatmore, see his *Terrorists, Anarchists, and Republicans*. Whatmore argues that the Enlightenment came to an end as a result of the rise of aggressive, large states in the final decades of the eighteenth century. Cf. Israel, *Enlightenment that Failed*. Israel's impressive book states that the enlightened legacy survived the French Revolution and continued into the first decades of the nineteenth century. However, his study describes the Enlightenment as 'failed', focussing on the radical Enlightenment as the true Enlightenment. The complex relationship between Enlightenment and Counter-Revolution is not fully explored here.

The historical Europeanists studied here, however, did not only use the works of the enlightened *philosophes*, but also those of their self-appointed contemporary critics. These eighteenth-century critics described themselves as '*anti-philosophes*', whose mission was to counter what they perceived as the pernicious contemporary enlightened philosophy of their time. Heeren, for instance, explained the decay and rot of the European system as the result of the spread of a 'false' philosophy in the eighteenth century. By caricaturing, especially, the French *philosophes* as atheists, egoists, and materialists, who contributed to the corruption and downfall of the European republic through their pernicious ideas, counter-revolutionary publicists helped shape the popular cliché of the purely secular and revolutionary French Enlightenment in later centuries.[44]

The thought of these contemporary opponents of the 'Age of Light' (*Siècle des lumières*) has long not been taken seriously by post-war historians of the Enlightenment.[45] Conventionally, the contemporary 'enemies' of the eighteenth-century *philosophes* were predominantly regarded by later historians of the eighteenth century as religious and apologetic reactionaries without any intellectual content. They were considered useful as worthy objects of study only for those who come from a religious tradition themselves. In more recent years, however, renewed scholarly, as well as contemporary political, interest in the historical phenomenon of the 'Counter-Enlightenment' can be observed.[46] These revisionist historians have attempted to study the *anti-philosophes* as part of the eighteenth-century Enlightenment rather than outside it: this study forms part of this revisionist approach.[47]

In the Anglo-Saxon academic world, the study of the 'Counter-Enlightenment' was famously put on the research agenda by Isaiah Berlin (1909–97). Writing in a Cold War context—his family had fled the Russian Revolution—Berlin discovered what he regarded as a 'pluralist' and modern 'Counter-Enlightenment' consisting of writers such as Hamann, Jacobi, Vico, Herder, Bonald, and Maistre.[48] Berlin contrasted these counter-enlightened writers, who, in his view, championed the 'incommensurability of values', with a proto-totalitarian view of the Enlightenment

---

[44] Schmidt, 'Inventing the Enlightenment', 421–3; Asal, 'The Contemporaneity of "Counter-Enlightenment"', 940–70; Lok, 'eeuw van ongeloof', 17–35.

[45] Gay, *Enlightenment* I. The anti-Enlightenment is still notably absent from authoritative studies on the Enlightenment as a phenomenon: Outram, *Enlightenment*; Edelstein, *Enlightenment*; Porter, *Enlightenment*.

[46] The word 'Counter-Enlightenment' or *Gegen-Aufklärung* did exist in the eighteenth century: Schmidt, 'Light, Truth and Counter-Enlightenment', 268–90.

[47] Lok, 'Vijanden van de Verlichting', 211–28. Cf. Lehner, *Catholic Enlightenment*; Burson, *Theological Enlightenment*. In his pioneering 1939 study of French Catholic thought of the eighteenth century, the American historian Robert Palmer underscored the extent to which apologists had adopted more secular enlightened ideas and genres in their defence of the Catholic Church. Palmer, *Catholics and Unbelievers*. Other older studies on France include: Monod, *Pascal à Chateaubriand*; Everdell, *Christian Apologetics*.

[48] Berlin, 'Counter-Enlightenment'; Berlin, 'Alleged Relativism'.

bent on homogenization and uniformity.[49] Berlin's analysis has been rejected by most, if not all, later historians.[50] His exclusively 'modern' interpretation of the Counter-Enlightenment was criticized by many researchers, who emphasized the historical otherness of eighteenth-century authors.[51] Darrin McMahon and Didier Masseau have, in their more recent works on French *anti-philosophie*, focussed on how historical authors have positioned themselves in an *anti-philosophe* tradition, rather than come up with a timeless definition themselves, as, for instance, Berlin did.[52] Masseau defined '*les contra-lumières*' above all as a 'polemical discourse'.[53] Overall, I have followed this discursive approach in this study.

The uses of history by these Enlightenment critics, as well as their contribution to the development of historical thought in this period, have, moreover, not been investigated at length. As the case of François-Xavier de Feller, the protagonist of the third chapter, demonstrates, *anti-philosophes* contested the dominance of *philosophe* authors in the field of history writing. Against the enlightened narrative of (European) history, writers like Feller opposed their own version of the past, drawing on older religious authorities. Nonetheless, even a radical and fierce *anti-philosophe* like Feller adopted enlightened arguments, as well as *philosophe* literary genres, such as the dictionary or the bimonthly scholarly journal, to combat the much-deplored enlightened spirit of the age.[54]

This study argues, to conclude this section, that the counter-revolutionary histories of Europe drew on the legacies of the *philosophes*, discussed in the next chapter, as well as on those of their self-declared contemporary enemies, the *anti-philosophes*, the topic of the third chapter. Many, but not all, of these publicists argued for some kind of a 'middle way' or new synthesis between enlightened 'philosophy' and the religious traditions. In almost all counter-revolutionary

---

[49] Berlin's Counter-Enlightenment consisted of 'a family of political and moral conceptions [...] based on the defiant rejection of the central thesis of the Enlightenment, according to which what is true, or right, or good, or beautiful, can be shown to be valid for all men by the correct interpretation of objective methods of discovery and interpretation, open to anyone to use and verify'. Berlin, 'Counter-Enlightenment', 19.

[50] Mali and Wokler, *Isaiah Berlin's Counter-Enlightenment*; Caradonna, 'There Was No Counter-Enlightenment', 51–69; Schmidt, 'Counter-Enlightenment: Historical Notes', 83–6. An exception is the Israeli activist and scholar Zeev Sternhell: Sternhell, *Anti-Enlightenment Tradition*. Sternhell, in contrast to Berlin, is very critical of the anti-Enlightenment, blaming many of Europe's twentieth-century catastrophes on the enemies of the Enlightenment, but his book suffers from many of the same ills as Berlin's publications, identifying two immutable and hostile strands of Enlightenment and Counter-Enlightenment. For an overview of the debate on the concept of 'Counter-Enlightenment': McMahon, 'What is Counter-Enlightenment?'; Norton, 'Myth of the Counter-Enlightenment'.

[51] Lilla, *Vico*.

[52] Masseau, *Ennemis des philosophes*; Masseau, *Dictionnaire des anti-lumières*. 'Rather than begin on high, with an abstract definition of what Enlightenment entailed, I begin on the ground, examining what hostile contemporaries themselves said about the *siècle des lumières* and its actuating principle, *philosophie*.' McMahon, *Enemies*, 10.

[53] 'Le couple antithétique "philosophe"/"antiphilosophe" fait lui-même l'objet de variations historiques.' Masseau, *Ennemis*, 43. The term '*anti-philosophe*' appeared at the same time that the *encyclopédistes* claimed the term *philosophe* for themselves. McMahon, *Enemies*, 205 n. 7.

[54] Lok, 'Feller'.

works, in Europe and beyond, an explicit *anti-philosophe* criticism can be found of a 'wrong' type of philosophy, usually associated with a decadent and corrupt eighteenth-century France, and Paris in particular.[55] This 'false' Enlightenment was criticized for its allegedly abstract character as well as its supposed 'atheism', eventually leading to 'anarchy' and 'despotism'. At the same time, most publicists emphasized that they were not opposed to Enlightenment or progress in history per se, provided it was the right kind of moral and religiously inspired Enlightenment.

5. Cosmopolitanism Against Revolution

The ambivalent attitude towards the Enlightenment by counter-revolutionaries can also be observed in their dealings with the legacy of eighteenth-century cosmopolitanism. Philosopher Kleingeld defines this concept as follows: '"Cosmopolitanism" consists of a wide variety of views in moral and sociopolitical philosophy. Despite their differences, all proponents of the cosmopolitan ideal share a view of a "nebulous core": the idea that all human beings are (or can and should be) citizens or members of a single community. Versions of cosmopolitanism vary depending on the notion of citizenship they employ and whether they take the notion of world citizenship literally or metaphorically.'[56]

The authors examined in this study did not just reject enlightened cosmopolitanism in its entirety, as is often suggested by students of historical cosmopolitanism in this period, but adapted it to fit their own purposes. Often, the counter-revolutionary Europeanists would decry what they regarded as the 'wrong' type of cosmopolitanism: atheistic, individualistic, rootless, and rebellious. They objected, however, in equal measure to an—in their eyes—excessive patriotism deemed 'fanatical', 'irrational', and regarded as a feature of the French Revolution. Instead, writers like Vogt, Müller, or Heeren—discussed in the following chapters— embraced a cosmopolitanism based on religious and moral foundations. From their perspective, a conflict between loyalty to the—local, regional, or 'national'— fatherland and to a supranational community simply did not exist. They also wrote various plans for the foundation of institutions beyond the regional or state level in order to attain the centuries-old dream of 'perpetual peace' in Europe and beyond.

---

[55] Lok and van Eijnatten, 'Global Counter-Enlightenment', 406–22.
[56] 'Cosmopolitanism challenges commonly recognised attachments to fellow citizens, the local state, and parochially shared cultures. In most versions of cosmopolitanism, the universal community of world citizens functions as a positive ideal to be cultivated. Also more radical strands existed in which all obligations towards local forms of political organisations are denied altogether.' Kleingeld, 'Cosmopolitanism'.

The origins of the cosmopolitan ideals in the Western world, such as the idea of 'human dignity', can be traced to the ancient world, particularly among the Greek philosophers, and later Roman, Stoa, which formed an important source of inspiration for counter-revolutionary authors.[57] Subsequently the cosmopolitan ideals of the Stoic writers were rediscovered by humanists in the early modern period.[58] In the early eighteenth century, cosmopolitanism came to stand for not just a specific philosophical tradition, but also an attitude of open-mindedness and impartiality, as well as an urbane lifestyle with extensive travelling and a wide range of social contacts.[59] The revival of Stoic and Cynic cosmopolitanism as a philosophy reached its culmination in the late eighteenth-century Enlightenment, with Immanuel Kant as its most important and innovative philosopher.[60] Other writers, such as the German Martin Wieland (1773–1813) defended a more traditional and aristocratic form of enlightened cosmopolitanism.[61]

Already from the early eighteenth century onwards, 'cosmopolitanism' was the object of criticism for its alleged rootlessness, selfishness, and lack of patriotism.[62] Most eighteenth-century self-proclaimed 'cosmopolitans' strived for a middle way between the ideals of patriotism and world citizenship, rather than discarding the *patria* altogether. The French Revolution is often described as a zenith of political cosmopolitanism, with radical cosmopolitan republicans, such as Anarchis Cloots, advocating the abolition of all existing states and the establishment of one, single world state.[63] However, Cloots was executed during the Terror, and after 1792, cosmopolitanism became a negative concept in revolutionary discourse, increasingly being supplanted by a militant patriotism. Counter-revolutionaries and moderate revolutionaries were declared 'enemies of the human race' and placed outside the community of man in accordance with their interpretation of natural law.[64] Nicolas de Bonneville, another cosmopolitan revolutionary and the protagonist of the next chapter, would also fall victim to revolutionary patriotism. The relationship between the cosmopolitan ideal and the French Revolution was thus highly equivocal.[65]

---

[57] Kleingeld, 'Cosmopolitanism'; Nussbaum, *Cosmopolitan Tradition*, 18–97. For a non-Western perspective: Pollock, 'Cosmopolitanism, Vernacularism, and Premodernity', 58–80; on 'cosmopolitan thought zones' outside the West, see the summary in Conrad, *What is Global History?*, 207–8.
[58] Bireley, *Counter-Reformation Prince*; Tuck, *Philosophy and Government*. According to Margaret Jacob, early modern people were particularly apt to 'experience people of different nations, creeds and colours with pleasure, curiosity and interest'. Jacob, *Strangers*, 1.
[59] Kleingeld, 'Cosmopolitanism'.
[60] Kleingeld, *Kant and Cosmopolitanism*. On the varieties of Enlightenment cosmopolitanism, see also: Robertson, *Enlightenment: Pursuit of Happiness*, 600–54.
[61] Albrecht, *Kosmopolitismus*, 82–94.
[62] Rousseau famously complained that cosmopolitans boast that they love everyone, 'to have the right to love no one'. Cited by Kleingeld, 'Cosmopolitanism'. Cf. Albrecht, *Kosmopolitismus*, 62–81.
[63] Poulsen, 'Cosmopolitan Republican'. [64] Edelstein, *Terror of Natural Right*.
[65] Pestel and Ihalainen, 'Revolution beyond Borders', 35–59; van den Heuvel, 'Cosmopolite', 41–55.

Most histories of (Western) cosmopolitanism end their narratives around the turn of the eighteenth and nineteenth centuries to signal a revival in the peace movement around 1900 and the First World War.[66] The Napoleonic wars allegedly inaugurated a new era determined by 'virulent nationalism and imperialism'.[67] Most of these historical studies seem to imply that cosmopolitanism is, by definition, a progressive and secular phenomenon. This limited focus has resulted in the neglect of the post-revolutionary decades and, perhaps, of the entire early nineteenth century as an age of cosmopolitanism, too. This general omission of counter-revolutionary and conservative perspectives is perhaps true for the history of international thought in general: scholars tend to focus on the progressive, revolutionary, and liberal forms of internationalism, while ignoring conservative, anti-liberal and counter-revolutionary forms of internationalism.[68]

This study argues that enlightened cosmopolitanism survived to a certain extent in the writings of counter-revolutionary Europeanists. Cosmopolitanism against the Revolution will be discussed in this study on the basis of five criteria. Firstly, I will research to what extent and how the authors described themselves rhetorically as 'cosmopolitans'. Secondly, I will determine more abstractly whether these writers viewed the world from a perspective beyond the local, regional, and national levels. To what extent did they see themselves as part of a larger community, for instance Europe or a global community? And if so, what did this community look like? Was it primarily a religious, legal, moral, or a civilizational commonwealth? And, very importantly, where did the boundaries of this cosmopolitan community lie, and who was excluded from it?

A third often-named characteristic of cosmopolitanism is the positive view of cultural diversity and a pluralistic outlook.[69] Heeren, for instance, valued Europe for its lack of cultural homogeneity and political centralism, qualities he associated with the Napoleonic Empire. Fourthly, I will briefly discuss to what extent ideas of 'world citizenship' can also be traced in counter-revolutionary writings. Several counter-revolutionary authors, such as Niklas Vogt, who features in the sixth chapter, saw the role of active citizens as vital for the functioning of a free and prosperous 'European republic', borrowing elements from classical republicanism.

---

[66] Jacob, *Strangers*; Belissa and Cottret, *Cosmopolitismes*; Belissa, *Repenser l'ordre Européen*; Stuurman, *Invention of Humanity*; Robertson, *Enlightenment: Pursuit of Happiness*, 600–54. An older work is Schlereth, *Cosmopolitan Ideal*. Cf. Scrivener, *Cosmopolitan Ideal*. Scrivener does not discuss the counter-revolutionary and conservative forms of cosmopolitanism in this period.

[67] Jacob, *Strangers*, 5.

[68] Recent studies on post-revolutionary cosmopolitanism, however, have partly corrected this constricted view. Kleingeld herself, in her study of the different varieties of late eighteenth-century German cosmopolitan thought, for instance, discerned a short-lived 'romantic' strand of cosmopolitanism in the work of the poet Novalis (Georg Philipp Friedrich von Hardenberg, 1772–1801) and his philosophical friend Friedrich Schlegel (1772–1829). Kleingeld, 'Romantic Cosmopolitanism', and Pestel, *Kosmopoliten*. See also: Lok, Pestel, and Reboul, *Cosmopolitan Conservatisms*, 4–8.

[69] Nussbaum, *Cosmopolitan Tradition*, 100–7; Jacob, *Strangers*, 1–12; Robertson, *Enlightenment: Pursuit of Happiness*, 648–54; Muthu, *Enlightenment against Empire*. Cf. Cooper, *Citizenship*. See also Chapters VI and IX.

A fifth and final criterion is the use of 'cosmopolitan' enlightened historical narratives of a developing European civilization in progressive stages in their account of history.[70]

By interpreting counter-revolutionary authors as 'cosmopolitans', a generally positive term for progressive intellectuals, as well as a negative marker for contemporary anti-liberals, my aim is not to paint an overly rosy picture of the opponents of the French Revolution.[71] Strict geographical, political, and cultural boundaries were put around the cosmopolitan designs for a counter-revolutionary new order. Most authors confined the reconstructed European republic or commonwealth to the Christian, and in some cases only Catholic, Orthodox, or Protestant, world. Although a peaceful and stable world system was the ultimate goal of many designs of a new European system, the authors simultaneously defended relentless warfare and violence to destroy the revolutionary legacies. Moreover, this new cosmopolitan order was based on ideas of inequality and exclusion.[72] Boundaries were also erected between Europe and the rest of the world, often reconfirming Europe's moral and cultural superiority and its imperial right to rule.[73]

6. The Age of Counter-Revolution

In recent decades the role of the Counter-Revolution in political and intellectual history has been re-evaluated. No longer regarded as juxtaposed to and placed outside the revolutionary mainstream of modern European history, the Counter-Revolution is increasingly understood by historians as an integral and important part of the revolutionary experience itself.[74] In the past, counter-revolutionaries were often regarded as insignificant and peripheral, anachronisms who lost out in the course of European progress. Their ideas were also not taken seriously and

---

[70] O'Brien, *Narratives*, 2.
[71] In the works of eminent social scientists and philosophers such as Kwame Anthony Appiah, Ulrich Beck, Gerard Delanty, Jürgen Habermas, and Martha Nussbaum, published since the fall of the Berlin wall, 'cosmopolitanism' has been propagated as an alternative to what seemed at the time as the outdated attachment to a world of nation states. Appiah, *Cosmopolitanism*; Beck and Grande, *Cosmopolitan Europe*; Delanty, *Cosmopolitan Imagination*. For an overview of contemporary cosmopolitan positions: Kleingeld, 'Cosmopolitanism'; Albrecht, *Kosmopolitismus*, 1–9.
[72] According to Glenda Sluga and Julia Horne, 'the history of cosmopolitanism illustrates vividly that gender, internationalism, immigration, imperialism, science, trade, globalism, and nations all have a claim on the history of cosmopolitanism'. Sluga and Horne, 'Cosmopolitanism: Its Pasts and Practices', 369–73.
[73] Pagden, 'Stoicism'. See for the nexus between Counter-Revolution and imperialism: Chapter IX.
[74] Already in the 1960s, French historian Jacques Godechot studied the Counter-Revolution as a European and even Atlantic phenomenon, responding to the remark by English historian Alfred Cobban in 1956 that 'the biggest gap in the history of the Revolution is, paradoxically, the history of the Counter-Revolution'. Godechot, *Counter-Revolution*. For more recent works that integrate the Counter-Revolution and the Revolution: Sutherland, *France 1789–1815*; Martin, *Contre-Révolution, Révolution et Nation*.

stereotyped as clichés without real content.[75] Together with the renewed scholarly interest in Counter-Enlightenment, the political thought of counter-revolutionary writers is now also being studied by those historians who do not primarily wish to defend and legitimize the counter-revolutionary ideas.[76]

Without condoning the counter-revolutionary political ideas themselves, this study also argues that counter-revolutionaries played a crucial role in the development of modern European and Western political and intellectual history.[77] The nineteenth century was not only the 'age of revolution', in the well-known phrase of Eric Hobsbawm, but in equal measure also a 'Century of Counter-Revolution'.[78] Similar to the subsequent waves of revolution, modern Europe was shaped by recurring restorations and reactions, which adapted to new political and social contexts as well as building on older precedents, but are overall far less investigated.[79]

In contrast to the political myth constructed by hostile revolutionaries, the 'Counter-Revolution' was not one unified phenomenon, organized by a small group of aristocratic plotters. Counter-Revolution consisted of a wide variety of opinions, which often contradicted each other. The word 'Counter-Revolution' emerged as a neologism at the beginning of the French Revolution.[80] 'Counter-Revolution', initially, did not simply imply turning the political clock back to the *ancien régime*. Rather, the term generally designated the process of combatting revolution. Within the broad spectrum of possible approaches towards revolution, the idea of 'countering' was politically highly flexible. Counter-Revolution could even be a left-wing political phenomenon. In different countries, moreover, the concept of 'Counter-Revolution' was shaped by specific national histories and experiences. For instance, in Great Britain, the idea of 'Counter-Revolution' was determined by the experience of the 'Glorious Revolution' of 1688. It was only over the course of the nineteenth century that the concept lost most of its ambiguous meaning and became the reactionary concept in the sense it is used today.[81]

---

[75] This was, for instance, the view of Godechot, who strictly separated the ideology of the counter-revolutionaries, which he believed irrelevant, from their political activism: Godechot, *Counter-Revolution*. A further weakness of this classic work is its implicit francocentric focus. Moreover, the book does not address the topic of historical Europeanism and the uses of history by counter-revolutionaries in an extensive manner.

[76] Annelien de Dijn, for instance, in her critical history of the Western idea of freedom, attributes a pernicious yet crucial role of counter-revolutionaries. De Dijn, *Freedom*.

[77] According to Jacob Burckhardt, Counter-Revolution, Reaction, followed by Restoration were recurring phases of any world historical 'crisis' and need to be studied jointly. Burckhardt, *Wereldhistorische Beschouwingen*, 216–29.

[78] Hobsbawm, *Age of Revolution*.

[79] On this topic, see Lok, Pestel, and Reboul, *Cosmopolitan Conservatisms*. See also: Schettini, *Invention of Catholicism*. For the post-1848 reaction: Clark, 'After 1848'; Caruso, *Nationalstaat als Telos?*; Sperber, *Europe, 1850–1870*.

[80] On the changing concept of 'Revolution': Baker, *Inventing the French Revolution*.

[81] Pestel, 'On Counter-revolution'; Pestel, 'Contre-révolution'. See more extensively Chapter IV.

A timeless definition of what Counter-Revolution is will therefore not be provided here. Authors have been labelled as 'counter-revolutionary' when they have clearly expressed their hostility and criticism towards what they regarded as the French Revolution and its legacy. Heeren, for instance, and as mentioned earlier, termed the French Revolution a 'great catastrophe'. It would, however, be misleading to typecast these authors hostile to the Revolution as simply reactionaries. Authors like Heeren saw themselves as 'moderates' who strived for a new middle way or synthesis between conserving an idealized past and reforming a corrupted system. While criticizing the wrong kind of philosophy, they usually situated themselves in the tradition of moderate Enlightenment, believing in the possibility of gradual progress. Not merely wishing to restore a distant world destroyed by Revolution, the counter-revolutionary authors dreamt of regenerating Europe in political as well as in moral, cultural, and spiritual terms. Far from opposing Revolution in unison, they adopted elements from the ideas of their political opponents. Moreover, counter-revolutionaries were often not ideologically consistent: supporting reaction and 'pure royalism' in one context, moderate reform in another, and sometimes even acting as liberals and radicals in yet another.[82]

This book adds to this new perspective on the intellectual legacy of the Counter-Revolution by focussing on the counter-revolutionary view of the European past and future. For the first time, the counter-revolutionary writing of European history has been studied from a transnational perspective, without, of course, claiming to have examined all possible sources of this vast subject. Next to well-known counter-revolutionary figureheads such as Joseph de Maistre, lesser-known authors, often thinker-agents straddling the lines between scholarship and administration, and their writings have been looked at in their intellectual and political context. Moreover, the undervalued and perhaps counter-intuitive but crucial role of counter-revolutionaries in the transmission and adaption of enlightened ideals, including strands of enlightened cosmopolitanism, for political purposes will be shown. Finally, the fundamentally 'European' and transnational character of counter-revolutionary thought will be demonstrated.[83]

7. Conservative Europeanism

The 'Counter-Revolution' is usually associated with the birth of the political ideology of 'conservatism', but this relationship needs to be nuanced. For the

---

[82] Arguably, this was true of Charles-Alexandre Calonne, see Chapter IV. On this topic, see also the forthcoming work of Maurizio Isabella on the history of the 1820s revolutions in global context.
[83] The European character of the Counter-Revolution has earlier been underlined by Godechot and Martin: Godechot, *Counter-Revolution*; Martin, *Contre-Révolution en Europe*. However, these authors do not study Counter-Revolution from the perspective of historical Europeanism.

years studied in this book, to speak of 'conservatism' as a coherent party ideology is mostly an anachronism. The word 'conservative' was first used in modern history during the Thermidor moment in the French Revolution.[84] These late eighteenth-century appearances of the word conservatism were saliently not anti-revolutionary in intent but instead supported the revolutionary legacy of 1789. Only after the re-establishment of the Bourbon monarchy and the appearance of the constitutional text *La Charte* of 1814 did the concept of conservatism emerge in Europe as a term for a political party and ideology, especially following the revolutions of 1830 and 1848.[85] Instrumental in this regard was Chateaubriand's journal entitled *Le Conservateur* (1818–20), founded to defend the monarchist constitution against liberals and 'ultra-royalists' alike, although the more abstract notion of '*conservatisme*' could be found in dictionaries only much later.[86]

In the continental context, the word 'conservative' often was a negative marker assigned by opponents.[87] One of the ideological founders of nineteenth-century Dutch political Protestantism, Guillaume Groen van Prinsterer (1801–76), refused to be called a 'conservative', because for him conservatism stood for a compromise with the principles of the French Revolution. He preferred the term 'anti-revolutionary'.[88] The notion of conservative can thus not simply be equated with 'anti-' or 'counter-revolutionary', although it is a truism to state that later 'conservatives' showed themselves generally hostile to the legacy of the French Revolution in some form. As Brian Vick remarked, 'all versions [of conservatism] were counter-revolutionary in the strict sense, but conservatives could and did disagree about the best way of combatting or preventing revolution'.[89]

In the twentieth century, 'typologies' of different strands of conservatism were designed. Most famously and still influentially, German sociologist Karl Mannheim (1893–1947) distinguished in the 1920s between an ahistorical 'traditionalism' and 'conservatism'.[90] Whereas 'traditionalism' was, according to Mannheim, a formal psychological characteristic of every individual's mind, 'conservatism', by contrast, was always dependent on a concrete set of circumstances such as the revolutionary period. For Mannheim, studying mainly German sources, 'traditionalism' was foremost unconscious, whereas 'conservatism' was

---

[84] Earlier uses of the word 'conservative' in the Latin classical and medieval Christian traditions can also be found. Vierhaus, 'Konservativ', 537.

[85] On Spain and Portugal: Herrero, *orígenes del pensamiento reaccionario español*; Escrig Rosa, 'Pasión racional, razón apasionada'; Herrera, *¡Serviles!*; Artola Renedo and Calvo Maturana, 'Declinaciones de la reacción eclesiástica', 437–69; Schmidt, 'Contra "la falsa filosofía"', 233–6; Luis, *Utopie reactionnaire*. On Central and Eastern Europe: Trencsenyi et al., *Modern Political Thought in East Central Europe*.

[86] *Dictionnaire de l'Academie française* of 1842, 268.   [87] Vierhaus, 'Konservativ', 565.

[88] Groen van Prinsterer, *Ongeloof en Revolutie*, 6. See also Chapter IX.

[89] Vick, *Congress of Vienna*, 235.

[90] Mannheim, 'Conservative Thought', 280–1. Rudolf Vierhaus later rightly argued against making an overly strict dichotomy as, in his view, traditionalism was also influenced by 'historical and social factors', whereas conservatism contained many 'pre-political' elements. Vierhaus, 'Konservativ', 532.

reflective from the beginning, since it supposedly arose as a counter-movement in conscious opposition to a highly organized, coherent, and systematic 'progressive' movement.[91] Conservatism was, in Mannheim's view, therefore, very much a modern phenomenon, arising as a response to the dynamism of the development of the modern state, the industrial economy, and society.[92]

The former *Ostforscher* Fritz Valjavec (1909–60), subsequently, argued fruitfully that early 'conservatism' in Germany consisted of more than a mere response to the French Revolution. Already in the late eighteenth century, the diverse origins of a conservative 'current' (*Strömung*) could be observed in the form of criticism of enlightened *philosophie*, the opposition to monarchical rational reforms, and the idea of an atheistic plot by illuminati and Freemasons. Valjavec differentiated between reactionary and reform-minded conservatives, such as Möser, Rehberg, Niebuhr, and Müller who strove for a moderate 'middle way' between the extremes.[93] As a result of the French Revolution, however, conservative ideas became increasingly politicized and widespread. A true German conservative political movement and ideology, according to Valjavec, developed only in the late nineteenth century after the revolutions of 1830 and 1848.[94] Valjavec, moreover, already underscored the essentially 'European' character of early conservatism.[95]

The American historian Klaus Epstein, in his influential 1966 study of German conservatism from the 1770s to the dissolution of the Holy Roman Empire, argued in a similar vein that the formation of conservative ideas had already taken place in the decades before the French Revolution. He was able to distinguish between three distinct ideal types of conservatism, depending on how they dealt with past and present: 'defenders of the status quo', 'reform conservatives', and 'reactionaries', personally sympathizing with the middle type. Epstein's influential typology has been criticized by later historians for too clearly demarcating separate and homogeneous sociological groups.[96] Epstein, furthermore, saw conservatism as

---

[91] On the concept of 'tradition': Pocock, 'Time, Institutions and Action', 187–216.
[92] Mannheim, 'Conservative Thought', 286. Panajotis Kondylis, by contrast, controversially dated the origins of the classic tradition of conservatism in the sixteenth-century aristocratic resistance against the centralizing tendencies of the absolutist states. Kondylis, *Konservatismus*.
[93] Valjavec, *politischen Strömungen*, 268–70.
[94] Valjavec, *politischen Strömungen*, 303–4. For an overview of German counter-revolutionary ideas in the 1790s, see also the chapter on 'The Rise of German Conservatism' in: Beiser, *Enlightenment, Revolution and Romanticism*. Beiser defined 'conservatives' as counter-revolutionaries who 'defended paternalism and the old social hierarchy' (282). Beiser, moreover, emphasized the heterogeneous character of counter-revolutionary German conservatism and stated that these conservatives were, in their own words, not opposed to Enlightenment *per se* but stood for a different kind of Enlightenment. The European dimension, regrettably, is here largely absent.
[95] Valjavec, 'europäischen Konservatismus', 138–55. The essay was originally published in 1954.
[96] The party of movement is rather simplistically defined as the party whose ambition was 'to transform society into a secular, egalitarian and self-governing direction'. Epstein, *Genesis*, 5. Cf. Palmer, *Democratic Revolution*.

directly related to the defence of particular economic interests.[97] New, and less rigorous, typologies and 'family resemblances' have since then been formulated by political scientists Michael Freeden and Jan-Werner Müller.[98]

A different approach was taken by American political scientist Samuel Huntington. He argued in 1957 that conservatism does not contain any substantial ideological core.[99] According to Huntington, in this 'situational definition', conservatism differed in this respect from all other ideologies, except radicalism. In essence, conservatism consisted of a defence and rationalization of any existing establishment or set of institutions. This study partially agrees with this situational definition, by arguing that counter-revolutionaries appropriated enlightened narratives for a new counter-revolutionary agenda, demonstrating their adaptability to the enlightened 'spirit of the age'. Huntington, however, ignores the extent to which conservatives were constricted in the expression of their views by older historical traditions and examples.

Twenty-first-century historical scholarship has shown itself to be increasingly critical of attempts by—mostly—social scientists to define a 'conservative' ideological essence or a coherent conservative tradition or typology through the ages. These revisionist scholars argue that such an idea is often a political myth constructed for political reasons, as we could, for instance, observe in the congress of 'conservative nationalists' in Rome in 2020.[100] Richard Bourke and Emily Jones have, for example, convincingly demonstrated that the representation of the eighteenth-century Whig politician Edmund Burke as the intellectual 'father' of an allegedly conservative tradition is a late nineteenth-century invention.[101] Other scholars have similarly emphasized that other early nineteenth-century conservative icons, such as Friedrich (von) Gentz and Joseph de Maistre, should be understood as exponents of a tradition of late Enlightenment cosmopolitanism rather than representatives of a reactionary and retrograde response to the French Revolution, or even worse, as early precursors of fascism.[102]

In his study of the Congress of Vienna of 1814–15, Brian Vick, furthermore, emphasized the blurred lines between early 'liberal' and 'conservative' writers, demonstrating the anachronistic character of such labels. He argued that the so-called conservative elite adapted much more to new trends, such as nationalism and liberal ideas, than previously thought.[103] According to Vick, we should 'shift

---

[97] Epstein, *Genesis*, vii. See for a somewhat controversial analysis of conservatism as the defense of socio-economic privileges: Robin, *Reactionary Mind*.

[98] Freeden, *Ideologies and Political Theory*; Müller, 'Comprehending Conservatism'.

[99] Huntington, 'Conservatism as an Ideology'. Cf. the American sociologist Albert Hirschman, who has analysed conservatism on a more abstract and rhetorical level: Hirschman, *Rhetoric of Reaction*.

[100] Bourke, 'What Is Conservatism?' According to Bourke, the political thought of the nineteenth and twentieth centuries remained comparatively immune from rigorously historicist procedure.

[101] Bourke, *Empire and Revolution*; Jones, *Edmund Burke*.

[102] Armenteros, *French Idea*; Cahen, *Gentz*; Green, '"Fiat Justitia"'.

[103] Vick, *Congress of Vienna*, 134–8, 235–8. Michael Broers has described post-revolutionary conservatism as an ideology above all aimed at stability, in contrast to reaction. 'Conservatism did

analysis away from ideal types of liberal and conservative ideologies to explorations of ideas, actual paths, and processes of development in the political contexts of the late eighteenth and early nineteenth centuries'.[104] He also underscored the importance of sociability and the study of networks. Socially, political camps were not exclusive: Gentz, Maistre, and Chateaubriand, turned into figureheads of conservatism by later generations, frequented the same dinners and salons as famous liberals and later icons of the 'liberal' movement, such as Benjamin Constant and Mme de Staël.[105] Also, liberals and conservatives used the same political vocabulary, 'making competing claims to key concepts that had established themselves as winners'.[106]

This study argues in line with this revisionist approach that the early 'conservatives' examined here were not mere reactionaries who romantically glorified the local and the national against revolutionary universalism, but that they should be considered part of one particular strand of Enlightenment. The historical Europeanists adapted (anti-)enlightened and cosmopolitan arguments for their counter-revolutionary agendas. They used words like 'moderate', 'middle way', 'reasonable', and 'impartial' to define their own political positions, rather than 'conservative'. The values these post-revolutionary publicists, despite their differences, shared, to some extent were (their idea of) order, balance, freedom, 'pluralism', the rule of law, a religiously inspired morality, and a positive take on historically grown institutions and the gradual progress of civilization. These values they considered under threat from the revolutionary barbarism that destroyed the historical institutions and traditions, inevitably leading to both state despotism as well as social anarchy.

This book also demonstrates systematically and, from a transnational perspective, for the first time the key role of European history writing as the vehicle through which counter-revolutionary and conservative ideas were articulated, as well as the importance of the new tradition of 'historical Europeanism'. Rather than only defending the local or the national against the rising tide of revolutionary universalism, the counter-revolutionaries studied articulated their own strand of internationalism.[107] This counter-revolutionary cosmopolitanism usually took the form of historical Europeanism, which erected its own cultural and political boundaries and constructed new hierarchies.[108] This transnational approach contrasts with views held by still influential historians, such as Klaus Epstein,

---

not so much stand between reaction and liberalism on a political kaleidoscope running neatly from right to left; rather it defined itself from both of them in a complex series of relationships.' Broers, *Europe after Napoleon*, 21.

[104] Vick, *Congress of Vienna*, 235.   [105] Vick, *Congress of Vienna*, 237.

[106] Vick, *Congress of Vienna*, 237. See also Vick, 'Transnational Networks', 197–218.

[107] My European transnational perspective on early conservatism, for instance, clearly differs from the comparative national perspective of Edmund Fawcett in his *Conservatism*.

[108] See Chapter IX.

that early conservatism and Counter-Revolution can, due to their nature, be studied only exclusively in a national, regional, or local context.[109]

8. Circulation of Concepts

The concepts 'Enlightenment' and 'Counter-Enlightenment', *'philosophie'* and *anti-philosophie'*, 'Revolution' and 'Counter-Revolution', are not merely neutral descriptive categories. They were, and are, rhetorical weapons forged in the political struggle of the post-revolutionary decades, but also by later generations. This holds true for the other key concepts and vocabularies in this study: 'reaction', 'restoration', 'conservatism', 'liberalism', 'moderation', etc. Even words like 'royalist' and 'republic' were defined differently from our contemporary understanding. These key words can be considered elastic concepts: different meanings were given to them in different national, linguistic, and historical contexts.[110] Often, political debates were fought over the exact meaning of concepts instead of over which words to use. In many ways, counter-revolutionaries shared much of the revolutionary vocabulary of their opponents, such as the emphasis on 'freedom' and 'liberty', but radically differed in their interpretation of them.[111]

Arguing for the 'otherness' of historical concepts is, of course, nothing new in intellectual history. Already in his seminal essay of 1969, Quentin Skinner rejected what he saw as the then dominant forms of studying the history of ideas: either by reducing ideas to their political or socio-economic context or as an endeavour to explore the timeless questions in classical texts.[112] This exploration follows Skinner's methodological insights as well as those of the famed 'Cambridge contextual school' in the sense that this book does not entail an intellectual biography of one author or a classic text, nor the study of one specific idea through time.[113] Instead, I will contextually analyse the transnational political vocabulary and concepts of a group of authors from different geographical and linguistic backgrounds at a specific moment in time, the decades around 1800.

Rather than merely reflecting change, I will demonstrate that these writings also contributed to the shaping of these historical and political orders. Exploring a wide variety of sources, I paint a canvas of the different elements of the counter-

---

[109] In Epstein's view, conservatism consisted of a 'specific defence of a concrete and ever-changing status quo, and it [is] therefore as variegated as the conditions which it defends'. Epstein, *Genesis*, 6–7. Cf. Greiffenhagen, *Dilemma des Konservatismus*; Muller, 'Introduction', 29. The conceptual history of liberalism is, in contrast to conservatism, extensively studied from a European perspective: Leonhard, *Liberalismus*; Freeden, Fernández Sebastián, and Leonhard, *European Liberalisms*.

[110] See for a study of 'Europe' as an 'elastic' concept in twentieth-century Dutch political history: de Bruin, *Elastisch Europa*.

[111] Lok, '"A Just and True Liberty"'. [112] Skinner, 'Meaning and Understanding', 48.

[113] Much has been written on the methodology of the 'Cambridge school'; see for an introduction: Whatmore, *What Is Intellectual History?* Cf. Skinner, *Foundations*.

revolutionary narratives of European order and history. By doing so, I will be able to discern to what extent individual authors fitted into a wider linguistic and ideological pattern and to what extent they diverged from commonly held political convictions.[114]

In this study, I will make use of the combined methodological insights from historiographical schools from various countries and languages. In addition to looking at Britain, France, Germany, and the United States, I will draw on lesser-known countries, such as Spain, Italy, the Netherlands, Luxemburg, and Belgium. This study thus also builds on the cultural turn in the study of the French Revolution since the 1980s, which led to an increased sensitivity to the discourse and political symbolism used by the revolutionaries and their opponents.[115] The Revolutionary Republic, the Napoleonic Empire, and the Restoration are increasingly studied from the perspective of legitimacy and political ritual, although valuable and well-written biographies of 'great men' based on extensive archival research are fortunately still being published. French historians have also written on the different vocabularies related to the French right, with specific attention to the interrelation of literature, poetry, and political theory.[116] Historian Pierre Serna, for instance, demonstrated very well how the political concept of the 'radical centre' was formed in moments of political change and regime change, building on older discourses, and how languages of radicalism and moderation interacted in this era.[117]

No other continental academic tradition has done more for the study of historical concepts than the German school of *Begriffsgeschichte*. This specifically German approach was developed in the post-war years, partly to come to terms with the legacy of the world wars as a process of 'semantic chastening' of the German languages of politics.[118] Between 1972 and 1997 Reinhart Koselleck co-edited, together with Werner Conze and Otto Brunner, the eight-volume *Geschichtliche Grundbegriffe*. This work, together with his later contributions, became the cornerstone of German and European conceptual history, the study of the changing semantics and pragmatics of concepts in their social and political contexts. One of the flaws of this approach was that it was profoundly influenced by a certain critical idea of modernity. Also, the relationship between historical

---

[114] On 'verbalisation as a political act' and historiography as political thought: Pocock, *Political Thought and History*, 33–50. Pocock specifically pointed to historiography as a neglected form of political thought.

[115] François Furet and Mona Ozouf are the best-known examples of this approach. Annie Jourdan has extensively written on the political culture of the French Revolution and the Empire, but also on the cultural transfer of the revolutionary sister republics, such as the Batavian Republic, fusing cultural and political history: Jourdan, *Révolution. Une exception française*; Jourdan, *La révolution batave*.

[116] On the terminology of 'the right' in the French context: Tort, *droite française*. For the word 'Reaction': Starobinski, *Action et réaction*; Compagnon, *antimodernes*. On French intellectual history in general: Lilti, 'Does Intellectual History Exist in France?'.

[117] Serna, *République des girouettes*.

[118] Müller, 'Conceptual History', 78. Cf. Richter, 'History of Political Languages'.

concepts and social history was never satisfactorily determined.[119] One of its main strengths is, nonetheless, the attention given to the close relationship between the meaning of concepts and the experience of time.

In recent decades, renewed attention has been given to the transfer of ideas and concepts. 'Cultural transfer' has become an influential approach to cultural history.[120] As this study also will show, ideas and narratives were not blindly copied from one geographical, temporal, or linguistic context to another, but were consciously adapted to the new circumstances, where they acquired new meanings. The historical Europeanism studied in this book combined common European with local and national traditions. The transfer of ideas was also greatly stimulated by the—often involuntary—mobility of people due to political upheaval, exile, proscriptions, and continent-wide wars.[121] Studying the transfer or 'circulation' of concepts is also one of the key methods of the emerging 'global intellectual history'.[122] However, the attention of most global intellectual and international historians has so far been directed to the transfer of progressive and liberal ideas; the circulation of ideas of the Counter-Enlightenment, Counter-Revolution, and Reaction has been relatively neglected.[123] As David Armitage has, for instance, pointed out, in contrast to global histories of the revolutionary decades, 'there is no synoptic account of the late eighteenth century as the age of global *anti*democratic *counter*-revolution'.[124]

9. The Protagonists

There is no question that the political and intellectual history of the (post-)revolutionary era was determined by individuals. Attempts to confine contemporaries within a specific and coherent ideological or party label, be it 'liberal', 'radical', or 'conservative', or a specific national identity, usually fail. Contemporaries were often highly eclectic in their choice of ideas and, from our perspective, often inconsistent, depending on the changing political circumstances. Modern

---

[119] Müller, 'Conceptual History', 74–93. The '*GG*' also relied extensively on elite discourses and less attention was placed on alternative concepts.

[120] Espagne and Werner, *Transferts*; Burrows, Dziembowski, and Thomson, *Cultural Transfers*; Muhs, Paulmann, and Steinmetz, *Aneignung und Abwehr*; Pestel, *Kosmopoliten*, 37–46.

[121] The modern, that is, the primarily political refugee, can be considered an invention of this revolutionary period. Cf. Aprile, *Siècle des exilés*; Jasanoff, 'Revolutionary Exiles'; Pestel, 'Age of Emigrations'; Reboul, *French Emigration*.

[122] Moyn and Sartori, 'Approaches to Global Intellectual History'. Cf. Pernau and Sachsenmaier, *Global Conceptual History*. On global history generally: Sachsenmaier, *Global Perspectives*; Conrad, *What Is Global History?*; Hunt, *Writing History in the Global Era*.

[123] See also: Lok, Pestel, and Reboul, *Cosmopolitan Conservatisms*.

[124] Armitage, 'Foreword', xx. Cf. Armitage and Subrahmanyam, *Age of Global Revolutions*; Bayly, *Birth of the Modern World*. For transnational study of the revolutionary decade: Koekkoek, *Citizenship Experiment*. See more extensively: Lok, Pestel, and Reboul, *Cosmopolitan Conservatisms*; Lok and van Eijnatten, 'Global Counter-Enlightenment'.

bureaucracies and institutions, such as ministries and universities, were beginning to develop, but individuals could still very much put their stamp on them. The different aspects of counter-revolutionary historical Europeanism will therefore be examined in this study through the prism of a select number of individual authors.

The writers studied here certainly did not form a coherent group or cohort. Nonetheless, it should be noted that Europe's political, intellectual, and literary elite at the beginning of the nineteenth century consisted of a surprisingly small network of people who were interconnected in various ways.[125] The writers did not live like reclusive scholars, writing in isolation, but were politically and socially active as civil servants, journalists, educators, clergymen, or advisors to princes. They could be called intermediary 'thinker-agents', connecting the world of philosophical ideas and the realm of power and practical politics.[126] Vogt, for instance, had been the teacher of Metternich, the architect of the Vienna Peace of 1815, Calonne was a former French minister, and Müller an Austrian officeholder, who dedicated his main work to his former teacher Heeren.

My protagonists were often prolific authors who published thousands of pages, in many cases repeating themselves or recycling older materials. Self-plagiarism was the norm rather than the exception. They used various media such as journals, magazines, letters, diaries, dictionaries, sermons, books, and pamphlets. These writings were often not intended to become works of timeless political thought but consisted of an immediate response to political events and interventions in heated contemporary public debates. These texts can truly be considered examples of 'ideas in action', in line with their mistrust of abstract philosophical speculation. The authors examined here, and their works, often despite their own intentions, also played a role in emerging forms of 'popular conservatism', bridging the gap between elite politics and political action at the other end of the social stratum.[127]

The protagonists who figure in this book usually occupied a grey area between scholarship, journalism, politics, and administration so typical of an era in which academic and professional specialization was only slowly and gradually becoming an ideal. Stefan Berger has pointed out that the interpretation of the early nineteenth century as the birth of modern historical scholarship is, to a certain extent, an unsupported cliché and must be regarded as a later projection.[128] History writing was still regarded by many as a branch of literature or rhetoric, not primarily as a scientific activity. Many histories of Europe were not published by professional academics, but by politicians, journalists, members of the clergy,

---

[125] Vick, 'Transnational Networks'.
[126] On the concept of 'thinker-agents': Kattenberg, 'Power of Necessity'.
[127] On popular conservatism: Philp, 'Vulgar Conservatism'; Neuheiser, *Crown, Church and Constitution*; te Velde and Haks, *Oranje onder*.
[128] Berger, *Past as History*, 80–139.

and independent aristocratic men of letters.[129] History was written by politicians and prominent civil servants, often in exile or temporarily out of office, and historians became statesmen.[130] Not only universities, but also academies, historical associations, edited journals, and source editions provided the institutional framework for the production of historical narratives. The continuing proximity of historiography and theology, as well as classical studies, will be shown here.[131]

All my case studies, finally, consist of male authors. The omission of female authors does not, of course, imply that women did not play a crucial role in the Counter-Revolution as a movement and belief system.[132] Alicia Montoya, for instance, has stressed the importance of female authors, such as Mme de Genlis (1746–1830), in the making of a more conservative and religious 'middlebrow' Enlightenment of the eighteenth and early nineteenth centuries.[133] In the aristocratic and counter-revolutionary salons, but also at peace congresses and in diplomatic networks in this period, upper-class women were omnipresent. Moreover, one of the protagonists, Niklas Vogt, wrote a history book which specifically targeted an exclusive female audience of educators and mothers.[134]

Furthermore, gender did play a significant role in the representation of the Counter-Revolution and the European past. One of the most influential accusations that the revolutionaries levelled against their ideological opponents was their 'effeminate' lack of masculinity and the corrupting presence of aristocratic women, who allegedly betrayed the patriotic cause. The authors in this study often took 'fatherly' authority as a model of firm but tempered and 'loving' wielding of power. This fatherly authority and masculinity were deemed typical of the European Republic, unlike the autocratic power of a Robespierre, Napoleon, or 'oriental' despot. A balanced European order should have a balanced household as its foundation.[135] Race and class, moreover, did not figure explicitly in the sources I have studied, although further research on the concept of 'race' in

---

[129] On interaction of literature and historiography in the early nineteenth century: Gossmann, *Between History and Literature*; Rigney, *Afterlives of Walter Scott*; Rigney, *Imperfect Histories*; Bann, *Clothing of Clio*.

[130] Crossly, 'History as Principle of Legitimation', 49–56; Mellon, *Political Uses of History*.

[131] Berger, *Past as History*, 87.

[132] Glenda Sluga has argued for a more prominent role for women as actors and thinkers of the international order, citing the example of Mme de Staël: Sluga, 'Women and the History of International Thinking'. Cf. Sluga, *Invention of International Order*. On gender in international thought in general: Owens and Rietzler, *Women's International Thought*. Moreover, Hannah Arendt devoted a biography to the Jewish cosmopolitan intellectual and *salonnière* Rahel Varnhagen (1771–1833): Arendt, *Rahel Varnhagen*. According to Arendt, assimilation was in essence the entry of the Jews in the 'European historical world', 368.

[133] Montoya, 'Marie Leprince de Beaumont'. Cf. Montoya, 'Middlebrow, Religion, and the European Enlightenment', online: http://h-france.net/rude/wp-content/uploads/2017/08/vol7_Montoya.pdf. On the scholarly debate on gender and Enlightenment: Outram, *Enlightenment*, 84–98. On conservatism and gender: Armenteros, 'From Centre to Periphery'.

[134] See Chapter VI.   [135] Lok and Scholz, 'Return of the Loving Father'.

counter-revolutionary and counter-enlightened thought would be desirable.[136] It is clear that values such as moderation and reasonableness were overall regarded exclusively as capabilities of (Northern) European, middle-aged males.[137]

Each chapter has a different protagonist who acts as a lodestar for discussing and highlighting a specific aspect of counter-revolutionary Europeanism. Subsequently, the chapter guides are in order of appearance: the French revolutionary Nicolas de Bonneville, the former Jesuit François-Xavier de Feller from Liège, the French minister turned *émigré* Alexandre de Calonne and his acquaintance the politician Edmund Burke, the 'German Montesquieu' Adam Müller, the history professors of Mainz and Göttingen, Niklas Vogt and Arnold Heeren and, finally, the papal theorist Joseph de Maistre and the Dutch anti-revolutionary politician Groen van Prinsterer. Through these individuals, different aspects of counter-revolutionary Europeanism will be explored, without claiming that individual authors were representative of counter-revolutionary historical Europeanism in its entirety.

As becomes clear from this list, not all European geographical regions have been covered extensively and with equal weight. Ideally, separate chapters had been included on protagonists coming from the Iberian Peninsula, Southern Italy, Central and Eastern Europe or the Scandinavian countries. On the one hand, this choice is pragmatical, partly the result of the lack of specific language skills and the necessity to restrict a potentially huge and limitless research subject. But it could also be argued that exactly in this moment, new hierarchies were created, designating which countries and states belonged to the core of European history and which to the periphery. Precisely around these years, a new historiographical core was formed of the great powers in Northwestern Europe, with France, Britain, and the German lands as the main drivers of European history.[138] Generally speaking, this study does not claim to be in any way comprehensive. Many other fascinating counter-revolutionary writers, such as the Swiss statesman and political philosopher Karl Ludwig von Haller (1768–1854) or the Spanish diplomat Juan Donoso Cortés (1809–53), could have been given their own chapter, but the book would have become too voluminous and the core argument would not fundamentally change by adding more case studies.

The study starts in the years preceding the Revolution, around 1780, when widespread worries about Europe's decline and corruption increasingly came to the fore. The main part of the book deals with the decades around 1800, when the disruptive revolutionary and Napoleonic wars made dealing with the problem of

---

[136] On the relation of race and religion: Kidd, *Forging of Races*. On the relation of race and the key concept of freedom: Stovall, *White Freedom*.
[137] See more extensively: de Haan and Lok, 'Introduction'. On race and the Enlightenment: Outram, *Enlightenment*, 67–83; Vartija, 'Colour of Equality'; Sebastiani, *Scottish Enlightenment*.
[138] On this problem of European historiographical hierarchies: Baár, *Historians and Nationalism*; Rodríguez Pérez, 'Being Eurocentric'; Drace-Francis, 'The Elephant on the Doorstep?'.

European order and history particularly urgent. The 1820s and 1830s, when the disillusion with the ability of the Vienna conference and the Restoration to truly regenerate and remoralize European civilization had set in, form the final years studied in depth, although the final chapter discusses some of the long-term legacies in the nineteenth and twentieth centuries. The chapters in this book are such that they could be divided into three parts. In the first part (Chapters 2–4) mainly francophone sources in the 1780s and 1790s, the years preceding and following the French Revolution, will be explored. The second part (Chapters 5–7) mostly deal with German-speaking writers, primarily, but not exclusively, from 1800 onwards. In the third and final part (Chapters 8–9) the Congress of Vienna as a failed moment of European renewal, the years 1815–20 and beyond, will be described and a cursory overview will be given of historical Europeanism in later centuries.

2
An Unfinished History

1. A Cosmopolitan Revolutionary

In 1789, the first year of the Revolution in France, the curious revolutionary Nicolas de Bonneville (1760–1828) published two volumes of his *Histoire de l'Europe Moderne*.[1] As he wrote in the introduction, the extraordinary events in France had made all existing history writing obsolete. As a result of the unprecedented political turning point he was experiencing, he realized that new books needed to be written which explained history from a revolutionary point of view. His new 'modern European history' consisted of a narrative of unfolding freedom, as well as of the failed attempts by its enemies, mainly Catholic clergy, to halt this development. The apotheosis of his historical narrative was evidently the unfolding of the Revolution in France in 1789, when freedom, reason, and light finally triumphed over superstition and despotic obscurantism.[2] Rather than summarize the histories of individual European states, Bonneville attempted in his *History* to capture 'the European spirit' in every century. This spirit could be distilled from the different national historiographies. His aim was to write a true 'European history', with his native France at centre stage.

Bonneville also wrote that his history books were intended for the education of children and young adults, who needed to be taught the importance of revolutionary values and ideas such as freedom, tolerance, the social contract, and natural law. Bonneville, however, did not write an entire new history from scratch. To a large extent his work was a translation of the English *History of Modern Europe* published between 1779 and 1786 by the enlightened Scottish historian William Russell (1741–93).[3] As Bonneville explained in his introduction, it had been necessary to adapt Russell's Scottish work for French audiences.[4]

Like other protagonists featured in this book, Bonneville's life was determined by the political events that occurred after the outbreak of the French Revolution. Bonneville was born in 1760 in Evreux (Normandy) as the son of a procurator. He left his home town after a scandal surrounding his enthusiastic views on the controversial works of Rousseau, and went to Paris to study linguistics and foreign

---

[1] Bonneville, *Histoire* I–II. [2] Bonneville, *Histoire* I, 33–4.
[3] [Anonymous, by William Russell], *History of Modern Europe*. Three further volumes, with the author's name, appeared in 1784, and the whole work was published in five volumes in 1786.
[4] Bonneville, *Histoire* I, 43–4.

Europe against Revolution: Conservatism, Enlightenment, and the Making of the Past. Matthijs Lok, Oxford University Press.
© Matthijs Lok 2023. DOI: 10.1093/oso/9780198872139.003.0003

languages with the financial support of the *philosophe* d'Alembert.[5] In Paris, he lived in a cosmopolitan and multilingual environment, regularly meeting Americans, Englishmen, and Germans, and conversing with them in English and German. In the 1780s, Bonneville worked as a translator of German theatre pieces and novels by Goethe and Schiller, among others.[6] In 1786, he travelled to England, where he became a member of a London Freemasons lodge and became acquainted with the work of Russell. While in England, Bonneville published a work on the supposed infiltration of Freemasonry by the Jesuit order. In 1788, on the eve of the revolution that would transform Europe and Bonneville's life, he returned to France.

In 1789, Bonneville immersed himself in revolutionary activities. He became an elector of the city of Paris, charged with provisions. In this capacity he proposed the formation of a Parisian '*garde bourgeoise*'. He conducted all kinds of activities, such as the publication of the journal *Le Tribun du Peuple*, with the aid of Mirabeau. In 1790, he established the *Cercle social*, a revolutionary forum that aimed to be an inclusive and open revolutionary society, in contrast to the more closed and exclusive revolutionary clubs such as those of the Jacobins.[7] In the organ of the *Cercle social*, *Bouche de Fer*, cosmopolitan ideals such as universal democracy and fraternity and the abolition of all states were voiced, until its publication was halted in 1791. Bonneville clearly was an exponent of early revolutionary cosmopolitanism, which was rejected as the revolution radicalized.[8] In 1791, Bonneville's magnum opus *De l'esprit des religions* was published with considerable success. After the closure of the *Cercle social* in 1791, Bonneville worked for several journals associated with the Girondins. He firmly believed that writers should play a leading part in the social and political transformations of his time.

After 1792, his life took a downward turn due to the political developments in France. During the Terror, Bonneville, under suspicion as a cosmopolitan Girondin, narrowly escaped the guillotine and probably returned to his native Normandy. Under Napoleon, Bonneville was suspected of oppositional activities and criticism of Napoleon. He was accused of comparing Napoleon to the English dictator Cromwell and was kept under strict police surveillance. In 1800, his printing press was confiscated by the authorities, precipitating his financial ruin, and he was charged with having translated Thomas Paine's proscribed publication *Maritime Pact*. In 1815, after the restoration of the Bourbons as kings of France, which did not bode well for him either, the former revolutionary emigrated to the United States. His wife and children had already been living there since 1802, with

---

[5] On Bonneville and Rousseau: Werner, 'Geschichtsauffassung', 225.
[6] Bonneville, *Le nouveau Théâtre allemand*; Bonneville, *Essais*.
[7] Furet, *Bonneville*; Brasart, 'Bonneville et le cercle social'; Moore, 'Poetry'; Kates, '*Cercle Social*'.
[8] Van de Heuvel, 'Cosmopolite', 9–49.

the aid of Bonneville's friend Thomas Paine, evidence of the extent of his international network. In 1819, Bonneville returned to Paris where he earned a meagre living in a bookshop until his death in 1828. In his final years he was apparently 'half mad' and suffered great financial difficulties. The heyday of Bonneville's cosmopolitan and revolutionary life was no doubt the first half of the revolutionary decade, the moderate first phase, when he also published most of his works. In the hostile political climate of the Napoleonic Empire and, subsequently, the Restoration monarchy, Bonneville became a peripheral person, 'a fire extinguished by misery and disease'.[9] Fortunes, however, revived for his son, Benjamin, who eventually became a general in the United States Army.

Most publications focus on Bonneville's revolutionary and literary activities and pay less attention to Bonneville as a historian of modern Europe.[10] Philippe Le Harivel defined Bonneville in his biography essentially as a 'pre-romantic' and as a freedom-loving revolutionary.[11] In her dissertation on Bonneville of 1981, the literary scholar Susanne Kleinert reassessed Le Harivel's interpretation. She argued that Le Harivel placed too much emphasis on Bonneville as an Enlightenment author. In her view Le Harivel did not sufficiently underscore the mystical and esoteric aspects of Bonneville's thought or show due appreciation for the diversity of his writings. Kleinert also highlighted the associative, opaque, and sometimes inconsistent character of Bonneville's works.[12] As we will see, the combination of enlightened history writing and the mystical yearning for spiritual renewal was not unique to Bonneville, but can be considered a typical feature of most European history writing in this period.

The aim of this chapter is fivefold. Firstly, I will sketch the construction of a canon of 'European historians' in the eighteenth century, as well as an enlightened narrative of European history. Secondly, I will demonstrate how this historical narrative and the notion of 'modern Europe' was adapted by Bonneville in 1789 for revolutionary purposes, showing the political malleability and politicization of enlightened historiography in the revolutionary decade. Thirdly, I will describe how the attempt to write a new revolutionary history of Europe, the narrative of Europe *for* the Revolution, was smothered by the political climate of the Terror. Fourthly, I will briefly discuss the revolutionary ideology, which so many counter-revolutionaries, who will be discussed in subsequent chapters, vocally objected to, but at the same time also silently, to a certain extent, copied. Fifthly, I will point to

---

[9] Cited in Le Harivel, *Bonneville*, 15.   [10] An exception is: Werner, 'Geschichtsauffassung'.

[11] 'Grand apôtre de la Révolution, ennemi de toute servitude comme de tout excès, il employa son talent à secourir ses contemporaines et à leur prêcher les principes de l'amour, de la liberté et de l'égalité.' Le Harivel, *Bonneville*, viii.

[12] For Kleinert, 'Bonneville steht zwischen Aufklärung und Romantik, allerdings nicht so, als könnte man ihn quasi als eine Mischung aus Voltaire und Chateaubriand erklären: er hat die verscheidenden Einflüsse zu einem eigenwilligen und selbständigen, wenn auch nicht geschlossenen Gedankengebäude verarbeitet.' Kleinert, *Bonneville*, 12–13. For Bonneville as a representative of the 'Super-Enlightenment', Moore, 'Poetry'.

the similarities between the interpretation of European history by revolutionaries and counter-revolutionaries alike, for instance related to the ideas of European freedom, pluralism. or moral and spiritual regeneration. These similarities are perhaps not surprising as authors from different political persuasions drew upon the same enlightened sources, as will be demonstrated in the next chapters. I have thus not selected Bonneville here to underscore his unique role in the French Revolution or to argue for the long-lasting influence of his work, but to explore the vagaries of European history writing in the revolutionary decade through the lens of his life and works.

The chapter title 'an unfinished history' can be interpreted in two ways. To begin with, as this book will demonstrate, the enlightened narrative did not end in the revolutionary decade but was adapted and used by publicists in the succeeding decades. Moreover, Bonneville's project of writing a *magnum opus* on European history would remain incomplete, which was perhaps exemplary of the fate of the revolutionary tradition of European and cosmopolitan history writing during the Terror. Instead, the project of writing a European history would be left to the self-proclaimed enemies of the revolutionary ideals.[13]

2. The Enlightenment and the Past

Historians have only relatively recently become interested in the relationship between the Enlightenment and the past. Following the critical verdict of nineteenth-century romantic historians, eighteenth-century historiographical writings were not valued for most of the twentieth century. Science and rational philosophy were supposed to be the hallmarks of the Enlightenment era, not history writing. The eighteenth century was seen, according to the romantic cliché, as a predominantly forward-looking and ahistorical age, obsessed with the idea of 'progress'. The development of a modern historical awareness in Europe was therefore long understood as a result of the rupture of the French Revolution and was usually situated in the romantic and historicist history writing of the early nineteenth century.[14] The ahistorical perspective of the Enlightenment contrasted, however, with the views of noted contemporaries: David Hume famously termed the eighteenth century as 'the historical age', and the German author Friedrich Nicolai wrote that 'history is carrying the torch of the Enlightenment'.[15]

Since the late 1970s, this ahistorical interpretation has been questioned, and the crucial role of the writings of eighteenth-century Enlightenment in historical

---

[13] See Chapter 9 for liberal variations of historical Europeanism.
[14] Fritzsche, *Stranded in the Present.* Cf. Berger, *Past as History*, 43.
[15] Cited in Berger, *Past as History*, 43.

thought has been more fully acknowledged.[16] Also, the supposed break between enlightened, on the one hand, and romantic and historicist, on the other, history writing has been nuanced. The extent to which, for instance, the historical work of the nineteenth-century historian Leopold von Ranke (1795–1886), 'alleged historicist father of modern history', was still very much indebted to enlightened historiographical traditions is now visible.[17] This study can be considered part of a, still ongoing, re-evaluation of the importance of enlightened historiography and its legacies from the, so far undervalued, counter-revolutionary perspective.[18] Part of this re-evaluation involves renewed attention to lesser-known authors, in line with the contextual approach of the Cambridge school sketched earlier.[19] In this chapter, we will examine the works of Bonneville, an author who is less known in his capacity of historian, as well as those of William Russell in the context of the formation of a canon of the authoritative historians of Europe.

However, we should take care not to overemphasize the 'modern' aspects of enlightened historiography: eighteenth-century historical thought was in many ways different from 'modern' historiographical practices.[20] Classical history, for instance, continued to have great relevance for enlightened historians. The outcome of the *Querelle des anciens et modernes* is no longer regarded as an unambiguous victory for the moderns.[21] As we shall see, for instance, in the next chapter, it would also be incorrect to state that providential and sacred history writing was simply set aside by more secular forms of historiography in the eighteenth century. Much enlightened European history writing, including that of Bonneville, contained an—often ignored—religious and providential aspect. Late eighteenth-century *anti-philosophes* such as François-Xavier de Feller, furthermore, attempted to revive the European historical narratives based on the Holy Writ by the seventeenth-century Bishop Bossuet and other Catholic historians as part of their struggle against the pernicious 'spirit of the age'.[22]

French scholars Antoine Lilti and Céline Spector, among others, have argued that during the enlightened eighteenth century, 'Europe' was conceived for the first time as a historical continent and a comprehensive European historical

---

[16] Bourgault and Sparling, 'Introduction', 1–22; Velema, 'Introduction: Enlightenment and the Past', 7–26; Berger, *Past as History*, 43–79; An older study is: Bödeker et al., *Aufklärung und Geschichte*. A pioneering work is: Reill, *German Enlightenment*.

[17] Iggers and Powell wrote in 1990 that 'it is significant that Leopold von Ranke, who was born in 1795 and whose work spanned much of the nineteenth century, had deep roots in the religious and intellectual world of the eighteenth century.' Iggers and Powell, *Leopold von Ranke*, 14.

[18] An exception for the Dutch context is: Boom, 'Against Enlightened Abstraction'.

[19] Velema, 'Introduction: Enlightenment and the Past', 43.

[20] De la Porte, 'History beyond the Nation'; Rotmans, 'Circles of Desire'. Rotmans underscored the 'pessimistic' character of Dutch Enlightened historiography: Rotmans, 'Enlightened Pessimism'.

[21] Edelstein, *Enlightenment*; Norman, *Shock of the Ancient*; Velema, *Omstreden Oudheid*; Raat, Velema and Baar-de Weerdt, *Oudheid in de Achttiende eeuw*.

[22] Griggs, 'Universal History', 219–47.

narrative was crafted.[23] The enlightened 'European civil society' of the eighteenth century formed, in their view, a new phenomenon marked by a rupture with the humanistic republic of letters.[24] In the eighteenth century, 'Europe' became the object of philosophical enquiry and knowledge as well as a historical narrative.[25] A crucial text in the crafting of this 'enlightened narrative' was, according to Lilti and Spector, Montesquieu's *L'Esprit des Lois*, the 'matrix of the enlightened reflection on Europe'. This text was read and cited by both *philosophes* and *antiphilosophes*, as well as by revolutionaries and their opponents.[26] The counterrevolutionary works studied here confirm the central role of Montesquieu's work, as well as the conservative interpretation of his ideas in the post-revolutionary decades.[27]

Enlightenment authors overall produced a history of European civilization as a narrative of the progress of society from the dynamic barbarism of the early Middle Ages to the advanced commercial and urban societies in the Northwestern Europe of the late eighteenth century. At the same time, *philosophes* usually did not directly debate Europe's essence: 'Europe' was often indirectly defined in contemporary debates on related topics such as the dream of attaining perpetual peace, the law of nations, universal history, the advantages of international trade, imperialism, and cultural progress. The central concept in all these histories is the notion of 'civilization', first coined in 1756 by Mirabeau in his *L'ami des hommes* (1756) and in English in 1767 by Adam Ferguson. 'Civilization' was a dynamic concept indicating a process: Europe was framed by the *philosophes* in terms of permanent historical change and continuing progress.[28]

Enlightened historians did not invent European history from scratch but could build on older humanist historiography. The origins of the 'idea of European history' could be found in the Italian Renaissance.[29] Italian political history was analysed by early sixteenth-century historians in a broader European context. Already in the dedication of his *Brief Account of Italian History* (from 1511 to 1527) Francesco Vettori (1474–1539) wrote: 'the historical events of our times are so closely bound together that you cannot speak of those of Italy alone and omit all other'.[30] The *History of Italy*, written in the 1530s and published in 1561 by the

---

[23] See for 'Enlightenment narrative' also: Pocock, *Barbarism and Religion II*.
[24] According to Lilti and Spector, the concept of Europe in the eighteenth century had three meanings: an institutional federal project to attain 'eternal peace', Europe as a market and trading place for 'commerce', and finally the notion of a 'European civilization'. Lilti and Spector, 'Introduction: l'Europe des Lumières', 1–9.
[25] Lilti, 'La civilisation est-elle européenne?', 142. For a similar argument: Pocock, *Barbarism and Religion* II.
[26] Lilti and Spector, 'Introduction: l'Europe des Lumières', 9.
[27] See also for a 'conservative' interpretation of Montesquieu: de Dijn, *Liberty in a Levelled Society?*
[28] Den Boer, 'Comparative History of Concepts'.
[29] Burke, 'Did Europe Exist before 1700?', 21–9; Hale, *Civilisation of Europe*; Wintle, *Image of Europe*.
[30] Cited in Hale, *Civilisation of Europe*, 37.

internationally oriented papal administrator Francesco Guicciardini (1483–1540), reached far into Europe and even into the New World to explain the effects of foreign invasion on the peninsula. Guicciardini's history was also read by a European audience as the book was translated into Latin, French, German, Dutch, Spanish, and English.

In the mid-sixteenth century a number of historiographical books appeared in Italy with 'Europe' in the title: Lodovico Guicciardini's *Commentary on the Most Notable Events in Europe* (1566), Pier Francesco Giambullari's *History of Europe* (1566), and Alfonso Ulloa's *The History of Europe* (1570).[31] Giambullari's posthumously published work deals only with the early Middle Ages, Guicciardini's book primarily concerned the Netherlands, and Ulloa's history mainly consisted of a series of political and military events.[32] However, it was increasingly acknowledged that the history of individual countries was bound up with that of others. Also, the late-humanist universal histories published in the late seventeenth and early eighteenth centuries contained narratives of European history and, to a certain extent, can be regarded as precursors of enlightened eighteenth-century historiographical tradition. The notion of a strict rupture between late-humanist and enlightened historiography, as put forward by Spector and Lilti, must therefore be nuanced. This humanist legacy, however, was usually not acknowledged by eighteenth-century authors, who, like the romantic authors who succeeded them, strongly distanced themselves from their predecessors.[33]

In the eighteenth century, however, a new reading of European history as the transition from medieval and feudal to modern, commercial social systems was shared in these enlightened histories, notwithstanding their differences.[34] European history was clearly demarcated from ancient history. The beginnings of European history were traced to the early Middle Ages after the collapse of the Roman Empire. A new central role was given to the 'Middle Ages', as an era characterized by superstition and oppression but by creative development as well.[35] In the High Middle Ages, feudalism became undermined by the development of cities, trades, states, education, and knowledge. The Catholic Church was analysed less from a polemical religious perspective, as had been done during the Wars of Religion, but more neutrally as an important historical actor in European history. For Voltaire and Robertson, as well as for the authors in this study, the sixteenth century, in particular, formed an important moment in the making of

---

[31] As John Hale has observed, 'these books cannot be considered integrated histories of Europe as they appeared on the map'. Hale, *Civilisation of Europe*, 37.

[32] On Giambullari: Dionisotti, *Europe in Sixteenth Century Literature*, 13–15.

[33] Pocock, *Barbarism and Religion* II, 1–25; Grafton, *What Was History?*; Clark, 'Dividing Time'; Grell, *L'histoire entre érudition et philosophie*; Bos, 'Historical Thought'.

[34] According to English literary scholar Karen O'Brien, a salient characteristic of the Enlightenment was 'the elaboration of a common descriptive model for the history of Europe through separately periodised ancient, medieval, early modern and enlightened modern stages'. O'Brien, *Narratives*, 11.

[35] Raedts, *ontdekking van de Middeleeuwen*.

modern Europe. This century witnessed the rise of a dynamic and pluralist European state system consisting of strong monarchies. The final stage of European history, according to these prominent Enlightenment historians, was the coming of modern societies in which commerce had refined manners and brought prosperity and freedom to an increasing number of people.[36]

A key source of inspiration for eighteenth-century 'philosophical history' was, in addition to Montesquieu's *Spirit of the Laws*, Voltaire's *Essai sur les Moeurs* (1756). Voltaire's history formed a crucial reference work for other enlightened historians of Europe: historians, such as Bonneville, commented positively, as well as critically, on this work.[37] In Voltaire's *Essai* European history had two essential characteristics: firstly, the development of a European state system and, secondly, the progress of civilization ('*moeurs*') from the early Middle Ages onwards. Already in the sixteenth century, conditions were created that would propel the cumulative development of modern European civilization: the decline of feudalism and the political role of the papacy, the balance of power among the great monarchies, the rise of commerce, and the refinement of the arts.[38]

Voltaire's work was a deliberate departure from the providential universal histories written in the Christian tradition, above all Bossuet's influential *Discours sur l'histoire universel* (1672).[39] In contrast to Bossuet, Voltaire put the supposed uniqueness of Christian Europe into global perspective by starting his *Essai* with Chinese history. The Enlightenment histories following Voltaire's model could, consequently, be considered a departure from traditional Christian historiography, in their questioning of the centrality of biblical and European history and opting for a 'universal history'. This type of Enlightenment history tended towards 'world history', as it aimed to understand the experience of all mankind in history.[40] However, the Eurocentric dimension of Voltaire's work should not be overlooked: most of the pages of Voltaire's *Essai* were devoted to European history. Moreover, he assumed the superiority and uniqueness of European civilization over all others, only citing different arguments from those chosen by Bossuet, such as progress and even race. Non-European societies were analysed by Voltaire to allow him to contrast their stagnation and lack of development with European dynamism. Voltaire's *Essai* can therefore be interpreted both as an enlightened criticism of the older Christian inspired historiography and as a new confirmation of its European bias by other means.[41]

---

[36] O'Brien, *Narratives*, 11–12.

[37] Voltaire started working on his 'general history' in 1741, and he published a first edition in 1756 to correct a pirated edition of 1753. Revised editions were published in 1768 and 1775 under the title of '*Essai sur les moeurs et esprit des nations*'. The edition of 1785 contains the last corrections by Voltaire. Lilti, 'La civilisation est-elle européenne?', 144; Pierse, 'Voltaire', 153–87.

[38] Lilti, 'La civilisation est-elle européenne?', 144–5.   [39] See also Chapter 3.

[40] Berger, *Past as History*, 46.   [41] Lilti, 'La civilisation est-elle européenne?', 156.

The extent to which enlightened history was 'national' in character is a matter of some debate. Karen O'Brien has underscored the European and 'cosmopolitan' dimension of eighteenth-century historiography. Stefan Berger and others, by contrast, have argued that much of the so-called universal history can in fact be reduced to national history, and then predominantly the national history of the 'main' nations. According to the German August Ludwig von Schlözer, for instance, only the 'main peoples' (*hauptvölker*) were the proper subject of history. His colleague at Göttingen, Johann Christoph Gatterer (1727–99) argued in his handbook of universal history of 1761 that the origins of nations were the true beginning of world history. Also, much history writing in the eighteenth century took the 'nation' as its main perspective: most universal ideals of progress and civility were nationally inflected.[42] In any case, the boundaries between national, regional, European, and universal history writing were fluid. Like the important Scottish historian William Robertson (1721–93), Voltaire started out as a 'national' historian: Voltaire published a history of Louis XIV, Robertson a history of Scotland. Then Voltaire published his famous *Essai* and Robertson his history of Europe during the reign of Charles V. Finally, both authors turned to colonial, imperial, and overseas histories. Robertson's *History of the Americas* (1777) was, for instance, a corollary of his work on European history.[43] In the eighteenth century, to sum up, the lines between world, European, and national history writing were porous.[44]

3. A Canon of European Historians

European history writing, however, cannot be reduced to solely national or universal history. In the eighteenth century a clearly demarcated transnational canon of historians of Europe came into being as part of the crafting of the enlightened narrative.[45] This process can be illustrated by Bonneville's 'Notice on the principal historians who have written on European affairs'. In this notice Bonneville discussed the merits, and especially the flaws, of the existing French, German, and British histories of Europe. By dwelling on the alleged shortcomings of the older works, he provided a justification for the publication of his own work on European history. This preliminary note was attached as an introductory essay

---

[42] Berger, *Past as History*, 47. Cf. Jensen, *Roots of Nationalism*.   [43] Smitten, 'Robertson'.
[44] See for the Dutch case: De La Porte, 'Verlichte Verhalen'.
[45] It would be worthwhile to quantitatively study the dissemination of histories of Europe in the European libraries. Alicia Montoya of Radboud University Nijmegen is currently undertaking a digital quantitative research project called 'Mediate', funded by the ERC, of the books read in the eighteenth century, examining auction catalogues among other sources. Unfortunately, the database was not sufficiently completed to allow for drawing conclusions regarding the dissemination of 'modern European histories' for this study. I thank her and Juliette Reboul, nonetheless, for giving me access to this fascinating and useful database in progress.

to his *History of Modern Europe* and was, to a large extent, based on Bonneville's earlier *Letter to Condorcet* of 1787, written during his stay in London.[46]

Bonneville credited the late seventeenth-century German scholar Samuel von Pufendorf (1632–94) with being the first 'historian of Modern Europe'.[47] Bonneville praised him for his 'immense erudition', eye for detail, and precision, but at the same time lambasted Pufendorf for his fondness of details, pedantry, and lack of a larger narrative.[48] His European history writing, in Bonneville's eyes, lacked 'grandeur' and should therefore be regarded primarily as a reference work ('*des secours prépares*') for those who have the ambition to write a true European history, such as Bonneville himself.[49] Voltaire's *Essai sur les moeurs*, in Bonneville's eyes, in many ways corrected the flaws of Pufendorf and put 'colour' and flesh on Pufendorf's bare 'skeleton'. Voltaire rightly paid attention to the character ('*moeurs*') of the European people and did not focus only on events, as had Pufendorf.

Voltaire, however, was also far from perfect in the eyes of the critical Bonneville: the great *philosophe* had made factual errors and, according to Bonneville, was far too positive about the absolutist kings of France, not shying away from 'deifying a despot'.[50] Bonneville described Voltaire's *Essai* for this reason as little more than a 'sad philosophical novel' (*un triste roman philosophique*).[51] Nonetheless, Voltaire's writings should also be regarded in the context of his age, Bonneville continued to write in a more understanding vein.[52] In essence, Voltaire was a 'friend of humanity' (*véritable ami de l'humanité*), siding with the right moral side of history. He should therefore be honoured for his struggle against the irrational 'fanaticism' of the Catholic Church. Above all, Voltaire's history was valued by Bonneville for its literary style as it taught the 'art of narrating with elegance and precision'.[53] So, in this historiographical introduction, Pufendorf and Voltaire were, on the one hand, praised by Bonneville, as precursors and 'fathers' of European history writing and, on the other, dismissed as flawed and outdated.

Bonneville, subsequently, mentioned—briefly and often derogatorily—the competing contemporary historical works of his French compatriots the

---

[46] Bonneville, 'Notice'. The notice was also integrally inserted at the start of the first volume of Bonneville's *Histoire*.
[47] Pufendorf, *Historie der vornehmsten Reiche*.
[48] 'On marche toujours et l'on n'avance point dans ces histoires confuses.' Bonneville, 'Notice', 6.
[49] Bonneville, 'Notice', 6.
[50] 'L'ouvrage n'est point perfectionné. Voltaire, en son Histoire générale, est plein de caprices, et, qui le croiroit, de préjugés!' Bonneville, 'Notice', 8, 10.
[51] Bonneville, 'Notice', 11.
[52] 'Ses fautes, en cette Histoire, sont grandes, mais ce sont les fautes de son siècle, d'un siècle qui n'etoit pas mûr pour la vérité.' Bonneville, 'Notice', 8.
[53] Bonneville, 'Notice', 12, 14.

Chevalier de Méhégan, the Abbé Millot, and the Abbé de Condillac.[54] Bonneville, overall, rejected these works for being judgemental or unsuitable for pedagogical purposes.[55] He blamed Méhégan, the author of *Tableau de l'Europe modern* (3 vol. 1766), for imitating the style of Bossuet (1627–1704), the bishop in the service of Louis XIV. It was the historian's responsibility to 'preserve reason', and Bossuet had only tried to destroy reason and to dictate cruel prejudices in the name of eternal providence, Bonneville wrote damningly.[56] The *Cours d'études* by the Abbé de Condillac, were motivated by '*bons principes*', but written without passion or love, and too much intended for a young prince and not for the children of the nation as whole.[57] Bonneville, subsequently, dismissed the popular pedagogical work of 'J.M. Schroekh' (Johann Matthias Schröckh, 1733–1808). His history allegedly consisted of no more than a mere collection of the histories of different countries, only of use for a German readership.[58] Bonneville, moreover, blamed Schroekh for not sufficiently praising the freedom-loving and religious practices of the Germanic tribes, 'our ancestors', and for not denouncing sufficiently the corrupting influence of the Catholic clergy.[59] For these reasons, Bonneville deemed Schroekh's six-volume work, *Algemeine Welt-Geschichte für Kinder* not suitable, at least not for French children in a revolutionary society.

Bonneville's essay provides insight into the construction of hierarchies between historiographical centres and peripheries.[60] Bonneville mentioned in his text only German, French, and British sources, leaving out all other national or linguistic traditions. Only historians from these three particular 'leading' nations, apparently, had, according to Bonneville, the authority to make decisions regarding what belonged to 'European history' and what did not. This emphasis on these three traditions presented a marked contrast with, for instance, the Italian dominance regarding European history writing in the Renaissance, but also the prevalence of Spanish and Dutch humanist scholarship in earlier centuries, let alone historians from Central, Eastern, or Northern Europe. Also, apologetic Catholic historians were, not surprisingly in view of his anticlericalism, mostly absent from Bonneville's overview or viewed only pejoratively. Bonneville devoted, for instance, only a few and very critical words to the influential universal history of the French bishop Bossuet, expelling providential and explicitly Catholic histories to the historiographical periphery.[61]

---

[54] 'S'il manquoit d'enthousiasme et de génie, comment peindroit-il, pour l'exemple des siècles futurs, les actions toutes divines des amis de l'humanité?' Bonneville, 'Notice', 16.
[55] Bonneville, 'Notice', 14–19.   [56] Bonneville, 'Notice', 15.
[57] Bonneville, 'Notice', 18–19.
[58] 'Ce n'est pas à un étranger à trouver mauvais un style qui plaît aux nationaux; mais en comparant le style de M. Schroekh, avec celui de nos bons ecrivains, il y a, j'ose le dire, une disparité prodigieuse: peu de création, presque point d'abandon, à peine quelques images quie aient de la fraîcheur.' Bonneville, 'Notice', 20. Schroekh, *Allgemeine Welt-Geschichte*.
[59] Bonneville, 'Notice', 22.
[60] On the problem of historiographical 'peripheries': Baár, *Historians and Nationalism*, 1–18.
[61] Bonneville, 'Notice', 15.

Bonneville ended his historiographical essay with an examination of the European history he valued most: the five-volume *History of Modern Europe* by the Scottish historian William Russell, published in the years preceding the Revolution for the benefit of educating 'young noblemen and gentlemen'.[62] To my knowledge Russell's work of 1779 was the first book ever entitled 'History of Modern Europe', instead of just 'History of Europe', a title already used in sixteenth-century Italy, as has been noted earlier. Bonneville's history started out as a simple translation of Russell's work, at the request of his publisher Durand, when he was residing in London. Bonneville praised Russell for finding a 'medium' between the 'dry chronological method' of Pufendorf and the 'desultory but captivating manner' of Voltaire.[63] Bonneville, moreover, highly estimated Russell's 'clarity, style, precision, elegance'.[64] Bonneville appreciated, in particular, the fact that Russell not only described the events, but also analysed the general 'progress of the arts and civilization' in every epoch of the European past, as he also intended to undertake. It had therefore not come as a surprise that Russell's history had received great acclaim in England in the 1780s and was now used in all prestigious public schools, such as Eton and Exeter.[65]

Despite his apparent popularity in the eighteenth and nineteenth centuries, even outside Britain, surprisingly few recent scholarly publications have been devoted to William Russell.[66] His work is often omitted in overviews of Scottish historiography.[67] Russell, admittedly, was not one of the most eye-catching members of the Scottish Enlightenment. He studied writing and arithmetic for ten months in Edinburgh in 1756, before becoming an apprentice of a bookselling and printing firm in that same city. In 1767, he left Scotland for London, in the hope of succeeding in a literary career. In the 1770s, he had some success with his literary writings and was able to make a living from his publications. He would achieve most fame as a historian. Like the more famous British enlightened historians, Russell also published histories on national and colonial themes, as well as on European history. His first work was *The History of America, from the First Discovery by Columbus to the Conclusion of the Late War* (1779). His *History of Ancient Europe, with a View of the Revolutions in Asia and Africa* (1793) consisted of a mere fragment. He was also commissioned to write a contemporary history of England, but he never started this project.[68]

Even Russell's highly praised *History of Modern Europe*, however, showed serious deficits, in Bonneville's opinion. Apart from the factual mistakes, Russell

---

[62] Russell, *History of Modern Europe*.   [63] Russell, *History of Modern Europe* I, Advertisement.

[64] 'De toutes les histoires des affaires de notre Europe, la plus utile et la plus estimée, est celle qu'on vient de publier en Angleterre.' Bonneville, 'Notice', 26.

[65] Bonneville, 'Notice', 25.

[66] On Russell's *History of Modern Europe*'s longevity as a textbook, see Peardon, *Transition*, 65.

[67] For instance: Allan, 'Identity and Innovation'. Mark Phillips briefly sketches him as a historian of manners: Phillips, *Society and Sentiment*, 152–4.

[68] Bayne, 'Russell, William (1746–1793)'.

was, in Bonneville's eyes, above all a compiler of older histories, often in erroneous translations. Russell may not have possessed genius himself, but he, according to Bonneville, reflected the genius of others such as Voltaire, Montesquieu, and the lights of the Scottish Enlightenment: Hume, Robertson, and Ferguson.[69] At the end of his discussion of Russell's work, Bonneville still had some kind words to spare for the effort and the 'zeal' of the 'compiler' Russell and the 'usefulness' of his far from perfect pedagogical history. Finally, Bonneville valued Russell for his extensive use of notes on, and references to, not primary sources but to other authorities and secondary literature, an apparent criterion of a trustworthy scholar as well as a relatively rare phenomenon in eighteenth-century European historiography.[70] Along with Russell, Bonneville's historiographical models were Montesquieu, Abbé de Mably, Gibbon, and the Scotsmen David Hume and William Robertson.

Bonneville, thus, did not set out to produce a mere translation and 'slavishly follow' Russell, as was his original assignment. In apparent agreement with his publisher Durand, he decided to adapt this work and publish the volumes under his own name, under the motto 'translating is creating'.[71] For instance, he did not publish his *History* as a series of letters to his son, the literary form Russell had chosen, which was common in the eighteenth century, but as a continuous argument in several chapters, 'in the manner of Voltaire'.[72] Bonneville's 'improvements' concerned both the style of the history and the correction of perceived errors. He also removed several alleged 'national injuries' to the French made by Russell, and thus intended to adapt and re-edit Russell's history for a French audience.[73]

This copying was justified, according to Bonneville, as the Scottish historians on whose work Russell had been able to build, had themselves, in their turn, copied the work of eminent French historians such as Montesquieu and Voltaire. Plagiarism was clearly not considered a great sin by him. As can be concluded from Bonneville's essay, the writing of history in the eighteenth century was a borderless and cosmopolitan business.[74] Bonneville's three-volume *History of Modern Europe* formed thus a perfect illustration of the 'travelling' of European historical narratives between different national traditions, prioritizing some national histories above others. Bonneville's example also showed how 'foreign'

---

[69] According to Bonneville, British historians base their work to a large extent on French authors, without acknowledging this debt, implicitly justifying Bonneville's unashamed use of Russell. Bonneville, *Histoire* I, Postscript, 43.

[70] On the development and meaning of the footnote: Grafton, *Footnote*.

[71] Bonneville, 'Notice', 29. Cf. Bonneville, *Lettre*, 45. On the topic of translation: Kontler, *Translations*.

[72] On epistolary form of Russell's *History*: Phillips, *Society and Sentiment*, 92–3.

[73] On the writing of French history before 1830: d'Auria, *French National Identity*. D'Auria does not discuss Bonneville's writings.

[74] Bonneville, 'Notice', 44.

histories were at the same time adapted to national contexts and to the taste of national audiences.[75]

Bonneville's model historian, however, is a paradoxical persona, reflecting the contrasting tendencies in Enlightenment historiography itself. On the one hand, he argued that these idealized historians should understand past events in the context of their own time.[76] He ridiculed Voltaire, for instance, for applying his prejudices to earlier times.[77] On the other hand, he dismissed historians he deemed insufficiently critical of the medieval Catholic Church. He believed, furthermore, that he had a duty, as a historian sympathetic to revolutionary ideals, to combat oppression and fanaticism in the present by analysing the European past. On certain pages Bonneville halted his historical narrative to directly address his fellow Frenchmen as Europeans and to exhort them to defend freedom and natural rights and to support the revolutionary effort against the treacherous clergy.[78] Moreover, he emphatically proclaimed that historians should be impartial and without national prejudice ('without fatherland or master'). At the same time, this cosmopolitan revolutionary apparently also felt the need to adapt his work to national audiences.[79] Finally, there was the ambivalent attitude towards historiography as a literary genre. Bonneville published novels as well as historiography. He, however, explicitly stated that he himself was not a novelist and underscored emphatically the differences between literature and history writing: only history, and not literature, was suitable for educating a new generation in times of revolution.[80]

4. Esoteric Europeanism

Bonneville's multivolume *History of Modern Europe* was originally intended as a part of a much larger project of publications. In his *Letter to Condorcet* of 1787, Bonneville set out his intention to complement his projected 'elementary history of our Europe' with a visionary essay on 'the prejudices of the Europeans'. In this essay on prejudice, he would 'open the eyes of the Europeans'.[81] Already in this pre-revolutionary text, dedicated to the anticlerical *philosophe* Condorcet, Bonneville painted a cosmopolitan and bright future for humankind, led by a

---

[75] 'Pour tâcher de rendre cette histoire moderne un peu plus le nôtre, j'aurai soin de parler toujours comme si j'écrivois en françois, d'après mes observations et mes idées, sans modestie.' Bonneville, *Lettre*, 46. Bonneville also elaborates on the problems of translation in his letter to Condorcet, Bonneville, *Lettre*, 13–15. Espagne and Werner, *Transferts*; Espagne, *transferts culturels*.

[76] 'Ne transportez pas dans son siècle des idées et des mœurs, et des espérances qui n'y étoient pas.' Bonneville, 'Notice', *Histoire* I, 9.

[77] Bonneville, *Histoire* I, 128–9.   [78] For instance: Bonneville, *Histoire* I, 332, 406.

[79] Bonneville, *Lettre*, 45. On Bonneville's cosmopolitanism: van den Heuvel, 'Cosmopolite', 9–10.

[80] Bonneville, *Histoire* I, v. Cf. Berger, *Past as History*, 43–79; Gossmann, *Between History and Literature*; Phillips, *Society and Sentiment*.

[81] Bonneville, *Lettre*, 16, 30; Werner, 'Geschichtsauffassung', 223–4.

European vanguard. Tyranny and dictatorship, the result of ignorance, would disappear in the near future. Superstition vanished when people chose to use their own judgement instead of relying on false authorities and impostors such as the Catholic clergy.[82]

In Bonneville's prophetic vision, unity and mutual understanding would eventually prevail among nations. The earth would awaken from its 'lethargic sleep' and the natural and racial equality of all men would be reinstated, including that of the Africans, Bonneville wrote hopefully.[83] A social contract beneficial to all would be established as the basis of a worldwide political community.[84] When the European nations realized their common interest, Bonneville continued, they would allow a 'man of genius' (*l'homme de genie*) to come forward to bring them happiness and prosperity and 'to devour the dark shadows where the demons hide'.[85] The 'enemies of humanity' would, in vain, try to extinguish the 'flame of reason', kindled by the likes of Voltaire, Rousseau, and d'Alembert.[86] Although he condemned atheists, he argued that they too should be tolerated and not persecuted in the future utopia.[87] The empirical evidence for the truthfulness of these prophesies was to be provided by Bonneville in his account of European history. Thus, already in the years preceding the Revolution, Bonneville pleaded for a spiritual regeneration of humankind and the restoration of liberty in Europe he believed was imminent. Also, his European history writing was closely aligned with more esoteric and religious beliefs.

For Bonneville, the Revolution of 1789 was the moment that his utopian vision would become a reality. Just as in the past large empires had suddenly and unexpectedly collapsed, the 'old regime' would disappear from the face of the earth. Kings had fallen, history had taught us, but the 'people' were eternal and just and would eventually emerge victorious.[88] Bonneville called on all Europeans to abolish or reform Europe's institutions and make them more just, free, and equal: 'the hour will come: the purified earth will no longer bring forth absolute kings, grand viziers, or priests'.[89] He was convinced that European history would eventually end happily: 'in the long run, it is always the case that the most righteous people, the most enlightened, the most attentive, the most generous

---

[82] The deceitfulness of the clergy forms also the crucial theme in Condorcet's *Esquisse d'un tableau historique des progrès de l'esprit humain*, the addressee of Bonneville's letter of 1787.

[83] Bonneville, *Lettre*, 33.

[84] Bonneville, *Lettre*, 20–30. On Bonneville's notion of progress as a synthesis of Rousseau, Voltaire, and Mably: Werner, 'Geschichtsauffassung', 227–9.

[85] Bonneville, *Lettre*, 19–20. On the Enlightenment idea of the 'genius': McMahon, *Divine Fury*, 67–112.

[86] Bonneville, *Lettre*, 36.   [87] Bonneville, 'Notice', *Histoire* I, 40.

[88] Bonneville, *Histoire* I, i–ii.

[89] 'Ce jour viendra: la terre épurée ne reproduira plus de rois absolus, ni de grands vizirs, ni de prêtres, (...).' Bonneville, *Histoire* I, 406.

will defeat tyranny and destroy superstition'.[90] With the coming of the French Revolution, according to Bonneville, the moment had finally arrived when centuries of struggle and oppression had at last ended and the original freedom of Europe would finally be restored. Bonneville thus did not interpret the Revolution of 1789 as an innovation but as a return to an older idealized past.[91]

Bonneville explained in 1789 that he planned to write a layered corpus of texts consisting of three parts. Each part was intended for a different audience. For Bonneville, insight into the mechanisms of European history was esoteric and mystical 'hidden' knowledge, to be revealed in layers to ever smaller circles of men, on the model of the Freemasons and secret societies.[92] The first part was a narrative of events in European history to be read by 'men of all classes'. This part was to become his *History of Modern Europe*.[93] The second pillar of his grand project consisted of a description of the progress made in the European 'history of the sciences and the arts', intended for the more cultivated and technical spirits. Bonneville projected, finally, a 'third part', consisting of 'a history of the human spirit in Europe'. This pillar entailed thematic essays on religion, legislation, language, commerce, and the encyclopaedia. This third and final part, summarized in a concluding essay entitled *Les pourquoi? Ou Récapitulation générale de 'histoire de notre Europe modern'*, was to be understood only by a small elite of 'sensitive and reflective human beings', virtually a new class of secular priests.[94]

Eventually, Bonneville would be able to achieve only a small part of his writing ambitions. His active participation in the revolutionary events, his membership in the *Cercle social*, and the turmoil of the revolutionary decade, as well as his habit of working on several projects at the same time, prevented the completion of most of his writing plans.[95] In the end, Bonneville published only three volumes of his incomplete political historical narrative of Europe. Although his history was supposed to cover all the centuries until 1789, he in the end did not venture beyond the Middle Ages. Of the intended second and third parts of his work, Bonneville published only the promised book on religion, *De l'esprit des religions* (1791).[96] In this rather opaque work, Bonneville combined his visionary revolutionary ideals with esoteric religion and mysticism. In the book he once again

---

[90] 'C'est toujours, à la longue, le peuple le plus juste, le plus éclairé, le plus attentif, le plus généreux, qui fait pâlir la tyrannie et terrasse la superstition.' Bonneville, Histoire I, ii.

[91] On the myth of the golden age in revolutionary republican thought: Edelstein, Terror. On the Enlightenment 'origin myth' as a means to establish an alternative tradition to the myths of Scripture and Divine-right monarchy: Edelstein, 'Super-Enlightenment', 15.

[92] On the esoteric and mystical dimension of Enlightenment thought: Edelstein, 'Super-Enlightenment', 1–34.

[93] Bonneville planned to divide his European history into four periods: (1) from the fall of the Roman Empire to the Peace of Westphalia (1648); (2) from Westphalia to the Peace of Aix-la-Chapelle (1748); (3) from 1748 to the Peace of Paris of 1763; and the (4) fourth period ended with the American independence of 1783. Bonneville, 'Notice', Histoire I, 35–6.

[94] Bonneville, 'Notice', Histoire I, 35.   [95] Werner, 'Geschichtsauffassung', 223.

[96] Bonneville, *esprit des religions*.

called for unity among the 'friends of truth' (*amis de la vérité*) and for the establishment of a universal federation of states that would end all conflict, attain perpetual peace, and celebrate the 'universal spirit of the nations'. Bonneville praised the Germanic tribes, and especially their spiritual leaders, the Druids, as the founders of European freedom and as models for the future regeneration of Europe.[97] To further promote a pan-European sense of belonging, he advocated the restoration of the medieval name of 'Franks' instead of Europeans for the inhabitants of the European continent.[98] Fighting ignorance and promoting knowledge and reason were to be his chosen means to defeat the spiritual tyranny of the priests and their helpers. In this work, he once again prophesied a spiritual regeneration of Europe under the leadership of a Christ-like genius, who would defeat the 'enemies of humanity', as part of a future renewal on a global scale.[99]

5. Modern versus Ancient History

Bonneville explicitly argued that his European history was meant to be more than a mere compilation of the history of individual countries: he believed that a new history of Europe should be written that superseded national histories. In his *History*, he aimed to capture the 'spirit (*esprit*) of Europe', in the vein of philosophical history writing. A good historian of Europe should, according to Bonneville, not only describe historical events but also have the ambition to explain the mechanisms behind them. This awareness of a deeper meaning of European history, almost in the sense of a divine revelation, can also be found in many counter-revolutionary histories of Europe. Bonneville, however, dismissed out of hand the direct intervention of providence in history, prevalent in most Catholic histories, such as the one by Bossuet, as superstitious. Instead of chronicling all individual events, Bonneville focussed on moments of political change, the revolutions, and turning points in modern European history, like the one he was personally experiencing in 1789.[100]

Bonneville did not hide the political agenda underlying his history. In the introductory notice, he stated that 'the revolutions which are going on at the moment, turn the attention of scholars towards history, a history which is so far

---

[97] Bonneville was not the only propagator of the 'Druid model' to replace Christian orthodoxy: Edelstein, 'Super-Enlightenment', 12.
[98] 'Européens, reprenez votre ancien nom de Francs, commun à tous les peuples. C'est un moyen de réunion bien doux, "presque insensible".' Bonneville, *esprit des religions*, 206.
[99] Bonneville's emphasis on the spiritual renewal of Europe seems to differ from most revolutionary imaginings of Europe, which usually entailed notions of a peaceful (con)federation of (democratic) republics based on the revolutionary and classical republican ideals: On revolutionary Europeanism: Serna, 'l'Europe, une idée nouvelle?'; Wahnich, 'L'Europe dans le discours révolutionnaire'; Jainchill, *Reimagining Politics*, 141–96; Ghervas, *Conquering Peace*; Pasture, *Imagining European Unity*, 39–44; Belissa, *Repenser l'ordre Européen*. See also Chapter 5.
[100] Bonneville, *Histoire* I, 48–9.

missing'.[101] The turning point of the revolutionary events required and even necessitated a new European history, according to Bonneville, based on the principles of natural law, toleration, and the social contract. His project of publishing a new history of Europe was his answer to what he perceived as a call from the 'voice of the people' (*la voix de tout un people*).[102] Bonneville's history provided, thus, a telling example of the close relationship between politics, especially political turning points, and the writing of European history.

Bonneville also reflected on the European focus of his historical account within the wider history of humanity. 'Europe', according to Bonneville, had been chosen as the subject of his history as this continent formed the 'main theatre of mankind'. Following Russell, Bonneville argued that the true character of 'man' was revealed on the 'European stage'.[103] Europeans were the universal humans, and European history was the essence of universal history. Bonneville, however, did not regard European history as isolated from the rest of the world, and he acknowledged the necessity sometimes to examine events in other parts of the world to get a general idea of the 'troubles in the universe'.[104] As well as demonstrating its universal character, Bonneville also, paradoxically, underscored the continent's uniqueness. Europe was different from the rest of the world, according to him, as it formed the only region on the globe where society is based on the idea of a social contract. For Bonneville, Europe therefore functioned as 'the asylum of liberty' in an overall unfree world.[105]

Bonneville's European history was not only Eurocentric, but also Francocentric, exemplifying the close relationship between French national and European history. Bonneville began his narrative with the history of the French monarchy, the 'most important monarchy' and main 'conserver of Europe', followed in rank by that of Spain. He also described the tribe of the Gauls as by far the most civilized of all Germanic tribes. From its beginnings in the early Middle Ages, the French monarchy had defended liberty and fought slavery.[106] Only in later ages had this monarchy become corrupted by power-hungry and pernicious monarchs, guided by their treacherous advisors, the Catholic clergy. The Revolution, in Bonneville's writings, was thus nothing more than an attempt to return to these pure and felicitous origins of the French state. For Bonneville, the so-called French Revolution was, in fact, a restoration of an older situation.

---

[101] 'Cependant les révolutions qui se préparoient en France, tournoient aussi les études vers l'histoire, vers une histoire qui nous manquoit.' Bonneville, 'Notice', *Histoire* I, 33–4.
[102] Bonneville, 'Notice', *Histoire* I, 33.
[103] 'L'Europe est le théâtre sur lequel on a toujours vu le vrai caractère de l'homme se déployer avec de plus grands avantages. C'est en Europe que le pacte social qui unit les fragiles individus, pour en former un corps indestructible, semble avoir atteint, dans tous les temps, un degré de force inconnu à toutes les autres parties du monde; son histoire exige donc une attention sévère.' Bonneville, *Histoire* I, 1–2.
[104] Bonneville, *Histoire* I, 3.   [105] Bonneville, *Lettre*, 22.   [106] Bonneville, *Histoire* I, 51.

Significantly, Bonneville gave his book the title *History of Modern Europe*, copying the title of Russell's work with the same title. The use of the words 'modern Europe' was, of course, not accidental but signified a specific agenda. 'Modern Europe' should not be confused with the twenty-first-century idea of modern or contemporary Europe. According to Russell and Bonneville, the history of 'Modern Europe' started with the collapse of the Roman Empire. Early and high medieval history in Bonneville's eyes was, therefore, also very much part of 'modern European history'. The concept of 'modern Europe' was, furthermore, explicitly construed by these historians against the idea of the superiority of 'ancient history' over 'modern history'.[107] In his *Letter to Condorcet*, Bonneville wrote mockingly of the 'useless' and 'outdated' ancient histories, still so often published in his own times, but unsuitable for the new generation:

> An elementary history of modern Europe is missing. We are flooded by ancient histories, in which we read [useless details such as] that the archbishop of Mainz was eaten by an army of rats and of dolls which embrace courtesans. (...) The years disappear quickly, and we lose precious time for which we can find better use, as the sage [Rousseau] has said.[108]

Bonneville approvingly quoted Voltaire who compared 'ancient history' with 'old medals' and 'modern history' with current coins: the first sat in cabinets, whereas the second circulated, to be used in commercial relations among people.[109] Bonneville also followed Voltaire's overall emphasis on the relevance of modern and contemporary history.[110] Modern history was appropriate for the new revolutionary man who preferred action and social engagement over quiet and private reflection.[111] So, the French Revolution resulted not only in a new political but also in a new historiographical world. Contemporary and modern history was to triumph over older forms of history writing, deemed reactionary and out of date. His disdain for ancient history, however, did not hinder Bonneville from

---

[107] On the '*Querelle des Anciens et des Modernes*' in eighteenth-century France: Edelstein, *Enlightenment*; Norman, *Shock of the Ancient*; Grell, *dix-huitième siècle et l'Antiquité*; Lecoq, *querelle des anciens et des modernes*.
[108] 'Une histoire élémentaire de l'Europe moderne nous manquoit. Nous sommes inondés d'histoires anciennes, dans lesquelles on trouve des Archevêques de Mayence [Mainz], mangés par des armées de rats, et des poupées qui embrassent des courtisans. Qu'un jeune homme ait une légère teinture de ces tems reculés. Les années s'envolent d'une aîle rapide: et l'on perd toutes les heures, a dit un sage, dont on pourroit faire un meilleur employ (in the original text it is 'emploi').' Bonneville, *Lettre*, 12. In a footnote, Bonneville identified the sage as the 'author of Emile' [Rousseau].
[109] Bonneville, *Lettre*, 13.
[110] Force, 'Voltaire and the Necessity of Modern History'; Lilti, 'La civilisation est-elle européenne?', 146–7.
[111] Bonneville, *Histoire* I, 2.

inserting manifold citations of classical historians such as Tacitus and Procopius, or using them as authorities on historical topics.[112]

The key moment in European history for Bonneville, following Voltaire and Robertson, was the end of the fifteenth and early sixteenth centuries. The sixteenth century did not represent a return of classical ideas, as humanist historians had argued, but instead it should be regarded as the moment a new and modern Europe was formed. Around 1500, 'Europe transformed' (*'Europe a change de face'*) and became a 'republic'. The new balance of power on which the modern republic was founded was far superior to what had existed in ancient Greece, according to Bonneville.[113] As a result of the invention and the dispersion of the printing press, the discovery of the Americas, increased communications, and the development of the arts, Europe had attained a far higher degree of perfection than was ever attained in either classical Greece or ancient Rome, Bonneville wrote confidently.

Bonneville explicitly denied that classical antiquity had left a large legacy in European culture, and above all emphasized the rupture between antiquity and modern Europe, as would many counter-revolutionary historians of Europe: 'almost nothing remains in our Europe of the laws, the morals, or the fine arts of the Romans'.[114] On the contrary, a modern and free Europe started to develop once the despotic and corrupt Roman world had collapsed.[115] Only after the fall of the (West) Roman Empire did 'the chaos of Europe' acquire a 'more solid form'.[116] Bonneville was surprisingly critical of the Roman Empire and its legacy, especially when considering the extensive uses of antiquity by the French revolutionaries.[117] For Bonneville, following Montesquieu, the civilization of the Roman Empire was false and despotic, as the Romans imposed their culture on other peoples by force. The political despotism and lack of freedom eventually corrupted Roman morals and ultimately led to the demise of the Roman Empire: 'Roman liberty' was, in fact, 'Roman despotism'.[118] Many counter-revolutionaries could not have agreed more.

Bonneville regarded the Roman Empire as the classical equivalent of the French *ancien régime* monarchy and the German tribes as predecessors of the French

---

[112] French counter-revolutionaries in response tried to appropriate ancient history for a counter-revolutionary agenda, arguing for a fusion of the classical and Catholic Christian legacies. Lok, '"berceau des muses"', 59–74.

[113] Bonneville, *Lettre*, 13. On the concept of the 'European Republic', see Chapter 6.

[114] 'Il ne resta presque rien dans notre Europe des lois, des mœurs et des beaux-arts des Romains.' Bonneville, *Histoire* I, 24–5.

[115] 'Ils établirent sur ses ruines de nouveaux gouvernements, de nouvelles mœurs; ils accomplirent la révolution la plus frappante dans l'histoire des nations.' Bonneville, *Histoire* I, 6.

[116] Bonneville, *Histoire* I, 3.

[117] Nippel, 'Images of Antiquity'; Parker, *Cult of Antiquity*; Raskolnikoff, 'adoration des Romains'; Mossé, *antiquité*.

[118] Bonneville, *Histoire* I, 6, note 2.

revolutionaries.[119] Intensely studying ancient history was therefore useless in Bonneville's eyes: ancient history has nothing to teach us except despotism and superstition. As a late contributor to the '*Querelle*' of the ancients and the moderns, Bonneville stated confidently that modern Europeans surpassed the ancient world in most respects, and would soon be superior in every way.[120] 'The history of modern Europe provides us with everything necessary to understand men and the Empires', he wrote confidently.[121] Tellingly, Bonneville devoted only a few meagre pages to ancient Greece and Rome in his history.

Underlying Bonneville's concept of 'modern European history' was, to sum up, an idea of a certain relationship between past and present.[122] For Bonneville, the present, in particular the revolutionary present, was superior to the ancient past, although he acknowledged a moment of freedom at the start of 'modern' European history after the collapse of the (West) Roman Empire.[123] The groundbreaking events of the Revolution resulted in the need for a new history of Europe. His emphasis was not on continuity and tradition, but instead on rupture, restoration, and change in history, and significantly also in history writing.[124] This distinct sense of the uniqueness and newness of 'modern Europe' and 'our modern times' (*nos temps modernes*) required a radical new history: Bonneville's mission was to fill this void.[125]

6. Germanic Liberty versus Clerical Tyranny

The central theme of the three published volumes of Bonneville's *History of Modern Europe* was the struggle of the proponents of liberty, popular sovereignty, and reason versus those who stood for ignorance, superstition, and despotism. The main culprits in Bonneville's work were the Catholic clergymen, and to far lesser extent their accomplices, the monarchs and the nobles, who assisted the

---

[119] On the liberty of the Germanic tribes in French thought: de Dijn, *Liberty in a Levelled Society?*, 11–39; Thom, *Republics, Nations and Tribes*; d'Auria, *French National Identity*.
[120] 'Pour tout homme sensible qui voudra sincèrement la méditer, avec la plus grande attention, elle doit être plus utile que le plus beau traité de morale que nous aient laissé les anciens: ces anciens qu'on admireroit sans doute un peu moins si on les connoissoit davantage: ces mêmes anciens que nous avons déjà surpassés en tant de choses essentielles, et que nous surpasserons en tout plutôt, qu'on ne pense.' Bonneville, *Lettre*, 19.
[121] 'L'histoire de notre Europe moderne fournira tout ce qui nous est nécessaire pour connoître les hommes et les empires.' Bonneville, *Histoire* I, 2.
[122] On the conceptual connection between 'Europe' and 'modernity' in the eighteenth century: Asbach, *Europa und die Moderne*.
[123] 'J'y ai réfléchi long temps, et je préfère au fond de mon cœur le siècle présent à beaucoup de siècles qui l'ont précédé.' Bonneville, *Lettre*, 31.
[124] 'Nous devons nous borner à l'histoire des révolutions mémorables, suivies des conséquences politiques ou civiles qui ont produit quelque altération dans le gouvernement ou dans les mœurs d'un peuple.' Bonneville, *Histoire* I, 49.
[125] Bonneville, *Histoire* I, 192.

Church out of short-sighted self-interest. Following Montesquieu and Boulainvilliers, Bonneville argued that freedom was originally brought to Europe by the Germanic tribes who destroyed the despotic and violent uniformity of the Roman Empire. They were effectively the founders of 'modern Europe'.[126] Bonneville's views also echoed those voiced by Mably in his *Observations sur l'histoire de France*, first published in 1765. In that work, Mably criticized the notion of the continuous existence of a French ancient constitution, underscoring the rupture with the past and the loss of freedom soon after it was introduced in France by the Franks.[127]

Bonneville wrote that the Germanic tribes 'established on the ruins [of the Roman Empire] new governments, new customs [*moeurs*]: they accomplished the most striking revolution in history'.[128] The decadent, effeminate, and cruel luxury of the Greeks and the Romans was sharply contrasted with the virtuous, manly, vigorous, and peaceful simplicity of the Germanic peoples, often referring to Tacitus's classic *Germania*.[129] In Bonneville's eyes, the Romans left almost no legacies in modern European history: the Germanic tribes started European history with a clean slate.

The collapse of the Roman Empire was a destructive as well as creative moment.[130] The virtuous Germanic tribes created early nation states and installed an early form of democracy, according to Bonneville, turning them into the forerunners of late eighteenth-century French revolutionaries. Also, the uniquely European representative and parliamentary systems, as well as 'universal liberty', were Germanic gifts to the modern Europeans. Bonneville praised the Lombard kings, for instance, for their religious toleration and respect for the freedom of conscience, not coincidentally also natural rights proclaimed by the French revolutionaries.[131] The early Saxon kings were the 'first citizens' among their fellow citizens, rather than absolutist monarchs ruling over their obedient subjects, and their executive powers were severely constricted by custom and law.[132] Slavery was outlawed by the Saxons as contrary to natural law, and their criminal

---

[126] Werner, 'Geschichtsauffassung', 336; Henri de Boulainvilliers (1656–1722) also defended the freedom of the Frankish people. For Boulainvilliers, it was primarily monarchy, and not in the first instance the clergy, that was responsible for the destruction of original freedom. De Dijn, *Liberty in a Levelled Society?*, 14–33. On Montesquieu's views on the French Constitution and the myths of German liberty: Carcassonne, *Montesquieu*.

[127] Mably, *Observations*. On Mably and the political debate on the French ancient constitution in the late eighteenth century: Baker, *Inventing the French Revolution*, 31–58. Cf. Wright, *Classical Republican*.

[128] 'Ils établirent sur ses ruines de nouveaux gouvernemens, de nouvelles mœurs; ils accomplirent la révolution la plus frappante dans l'histoire des nations.' Bonneville, *Histoire* I, 6.

[129] On the reception of Tacitus's *Germania*: Krebs, *Dangerous Book*; Leerssen, *National Thought*; Thom, *Republics*. It remains remarkable that the thesis of the Germanic origins of modern Europe, which later would become so crucial to right-wing and nationalist German history writing in the nineteenth and twentieth centuries, was championed here by an ardent French revolutionary author inspired by the Enlightenment legacy.

[130] 'Toute Europe changea de face.' Bonneville, *Histoire* I, 25.   [131] Bonneville, *Histoire* I, 95.

[132] Bonneville, *Histoire* I, 151–3.

laws were enlightened, mild, and just. The Germanic tribes, however, were eventually weakened by their internal quarrels and civil wars. Nonetheless, they left a lasting legacy of a new European order and a spirit of freedom and independence that could never entirely be suppressed by the 'obscurantists' in the centuries that were to follow.[133] Even medieval feudalism, although a deeply flawed and unjust system, never became as despotic and 'degrading to mankind' as once the Roman Empire had been.[134]

Although the Germanic tribes laid the original foundations of Europe, 'modern history' truly started for Bonneville with Charlemagne, essentially a 'French' king. Bonneville's interpretation of Charlemagne was highly ambivalent. On the one hand, *Carolus Magnus* was hailed as a bringer of civilization and material progress, restoring order after the chaos of the seventh century. On the other, Bonneville chastised him for his despotic style of government and his indulgence of the priest class. The historian mocked those writers who still lamented the collapse of the Carolingian Empire: Charlemagne had aimed for the establishment of a universal and despotic empire, on the model of Byzantium, that would have been detrimental to Europe's original freedom.[135]

In the following centuries, the papacy adopted Charlemagne's ambition of establishing a universal and centralized European monarchy. In trying to achieve this ambition, the papacy attempted to destroy Europe's liberty, corrupting the original purity of the Christian faith and early Church. Celibacy, for instance, was for Bonneville only a later creation to impress the common people by extolling the holiness and moral superiority of the clergy. The Catholic Church was, for Bonneville, the natural successor to the despotic and persecuting Roman Empire via the example of Charlemagne.[136] Bonneville explained the origins of the temporal power of the pope as emerging out of the power struggles on the Italian peninsula rather than being derived from a gift of Constantine with divine approval. Even more 'odious' than the temporal power, no different from that of any monarch, was, according to Bonneville, the hypocrisy and tyranny of the spiritual power of the Church, through which the papacy tried to enslave the minds of the Europeans more effectively than the worldly powers ever could have done. Opposite the despotic Roman clergy, Bonneville placed the mystical Germanic Druids, who were able to unite religious functions with a cult of freedom and tolerance.[137]

In contrast to his views on the Catholic Church, Bonneville's stance towards Islam was generally positive. Mohammed had established in Mecca an ideal and enlightened spiritual and temporal monarchy. He was seen by Bonneville as a

[133] Bonneville, *Histoire* I, 39. [134] Bonneville, *Histoire* I, 44.
[135] Bonneville, *Histoire* I, 167–222.
[136] Bonneville's views on universal monarchy show resemblances to Montesquieu's *Réflexions sur la monarchie universelle*.
[137] Bonneville, *Histoire* I, 286.

prince who brought enlightenment and progress to his people. Islamic rule in Spain and its high level of civilization was especially praised, and juxtaposed with the Christian rule that followed in that country. Post-Reconquista Spain, by contrast, was depicted as a violent and persecuting country dominated and oppressed by a particularly monstrous class of treacherous and deceitful priests and monks.[138]

In his narrative of events, Bonneville concentrated mainly on French, English, German, and Italian history as the national histories crucial to capturing the 'European spirit'. Scandinavia received scant attention but abundant praise as the 'source of European liberty'. Instead of ferocious and cruel warriors, the Normans, educated by the Druids, were, for Bonneville, enlightened 'deists' with civilized and tolerant manners and customs, almost the ideal modern Europeans.[139] Whereas Southern Europeans tended towards establishing a hegemonic monarchy and enslaving themselves under papal rule, the freedom-loving Germanic people of the far North, 'the temple of nature' and sanctuary of uncorrupted peoples of pure Germanic stock, fiercely defended Europe's liberty and natural rights.[140]

Eastern Europe, especially the 'backward' and decadent Byzantine Empire, the symbol of 'oriental and Asian luxe', was generally not seen by Bonneville, invoking the works of Montesquieu, as part of European history. The Byzantine Empire was believed to be even more under the sway of treacherous and plotting monks than its Western counterparts. In Byzantium, theology trumped science and reason on all fronts.[141] Bonneville thus effectively reduced 'Europe' to Latin Christianity, excluding the Orthodox and oriental Christian worlds.[142] The history of Hungary, Spain, Poland, and Sweden was discussed briefly and cursorily by him. In all the histories of these European countries the central theme for Bonneville was the struggle between tyranny and freedom, between light and darkness, and between ignorance and reason.[143]

In the second volume, Bonneville dealt with the struggle for supremacy between the pope and the emperor in the High Middle Ages, the Crusades, and even the history of the Arab world and the rise of the Turks. The Catholic clergy once again was cast in the role of fanatical evil genius, hovering in the shadows and secretly instructing the greedy and power-hungry monarchs to impose a despotic and obscurantist rule over their peoples.[144] The Crusades were interpreted by Bonneville essentially as an attempt by the papacy to establish a universal theocratic monarchy in Europe:

---

[138] Bonneville, *Histoire* I, 70–5. [139] Bonneville, *Histoire* I, 347.
[140] Bonneville, *Histoire* I, 273. [141] Bonneville, *Histoire* II, 155.
[142] Bonneville, *Histoire* I, 16. [143] Bonneville, *Histoire* I, 379–80, 399–400.
[144] 'Que la politique des prêtres a voilé de crimes! (...) Sans les conseils pervers des prêtres, il est probable qu'il n'eût point déchiré le cœur d'un bon père.' Bonneville, *Histoire* II, 223.

In the history of the crusades, one sees above all the hand of the popes, working in the shadows to achieve the project of a universal monarchy: their ambition is to construct a church on the Greek [Byzantine] model; they hope to destroy the freedom of Europe and to chain reason.[145]

The Crusades were also characterized by the worst excesses of 'fanaticism' and intolerance, as exemplified by the cruel and bloody violence committed against the Jews for no reason.[146] In contrast to most other historians of Europe of his time, and contrary to his earlier remarks on Europe's unique liberty, Bonneville argued here, inconsistently, that the differences between the histories of Europe and Asia should not be overdrawn: both continents were characterized by political fragmentation and lack of unity, resulting in endless and meaningless civil wars.[147]

Much attention was devoted to English history, which was not surprising as Bonneville's history was essentially based on work by a British historian. The Germanic and anti-Roman myth was a major theme in Russell's history. The wise and enlightened King Alfred, who ruled from 871 to 899 according to natural law principles, was credited by Bonneville with the establishment of British judicial institutions and the tempered monarchy, as well as with the foundation of British naval might. He also stimulated the arts and sciences, as well as commerce and trade. Bonneville turned the enlightened rule of Alfred into a shining example for other European rulers, including his own French king, Louis XVI. The invasion of England by the power-hungry and despotic William the Conqueror in 1066, with the blessing of the pope, was termed by the French historian a disaster for the freedom-loving Anglo-Saxons, as well as a major turning point in modern European history.[148]

In the short run, the invasion of 1066, which Bonneville generally condemned, led to a diminution of freedom and the corruption of morals as a result of the lack of liberty on the British Isles. In the long run, fortunately, in the eyes of Bonneville, the invasion resulted in the Magna Carta of 1215 and the establishment of the English representative institutions, turning England into the home of 'the freest people in the world'.[149] The English political system, originating in the early Middle Ages, consequently became a model of liberty for the whole of Europe.[150] At the end of the second volume, Bonneville cited the rights supposedly accorded to the English people by their king in the Magna Carta: no reader would have missed the similarities with the revolutionary Rights of Man of 1789.

---

[145] 'Dans l'histoire des croisades, on sent partout la main des pontifes, travaillant, dans les ténèbres, à consommer le projet d'une Monarchie universelle; ils en vouloient à l'Eglise grecque; ils voulaient anéantir la liberté de l'Europe, et enchaîner la raison.' Bonneville, *Histoire* II, 272.
[146] Bonneville, *Histoire* II, 314.   [147] Bonneville, *Histoire* II, 139.
[148] Bonneville, *Histoire* II, 105.   [149] Bonneville, *Histoire* I, 404.
[150] Bonnevillle, *Histoire* II, 299–300.

The ideals of the French Revolution were thus not described as a new or 'revolutionary' development by Bonneville, but instead as a 'restoration' of an older liberty. This original liberty was injected into European history by the Germanic tribes. European history in essence consisted for Bonneville of a perpetual struggle between those who defended freedom and progress and those who strived to undermine through ignorance and superstition. Mainly the Catholic Church and their monarchical collaborators repeatedly attempted to 'extinguish' the 'light' of reason and to return the continent again to the 'shadows'.[151] Nineteenth-century historians such as Guizot would revisit this 'conservative' interpretation of the French Revolution not as a rupture in time, but as a return to an original free state that had become corrupted by the enemies of liberty.[152]

7. Perjuring Kings

The third and last, and also not coincidently by far the shortest, volume of Bonneville's incomplete *History of Modern Europe* was published three years later, in 1792. In the meantime, France had become a republic in a climate of war, radicalization, and increasing suspicion of counter-revolutionary plots. The language of optimistic cosmopolitanism of the early years, perfectly embodied by Bonneville, had been gradually replaced by a militant patriotism and grim discourse of martyrdom for the *patrie* in danger. The differences between the political circumstances in 1789 and 'Year I of the [revolutionary] Republic' (1792) could be clearly observed in the opaque introduction to this third volume. In this preliminary essay, entitled 'kings who commit perjury' (*les rois parjurés*), Bonneville wrote that he rejoiced that the French kings, 'who had committed perjury for over eight hundred years', had now fallen from their throne. These kings should be dealt with mercilessly, Bonneville advocated, otherwise another tyrant would rise to snatch away the freedom of the people.[153] The only sovereign left in 1792 was the nation: the national will was the only source of law for Bonneville.

This introduction perfectly exemplified the malleability of European history, adapting the historical narrative to new political contexts in the fast-changing political climate of the radicalizing revolution in France. Bonneville also demonstrated the relevance of his medieval history for current events, although in the end it was not sufficient to keep him safe as a Girondin during the phase of the Terror after 1792. Bonneville, in the introduction, cited at length the tribunal of the English king Charles I, who was beheaded in 1649. Long citations of the

---

[151] Bonneville, *Histoire* I, 335.   [152] See Chapter 9.   [153] Bonneville, *Histoire* III, vi.

indictment of the king's main accuser Oliver Cromwell were quoted *verbatim*. During the trial, Cromwell had accused the English king of treason and tyranny. The deeds of the French king Louis XVI and his son, Louis XVII, were in Bonneville's eyes even worse than those of their English counterpart. Bonneville, furthermore, wrote that he had published this new volume of his *History of Modern Europe* to give evidence of the perjury of French kings in medieval history. These historical sources added weight to the accusations against Louis XVI, who would be executed the following year.[154] British medieval history formed in this respect a counterpoint to French history. The example of King John 'Lackland' (1166–1216) demonstrated, according to Bonneville, that it was in principle possible for a king to accept the people's representation and combine liberty with monarchy, unlike the deeds of Louis XVI.[155]

Full of disapproval and disgust ('*dégout*' and '*horreur*'), Bonneville described— once more—the struggle between the emperor and the pope in this volume. Instead of an impartial and peace-loving mediator, as depicted by Joseph de Maistre's argument in *Du Pape* (1819), the medieval papacy was a power-hungry, greedy, and warmongering institution, ready to stir up military conflict for its own benefit.[156] In sharp contrast to the aggressive behaviour of both the pope and the emperor, the Hanseatic League of cities, for Bonneville, stood for 'reason', 'peace', and 'freedom'. Interestingly in the context of the developing Terror and the abolition of the monarchy, Bonneville wrote rather positively about a few medieval French kings. Bonneville provided, for instance, a positive description of the first French king, Hugo Capet. He praised the king for his prudence and 'moderation'. Louis IX, 'Saint Louis' (1214–70), furthermore, was presented as a 'good' and 'patriotic' king who was basically misled by deceitful clergy into starting religious persecutions and committing himself to the Crusades against Islam.[157]

His description of the power struggles in Spain between Muslims and Christians was salient, with the Moors being depicted by Bonneville as reasonable and open-minded and the Christians as intolerant fanatics.[158] Just as he did in his book on the *Spirit of the Religions* (1791), Bonneville urged the Europeans to call themselves henceforth 'Franks', as this name stood for Germanic freedom and represented Europeans as the 'true friends of humanity'. Because the word 'Europe' had its origins in the classical world, Bonneville rejected it as not associated with freedom, the gift of the Germanic tribes.[159]

The developments in medieval Britain were of the utmost importance in 'these modern times'.[160] For the first time in modern history, Bonneville wrote following Russell, after 1215 the people in Britain received a voice in their representative

---

[154] Bonneville, *Histoire* III, xliii.
[155] Bonneville, *Histoire* III, xliii.
[156] See Chapter 8.
[157] Bonneville, *Histoire* II, 45–8.
[158] Bonneville, *Histoire* III, 104–23.
[159] Bonneville, *Histoire* III, 124.
[160] Bonneville, *Histoire* III, 124.

institutions. Bonneville believed that all other European countries would eventually follow England's example. The will of the free peoples would always triumph over fanaticism and tyranny, Bonneville reiterated. Equality and freedom went, for him, hand in hand with representative institutions. Surprisingly for someone caught up in the middle of a radicalizing revolution, he argued here that revolutions were unnecessary when representative institutions could be installed by peaceful means.[161] European history's main narrative was a story of unfolding freedom and progress, first in England, then in the rest of Europe, and finally, the world.

At the end of the third volume, Bonneville connected the medieval past with contemporary politics: the constitutional developments that had begun in medieval England would eventually spread all over Europe: in the future the Third Estate, as the representative of 'the people', would establish a constitutionally enshrined freedom, Bonneville wrote, directly addressing his contemporary readers.[162] However, he did not ignore the dark sides of English medieval history. For instance, he described at length the attempts by tyrannical English kings to suppress the freedom of the Celtic Scots and the Welsh. Not surprising for a book based on a work by a Scottish historian, Bonneville paid much detailed attention to the wars between the English and the Scots in the Middle Ages, both free Germanic nations. Bonneville refused to take sides in this conflict and showed himself to be sympathetic towards the rulers of both countries.[163] Bonneville, furthermore, decried the relentless persecutions of the Jews in the Holy Roman Empire as important examples of the religious intolerance and immorality of the Holy Roman emperors.

The third volume ended with another struggle of a freedom-loving people against a tyrannical ruler. Bonneville recounted at length the fight of the Swiss, that noble and free 'Celtic' people, against the tyrannical and hegemonic schemes of the Habsburg rulers of the Holy Roman Empire. Obviously, Bonneville saw in the successful Swiss revolt of 1308 the precursor of the French Revolution in his own time, as almost every historical event in his European history had become a revolutionary struggle.[164] Bonneville's optimistic vision of a straightforward victory of freedom over obscurantist despotism was not realized. His grand project of writing a larger cosmopolitan history of Europe became smothered by a political climate of radicalization, war, and attempts to reimpose order. The incomplete state of his works offered a telling example of the ending of a nascent revolutionary cosmopolitan tradition of European history writing. From 1792, counter-revolutionaries would take the initiative in the construction of a European past for their own purposes.

---

[161] Bonneville, *Histoire* III, 129. [162] Bonneville, *Histoire* III, 151.
[163] Bonnevillle, *Histoire* III, 200–1. [164] Bonneville, *Histoire* III, 227.

8. Conclusion: A Revolutionary Narrative

In the eighteenth-century Europe became predominantly understood as a 'historical' concept, the result of a centuries-long historical institutional evolution. A canon of European historians was established, as we could observe in Bonneville's writings, consisting mainly of German, French, and English historians, representing the leading nations and excluding other national historiographies. In this historiographical sense, new centres and peripheries were shaped, which continue to this day. As the example of Bonneville's *History of Modern Europe* demonstrated, this enlightened historiography was essentially a transnational endeavour. Bonneville based his history on the works of the Scot, William Russell, who was himself inspired by Montesquieu and Voltaire, among others.[165] At the same time, despite Bonneville's exhortation that true and impartial historians should have neither a master nor a fatherland, he clearly adapted Russell's original text to the tastes of a French national audience.

In the 1790s, this historical narrative became increasingly politicized by the impact of the French Revolution. Bonneville explicitly wrote that the new political regimes made a new and modern history imperative, particularly to educate the new generations, as was Bonneville's intention. Along with the *ancien régime*, the dominance of ancient history had to be abolished in order to create a more just and freer society. Bonneville appropriated the enlightened historians for his own revolutionary agenda, overemphasizing no doubt the revolutionary potential of older enlightened historiography. European history was on the side of the revolutionaries, Bonneville argued. As we shall see in the coming chapters, the counter-revolutionaries refuted this revolutionary interpretation of the European past. At the same time, they made use of the same narrative of Germanic freedom as Bonneville. In the counter-revolutionary narratives, however, the revolutionaries were cast as the new Romans, destroying the original European liberty and establishing despotism, and ignorance.

Bonneville's European history writing was part of a much larger cosmopolitan programme of publications, facilitated by his knowledge of foreign languages and extensive travel. Bonneville advocated perpetual peace and international collaboration and criticized what he regarded as national prejudices. Interestingly this enlightened cosmopolitanism, championing reason, progress, and knowledge, was strongly infused by mystical beliefs, extolling, for instance, the eternal wisdom of the Germanic Druids. Studying European history revealed a deeper meaning and esoteric truth about humankind, that could be understood on different hierarchical levels by ever-smaller consecrated elites. Also, Bonneville prophesied the coming of a 'saviour' that would inaugurate a new era of spiritual renewal and

---

[165] See also Kontler, *Translations*.

end an age of decline and corruption. As we shall see, many of these religiously and mystically inspired ideas of spiritual renewal and of moral and cultural regeneration formed also key elements of the intellectual world of counter-enlightened and counter-revolutionary Europeans. The intellectual boundaries between revolutionary and counter-revolutionary Europeanisms were porous.[166]

---

[166] An earlier and shorter version of this chapter has been published as Lok, 'Revolutionary Narrative'.

3
The Philosopher's Apprentice

1. History against Philosophy

> Has history not been sufficiently humiliated for it to be spared further outrage? Is there still a piece [of history] left that the breath of lie has not dishonoured, that calumny and the contemporary unnatural philosophy has not disfigured, for it to be mistreated at the hands of a certain mister Bonneville?[1]

This damning verdict on Bonneville's *History of Modern Europe* appeared in the *Journal historique et littéraire* of 1 July 1789. The author was François-Xavier de Feller (1735–1802), a former Jesuit and anti-Jansenist Catholic publicist. Feller's criticism would not have come as a surprise to Bonneville. Feller was a self-proclaimed '*anti-philosophe*' whose life's mission was to fight what he deemed to be a pernicious contemporary 'philosophy' that undermined all religious and, eventually, also all political authority. For Feller, Bonneville's history books stood for what he observed to be a perversion of historical writing, and the intellectual climate in general, by enlightened *philosophie*.[2] This philosophy was the scourge of his century and at the origin of all contemporary society's ills, or so Feller believed.

Feller often used historical arguments in his many publications to fight 'philosophy' and to defend the Catholic tradition and doctrine against criticism. He tried to counter what he saw as the contemporary corruption of the sacred art of history writing by atheistic rebels such as Bonneville. In his view, at the hands of 'a multitude of broddlers' [the *philosophes*] history underwent 'a triste metamorphosis' in the eighteenth century, turning a once glorious discipline into 'a storehouse of corruption and mistakes'.[3] Feller's aim was to safeguard the weapon of secular history writing for the good cause: the defence of the Church and the Catholic tradition.

---

[1] 'L'histoire n'est-elle donc pas assez ravalée pour qu'on ne raffine pas sur les outrages reçoit? En reste-t-il encore quelque morceau que le souffle du mensonge n'ait point flétri, que la calomnie & la dénaturante philosophie du jour n'a point défiguré, qui soit réservé à l'opération d'un monsieur Bonneville?' *Journal Historique et Littéraire* (henceforth *JHL*), 1 July 1789, 344–5.

[2] Feller was also very critical of the work of the German historian Schroekh and that of Edward Gibbon. In his review, Feller wrote maliciously that Gibbon's *Decline and Fall of the Roman Empire* added little new to Montesquieu's older work and contained many errors. *JHL*, 15 August 1789, 587–9.

[3] *JHL*, 1 November 1789, 351.

Feller was not alone in his endeavour to use history to combat allegedly atheistic philosophical writings. In the eighteenth century, the Catholic tradition lost much of its self-evidence, or so many Catholic apologetic publicists feared.[4] To a certain extent this was not a new phenomenon: the foundations of the Catholic tradition had earlier already been shaken and reconfirmed by the humanist textual criticism of the Reformation and Renaissance.[5] The critical enlightened philosophy of the eighteenth century, however, presented a whole new challenge. Eighteenth-century Catholic apologists, advocates of the Catholic doctrine and Church, turned to the historical method to defend and legitimate what they understood to be the tradition.[6] Most Catholic writers were 'modern' enough to accept the new critical method made popular by Bayle and others as valid, but evidently not willing to dismiss Christian revelation as false. A minority of authors, such as the eccentric Jesuit Jean Hardouin and his follower Isaac Berruyer, even used historical scepticism to question the authenticity and intelligibility of all historical documents and thus to legitimize the authority of the Church to decide what was historical truth. Ancient documents inconvenient to the Church could, in this way, be disposed of. Tradition was, thus, paradoxically vindicated by the new critical method of history.[7]

The majority of Catholic authors, however, tried to prove the biblical revelation by establishing historical facts.[8] Historical research was increasingly regarded in the eighteenth century as an important means to demonstrate religious truth, similar to the study of the book of nature.[9] Authors such as Abbé Gauchat regarded the Bible as a historical work, whose truthfulness could be demonstrated by source criticism and historical methods. 'it [the Bible] teaches us certain [historical] facts which bear on the designs and works of the lord', he wrote.[10] The Holy Scripture formed, however, a unique historical source as it was to remain the only historical source for the events it described.[11] Comparing biblical events with older histories such as the history of China, and consequently stating

---

[4] In his seminal *Catholics and Unbelievers* (1939), the American historian Robert Roswell Palmer distinguished 'history' from 'tradition'. Tradition 'enters the past not by going directly to what we call sources but by appealing to a social memory which, because of the overlapping of generations, is continuous and unbroken'. Historical evidence served only to confirm social memory in traditional narratives. Tradition assumed that each generation would hand on unaltered the knowledge that it had received. Palmer, *Catholics and Unbelievers*, 54–60.

[5] Cameron, 'Turmoil of Faith', 145–73; Po-Chia Hsia, *Catholic Renewal*; on the concept of 'tradition': Pieper, *Tradition*.

[6] This enterprise in the end was doomed to failure, according to Palmer. 'By the eighteenth century something of the historical spirit had entered the minds of many people who were not aware that it might undermine tradition'. Palmer, *Catholics and Unbelievers*, 60.

[7] Palmer, *Catholics and Unbelievers*, 65–76.   [8] Palmer, *Catholics and Unbelievers*, 77.

[9] On the 'book of nature': Jorink, *Reading the Book of Nature*; Palmer, *Catholics and Unbelievers*, 23–52, 206–24.

[10] Cited in Palmer, *Catholics and Unbelievers*, 63.

[11] On the *anti-philosophe* conception of knowledge: Armenteros, *French Idea*, 82–114; Palmer, *Catholics and Unbelievers*, 77–102; Lok, 'Vuursalamanders'.

that Chinese and Indian civilizations pre-dated Hebrew history, as the *philosophes* had done, was, however, mostly out of the question for these Catholic propagandists.

Thus, in the decades preceding the French Revolution, secular historical reasoning was instrumentalized and adapted by apologists defending the Catholic tradition. So far, this use of history writing by *anti-philosophes* has received surprisingly little attention from the growing numbers of scholars studying the Enlightenment and the past.[12] The role of the self-proclaimed enemies of the Enlightenment in the development of historical thinking in the eighteenth century has almost entirely been ignored, leaving important lacunae in the study of the history of modern historical thought.[13] Furthermore, the response of the contemporary opponents of the *philosophes* to the enlightened narrative of European history has hardly been studied, not even by Palmer. To what extent did, for instance, the pre-revolutionary *anti-philosophes* adopt or reject this enlightened historical narrative, and in what way did the past more generally figure in their defence of the tradition?

In this chapter, the uses of the European past by contemporary opponents of enlightened philosophy will be examined, using François-Xavier de Feller as lodestar. Few *anti-philosophes* exemplified so well the transnational character of the Counter-Enlightenment as Feller. In the next sections, Feller will be interpreted as a 'Christian cosmopolitan' in the Pauline-Cynic tradition, and he is situated in the larger context of the 'counter-enlightened international'. Consequently, we will see how Feller imagined European civilization and how he tried to revive the providential universal history of Bossuet in his *Dictionnaire historique*. Then it will be shown how Feller fought enlightened philosophy in the pages of his *Journal*, and we will discuss the role of revolution in Feller's anti-enlightened historical narrative. The last sections entail a comparison of his views on the decline and corruption of European civilization with those of a French literary scholar, Rigoley de Juvigny, to provide a fuller perspective on the varieties of anti-enlightened Europeanism, and concluding remarks.

The title of this chapter referred to a poem entitled 'the modern philosopher's apprentice', printed in the 15 April 1789 issue of Feller's historical and literary *Journal*.[14] In this poem, a servant turned into a thief, stealing his master's money, because he had lost all respect for property and rank as a result of philosophical ideas taught him by his master. The eighteenth-century philosophers were, for the

---

[12] For the Enlightenment and the past, see Chapter 2.
[13] In his article on the idea of progress of *philosophes* and 'reactionaries', François-Emmanuël Boucher in his contribution to Brill's *Companion to Enlightenment Historiography*, for instance, pays attention only to post-revolutionary enemies of philosophy, not to the pre-revolutionary *anti-philosophes*. Boucher, 'Philosophes', 373–400. An exception is Chadwick, *From Bossuet to Newman*, especially 21–95.
[14] *JHL*, 15 April 1789, 590.

anti-philosophes, comparable to the sorcerer's apprentice, the character from Goethe's ballad of 1797.¹⁵ Goethe, not coincidentally, wrote his poem on human hubris and the overestimation of human capabilities in the years immediately following the Terror. At this time the optimism and the idealism of the early Revolution had transmuted into a violent regime that seemed out of control. By teaching the 'common people' dangerous philosophical ideas, the modern *philosophes* eventually had lost control, and society had descended into violent chaos, publicists like Feller claimed, like the apprentice who could no longer control the 'sorcery' once he had begun to make use of it.

2. An Anti-Enlightened Cosmopolitan

Feller formed part of the caste of priests who were, in Bonneville's eyes, responsible for the superstition and ignorance that had enslaved humanity for so long. He was born in Brussels in 1735 to a family with roots in Luxembourg. His father had held important offices in the Habsburg Netherlands, and he had been ennobled in 1741. François-Xavier studied at the Jesuit college in Luxembourg, followed by a study of philosophy and theology in Rheims. In 1764, he was consecrated as a priest. In 1771, Feller established residence in the prince-bishopric of Liège, then part of the Holy Roman Empire, which at that time did not belong to the Southern Netherlands. In Liège, he taught at a college. After the dissolution of the Jesuit order in 1773 by Pope Clement V, Feller was forced to become a full-time journalist and publicist.¹⁶ The dissolution of his order came as a tremendous shock and strengthened Feller in his conviction that philosophical ideas formed a mortal threat to the Catholic Church.¹⁷ Although Liège remained his main residence, Feller consequently led a travelling life, often staying with friends in different places all over Europe.

In the 1780s and early 1790s, Feller actively participated in the struggle against the reforming policies of the enlightened Habsburg Emperor Joseph II in the Southern Netherlands, a ruler he had originally greeted with high hopes. Whereas later Feller would condemn the French revolutionaries as the main apostles of enlightened philosophy, in the 1780s the main threat to the Church and Belgian traditional liberties came in his eyes from the Habsburg Emperor—a *philosophe*.¹⁸ As a result of his oppositional activities, he was censured and persecuted by the authorities. Not only *philosophes*, but also their enemies clearly had to fear government prosecution in the eighteenth century. Feller's relationship with the

---

¹⁵ Goethe, '*Zauberlehrling*', 32–7. ¹⁶ Burson and Wright, *Jesuit Suppression*.
¹⁷ Sprunck, 'Feller', 134–5; Wagner, 'Feller, François-Xavier de', 550–8.
¹⁸ On the Belgian Revolt, see pp. 91–2.

papacy was complicated as well: he was a fierce advocate of papal authority, but he also criticized the pope for not doing enough to counter the spread of philosophical ideas and he felt insufficiently appreciated by the Church hierarchy. Feller's oppositional stance towards several authorities is a reminder that the anti-Enlightenment cannot be simply equated with a conservative defence of the powers that be.

Eventually, Feller was caught up between the hostile Habsburg government, on the one hand, and the French revolutionaries, on the other. In 1792, he temporarily left Liège after the first revolutionary invasion in that princedom. He went to the provincial town of Maastricht in the south of the Dutch Republic, where he was able to publish his *Journal historique et littéraire*, the scholarly periodical he had edited since 1773. The restoration of Habsburg rule did not improve his situation much: his *Journal* remained proscribed by the authorities, and several publications hostile to Feller were published. In 1794, he had to leave Liège and the Southern Netherlands for good after the second invasion of French revolutionary troops, and, like so many counter-revolutionaries, he became an exile and a refugee.[19] He fled to the Holy Roman Empire and eventually died in exile in Regensburg in 1802.[20]

Feller belonged to a larger group of Catholic publicists from the Southern Netherlands who opposed the reforms of the Habsburg government, such as Henri-Ignace Brosius, Johannes Josef van den Elsken, and Pieter Simon van Eupen. These anti-reformists developed their own variation of Christian cosmopolitanism inspired by the writings of St Paul and his tactical appropriation of the Cynic 'philosophy of life', as represented by Diogenes of Sinope.[21] These publicists opposed their version of Pauline–Cynic cosmopolitanism to the Stoic cosmopolitan ideals that underlay the official enlightened Josephist state in the Southern Netherlands. It also allowed them to model themselves on the apostolic martyrdom of the first Christians, with the Habsburg authorities in the role of persecuting Romans. This Cynic–Christian cosmopolitanism was not founded on the idea of a larger political community, but instead on a rejection of the worldly political community and the pursuit of worldly glory. These Catholic activists imagined an otherworldly moral universal community, advocating a public display of spiritual ethics and beliefs and the embrace of poverty and frugality.[22]

Feller also led a life typical for an eighteenth-century cosmopolitan. He travelled widely in Central and Eastern Europe and Italy, using the Jesuit networks within the Habsburg Empire that continued to exist after the order's dissolution. He befriended Hungarian and other Central European nobles. His posthumously

---

[19] On this theme: Philip and Reboul, *French Emigrants*.
[20] Sprunck, 'Feller', 182–99.   [21] Shea, *Cynic Enlightenment*.
[22] Van Dam, 'Christian Cosmopolitanism'; van Dam, 'Enlightened Reform'.

published *Voyages* are a striking example of anti-philosophical travel literature, an interesting counterpoint to the connection, too often taken for granted, between Enlightenment and voyages.[23] He also published a rather Eurocentric geographical dictionary in which social and physical geographical information was mingled with his own political and religious views. In the entry on Bengal, for instance, he scornfully remarked that *philosophie*, while destroying Europe's more developed national cultures, had been completely unsuccessful in eradicating the practice of human sacrifice in Asian countries.[24]

The European character of Feller's life and work was perhaps also reflected in the fact he was claimed by different countries as one of their own. He, for instance, received entries in Belgian, Dutch, Luxembourgish, French as well as German national biographies. His Luxembourg hagiographic biographer Sprunck proudly identified him as a Luxembourger and praised him as the 'ancestor of Luxembourg journalism'.[25] As we shall see, along with his cosmopolitan outlook, Feller had strong regional roots in the Southern Netherlands and Liège, perfectly combining an anti-enlightened form of Christian and anti-Jansenist cosmopolitanism with a Southern-Netherlandish, anti-Habsburg, Catholic patriotism.

The *Journal historique et littéraire*, which Feller edited from 1773 until his exile in 1794, formed an important pillar of a transnational *anti-philosophe* public opinion. His audience extended widely beyond the borders of his own country, forming an intellectual link between France and the Holy Roman Empire.[26] In a polemical style, Feller used his journal to attack philosophical ideas across a wide range of disciplines, from literature and politics to mineralogy, penal law, mining, and botany. No neutral or impartial knowledge seemed to exist in this ideological war of the eighteenth century. Feller turned even a scientific debate on the question whether salamanders could survive in fire into an attack on *philosophie*.[27] The *Journal* is also of wider interest as we can follow the long-term and continuous evolution of anti-philosophical ideas from the early 1770s, to the radicalization of the French Revolution and the foundation of the revolutionary Republic in 1792. Furthermore, by reporting in the *Journal* events that happened in different European countries, including the Russian and the Ottoman Empires, Feller created an idea of European civilization through continent-wide news coverage.[28]

---

[23] Feller, *Itinéraire*.   [24] Feller, *Dictionnaire géographique* I, 138.

[25] Sprunck, 'Feller', 123. Sprunck emphasizes that Feller was a true native of Luxembourg ('Feller est d'authentique souche Luxembourgeoise', 125).

[26] According to McMahon, the magazine was 'a refuge and intellectual clearing house for Jesuits, the journal united numerous contributors in a continent-wide war against incredulity, fusing literary criticism with cultural commentary and militant *dévot* piety. (...) the journal followed French and pan-European affairs intently, making the fight against the *philosophes* its raison d'être, a truly international concern.' McMahon, *Enemies*, 107.

[27] *JHL*, 15 March 1789, 403–7. See, more extensively: Lok, 'Vuursalamanders'.

[28] Eastern Europe for Feller is clearly not a significant 'other': cf. Wolff, *Inventing Eastern Europe*.

3. Counter-Enlightenment International

Since the turn of the twenty-first century, 'enemies of Enlightenment', such as Feller, have been the subject of renewed scholarly interest.[29] In his book *Ennemis des philosophes*, French literary scholar Didier Masseau, for instance, painted a broad canvas of a diverse and differentiated *anti-philosophe* public opinion in late *ancien régime* France. This country was seen by contemporaries as the intellectual centre not only of the Enlightenment but also of the Counter-Enlightenment.[30] The *anti-philosophes* regarded themselves as the true heirs of the humanistic republic of letters, reconciling the classical heritage with Catholic doctrine. This republic was, in their view, now sadly corrupted by immoral and atheistic *philosophes*. The relationship between the *philosophes* and the self-proclaimed *anti-philosophes* was highly ambivalent. To a certain extent *anti-philosophe* sociability constituted a separate sphere from the social world of the *philosophes*, but often the *philosophes* as well as their 'enemies' frequented the same salons and learned institutions.[31]

Self-confessed *anti-philosophes*, despite their differences, all shared a distaste for what they regarded as the overly abstract theories of the *philosophes* and their arrogant and immoderate belief in the possibilities of human reason, such as was demonstrated in the poem of the philosopher's servant.[32] At the same time, many arguments and ideas, usually associated with the Enlightenment, could also be found in the *anti-philosophes*' publications. For instance, the notions of 'freedom', 'civilization', 'reason', and 'progress' were much in use in *anti-philosophe* writings, although they were used for a different agenda and acquired an entirely different meaning. But it should be noted that *philosophes* and their opponents often shared the same conceptual language. Furthermore, typical *philosophe* literary forms such as the dictionary, theatre pieces, journals, and novels were used by the *anti-philosophe* authors, such as Feller, as well.[33]

For these reasons, it has been argued that the term 'Catholic Enlightenment' is much more appropriate to describe the writings of eighteenth-century Catholic authors than 'Counter' or 'anti-Enlightenment'.[34] Most eighteenth-century publicists, Catholic or Protestant, claimed indeed that they were not against Enlightenment (*Siècle des Lumières*) per se, but they objected to the wrong kind of Enlightenment, by which they meant an abstract Enlightenment completely

---

[29] '*Anti-philosophie* so-called was a powerful cultural movement of the eighteenth century, albeit one remarkably neglected by modern historians.' Israel, *Democratic Enlightenment*, 140.

[30] For the problem of centre and periphery in the (Counter-)Enlightenment, see Lok and Montoya, 'Centre and Periphery'.

[31] Masseau, *Ennemis*, 67–108. Cf. Masseau, *Dictionnaire*.

[32] Masseau, *Ennemis*, 45.   [33] Masseau, *Ennemis*, 273–320.

[34] Lehner, *Enlightened Monks*; Lehner, *Catholic Enlightenment*; Burson and Lehner, *Enlightenment and Catholicism*; Lehner and Printy, *Companion to the Catholic Enlightenment*. For the concept of the 'religious Enlightenment': Sorkin, *Religious Enlightenment*.

separated from religion. It is also true that, especially in the first half of the eighteenth century, Catholic as well as Protestant authors strove for an incorporation of the new contemporary scientific insights into Catholic teachings and promoted the reconciliation of science and revelation as well as that between reason and faith.[35] Furthermore, from the middle of the eighteenth century onwards, diverse authors such as David Hume, Jean-Jacques Rousseau, and Johan Gottfried Herder also became increasingly critical of the 'abstract' ideas and absolute faith in the universal applicability of reason of the 'arrogant' (French) *philosophie*, complicating the concept of Counter-Enlightenment as well as that of Enlightenment.[36]

However, by placing too much emphasis on the reconciliation between science and religion, the scholarly proponents of the 'Catholic' or 'religious' Enlightenment seem to downplay the fact that, in the late eighteenth-century, apologists such as Feller, especially from the 1770s onwards, explicitly framed themselves as radical and uncompromising opponents of *philosophie*. This uncompromising stance was often combined with the tacit appropriation of the instruments as well as the ideas of their opponents, as the case of Feller also demonstrated. Thus, the concept of 'Counter-Enlightenment' will still be used here, but exclusively in the sense of a self-proclaimed *anti-philosophie*, as the term was used by eighteenth-century contemporaries themselves.[37]

The term 'Counter-Enlightenment' was particularly apt for the intellectual climate in France in the later eighteenth century. An accelerating process of polarization resulted in the formation of two increasingly opposed and self-conscious ideological camps: the *parti philosophique* and the *parti anti-philosophique*. An important turning point in this evolution was the so-called Prades affair (1751–3), a scandal surrounding a thesis defended at the Sorbonne by the theology student Jean-Martin de Prades.[38] The Prades affair became the focal point of existing struggles between Jansenists and Jesuits, between court factions, as well as between the king and the parliaments, and finally between the *philosophes* and their enemies. As a result, Catholic doctrine became defined more sharply, leaving less room for the incorporation of new discoveries.[39] The publication of Rousseau's *Émile* in 1762 and Voltaire's *Dictionnaire philosophique* (1764) provoked many Catholic refutations.[40] The quest to reconcile faith and

---

[35] For the Netherlands: van der Wall and Wessels, *veelzijdige verstandhouding*.

[36] Israel, *Democratic Enlightenment*, 93–109, 209–332.

[37] 'What united them, however, was their tendency to engage in a process of radical simplification and reification, presenting the social and political order in Manichean, either/or terms.' McMahon, 'What is Counter-Enlightenment?', 41.

[38] After a complex religious as well as political struggle, the Jansenist-dominated *Parlement* of Paris took control of the Sorbonne and discredited the Jesuit order, which was eventually banished by the French king in 1762–4. Burson, *Theological Enlightenment*; Masseau, *Ennemis*.

[39] The Sorbonne, now controlled by Jansenists, turned against the *Encyclopédie*. Montesquieu's *L'esprit des lois* (1748) as well as Helvétius's *De l'esprit* (1758) were censored.

[40] On the complex relationship between *anti-philosophie* and Rousseau: McMahon, *Enemies*, 34–5, 51–2, 99; Garrard, *Rousseau's Counter-Enlightenment*.

reason, however, had not ended, and moderate Catholics such as Madame de Genlis (1748–1830) continued to publish works that condemned atheism but used reason to support religion.[41] This alleged rise of atheism should not be overestimated: on the eve of the Revolution, most Frenchmen as well as the clergy regarded themselves as loyal Catholics.[42]

A shortcoming of most studies on the Counter-Enlightenment, however, is that they understand anti-philosophy almost exclusively—and anachronistically—within a national framework.[43] Darrin McMahon, by contrast, pointed to the international dimension of Enlightenment criticism. He argued that in the eighteenth century an *antiphilosophe internationale* came into being: France not only inspired a transnational enlightened culture but was also an exporter of Francophone Enlightenment criticism. All over Europe, but also in the Americas and even beyond, French *antiphilosophe* texts circulated and were adapted to local usage.[44] This travelling of *antiphilosophe* texts extended to Catholic as well as to Protestant countries. The idea of a plot by a small sect of intolerant and fanatical *philosophes*, determined to destroy established religion, was widespread, for instance, throughout Europe even before the French Revolution.[45] Through the reception of French works, a European and even global *anti-philosophe* public opinion with its own heroes and infrastructure, including as the scholarly journal, developed in the late seventeenth and eighteenth centuries. This anti-enlightened public sphere could partly built on older Counter-Reformation practices and ideas.[46] François-Xavier de Feller was a typical representative of this transnational Catholic and ultramontanist Counter-Enlightenment, with firm local roots in the Southern Netherlands and Liège.[47]

---

[41] Montoya, 'Madame de Genlis', 2.

[42] Plongeron, *Théologie et politique*; McManners, *Church and Society*; Aston, *French Bishops*; van Kley, *Religious Origins*.

[43] For instance: Weiß, 'Obscuranten'; Masseau, *Ennemis*.

[44] McMahon, *Enemies*, 106–15; McMahon, 'Century of Lights', 81–104. Also, Jonathan Israel analyses *anti-philosophie* as a transnational and transconfessional 'European' phenomenon: Israel, *Democratic Enlightenment*, 140–71. See, furthermore, the various contributions in Lok and van Eijnatten, themed issue on the 'Global Counter-Enlightenment'. Older studies that emphasize the European dimension of *anti-philosophie* in Spain and Italy are: Herrero, *pensamiento reaccionario*; Prandi, *Cristianesimo offeso e difeso*. A recent study: Calderon, *Olvido y Memoria*.

[45] Weiß emphasizes, for instance, the heterogeneous character of the German 'Counter-Enlightenment'. They argue that, around 1770, a new self-proclaimed criticism of the 'Enlightenment' came into being. In the 1780s, this current of Enlightenment criticism developed and became more systematized as a result of the discovery of the Illuminati order and the Prussian religious edict, and in the 1790s in the context of the French Revolution. Albrecht and Weiß, 'Einleitende Bemerkungen', 16–35.

[46] On the continuity of eighteenth-century Catholic publicists and the Counter-Reformation: Lehner, *Catholic Enlightenment*, 4.

[47] As McMahon noted: '[Feller] wrote the international language of French, directing his most pointed criticism at the French philosophes themselves, warning of their pernicious effects throughout Europe. All of this helps to underscore the fact that Catholic enemies of the Enlightenment conceived of themselves as genuinely "Catholic" community in the eighteenth century, an international alliance engaged in an international struggle.' McMahon, *Enemies*, 107–8. An important aspect of Feller's transnationalism was his role within 'an ultramontanist international', as described by Vanysacker, *Erudite Activities*, and Vanysacker, *Cardinal Giuseppe Garampi*.

4. The Gentle Continent

In his paradoxically titled *Catéchisme philosophique*, first published in 1773 under the pseudonym 'Flexier de Réval', Feller's views on European history could only be found in an indirect and implicit manner. The truth of Catholic doctrine was defended in this 'Catechism' by using arguments mainly drawn from natural philosophy, not yet historical science.[48] In this work, he made the interesting sceptical observation that biblical history was not fundamentally different from modern worldly history: both types of history rest on incomplete and imperfect sources. If we start doubting the historical truth of the biblical events, we could just as well stop believing in the existence of the sixteenth-century French king Henri IV, and treat him as a fable as well.[49] The title of 'philosophical catechism' already indicated that the work was both a traditional defence of Catholic doctrine, a catechism, and a contemporary response to the challenges posed by the *philosophes*.[50] In this publication, the Catholic faith was propagated on the utilitarian and sociological grounds that it was first and foremost 'useful' (*utile*) and brought 'happiness' (*bonheur*) to the people.[51] Philosophical 'atheism', on the other hand, had a negative impact on social life: it destroyed social ties and drove people to commit suicide.

In the *Catéchisme*, Feller, furthermore, extensively reflected on what he regarded as the essence of 'Europe', providing insight into the counter-enlightened imagining of this continent. In the entry on 'Europe' in the *Dictionnaire géographique*, the continent is described by Feller as the most civilized and advanced continent due to its religion and development. Feller proudly supported European expansion in other parts of the world.[52] Appropriating Montesquieu for a radical Catholic agenda, Feller argued that 'moderation' constituted the essential element of European society, an argument that could also be found in the revolutionary history of his ideological opponent Bonneville. In contrast to the rest of the world where despotic and unbounded power was the norm, the political power of the princes was constrained in Europe and their standards were softened and less cruel than elsewhere.[53] In this sense, the idea of a salient European 'moderation', as most prominently articulated by Montesquieu, can be found in

---

[48] Flexier de Réval, *Catéchisme philosophique*, 1773 (first edition; I have also used here the second edition of 1777 and the new edition of 1828).

[49] 'Rejeter l'histoire de Jésus-Christ, parce qu'elle est rapportée par quelques anonymes, & que tous ceux qui en parlent n'ont pas une égale autorité, c'est comme si je traitois de fable l'histoire de Henri IV, parce que telle lettre qui porte le nom de Sully, n'est peut-être pas de ce ministre.' Flexier de Réval, *Catéchisme philosophique* (1777), 359.

[50] On the literary form of the 'philosophical catechism': Masseau, *Ennemis*, 296-7.

[51] On the enlightened idea of happiness: McMahon, *Happiness*.

[52] Feller, *Dictionnaire géographique*, 401-2.

[53] See, for Feller praising the virtue of moderation: *JHL*, 1 June 1789, 215. Cf. Montesquieu, *Spirit of the Laws*, 118. On Montesquieu as a political philosopher of moderation: Craiutu, *Virtue for Courageous Minds*, 33-68. For Craiutu, Montesquieu is important because, for him, moderation is no longer an individual virtue, but an essential feature of a type of government, above all a pluralist and

the writing of *philosophes* and *anti-philosophes*, revolutionaries and counter-revolutionaries alike, and was thus instrumental in providing legitimation for completely contradictory political projects.

Europe's uniqueness could, for Feller, in part be explained by the geographical irregularities of the European '*géocosmie*': 'the varied manner in which the sea embraces and divides the continent, the winding of its rivers, the multitude of its gulfs and bays, which form the soul of navigation and one of the great bonds of general society'.[54] Feller's geographical reflections evidently echoed the famous third part of Montesquieu's *De l'esprit des lois* (1748).[55] In this book, Montesquieu promulgates his influential theory of the influence of climate and other geographical factors on the shaping of national and continental characters. According to Montesquieu, Europe's moderate character is above all formed by the 'temperate' climate zone.[56] Geography, Feller agreed with Montesquieu, also explained why in Europe a plurality of smaller and medium-sized states existed, in his eyes a guarantee of freedom, whereas in Asia the great plains facilitated large and usually despotic empires.[57]

Feller continued to argue, and here his views started to diverge from Bonneville's, that the main explanation for Europe's moderation could be found in its Christian religion. Catholic Christianity made European governments in general more stable and revolutions less bloody than in ancient times or in other parts of the world.[58] To support this analysis, Feller again selected citations from Montesquieu: 'the Christian religion is remote from pure despotism; the gentleness so recommended in the Gospel stands opposed to the despotic fury with which a prince would mete out his own justice and exercise his cruelties'.[59] The moderate exercise of power by Christian European princes stood in contrast to the cruelty of Islamic and other oriental rulers. Catholic Christianity was, for Feller, a promotor of mild manners. Feller thus described the Catholic Church in his book as an enlightened 'civilizer', as would later counter-revolutionary authors like Chateaubriand and Maistre.[60] The introduction of Christianity into Ethiopia, to

---

complex constitution. Craiutu, however, pays little attention to the relationship Montesquieu draws between Christianity and moderation in the *Spirit of the Laws*. See also: Spector, *Montesquieu*; de Dijn, 'Was Montesquieu a Liberal Republican?'.

[54] 'La manière variée dont la mer embrasse et partage le continent, la tortuosité de ses rivages, la multitude de ses golfes et de ses baies sont l'âme de la navigation, et un des grands liens de la société générale. Le centre de l'Afrique, de l'Asie, de l'Amérique méridionale est inculte et désert, tandis que l'Europe, entrecoupée et divisée par la mer, est généralement florissante, et qu'il en est de même à proportion (laissant à côté d'autres causes) des Indes et de l'Asie méridionale, de l'Afrique et de l'Amérique septentrionale, des Archipels, des îles et presqu'îles.—Les irrégularités de la géocosmie, la figure anomale, brusque et bizarre des rivages et des mers, forment, ainsi que les montagnes et les fleuves, des limites naturelles pour les régions et les nations'. Flexier de Réval, *Catéchisme philosophique* (1828), 54.

[55] 'Ce paradoxe qui a été réfuté victorieusement par l'Auteur de l'Esprit des Lois, n'a réellement besoin d'autre réfutation que lui-même.' Flexier de Réval, *Catéchisme philosophique* (1777), 439.

[56] Montesquieu, *Spirit of the Laws*, 280.
[57] Montesquieu, *Spirit of the Laws*, 283. See also, more extensively, Chapter 6.
[58] Flexier de Réval, *Catéchisme philosophique* (1777), 432.
[59] Montesquieu, *Spirit of the Laws*, 461.   [60] See Chapter 8.

provide another example, prevented, in Feller's eyes, despotism in that region and brought 'European morals and laws' into the heart of Africa, despite the unfavourable climate and geography.[61] So 'moderation' was not only confined to the European continent, but could also be exported along with the Catholic faith: religion, not geography or climate, was for Feller the ultimate determining factor.

In his *Philosophical Catechism*, Feller thus made an eclectic use of enlightened authorities for his *anti-philosophe* and Catholic redefinition of European civilization. During the French Revolution, Feller would invoke Montesquieu's authority several times as ammunition against the French revolutionaries, who also made use of him in their turn.[62] Feller also, more surprisingly perhaps, cited approvingly, Jean-Jacques Rousseau and his views on the beneficial effects of organized religion on society. This referencing showed that the Genevan republican and later revolutionary icon also served as an intellectual authority for the Counter-Enlightenment in the late eighteenth century.[63] However, Feller attacked other iconic *philosophes*. He radically turned against the cultural relativism he associated with Voltaire ('*ce Grand papa de la philosophie*') and other *philosophes* such as Bayle. The positive view of China and its history in Voltaire's *Essai* came in for particular ridicule by Feller. According to him, the Chinese were 'idiots' (*imbéciles*) compared to the Christian Europeans, and he mocked the idealization of China and its supposedly continuous ancient history by the *philosophes*. Chinese older history writing, like the history of ancient Egypt, India, and Babylonia, was nothing but an 'assemblage of fables', contrasting sharply with the—in Feller's eyes—undeniable historical truths of the biblical texts.[64] His Catholic cosmopolitanism in this work had clear boundaries.

5. A Historical Dictionary

Feller's idea of European history was more clearly articulated in his influential and bestselling 'historical dictionary' (*Dictionnaire historique*) of 'men who gained a reputation through their genius, talents, virtues, and errors since the beginning of the world until the present day'. The first of the eventual six volumes of the dictionary was published in 1781, with several revised re-editions in different

---

[61] Flexier de Réval, *Catéchisme philosophique* (1777), 432.   [62] *JHL*, 15 September 1789, 114.

[63] 'Nos gouvernements modernes, dit J.J. Rousseau, doivent incontestablement au Christianisme leur plus solide autorité & leur révolutions moins fréquentes. Il les a rendu eux-mêmes sanguinaires; cela prouve par le fait, en les comparant aux Gouvernements anciens. La Religion mieux connu, écartant le fanatisme, a donné plus de douceur aux mœurs chrétiennes.' Flexier de Réval, *Catéchisme philosophique* (1777), 245. On Rousseau as a counter-enlightened authority: Garrard, *Rousseau's Counter-Enlightenment*; McMahon, *Enemies*, 34–5, 51–2, 99.

[64] Feller even criticized the Jesuits for being too credulous of the historical myths regarding the Chinese emperors. *JHL*, 1 May 1776, 18.

countries and languages in the late eighteenth and early nineteenth centuries.[65] Feller regarded his multivolume dictionary as the synthesis of his knowledge and ideas, although he had difficulties in completing the enormous work.[66] The dictionary, when it came out, was immediately forbidden by the censor of Liège, despite Feller's appeals to the papacy. Feller often complained—not without justification—that state censorship in the Austrian Netherlands was friendlier to the *philosophes* than to their opponents.[67]

It is not surprising that Feller chose the literary genre of the dictionary as it was one of the most prestigious forms of writing in the eighteenth century.[68] The use of the dictionary to advance the *anti-philosophe* agenda formed a good example of the copying of literary genres of the *philosophes* by their self-proclaimed opponents. In response to the publication of Pierre Bayle's *Dictionnaire historique et critique* (1697) and Voltaire's anticlerical *Dictionnaire philosophique* (1764), three Catholic dictionaries were published in France by Catholic apologists: the *Dictionnaire antiphilosophique* by Abbé Chaudon (1767), the *Dictionnaire philosopho-théologique portatif* (1770), and Nonotte's *Dictionnaire philosophique de la religion* (1772). The most respected apologist, Nicolas-Sylvestre Bergier (1718–90), published his own *Dictionnaire de théologie* in the years before and during the Revolution (1788–90). Feller's dictionary should thus be seen as part of this genre of late eighteenth-century anti-philosophical dictionaries. The portable anti-philosophical dictionary became a true 'vademecum of orthodox thought'.[69]

In his *Dictionnaire*, Feller targeted his fellow clergymen such as the Jansenists, the Jesuits' main adversaries, as much as *philosophes* such as Bayle, Voltaire, and the *Encyclopédistes*. In the preface, Feller legitimized his own work by pointing out the deficiencies of existing biographical dictionaries. The dictionaries currently in use, according to Feller, contained either factual mistakes or national prejudices. Other dictionaries were too positive about *philosophie* or inspired 'hatred of Christianity'. Some Catholic dictionaries even erred in being 'too fanatical' and 'too enthusiastic' in their fight against atheism.[70] Feller's book, he claimed, was by contrast based on 'good principles' (*bons principes*), and intended as an impartial service to 'religion, the arts and letters and historical truth'.[71]

---

[65] The editorial history of the *Dictionnaire historique* is complicated. In the eighteenth century, two editions were published in both Liège and Augsburg: the first one in 1781–4 (in six volumes), the second in 1789–94 (Augsburg, 8 volumes with supplement) and '1797' (Liège, 8 volumes). The first nineteenth-century editions were published in 1818 in Liège (8 volumes) and Paris (16 volumes). In 1832, 1836, 1847, and 1866, other French versions followed under the added title of 'Biographie universelle'. Also English, Italian, and Dutch translations were published.
[66] Sprunck, 'Feller', 148.
[67] See, for the context of the writing of the *dictionnaire*: Sprunck, 'Feller', 145–7.
[68] In 1697, Pierre Bayle, for instance, published his influential *Dictionnaire historique*.
[69] Masseau, *ennemis*, 287; Rétat, 'L'âge des dictionnaires', 186–94.
[70] Feller, *Dictionnaire historique* (1781), 'avertissement de la première édition'.
[71] Feller, *Dictionnaire historique* (1781), 'avertissement de la première édition'. Masseau, *Ennemis*, 288–9.

The dictionary consisted of a collection of hundreds of biographies of—mainly—men who had played a role in ancient, European, and, to a lesser extent, Near Eastern history. Life descriptions of biblical figures can be found indiscriminately next to biographies of medieval Islamic philosophers and seventeenth-century European statesmen. Although Feller's style as a compiler of the historical dictionary was far less polemic than in the *Journal historique et littéraire*, the dictionary certainly was intended as an instrument in the war against 'incredulity'. Catholic clergymen were praised, whereas *philosophes* and Protestants generally received a negative press. Arabs and Muslims were often treated surprisingly neutrally, sometimes even positively. Feller wrote, for instance, that he regarded the Arabs as more civilized than most European peoples who were deemed corrupted by philosophy.[72] This positive assessment of Arab cultures contrasts with his uncompromising Catholic Eurocentrism in his other writings, demonstrating that Feller used a different rhetoric for different audiences and his views were not always consistent throughout his *oeuvre*.

The Arab medieval philosopher Averroes, who was revered by the *philosophes*, was, by contrast, blamed by Feller for mutilating Greek classical texts by making mistakes in translating them and for his supposedly anti-Christian mentality.[73] As the entry for the *philosophe* d'Alembert demonstrated, Feller criticized not just the ideas of the *philosophes*, but also tried to use ad hominem arguments to discredit his opponents, as was the custom at this time.[74] D'Alembert's ideas were not just harmful in their content: the *philosophes* also had no morals or character at all, according to Feller. The *philosophes* even failed at being true villains. Precisely because the dictionary claimed to offer a merely neutral biographical description and was widely used as a reference work, it formed an effective instrument in the ideological war against *philosophie*.

The biographical entries were preceded by an extensive essay on the 'chronology of universal history' (*chronologie de l'histoire universelle*). This essay consisted of an explicit refutation of the Enlightenment narrative of European history. In the preliminary chronology, Feller pleaded wholeheartedly for a return to the providential history of the seventeenth-century bishop Jacques-Bénigne de Bossuet.[75] Bossuet's *Discours sur l'histoire universelle* (1681) was praised by Feller as an alternative to the historical narrative of the *philosophes*.[76]

---

[72] The rather neutral, and sometimes even positive, tone is also striking in the entries on the Arabic world in Feller's geographical dictionary. Feller, *Dictionnaire géographique*, 65.

[73] Feller, *Dictionnaire historique* (1797) I, 'Averroes', 438.

[74] Feller, *Dictionnaire historique* (1797) I, 127-9.

[75] Catherine Maire has shown how Bossuet effectively came to agree with Jansenist historians like Duguet and Fleury about the Apocalypse that was at hand, informing his own providentialist outlook. Cf. Maire, *De la cause de Dieu à la cause de la Nation*, 174-5. Feller's appropriation of such Jansenist-Augustinian tropes was thus anything but straightforward. Cf. van Dam, 'Enlightened Reform', 287.

[76] Bossuet, *Discours sur l'histoire universelle*. Feller also referred to Bossuet regularly in his journal (*JHL*), for instance, in the issue of 15 January 1789, 87. In the *Dictionnaire historique*, he wrote regarding Bossuet's *Discours*: 'on ne peut se lasser d'admirer la rapidité avec il décrit l'élévation & la

Bossuet wrote his universal history as part of the attempt to legitimate the absolutist rule of the French king Louis XIV.[77] The bishop had started his 'universal history' with the biblical narrative, from which all human political history until the present flowed. Providence for Bossuet was also the ultimate cause and explanation of all events in human world history. The rise and fall of once-mighty empires, due to divine intervention in Bossuet's narrative, made it abundantly clear that all human history was temporary, and that no human endeavour could endure forever. Feller, at the end of his introductory chronology, cited Bossuet approvingly when he stated that only God, the ultimate cause of all historical development, was himself eternal and unchanging.[78] The truth of the Catholic doctrine was regarded by Bossuet and Feller as universal and timeless, and contrasted with the religious belief of the heretics, which was situated in particular times and places.[79]

The reception of the *Dictionnaire* was not without controversy, which was not surprising given his resistance to the Habsburg authorities in the Southern Netherlands and his own polemical style in the *Journal*. On the occasion of the second edition of the historical dictionary, a hostile pamphlet appeared, calling the dictionary 'the tomb of the reputation of the ex-Jesuit Feller'. Not content with spreading falsehoods in his *Journal*, Feller had now produced work lacking in accuracy, according to the anonymous critic, trying to undermine the credibility of the dictionary. The dictionary was, in the latter's eyes, also a clear case of plagiarism.[80] Feller was, according to his critics in the polarized opinion of late 1780s' publications, far too negative about the rule of the princes and too positive about the track record of the papacy. Above all, Feller's dictionary was regarded in the eyes of his critics as a typical propaganda instrument of the much-maligned Jesuit order, 'that turbulent order of Machiavellists, which vomits monsters whose incendiary maxims have brought disorder everywhere they appear'.[81]

---

chute des empires, les causes de leur progrès & celles de leur décadence, les desseins secrets de la Providence sur les hommes, les efforts cachés qu'elle fait jouer dans le cours des choses humaines'. Feller, *Dictionnaire historique* (1781), 483.

[77] On the absolutist history writing of Bossuet and its reception: Goulemot, *règne de l'histoire*.

[78] 'Par-là se vérifie, ce que dit l'Apôtre, que Dieu est le seul puissant, Roi des Rois et Seigneur des Seigneurs (1 Tim 6); qui voit tout changer sans changer lui-même, et qui fait tous les changements par un conseil immuable; qui donne et qui ôte la puissance; qui la transporte d'un homme à une autre, d'un peuple à un autre, d'une maison à une autre, pour montrer qu'ils ne l'ont tous que par emprunt, et qu'il est le seul en qui elle réside naturellement.' Bossuet, *Discours sur l'histoire universelle*, 3e part, n. 7) as cited by Feller, 'Chronologie de l'histoire universelle', 128.

[79] Chadwick, *Bossuet to Newman*.

[80] 'Le nouveau Dictionnaire des hommes illustres est le tombeau de la réputation de l'Ex Jésuite Feller son auteur, qui n' a fait que tronquer, falsifier un ouvrage qui n'est pas de lui; non content d'avoir long-tems trompé, par son Journal de Luxembourg, le public qu'il trompe encore par son Journal historique & littéraire, il a cru, sans doute, que ses impostures qu'il débite avec une impudence révoltante, auroient pu ensevelir dans les ténèbres de l'oubli, ou du moins rendre douteux, des faits historiques trop attestés pour sauver par ce moyen coupable, l'honneur de la Cour de Rome (...).' *Apologie du Décret du Gouvernement-Général*, 1.

[81] *Apologie du Décret du Gouvernement-Général*, 13.

However, Feller had, in this respect at least, the last laugh: his dictionary would have a long afterlife with many, augmented and corrected, posthumously published re-editions from 1818 onwards. Several translations appeared, including in Dutch and Italian, demonstrating the transnational character of Feller's thought and perhaps of *anti-philosophie* in general.[82] The editions in other languages, however, were much more than merely literal translations. Just as Bonneville changed Russell's history for a French audience, so Feller's dictionary was adapted to different national and historical contexts. The editor of the Italian edition of 1830, for instance, praised Feller for his insight and his efforts 'to oppose the overflowing of false doctrines that perverted the world'.[83] However, as Feller had died in the middle of the revolutionary turmoil in 1802, new names had to be added, later editors explained. Also, more Italian lives were inserted to be relevant for Italian-speaking audiences.[84] So Feller's anti-philosophical dictionary, with his providential account of world history, travelled around Europe, a perfect illustration of the mobility of the ideas of the enemies of the Enlightenment across national boundaries.

6. Providential Chronology

In his introductory chronological essay to his historical dictionary, Feller, building on Bossuet as had many others, provided his own narrative of human history, which fundamentally differed from the enlightened narrative of the *philosophes*.[85] He started his own 'universal history' in 4004 BC. By choosing the biblical creation as a point of departure, Feller rejected Voltaire's focus on the history of China in his *Essai* as the beginning of human worldly history. The marriage of Adam and Eve was described by Feller as the origin of a human social order. The 'Fall of Man' introduced evil into history, and God consequently almost destroyed his creation. After the Flood, the descendants of Noah spread over the earth, and God designated the tribe of Abraham to be his chosen people. With God's selection of Israel, proper human history characterized by political revolutions started, according to Feller.[86] A summary of the history of Israel was depicted in a table inserted in his dictionary.

---

[82] In 1828, also, a Dutch translation of the *Dictionnaire historique* appeared under the title of *Geschiedkundig Woordenboek*.

[83] 'L'Opera pertanto che ci proponiamo di fare italiana con questa prima versione, è in molto parte lavoro del dotto gesuita che nell'ultima metà dello scorso secolo ebbe il coraggio ed il merito con ogni maniera di scritti, e principalmente col suo Dizionario storico, di opporsi argine saldo allo straripare delle false dottrine che pervertirono prima indi insanguinarono tanta parti di mondo.' Feller, *Dizionario Storico* I, preface.

[84] Later additions were marked with a symbol for readers to note the difference between the original articles by Feller and later additions by Italian editors.

[85] On the reception of Bossuet: Goulemot, *règne de l'histoire*.

[86] Feller, 'Chronologie de l'histoire universelle', 1–5.

The histories of the ancient empires of Egypt, Assyria, Babylon, the Persian Empire, and the ancient Greeks were described in a fairly neutral way, without any indication of either admiration or disapproval. Like Bossuet in his universal history, Feller presented an Augustinian narrative of human beings who tried in vain to amass earthly riches and glory: all great empires finally collapsed, and all 'great men' were forgotten soon after their deaths. Universal history for Feller was above all a lesson in human hubris and the transience of earthy strivings, in contrast to the eternal and spiritual world. Feller used the term 'revolution' in the classical meaning of turning, an ever-recurring process of rise, greatness, and the fall of states and empires.[87] European history was thus interpreted by Feller in a continuous line with the sacred history of Holy Scripture. Feller's essay is an important reminder that providential universal history, as prominently written in the seventeenth century, did not just disappear in the eighteenth century to be replaced by more secular Enlightenment narratives. Instead, it was revived by authors such as Feller in the context of the eschatological fight against atheistic philosophy.

In contrast to many other French *anti-philosophes*, Feller did not particularly glorify the Roman Empire, as we have seen.[88] Feller chastised the Roman world for its excessive, immoral, and frivolous character. However, he conditionally admired some Roman authors, such as the Stoic cosmopolitan Seneca, who was, in Feller's eyes, unjustly claimed by contemporary *philosophes* as one of their own.[89] Augustus was termed an '*heureux tyran*', a mild and able administrator but morally corrupt and too lenient in his treatment of his wife, a veritable sin in Feller's view.[90] The homosexual love of Hadrian for Antinous, Feller saw as evidence of the depravity of a Roman emperor admired by the eighteenth-century *philosophes*.[91] On the whole, in Feller's eyes, the Platos, the Ciceros, the Homers, and the Demosthenes of the pagan world were 'eclipsed' in every aspect, literarily as well as intellectually, by the biblical evangelists. The Roman Empire was, for Feller, in essence not different from all the other great empires of the ancient world. Its decline started with the reign of the son of Theodosius: due to Roman decadence barbaric tribes were able to penetrate the borders and to establish themselves in the Roman provinces, forming the kernels of the later modern European nations, and starting modern European history. Constantinople was constructed as a new Rome, but instead of acting as a monument to human glory, it turned out to be another tale of human hubris and immorality.[92]

---

[87] Feller, 'Chronologie de l'histoire universelle', 22. Cf. Baker, *Inventing the French Revolution*.
[88] On the idea of antiquity of the French *anti-philosophes*: Lok, 'berceau des muses'.
[89] 'La plupart des écrivains modernes se sont donné la liberté de peindre cet homme célèbre non d'après sa conduite qui etoit la seule manière de le faire connoitre, mais d'après leur imagination & selon l'estime plus ou moins grande qu'ils avoient conçu de ses ouvrages.' *JHL*, 15 June 1776, 238–9.
[90] Feller, *Dictionnaire historique* (1797) I, 'Augustus', 439–41.
[91] Feller, *Dictionnaire historique* (1797) I, 'Antinous', 256.
[92] 'Mais tel est le sort des choses humaines: cette ville superbe fut sujette aux pestes, aux famines, aux tremblements de terre, aux feux du ciel, aux incursions des Barbares; et il ne s'est passé aucun siècle, depuis sa fondation, qu'elle n'ait été désolée par tous les fléaux.' Feller, 'Chronologie de l'histoire universelle', 75.

Feller regarded the centuries between the fall of the Roman Empire and the Renaissance in the tradition of humanist scholarship as the 'Dark Ages'.[93] The romantic infatuation with the Christian Middle Ages was still mostly absent from Feller's works. However, the Christian Church clearly was, for Feller, not an important cause of cultural backwardness, as it was depicted by Bonneville, but, on the contrary, served as a lonely beacon of light and civilization in an otherwise barbaric era. The Church had at least preserved part of the sciences and culture that would otherwise have been buried under the ruins of the Roman Empire.[94] Also, in the Catholic version of the 'Germanic myth', Feller credited the Germanic peoples with preserving the Christian faith.[95] Feller made a sharp contrast between the vain striving for power and riches by secular rulers, and the role of the papacy in medieval Europe. Feller, foreshadowing the European histories of, for instance, Joseph de Maistre, described the popes as exceptionally wise rulers who spread civilization and enlightenment all over the known world.[96]

The political independence of the pope was, for Feller, a necessary condition for his functioning as a mediator between princes as well as for his role as a spiritual leader. Feller even referred to Voltaire's analysis that the popes of Avignon were too dependent on the French king to be able to act as good Church leaders. The Byzantine patriarchs, who were too obedient to the Eastern Christian Emperor, were regarded as another negative example of religious authorities submitting to secular leaders. Feller even cited David Hume to support his claim that the Catholic Church was the main force behind the development of European civilization, incorporating even the works of this Protestant sceptic into the Catholic apologetic arsenal.[97] Although Feller mentioned the early Church councils as important and useful institutions, they, without any doubt, stood in the shadow of the papacy, as the rightful embodiment of the one true Christian and Catholic universal Church.[98]

In contrast to the history writing by the *philosophes* as well as some *anti-philosophes*, and to a certain extent the entries in his own historical dictionary, Feller almost entirely omitted Asian, African, and American history from his 'chronology of universal history'. He briefly paid attention to the rise of Islam and the history of the Arabic and Persian Empires. Islam was defined in his introduction as a 'sect' and Mohammed as a 'dreamer'. A salient characteristic of the

---

[93] On the Enlightenment and the medieval past: Montoya, *Medievalist Enlightenment*.
[94] 'Sans la Religion Chrétienne les Sciences eussent été ensevelies sous les ruines de l'Empire romain.' Flexier de Réval, *Catéchisme philosophique* (1777), 447.
[95] *JHL*, 1 December 1789, 544.
[96] The legitimation for the papal temporal rule was defended by Feller in a traditional way by referring to the 'gift of Constantine', who had appointed the pope as his political successor when he left Rome for Constantinople. Feller, 'Chronologie de l'histoire universelle', 58–70.
[97] Feller, 'Chronologie de l'histoire universelle', 59.
[98] Feller, 'Chronologie de l'histoire universelle', 58–70.

Islamic Empires was the fact that religious and secular political powers were concentrated in the same hands, resulting in oriental despotism. In the Christian world, by contrast, political and religious authorities were autonomous and separate. Again echoing Montesquieu's *Spirit of the Laws*, Feller underscored the importance of political and religious polycentrism between secular and sacred power as a source of unique European moderation and freedom.[99] However, he strongly disapproved of the religious pluralism that resulted from the religious schisms and the Reformation era: whereas the Catholic Church stood for universal truth and peace, the 'sects' that split from Rome have sown only discord, rebellion, and violence, a standard Catholic argument since the Counter-Reformation.[100]

The last part of the essay on universal history was devoted to the history of the different European countries. Feller, in this essay at least, did not have an idea of 'European history' as more than the sum of the individual histories of the different European nations. He did not refer to a 'European spirit' in a particular age, as, for instance, Bonneville and other enlightened historians had done. Feller started each national history with a short description of the specific characteristics of a European country, which dovetailed very well with eighteenth-century Jesuit protonationalism, followed by an overview of the monarchs and their deeds. His national history was, above all, traditional dynastic history. The history of France was regarded by the Francophile Feller as a *primus inter pares* of all European national histories. Feller described how the imperial authority of Charlemagne, which he praised for bringing about peace in Europe while at the same time preserving the liberties of the Church and the rights of the people, first transferred to France, and was later lost to the Germans.[101] He showed himself fairly impartial in his description of the national histories. However, the history of the Republic of the United Provinces was singled out by Feller as that of a particularly devious state. The sixteenth-century revolt against Spain was, in the eyes of Feller, caused by the 'natural effect of fanaticism' of the Protestants, guided by their despotic leader William of Orange. The Republic's hereditary officeholder, the stadtholder (*stadhouder*) of the House of Orange, was compared to a Roman dictator.[102]

---

[99] Feller, 'Chronologie de l'histoire universelle', 82–3. See also the preceding section.

[100] 'Ces sectes, quoique séparées aujourd'hui de l'Eglise de Rome, sont des preuves de son universalité; c'est dans son sein qu'elles ont appris Jésus-Christ. Elles ont été attachées à l'arbre, avant que d'en être arrachées. 2. Elles font toutes resserrées dans quelques provinces de l'Europe. Aussi divisées entr'elles qu'ennemies de la Catholicité, elles ne se sont jamais empressées à gagner du terrain, sinon par des guerres & les rébellions qu'elles ont excitées dans les États où elles ont trouvé accès.' Flexier de Réval, *Catéchisme philosophique* (1777), 590.

[101] In his *Dictionnaire*, Feller praised Charlemagne as a genius and a model of a Christian prince, a combination of a wise administrator and a good Christian, living in a barbaric age: 'ses lois sur les matières tant civiles qu'ecclésiastique sont admirables, surtout pour un temps moins éclairé que le nôtre (…) L'empire se maintint par la grandeur du chef.' Feller, *Dictionnaire historique* (1782) II, 'Charlemagne', 142. Feller viewed Charlemagne above all as a *French* king.

[102] Feller, 'Chronologie de l'histoire universelle', 117–18.

7. War against Unbelief

In the *Journal historique et littéraire*, Feller used a much more polemical style than in his historical dictionary and he was able to respond more directly to contemporary events.[103] The *Journal* fiercely criticized well-known (French) *philosophes* such as Voltaire, Raynal, and Buffon, but at the same time invoked authors such as Rousseau, Hume, and Montesquieu as authorities in the service of the *antiphilosophe* cause. Feller praised Catholic apologists, such as Barruel and Bossuet, but also viewed negatively others, especially Jansenists, the old adversaries of the Jesuits within the Catholic Church, or other publicists with anti-Jesuit leanings.[104] In certain cases, Feller accepted the historiographical verdict of the *philosophes*. For instance, regarding Emperor Charles V, Feller cited Voltaire's judgement and praised Robertson's account of his life, despite Robertson's enlightened and Protestant background.[105]

Like Bonneville, Feller devoted most of his reflections to contemporary history. 'Modern' history was, in the eyes of Feller, characterized by the pernicious rise of *philosophie*, a phenomenon Feller interpreted essentially, as we have seen, in religious terms as 'atheism' or 'unbelief' (*incrédulité*).[106] Although the omnipresence of *philosophie* was the hallmark of 'our modern age' (*nos temps modernes*), its roots were for Feller much older. Already in the ancient world, precursors of the eighteenth-century *philosophes* could be found among the classical philosophers. A more recent manifestation of perennial unbelief was the Reformation, and the rise of the Protestants and their successors, the Jansenists.[107] According to Feller, there hardly existed any difference between a Jansenist, a Protestant, or a Muslim: all were schismatic enemies of the universal and one true Catholic Church.[108]

In his many reviews of recently published books, Feller pointed to the political and social effects of the rise of *philosophie*. In accordance with the common defence of eighteenth-century Catholic apologists as well as Rousseau, Feller argued that religion is the basis of all social order. In the issue of 15 January 1789, he wrote

---

[103] Although several collaborators were attached to the *Journal*, such as Bernard de Saive, Jean-Noël Paquot, Henri-Ignace Brosius, Jean-Henri Duvivier, l'abbé Hacquet, and possibly Ignace-Xavier Hubens, Feller was the sole editor. Sprung, 'Feller', 139.

[104] Feller's review of Barruel's *Les Helviennes*, for instance, was very positive: 'Les *Lettres* de l'abbé Barruel (...) ont eu, comme elles le meritoient, le plus brillant succès. Les philosophes qui y font attaqués par les armes de la raison & du ridicule tout ensemble, n'ont pas reçu encore de coup plus vigoureux.' *JHL*, 1 November 1789, 323. According to Feller, Barruel demonstrated very well that *philosophie* was not only evidently false, but also had disastrous social consequences.

[105] 'Elle [Robertson's history] est écrite avec autant de vérité qu'on peut en attendre d'un Protestant & d'un philosophe du 18ᵉ siècle, qui écrit l'histoire d'un prince catholique et pieux.' Feller, *Dictionnaire historique* (1782) II, 148.

[106] On the concept of 'modern history', see Chapter 2.   [107] *JHL*, 1 April 1790, 530–44.

[108] *JHL*, 15 May 1790, 169.

a society of which citizens forget the religious principles, cannot subsist: the moral disorder would inevitably lead to a political revolution. Kings of the earth, reflect on this important truth! Religion, much more powerful than armies and soldiers, forms the basis of your power, discards the factions and the rumours, and enables your empire to flourish, renders your legislation beneficial and makes your people happy.[109]

Philosophie undermined religion and thus threatened the political system, and society as a whole, by turning human beings into immoral wild beasts devouring each other or killing themselves out of despair. Due to the spread of *philosophie*, men lost respect for property and became thieves, as in the tale of the philosopher's apprentice.[110]

Feller explicitly conceptualized *philosophie* and the destruction it caused as a pan-European and even global phenomenon. The struggle against atheism should therefore be fought not just in one country, but 'in the four quarters of the world'.[111] 'Europe' was the main theatre of this apocalyptic battle between the forces of (Catholic, Christian) religion and its incredulous adversary in the guise of modern *philosophie*. The specific emphasis on the international dimension of *anti-philosophie* can also be found in the later counter-revolutionary classic *Mémoires pour servir à l'histoire du jacobinisme* (1797), by Feller's fellow former Jesuit, the Abbé Augustin Barruel. Feller referred to the publications by Barruel approvingly on many pages of his *Journal*. According to Barruel, the *philosophes* were connected through a secret international network covering all Europe's corners. They received support from despotic monarchs such as Catherine of Russia and the Prussian king Frederick. The plot against organized religion was, in the eyes of its opponents, a supranational phenomenon and could be fought only by a united and universal Catholic Church, which, also by definition, transcended national boundaries.[112]

---

[109] 'Une société dont les citoyens oublient ou méconnaissent les principes religieux, ne peut point subsister: ce désordre moral doit nécessairement amener une révolution politique. Rois de la terre, méditez sur cette grande vérité! La religion, plus forte que les armées & les soldats, affermira votre puissance, éloignera du trône les murmures & les factions, rendra votre empire florissant, votre législation salutaire & vos peuples heureux.' *JHL*, 15 January 1789, 93.

[110] 'Allez donc, philosophes barbares, allez, répandez-vous dans les carrefours & les temples, pour annoncer aux peuples qu'il n'existe ni crime, ni vertu, ni juste ni injuste. Quand vous feriez ces monstres ennemis par leur nature de tout le genre humain, quand, fortis de l'abime ou la main du très haut les enchaine, pour nous mettre à l'abri de leur jalouse fureur, vous auriez dans vous seuls toute leur haine: quel moyen plus perfide & plus efficace auriez-vous inventé pour détruire les hommes, pour dissoudre à la fois tous les nœuds qui font le bonheur du père, de l'époux, de l'épouse, des enfants, la tranquillité des familles, la sureté, les charmes de la société, la base des empires?' *JHL*, 1 November 1789, 338–40.

[111] *JHL*, 15 April 1790, 634.

[112] Barruel, *Mémoires*. A hagiographic biography: Riquet, *Barruel*. For a criticism of Barruel's conspiracy theories by the counter-revolutionary Mallet du Pan, who also regarded the Revolution as the consequence of philosophy: Burrows, 'Counter-revolution, Conservatism and Conspiracy', 88–107.

Events in modern European history clearly demonstrated for Feller the causal relation linking *philosophie* to rebellion and the breakdown of the social order. An early example of the political effects of the spread of *philosophie* was, for Feller, the sixteenth-century Dutch Revolt, when the spread of Protestantism led to a revolt against the lawful monarch Philip II of Spain. This revolt led to the establishment of the ungodly and monstrous Dutch Republic, an early sanctuary of radical atheism in the heart of the European continent.[113] In more recent history, Feller explained in his comments in the news section of his journal, the outbreak of both the American and the French Revolutions was caused by philosophical atheism. In contrast to Edmund Burke, for instance, who also famously juxtaposed the American and French Revolutions, Feller emphasized the similarities between the two political events.[114] Feller placed particular blame on the works of Guillaume Thomas Raynal (1713–96), Feller's most cited adversary, on the history of European colonization, for the outbreak of the American revolt against England.[115] For Feller, ideas, not economic or political factors, made revolutions.

Feller painted a contrast between the 'moderate' and 'reasonable' English king George III (1738-1820), on the one hand, and the 'fanatical' American rebels on the other. The new American republic had become a state dominated by what he deemed a 'murderous liberty'. In his *Journal* he called for European solidarity against what he perceived as American despotism. For Feller, all the European peoples are united by unbreakable bonds and by common interests and political convictions. He prophesied, not incorrectly as it would turn out, that in the future America would one day dominate 'old Europe', 'the most noble part of the globe'. He also predicted, less correctly, that European migrants would be treated as 'slaves' in the New World.[116] The American Revolution clearly inspired a strong sense of European patriotism and an awareness of a common European destiny in the ex-Jesuit. He was also aware of the international impact of the American Revolution: by aiding the American revolutionaries in their struggle, the French king, like the sorcerer's apprentice from Goethe's ballad, had brought the French Revolution upon himself.

In contrast to France and other European countries where *philosophie* was spreading, Spain presented, for Feller, a model country, a modern counter-enlightened Jerusalem. This *anti-philosophe* utopia, relatively immune to irreligion, was, for Feller, a 'consoling spectacle for those who still wished to see virtue and happiness on earth'.[117] Feller was delirious about the Spanish monarchs in his

---

[113] Feller is, in this respect, ironically, in agreement with historians who emphasize the radical nature of early Dutch Enlightenment thought. Cf. Israel, *Radical Enlightenment*; Jacob, *Radical Enlightenment*.
[114] See Chapter 4.   [115] Raynal, *Histoire des établissements et du commerce dans les deux Indes*.
[116] Sprunck, 'Feller', 224–5.
[117] 'C'est surtout dans le peuple qu'elle [religion] est sensible: & l'on peut dire que dans les provinces ou la corruption & les égarements du philosophisme n'ont pas encore pénétré, l'Espagne offre un spectacle bien consolant pour ceux qui aiment encore à voir la vertu & le bonheur sur la terre'. *JHL*, 15

Dictionnaire as well. He defended the Spanish conquests in the Americas with fervour, attacking the alleged prejudices of the *philosophes*, such as Raynal and Diderot, against Spanish imperialism. Feller praised the Spanish government for taking measures to prevent the spreading of 'French anarchy' to Spain. Feller even defended slavery in the Spanish colonies with the argument that the African slaves were much happier under their Spanish masters than they could ever hope to be in their native lands. He mocked the English antislavery movement, which he believed was hypocritical, and not at all interested in the plight of the slaves, but motivated only by hatred of the Catholic Church.[118] For him the true goal of the antislavery activists, inspired by atheism, was to undermine the Church and the natural social order.

8. Philosophy and Revolution

For Feller, who greatly admired France, the heyday of French culture and freedom was '*le beau siècle*', the late seventeenth century. In this respect Feller wholeheartedly agreed with his *philosophe* adversary Voltaire, with the difference that, for Voltaire, the seventeenth century was admirable for its aesthetic and literary taste, and for Feller, it was so for its religion. Catholic religion and morality supposedly formed the basis of French political and literary greatness as well as French foreign policy under the reign of Louis XIV.[119] The revolutionary depiction of *ancien régime* France as a time of oppression and darkness was, for Feller, a complete fabrication and revolutionary fantasy.[120] In the eighteenth century, by contrast, France had declined primarily as a result of the corrupting influence of philosophy, supported by a foolish and infatuated nobility and a monarchy which acted against its own self-interest. As early as January and February of 1789, Feller predicted that the meeting of the Estates-General in May would lead to the end of the existing social and political order in France.[121]

On the eve of the revolution, Feller called upon his readers to 'adore the judgements of God' and 'to respect the shadows of the future' which was known only to divine providence. In apocalyptic style, he wrote that in the Bible it was announced that a time will come when the rule of the law is extinguished, and

---

April 1789, 576. Also: *JHL*, 1 December 1789, 516. In his historical dictionary, Spanish monarchs usually are praised. Philip II, for instance, was called a 'genius' and in his time 'the principle personage in Europe'. Feller, *Dictionnaire historique* (1783) V, 345.

[118] *JHL*, 15 June 1789, 250; *JHL*, 1 February 1790, 170–2.

[119] *JHL*, 1 June 1789, 185. Works critical of Louis XIV, such as the memoirs of the Count Saint-Simon, were laughed off by Feller with the argument that the author was a Jansenist and a secret Protestant. On the positive evaluation of the foreign policies of Louis XIV: *JHL*, 15 November 1789, 403–8.

[120] *JHL*, 15 March 1790, 463.   [121] For instance, *JHL*, 15 August 1789, 538, 556.

'unbelief will raise its voice and will spread into the extremities of the earth'.[122] Paris was described as a particularly immoral place to which the young swarmed, and then became corrupted. Feller attributed to the theatre an especially pernicious role in spreading 'libertinage' and corrupting the people. The fact that many theatres had burned down in recent years, causing many casualties, could only be seen as a case of wise divine intervention, he wrote in his journal.[123] The fears of the *anti-philosophes* were to be exonerated by the revolutionary events and gained a much wider currency after 1794.[124] In nineteenth-century re-editions of the eighteenth-century *anti-philosophe* texts, Feller's works were praised for their foresight and regarded as more topical than ever.[125]

The unfolding of the Revolution in France from 1789 onwards indeed confirmed Feller in his belief that the destruction of an old constitution inevitably led to political and social chaos.[126] The events in revolutionary France, reported in the *Nouvelles* section of the *Journal*, were framed by Feller in a narrative of increasing chaos, the breakdown of social structures, and the rise of violence due to the attack on the institutions of the *ancien régime*, as prophesied in the Holy Scripture. Like his contemporaries, he believed that he was living in a unique and baffling period in history: 'events, catastrophes and revolutions succeed each other with such speed, that no one can make an idea of it or have witnessed them at all. It is difficult to find a parallel in history.'[127] This sense of disorientation and historical blindness was at the same time for Feller a crucial aspect of an apocalyptical theology, framing the French Revolution as the beginning of the end of human history.[128]

The meetings of the Estates-General were, according to Feller, characterized by dissent and division. Feller argued that the Third Estate was more motivated by irreligion than by a desire for justice or independence from the king.[129] Feller also fundamentally disagreed with the notion of human rights claimed by the revolutionaries: legal equality would lead to destruction of all order but also went against natural law.[130] Minister Jacques Necker (1732–1804) was, in Feller's eyes, the evil

---

[122] 'Adorons les profonds jugements de Dieu! Respectons les ténèbres d'un avenir dont ik possède le secret. Soit que nous touchions à cette époque fatale, si clairement annoncée dans l'Evangile, de l'extinction presque générale de la foi (a), soit que les épreuves présentes & l'espèce de nuage qui entoure ce divin flambeau, nous préparent à une lumière plus éclatant & à de nouvelles conquêtes: il n'est que trop certain que les jours font mauvais (b), que l'impiété élève sa voix jusqu'au ciel & la fait retentir jusqu'aux extrémités de la terre.' *JHL*, 1 February 1789, 162.
[123] *JHL*, 15 April 1789; *JHL*, 1 November 1789, 348.   [124] McMahon, *Enemies*, 95.
[125] [Feller], *Mélanges de politique, de morale et de littéraire*, avertissement.
[126] As the case of Feller's *Journal Historique et Littéraire* demonstrates, a certain ideological continuity between *anti-philosophie* and Counter-Revolution existed, although many counter-revolutionaries started out as *philosophes* as well. Masseau, by contrast, argued that a radical rupture existed in terms of ideas and people between late eighteenth-century *anti-philosophie* and the Counter-Revolution. Masseau, *Ennemis*, 27.
[127] *JHL*, 1 August 1789, 538.
[128] [Feller], *Mélanges* III, 470–1. I thank Michiel van Dam for this suggestion.
[129] *JHL*, 1 April 1789, 547.   [130] *JHL*, 1 September 1789, 59.

genius who orchestrated many of the revolutionary machinations. The partisans of the new constitution, while claiming to act in the name of freedom, did nothing but spread the 'fruits of fanaticism' and chaos on purpose. The true goal of the members of the *Assemblée Nationale* was to get their hands on Church property, following the example of the English king Henry VIII, 'the English Nero'.[131] Feller accused the revolutionaries of creating an 'exaggerated and purely Romanesque' myth of the Bastille prison as a symbol of the oppression and abuse of power of the *ancien régime* monarchy.[132]

Feller also supported the idea, so widespread among counter-revolutionaries such as Barruel, that the Revolution was, in essence, a plot by a small group of scheming *philosophes*. It formed the climax of a century of dark philosophical plans to destroy the Catholic Church and the social order.[133] The ordinary people, kept in the dark by revolutionary leaders regarding the true motivations of the Revolution and unleashed from all traditional constraint, were on the loose, creating havoc all over the country. In the issue of 1 July 1789, Feller, negatively echoing Bonneville's view of the genius, predicted the rise of an all-powerful person who would destroy traditional religion. On the ruins of the old cult an entirely new religion would be founded.[134] The revolutionaries, for Feller, achieved exactly the opposite of what they claimed they were fighting for: instead of liberty it brought despotism, instead of fraternity—war and violence, instead of happiness—misery. '*Philosophie*', Feller summed up, 'whilst at the same time fighting against despotism, plunges the unhappy persons that believe in its message into much more horrible and harmful troubles than it pretends to heal'.[135]

However, not all revolts were to be condemned. Feller actively supported and participated in the resistance of the Southern Netherlands against the centralizing policies of the Habsburg Emperor Joseph II.[136] Joseph tried to reform religious education and to close monasteries, which he deemed useless. In this particular case, it was not the revolutionaries but the monarch who tried to spread *philosophie* and who turned out to be an enemy of religion, in Feller's perspective. By contrast, the so-called rebels were, in Feller's eyes, defending their ancient liberties

---

[131] *JHL*, 1 November 1789, 382, annotation b.

[132] 'Il faut bien se garder d'adopter les idées fausses & calomnieuses de l'auteurs touchant Louis XIV, les lettres de cachet, la Bastille & la cruauté raffinée des officiers employés dans cette prison d'état. Tout cela est purement romanesque & imaginé pour exagérer les abus du pouvoir (...).' *JHL*, 15 December 1789, 567.

[133] *JHL*, 1 November 1789, 381. On the notion of the revolution as a plot by a sect of *philosophes*: McMahon, *Enemies*, 57–73.

[134] *JHL*, 1 July 1789, 335.

[135] 'La philosophie, en même temps qu'elle repousse le despotisme, plonge les malheureux qui croient en ses leçons, dans des malheurs plus affreux encore & plus redoutables que ceux qu'elle prétend guérir.' *JHL*, 1 August 1789, 538.

[136] Polasky, *Revolution in Brussels*; Judge, '"Qu'allons-nous devenir?"'; Roegiers, 'Brabantse omwenteling'; Koll, '*belgische Nation*'; on Belgium in the Napoleonic age: Deseure, *Onhoudbaar Verleden*.

and their religion against their irreligious and despotic overlord. This tyrant did not respect traditional rights and could thus be considered a dangerous revolutionary himself. Full of patriotic fervour, Feller sharply contrasted the French youth corrupted by *philosophie* with the pious and virtuous Belgians, the true carriers of the threatened Catholic faith in Europe.

In the Southern Netherlands, loyal Catholics could be regarded as good patriots. Instead of stimulating national feeling, *philosophie* destroyed all sense of patriotism, as the French had demonstrated, according to Feller. For Feller, *philosophie* is, by definition, antinational, incapable of serving a higher common goal.[137] For him, anti-Jansenist and anti-enlightened Catholic cosmopolitanism and South-Netherlandish patriotism seamlessly overlapped.[138] Feller was confident that the horrific example of the cannibalistic fate of revolutionary France would prevent the spreading of philosophical ideas in the Southern Netherlands.[139] For Feller, the Brabant Revolt had a significance far beyond the local: in the Southern Netherlands the rise of unbelief would be stopped with the aid of divine providence, and the revival of religion in Europe would commence. The Belgian revolt for Feller became a turning point of biblical proportions in the larger apocalyptic narrative of European and global history.[140]

In all his writings on revolution and philosophy, in the United States, France, or Brabant, the concept of liberty took centre stage in Feller's thought.[141] Feller did not reject human freedom out of hand, but instead used the vocabulary of liberty to counter the argument made by his ideological revolutionary enemies. In the issues of the *Journal historique et littéraire*, a description of two kinds of liberty can be found.[142] Feller discerned a 'false' or 'murderous' liberty, the chimerical

---

[137] 'Le François ne se reconnait plus à l'air français: ses traits, son caractère, son œil n'inspirent plus la confiance.' *JHL*, 15 April 1790, 569.

[138] Van Dam, 'Christian Cosmopolitanism'; van Dam, 'Een spirituele revolutie?'. Cf. Roegiers, 'At the Origin of Revolution', 325; Trousson, 'L'abbé F.-X. de Feller et les "philosophes"'.

[139] 'L'exemple de la France qui se détruit & dévore elle-même, est pour eux un excellent préservatif contre les assassinats philosophiques.' *JHL*, 15 February 1790, 283. In this issue Feller explained his views on the Belgian revolution to a Hungarian nobleman.

[140] *JHL*, 15 April 1790, 607–24. Cf. van Dam, 'Christian Cosmopolitanism'. On the Belgians as the 'chosen people': Polasky, 'Providential History in Belgium'.

[141] Sociologist Karl Mannheim has argued that early-nineteenth-century German conservatives, compelled by political necessity, developed a 'concrete and qualitative idea of liberty' to distinguish it from the revolutionary egalitarian abstract concept. Early Romantic conservatives then supposedly detached this qualitative idea of liberty from the individual and transferred it to larger collectives, the organic communities of the estates, the state, or the nation. Feller's idea of liberty, however, cannot be regarded as 'romantic' as he did not conceive of freedom in terms of a unique and singular development of individuals and collectives, but instead primarily as the moderation of state power by history and religion. Mannheim, 'Conservative Thought', 292–5. Feller thus did not fit into the counterrevolutionary idea of liberty, as analysed by de Dijn: de Dijn, *Freedom*, 231–76.

[142] Feller's anti-enlightened idea of freedom can be traced to sixteenth-century Counter-Reformation thought. Already in Catholic tracts in the sixteenth century, the idea was attacked that a state should be governed only on the basis of consideration of political power and reason of state associated with Machiavelli. *JHL*, 1 March 1789, 325. On the topic of Catholic anti-Machiavellism: Bireley, *Counter-Reformation Prince*; Kattenberg, 'Power of Necessity'. So far Protestant and Catholic anti-Machiavellism in the eighteenth and nineteenth centuries has not been sufficiently researched.

ideology of destructive political revolutions, from a true freedom in accordance with religion and tradition. Abstract concepts of freedom, individual rights, the idea of popular sovereignty, and religious toleration would lead to a society without morals that would eventually disintegrate into chaos. The liberty of the press, a degenerate form of tolerance in Feller eyes, invoked by magistrates and lawyers, had invited a deluge of seditious pamphlets and scandalous brochures. Even worse, unbelief would lead to unhindered state power and an 'empire of despotism'.[143] According to Feller, British imperialism was more oppressive than the colonial empires of the other European countries, precisely because England was a so-called free state with its origins in a revolution against a legitimate overlord.[144] The most terrible despotism thus 'wears the mask of liberty'.[145]

9. The New Dark Ages

The continent-wide—and even global—war against the dangerous rise of philosophy also had a strong cultural and literary dimension. In many articles in his *Journal*, Feller related the rise of 'atheistic' philosophy to the development of the arts and sciences in Europe, and France in particular. For him, following Voltaire, the seventeenth century had been the zenith of cultural development when a 'great number of French authors such as Corneille, Racine, Molière, Boileau & la Fontaine (…) flourished under the absolute authority of Louis XIV'.[146] Only under an absolutist as well as a Catholic monarchy could the arts thrive. Looking backward in time, Feller explained the cultural Renaissance in the sixteenth century by the encouragement and the protection of the arts by Pope Leo X and the French king Francis I. In the century following the death of 'Louis le Grand' (Louis XIV), literature and the arts had consequently declined and fallen into disrepair.

The prime cause of the contemporary sterility of French literature was undoubtedly, in Feller's eyes, the sect of the '*encyclopédistes*'. The sceptre over the 'literary empire' was now in the hands of the prince of the *philosophes*, Voltaire, the despotic 'patriarch of our literature'.[147] In an 'epistle on modern literature and the strengths of antiphilosophical criticism', published in the *Journal* issue of 1 July 1776, the profound decadence and deep obscurity of French letters is bemoaned.[148]

---

[143] 'Je vois avec douleur profaner ce saint nom de liberté par la plupart de ceux qui l'invoquent. On cherche la liberté dans l'indépendance. Elle n'est que dans la règle. Supprimez toutes ces gênes des loix, qui dirigent les mouvements de la liberté & en répriment les écarts, vous établirez la plus cruelle des tyrannies, la plus hideuse des servitudes.' *JHL*, 1 November 1789, 394.

[144] 'La domination d'un peuple libre est encore plus dure que celle d'un despote.' *JHL*, 1 May 1776, 6.

[145] *JHL*, 15 November 1789, 466.   [146] *JHL*, 1 July 1776, 323.   [147] *JHL*, 1 June 1776, 178.

[148] 'Dans cette effroyable abondance, de froids & stériles écrits, dont les objets & l'affluence, annoncent moins de nos esprits, les progrès que la décadence. Moins leur force que leur enfance, et nous exposent au mépris, en étalant notre opulence: dans cette foule de journaux, dont le déluge nous inonde, et qui tombent, à peine éclos, dans une obscurité profonde.' *JHL*, 1 July 1776, 399.

Furthermore, the dominance of the *encyclopédistes* had resulted in a feeble cultivation of the sciences in eighteenth-century France. In comparison to the depths and profound physical, geometrical, and mathematical knowledge of the Germans and the English, French science had become shallow: abstract theories were proposed by French scholars to hide what is, in essence, scientific '*charlatanerie*'.[149]

Feller was not alone in his European cultural pessimism on the eve of the Revolution. Notions of cultural decline and decadence were also widespread in the writings of Feller's adversaries, the *philosophes*, although obviously their solutions differed widely from those of their self-proclaimed opponents. In their eyes, it was the lack of progress and *philosophie*, not the spreading of it, that was causing France's cultural decline.[150] Also, other *anti-philosophes* decried the cultural decadence of France and Europe. Jean-Antoine Rigoley de Juvigny (1709–88), honorary councillor of the *Parlement* of Metz and a member of the Academy of Sciences in Dijon, provided an example of a different strand of anti-enlightened cultural pessimism. Rigoley differed from Feller in the sense that he approached the topic of cultural decline less from the perspective of rising unbelief, as had Feller, and more from the perspective of the neglect of the classical legacy and literary tradition. By putting the works of Rigoley next to those of Feller, we can observe different variations of *anti-philosophe* writing on cultural decline.[151]

In his treatise *De la décadence des lettres et des mœurs, depuis les Grecs et les Romains jusqu'à nos jours* (1786), Rigoley argued that it was above all the neglect of humanist classical studies that resulted in the literary collapse of France. The so-called century of lights was, for him, an age of literary decline and corruption of morals, caused by the forgetting of classical models.[152] For Rigoley, the cultural history of mankind is not a story of continuous progress, but, on the contrary, a tale of high cultural achievement followed by the inevitable decline when classical models are no longer followed and the tradition is lost. By chronicling the zenith and nadir of European cultural history, Rigoley provided an interpretative framework for the literary low point at which France and Europe found itself towards the end of the eighteenth century. His work was thus indicative of the pessimistic cultural climate that characterized the last decades of the eighteenth century.[153]

Ancient Greece was for Rigoley, in sharp contrast to Feller, the 'veritable cradle of the muses', Homer was the 'greatest philosopher' that ever lived, Herodotus the 'most perfect' of all historians, and Plato the 'most eloquent' of all philosophers.[154]

---

[149] *JHL*, 1 June 1776, 180.   [150] Mortier, 'L'idée de la décadence littéraire'.
[151] On the rise of cultural criticism in the eighteenth century: Jung, *Zeichen des Verfalls*.
[152] 'Malgré le titre superbe de Siècle des Lumières, dont notre Siècle se décore, nous n'avons jamais été plus fondé à nous plaindre non seulement de la décadence des lettres et du Goût, mais même de la corruption des mœurs. A quoi devons-nous en attribuer la cause, si n'est au vice de notre éducation, a la faiblesse de nos études, à l'oubli des modèles de l'Antiquité savant, aux écarts enfin dans lesquels le Bel-Esprit & une philosophie insensée & trompeuse ont entraîné la génération présente?' Rigoley de Juvigny, *décadence des lettres*, 1–2.
[153] Cf. Rotmans, 'Enlightened Pessimism'.   [154] Rigoley de Juvigny, *décadence des lettres*, 4–23.

However, after Demosthenes, the ancient Greeks no longer followed their own classical models and their culture declined. A new high point of cultural achievement was reached in Rome with the coming of the Augustan age in the first century AD. But under Emperor Augustus, the rot set in as the Romans, who had become too arrogant and proud, no longer respected tradition and tried to introduce innovations instead. Whereas Feller still valued Seneca, for Rigoley the Roman philosopher embodied human hubris and depravity, 'and thus eloquence was corrupted'.[155]

The question to what extent the ancient pagan philosophers were precursors of the contemporary *philosophes* was a matter of debate among the *anti-philosophes*.[156] Feller, for instance, interpreted the works of most ancients as early manifestations of *philosophie* and condemned them. Others, such as Rigoley and Barruel, on the contrary, stated that the often-drawn parallel between ancient philosophers and their contemporary counterparts was another aspect of the *philosophe* plot.[157] They consciously rejected the cultural appropriation of ancient writers by the radical Enlightenment. Eighteenth-century *philosophes*, in their eyes, wrongly identified themselves with the great minds of the ancient world from Socrates to Marcus Aurelius.[158] For many *anti-philosophes* and later counter-revolutionaries, most classical philosophers were firmly on the side of the Catholic Church and its fight against incredulity, notwithstanding their disapproval of the social and political effects of abstract philosophy in antiquity.[159] So, both the *philosophes* and their enemies claimed the classical authors.

Bonneville, Feller, and Rigoley all believed in the Gallic origins of modern France and Europe. They, however, had a different version of the Germanic achievements and mirrored their own beliefs in the imagined tribal societies. Whereas, for Bonneville, the ancient Gauls stood for revolutionary freedom and, for Feller, the Gauls were the defenders of the Catholic religion, the importance of Gaul for Rigoley lay first and foremost in the preservation of the classical

---

[155] Rigoley de Juvigny, *décadence des lettres*, 194. Feller's appreciation of Seneca was conditional though; while Stoicism stood in closer proximity to truth than enlightened philosophy, it was still trumped by Christian morality. Cf. Feller's discussion of Maupertuis in: Flexier de Réval, *Catéchisme philosophique* (1777), 460–6. I thank Michiel van Dam for this suggestion.

[156] The image of antiquity and the classics in *anti-philosophe* thought is a much-understudied topic. Historians of *anti-philosophie*, such as Darrin McMahon, focus primarily on the religious dimension of *eranti-philosophe* thought. McMahon, *Enemies*. Scholars of the image of antiquity in eighteenth-century France, however, usually study exclusively the *philosophes*. Cf. Gay, *Enlightenment* I, 31–126; Parker, *Cult of Antiquity*; C. Grell, *dix-huitième siècle*.

[157] Barruel, *Mémoires* (1803), 278. According to Barruel, Voltaire differed from the classical *philosophes* in the sense that the classical authors at least had an idea of a (false) God, whereas Voltaire believed in no God whatsoever.

[158] According to Peter Gay, 'through the noise of antique debates, the philosophers heard a certain ground tone, a tone of confidence in rational enquiry, of contempt for superstition or naiveté, in a word, or reliance on critical philosophy'. Gay, *Enlightenment* I, 126. At the same time the *philosophes* distanced themselves from the classical authors.

[159] Lok, 'Oudheid', 67–71.

tradition.[160] For the Dijon academic, the Gauls were essentially a conservative people who achieved the perfect symbiosis of the classical legacy and the Christian religion. The reign of Charlemagne was, for Rigoley, another example that Christianity and ancient civilization should not be seen as opposites, as the *philosophes* had argued, but were indeed complementary. As with Feller, Rigoley's appreciation of the Church did not translate into a positive judgement on the Middle Ages, seen by him also as a barbaric period dominated by fables, immoral love stories, and frivolous chivalry.

During the Renaissance, in Rigoley's narrative, the classical models were rediscovered and perfected, above all in the 'Golden Age' of French culture under Louis XIV, 'the century of talents'.[161] Rigoley drew clear historical parallels between seventeenth-century France and Augustan Rome, both high points of literary and cultural development, stimulated by strong monarchy and the reverence for classical models. However, as in the Augustan age, arrogance caused the neglect of tradition and ushered in the decline: 'always the *Bel-esprit* has been the precursor of false philosophy, and we will not hesitate to demonstrate how disastrous this alliance [of *bel-esprit* and philosophy] has been to letters, taste (*gout*) and morals (*mœurs*)'.[162] The alleged '*siècle des lumières*' was for Rigoley nothing more than the coming of a new dark ages.

Although Rigoley's primary concern was the classical tradition, he firmly connected this legacy to the Catholic Church. A particular blow to classical education was, in his eyes, the decline in Catholic education and in particular the dissolution of the Jesuits, a traumatic event for Feller personally as well. The Jesuits were truly the inheritors of the ancient world for Rigoley. The only possible solution to the cultural crisis of the classics, caused by the rise of philosophy, was to improve the schooling for the young. Pedagogy should be firmly based on the twin pillars of Revelation and (a selection of) the classical authors, a symbiosis that had been reached by the classical French authors of the age of Louis XIV. As a true traditionalist, Rigoley ended his treatise by decrying the attack on tradition and the pedagogical wisdom that had been accumulated over the centuries in exchange for 'frivolities, trivial reflections, and errors'.[163]

The appeal to the classical tradition by French conservatives did not end in 1789 but was reinforced by the events of the revolutionary Terror, which was itself partly inspired by ancient models. In his opening speech for the *Lycée républicain* on 1 December 1796, Jean-François de la Harpe (1739–1803) discussed what caused the 'revolutions of the human spirit'.[164] Why is the 'torch' of cultural achievements in some cases extinguished forever and in other cases several times rekindled?, La Harpe wondered. He found his answer in the blind veneration for

---

[160] On the concept of 'antiquity' in eighteenth-century French thought: Grell, *dix-huitième siècle*.
[161] Rigoley, *décadence des lettres*, 340.   [162] Rigoley, *décadence des lettres*, 332.
[163] Rigoley, *décadence des lettres*, 501.   [164] Harpe, *état des lettres en Europe*.

cultural innovation (*l'amour aveugle de la nouveauté*) that destroyed all cultural achievements.[165] The recovery of classical civilization during the Renaissance had been undermined by the *philosophes*, 'the barbarians of the eighteenth century', and finally destroyed by the revolutionaries.[166] De La Harpe wrote that he had become a counter-revolutionary as the Revolution had destroyed not just the arts and the letters, but that 'the revolutionary spirit is diametrically opposed, not only to the republican government, but to any government whatsoever'.[167] De La Harpe's views were all the more salient as he underwent a conversion during the Revolution: before the Revolution, he was a *philosophe*, heavily criticized by Feller in the pages of his *Journal*.[168] As a result of the Terror, the former *philosophe* became one of their staunch enemies, as did many others.

10. Conclusion: Counter-Enlightened Pessimism and Renewal

In the increasingly polarized decades preceding the French Revolution, a self-conscious transnational anti-enlightened movement came into being, fiercely criticizing the 'century of lights'. Self-proclaimed *anti-philosophes* fought an apocalyptic battle against the forces of unbelief, often appropriating ideas and literary forms, such as the dictionary or the journal, of their ideological opponents. *Anti-philosophe* texts were circulated and adapted to different national and linguistic contexts. As the case of Feller demonstrated, this Francophone anti-Enlightenment was distinctly cosmopolitan in character, albeit strictly confined to the Catholic world. Feller was not always consistent in his discourse, as could be observed in the contrast between his relative sympathy for the Arab peoples in his *Dictionary*, on the one hand, and his polemical and intolerant defence of universal Catholicism in his *Journal*, on the other.

History writing was one of the select fields in which the ideological battle between the *philosophes* and *anti-philosophes* was waged. Feller's aim was to cleanse contemporary history writing of *philosophe* dominance and roll back the philosophical offensive. It has been shown in this chapter that the biblically inspired universal history in the tradition of Bossuet did not disappear in the late eighteenth century but was revived by Feller and others. Modern European history was for Feller in essence not a different kind of history from history as described in Holy Writ. Jewish and Islamic history, as well as the history of the Near East in general, formed part of Feller's 'universal history', while Eastern and Southern Asian, American, and African history was mostly excluded. Instead of a

---

[165] Harpe, *état des lettres en Europe*, 2.
[166] 'Ombres illustres [of the classical civilization], que j'aime évoquer ici (. . .), voilà donc ce qu'ont anéanti les barbares du dix-huitième siècle, qui se sont nommés Philosophes!' Harpe, *état des lettres en Europe*, 19.
[167] Rigoley, *décadence*, avertissement.   [168] For instance, in the *JHL* issue of 15 June 1776.

story of linear progress over the long term, these *anti-philosophe* narratives thus contained a more cyclical narrative of rise, and especially decadence and fall. At the same time, Feller depicted the Church as an enlightened civilizer, stimulating the arts and the sciences, and thus bringing progress as well as softening the behaviour of modern man.

A profound European cultural pessimism, due to the rise of what was perceived as an 'atheistic' philosophy, was expressed in *anti-philosophe* public opinion in the decades preceding the Revolution. All around him, Feller observed the rise of the *philosophes* and their pernicious influence ('*le jour de la ruine est proche*'). The loss of traditions was bemoaned, and the idea defended that without religion and a strong absolutist ruler, the arts and sciences could not flourish. Above all, Feller argued that philosophy and the consequent revolutions destroyed freedom and inaugurated the rule of despotism. The perception of a struggle between 'religion' and 'unbelief' was described by apologists such as Feller, Barruel, Rigoley, and La Harpe very much in European and global terms, with France as its main stage. Also, the revolutionary events were described in eschatological and apocalyptic terms, signalling the end of normal history and human time.[169]

Rather than being merely conservative defenders of the existing order, *anti-philosophes* pleaded for a radical renewal of this fundamentally corrupt and decaying society. Feller, Rigoley, and other *anti-philosophes* propagated a thorough reform of education on religious, traditional, and moral bases as the only possible way of avoiding the coming of a new dark age. Feller's adversaries were not only the revolutionaries and their ideologues, but also the Habsburg government of the Southern Netherlands, and to a lesser extent the accommodating and passive Church hierarchy itself. Foreshadowing later publications by Joseph de Maistre and other counter-revolutionaries, Feller hinted that providence might interfere to cleanse Europe and to restore the Catholic faith to its central place. The intense yearning for European spiritual and moral renewal clearly pre-dated the revolutionary events of 1789.

---

[169] Feller wrote: 'le jour de la ruine est proche & les temps se hâtent d'arriver'. *JHL*, 1 July 1789, 331.

4
Crusaders for Moderation

1. A Boundless Perspective

(...) Europe, at this critical juncture, opens, to the members of the British senate, the most extensive field for speculation; it presents, to their consideration, objects the most interesting, and scenes the most extraordinary: it offers a boundless perspective, and a horizon, on all sides, clouded, and obscured. Never was it more important to dive into futurity, and never did futurity seem more impenetrable; never therefore was it more excusable to be lost in conjectures. When every occurrence is improbable, it can excite no surprise that its consequences cannot be anticipated.[1]

These words were written in 1795 by the French exile Charles-Alexandre de Calonne (1734–1802) in his treatise *Tableau de l'Europe*. In this treatise Calonne, a former minister of Louis XVI then residing in exile in London, gave his views on the current political situation in Europe for the benefit of a British as well as continental readership. He emphatically opposed, in particular, the conclusion of a peace treaty by Britain with the French revolutionary Republic, established in 1792. As the citation showed, Calonne, like Feller, expressed a sense of profound bewilderment over the course of recent European history: history no longer seemed to follow a 'normal' trajectory. Time had become completely unpredictable: everything seemed possible now, a 'boundless perspective' had opened up. This was also the moment when the decisions taken by statesmen would determine the course of history for future generations.[2]

In the 1790s, in response to international developments and war, counter-revolutionaries like Calonne increasingly turned to the urgent problem of the ordering of Europe in their publications. Between 15 March 1792 and February 1793, according to French historian Marc Belissa, a conscious break was made by

---

[1] Calonne, *Political State of Europe*, 1–2. The original French version: 'Le tableau de l'Europe, en ce moment où les séances du Parlement d'Angleterre viennent de se rouvrir, présente au réflexions politiques de ses membres, le champ le plus vaste & le plus intéressant, mais en même temps la perspective la plus trouble & la plus chargées de nuages. S'il n'y eût jamais plus de motifs pour désirer de pénétrer dans l'avenir, jamais aussi l'avenir ne fut plus impénétrable & jamais on ne fut plus excusable de s'égarer dans les conjonctures.' [C. de Calonne], *Tableau de l'Europe*, 3. By 'senate' Calonne meant the 'House of Lords'.

[2] Cf. Koselleck, *Vergangene Zukunft*. See also Chapter 1.

the revolutionaries with the pre-revolutionary international politics of Minister Vergennes (1719–87), which until then had prevailed even during the early years of the Revolution. The *ancien régime* diplomats were consequently replaced by revolutionary men.[3] Vergennes' unpopular Austrian alliance received particular scrutiny. The start of the war in April 1792, and above all the fall of the monarchy on 10 August in that same year, made contemporaries realize that the old European order, 'the old edifice', had broken down.

The worsening of the international situation and the entry of Spain and Great Britain into the war against the revolutionary Republic in February 1793 resulted in the suspension of all diplomatic ties between revolutionary France and most other European states. The unexpected military successes of the French Republic in the summer of 1794 and in the winter of 1794–5 in the Netherlands and in Spain, led to a breakdown of the first coalition. In 1795, a general feeling spread among diplomats and statesmen such as Calonne that the old European order no longer functioned and needed to be mended. The key question was what role, if any, the revolutionary Republic, which was based on such different principles from the monarchical states, should play in the existing monarchical order.[4]

After the Thermidor *coup d'état* (27 July 1794), the revolutionary Republic transformed into a more moderate regime and the radical phase of the Revolution had come to an end, or so the revolutionary leaders claimed.[5] The new Directory regime tried to maintain stability and to prevent a return of the revolutionary Terror that had shocked European society to its core. In public opinion in the different countries, pleas could be heard in favour of a permanent peace treaty with this Thermidor regime, a de facto acceptance of the legitimate existence of the revolutionary Republic among the European monarchical states.[6] Spain, Tuscany, and finally also Prussia, started peace negotiations. On 5 April 1795, a peace treaty was signed at Basel between France and Prussia. This peace agreement was followed by the Treaty of The Hague with the newly installed Batavian Republic, and a treaty with Spain on 22 July 1795. The war continued, however, with Austria, Great Britain, and some of the German states. On 18 October 1797, a truce was also signed between France and the Habsburg Empire after the resounding victories of the revolutionary general Bonaparte in Italy. Negotiations started at Rastatt to discuss a general peace for the Holy Roman Empire, which would

---

[3] Belissa, *Repenser l'ordre Européen*, 43.
[4] 'La Révolution menace non seulement l'homogénéité et les principes de la société des États mais aussi des formes de régulation (droit publique et équilibre) et les rapports de force au sein de cette société.' Belissa, *Repenser l'ordre Européen*, 48.
[5] Baczko, *Comment sortir de la Terreur*; Jainchill, *Reimagining Politics*.
[6] Belissa, *Repenser l'ordre Européen*, 21–4.

eventually fail. On 12 March 1799, the war of the Second Coalition had begun, which was ended with the Treaty of Amiens in 1802.[7]

In the eyes of concerned contemporaries, the revolutionary wars had shattered the old international system that had existed in the eighteenth century since the Peace of Utrecht of 1713. Revolutionaries, as well as their enemies, discussed the shape of this new international order that would take its place. Charles-Alexandre de Calonne and Edmund Burke (1730–97) were both prominent writers on the problem of a restored international order. These protagonists of this chapter were not 'historians' in a restricted sense of the word, but these political actors used European and national history in the articulation of their political views, thus contributing to the construction of the idea of a 'historical Europe'. The contacts and conversations between Calonne and the British politician and man of letters Burke offer a striking example of the possibilities, as well as limitations, of the transnational conversation on the international system, and the Counter-Revolution in general.

Although recently important studies have been published on the *monarchiens* and other French 'moderate' counter-revolutionaries, few publications have appeared on Calonne since the 1960s.[8] I will argue that despite the vagaries of Calonne's political life, his views on the French political system were more or less coherent throughout his career, as Calonne also claimed himself. Also, I will extensively emphasize the transnational context of Calonne's cosmopolitan life and thought, situating him outside the French national context. More generally, I will argue that the different traditions of counter-revolutionary thought were not isolated but influenced each other, often through exiles such as Calonne who acted as intermediaries. Burke, by contrast, has not suffered from lack of scholarly attention. As a result of renewed scholarly attention to the imperial as well as the Atlantic dimension of Burke's thought, the important European historical dimension of his historical works has been somewhat overshadowed.[9]

Calonne's *Tableau* of 1795 formed part of a wider stream of publications on the future order of Europe, which came out during the Directory regime (1795–9), by self-proclaimed counter-revolutionaries. So far, much more attention in the scholarly literature has been given to the pro-revolutionary views of attaining 'perpetual peace' by building some kind of a (con)federation of revolutionary republics.[10] It is less known that in response to the revolutionary events, also

---

[7] Belissa, *Repenser l'ordre Européen*, 135–54; Schroeder, *Transformation of European Politics*, 100–76; Blanning, *Pursuit of Glory*, 611–37; Blanning, *French Revolutionary Wars*; Jourdan, *Nouvelle histoire*. On the impact of war on European society: Blaufarb, Forrest and Hagemann, Palgrave Macmillan series 'War, Culture and Society'.

[8] An important study on Calonne and the Assembly of Notables of 1787 in German is: Klesmann, *Notabelnversammlung 1787*.

[9] Burke, *Writings and Speeches*.

[10] Serna, 'l'Europe, une idée nouvelle?', 1–16; Wahnich, 'L'Europe dans le discours révolutionnaire', 11–28; Belissa, *Repenser l'ordre Européen*. See also Chapter 2.

counter-revolutionaries 'invented' their idea of Europe and European history, partly building on pre-revolutionary *philosophe* as well as *anti-philosophe* narratives. Dreams of perpetual peace could also be found among the counter-revolutionaries, although their means to achieve it were different from those on the revolutionary side of the political spectrum.

The key concept in the counter-revolutionary rethinking of Europe in the late 1790s, and the individual countries that constitute it, was the notion of the 'ancient constitution'. Of course, the idea of the 'ancient constitution' was not a new idea in the revolutionary decade. 'Ancient constitution' formed a very broad and malleable concept, which was interpreted in many different ways in different national and intellectual traditions.[11] The concept, however, gained new political urgency as a result of the impact of the French Revolution and the revolutions elsewhere in Europe. Rather than being mere reactionaries, the authors studied in this chapter advocated not a blind return to a previous order in the distant future, but instead argued for an improved and reformed version of this older—usually unwritten—ancient constitution, both on the level of the state and the European state system.

In the counter-revolutionary discourse of the protagonists, the ancient constitution above all guaranteed a 'moderate' exercise of power in line with the rule of law, as well as a unique liberty, characteristic of European monarchies since their foundation. These unique features of the political system of Europe were, however, threatened by revolutionary radicalism, which would eventually result in despotism as well as anarchy. So far, most research on the concept of the ancient constitution in different European countries has focussed on the exclusive national context; the idea that ancient constitutions of individual states formed part of a wider European institutional context, the topic of this particular chapter, has been less explored.

In the next section, the life and writings of Calonne, the years until 1795, will be described and analysed, followed by paragraphs on Calonne's interpretation of the concept of the 'Counter-Revolution'. Then the émigré community and the counter-revolutionary transnational public sphere will be discussed from the perspective of Calonne's journal *Courier de Londres*. Subsequently, the relationship between Calonne and Edmund Burke and their idea of a European 'commonwealth' will be explored. The last sections deal with the transnational post-Terror debate on a new European order and Calonne's intervention in this debate. The conclusion revisits the reinvention of the idea of the 'ancient constitution' and 'moderate monarchism' in a European and transnational context.

---

[11] Pocock, 'Burke and the Ancient Constitution'; Pocock, *Ancient Constitution*; Burgess, *Politics of the Ancient Constitution*; van den Bossche, *Enlightened Innovation*; Deseure, 'De lange schaduw'; Velema, *Enlightenment and Conservatism*; Boom, 'Against Enlightened Abstraction'; Kondylis, *Konservatismus*; Epstein, *Genesis of German Conservatism*; Baker, *Inventing the French Revolution*; Carcassonne, *Montesquieu*.

2. From Office to Exile

Calonne's life and writings exemplified the ideological continuity between pre-revolutionary enlightened reform and counter-revolutionary activism in the 1790s. Calonne came from a rising family from the North of France—his father was a member of the provincial *parlement*. He himself was born in 1734 in Douai, a Flemish town that had been incorporated into the French kingdom as recently as 1668, as a result of the conquests of Louis XIV. He was an excellent student at a college founded by Cardinal Mazarin in Paris to groom talented youngsters of the newly acquired territories for the service of the French state. After a short stint as a lawyer in Douai, he quickly became, subsequently, *avocat general* at the *Conseil superieur de Artois* in 1758, *procureur* and *maitre de requêtes* at the *Conseil d'État* in 1762, the incubator of administrative talent. From 1766 to 1783, he acted as intendant first at Metz, like Douai a relatively recently annexed city, and in Lille, an important administrative post. In these functions he developed into an experienced royal administrator and was able to build an extensive network in Paris, only two days' travel from Lille.[12]

Calonne reached the zenith of his administrative career in November 1783, when the king made him controller-general (*contrôleur general*), the equivalent of the functions of minister of the interior, finance, and economy all in one.[13] As a sign of royal favour, Calonne was made minister of state with the privilege to attend all royal councils, thus effectively becoming the key official in the royal government. Calonne's task as controller, however, was daunting as the financial problems facing the monarchy were enormous. The recent wars of American independence had put a great strain on finances, as had the many public works undertaken by the monarchy. The financial difficulties of the French monarchy were also structural: too many sections of the population claimed tax exemptions and French finances were badly organized. To overcome the resistance of established and privileged groups against his reforms, and to ask for new loans, Calonne, at the beginning of 1787, organized a 'meeting of notables' (*Assemblée des notables*) on the model of a seventeenth-century precedent, somewhat naively trusting that the authority of the king would be sufficient to overcome all opposition to his reforms.

In his speech to the 130 notables assembled at the Versailles palace on 22 February 1787, Calonne outlined his vision for a reformed French state.[14] In contrast to his predecessor Jacques Necker (1732–1804), Calonne painted a sombre picture of the 'very critical state' of the French finances to create a sense

---

[12] Lacour-Gayet, *Calonne*, 11–45. Another literary biography is: Jolly, *Calonne*.
[13] Lacour-Gayet, *Calonne*, 46–7.   [14] Klesmann, *Notabelnversammlung*.

of urgency in order to be able to undertake his reforms.[15] In this speech, we can already read many ideas on the state and the constitution that Calonne would defend his entire life, although their meaning would fundamentally shift over time due to evolving political circumstances. Calonne compared the mission of Louis XVI with the reform of the French state under the sixteenth-century king Henri IV (1553–1610). This model king had created the absolutist monarchy in the aftermath of the French Wars of Religion, foreshadowing the important role the image of Henri IV later would play during the Restoration rule of Louis's brother as Louis XVIII (1814/15–24).[16] Calonne proposed the reform of historic tax exemptions currently enjoyed by many social groups and a more even and fairer distribution of the taxes. Also, a stronger executive government would diminish the powers of the provincial *parlements*.[17] To encourage trade, Calonne argued in the spirit of the political economists of the Scottish Enlightenment that customs barriers should be removed and commerce be allowed to flow freely in order to raise tax income. In many ways Calonne's reform programme was a typical example of eighteenth-century enlightened absolutism.[18]

Not surprisingly, many notables were not very enthusiastic about Calonne's 'revolutionary' proposals and mounted a campaign to have this alleged 'radical' removed from office. With the aid of members of the court, they accused the controller of royal 'despotism' and of overstepping the boundaries of his office and, ironically, acting as a revolutionary. Calonne's opponents successfully convinced the king to let him go. As result of the disfavour of the king and court, Calonne felt obliged to leave France, under the threat of prosecutions and lawsuits, and to go into exile in order to be able to work for his—in the end unsuccessful—rehabilitation. Unlike most émigrés, Calonne thus did not originally flee France as a result of the revolutionary events, and Calonne questioned his status as the 'first' émigré in the legal sense, whenever it suited him politically and privately.[19] The failure to reform the state's finances set the course for the outbreak of the Revolution two years later.[20] For the rest of his life, Calonne felt almost desperately compelled to justify his choices as controller in the key year 1787.

---

[15] 'Lorsqu'à la fin de 1783 le Roi daigna me confier l'administration de ses finances, elles étoient (…) dans l'état les plus critique.' [Calonne], *Discours* (1787), 6.
[16] [Calonne], *Discours* (1787), 26–7. Cf. Susane, *tactique financière*.
[17] [Calonne], *Discours* (1787), 28.
[18] Blanning, *Pursuit*, 294–304. Lacour-Gayet, *Calonne*, 125–67; Klesmann, *Notabelnversammlung*, 371–3.
[19] In a document without date, Calonne argued, no doubt unsuccessfully, that he was mistakenly placed on the émigré list. As part of an attempt to seek reconciliation with the French revolutionary or consular regime, Calonne downplayed his counter-revolutionary activities and fervour. He wrote that he had to leave France in 1789 because of reactionary opposition to his reforms, and that he had played little role in the movement of the princes. He falsely claimed that his travels over the last years had been for touristic purposes only. This document showed Calonne's adaptability in presenting himself as a counter-revolutionary, in the French tradition of the '*girouette*'. Archives Nationales, Fonds Calonne, 297 AP/3, no. 124–38, 'Objet d'examen'. Cf. Serna, *République des Girouettes*.
[20] Lacour-Gayet, *Calonne*, 218–44; Goodwin, 'Calonne', 329–77, 202–34.

In the spring of 1789, Calonne, now living in England, campaigned to be elected to the Estates-General as part of his strategy to return to high office. In his *Lettre adressé au Roi* of 9 February 1789 he once again aired his views on the need for reform of the French state. Calonne argued that, following the example of the kingdom of Prussia, France should have a written constitution as well. This new constitution, however, should above all be based on the existing unwritten French constitution and not form a blueprint for an entirely new political system, as some hotheads had proposed. In addition to the reform of old abuses, which Calonne already had criticized in his speech to the notables, the former controller-general argued for the establishment of a new Estates-General that was to be composed of two chambers, after the British model.[21] In the French equivalent of the House of Lords, the nobles and the clergy, who were allowed to retain their old privileges, deliberated on the country's affairs. He criticized the proceedings of the Estates-General of May 1789 as being too democratic and allowing too much popular participation. He predicted, rightly as it turned out, that the meeting of the Estates-General in its current form would lead to the end of the old political order.[22] The Estates-General was subsequently converted into the National Assembly and in 1792 into the republican Convention. In the years between 1789 and 1792, a complex process of radicalization took place in France that culminated in the establishment of a revolutionary Republic in September 1792 and the beheading of the French king on 21 January 1793.[23]

After the attempt to become a member of the Estates-General failed, Calonne turned against the Revolution and started to work as a lobbyist for the international Counter-Revolution, led by the brothers of Louis XVI. He left London in November 1790 to go to Turin to offer his services to the exiled French princes, who at that time dwelt at the court of the king of Sardinia, after having brought their case to the attention of the British court earlier. On both sides the expectations were high: the princes expected Calonne to solve their huge financial problems and Calonne hoped that he in his turn would be restored to high office when the princes returned triumphantly to France in the near future.[24] In the following years, Calonne worked tirelessly for the cause of the exiled princes: lobbying, publishing, letter writing, and organizing, often with little effect. He travelled all over Europe in an attempt to gain support for the princes. This certainly was not an easy task: the efforts to stir up Europe's monarchs against the Revolution, and thus also work against Louis XVI, who was, in the eyes of most, the legitimate king, were usually met with a cold shoulder. Also, the

---

[21] Later Calonne denied that he had wished to impose an alien British constitutional model on the French. Calonne, *Political State of Europe*, 131.
[22] [Calonne], *Discours* (1787). Cf. Beik, *French Revolution*, 15–17.
[23] Furet, *Révolution* I, 81–180; Martin, *Contre-Révolution, Révolution et Nation*; Edelstein, *Terror of Natural Right*; Tackett, *Coming of the Terror*; Linton, *Choosing Terror*; Jourdan, *Nouvelle histoire*.
[24] Parrel, *papiers de Calonne*.

organization of the princes was plagued by a chronic lack of funds and overall incompetence.[25]

As part of the campaign to win European hearts and minds for the Counter-Revolution, as well as improving his own standing and profile, Calonne published a treatise on the state of France in October 1790, *L'état de la France*. This work was translated shortly after into English as the *Considerations on the Present and Future State of France* (1791).[26] The work went through several editions and was widely read and commented upon in France as well as in England. The publication of Edmund Burke's *Reflections on the Revolution in France* in 1790 stimulated interest in Calonne's now uncompromising anti-revolutionary work in Britain and beyond.[27] In the preface of this work, Calonne devoted a few lines to his own fate as an exile who had suffered hardship as a result of his self-sacrificing choice to remain loyal to the king of France, despite having been disgraced.[28] He, not very convincingly, also described himself as someone who was now much happier not having to carry the weight of an important office. According to Calonne, the representatives, first of the Estates-General, and then of the National Assembly, had betrayed the French nation.[29] In the name of freedom and equality, the revolutionaries had implemented measures that in effect brought despotism and chaos to France.[30]

In the middle of the failed allied invasion of France of 1792, Calonne also fell out of grace with the princely court in exile in Coblenz. This second time the disgrace was final. Due to court intrigues and the machinations by rivals, Calonne had to offer his resignation on 13 September 1792. This second fall from grace inaugurated the final years of Calonne's life. Calonne had become an isolated figure, disliked by all parties, 'distrusted by the princes, despised by the queen, hated by the revolutionaries and ignored by Orléanist faction'.[31] Troubled by financial difficulties and harassed by his debtors, Calonne was forced to leave the English capital, and he travelled via Spain to Italy. The ambitious former minister, however, was not suited for life exclusively in the private sphere and continued to yearn for a new role on the international political stage.

---

[25] Lacour-Gayet, *Calonne*, 275–430. Chateaubriand in his later memoirs would also paint a negative picture of the activities of the exiled princes: Chateaubriand, *Memoirs from Beyond the Tomb*, 160–80.

[26] Calonne, *Considerations*. The French original: Calonne, *l'état de la France: présent et à venir* (1790); followed by Calonne, *état de la France: Tel qu'il peut et qu'il doit être* (1790). A summary was subsequently published under the title *Esquisse de l'état de la France* (1791). According to Paul Beik, the changes made in the supplementary pamphlet of November 1790 (*De l'état de la France, Tel qu'il peut et qu'il doit être*) 'were all accompaniments of the author's physical transfer from England to the continent and his new position as minister of emigration'. Beik, *French Revolution*, 45–6.

[27] On the reception of *L'état de la France* in France and Britain: Lacour-Gayet, *Calonne*, 297–301. See also the section on Calonne and Burke (C4S6).

[28] On the self-fashioning of the *émigrés*: Reboul, *French Emigration*.

[29] 'How fatal is the art of deceiving the people! And what an execrable use has been made of it, within a year past, by the disturbers of France!' Calonne, *Considerations*, xv.

[30] On the francophone counter-revolutionary conception of freedom: Lok, 'Just and True Liberty'.

[31] Lacour-Gayet, *Calonne*, 440.

He frantically kept writing letters to monarchs and officials and publishing memoirs hoping to return to the centre of political action. Restlessly travelling through Europe, Calonne desperately tried to get accepted at the courts of Madrid, Naples, London, and Saint Petersburg. He even considered retiring to the Crimea, which was governed for the tsar by the later French prime minister Richelieu. His attempts to return to office, however, were unsuccessful.[32] Eventually, after having been erased from the list of proscribed émigrés, Calonne returned to Consulate France in 1802. He died in October of that year, before being able to obtain a post in the Napoleonic administration.

3. Daughters of Thessaly

The question to what extent Calonne's thought can be termed 'counter-revolutionary' is not easy to answer. The interpretation of the concept 'Counter-Revolution' has shifted fundamentally in recent scholarship.[33] Older studies, often written from an ideological point of view, positioned a clearly demarcated and coherent 'Counter-Revolution' against a similarly defined 'Revolution', in a way reifying the Jacobin usage of these concepts.[34] Revisionist historians, by contrast, regarded both concepts as different aspects of the same historical phenomenon.[35] According to French historian Jean-Clément Martin, the idea of a centrally organized 'Counter-Revolution' was a myth concocted by the revolutionaries in order to promote unity in their own ranks. Only during a short moment in 1793–4, did a temporary alliance in Western France between nobles and popular resistance against the revolutionary central state come into being. However, this so-called *Vendée* started as a revolt of soldiers and was never a centrally controlled movement. Despite British military support, the *Vendée* was defeated by the revolutionary troops in the fall of 1793 due to internal divisions.[36]

Conceptual historians have, furthermore, demonstrated that 'Revolution' and 'Counter-Revolution' were heterogeneous, contingent, and elastic words: they did not possess an uncontested and stable content.[37] Friedemann Pestel has argued for

---

[32] Lacour-Gayet, *Calonne*, 431–59.
[33] On the history of the term 'Counter-Revolution': Pestel, 'Counter-revolution'; Pestel, 'Contre-révolution'; Pestel, *Kosmopoliten*, 131–42.
[34] For instance: Roberts, *Counter-Revolution in France*.
[35] Donald Sutherland has also argued that Revolution and Counter-Revolution should be studied together, but mainly focussed on social groups: Sutherland, *France 1789–1815*.
[36] Martin, *Contre-Révolution, Révolution et Nation*, 171–96; on Counter-Revolution as popular resistance: Middell, *Widerstände gegen Revolution*. On the semantic problem of integrating popular resistance to the revolution into the concept of Counter-Revolution: Pestel, 'Counter-revolution', 68.
[37] 'Nous savons désormais que l'affrontement entre révolution et contre-révolution est un processus dans lequel les protagonistes, et particulier les contrerévolutionnaires, ont adapté leur pratiques, leur langage et leur discours aux armes de l'adversaire afin de se rendre davantage intelligibles.' Artola Renedo and Luis, 'contre-révolution', 1.

a radical, discursive approach to the concept of 'Counter-Revolution'. According to him, 'a semantically informed approach' allowed for more focus on the actor and the rhetorical use of this word. For instance, in 1787 the opponents of Calonne labelled his reform measures as a 'revolution'.[38] During the preparations for the meeting of the Estate-General, the word 'reaction' was used by critics for those who defended the model of 1614 for the meeting of the Estates.[39] Also, the concept of 'Counter-Revolution' had a strong temporal dimension: the word never referred to the present of the revolution, nor to the pre-revolutionary past, but always to the future. Furthermore, 'Counter-Revolution' remained a 'void category', as the word did not provide the discursive framework for an eventual return to the *ancien régime*, in contrast to the language of the *'ancienne constitution'*.[40]

As a result of the political polarization of the years 1789–92, the ideological demarcation of who and what belonged to the Revolution became ever more narrowly defined.[41] The word 'Counter-Revolution' was often used as a pejorative predicate by revolutionary factions to discredit and exclude other revolutionary groups, legitimizing persecution and exile. In revolutionary discourse, a large panorama of very differentiated groups, such as the right-wing press, moderate monarchists (*monarchiens*), émigrés supporting the exiled princes, and combatants in the civil war in the South, were lumped together as 'counter-revolutionaries'.[42] Until 1792, King Louis XVI was seen as part of the 'Revolution', but after his flight to Varennes he increasingly was set aside as an 'anti-revolutionary' and placed outside the national revolutionary community.[43] The émigrés were further catalysts in the polarization between Revolution and Anti-Revolution, as was the outbreak of the war between revolutionary France and the allied powers in 1792. The refusal of the pope to agree to have priests take the oath supporting the constitution, moreover, led to an increasing anti-Catholic definition of the Revolution.

Thus from 1792 onwards, a hostile discourse was constructed on the rhetorical combination of 'Counter-Revolution', 'monarchy', 'émigrés', and the 'enemies of the nation', cemented by the military victory of the revolutionary troops over their opponents. Counter-revolutionaries were not only regarded by the revolutionaries as political opponents, but also as 'enemies of humanity' who had put themselves outside the boundaries of natural law.[44] In 1794, a rhetorical middle way between 'Revolution' and 'Counter-Revolution' ceased to be a viable political option.[45]

---

[38] Martin, *Contre-Révolution, Révolution et Nation*, 22–6.
[39] Starobinski, *Action et Réaction*.
[40] Pestel, 'Counter-revolution', 73–5.
[41] On the right-wing press in Revolutionary France: Popkin, *Right-wing Press*.
[42] Montlosier, *Nécessité d'une contre-révolution*.
[43] Martin, *Contre-Révolution, Révolution et Nation*, 59–104.
[44] Wahnich, *impossible citoyen*; Edelstein, *Terror of Natural Right*.
[45] Martin, *Contrerévolution, Révolution et Nation*, 147–98.

The winter of 1794, however, marked a conceptual as well as a political turning point. The extremely narrow definition of 'Revolution' and the all-encompassing concept of 'Counter-Revolution' contributed to the downfall of the radical regime and the persecution of Robespierre himself as a 'counter-revolutionary'.[46] After the Thermidor coup the definition of what belonged to the 'Revolution' in revolutionary discourse became again more inclusive.

This complexity and ambiguity regarding the use of the concept of 'Counter-Revolution' can be perfectly observed in Calonne's publications. The word itself did not appear often in his writings. Calonne struggled with the notion, and he was in general unwilling to describe himself as a 'counter-revolutionary'. As we saw, in 1787 he was still regarded as a radical revolutionary by his opponents at the Assembly of Notables. There was no doubt, however, that he explicitly rejected the revolutionary order in 1791. As he wrote in his *Considerations*:

> since it is evident that present state of things [The Revolutionary regime] is detestable, and since it is equally demonstrated that the progress of the present arrangement can lead to no salutary amendment; it is necessary, and urgently incumbent on us, to seek, in another order of things, the means which may restore to France her vitality, power and tranquillity; rescue her from the abyss in which she is plunged; and give her, once more, a Law, a King and a Constitution.[47]

Calonne, however, did not support just any kind of Counter-Revolution. He pointed out that he stood for a specific kind of 'Counter-Revolution':

> But, to effect this, what is necessary?—A Counter-Revolution? Yes, if by this word is meant the united efforts of all good citizens to restore order to France; to banish anarchy, to put an end to the tyrannical usurpation of a handful of demagogues, who govern the kingdom, or rather who prevent it from being governed; to restore to the King that authority which belongs to every monarch, and which is necessary in every well-regulated state; and, lastly, to enable the Nation to recover its rights, and to secure to it the free exercise of that power which it could alienate (…).[48]

Calonne emphatically disapproved of the Counter-Revolution as a pure reaction. His answer to the question of whether a 'Counter-Revolution' was necessary consisted of the following words:

---

[46] On the uses of 'Counter-Revolution' by left-wing persons and groups: Pestel, 'Counter-revolution', 64–7.
[47] Calonne, *Considerations*, 476.   [48] Calonne, *Considerations*, 476.

NO, if the consequence of a Counter-Revolution must be to revive ancient abuses, to strip the Nation of its lawful privileges, and to deprive it of that just measure of liberty which it ought to enjoy; of the advantages which the King himself had secured to it, and of that inestimable blessing, a good and permanent constitution.[49]

Like Bonneville and Feller, Calonne invoked the authority of Montesquieu to explain his political and constitutional views. In Calonne's case, Montesquieu was called upon to support his thesis that the balance of powers no longer existed under a revolutionary government: 'the same principle which requires the division of powers to constitute national liberty, requires their equilibrium to maintain it'.[50] Calonne, furthermore, criticized the revolutionary constitution of 1791 for its inconsistency. The constitution gave the king the right to declare war and peace, but at the same time the consent of the legislative assembly was required, making a constitutional stalemate almost inevitable.

The crucial mistake made by the National Assembly in Calonne's eyes was that the representatives had destroyed the old institutional structures in order to build a new order: 'can they be so little versed in political science, as not to know that governments are formed and completed by time, but they cannot be created at once?'[51] By destroying the old order, the revolutionaries had created total anarchy and social dissolution. Instead of regenerating the kingdom, the revolutionaries brought it to ruin.[52] Indeed, 'in the sense of the Revolution, to regenerate is to annihilate'.[53] The revolutionaries reminded Calonne of the daughters of the king of Thessaly, who killed their father and boiled his mangled limbs fondly believing they might thus renew his youth.

Calonne, not surprisingly for someone who had been in charge of the finances of the French state, also devoted many pages of his *Considerations* to the economic and financial effects of the Revolution. The main economic effect of the Revolution had been, in his eyes, the impoverishment of France.[54] The infringement of economic rights, especially property rights, was, in Calonne's view, closely linked to the disappearance of political freedom and the end of the rule of law. The royal prerogative, according to Calonne the main 'bulwark of public liberty', had almost been annihilated.[55] The equilibrium between monarchy and legislative power, the prerequisite of free and moderate government, had been disturbed by the usurpation of power by the National Assembly. The traditional 'intermediate power' between the monarchy and the people, the aristocracy, had been

---

[49] Calonne, *Considerations*, 476.
[50] Calonne, *Considerations*, 198, 206. Cf. Beik, *French Revolution*, 43–5.
[51] Calonne, *Considerations*, 1.   [52] Calonne, *Considerations*, 4.
[53] Calonne, *Considerations*, 404–5.   [54] Calonne, *Considerations*, 128–30.
[55] Calonne, *Considerations*, 189.

destroyed by the revolutionaries, making way for the tyranny of the many, which was worse than the despotism of a single king.[56]

Calonne thus did not justify the monarchy with an appeal to *droit divin* and the historical right to rule of the Bourbon dynasty, but instead defended the monarchy on the grounds of a 'modern' discourse based on the enlightened concepts of liberty, progress, property, moderation, and the rule of law, the very vocabulary also used by his revolutionary opponents.[57] In opposition to these allegedly counter-revolutionary ideals, Calonne posed the 'revolutionary' antipodes of 'slavery', 'fanaticism', and 'arbitrariness'. Instead of protecting rights, the Revolution had unashamedly infringed on the rights of French citizens. Not only political and religious rights, but also property rights, the basis of a just system and rule of law, had not been protected by the revolutionaries. Just as Feller had argued in his *Journal*, Calonne wrote that the Revolution had led to an essentially lawless society in which only despotism could flourish.

At the end of *Considerations*, Calonne gave a 'moderate' answer to the questions: 'what ought to be done? What can be done? How is it possible to avoid the danger of extremes, and the violence of a new concussion?'[58] Calonne's idea of a 'Counter-Revolution' was thus his own middle way between reactionary royalism and revolutionary radicalism. He pleaded for a return to the original reform-minded Estates-General of May 1789, and urged the deletion of every law and measure taken since then that did not accord with the instructions given by the king. The former controller outlined a project for 'a constitution which should be founded on the ancient bases of the French monarchy, and which only proscribed its abuses'.[59] In seventy-six articles Calonne proposed his version of a constitution for France with conservative and monarchical as well as Catholic features, but also with—what could be anachronistically termed—early 'liberal' characteristics. These included the abolition of tax exemptions and a more equal distribution of taxes, the reform of legal abuses, a more rational design and functioning of the state, and the joint government of king and legislative assembly (in combination with a royal prerogative), derived from eighteenth-century reform projects.[60]

---

[56] Cf. de Dijn, *Liberty in a Levelled Society*.   [57] Lok, 'Just and True Liberty'.
[58] Calonne, *Considerations*, 442.
[59] Calonne, *Considerations*, 474. Calonne could build on the discourses of the French ancient constitution rearticulated in the political crises of the 1750s: Baker, *Inventing the French Revolution*, 34.
[60] Calonne, *Considerations*, 445–57. On the *monarchiens* and the early revolution: Pestel, *Kosmopoliten*, 97–106. Calonne was not alone in his liberal defence of the French monarchy. The female author Robert de Lézardière—who was, like Calonne, inspired by Montesquieu in her *Théorie des lois politiques de la monarchie française*, 4 vol., composed in the 1780s and published for the first time in 1791—extolled the freedom of the French ancient constitution as the generous legacy of the Franks, but, in her case, to support a liberal monarchy. Signoret-Serrano, 'idées politiques'; Armenteros, 'From Centre to Periphery' and, Armenteros, 'Royalist Medievalisms'.

4. The Exile Press

The 'Counter-Revolution' of the 1790s was a distinctly transnational and European phenomenon.[61] At the same time, it was also true that the revolution against the revolution differed in character in various countries and political contexts.[62] According to the French historian Jean-Clément Martin, the 'Counter-Revolution' should be seen as a 'generic matrix', in which local circumstances could be projected and adapted to regional and national contexts.[63] In France, the revolutionaries were, for instance, able to frame the Counter-Revolution as an anti-national movement, whereas in Spain and, as we have seen, in the Southern Netherlands, the Counter-Revolution was understood in terms of a national and patriotic resistance against the foreign import of French revolutionary innovations. Also translating the concept of 'Counter-Revolution' into different linguistic and national contexts led to semantic problems.[64]

The embodiment of this 'transnational Counter-Revolution' was no doubt the community of émigrés, who had fled—or were forced to leave—revolutionary France and were dispersed across Europe and the New World.[65] Historians have argued that these exiles were the first European political refugees, marking a break with primarily religiously motivated exiles of the early modern period, but tied to earlier waves of refugees such as the Huguenots.[66] Like all refugees, none of the émigrés had originally expected to live a large part of their lives outside their home country.[67] Most of them, such as Calonne, regarded their exile as a temporary phenomenon and expected to return home in the near future. Their 'cosmopolitanism' and international outlook were thus forced upon them by revolutionary circumstances. They were, in the words of Jacques Mallet du Pan, 'reluctant cosmopolitans' (*cosmopolites malgré eux*).[68]

The émigré communities, scattered around the continent and even beyond, constituted an international society in opposition to the existing revolutionary one. London, Coblenz, and Saint Petersburg, and many smaller cities, became

---

[61] Rance, 'Contre-revolution', 182–92; Martin, *Contre-Révolution en Europe*. Older studies are: Godechot, *Counter-Revolution*; Palmer, *Democratic Revolution*, 377–99, 473–504, 779–84. See also Chapter 1.

[62] Martin, 'Introduction', in Martin, *Contre-Révolution en Europe*, 9.

[63] Martin, 'Introduction', in Martin, *Contre-Révolution en Europe*, 12.

[64] Pestel, 'Counter-revolution', 68–73.

[65] On the terminology of 'émigré', 'refugee', 'emigrant', and 'exile': Reboul, *French Emigration*, 1–6; Cf. Rapport, *Nationality and Citizenship*.

[66] Pestel, *Kosmopoliten*, 16–17.

[67] Carpenter, *Refugees*; Carpenter and Mansel, *French Émigrés in Europe*. On Germany: Höpel, *Emigranten*; Rance, 'émigration nobiliaire'. On the Dutch Republic: Gaspar, *vlucht voor de guillotine*. From a comparative perspective: Jasanoff, 'Revolutionary Exiles'.

[68] Jacques Mallet du Pan to Johannes von Müller, 6 December 1797. Cited in Pestel, *Kosmopoliten*, 20.

nuclei of émigré communities.[69] They became 'European spaces' with their own social life organized around salons, news outlets, and societies, presenting an alternative counter-revolutionary Europe to the world of the revolutionary sister republics.[70] The rupture of the Revolution should be nuanced as well: to a certain extent, counter-revolutionaries could build on pre-existing international networks of *anti-philosophes* and religious orders, as we have seen in the case of François-Xavier de Feller, and the pre-revolutionary aristocratic salon life.[71] In his *Le mouvement des idées dans l'émigration française* (1924), the French literary scholar Fernand Baldensperger, writing in the aftermath of the First World War, discussed the experience of exile, the interpretation of the recent past of the Revolution, and visions of the future of European civilization.[72] Although Baldensperger's book forms, in many ways, a work of an older history of ideas, only examining a few 'great' authors such as Maistre, Chateaubriand, and Mme de Staël, his temporal approach is still topical.[73]

Older studies have examined the émigrés predominantly from a political perspective. Depending on the political background of the historian, the émigrés were either described as traitors of the French nation or presented as innocent victims of a cruel and barbarous Revolution. Since the 1980s, a less politicized historiography of the émigrés has come into being.[74] It has become clear that no coherent and ideologically homogeneous emigrant factions existed in the 1790s. The formerly held interpretation of a rigid ideological dividing line between 'liberal' and 'moderate' *monarchiens* versus 'ultraroyalist' and 'pure' émigrés before the Napoleonic era has increasingly been called into question.[75] In many ways the image of the émigré was shaped by first of all the émigrés themselves, as can also be observed in the case of Calonne, followed by their enemies in revolutionary France and by the host nation. In Britain, for instance, much more attention was given to intransigent émigrés than to moderate ones, and more to noble than non-noble refugees.[76]

---

[69] Henke, *Coblenz*. So far, much attention has been given to the spatial and geographical dimensions of Enlightenment and Revolution; this is far less true of Counter-Enlightenment and Counter-Revolution: Withers, *Placing the Enlightenment*.

[70] Pestel, *Kosmopoliten*, 489–502.   [71] McMahon, *Enemies*; Chappey, 'anti-lumières', 165–80.

[72] Baldensperger, *mouvement des idées*. Baldensperger wrote his book around the First World War, no doubt discerning parallels between the revolutionary wars with their forced movements of peoples and his contemporary situation. Also, intellectuals dreamed of regenerating a corrupt European civilization in both periods.

[73] The revolution was interpreted by most émigrés in one of two ways: either as a random event without broader significance ('*la force des choses*'), a kind of classical '*fatum*' which mere humans could not influence. Or the revolution was seen, most notably but not just by Joseph de Maistre, in a mystical vein as the result of divine intervention, as part of a larger plan for human history. Baldensperger, *mouvement des idées* II, 65–97.

[74] See for a critical overview of the literature on the *émigrés*: Reboul, *French Emigration*, 3–20; Pestel, *Kosmopoliten*, 25–31. The classic study is Daudet, *Histoire de l'émigration*.

[75] Burrows, *Exile Journalism*, 224–6; Pestel, *Kosmopoliten*, 37.

[76] Reboul, *French Emigration*, 61–90.

An important role in this transnational émigré community and its contact with the host nations was played by the exile press. The exile journals functioned as important sources of information on the events in continental Europe for both the British public and the British government. Émigrés tried to influence British policy by, for instance, depicting support for the Counter-Revolution in France as being much stronger than it was in reality. In the Napoleonic era, the remaining—and increasingly radical—French émigré journalists played an important role in the production of anti-French propaganda. The relationship between the exiled journalists and the British government was, however, complex: at certain moments, the administration and the journals collaborated, at other times they were adversaries.[77]

Calonne played a central role in the London-based French exile press. He secretly acquired a share in the biweekly journal *Courier de Londres*.[78] This periodical was founded before the Revolution in 1776 as '*Le Courier de l'Europe*', a Francophone journal published in London. This most successful and durable of all the émigré papers, survived until 1826. From 1 November 1793 to 28 December 1798 the journal was edited by Charles-Alexandre's brother, Jacques-Ladislas-Joseph de Calonne (1743–1822).[79] The *Courier* had a relatively large and constant number of readers and played an intermediary role between French and British public opinion and diplomatic relations. The journal lent itself to ever-changing political agendas, demonstrating the malleability of these kinds of journals, as well as of their contributors. The magazine had first showed itself critical of the French monarchy in 1776–83, then, subsequently, became a mouthpiece for constitutional monarchy in 1784–91. From 1791–2 the journal turned against the Jacobins and evolved subsequently into the organ of various, shifting émigré groups from 1793 onwards.[80] The paper thus adapted to the phases of emigration: from an uncompromising anti-revolutionary and royalist *pur* position during the Terror, the paper followed a more moderate line from 1795 onwards, influenced by the political views of its owner Calonne, although it should be stressed that the paper, to a certain extent, kept its editorial independence. The journal—not without justification—was considered by critical contemporaries as inconsistent and mercenary, changing with every new political wind.[81]

---

[77] Burrows, *Exile Journalism*.

[78] The *Courier de Londres* appeared from 1776 to 1820. The journal appeared under the names 'Courier de l'Europe' (1776–88, English edition and 1778–92 continental edition), 'Courier de Londres' and 'Gazette de la Grande Bretagne' (1805–7). The original papers are preserved in the Bodleian library of the University of Oxford. On the turbulent editorial history, see: Burrows, *Exile Journalism*, 233–4.

[79] The moderate royalist publicist Montlosier was the main editor until 1802. Burrows, *Exile Journalism*, 233.

[80] Burrows, *Exile Journalism*, 18–19; Proschwitz and Proschwitz, *Beaumarchais et le Courier de l'Europe*.

[81] Burrows, *Exile Journalism*, 19–20.

Although the journal claimed to be an independent and impartial news source on current events in revolutionary Europe, in its reporting a counter-revolutionary 'bias' can clearly be observed. The journal often pointed to the allegedly chaotic nature, cruelty, and bloody results of revolutionary policies. Usually, the supposed lack of popularity of the revolution among common Frenchmen and Europeans was emphasized, exaggerating the support for a monarchical restoration in France.[82] The development of the revolt of the *Vendée* was, furthermore, extensively reported upon, and proclamations of the French king-in-exile Louis XVIII were published in their entirety. When writing about the Batavian Republic, the editors falsely claimed that the Batavian revolution was not at all popular and that the House of Orange still enjoyed the overwhelming support of the people in the former Dutch Republic.[83] By their negative reporting on the supposed lack of revolutionary fervour among the common people, the *Courier* played a role in misleading British official minds regarding the situation in Europe, influencing policy decisions such as military interventions on the continent.[84]

The editors, however, made no secret of their political sympathies. In response to a letter from a reader, the editors stated in an editorial that they were indeed royalists and defended the old constitution of France (*la constitution antique de la France*).[85] At the same time, they insisted that they were not reactionary 'extremists': they stood firm for an 'impartial moderation' and claimed not to belong to any faction. Furthermore, the editors claimed that the common interest would always prevail above particular, hence the journal's motto '*Tros Tyriusve mihi nullo discrimine agetur*' (Trojan and Tyrian will be treated by me with no distinction), which was translated by the editors as 'accessible to all parties without being influenced by anyone'. Notwithstanding this lip service to impartiality, the critics of Charles-Alexandre Calonne usually received a strong reply. Also, Calonne was given ample editorial space to defend his publications.[86]

The journal devoted many pages to in-depth reflections on the French Revolution and thus stimulated the development of counter-revolutionary political thought. Excerpts were published from counter-revolutionary books, such as from *Les mémoires pour servir à l'histoire du Jacobinisme* (1797) of Abbé de Barruel.[87] Attacks on eighteenth-century *philosophes* such as Diderot can be

---

[82] For instance: *Courier de Londres*, vol. 37, no. 27 (3 April 1795), 209, reported on the French armies in Italy, emphasizing the lack of moral and revolutionary conviction of the French soldiers. Cf. Burrows, *Exile Journalism*, 144–78.

[83] *Courier de Londres*, vol. 37, no. 27 (3 April 1795), 247.

[84] Burrows, *Exile Journalism*, 142–3, 222.

[85] *Courier de Londres*, vol. 37, no. 37 (28 April 1795), 270.

[86] When Calonne won a court case against his debtors, this news was joyfully announced. *Courier de Londres* vol. 43, no. 10 (1798), 115. Calonne's attempts to exercise direct control over the editorial content of the *Courier*, however, were not always successful. Burrows, *Exile Journalism*, 88–9.

[87] *Courier de Londres*, vol. 40, no. 45 (1796), 359.

found, continuing the tradition of pre-revolutionary *anti-philosophie*.[88] Also, more detailed pieces on unfolding revolutionary events were published, usually anonymously, in the '*Mélanges*' section. Calonne's treatise *Tableau de l'Europe*, for instance, appeared first as a series of short articles in the fall of 1795, followed by responses from readers.[89] The *Courier de Londres* offered thus a limited platform for discussion among those in favour of a return of the monarchy in France. Also, through its European outlook, dispersion, and network, the *Courier* constituted an example of the dynamics of counter-revolutionary internationalism and Europeanism.[90]

5. The European Commonwealth

A fervent supporter of the émigré community in Britain was the member of Parliament Edmund Burke. Like Calonne, Burke was not a born counter-revolutionary. A journalist and man of letters with Irish roots, originally (in)famous for his writings on aesthetics, he became a member of parliament for the Whig party. As a member of the House of Commons, he strived for a conciliatory and moderate approach towards the American rebels, and he famously argued for the impeachment of Warren Hastings, the governor of British Bengal, whom he accused of tyranny and corruption. Only at the end of his long career did Burke publish his *Reflections on the Revolution in France* in 1790 to counter, in his eyes, the pernicious sympathy for the French revolutionaries in England.[91] Calonne and Burke did not write out of sheer intellectual curiosity, but rather responded as 'thinker-agents' primarily to political events.[92]

New scholarship has convincingly questioned the widespread interpretation of Burke as the ideological architect of modern conservatism. The 'conservative' Burke is now considered primarily a twentieth-century invention, the result of a long process of reinterpretation.[93] Richard Bourke has argued against the use of

---

[88] In *Courier de Londres*, issue number 42 of volume 40 (1796), the editors, for instance, criticized the re-edition of the works of Diderot and claim that his publications were also responsible for the outbreak of the French Revolution (343–4). See also McMahon, *Enemies*.

[89] The first contribution appeared in issue number 34 of volume 38 (1795). Strangely, this particular issue is missing from the only copy in the Bodleian library.

[90] The editors, however, were also keenly aware of the limits of their newspaper. As the editor sighed: 'La nature de cette feuille & la multiplicité des événements, laissant & peu de place & peu de temps aux réflexions.' *Courier de Londres*, vol. 43, no. 10 (1798), 78.

[91] The life and works of Edmund Burke have generated an enormous number of publications. A selection: Bourke, *Empire and Revolution*; Lock, *Edmund Burke*; Bromwich, *Intellectual Life*; Dwan and Insole, *Cambridge Companion*; Hampsher-Monk, *Political Philosophy*; Hampsher-Monk, *Impact of the French Revolution*. On the political context of British counter-revolutionary conservatism: Schofield, 'Conservative Political Thought'; Thompson, 'Britain and the French Revolution'; Philp, 'Vulgar Conservatism'.

[92] Bourke, *Empire and Revolution*, 677.

[93] Claeys, 'Nineteenth Century Appraisals', 75–90; Jones, *Edmund Burke*.

anachronistic labels such as 'liberal' and 'conservative' to describe Burke's thought, and interpreted him chiefly as an eighteenth-century enlightened reformer.[94] Bourke described him as an exponent of the moderate Enlightenment, above all preoccupied with the problem of preserving the 'spirit of liberty'.[95] Burke believed in a historically grown constitution that acted as a guarantee of this freedom. On the basis of this interpretation of the historical constitution, Burke turned against all phenomena he considered tyranny, usurpation, and belonging to the 'spirit of conquest'. Thus, Burke supported the British 1688 'Glorious Revolution' against the despotic King James II, as well as the American revolutionaries against the despotic British rule in the colonies. Also, he accused the British imperial government in India of abuse of power, although he did not, in general, question imperialism as a system, and of neglecting to respect and build on the historically grown Indian constitution.[96] He, moreover, like Feller, was sympathetic towards the revolt of the Southern Netherlands against the centralizing Habsburg reforms.[97]

The French revolutionaries, by contrast, did not—in his view—restore a threatened legal order, but destroyed the existing French constitution, and therefore embodied the 'spirit of conquest' instead of liberty.[98] Although Burke did not oppose reform per se, he, like the other counter-revolutionaries in this study, abhorred the sudden rejection of this age-old historically grown system of institutions by the French revolutionaries and the construction of a political system *ex nihilo*. As he wrote in his *Reflections*: 'the very idea of the fabrication of a new government is enough to fill us with disgust and horror'.[99] The French Revolution destroyed the rule of law and a thriving commercial society that had arisen from its feudal origins, inaugurating a new era of 'the most coarse, rude, savage and ferocious' manners, basically destroying every possible form of order, civilization, and morality.[100]

Burke's fight against the revolutionaries was, in his view, therefore not just a conflict between opposing interests, but an ideological struggle between two incommensurable world views. By trying to annihilate an imperfect but flourishing European civilization, characterized by the spirit of religion and chivalry,

---

[94] Bourke, *Empire and Revolution*; Bourke, 'What Is Conservatism?'.
[95] 'Burke's achievement was to analyse the conditions of freedom in minute practical and constitutional detail.' Bourke, *Empire and Revolution*, 1. Bourke's emphasis on Burke's colonial, Atlantic, and British positions, however, in my view, has somewhat overshadowed the European dimension of his thought.
[96] Bourke, *Empire and Revolution*, 16–24.   [97] Jennings, 'Burke', 94.
[98] On Burke's (lack of) knowledge of (revolutionary) France and the French language: Mitchell, 'Introduction', 1–5.
[99] Burke, *Reflections*, 32. Hampsher-Monk, *Political Philosophy*; Hampsher-Monk, 'Reflections'.
[100] Burke, *First Letter*, 311. The interpretation of the French Revolution as a worldwide onslaught upon civilization was widely shared by British conservatives. Schofield, 'Conservative Political Thought', 621–2.

revolutionary France had placed itself outside of civilized Europe.[101] France under the Revolution resembled more an Asian or African despotism than a European state. Burke's struggle against the Revolution was, first and foremost, a defence of the idea of a European order against chaos and destruction.[102] His thought is usually interpreted as the product of a uniquely British or English tradition. Without denying the specific British context of Burke's writings, it should be stressed that similar ideas can be found in the works of counter-revolutionary authors in other countries. Burke's counter-revolutionary works resonated with many continental counter-revolutionary publicists, such as Calonne. However, they did not blindly copy his ideas but independently developed their political thought in their own national, religious, and linguistic contexts.

The publication of Edmund Burke's *Reflections on the Revolution in France* in November 1790, a work read and widely discussed by the governing classes, inaugurated a public debate in Britain on the events in France that so far had not taken place. As Scottish jurist, Whig politician, and historian James Mackintosh (1765–1832) put it:

> Before the publication of Mr. Burke [*Reflections*], the public was not recovered from that astonishment into which they are plunged by unexampled events, and the general opinion could not have been collected with precision. But that performance divided the nation into marked parties. It produced a controversy which may be regarded as the trial of the French Revolution before the enlightened and independent tribunal of the English public.[103]

From 1792 onwards, under the influence of the radicalization of the Revolution, British public opinion increasingly started to share Burke's view that the Revolution was a threat to Britain and its political system.[104] Yet, at the beginning, Burke did not receive much support for his call to international action against the revolutionary doctrines. The revolt against the French king was regarded by European statesmen as an ideal opportunity to weaken a competitor. They were more concerned about the schemes of their potential coalition partners than about the intentions of revolutionary France.[105]

---

[101] 'Europe undoubtedly (...) was in a flourishing condition the day on which your revolution was completed'. Burke, *Reflections*, 80.

[102] 'The political order that Burke set about vindicating was conceptualised in two dimensions: first, in terms of Britain's religious and political establishment; and second, in terms of principles underlying European politics. These two concerns were related to one another, since the situation in Europe, it seemed to Burke, was adversely affecting the interests of Britain. In practical terms, Europe here meant the monarchy of France, although Burke associated the revolutionary attack on property and religion with a general assault on the heritage of post-feudal Christendom.' Bourke, *Empire*, 679.

[103] Mackintosh, *Vindicae Gallicae*, 375. On the reception of the *Reflections* in France and England: Mitchell, 'Introduction', 13–23.

[104] Schofield, 'Conservative Political Thought', 603.

[105] Belissa, *Repenser l'ordre européen*, 41–2.

In later writings, the European and international dimensions of Burke's thought receive even greater emphasis. Like Calonne, Burke fiercely opposed the reluctance to go to war and the increasingly popular desire to make peace with the revolutionary Republic after 1795. In his *First Letter on a Regicide Peace* (1796), published shortly before his death, Burke further elaborated his ideal of a historically grown European order.[106] For a long time, he wrote, Europe was a 'Commonwealth',

> in which communities, apparently in peace with each other, have been more perfectly separated than, in later times, many nations in Europe have been in the course of long and bloody wars. The cause must be sought in the similitude throughout Europe of religion, laws and manners. At bottom these are all the same. [...] The nations of Europe have had the very same Christian religion, agreeing in the fundamental parts, varying a little in the ceremonies and in the subordinate doctrines. [...] When a man travelled or resided for health, pleasure, business or necessity, from his own country, he never felt himself quite abroad.[107]

The French revolutionary Republic, however, willingly broke with this commonwealth:

> Instead of the religion and the law by which they were in a great politick communion with the Christian world, they have constructed their Republick on three bases, all fundamentally opposite to those on which the communities of Europe are built. Its foundation is laid in Regicide, in Jacobinism and in Atheism; and it has joined to those principles, a body of systematick manners, which secures their operation.[108]

The 'violent breach of the community of Europe' and even 'a schism with the whole universe' by the revolutionaries could only be responded to by military means. For the *casus belli*, Burke used Roman private law as well as arguments drawn from natural law.[109] As he wrote: 'we are at war with a system, which, by its essence is inimical to all other governments (...) It is with an armed doctrine, that we are at war.'[110] A war against this politically anomalous 'monster' was therefore entirely justified as well as obligatory for the European powers.[111]

---

[106] Hampsher-Monk, 'Counter-Revolutionary Writings'. The 'letter' was not originally intended for publication, but as a memorandum privately sent to policymakers.
[107] Burke, *First Letter*, 316–17. Cf. Bourke, *Empire and Revolution*, 911–13.
[108] Burke, *First Letter*, 308.   [109] Burke, *First Letter*, 280, 318.
[110] Burke, *First Letter*, 266.
[111] On Burke's view of international relations: Hampsher-Monk, 'Editor's introduction', xxxiv–xxxv; Vincent, 'Edmund Burke'; Armitage, 'Edmund Burke and Reason of State'.

Burke's reception on the European continent varied considerably and should not be overstated.[112] Burke's *Reflections* were not well received in France, where the treatise of the Protestant English Whig politician was not appreciated, neither by Catholic counter-revolutionaries, nor by revolutionaries and liberals. In contrast to Burke, who regarded the Revolution as a sudden spontaneous eruption into the European body politic that could not be predicted, French Catholic counter-revolutionaries, as well as liberals, believed that the Revolution had its roots in centuries-old French and European history, dating back to the Reformation or at least the eighteenth century. Burke was notoriously absent from most French histories written in the nineteenth century.[113] The Englishman, however, maintained a good relationship with the brothers Antoine and Claude-François de Rivarol.[114] In Spain, Burke's works were banished altogether, as the Spanish government believed that the best way to prevent the spreading of dangerous revolutionary ideas was to forbid all works on the Revolution by proponents as well as critics.[115] Germany probably was the most fertile ground for Burke's *Reflections*, but, also here, his text was criticized and adapted to the local and regional context.[116]

6. Crusaders against Revolution

To what extent did the encounters between Burke and Calonne in 1790 exemplify the transnational character of counter-revolutionary thought? Colin Lucas has warned against drawing overly hasty conclusions. According to him, the expressions of sympathy between Burke and Calonne, and other French émigrés, were superficial and did not mean much. He emphasized that Calonne and Burke came from different national traditions and could read one another's texts only through a national lens. Also, the émigrés increasingly understood that Burke, despite his rhetoric and prominence, was not able to fundamentally change the course of British policy towards the French Republic. Nonetheless, he was celebrated as a hero of the emigrant cause by the French exile community, due to his tireless activities on their behalf.[117]

---

[112] The edited volume by Fitzpatrick and Jones is useful in examining the European reception of Burke, but their overview is not systematic enough, and the quality of the contributions varies widely. Fitzpatrick and Jones, *Reception of Edmund Burke*. According to Hampsher-Monk, the publication of the *Reflections* was hugely successful in terms of the number of copies sold. Hampsher-Monk, 'Reflections', 198.

[113] Gengembre, 'Burke', 916–23.

[114] Jennings, 'Burke'; Bourke, *Empire and Revolution*, 743–53.

[115] Simon Schuhmacher, 'Burke's Political and Aesthetic Ideas'.

[116] Kontler, 'Varieties of Old Regime Europe'. See also Chapter 5.

[117] Lucas, 'Edmund Burke and the *Émigrés*'. Richard Bourke also emphasized disagreements between Calonne and Burke: Bourke, *Empire and Revolution*, 761–2. Reboul, *French Emigration*, 162.

Although Lucas is no doubt right that the émigrés and Burke lived in different political and cultural worlds, and often misunderstood one another, his complete rejection of any significance of the contacts between Burke and Calonne is probably going too far. The two men read and appreciated each other's work and were to a certain extent influenced by each other's texts and conversations.[118] Despite coming from very different national traditions, one from a British parliamentarian tradition and the other from a French centralized bureaucratic tradition, many similarities can still be discerned between their views. Both men stood for the defence of a historically grown and continuously developing constitution that acted as a guarantee of the 'spirit of liberty'. This was true in their respective countries, but also within the wider frameworks of a larger European 'commonwealth'. Both agreed on the idea of 'moderation' as a key counter-revolutionary concept, to be contrasted with revolutionary fanaticism and destructiveness, although their understanding of what moderation entailed differed.[119]

Calonne and Burke were certainly regarded by contemporaries as like-minded spirits.[120] In his *Vindicae Gallicae* (1791) James Mackintosh attacked Burke and Calonne simultaneously, mocking their claims to be 'moderates'.[121] According to Mackintosh, both Calonne, 'an exiled robber living in the most splendid impunity' and his 'co-adjutor' Burke called themselves 'moderate', but in reality they belonged to the radical 'Counter-Revolution'.[122] Calonne's work *Consideration on the Present and Future State of France* was dismissed as a 'manifesto of counter-revolution', whose 'object is to inflame every passion' and 'probes the bleeding wounds' of princes, nobility, the priesthood, and the great judicial aristocracy.[123] In his defence of the French Revolution and its British supporters, Mackintosh described both Calonne and Burke as anachronistic 'crusaders' for an imaginary *ancien régime*, out of touch with the modern world.[124]

> They [Calonne and Burke] neglect the progress of the human mind subsequent to its adaption, and when, as in the present case, it has burst forth into action, they regard it as transient madness, worthy of only pity or derision. They mistake it for a mountain torrent that will pass away with the storm that give it that gave it birth.[125]

---

[118] See for a similar argument: Klesmann, *Notablenversammlung*, 294–305.
[119] Letter from Calonne to Burke, 6 May 1791. *National Archives* (London, Kew): PRO PC1/127 (Calonne papers): 248.
[120] As John Trevor wrote to the Duke of Leeds (Turin, 21 November 1790): 'J'ai lu le livre [*L'état de France*] de M. de Calonne. Il me parait parfaitement bien écrit. Le livre de Mr. Burke et le sien peuvent se traduire l'un par l'autre'. Cited in Lacour-Gayet, *Calonne*, 301.
[121] Later Mackintosh took a more sceptical and even counter-revolutionary stance towards the revolution in his writings on international law: Pitts, *Boundaries*, 124–34.
[122] Mackintosh, *Vindicae Gallicae*, xi–xii. Cf. Hampsher-Monk, *Impact of the French Revolution*.
[123] Mackintosh, *Vindicae Gallicae*, xii.
[124] On the use of the metaphor of the 'crusade' in the Catholic counter-revolution: Schettini, '18th-Century Crusaders'.
[125] Mackintosh, *Vindicae Gallicae*, 11.

Comparing Calonne with Burke, Mackintosh believed Calonne was the more methodological of his two adversaries and had a better understanding of the workings of French representative institutions. Also, he thought that Burke derived his analysis of the revolutionary finances mainly from Calonne's—in his view fraudulent and misleading—figures.[126] Mackintosh himself did not believe that the French Revolution was flawless—later he would take a much more critical, and even counter-revolutionary, stance—and he particularly condemned the revolutionary violence. In his 1791 work, however, he still supported the revolutionary project. The French Revolution was, for him, primarily an attempt to give France a more modern and reasonable political system, comparable to the British Glorious Revolution of 1688. Mackintosh also mocked Calonne's political ambitions, 'confident in the protection of all the monarchs of Europe, whom he [Calonne] alarms for the security of their thrones, and having insured the moderation of the fanatical rabble, by giving out among them the savage war-whoop of atheism, he already fancies himself in full march to Paris (...)'.[127]

Mackintosh's typology of Calonne's and Burke's political views as radical and reactionary 'manifestos of counter-revolution' was misleading, as we have seen. But his representation of their collaboration as brothers-in-ideological-arms and 'co-adjutors' was stereotyped as well. Their relationship was more complicated than Mackintosh depicted, and misunderstandings and problems of translation occurred in their conversations. On 23 October 1790, at his request, Calonne's wife sent a copy of his *L'état de France* to Burke, with a note by Calonne saying that it was unfortunate that he had not been able to read Burke's work before publishing his own book. In his response Burke wrote that he was very much in agreement with Calonne's views and shared his astonishment over the absence of resistance in France against the revolutionaries and the lack of resilience of the 'ancient institutions'. Although the ancient constitution was not without its flaws, Burke argued that sometimes the 'abuse of powers' should be borne by true patriots in an 'old and venerated constitution'.[128] Already in November 1790, Burke had started to incorporate some of the arguments of Calonne into later editions of the *Reflections*.[129] He claimed that 'indeed Mr. de Calonne's work supplies my deficiencies by many new and striking arguments on most of the

---

[126] Burke praises Calonne and his interpretation of the finances of the *ancien régime* monarchy in his *Reflections*: Burke, *Reflections*, 136–8.
[127] Mackintosh, *Vindicae Gallicae*, xii.
[128] Edmund Burke to Charles-Alexandre de Calonne, 25 October 1790, in Burke, *Correspondence* VI, 140–1. According to the editors, Burke and Calonne may have met before exchanging their treatises.
[129] Burke accepted Calonne's interpretation of the French revolutionary system in 1789 as a 'démocratie royale', a form of popular government with only a mere shadow of a monarchical system, without following his suggestion that the reform of the French state should be undertaken on the basis of the *Cahiers de doléances*. Bourke, *Empire and Revolution*, 762. Cf. Burke, *Reflections on the Revolution in France: A Critical Edition*, appendix I, 420–2.

subjects of this Letter', and in particular regarding the revolutionary constitution and finances.[130]

In his letter to John Trevor in January 1791, Burke showed himself to be more critical of Calonne's ideas: the former minister put, in Burke's view, too much faith in written constitutions, in contrast to the unwritten English common law, and was far too optimistic about the 'moderate' instincts of the French people and their leaders:

> I have a very high opinion of Mons. de Calonne. His book, upon the whole, must do great service. I wish, indeed, that he had hinted less about [constitutional] arrangements to be made in consequence of success. He speaks as if commissaries had been appointed to settle these differences. But I conceive things are very far from such a state. The matters he proposes will never be understood by the seduced common people; and, as to the leaders, he must think much better of their moderation than I do, if he thinks that anything but their present dominion will serve them. Theoretic plans of constitution have been the bane of France; and I am satisfied that nothing can possibly do it any real service, but to establish it upon all its *ancient bases*.[131]

Burke was also critical of the supposed attempts by Calonne and other French emigrants to impose the English bicameral system in France, as the British institution 'is not what it appears on paper', but mostly worked implicitly and by acquired habit over the ages, something Calonne apparently did not sufficiently grasp, in Burke's eyes. For Burke, it was impossible for France to adopt elements of the historically grown and unwritten English constitution.

On 9 February 1791, Calonne wrote Burke from Venice that he was in complete agreement with Burke, in particular with his views regarding the ancient constitution, perhaps purposefully overlooking their differences on this subject. Calonne, in contrast to Burke, had always advocated a written French constitution based on ancient principles. He also complained about the French translation of Burke's *Reflections* and mused upon the impossibility of translating a text from one language to another, echoing the counter-revolutionary aversion to universal ideas and concepts.[132] In his letter of 28 May, Burke advised Calonne against any form of negotiation with the revolutionary regime. In July of 1791, Calonne approached Burke again in an anonymous letter, when he attempted to win the British prime minister Pitt for the cause of the exiled princes. Burke first refused to

---

[130] Burke, *Reflections*, 190. Burke included references to Calonne's *De l'État de France* in the third edition of the *Reflections* of 16 November. Hampsher-Monk, 'A Note on the Texts of Reflections and the Letter on a Regicide Peace', lviii; Burke, *Writings* VIII, 233–4.

[131] Edmund Burke to John Trevor, January 1791, in *Electronic Enlightenment*. http://www.e-enlightenment.com/item/burkedOU0010291a1c/ (accessed 16 July 2018).

[132] Calonne to Burke, 9 February 1791, in Burke, *Correspondence* VI, 221–3.

speak to the anonymous author, but when Calonne revealed himself, a meeting took place during which Burke promised to aid Calonne and even send his son Richard to the princely headquarters in Coblenz.[133]

From this point onwards the relations between the two men began to deteriorate. In his letter of December 1791, Burke complained to Calonne that he did not appreciate the work Burke and his son had done for the cause of the Counter-Revolution. Burke had done all he could under the present circumstances, and Calonne should expect no more from him, Burke wrote, clearly irritated.[134] Few letters seemed to have been exchanged afterwards.[135] This excursion into the brief moment of contact between the member of parliament Burke and exiled minister Calonne demonstrated that the two men often misunderstood and fell out with each other, but also that a transnational counter-revolutionary conversation took place, as was acknowledged by both Calonne and Burke in their writings. This exchange of ideas influenced no doubt the development of a transnational counter-revolutionary vocabulary.[136]

7. A Decisive Moment

The fall of the radical revolutionary regime after the coup of Thermidor (July 1794), and the installation of the more moderate Directory in 1795, formed an important turning point in the eyes of the counter-revolutionaries. For royalists, the restoration of the French monarchy and the undoing of the revolutionary legacy after the nightmare of the Terror became suddenly a realistic possibility, or so they believed. The question, furthermore, was posed as to what role this militarily powerful republican state should play in the international arena, and whether it was possible and wise to start peace negotiations. Counter-revolutionary authors, including Calonne, published a flood of writings in the Thermidor years, in which they gave their views on the past, current, and future state of Europe. Their European conversation was very much a transnational one. In the last five years of the eighteenth century, a counter-revolutionary conception of Europe and its role in the world was formulated by a host of authors in response to current affairs. These views were not merely reactionary opinions but often consisted of dynamic and sometimes forward-looking views on the evolution and progress of European history and civilization.

---

[133] Calonne to Burke, Burke to Calonne, c.20 July 1791, in Burke, *Correspondence* VI, 300–2. For an account of Richard Burke's mission: Lock, *Edmund Burke* II, 391–3.
[134] Burke to Calonne, December 1791, in Burke, *Correspondence* VI, 473–5; Lacour-Gayet, *Calonne*, 376–7.
[135] Copeland and Shunway Smith, *Checklist of the Correspondence of Edmund Burke*, 127.
[136] Cf. Klesmann, *Notabelnversammlung*, 294–305.

The year 1795 was also, for the editors of the *Courier de Londres*, 'a decisive moment', a unique historical opportunity for the forces of the Counter-Revolution to restore 'European tranquillity' and determine the French as well as the European future.[137] So far, the royalists, the editors wrote, had worked against the historical momentum and their endeavours had consequently failed as a result of this hostile public climate. The counter-revolutionaries, in past years, had looked backwards when instead they should have looked towards the future, the *Courier* castigated. The Revolution had shown its true face in the days of the Terror. The Directory, which had succeeded the terrorist regime, satisfied nobody. According to the *Courier*'s optimistic reports, royalism was more widespread in France than ever.[138] A restoration could succeed in France at this time, if the émigrés would make no more mistakes, ignore their former differences, and jointly work together for the re-establishment of the monarchy. The monarchists therefore must forget '1789' and '1792' and look towards the future and realize that they were living in '1795'.[139]

This optimistic temporal vision was apparently also shared by Louis XVIII, the main pretender to the French throne after the death of his young nephew Louis XVII in a revolutionary prison. In his first declaration of Verona of 7 July 1795, published in its entirety in the *Courier de Londres* of 28 August 1795, Louis XVIII set the agenda for a restoration in France.[140] In the declaration, he claimed that a monarchical restoration should primarily be built on the foundations of the 'ancient constitution'. Only this 'ancient and wise constitution' (*cette antique et sage constitution*) could guarantee French 'liberty' and the rule of law. The revolutionary mania for innovations (*manie de nouveautés*) had clearly resulted in anarchy and despotism. Louis conceded that this so-called antique constitution was not perfect and that improvements needed to be made, but this could only be done in the context of peace. Louis called upon the French to return from the revolutionary path and once again follow the banner of the dynasty that had ruled France for more than fourteen centuries. He promised an amnesty to all those who had collaborated with the Revolution, after the emblematic example of his sixteenth-century predecessor Henri IV. The Revolution itself was described as a plot of a small band of atheists; the majority of the French were simply misled by devious plotters.[141]

This 'decisive moment' for the royalist counter-revolutionaries, however, was in danger of being lost as a result of impending peace negotiations with the French

---

[137] Cf. the quotation of Calonne at the beginning of this chapter (p. 99, n.1).
[138] *Courier de Londres*, vol. 37, no. 32 (21 April 1795), 254–6.
[139] *Courier de Londres*, vol. 37, no. 34 (28 April 1795), 270.
[140] On the context of this declaration: Mansel, *Louis XVIII*, 110–14. According to Mansel, between 1795 and 1800 'Louis issued declarations which are monuments of silliness and which helped to delay the Restoration' (110). In many ways, however, the Verona declaration foreshadowed *La Charte* of 1814.
[141] *Courier de Londres*, vol. 38, no. 7 (28 August 1795), 132–5.

Republic. After the losses of the allied coalition against the revolutionary army at the Battle of Fleurus on 26 June 1794, and the separate peace of the allies with the French Republic, the British government was increasingly interested in peace negotiations with the French Republic.[142] William Eden, Lord Auckland (1744–1814), a close associate of the British prime minister Pitt, gave arguments for a peace with France. Although Auckland, in principle, opposed the Revolution, he wrote in an influential memorandum that peace negotiations were in the best interests of Great Britain, as attempts to build a European counter-revolutionary alliance had clearly failed. Also, the pragmatic Auckland believed that the French Republic was currently too powerful to be defeated, but he thought that the political anomaly could be integrated into the European state system.[143]

Auckland found a fierce and principled opponent in Edmund Burke. In response to the British political debate on the peace negotiations, Burke composed his (eventually) four *Letters on a Regicide Peace*. Although Burke regarded the Revolution as a unique event in world history, he regularly referred to the historical example of the coalition under King-stadtholder William against Louis XIV. In many ways, the situation in 1697–1713 had been, in his eyes, much more difficult, as England had then been much weaker and less developed than it was in the 1790s.[144] Burke especially praised the role of King William, who had led the war against the French king in the face of hostile public opinion.[145] At the end of the eighteenth century, however, the stakes were much higher: whereas in the late seventeenth century the war was waged over who should be king, in the late eighteenth century the question was whether there should be a king at all.

Burke also castigated the passive and weak attitude of the European crowned heads as well as the conciliatory mood of English public opinion.[146] Allowing revolutionary France to exist would inevitably lead to further corruption and the spread of contagious revolutionary ideas, eventually producing a crisis of power in Britain itself. It was impossible to conclude a peace agreement with France, as this republic could not be trusted. England had, in Burke's view, an existential mission to lead the European and even universal fight against the Revolution. England was 'the great resource of Europe', 'not in a sort of England detached from the rest of the world, and amusing herself with the puppet shew of a naval power, but in that

---

[142] In 1796 and 1796, James Harris, Earl of Malmesbury (21 April 1746–21 November 1820), was in Paris to unsuccessfully negotiate with the Directory on behalf of the British government.

[143] Published as William Eden, baron of Auckland, *Some Remarks on the Apparent Circumstances of the War*. On the context: Burke, *Writings and Speeches* IX ('Part I: the Revolutionary War, 1794–1797'), 19–27; Blanning, *French Revolutionary Wars*; Mori, *William Pitt and the French Revolution*.

[144] Burke, *First Letter*, 297.

[145] 'In spite of his people he resolved to make them great and glorious; to make England, inclined to shrink into her narrow self, the arbitress of Europe, the tutelary angel of the human race.' Burke, *First Letter*, 302.

[146] 'I do not know of a more mortifying spectacle, than to see the assembled majesty of the crowned heads of Europe waiting as patient suitors in the anti-Chamber of Regicide'. Burke, *First Letter*, 272.

sort of England, who considered herself as embodied with Europe'.[147] Only as part of a European coalition would England stand a chance against France, but at the same time, resistance against France was futile if it were not led by England.[148] This sense of defending European civilization and the 'liberties of mankind' against revolutionary barbarism later was shared by the British members of parliament during the revolutionary and Napoleonic wars. International law was harnessed by the British as part of their struggle against the revolutionary Republic.[149]

French émigrés intervened as well with their own publications, hoping to influence British and European public opinion.[150] They, like Burke, believed that the handling of the revolutionary political anomaly determined the future, not only of France, but also of Europe and even the world. European historical narratives played a key role in these counter-revolutionary reflections on a future European order. In his *Réflexions sur la paix adressées à Pitt et au Français* (May 1795) the Genevan exile Francis d'Ivernois (1757–1842) argued against a peace with the Republic based on the argument that only a defeated France, returned to its pre-1792 boundaries, could restore the traditional 'balance' that had been the 'palladium' of European civilization over the last centuries. This balance had enabled the 'European republic' to halt foreign invasions and build a free and enlightened society since the sixteenth-century Reformation.[151] As a citizen of Geneva, he had seen with his own eyes the devastation that resulted from French dominance.[152] In a comparison of the finances of France and Britain, d'Ivernois concluded that the revolutionary regime was on the brink of financial bankruptcy and could collapse any moment. Only a peace treaty would provide an opportunity for the revolutionaries to recover their fortunes.[153]

Abbé Dominique Frédéric Dufour de Pradt (1759–1837), at that time living as an exile in Hamburg, also argued that the expansive revolutionary Republic had destroyed the traditional balance of power, as established in the

---

[147] Burke, *First Letter*, 262.
[148] 'We may consider it a sure axiom that as on the one hand no confederacy of the least effect of duration can exist against France, of which England is not only a part, but the head, so neither can England pretend to cope with France but as connected with the body of Christendom.' Burke, *First Letter*, 262.
[149] Pestel and Ihalainen, 'Revolution beyond Borders'.
[150] For instance: [Maisonfort], *De l'état réel de la France à la fin de l'année 1795*.
[151] 'Cet admirable balancement des forces de l'Europe a été depuis deux siècles le palladium de la civilisation. C'est à lui, c'est à son maintien, que cette vaste & riche République a dû de n'avoir plus été inondée par des irruptions dévastatrices; c'est seulement depuis qu'elle l'a découvert, qu'elle a pu, ainsi que la Grèce, durant la pondération de ses forces, se livrer avec quelque sécurité & avec de si brillans succès aux jouissances de la paix; aux arts qu'elle fait naître, & aux sciences qu'elle protège. C'est depuis cette grande découverte, accompagnée & favorisée de celle de la Réformation, que l'Europe a cessé d'être barbare. Enfin, c'est à la faveur de cet équilibre que les peuples Chrétiens prenaient chaque jour un élan plus rapide vers le bonheur, les lumières & la liberté' (...).' D'Ivernois, *Réflexions sur la guerre*, 24.
[152] D'Ivernois, *Réflexions sur la guerre*, 5.
[153] On the European balance or equilibrium, see also Chapters 5 to 8.

Peace of Westphalia. Before the Revolution, according to Pradt, a true 'European community' had existed, where 'the frequent mutual contacts between the different peoples had led to a proximity of manners and hearts, as well as the communication of words and ideas'.[154] The coming of the Revolution and the revolutionary wars had brutally 'molested' this calm and enlightened community, replacing it with turmoil, war, and ignorance, Pradt noted nostalgically. Allowing France to keep her territorial conquests in a general peace would lead to a permanent imbalance on the European continent. In contrast to d'Ivernois, he did not believe that the *ancien régime* balance could be restored, as it had not functioned properly in the decades preceding the Revolution. Instead, he proposed the reinforcement and enlargement of the states surrounding France, and he suggested the establishment of a new state consisting of the former Dutch Republic, the Austrian Southern Netherlands, Liège, and parts of the Holy Roman Empire, foreshadowing the construction of the United Kingdom of the Netherlands in 1815.[155]

Jean Gabriel Maurice Rocques, Comte de Montgaillard (1761–1841) in his *Necessité de la guerre et dangers de la paix* (October 1794) also argued that negotiating with the French Republic would not lead to an enduring peace, and that only a military defeat would. For the Directory, peace negotiations were a strategy to ensure the survival of the revolutionary regime in order to spread its anarchy and corruption all over the globe. Signing a peace deal would be signing the death warrant of the European monarchies, as Montgaillard agreed with Burke that the struggle with this Republic was unlike any other war in history.[156] As France was the key to peace in Europe and even throughout the globe, the French regime needed to be overturned as soon as possible. Generations of young Frenchmen and Frenchwomen were growing up without any memory of, or personal experience with, the monarchy, making it increasingly hard to restore the Bourbon dynasty. Eventually, it would no longer be possible to reverse the revolutionary legacy, Montgaillard feared.[157]

Another pamphlet that underlined the threat of the French Revolution is the aptly named *The Dangers which Threaten Europe* of 1795. This work was a translation of the French original written in 1794 by Jacques Mallet du Pan (1749–1800). Like d'Ivernois, Mallet du Pan was originally from Geneva, where he had been influenced by Voltaire in his youth, moving to Paris to pursue a

---

[154] 'La fréquentation mutuelle entre les différents peuples, devenue plus commune et plus facile, avoit rapproché les mœurs et les cœurs, étendu la communication de la parole et des idées, et fondu, pour-ainsi-dire, tous les habitans de l'Europe dans une seule communité, au milieu de laquelle il etoit impossible de trouver absolumens étrangers.' [Pradt], *Antidote au Congrès de Rastadt*, 4–6.

[155] [Pradt], *Antidote au Congrès de Rastadt*, 74–106.

[156] 'Cet acte serait la sentence de mort de tous les gouvernements qui le signeraient, & il n'en est aucun contre lequel, la Révolution Française ne s'en fit, bientôt, une armée. Les capitaines d'Alexandre ne signèrent que le démembrement de sa puissance, les empires restèrent; mais les maitres de l'Europe consacreraient, l'abdication de toute la leur & la Royauté, l'ordre & les loix seraient des lors sans propriété, comme sans azyle, sur le Globe.' Montgaillard, *Nécessité de la Guerre*, 20.

[157] Montgaillard, *Nécessité de la Guerre*, 13.

journalistic career. During the Revolution, he sided with the royalists and worked for the exiled princes, gaining a reputation by the publication of his widely read essay on the causes of the French revolution, the *Considérations sur la nature de la Révolution de France, et sur les causes qui en prolongent la durée* (1793).[158] Mallet du Pan became a key player in the transnational and pan-European conservative networks of the 1790s, corresponding with other counter-revolutionary authors such as Gentz. In the pamphlet of 1794/5 he left not a doubt regarding the mortal danger of the Revolution for European civilization:

> It is a deadly war (…), the monster of anarchism must perish, or Europe must expect soon to see the downfall of all thrones; the dissolution of every tie of subordination and friendly intercourse; the annihilation and contempt of all religion; the subversion of all rectitude; the violent usurpation of all property; and the massacre of all its inhabitants.[159]

Mallet du Pan had no doubt that the Revolution would eventually fail, 'because it is built on quicksand'.[160] But before this joyous event could take place, Europe would be completely in ruins and suffering from a catastrophic loss of life. Similar to other moderate publicists, Mallet du Pan was also critical of the counter-revolutionary campaign of 1794. The divided crowned heads of Europe were, in his view, mostly pursuing their own short-sighted interests, and they failed to win the hearts of the French, solely relying on military powers and making horrendous tactical mistakes, which explained the success of the revolutionary armies.

A final conciliatory voice among the émigrés was, to conclude this overview, François Dominique de Reynaud, Comte de Montlosier (1755–1838), the co-editor of the *Courier de Londres*. In his *Vue sommaire sur les moyens de paix* (1796), Montlosier argued for a 'return to order' (*retour de l'ordre*) on the basis of national reconciliation, rather than a military victory over the French Republic. Even should the allied coalition win the war, France would become a 'volcano', endlessly erupting in revolutionary revolts out of resentment over the humiliating defeat and posing a permanent threat to its neighbours. The suffering of the French people will end only when those who command the armies realize that peace is in their best interests. The French yearned for peace and would accept a moderate and national monarchy, as they realized that the republican alternative was not a realistic option in the long term.[161]

---

[158] On Mallet du Pan as a cosmopolitan counter-revolutionary journalist: Burrows, *Exile Journalism*; Burrows, 'Counter-revolution, Conservatism and Conspiracy'.
[159] Mallet du Pan, *Dangers which Threaten Europe*, 3–4.
[160] Mallet du Pan, *Dangers which Threaten Europe*, 11–12.
[161] Montlosier, *Vue sommaire sur les moyens de paix*. This pamphlet was to be read together with another work in which Montlosier argued that international peace was possible only if 'moderation' prevailed in domestic politics: Montlosier, *Des effets de la violence et de la modération*. On Montlosier: Beik, *French Revolution*, 33–5, 93–8; Pestel, *Kosmopoliten*; Piguet, '"Contre-révolution"'.

8. Conquering the Spirits

In his *Tableau de l'Europe* of 1796, first published as a series of articles in the *Courier* from October to December 1795, Calonne shared the criticism of Burke and many émigrés of a peace agreement with the French Republic. The Directory consisted, in Calonne's view, of former Jacobins, who had changed tactics to spread their revolutionary ideas on the European continent by other means. Calonne described them as 'chameleons' who only appeared as moderates, but secretly still retained their fanatical revolutionary ideals. It was, in his view, therefore, also impossible to reach a permanent peace agreement with this regime. The constitution of 1795 was, like the former revolutionary constitutions, based on 'false' and abstract universal human rights, detached from national customs and traditions. The constitution of 1795 was still too 'democratic' to be stable, allowing too many people from all social strata to participate in politics.[162]

The tone of his *Tableau*, translated for British audiences in English as *The Political State of Europe at the Beginning of 1796*, however, was markedly different from that of the *L'état de la France* of 1790 and its English translation, the *Considerations* of 1791.[163] In 1796, turning back the clock to the spring of 1789 as if the Revolution had never happened no longer appeared to be a realistic option. A threshold had clearly been crossed in the minds of the counter-revolutionaries. Calonne argued that the previous strategy of the allied forces to defeat the revolution with military force had been a dismal failure. The European great powers had intervened too hesitantly at the beginning, and when they finally understood the danger that the Revolution presented to the European monarchical order, their military commanders acted incompetently. Instead of directly attacking the revolutionary capital, Paris, they lingered in the provinces. More essentially, the strategy to destroy the revolution by military force only was essentially flawed. The military struggle so far had therefore reinforced the Revolution instead of weakening it.[164]

---

[162] Calonne, *Tableau* 1796, xxxviii.

[163] As Calonne explained in the preface of his book, he did not originally plan to publish a treatise. He first published several articles in the *Courier de Londres*, edited by his brother l'abbé de Calonne. Several of these articles were published anonymously as *Tableau de l'Europe en novembre 1795, et pensées sur ce qu'on a fait & qu'on n'auroit pas dû faire*. As it was generally known that Calonne was the author and many mistakes had occurred in the first edition, Calonne decided to publish an expanded and revised edition in 1796 under his own name. This edition was also translated into English as *The Political State of Europe at the Beginning of 1796; or Considerations on the Most Effectual Means of Procuring a Solid and Permanent Peace*. Translated from the French by D. St. Quentin, A.M. (London: Debrett; Murray and Highley; and Richardson, 1796). Lacour-Gayet, *Calonne*, 466–81. Cf. Beik, *Revolution*, 94.

[164] 'La pression extérieure a tendu tous les ressorts de réaction; la nécessité de défendre ses foyers a enflammé le patriotisme contre la cupidité; la destruction même de toutes les branches d'industrie a produit des nuées de combattants: le besoin a créé des soldats; la guillotine les a fait marcher; le fanatisme les a rendus intrépides; les succès en ont fait des héros.' Calonne, *Tableau de l'Europe* (1796), 3.

The revolutionary Republic, Calonne agreed with Burke, was unlike any other state that ever existed in history. This French Republic could not be compared to the classical republics such as ancient Rome or Greece, but it was also entirely different from contemporary 'modern' republics such as the United States. Experience in former wars was therefore useless when dealing with this particular revolutionary Republic. It was, according to Calonne, also chimerical, as d'Ivernois had argued, to think that the Republic would collapse under the weight of its economic and financial problems. This Republic did not act according to normal economic laws: the revolutionaries were 'economists of the blood of their people' (*économes de sang de leur peuples*), driven by ideological fervour instead of rational interests, and willing to ask any sacrifice from their citizens. Calonne, claiming not to be an alarmist himself, warned against the underestimating of revolutionary France by the '*tranquilliseurs*', approvingly citing an unnamed 'English author' (probably Edmund Burke) who shared his opinions.[165]

Calonne believed that democracies were more prone to making war than monarchies and aristocracies and were averse to peace. No durable peace could be made with this regime, which regarded the end of hostilities as a means to further their revolutionary agenda and to eventually bring down all European monarchies. In his treatise, Calonne urged the British government, in his view the only true pillar of the European Counter-Revolution, to stand firm and not be lured into a peace agreement which was detrimental to Britain as well as Europe as a whole. A regime change in France itself was the key to peace in Europe and a stable European order.[166] Calonne, however, advised against attempts to end the Revolution solely by a military defeat, as Burke, d'Ivernois, and Montgaillard had proposed. Humiliating the French militarily would result only in a new revolution. Calonne therefore argued that the struggle against the Revolution should not be waged with weapons only, but also with ideas, 'a war of [public] opinion'.[167]

Instead of trying to crush France militarily, which had turned out to be impossible, the allied coalition should offer the French a reasonable alternative: a moderate constitutional monarchy. This proposed monarchical constitution should be in accordance with France's historically grown laws and customs. Calonne advocated a 'mild government, which did not clash with prejudices too deeply rooted; which did not destroy hopes too fondly fostered, and which did not excite fears that might alarm and necessarily dissuade; of a government which allowed the just expectation of a rational liberty, secured by fixed and determinate laws'.[168] Calonne, however, emphatically stated that he did not wish for the

---

[165] Calonne, *Tableau de l'Europe* (1796), xxxv, xxxviii.
[166] Calonne, *Tableau de l'Europe* (1796), liii.
[167] 'Le plan à suivre dans une guerre, qu'on peut appeler, guerre d'opinion, devoit être de joindre la persuasion à la force; d'éclairer d'une main ceux que l'on combattoit de l'autre; de s'attacher & conquérir les esprits autant au moins qu'à conquérir.' [Calonne], *Tableau de l'Europe* (1795), 8.
[168] Calonne, *Political State of Europe*, 139.

European powers to impose a foreign and alien constitution upon the French, although he had proposed this in earlier works.[169]

Offering a positive alternative to the Revolution was all the more realistic as the public mood had changed in France after the Terror, as it seemed to the optimistic Calonne. He observed a general discontent among the French. Many French people, furthermore, in Calonne's eyes, feared that their possessions were not safe and their property rights could be infringed upon by the state: 'can France forget, that the first principle, and the first effects of the revolution have been to respect no kind of property?'[170] For Calonne, the protection of property formed the basis of all political communities: 'Oh property! Thou sacred right, generating principle of civil society, and necessary attribute of social order!'[171] In the state of nature, no rights of man existed. Men united because they needed to protect their property, and so political communities came into being and rights were created. The flaw of the French revolutionaries was that they severed the abstract concepts of liberty and equality from property rights following the ludicrous notions of Jean-Jacques Rousseau.

The British in their constitution, Calonne noted approvingly, regarded liberty as inseparable from the guarantee of concrete property rights. The confiscation of possessions belonging to the émigrés was, according to Calonne, a perfect example of the revolutionary disregard for property rights.[172] Like Burke, Calonne argued that resistance against the revolutionary republic was required not only on the basis of natural and public law, but also based on arguments drawn from private property law: 'we maintain, that the interest of all men of property in the world, the common and reciprocal rights of all nations demand an universal resistance, to prevent so daring a violation of the right of property from passing into a law in any constitution whatever'.[173]

Many French people were concerned about the dismal state of French finances and worried about economic problems. Calonne emphasized economic arguments for a restoration of the monarchy: monarchy equalled prosperity and trade whereas the Revolution clearly stood for poverty. Also, taxes were much lower under the supposedly despotic *ancien régime* monarchy than under this democratic government. By imposing an excessive tax on the French people without its consent, the revolutionary government demonstrated its despotic character.[174] The final 'motor of discontent' for Calonne was religion. According to Calonne, tapping into the *anti-philosophe* tradition, the Revolution essentially stood for 'atheism' and 'unbelief', whereas most Frenchmen were convinced of the existence of a supreme being. Most Frenchmen, Calonne believed, also thought

---

[169] Calonne, *Political State of Europe*, 131.
[170] Calonne, *Political State of Europe*, 145.
[171] Calonne, *Political State of Europe*, 149.
[172] Calonne, *Tableau de l'Europe* (1796), 155–69.
[173] Calonne, *Political State of Europe*, 157.
[174] Calonne, *Political State of Europe*, 159–73.

that some form of organized religion was necessary to maintain social order.[175] Like Burke, Calonne believed that politics should not appeal only to reason:

> The same interest of true policy likewise requires, that particular attention should be paid to exterior worship, and that the government should see it countenanced and respected. Men in general require sensible images; they must have symbols and visible rites to bind them to their spiritual duties. The sentiments of adoration, of gratitude and submission, which they owe to the eternal, would not make on their minds a lively and durable impression, if they were not excited and mutually communicated by external signs.[176]

Calonne ended his treatise with an utterly dark scenario should his advice not be heeded. Even were England to succeed in crushing the French armies and imposing a new regime, this would not lead to a durable peace. Like Montlosier, Calonne prophesied that France would become an unstable 'volcano', with periodic revolutionary eruptions.[177] A Bourbon monarchy established by foreign arms would never be legitimate in the eyes of the French people. Also, the European balance would again be destroyed, with Habsburg Austria as the new hegemon, and England, finally, would lose its most valuable market.[178]

The anonymously published *Tableau* met with a hostile reaction from more radical *royalistes purs* or 'ultraroyalists'. They regarded Calonne's self-proclaimed 'moderate' tone as treason to the royalist cause. They wrongly accused him of no longer supporting the French ancient unwritten constitution.[179] Following the publication of the *Tableau*, the Count of Artois, the king's brother and future Charles X, broke definitively with his former advisor.[180] In response to Calonne's criticism, d'Ivernois published a treatise, in which he gave much more evidence for his earlier financial claims, expressing his unpleasant surprise at being targeted in such a personal manner by the former controller-general.[181] In articles in the *Courier de Londres*, Calonne responded in turn to his British as well as French critics.[182] He was particularly hurt by the criticism that he had changed positions and that his interpretation of 'ancient constitution' was inconsistent. Calonne claimed that the situation in 1789 was entirely different than in 1795. His principles by contrast had always stayed the same, he argued; he had consistently defended the idea that 'the monarchical powers should be regulated and tempered by fundamental laws, (...) guaranteed by a solemn constitution, and preserved by

---

[175] Calonne, *Tableau de l'Europe* (1796), 169–98.
[176] Calonne, *Political State of Europe*, 180–1.
[177] On Calonne and the *monarchiens*: Pestel, *Kosmopoliten*, 120, 134, 156–8, 160–2, 170, 224, 372.
[178] Calonne, *Tableau de l'Europe* (1796), 225–35.
[179] On the concept of the French ancient constitution: Beik, *French Revolution*, 1–13; de Dijn, *Liberty in a Levelled Society?*, 14–20; Pestel, *Kosmopoliten*, 71–5; Baker, *Inventing the French Revolution*.
[180] Burrows, *Exile Journalism*, 159; Lacour-Gayet, *Calonne*, 465–71.
[181] D'Ivernois, *État des Finances*.   [182] *Courier de Londres*, vol. 39, no. 2 (5 January 1796), 14.

sufficient and efficacious laws (...)'.[183] However, Calonne decidedly disagreed with many 'pure royalists' in the sense that he believed that the ancient constitution was not fixed at a certain point in time, but evolved in response to changing political circumstances.

In the preface to his *Tableau*, Calonne presented himself above all as 'moderate'.[184] He rejected the Revolution, which for him stood for fanaticism and arbitrariness as well as despotism. But he also explicitly distanced himself from the royalists he deemed 'pure royalists (*royalistes purs*)'. It was precisely the 'fanaticism' of certain émigrés that had contributed to the failure, so far, to undo the Revolution and had undermined the support of the French people for the cause of the monarchy. The choice for Calonne was between reconciliation or defeat.[185] He rightly knew, however, that this would not make him popular among the more intransigent members of the French émigré community: 'if by this explicit declaration I lose for ever the favourable opinion of those, who pique themselves on an inflexible pertinacity in their principles, and shudder with horror at the mere mention of the word reconciliation, I pity their blindness more than I regret their alienation from me (...)'.[186] By the end of the 1790s, Calonne had become an isolated and lonely figure, disliked by all parties.[187] Many of his ideas of a moderate monarchy, based on the principles of reconciliation, forgetting, property, prosperity, and stability, as an attractive alternative to the radicalism of the revolutionaries and pure royalists alike, would be claimed by the restored Bourbon monarchy in the spring of 1814.[188]

9. Conclusion: Ancient Constitution and European Commonwealth

In response to the shocking events of the Revolutionary wars, those opposed to the French Revolution felt the need to make their ideas explicit. The formulation of ideas of a renewed European order, by 'thinker-agents' such as Calonne and Burke, was not a mere intellectual exercise, but formed a reaction to concrete political events, such as the peace negotiations with the French Republic in 1795.

---

[183] 'Le pouvoir monarchique doit être réglé et tempéré par les loix fondamentales, qui soient fixes et établies constitutionnellement, consignés dans un code solennel, et préservés par les mesures suffisant efficaces, de la mutabilité à laquelle elles etoient sujettes, quand il dependoit entièrement de la volonté du roi de les maintenir or d'y déroger.' *Courier de Londres*, vol. 39, no. 2 (5 January 1796), 15. These sentences can also be found in the appendix to *Tableau de l'Europe*.

[184] See more extensively on moderation and counter-revolution: Lok, '"The Extremes"'.

[185] '(...) je conseille (...) le rapprochement de tous les partis, et leur ralliement à l'établissement constitutionnel d'une monarchie sagement tempérée, que je n'envisageais à ces différents époques que comme une chose infiniment désirable, étant devenu tellement nécessaire qu'il n'y a plus d'autre ressource, et qu'il faut présentement ou se concilier, ou périr.' Calonne, *Tableau de l'Europe* (1796), xv.

[186] Calonne, *Political State of Europe*, x.   [187] Lacour-Gayet, *Calonne*, 440.

[188] See also Chapter 8.

In the 1790s, a pan-European dialogue, hostile to the revolutionary experiment, came into being on the reconstruction of a European order. European history played a key role in this transnational conversation. Counter-revolutionaries had to define explicitly what they believed should have stayed unsaid and self-evident. Most counter-revolutionary authors agreed that a 'moderate' monarchy should be restored in France, on the basis of the 'ancient constitution', as the means to bring peace and stability to Europe, rather than using the more problematic concept of the 'Counter-Revolution'. As a result of the revolutionary wars, for these authors in the 1790s, the problem of the national constitution became intrinsically bounded to the question of a European and international order.

There was, however, much disagreement among the authors discussed in this chapter about what constituted this 'ancient constitution'. As Montlosier pointed out in his *Vue sommaire*, a fundamental debate was conducted over the origins of the French constitution among its proponents: some authors believed that it took its final shape under the government under Louis XIV, while others pointed to Clovis or the Germanic tribes as the true founders of the French constitution. The counter-revolutionary authors were no less divided over what institutions belonged to this French ancient constitution: the Estates-General, the provincial *parlements*, or exclusively the monarchy. Montlosier wrote mockingly that the confusing and ambiguous character of the concept of the ancient constitution was its greatest merit in the eyes of its advocates, as it could be adapted to new circumstances.[189]

Despite accusations of inconsistency, Calonne argued that he had continuously defended the same views on the French constitution since the days he organized the Assembly of Notables in 1787. Rather than creating a new system from scratch, the government of France should be governed along the lines of its ancient constitution. However, this did not imply that all constitutional change should be rejected. Calonne argued in all his writings that the French ancient constitution was not fixed at a certain point in time, but evolved in response to changing circumstances, and should acquire a written form as well.[190] Calonne also put forward ideas that would, in the next century, be labelled as 'liberal', such as the defence of property and individual rights.

This concept of the ancient constitution formed the basis of the post-revolutionary reconstruction of an essentially moderate monarchy, characterized by restricted use of power, civil freedom, and the rule of law. In the *Tableau*, Calonne situated himself in the middle between uncompromising royalists, on the

---

[189] 'On voit quelle confusion de vues, d'idées et de langage, se trouve parmi prôneurs de la constitution de quatorze siècles; mais c'est cette confusion même qui a été précieuse à ses inventeurs.' Montlosier, *Vue sommaire sur les moyens de paix*, 11–13.
[190] I therefore disagree with Simon Burrows' assessment that 'Calonne categorically denied that *ancien régime* France had a constitution'. This view echoes, in my opinion, too much the interpretation of Calonne's royalist '*pur*' enemies. Burrows, *Exile Journalism*, 159.

one hand, and radical revolutionaries, on the other. As both Calonne and Burke argued against peace negotiations with the Directory and advocated continuing warfare against the revolutionary Republic, the extent of their moderation can, of course, be questioned. Their moderate attitude was also mocked by contemporary critics such as Mackintosh, who claimed that under the guise of moderation, Burke and Calonne were essentially militant 'crusaders' of a radical Counter-Revolution.

Calonne's unforeseen and unwanted experience of exile shaped his cosmopolitan world view, as well as that of many other émigrés. As the contacts between Calonne and Burke showed, a transnational conversation came into being among the opponents of the Revolution, and ideas were shared, if only briefly and imperfectly. The writers discussed in this chapter shared the Enlightenment narrative of the long-term social, institutional, and economic development of European progress and civilization. In contrast to Bonneville, who harnessed 'modern European history' to support the Revolution, both Calonne and Burke, despite their different French and English perspectives, used the narrative of European and national history as an argument against the Revolution. In their views, the continuously evolving institutions of Europe since medieval times had guaranteed liberty and the rule of law. By abruptly breaking with historic institutions, the revolutionaries had situated France outside of the European civilized commonwealth, and thus outside of European history.

5
Equilibrium against Empire

1. Anti-Imperial Pluralism

After his successful coup of the '18th of Brumaire' (9 November 1799), the Corsican revolutionary general Napoleon Bonaparte became consul for life in 1802 and crowned himself emperor in 1804.[1] Counter-revolutionaries, as well as later historians, differed widely in their interpretation of this newly established Napoleonic 'Empire'. Some counter-revolutionaries, such as Chateaubriand, believed hopefully that deep down Napoleon was also a counter-revolutionary himself who would bring a halt to the Revolution and restore a monarchical order.[2] Many self-declared opponents of the Revolution, for ideological as well as for opportunist reasons, thus took office in this pan-continental Empire, or, like Calonne, tried to do so unsuccessfully.[3] Other counter-revolutionaries regarded Napoleon as essentially a Jacobin revolutionary in disguise whose aim was to destroy the final vestiges of the *ancien régime*. These publicists lamented that they earlier had predicted that the Revolution would end in a violent despotism, and that Napoleon proved them right.[4]

In the posthumously published *Mémorial of Saint Helena*, the Napoleonic Empire was above all vindicated by Napoleon himself as a civilizing enterprise, imposing uniform and enlightened regulations and laws on a grateful European continent.[5] From 1804 onwards, the Napoleonic Empire was increasingly presented as a pan-European enterprise rather than a merely French one. Napoleon was depicted in official discourse as a (West) European emperor, who defended the lands of Charlemagne against the commercial aggression of the British, on the one hand, and the Russian Eastern hordes, on the other. The continental blockade reinforced, often *à contre-coeur*, a continental European identity. Napoleon legitimized his Empire as an enlightened administration that would rule Europe in accordance with the principles of reason, peace, and progress through a strong and efficient government.[6] The British historian Stuart Woolf has argued that this

---

[1] Lentz, *Grand Consulat*; Lentz, *Nouvelle Histoire du premier Empire*; Broers, *Napoleon*, vol. I; Broers, Hicks, and Guiméra, *Napoleonic Empire*.
[2] See also Chapter 6.   [3] Woloch, *Napoleon and His Collaborators*; Lok, *Windvanen*.
[4] See also Chapter 2.   [5] Casas, *Mémorial de Saint Hélène*.
[6] On the legitimation of the Napoleonic Empire: Jourdan, 'Napoléon et la paix universelle'; on the 'French' character of the Empire: Woolf, 'French Civilisation and Ethnicity'.

Empire was indeed a first attempt at European integration.[7] Woolf, moreover, believed that the Empire had a fundamental influence on shaping European identity vis-à-vis the rest of the world, resulting in a more Eurocentric writing of European history and a reinforced distinction between Europe and the other parts of the globe, justifying nineteenth-century imperial conquest.[8]

Napoleon's imperial project undoubtably provided a strong impetus for the rewriting of the European past. In response to this pro-Napoleonic propaganda, critical histories of Europe were written that presented an alternative vision to this enlightened imperialism. In his history of the European state system, Arnold Heeren, as we saw in Chapter 1, painted a picture of a historical tradition of European political pluralism that was all but destroyed by the despotic rule of this new Napoleonic universal monarchy. In the next three chapters, I will examine European histories that were published in response to the rise of this new European Empire. I will focus, in particular, on sources in German. Although European histories were published in other national and linguistic contexts as well, the German sources in this decade are especially abundant. Moreover, it was German authors who articulated the idea of Europe as a pluralist continent, whose unique freedom was the result of centuries of political and cultural fragmentation and lack of centralization, and who presented the German Empire and the German Nation as the crucial building blocks of this system.[9]

The key concept in most of these—anachronistically termed—'pluralist' histories was 'balance' or 'equilibrium' (*Gleichgewicht* in German). These eulogies of the European 'balance' were usually combined with a positive assessment of the alleged political, cultural, and economic contrasts, deemed typical of European history. This typical European equilibrium allegedly existed in different forms over many centuries, withstanding all attempts to establish a universal empire that would stifle Europe's unique diversity within a common Christian and institutional frame.

This German emphasis on the pluralist character of European history can no doubt partly be explained by the fact that, for German authors, European history was closely related to the history of the Holy Roman Empire, dissolved under pressure from Napoleon in 1806.[10] For German authors, questions of European order were seen in the context of the problem of reform of the Holy Roman

---

[7] Woolf, *Napoleon's Integration of Europe*.

[8] 'A European view of the extra-European view was consolidated which drew on earlier perceptions, but transformed them into a radically different unifying concept of European civilization and progress which allowed the classification, and justified the material exploitation of the rest of the world. Secondly, a distinctive conviction was forged of what constituted the essence of Europe's superiority, based on the division of its land mass into nation states and the role of the rational state in furthering progress.' Woolf, 'Construction of a European World-View', 74.

[9] For the concept of 'pluralism', see also Chapters 1 and 6.

[10] On the Holy Roman Empire: Stollberg-Rilinger, *Heilige Römische Reich*; Duchhardt, *Altes Reich*.

Empire of the German Nation.[11] Parallel to their idea of Europe, German-speaking authors also underscored the lack of centralization of the German Empire, the *Kleinstaaterei*, as its unique feature.[12] As we shall see in the next chapters, German authors used the pluralist narrative of European history both to legitimize as well as to criticize the Napoleonic Empire. The sources they used, however, were not only German in origin, but were also part of a transnational pluralist European tradition. For instance, Montesquieu, but also the works of the Scottish historians, in particular Robertson, greatly influenced these German pluralist narratives.

This counter-revolutionary emphasis on Europe as a balanced and diverse continent was, however, not confined to German sources alone. The theme of regarding one's own country as the embodiment of the European 'unity in diversity' can be found in different national manifestations, for instance in the French, Swiss, Spanish, British, Dutch, and Belgian historiographical traditions.[13] Montesquieu, whose anti-imperial Europeanism inspired both Feller and Calonne in their own way, would also provide an important authority for the German authors studied in these chapters.[14] Pluralist ideas of Europe were also articulated in Francophone publications in the Thermidor debate on a new international order. In his *Réflexions sur la paix adressées à Pitt et au Français* (May 1795) Francis d'Ivernois, for instance, argued that only the military defeat of France, and the return to its pre-1792 boundaries, could restore the traditional political balance of European states. This 'balance' (*équilibre, balancement*) was, according to him, the 'palladium' of European civilization. It was only as a result of this international balance, 'accompanied and stimulated by the Reformation', that the 'European republic' had been able to build a free, happy, and secure enlightened society and to halt all Asian invasions over the course of centuries.[15] D'Ivernois' critical views on the hegemony of one state and his enthusiasm about the 'balance of the forces' were no doubt influenced by his Swiss background—Switzerland being a small and partly Protestant country surrounded by larger monarchies, and itself constituting a balance of separate entities.[16]

In the following three chapters, I will discuss the reflections of self-proclaimed 'German' counter-revolutionaries on Napoleon's Empire from the perspective of 'cosmopolitanism'. I will argue in these chapters, that instead of disappearing,

---

[11] Burgdorf, 'Imperial Reform'.   [12] Berger, 'Building the Nation', 247–308.
[13] Berger, *Past as History*, 95–101.   [14] See also, for a more extensive discussion, Chapter 6.
[15] 'Cet admirable balancement des forces de l'Europe a été depuis deux siècles le palladium de la civilization. C'est à lui, c'est à son maintien, que cette vaste & riche République a dû de n'avoir plus été inondée par des irruptions dévastatrices; c'est seulement depuis qu'elle l'a découvert, qu'elle a pu, ainsi que la Grèce, durant la pondération de ses forces, se livrer avec quelque sécurité & avec de si brillans succès aux jouissances de la paix; aux arts qu'elle fait naître, & aux sciences qu'elle protège. C'est depuis cette grande découverte, accompagnée & favorisée de celle de la Réformation, que l'Europe a cessé d'être barbare. Enfin, c'est à la faveur de cet équilibre que les peuples Chrétiens prenaient chaque jour un élan plus rapide vers le bonheur, les lumières & la liberté (...).' D'Ivernois, *Réflexions sur la guerre*, 24. See also Chapter 4.
[16] Karmin, *Sir Francis d'Ivernois*.

cosmopolitan ideals survived and were adapted by counter-revolutionaries for their own agendas.[17] This emphasis on post-revolutionary cosmopolitanism is not self-evident, as we saw earlier: most histories of cosmopolitanism identify the eighteenth century as the heyday of the cosmopolitan age, which supposedly ended in the revolutionary and Napoleonic wars, leading to the rise of virulent nationalism. Pauline Kleingeld and Andrea Albrecht, studying German sources, have argued for a more inclusive definition, allowing for a plurality of cosmopolitanisms.[18] They, as well as others, also concluded that for the German case, patriotism and cosmopolitanism were regarded by contemporaries not as opposites but as complementary notions.[19] Until the later nineteenth century, and in the case of Friedrich Meinecke even later, a symbiosis of cosmopolitanism and patriotism was regarded as a particular quality of the German nation.[20]

The Münster historian Heinz Gollwitzer, in his study *Europabild und Europagedanke* of 1951, moreover, gave a comprehensive description of the German Europeanism of the early nineteenth century. In that book, Gollwitzer traced German European ideals in the eighteenth and nineteenth centuries, situating German history in an older tradition of enlightened and pluralist Europeanism.[21] In his influential book *Die Entstehung der politischen Strömungen in Deutschland: 1770–1815*, Fritz Valjavec (1909–60) argued that liberalism and conservatism were not foreign Western imports but had grown on German native soil.[22] He also stated that the roots of German conservativism and, above all, liberalism could be found in the eighteenth-century German Enlightenment. German political history, therefore, according to Valjavec, did not follow a trajectory different from that of other Western European countries.[23] Here I will situate German ideas of European history in a wider international context and interpret them as part of a transnational endeavour transcending the German-speaking world. Furthermore, the conceptual differences between post-revolutionary

---

[17] According to Fillafer and Osterhammel, 'cosmopolitanism was an ambiguous concept: it could possess strong imperial contours, encapsulating a civilising and pacifying mission; in the German context, it could also refurbish the *Reichsidee* in the sense of a *translation imperii*'. Fillafer and Osterhammel, 'Cosmopolitanism', 121. Cf. Horstmann, 'Kosmopolit'; Kleingeld, 'Six Varieties'. See also Chapter 1.

[18] Albrecht, *Kosmopolitismus*, 341.

[19] Albrecht, *Kosmopolitismus*; Kleingeld, *Kant*; Fillafer and Osterhammel, 'Cosmopolitanism'. Cf. Weichlein, 'Cosmopolitism, Patriotism, Nationalism'.

[20] Friedrich Meinecke (1862–1954) famously made use of the concept of European dialectic in his post-war book *The German Catastrophe* (*Die Deutsche Katastrophe*) of 1946. In this book, in many ways, he continued the argument of his earlier famous work of 1908, *Cosmopolitanism and the National State* (*Weltbürgertum und Nationalstaat*), adapting his positions to the new context of the post-war years. Meinecke, *Cosmopolitanism and the National State*, 21; Meinecke, *deutsche Katastrophe*, 172. Cf. Schulze, *Geschichtswissenschaft*, 46–76; Krol, 'geweten van Duitsland', 35–63. See also Chapter 9.

[21] Gollwitzer, *Europabild*.

[22] See also Chapter 9 for an examination of Gollwitzer and Valjavec as (post-)war historians.

[23] Valjavec, *politischen Strömungen*.

enlightened and romantic cosmopolitanism, often overdrawn in the scholarly literature, will here be nuanced.[24]

In the next section of this chapter, I will briefly discuss the eighteenth-century interpretations of the idea of the European balance, followed by a short overview of the revolutionary debate on the means to achieve 'perpetual peace' in Europe. This brief overview will provide the context for the analysis of German counter-revolutionary European ideals. I will then discuss the response by Friedrich Gentz to this debate on attaining peace and his use of the European past. Subsequently, I will examine the main case study of this chapter, Adam Heinrich Müller (1779–1827). I will argue that, instead of being a romantic reactionary or proto-national-socialist, as he usually has been made out to be, he should be regarded as a counter-revolutionary cosmopolitan in the moderate enlightened tradition, and that European history formed the main framework through which he expressed his political ideas.

2. The Enlightened Equilibrium

The 'balance of power' has long been a topic of scholarly discussion among historians of the international system.[25] In recent years, researchers have shifted from the idea of the balance as a neutral and purely analytical notion to the interpretation of the concept as an essentially prescriptive concept. Historians have increasingly paid attention to how historical actors themselves made use of the word as part of their rhetorical and political strategies.[26] So far, less systematic attention has been given to the European equilibrium as part of a larger narrative of European history with a long historiographical afterlife.[27] Rather than an abstract theory, theorists of the state system usually retorted to a narrative of historical events to explain the mechanisms of the equilibrium. Precisely because this balance was not seen as an abstract, but essentially as an empirical and historical notion, the idea was attractive for the counter-revolutionaries. As we shall see in this chapter, the enlightened notion of the balance was reinvented by counter-revolutionaries to be used as a rhetorical weapon. It provided an alternative idea of European order to the revolutionary schemes of a republican federation and the Napoleonic imperial idea, framed as part of a larger pluralist narrative of European history. Most counter-revolutionaries, however, did not argue for a full restoration of the balance that supposedly had existed in the

---

[24] For instance, by Gollwitzer, *Europabild*, 103–78.
[25] See for an overview of the literature: de Graaf, *Terreur*, 87–98 and notes, 417–19. A selection of works on the balance in international history are: Duchhardt, *Gleichgewicht der Kräfte*; Gruner, *Gleichgewicht in Geschichte*; Schroeder, *Transformation*; Dehio, *Gleichgewicht oder Hegemonie*.
[26] De Graaf, *Terreur*, 87–8. Cf. Haas, 'Balance of Power'.
[27] An exception: Muhlack, 'Europäische Staatensystem'.

pre-revolutionary decades, but instead pleaded for the reconstruction of an improved version of the *ancien régime* equilibrium.

The concept of the political balance of power originated in the Italian Renaissance and in humanistic political thought in the sixteenth and seventeenth centuries.[28] The balance also figured prominently in eighteenth-century international thought.[29] One of the first to formulate the 'pluralist' idea of European history in the German lands was the seventeenth-century philosopher Gottfried Wilhelm Leibniz (1646–1716). Leibniz no longer required the idea of universal monarchy to underpin European Christianity. Leibniz's *Reichspatriotismus* ('imperial patriotism') was no longer utopian and retrospective, according to Gollwitzer, but 'modern' and aimed at the prevention of the establishment of an imperial monarchy.[30] Already in Leibniz's thought we can observe a close connection between the idea of a fragmented Europe (*Vielvalt*) and Europe's imperial dominion of the world.[31] Leibniz divided the world among the European nations. Europe, China, and India could coexist in some kind of 'harmony' of high cultures, although Europe's ultimate superiority was based on the only true Christian tradition.[32]

In mid-eighteenth-century Germany, theories of *Gleichgewicht* gained prominence among German students of Europe and its political system. Especially in Göttingen, the 'balance' was studied in a systematic and historical manner that marked a rupture with seventeenth-century treatises.[33] From a mere power doctrine, the 'balance' became an enlightened idea in accordance with the principles of rationality, utility, and progress. Legal scholars, especially, developed an enlightened doctrine of the equilibrium. In 1744, Ludwig Martin Kahle, for instance, published a dissertation in which he attempted to make the balance theory the foundation of international law.[34] Despite their scientific-objective pretensions, the Göttingen scholars wrote in accordance with an older Protestant tradition, in which Britain was regarded as the cornerstone of the balance theory. In 1741, Göttingen professor Jan Jacob Schmauß, in his *Historie der Balance von Europa*, gave a more scientific as well as historicized interpretation of the balance theory.[35]

---

[28] Muhlack, 'Europäische Staatensystem', 314; Kaeber, *Idee des europäischen Gleichgewichts*; Meinecke, *Idee der Staatsräson*. The origins of the balance metaphor in the Middle Ages: Kaye, *History of Balance*.
[29] On the eighteenth-century idea of the balance: Bernardi, 'équilibre européen'; Anderson, 'Theories of Balance of Power', 183–98; Alimento and Stapelbroek, *Commercial Treaties*.
[30] 'Entsprechend seiner philosophischen Überzeugung und im Gegensatz zu der im Prinzip streng unitären Tendenz Campanellas suchte Leibniz jedoch die Synthese im Inneren der Vielheit, nicht die Uniformität auf Grund der Auflösung der Mannigfaltigkeit. Leibniz's politisches Denken bejahte den Europäischen Pluralismus.' Gollwitzer, *Europabild*, 44.
[31] See also Chapter 8.   [32] Gollwitzer, *Europabild*, 45.
[33] For the Göttingen school, see also Chapter 7.   [34] Kahle, *bilance de l'Europe*.
[35] Gollwitzer, *Europabild*, 74; Koskenniemi, *Uttermost Parts*, 880–3.

Over the course of the eighteenth century, German academics started to distinguish two different balance systems within the wider 'European republic'. Scandinavia, Poland, Russia, and Prussia were considered part of the 'Northern balance', the rest of Europe belonged to the 'Southern balance'. The fact that both balances were seen to be on an equal footing underscored the renewed importance of Northern Europe as a theatre of warfare and international relations. Prussian authors ascribed a key role for Prussia as the guarantor, not only of the Northern balance, but also as an intermediary between the Northern and the Southern European balance systems. Through its central role in the two balances, Prussia, in the eyes of its defenders, such as Herzberg, was the key player in the European republic. It was Prussia's national mission, determined by nature and providence, to maintain this European balance. Arnold Heeren, in his history of the European state system, continued to make the division between the Northern and the Southern state systems, although he considered the Congress of Vienna to have unified the two systems into one new state system.[36]

The doctrine of the European balance was generally accepted in the eighteenth century among academics and statesmen alike. Scholars provided an objective scientific legitimation for a prescriptive theory that could be adapted to many different political agendas. However, the doctrine also had its contemporary opponents. The cameralist J.H.G. von Justi, serving the Prussian monarchy, decried the 'chimera' of an abstract theory of balance: instead, he argued that balance, or even the idea of a European republic, was a fiction, and used as a mask for naked power politics. Justi and other 'sceptic-realist rationalists' believed eighteenth-century Europe consisted of a theatre of 'barbaric freedom', determined by the power plays of the great states. According to his pessimistic vision of human nature, and in particular of the character of kings, every form of order, such as balance, merely offered an excuse or legitimation of a certain political agenda.[37]

3. 'Perpetual Peace' and Its Discontents

After 1792, the enlightened idea of the European equilibrium became politicized as a result of the revolutionary wars.[38] Counter-revolutionaries responded to revolutionary proposals to bring 'perpetual peace' to Europe and the world through the establishment of a federation of states with common institutions

---

[36] See Chapter 7.
[37] Justi, *Chimäre des Gleichgewichts*. On Justi: Gollwitzer, *Europabild*, 75–6, 80–1; Burgdorf, 'Justi'; Koskenniemi, *Uttermost Parts*, 891–901.
[38] See also Chapters 3 and 4.

based on the principles of the French Revolution.[39] The most influential articulation of this ideal was Immanuel Kant's (1724–1804) *Zum Ewigen Frieden* (Towards Perpetual Peace), first published in 1795.[40] In these debates over achieving perpetual peace, narratives of European history were reinvented and older enlightened ideas of the European past were brought to the fore in a new political context.

The publication of *Towards Perpetual Peace* was the outcome of a discussion that had started with the publication of Kant's earlier essay 'On the Common Saying: That May Be Correct in Theory, but It Is of No Use in Practice' in September 1793. In this essay, Kant, after earlier refusing to take sides, sided with the revolutionary cause and argued for an egalitarian conception of civil liberty. The publication of this essay led to a discussion between Kant and his critics, among them Friedrich von Gentz (1764–1832), August Wilhelm Rehberg (1756–1836), and Justus Möser (1720–94), although Kant did not explicitly name his adversaries. These critics did not overall disagree with Kant over the significance of the concept of freedom but primarily disputed Kant's interpretation and the political implications of his view on liberty.[41]

In the *Towards Perpetual Peace* text, Kant made more explicitly public his support for the principles of the French Revolution. He pleaded for an ever-expanding union of states with similar 'republican' constitutions, defined primarily as the rule of law that was, in principle, compatible with constitutional monarchy.[42] Kant's fictitious opponent was the 'practical man' who might well have been an amalgam of Gentz, Möser, and, above all, Rehberg. Laws must, according to Kant, be constructed on a formal principle and only then implemented in reality, instead of letting principles be determined by practical purposes. In this work, he judged the military victory of the French Republic as offering advantages for humanity, international law, and peace.[43]

Kant's work was a key source of reference for all those who thought about a new European order in the decades after its publication in 1795, whether they approved of his text or not.[44] *Towards Perpetual Peace* was widely acclaimed by French pro-revolutionary journals, such as *Le Moniteur*, and discussed by French intellectuals such as Sieyès and the *idéologues*. However, it was in Germany where Kant's text received the most attention. Kant's text was at first abundantly praised

---

[39] On the peace tradition: Belissa, *Repenser*, 389–91; Kulessa and Seth, *Europaidee*; Ghervas, 'Paix par le droit'; Ghervas, *Conquering Peace*; Heater, *Idea of European Unity*; Burgdorf, 'Imperial Reform', 401–8.
[40] Kant, 'Zum ewigen Frieden'; Kant, *Perpetual Peace*.
[41] Maliks, 'State of Freedom'; Green, 'Fiat Justitia'.
[42] Maliks, 'State of Freedom', 199. On Kant's *Perpetual Peace*, a vast literature exists: Kleingeld, 'Kant's Cosmopolitan Law', 72–90, and note 1. See also: Kleingeld, *Kant and Cosmopolitanism*, in particular 43–71.
[43] On the complex relation of Kant to the French Revolution: Green, 'Fiat Justitia'.
[44] Belissa, *Repenser*, 391; Kleingeld, *Kant*, 43–71; Koskenniemi, *Uttermost Parts*, 901–24.

by Rhineland intellectuals. Joseph Görres (1776–1848), for instance, invited the French Directory to realize Kant's vision. Friedrich Schlegel, moreover, wrote that only a universal republicanism could realize the project to attain perpetual peace. Johann Gottlieb Fichte also regarded the project to establish a republic of multiple European states, analogous to the North American republic, as a realistic perspective. The revolutionary wars were blamed on the despotic European monarchies who selfishly opposed the revolutionary project to establish a peaceful new order.[45]

The year 1798 marked the apogee of Kant's popularity and enthusiasm for the realization of his peace plan. Thereafter, the tide turned and optimism for the swift realization of a perpetual peace faded.[46] The Peace of Lunéville of 1801 inspired fears in the hearts of many about the coming wars in the new century. According to the French historian Marc Belissa, between 1798 and 1804 an 'enlightened cosmopolitanism' was replaced in the minds of German intellectuals by the romantic 'monarchical and national state'.[47] However, Belissa's interpretation of a radical change around 1800 in the German lands, and in Europe more generally, from enlightened cosmopolitanism to romantic monarchical nationalism, is overdrawn. Enlightened notions of the *Gleichgewicht* (balance) and cosmopolitan interpretations of the European and world state system were still being published in the first decades of the nineteenth century.

4. A Counter-Revolutionary Balance

A prominent critic of the Kantian ideal of a federation based on republican principles was Friedrich (von) Gentz, a former pupil of Kant himself *nota bene*. Gentz was not just a romantic reactionary striving to restore a lost *ancien régime*, as the older historiography would have it. As Raphaël Cahen, Jonathan Green, Brian Vick, and others have argued, he should instead be regarded as part of the tradition of a moderate, 'prudential', and late cosmopolitan Enlightenment.[48] Rather than merely defeating the Revolution, Gentz—in his own words—hoped for the reconciliation of the two worlds of the Revolution and the old order. Although he explicitly chose the side of the enemies of the Revolution, he was also deeply critical of the European monarchies and their policies. Only by reforming

---

[45] Belissa, *Repenser*, 392–6.
[46] *Towards Perpetual Peace* was, however, still referred to, admiringly as well as critically, in the debates on a new European order in 1814–15. See Chapter 8.
[47] Belissa, *Repenser*, 397–8.
[48] Cahen, *Gentz*; Green, 'Fiat Justitia', 35–65. Gollwitzer in his *Europabild* (1951) already interpreted Gentz primarily as the exponent of an Enlightened cosmopolitan and rational eighteenth-century tradition. Gollwitzer, *Europabild*, 183–93.

and modernizing the European monarchies could the Revolution be contained, Gentz thought.

Gentz, who was born into a Protestant family in the Prussian Silesian city of Breslau and studied in Köningsberg, had originally greeted the outbreak of the Revolution with approval, as had many of his fellow Germans. In 1792, working as a civil servant in the service of the king of Prussia, he became a critic of the revolutionary ideals, after having read the works of Edmund Burke, Mallet de Pan, and Francis d'Ivernois. Gentz, however, would never reject the revolutionary legacy entirely.[49] He acquired fame as the translator of Edmund Burke's *Reflections on the Revolution in France* into German, adapting and augmenting the book to suit German audiences in a climate increasingly hostile to the Revolution.[50]

In December 1800, Gentz wrote a scathing criticism of *Zum ewigen Frieden* in the *Historisches Journal*, a journal he edited with Austrian subsidies.[51] In Gentz's article, Kant's ideas were both attacked and built upon. In this contribution, Gentz critiqued the peace plan of his former teacher as a dangerous and unrealistic chimera. At the same time, Gentz also agreed with Kant that a new European order was required. However, he, unlike his old mentor, underscored that the principle of reason of state should not be left out of this design, and he argued that the halting of all wars was not a desirable end in itself.[52]

In 1801, he further developed his idea of the balance of power as a model of international order in his *Über den Ursprung und Charakter des Krieges gegen die Französische Revoluzion*.[53] In this treatise 'on the origin and character of the war against the French Revolution', Gentz wrote that the allied coalition had been entirely justified in intervening militarily in revolutionary France. Although the sovereign rights of an individual European state were an important principle of the old state system, and not every attempt to reform a constitution could be termed a revolution, the events in revolutionary France were so radical in nature that intervention had become a duty for the other European powers. The violence and anarchism that had characterized the Revolution in France from the start, had destroyed the 'European republic'. This republic consisted of a great political confederation (*Bund*), characterized, as in Burke's view, by a 'common geographical position, manifold relations, a uniformity of morals, laws, way of life and

---

[49] Cahen rejected the idea of the sudden transformation of Gentz from a revolutionary sympathizer into a radical counter-revolutionary and emphasizes the continuity in his thought as a 'moderate' striving to reconcile the new and the old orders; in the years 1799 and 1800, a radicalization of Gentz's counter-revolutionary stance and an increased criticism of revolutionary natural law can be observed, but not a true rupture within his thought. Cahen, *Gentz*, 203–6, 224–5.

[50] Cahen, *Gentz*, 109–12, 405; Green, 'Friedrich Gentz's translation'; Kontler, 'Varieties'.

[51] According to Jonathan Green, Kant's debate with Gentz was a debate within the German Enlightenment: 'a debate not over *whether* to enlighten, but *how*'. Green, 'Fiat Justitia', 41. On Gentz and Kant: Kleingeld, *Kant*, 67–8; Cahen, *Gentz*, 160–4.

[52] Gentz, 'Über den Ewigen Frieden'.   [53] Gentz, *Ursprung*.

culture'.[54] Only the abrupt revolutionary reversal of all laws and norms that had hitherto existed, undermining the foundations of the entire international system, made military intervention by other countries legally and morally justified. Like Calonne, Gentz was at the same time also highly critical of the errors of judgement and failures of the allied armies in their struggle against the revolutionary armies in the 1790s.

In the same year, Gentz published another treatise on the state of Europe before and after the French Revolution (*Von dem politischen Zustande von Europa vor und nach der Französischen Revolution*).[55] In this work, he responded to the claim made by the French senior civil servant Alexandre d'Hauterive (1754–1830) that it was Britain, not France, that had destroyed the European state system through its ambition to achieve hegemony through commercial means. D'Hauterive presented the French Republic in a moderate vein as the protector of the European state system against British aggression, distancing himself from the vision of a federal order voiced by radical revolutionaries.[56] Gentz responded by arguing that commercial rivalry was essential to the old state system now destroyed by revolutionary France. Both d'Hauterive and Gentz drew upon eighteenth-century enlightened notions of the state system and commerce to support their own arguments.[57]

Gentz extensively redeveloped his concept of the balance in a further work, entitled *Fragmente aus der neuesten Geschichten des Politischen Gleichgewichts in Europa* (1806). This book, translated in the same year as *Fragments upon the Balance of Power in Europe*, is widely considered Gentz's magnum opus.[58] Gentz had by now left the service of the Prussian state and had become an anti-Napoleonic publicist employed by Austria. He could build on an extensive European network of correspondents consisting of diplomats, scholars, and writers. At the time of writing this work, he was travelling around Europe under the surveillance of Napoleonic agents. In the *Fragments*, Gentz argued that Europe found itself in a profound crisis or 'political illness' (*die politische Krankheiten Europa's*).[59] The traditional system of states had been destroyed and Napoleon's universal monarchy was a mortal threat to Europe's future. The Holy Roman Empire had been dissolved under pressure from Napoleon, ending a thousand years of institutional history.[60] The Treaty of Lunéville of 1801 was, for Gentz, not a true and balanced peace, but a treaty that worked to Napoleon's advantage only. He, therefore, as Burke and Calonne had done earlier, exhorted the European

---

[54] Gentz, *Ursprung*, 19.
[55] Gentz, *politischen Zustande von Europa*. In 1804, an English translation was published. Cf. Cahen, *Gentz*, 164–9.
[56] [Hauterive], *état de la France*.
[57] Nakhimovsky, '"Ignominious Fall"'; Forsyth, 'Old European States-System'.
[58] Cahen, *Gentz*, 55. The book was immediately translated into Swedish, French, and English. The English version is: Gentz, *Fragments upon the Balance of Power in Europe*.
[59] Gentz, *Fragmente*, iii.   [60] Klinger and Hahn, *Jahr 1806*; Hartmann, *Heilige Römische Reich*.

monarchs to cast off their lethargy and pacifism, and to fight against the Napoleonic threat. Gentz saw a special missionary role for the Germans in defeating the Napoleonic Empire and restoring European freedom.[61]

In the *Fragments*, Gentz extensively discussed his idea of the political balance (*politischen Gleichgewichts*).[62] For him, the political balance or *balance du pouvoir* formed an international system in which the states 'guarantee the independence and rights of one state against harm done by another state'.[63] This balance is not based on some abstract notion of equality, which supposedly formed the ideological foundation of the Kantian federation. Each European state had, for Gentz, a different position within a larger system: their particular rights and autonomy were protected by the commonwealth, but they could not claim equal rights. Also, the different states all had different national characters and, consequently, unique legal systems, of which Gentz approved. They, nonetheless, all formed part of a larger state system or 'republic' based on the principle of the rule of law. Gentz framed his idea of 'equilibrium' in a longer historical narrative: the political balance was the main explanation of the extraordinary development and progress of Europe since the sixteenth century, and therefore was beneficial to all mankind, according to Gentz, citing his cousin Ancillon as well as David Hume and Edmund Burke as authorities.[64]

In the first decade of the nineteenth century, however, the balance was destroyed by the latest version of the 'universal monarchy' that was the Napoleonic Empire. The roots of this decay of the international system for Gentz were, however, much older. The Lunéville treaty was only the capstone of the gradual destruction of the balance of power. According to Gentz, it was the Polish partition of 1772 and the accompanying lust for power, demonstrated by the great powers, where the rot had begun to set in. From 1772 onwards, the great powers 'slept' and no longer realized the advantages of the historically grown political balance. The partition of Poland unwittingly provided the pretext for the French conquest of large parts of Europe: the revolutionaries legitimized their usurpations by pointing out that they had been left out of the earlier partition by the Eastern monarchies. The subsequent revolutionary wars had destroyed the system and led to the subjugation of the German lands by foreign conquerors.

Gentz thus rejected the interpretation of the Napoleonic Empire as a counter-revolutionary regime, as, for instance, Niklas Vogt would argue.[65] Instead

---

[61] 'Europa is durch Deutschland gefallen: durch Deutschland muß es wieder emporsteigen.' Gentz, *Fragmente*, xlvi.
[62] See also: Cahen, *Gentz*, 227–35.
[63] 'Das was man gewöhnlich politisches Gleichgewicht (*balance du pouvoir*) nennt, ist diejenige Verfassung neben einander bestehender und mehr oder weniger mit einander verbundener Staaten, vermöge deren keiner unter ihnen die Unabhängigkeit oder die wesentliche Rechte eines andern, ohne wirksamen Widerstand von irgend einer Seite, und folglich ohne Gefahr für sich selbst, beschädigen kann.' Gentz, *Fragmente*, 1.
[64] Gentz, *Fragmente*, 11. See also Chapter 6.   [65] See Chapter 6.

Napoleon for Gentz was the inheritor of the revolutionary ideals. His empire was characterized by a despotic power which knew no boundaries. Gentz contrasted the new revolutionary despotism of Napoleon with the Austrian state, his model of a traditional 'moderate' European monarchy. The Austrian monarchy did not enforce the different components of its empire in uniformity, but instead acknowledged and protected the diversity of its component parts. Traditional provincial and local rights, as well as the noble and clerical orders, acted as breaks on monarchical power in Vienna, Gentz wrote lyrically. Also, in Austria the monarchs listened to public opinion, which acted as a bridle on the power of the state.[66] However, Gentz did not always sing the praises of the Habsburgs: he was also critical of what he regarded as the conservativism of the European monarchies. Reforming the administrations of the monarchical states along the lines of an enlightened programme was the only sure way to defeat the spectre of the Revolution, Gentz, like Calonne, argued.[67]

Gentz believed, like many other counter-revolutionary publicists, that the abstract ideals of the Revolution had, above all, resulted in a new all-powerful universal empire which had more in common with an oriental despotism than with a moderate European monarchy.[68] And just as Napoleon would not allow counterweights in the internal affairs of the French state, he would destroy all balancing forces in the field of international affairs. It was therefore a dangerous illusion, prevalent among the European crowned heads, Gentz argued in a vein similar to that of Burke and Calonne earlier, that they could make a stable peace with a revolutionary state. Gentz ended optimistically: not all was lost. Europe, guided by the awakened Germans, could defeat the despotic Napoleonic Empire and restore the old European 'commonwealth' in a new form. The timing of Gentz's work was not perfect: military victories had made Napoleon all powerful, and Prussian and Austrian cabinets did not wish to oppose him. Gentz would return to Vienna only in 1809 to work for Metternich, when the political tide was slowly beginning to turn to his advantage. From 1812 onwards, Gentz was able to put into practice his ideas of a regenerated new European order as an actor in the diplomatic conferences in the post-Napoleonic era.[69]

5. A German Montesquieu

Gentz developed his ideas on the regeneration of the European state system in close cooperation with his younger friend and pupil Adam Heinrich Müller (1779–1827), although their views differed in important respects.[70] Even more

---

[66] Gentz, *Fragmente*, 59–83.　　[67] Cahen, *Gentz*, 212–16.　　[68] Gentz, *Fragmente*, 62–6.
[69] Cahen, *Gentz*, 261–395. See Chapter 8.　　[70] Cahen, Gentz, 205–6.

than Gentz's, Müller's reputation has suffered at the hands of posterity.[71] In the nineteenth century, Müller was depicted by his liberal critics as an illiberal and anti-enlightened reactionary. Especially after the First World War, several publications on Müller appeared, in line with the wider renewed interest in early nineteenth-century conservatism.[72] Most well-known is Carl Schmitt's critical description of Müller as a representative of moralizing and utopian 'political romanticism'.[73] Others, such as Friedrich Meinecke, have described Müller primarily as a representative of a conservative and national organicist view of the state.[74] This national, anti-enlightened, and reactionary-conservative interpretation would consequently blacken Müller's reputation after the Second World War, when he came to be regarded as one of the intellectual authors of the German anti-liberal *Sonderweg*. In accordance with recent attempts to rescue Müller from his anachronistic reputation as a nationalist and arch-reactionary, I interpret his works, in particular his *Die Elemente der Staatskunst* ('The Elements of Statecraft') (1809), as a telling example of counter-revolutionary enlightened cosmopolitanism, without, of course, being willing to downplay the darker sides of his ideas.[75]

Müller (1779–1829) was born in Berlin. Originally, he intended to study theology, but from 1798 until 1801 he devoted himself in Göttingen to the study of law, philosophy, and natural science. His took classes from Arnold Ludwig Heeren and even dedicated his *Elemente* to this former teacher. Early in life he formed a close friendship with Gentz, fifteen years his elder. This friendship would determine his intellectual life as well as his professional career. Müller tried a short stint as a civil servant, followed by an itinerant life as a tutor, publicist, and courtier in different European countries. He converted to the Catholic faith in 1805. From 1805 to 1809, Müller lived in Dresden, where he gave his lectures that would form the basis of his *Elements*. In 1813, he entered the Austrian civil service. He took part in the peace conferences of Vienna (1814–15), and the Congress of Carlsbad (1819) where he was responsible for the drafting of the repressive, infamous 'Carlsbad decrees'. At the request of Metternich, he was ennobled as Ritter von Nittersdorf in 1826 and died in Vienna in 1829.[76]

---

[71] On the historiography of Adam Müller's works: Green, *German Readers*, 172–5 and more generally: 18–74. According to Benedikt Koehler, interest in Adam Müller and the problem of 'political romanticism' resurfaced in German historiography in times of political transition, such as 1848 and 1918. Koehler, *Aesthetik der Politik*, 12.

[72] See Chapter 9.

[73] Schmitt, *Politische Romantik*. On Müller as a 'political romanticist': Baxa, *Adam Müllers Philosophie*; Reinhold, *Staatslehre Adam Müllers*; Braune, *Edmund Burke in Deutschland*; Busse, *Lehre vom Staat*. On the Müller debate in the Interbellum: Green, *German Readers*, 18–38.

[74] Meinecke, *Weltbürgertum und Nationalstaat*, 113–41. Meinecke also emphasized the European dimension of Müller's thought.

[75] Cf. Green, *German Readers*. Benedikt Koehler attempted to revive Müller's reputation in the 1980s: Koehler, *Aesthetik der Politik*.

[76] Baxa, *Adam Müller*.

In his first, rather abstract, philosophical work *Die Lehre vom Gegensatze* (1804) or the 'doctrine of contradictions', Müller turned unequivocally against the French Revolution. By destroying the traditional balance of power, the Revolution brought about the authoritarian leadership of one person, Müller argued, without explicitly referring to Napoleon.[77] Instead of imposing an artificial revolutionary unity, the conundrum of the current political situation in Europe could be resolved, according to Müller, only by a 'doctrine of contradictions'. Building on the insights derived from the natural sciences and mathematics, he opposed what he regarded as the revolutionary as well as Napoleonic emphasis on 'unity', a principle he associated with oppression and artificiality. This revolutionary unity was contrasted with a 'positive' counter-revolutionary 'diversity' ('*Verschiedenheit*' or '*Mannichfaltigkeit*'). A weak balance (*Gleichgewicht*) of opposing forces would, in the natural and in the political world, eventually turn out to be stronger than an enforced 'unity'.[78]

Müller, furthermore, wrote that human society can develop only by building a synthesis out of 'opposing elements' such as nature and culture, feelings and reason, or reason and religion. Germany, for Müller, was therefore superior to France, as Germany united both art and nature in a new synthesis, whereas in France art and nature were merely in opposition.[79] Referring to Edmund Burke, Müller argued that the state should be based not only on the principle of reason, but that aesthetics and feelings also played an important part in politics. Rather than operating as a mere machine, the state should also be considered a work of art.[80] Although the essay was not well received—even his friend Gentz confessed that he had not truly understood it—his publication on the doctrine of contradictions laid the philosophical groundwork for Müller's later political works.[81]

Müller's *Lectures on German Science and Literature* (*Vorlesungen über die deutsche Wissenschaft und Literatur*) were published in 1806, shortly after the dissolution of the German Empire. His aim was to install a renewed confidence among his fellow Germans, by turning Germany's weakness—the absence of a strong state comparable to France—into its main strength. Germany's advantage did not lie in a strong centralized empire, but in the blossoming of literature and science. Germany's cultural achievements Müller deemed superior to those of the French: French culture was 'concentrated' and 'uniform' whereas German culture was 'diverse' and plural.[82] Also, German culture was more than just one national culture among many: it possessed a universal dimension. For Müller, as a result of its diversity, German culture could be considered to represent humanity's culture and civilization as a whole.[83]

---

[77] Müller, *Lehre vom Gegensatze*, xii.
[78] Müller, *Lehre vom Gegensatze*, 51.
[79] Müller, *Lehre vom Gegensatze*, 72.
[80] Müller, *Lehre vom Gegensatze*, 100–18.
[81] Green, *German Readers*, 185–6.
[82] Müller, *Vorlesungen*, ii–iii.
[83] Müller, *Vorlesungen*, 40.

Also, Germany played a uniquely central role in European politics, according to Müller. In opposition to the French, who simply aimed to control and dominate the continent politically as well as culturally, the Germans only influenced and stimulated other national cultures, without suppressing their uniqueness or destroying their freedom. Germany could thus be considered the 'mother' of Europe. Most European nations, moreover, found their origins in the Germanic tribes. German princesses were seated on all European thrones. Germany was thus Europe's 'fortunate middle land' (*Glückliche Mittelland*), whose natural role and duty was to mediate between other European nations, as well as between those who follow the Catholic and Protestant religions.[84]

Müller drew a parallel between Germany's position in Europe and Europe's position in the world. Just as it was Germany's role to be a mediator in Europe, it was Europe's destiny to play the middleman on the global stage, rather than exert imperial control over the other continents. Although Müller expressed sadness and melancholy over the destruction of Europe's modern culture and society as a result of the Revolution, he also wrote confidently that a new, improved, and free civilization would be created under German leadership.[85] Thus the national, European, and universal discourses overlapped seamlessly in the counter-revolutionary thought of Müller.

In 1809, Müller published his magnum opus, *Die Elemente der Staatskunst*.[86] This book consisted of thirty-six chapters, based on the lectures (*Vorlesungen*) he gave at the court of the Prince of Saxe-Weimar. Napoleon was not explicitly mentioned, due to the political sensitivity of the topic—Saxony was a formal ally of Napoleon—but the work clearly formed a critical reflection on his Empire. In the foreword, Müller wrote that he had modelled his book on Montesquieu's *Spirit of the Laws* of 1748.[87] On the one hand, he fully supported Montesquieu's insights regarding the essentially national character of laws, constitutions, and morals, and the impossibility of imposing general models on different countries. Also, he approved of Montesquieu's criticism of the oppressive Roman Empire and the positive influence of the freedom-loving German tribes. Müller, furthermore, appreciated Montesquieu's work on the decline and fall of Rome, *Considérations sur les causes de la grandeur des Romains et de leur décadence*, even more than the *Spirit of the Laws*.[88]

On the other hand, Müller was critical of the alleged lack of attention given by Montesquieu to the historical development of laws and his supposedly static views of constitutions.[89] Moreover, he regarded Montesquieu's concept of the separation of powers as overly artificial. Furthermore, he condemned the supposed atheism

---

[84] Müller, *Vorlesungen*, 12, 25–6.   [85] Müller, *Vorlesungen*, 36.
[86] Müller, *Elemente* (1936). Original text: Müller, *Elemente* (1809). When I use the original edition, I will add the year of publication (1809), other references are to the 1936 edition.
[87] See for a conservative reading of Montesquieu's work: de Dijn, 'Controversial Context'.
[88] See Chapter 2.   [89] Müller, *Elemente* (1809) vol. I, x–xi.

of Montesquieu and saw him pejoratively as a prophet of the catastrophic French Revolution.[90] Müller's self-proclaimed aim in *The Elements* was not to reject the ideas of this eighteenth-century French author altogether, but to improve Montesquieu's work and to adapt his insights to a new age. Müller's own time, having gone through the—in his eyes—horrific revolutionary experience, was more aware of the pernicious effects of radical *philosophie* than Montesquieu had been in his. Also, Müller wrote his book on post-revolutionary statecraft in a different national context, the German one.[91] Montesquieu was not the only foreign reference used by Müller: he also referred to eighteenth-century British authors such as Edmund Burke, 'the greatest statesman of all times', and more critically, to Adam Smith and other Scottish political economists.[92]

In the preface, Müller described his own position as that of a 'moderate' and as a man of the 'middle'.[93] He considered himself a critic of revolutionary chimeras, but also fashioned himself as an opponent of a reactionary nostalgia for a distant past or an overzealous patriotism. He ascribed to himself the characteristics he had earlier attributed to Germany as a whole: a 'middle man' and a 'mediator'.[94] Like Calonne, Gentz, and Burke, he allowed for a moderate degree of change and progress in accordance with a gradual historical development. It would also be wrong to conclude from the revolutionary experiment that all constitutions were flawed and that nations could never be influenced by man-made laws.[95] Müller's main goal in studying political history was to learn from past experiences how to combine individual freedom with law and order for the benefit of society and mankind.[96]

Müller regarded his *Elements* as the right synthesis between practical politics, on the one hand, and abstract philosophy, on the other. Müller condemned the impractical dream of *philosophes* and *schwärmer*, but also the narrow utilitarian and provincial views of the civil servants and bureaucrats of the small principalities who were only interested in administrating their states on a small scale. True statesmen united experience with a wider vision. Precisely by reconciling theory and practice, extremist and fanatical views from the right as well as the left could be moderated. Models for Müller were, in his own words, the inevitable Burke, as

---

[90] Müller, *Elemente* (1809), vol. I, xiv.
[91] 'Wenige Bücher der Welt möchten sich an Gelehrsamkeit und Kunde aller Gesetze und Verfassungen diesem Buche an die Seite stellen lassen.' Müller, *Elemente* (1809) I, viii–ix.
[92] Müller reserved most praise for Edmund Burke, who he believed was more appreciated in Germany than in his native Great Britain: Müller, *Vorlesungen*, 149–50. Cf. Green, *German Readers*. I will not discuss here Müller's extensive comments on, and his criticism of, the work of Adam Smith. Political economy formed an important and integral part of Müller's thought. I thank David Reuter for his assistance with the research for this chapter on Müller.
[93] Cf. Lok, '"Extremes"'.   [94] Müller, *Elemente* (1809) I, vi.
[95] 'Das sind zwei gleich verderbliche Extreme: denn Völker und Gesetze bilden sich immer und allenthalben gegenseitig; allein und abgesondert vermag weder der Wille der Völker, noch die Güte der Gesetze etwas.' Müller, *Elemente* (1809) vol. I, viii.
[96] Müller, *Elemente* (1809) vol. I, xiv.

well as the seventeenth-century Dutch lawyer and humanist Hugo Grotius.[97] So, whereas posterity interpreted Müller as a reactionary, and even an early far-right radical, Müller regarded himself and his works as part of a moderate (Counter-) Enlightenment tradition. His project was, again in his own words, to improve as well as build upon the work of Montesquieu to fight a revolution deemed out of control and destroying all boundaries, and to find a 'middle way' between radical ideological positions, as well as between theory and practice.[98]

6. A Christ-centred Cosmopolis

Building on the matrix of the *Spirit of Laws* and Montesquieu's other works, Müller in his *Elemente* gave a descriptive as well prescriptive account of what constituted 'Europe'. He began with an examination of the philosophical foundations before analysing the legal, historical, economic, and religious characteristics of the European commonwealth (*Gemeinwesen*). In the first lecture, he contrasted the 'dead' *philosophe* and revolutionary concepts (*Begriffe*) with what he regarded as living counter-revolutionary 'ideas' (*Ideeen*). This typology allowed him to make a distinction between a wrong or 'dead' concept of freedom, effectively the abstract and timeless interpretation of liberty he associated with the French Revolution, and the just or 'living' articulation of the—counter-revolutionary—historical idea of freedom. This living idea of freedom Müller, for instance, found in the work of Edmund Burke.[99]

Müller decried, like all counter-revolutionaries, the revolutionary fallacy that a state could be constructed *ex nihilo*. Constitutions and state institutions were, in his view, shaped by the combined forces of nature and Divine Providence over the course of many centuries. Müller also contrasted the revolutionary idea of the 'mechanic' state with the counter-revolutionary state as a dynamic organism.[100] Also, the state should not merely be an instrument of a powerful leader, such as was the case in the Napoleonic Empire. Napoleon's rule contradicted the European tradition that the power of kings and emperors was bounded by historically grown rights, laws, and customs, which the ruler could not simply bend to his will. The American historian Leonard Krieger even credited the 'reactionary' Müller with the invention of the German concept of the

---

[97] Müller, *Elemente*, 3–34.

[98] The counter-revolutionary idea of the state was further developed by the Swiss lawyer, statesman, and philosopher Karl Ludwig von Haller, culminating in his influential magnum opus *Restauration der Staats-Wissenschaft*, published in six volumes between 1816 and 1834. Haller juxtaposed the 'patrimonial state' with the revolutionary polity. Both Müller and Haller were critical of the 'revolutionary' legacy of Roman Law on the European legal tradition. Müller and Haller, in their turn, were criticized as joint figureheads of reactionary statecraft no longer in tune with modern times. Cf. Roggen, 'Restauration'; Kapossy, 'Haller's Critique'; Kapossy, 'Words and Things'.

[99] Müller, *Elemente*, 18–19. Cf. Lok, 'Liberty'.   [100] Busse, *Lehre vom Staat*.

'*Rechtsstaat*', an ambiguous concept that could be used for various political agendas.[101] Furthermore, Müller was critical of the revolutionary idea of positive law as the only source of civil law: laws in his view were the result of a long development and could not be changed overnight by the whims of an elected national assembly.[102]

In analogy to the functioning of families, the state was, for Müller, ideally founded on the idea of balance (*Gleichgewicht*). Families formed a unity without being of one mind: different interests and opinions coexisted among family members without destroying the family as a unit. Ideally, the state, again in analogy to Müller's idealized and gendered idea of the family, kept a balance between youthful action, on the one hand, and the calmness and composed reflection of the elderly, on the other. Like families, states need to combine the vigour of the male family members with the perceived sociability and sense of religion of the females. Precisely this 'variety in unity' concerning age and gender, made European families and states unique and superior from a global perspective. More than any other European state, Great Britain was regarded by Müller, not as a unique state *sui generis*, but as the most outstanding representation of this larger European unity-in-diversity principle.[103]

Müller, in opposition to the French revolutionaries' allegedly dangerous naivety, did not believe that an ideal political system could ever be constructed by mortal men. Every constitution had its flaws, Müller wrote in agreement with Feller, and no permanent constitutional solutions could be found. Constitutions therefore needed to be adapted to changing circumstances. Consequently, he was in favour of neither a pure monarchy nor a pure republic: an ideal state was in Müller's eyes, again following the lead of Montesquieu, a mixed constitution with both monarchical and republican elements.[104] In the end he preferred a monarchy over a republic, as he believed that monarchies were overall more respectful of the rule of law (*Rechtsstaat*) and more stable over the long term. He also pleaded for an important role for the nobility in the functioning of the state as an intermediary power between the individual and the collective interest.[105] He pointed to the House of Lords as a model for other European countries, although this British institution could not simply be copied and needed to be adapted to local and national contexts.

After having discussed the principle of balance at the level of families and the state, Müller applied the metaphor to the European level as well. Europe was regarded by Müller as a unique and superior continent, shaped—in the vein of

---

[101] Krieger, *German Idea*, 253–5. '(...) the doctrine of the *Rechtsstaat* represented the classic attempt to by-pass constitutional conflict and to bind all political authorities, traditional and representative alike, in the common service of civil freedom. The *Rechtsstaat* was born and remained an idea of conservation as well as liberalization.' Krieger, *German Idea*, 261.
[102] Müller, *Elemente*, 21–34.   [103] Müller, *Elemente*, 63–4.   [104] Müller, *Elemente*, 111.
[105] De Dijn, *Liberty*.

Montesquieu—by geography and natural boundaries. The European political system rested on a dynamic balance (*Gleichgewicht*) of power consisting of five empires, instead of one all-powerful state, as was the case elsewhere on the globe. These five empires were France, England, Germany, Spain, and Italy. Müller excluded Russia and the Ottoman Empire from this European state system.[106] Each of these 'European' empires formed worlds on their own, each imperial world itself the result of a particular dynamic of 'contrasting forces' and internal contradictions. The other, smaller, European countries did not exist independently but formed the periphery of these five imperial nuclei, like planets orbiting around the sun. European civilization was, for Müller, the result of the rivalry between these imperial worlds within a common cultural framework. Despite their internal differences and struggles, Europeans felt part of a commonwealth due to their common history, mutual enemies, and the Christian religion.[107]

Müller explicitly opposed the ideals of perpetual peace as defended by Kant and other pro-revolutionary authors. Human beings in his eyes were not only peaceful creatures, but also by nature competitive and power-hungry animals. 'Perpetual peace' would, therefore, inevitably lead to weakness and hypochondria, eventually resulting in unhappiness and despair. War and battle were, in Müller's eyes, moments of creation and progress as well as destruction and death. Only during wars did states reveal their true character and would their future be determined. Uniting the five European empires in a single federal republic or a universal empire (such as attempted by Napoleon) would thus destroy Europe's unique dynamism, resulting in stagnation, despotism, and catastrophe.[108]

Müller traced the origins of the European institutions back to two different, and in his eyes even contrasting, sources: Ancient Israel and classical Greece. Israel's laws differed from the Greek ones in the sense that in Israel there was only one major lawgiver, Moses, versus the pluralist variety of legal systems and lawgivers in ancient Greece. Furthermore, Mosaic law was, according to Müller, characterized by the dominance of private law, whereas public law prevailed in the law systems of Greece. Moreover, Jewish law was essentially monarchical in character, whereas in Greece the republican form was the norm. After Moses, the Jewish constitution, Müller wrote regretfully, had lost its noble, warrior aspect, and had become passive and otherworldly. Nonetheless, the Mosaic law would eventually form an important foundation of European feudal law in the Middle Ages.[109] With this emphasis on the influence of the Judaic legacy on European civilization, Müller stood aside somewhat from most other historical Europeanists who focussed more on the classical and the Germanic legacies.

Müller criticized ancient Greece for its divisiveness and its sacrificing of the individual to the public good. He was also highly critical of slavery in the ancient

---

[106] Cf. Pitts, *Boundaries*.   [107] Müller, *Elemente*, 122–3.   [108] Müller, *Elemente*, 124–5.
[109] Müller, *Elemente*, 133–42.

world. Nonetheless, the Greek legal inheritance was an essential component of what would later become the European institutions. In many ways, for Müller, the world of Greek city states mirrored the modern European state system.[110] The Greek legacy of Stoic cosmopolitanism formed in his eyes the basis of the Christian commonwealth. It was precisely this duality, contrasting as well as complementary, of Jewish law—exclusive, religious, private, monarchical, noble, and 'Asian'—and Greek laws—inclusive, political, public, republican, civic, cosmopolitan, and 'European'—that would later determine the unique development of modern European legal civilization.[111]

Müller, like Montesquieu, was far less enthusiastic about Roman legal inheritance. In contrast to Greek and Jewish laws, which were based on the principles of freedom and religion, Roman law reflected Rome's military conquests and yearning for domination. The Romans were not a creative people but instead developed their culture by incorporating the cultural achievements of other nations. Roman laws were founded on the principles of oppression and despotism: the rudimentary freedom that was present in early Roman history had rapidly vanished when the Roman state expanded. Müller criticized Roman law especially for its radical separation of private law and public law. The result was an individualistic and materialistic legal system that formed a direct precursor of the laws of the French Revolution. This lack of liberty, as well as the oppressive uniformity, contrasted with the 'great doctrine of contradictions' (*Die große Lehre von der Gegenseitigkeit aller Verhältnisse des Lebens*), Müller's primary principle, and would eventually lead to Rome's decline and fall.[112]

Medieval feudal law, by contrast, was highly praised by Müller.[113] In feudal law, private law was not cut off from public law, as in Roman law, but combined. Feudal law, moreover, was less individualistic, and more suitable for protecting the community, rather than the individual. Also, by building on Mosaic law and early Christianity, feudal law had a clear religious foundation, which Roman—and revolutionary—law lacked. As a result, power was not absolute in this unique European feudal legal system: legal tradition and religion acted as barriers to royal power, resulting in a *Rechtsstaat*. Instead of a stifling uniformity, medieval states supposedly consisted of a harmonious balance between the three orders of nobility, clergy, and the third estate. Rather than proclaiming abstract equality, the different orders in society all over Europe lived harmoniously side by side as part of an organic whole.[114]

---

[110] Müller, *Elemente* (1809) II, 42, 226–7.   [111] Müller, *Elemente* (1809) II, 44–5.
[112] Müller, *Elemente* (1809) II, 70–1.
[113] Müller was critical of Spittler and his 'prorevolutionary' *Staatengeschichte*, which he deemed too positive about the Roman Empire and too negative about feudalism. Müller, *Elemente* (1809) II, 92. See Chapter 7.
[114] Müller, *Elemente*, 163–74.

Müller's romantic idealization of a medieval past was clearly different from the views of eighteenth-century *anti-philosophes* such as Feller, who generally showed a lack of interest in the Middle Ages. The success of the British constitution, untouched by the influence of Roman law, was evidence of the superiority of these medieval feudal laws. However, this admirable legal system was threatened by the return of individualistic and materialistic Roman concepts as a result of the French Revolution. Müller drew inspiration from what he regarded as the distinctly European historical legal system, but he did not advocate a full restoration of medieval feudal law. He believed that the advantages of feudalism should be preserved in a new counter-revolutionary legal system that was to be adapted to modern times.[115]

The book ended with an appeal for the restoration and regeneration of the European state system and the principle of 'balance' as the cornerstone of the European commonwealth. This pre-revolutionary balance had been undermined in the eighteenth century as a result of the spread of atheistic materialism and an amoral ideology of power, Müller argued in classic *anti-philosophe* vein. The destruction of the international system by the Revolution also presented for him a unique opportunity to construct a new balance. This new balance should be organized in accordance with Müller's idea of historical progress: From the domination of private law in the classical and medieval worlds, via the emphasis on public law of the (early) modern state, a new synthesis between public and private law would occur in the foreseeable future. This prophesied future would bring a new 'middle way' between private and public interests. Fusing political philosophy with Christian revelation, Müller believed that Christ's death not only made the redemption of the individual possible, but also the redemption of the state and the political community.[116] Müller argued for a religious reconciliation between Catholicism and Protestantism as the basis for this new Christian-inspired European order, without actually advocating a merger between the two faiths.[117]

At the end of the book, Müller pleaded for what could be termed a variation of Christian cosmopolitanism. Müller tried to convince his compatriots that they were more than just a collection of individuals and that they formed part of a wider European and even worldwide community. Individuals as well as states should, consequently, not only follow their own short-term interests, but they should also serve the common goals of humanity as a whole.[118] Müller's idea of humanity was not constricted by geographical or national boundaries, but primarily by religious ones. Müller's idea of a 'world community' and political federation (*Staatenbund*) was to be structured according to the principles of the

---

[115] Müller, *Elemente*, 199–207.   [116] Cf. Chapter 8.   [117] Müller, *Elemente*, 401–10.
[118] 'Das Interesse der Völker ist, daß jeder Einzelne dem Ganze diene, jeder Mensch, jeder Staat dem Ganzen der Menschheit.' Müller, *Elemente* (1809) III, 294.

universal Christian religion and the particular nation state to which each individual belonged. Müller explicitly preferred a Christian cosmopolitanism over what he regarded as an outdated and narrow-minded patriotism, which had, in his view, belonged to the ancient world rather than the modern age.[119]

In the pre-Christian world, nations had fought to destroy and enslave one another. The Romans and the Jews had not possessed a conception of an international or human community. The Romans had destroyed Israel as an independent state without any afterthought. Only with the coming of Christianity in late antiquity did nations begin to acknowledge other states as independent entities having equal standing. Only within the framework of the Christian religion did it become possible to conceive of a 'world community of nations'.[120] With the birth of Christ, all pernicious ambitions of a secular 'universal monarchy' had become futile and void: the only possible universal empire was a sacred and otherworldly one. The Saviour had shown the peoples of the earth how to form an international world federation (*Bund*).[121] A federation of states could thus be formed only with Christ at its centre and as overlord of all national and federative life, and not through a violent revolution, as the French had miserably attempted in recent years.[122]

This Christ-centred cosmopolitanism was clearly juxtaposed by Müller to the 'wrong' revolutionary cosmopolitanism, which he deemed abstract, atheistic, and overly individualistic. The revolutionary idea of a world federation based on abstract, general, and non-Christian principles was a dangerous fiction and could exist only in times of war and large-scale violence.[123] When peace prevailed, nations would follow their own interests and new violent international conflicts would inevitably occur.[124] The Catholic convert Müller blamed the decline of this Christian world community, in existence since late antiquity, on the rise of

---

[119] 'Wir fühlen, es gibt keine bloßen, reinen Patriotismus mehr, wie ihn die Alten nährten; ein gewisser Kosmopolitismus geht ich zur Zeite, und mit Recht; denn es kommt auf zwei Dinge an: auf das Vaterland und auf den Staatenbund, deren eins abgesondert für sich ohne das andere nicht mehr begehrt werden kann.' Müller, *Elemente*, 421.

[120] 'Über diesen Ruinen [of the Roman Empire] erhob sich das heilige, verachtete Banier der christliche Religion, und um dasselbe sammelten sich jugendliche und alternde Völker des Orients und des Occidents: alle verstanden einander in jenen Dingen, welche allen gemein sind, und daher allein ein Band unter den Völkern der Erde abgeben können, während alle andern Sammelplätze der Macht und des Irdischen Glanzes sich mit Turme vergleichen lassen, der den Völkern zu einem Vereinigungs-punkte dienen sollte, und unter dessen Bau sie sich entzweiten, ihre Sprache verwirrte, und jeder Einzelne, was zu thun und zu lassen und zu wünschen sey, völlig vergaß.' Müller, *Elemente* (1809), III, 291. Cf. Müller, *Elemente* (1809) III, 274–5.

[121] 'Also hören die Träume der Universalherrschaft, oder einer wirklichen Verpflanzung der göttlichen Macht auf Erden, mit Christus auf: an ihre Stelle tritt in Knechtsgehalt, ohnmächtig und arm, ein Mittler, der Ein für allemal den Willen Gottes ausdrückt, bis zum machtvollsten Tode allen Triumph der Weltlichen Macht gänzlich vereitelt, den Untergang jeder möglichen weltlichen Universal Herrschaft als unvermeidlich zeigt, und zugleich den Völkern das Geheimnis ihres großen Bundes vollständig und klar hinterläßt.' Müller, *Elemente* (1809) III, 290.

[122] 'Der Mittelpunkt und Herrscher alles nationalen und föderativen Lebens wird er bleiben, wie es in denen Zeiten gewesen ist.' Müller, *Elemente* (1809) III, 300, 326.

[123] Müller, *Elemente* (1809) III, 292.   [124] Müller, *Elemente*, 411.

Protestantism. The coming of Protestantism in the sixteenth century had resulted in an increasing formalization of the rules of conduct between nations, undermining the spiritual character and divine aspect of the international community, eventually leading to its destruction in the revolutionary era.[125] Müller, however, believed it was possible to restore this early Catholic-Stoic world community to a new and dynamic footing in the form of a Christ-centred federation and to regenerate European civilization morally as well as spiritually.

7. Romantic Cosmopolitanism

Müller's plea for a renewed European and world order inspired by an idealized view of medieval feudalism did not stand on its own. At the turn of the century, a variety of German writers pleaded in different ways for European political, cultural, and spiritual regeneration. The best-known representative of this post-revolutionary German Europeanism was no doubt the poet Novalis (Georg Philipp Friedrich von Hardenberg, 1772–1801). In response to Kant's and Fichte's ideas on a new international order, which he regarded as too abstract and legalistic, Novalis, and other 'Jena romantics', developed alternative ideals for an international community. Novalis's ideas on a new world order found their clearest expression in an essay presented to the romantic circle in Jena in November 1799. This text was posthumously published in 1826, under the title 'Christianity or Europe: A Fragment'. In this essay, Novalis pleaded for the restoration of the moral and cultural unity that had supposedly existed in Christian medieval Europe. The poet envisioned a world community based not only on legal relations and self-interest, the alleged federation of *philosophie*, but also on deeply felt moral and spiritual bonds modelled after the ideal of the family.[126] Novalis's emphasis on a renewed political and public morality echoed older enlightened views on this topic and was also typical for the new romantic literary school.[127]

Like Müller's *Elemente*, Novalis's text has, since its publications, been interpreted in many different ways, ranging from a reactionary, theocratic, and even national-socialist manifesto to a left-wing critique of modern technocracy. Philosopher Pauline Kleingeld convincingly interpreted Novalis's essay as an articulation of what she termed 'romantic cosmopolitanism'.[128] Rather than a reactionary argument for the restoration of medieval society, *Christianity or Europe*, according to Kleingeld, consisted above all of a plea for cultural, moral, and spiritual renewal. 'Christianity' was, for Novalis, not the actual and historical Catholic Church, but stood for him as the representative of a spiritual ideal for

---

[125] Müller, *Elemente* (1809) III, 275. [126] [Hardenberg], *Novalis Schriften.*
[127] Uerlings, 'Europa der Romantik', 46. [128] Kleingeld, 'Romantic Cosmopolitanism', 272.

future renewal. Using the example of Novalis, Kleingeld argued for a broadening of the concept of cosmopolitanism outside the traditional confinements of eighteenth-century Enlightenment, and to include also early nineteenth-century romantic versions.[129]

Another example of a romantic cosmopolitan call for European cultural renewal in the first decade of the nineteenth century was the journal *Europa*.[130] This journal was edited by the brothers Friedrich (1772–1829) and August Wilhelm Schlegel (1767–1845) in Paris between the spring of 1803 and December 1804.[131] The journal was founded in a hostile climate. Paris under the Napoleonic Consulate was not very favourably inclined towards German idealist philosophy, which was regarded as unpractical, too abstract, and potentially subversive. Also, the Napoleonic dominance of the German states at the beginning of the nineteenth century left little room for ideas of German missionary leadership in Europe. In the contributions to the journal, a very bleak picture was painted of contemporary European culture. As a result of the influence of French Enlightenment, European culture had become superficial, decadent, and sterile. European art and culture consisted of mere individual expressions, the articles of the journal lamented, instead of expressions of national and communal feelings. The Schlegels were also disillusioned with the results of the French Revolution, which had, in their eyes, failed to create a new European culture. Instead, they believed the Revolution had only imposed the materialist Enlightenment by arms.[132]

The predicament of Europe was clearly expressed in the well-known contribution *Reisen nach Frankreich* (Journey to France), an account of a journey from Saxony to France. The German lands were nostalgically painted as a former great culture in decline. The view of the Rhineland made the author aware of the missed opportunities for European unity and the decline of the German nation, which he compared to the Arab world, where longing for a past greatness was also widespread.[133] As the author crossed the German–French border, the landscape changed: the ancient forests and dramatic landscapes disappeared, the countryside became more ordered. France struck the traveller as a superficial and sterile culture without creativity or spiritual depth. The outwardly glittering metropolis of Paris paled in comparison with the ensemble of smaller German cities, which

---

[129] See also Chapter 1. On romantic cosmopolitan monarchism, see also: Leerssen, 'Romancing the Monarchy', 283–306.

[130] Henri Chélin regarded the journal in essence as the expression of German cultural nationalism rather than an articulation of a European ideal: Chélin, *Friedrich Schlegel's Europa*. Herbert Uerlings, by contrast, argues that the journal articulated a European ideal, a programme for future cultural renewal that went beyond nationalism. Uerlings, 'Europa der Romantik'. I concur with Uerlings' interpretation. Also, Ernst Behler, in his introduction to the reprint of the journal in 1963, emphasized the cosmopolitan character of the journal. Cf. Schulz, 'Kosmopolitismus und Nationalismus'. On the choice of the title 'Europa': Chélin, *Friedrich Schlegel's Europa*, 97–9.

[131] Leerssen, *Encyclopedia*, 521–4; Behler, *Zeitschriften*; Mix and Strobel, *Europäer*.

[132] Schlegel, 'Über Literatur', 57–73. [133] Schlegel, 'Reise nach Frankreich', 13–17.

breathed a quiet spirituality. In France, deep sentiments were suppressed or turned violent when they were not controlled, as was demonstrated by the St Bartholomew's Day Massacre of 1572. The reader was left in no doubt that French dominance was to blame for the sorry state of Germany and Europe. Only the French imperial army, due to its ambition and success, was praised by the author for its vigour and dynamism, although this admiration was qualified by the observation that the imperial army stood apart from the French nation and that most of its soldiers were not born Frenchmen.[134]

In the quest for cultural renewal, the Schlegels, like Novalis, looked towards an idealized non-historical medieval past. In contrast to modern society, medieval Christianity was allegedly characterized by community, religiosity, morality, and tradition. The Schlegels also did not advocate a reactionary return to an imagined medieval past. Instead, the medieval past could function as a source of inspiration for the future regeneration of European culture. The medieval Crusades were seen as an admirable example of European dynamism and renewal, worthy of emulation by nineteenth-century Europeans. Friedrich Schlegel also argued for the reappraisal of the classical heritage, according to him, scorned by insensitive eighteenth-century *philosophes* and their false notion of modernity. Cultural renewal was the key to the regeneration of European civilization as a whole. The editors insisted that Europe formed an organic whole and that the German nation was only a part of this wider organic unity. The main division of Europe was, for these romantic authors, not between its eastern and western parts, but between its northern and southern parts, which each had their own 'individual' characters.

In the comparison between Asia and Europe, Europe's pluralism was both a strength and a weakness: Asia, in particular India, was deemed superior to Europe due its rich spirituality. Also, Asia formed a unity in the way Europe did not. For instance, in India there supposedly existed a continuous tradition from antiquity until the present. In Europe, by contrast, history was characterized in the pages of *Europa* by a certain rupture between the classical world and modern Europe. The attempt by the Catholic Church to bridge the classical and the post-classical worlds had eventually been unsuccessful.[135] Internal divisions (*Trennung*) had so far prevented Europe from flourishing culturally. Without a fundamental European regeneration, it was deemed more likely that Asia would one day dominate Europe rather than the other way around.[136] However, the current deplorable state of Europe, as well as its internal divisions, also contained seeds for regeneration and renewal through a synthesis between Orient and Occident, which the authors hopefully expected in the near future.[137]

---

[134] Schlegel, 'Reise nach Frankreich', 20–8.
[135] Schlegel, 'Reise nach Frankreich', 33.
[136] Schlegel, 'Reise nach Frankreich', 37.
[137] Schlegel, 'Reise nach Frankreich', 38; Schlegel, 'Über Litteratur', 83.

8. Conclusion: European Regeneration and National Renewal

Despite the profound differences between, on the one hand, Gentz and Müller, with their focus on legal and political institutions, and, on the other, the 'romantic Europeanists' with their emphasis on literary and spiritual renewal, they also shared convictions, as well as social networks. First of all, a common hostility can be discerned towards an allegedly superficial and materialistic French *philosophie*, the wrong kind of Enlightenment, as well as towards the revolutionary legacy, whether as inherently despotic or as a failed attempt to renew Europe. Secondly, all these authors pleaded for the regeneration of a European system and civilization. They were convinced that the spiritual Germans, rather than the exhausted and corrupted French, were the ones to lead this continent-wide renewal. As Müller argued, Germans had no ambition to impose cultural and political uniformity but were, in contrast to the French, precisely respectful of (national) cultural diversity and difference, so characteristic of Europe. Thirdly, they all shared a 'cosmopolitan' outlook in the sense that individuals were regarded by these authors as belonging to a larger human community beyond the local, the regional, or the national. In the journal *Europa*, as well as in other German Europeanist texts studied here, German cultural nationalism and cosmopolitan Europeanism were not framed as opposites but in many ways were seen as complementary.[138] Nationalism per se was, mistakenly, regarded by Müller as a phenomenon of a different and bygone age.

Different varieties of this post-revolutionary German cosmopolitanism, however, should be distinguished: Müller underscored the Christian and Catholic character of the new cosmopolis, excluding those outside the Christian and Catholic Church. Gentz, who remained a Protestant all his life, was, by contrast, wary of too much focus on the spiritual, focussing on the functioning of balanced institutions instead. Almost all counter-revolutionary writers continued to be influenced—sometimes *à contre-coeur*—in one way or another by Kant's ideal of bringing perpetual peace and order to Europe, although they differed on the means to achieve this goal.[139] The counter-revolutionary publicists could also be considered cosmopolitans in the sense that the European—rather than a restricted national—past formed the main framework in which the self-proclaimed German-speaking counter-revolutionaries developed their ideas.

The new European and world order was to be based on the idea of a dynamic historical continuity of existing institutions and beliefs. In many ways, enlightened historical narratives and enlightened cosmopolitan ideals were adapted by a variety of self-declared opponents (or disillusioned supporters) of the French

---

[138] On development of romantic cultural nationalism: Leerssen, *National Thought*; Leerssen, *Encyclopedia*.
[139] See more extensively Chapter 8.

Revolution and the subsequent Napoleonic Empire to suit new political contexts. Gentz and Müller, despite their profound differences, did not regard themselves as reactionaries, but fashioned themselves instead, as did the other protagonists in this study, as reasonable 'moderates' who stood for the correct middle way between revolutionary destructiveness and Napoleonic despotism, on the one hand, and excessive reactionary 'melancholia', on the other. Both authors believed that the *ancien régime* monarchies needed to be reformed in order to be preserved and both argued against a full-scale restoration they deemed out of date and irrational.

The turn of the century thus did not mark a sudden break with an eighteenth-century cosmopolitan Enlightenment, but instead enlightened historical and cosmopolitan narratives survived into the nineteenth century and were reconfigured and adapted to new political contexts. By focussing on the survival of enlightened cosmopolitanism in the historical writings by counter-revolutionary publicists and statesmen, we are able to nuance the persisting picture of a sudden rise of a dominant romantic nationalism in response to the French Revolution and the Napoleonic wars. In the next two chapters, we will examine in more detail two 'European' historians, the Catholic Niklas Vogt and the Protestant Arnold Heeren. These scholars appropriated the enlightened historical and pluralist narratives for entirely different political agendas: Vogt to support the Napoleonic Empire, Heeren to undermine it.

6
The Pluralist Republic

1. The European Republic

Between 1787 and 1792, the Mainz historian Niklas Vogt (1756–1836) published a multivolume work entitled *On the European Republic* (*Über die Europäische Republik*). In five separate parts Vogt analysed the 'European republic' from different perspectives. He described 'Europe' successively as a system of independent states, a political and constitutional regime defined by moderation, a mixed political economy, a diverse assemblage of morals, laws, and religious beliefs, and finally as a military balance (*Gleichgewicht*).[1] Within this wider European 'republic', cities, provinces, states, empires, as well as religious communities, were able to develop in their own individual way. This unique European pluralism was determined by climate and steered by providence and destiny.[2]

In this chapter, we will see how Vogt's idea of Europe as a 'pluralist republic' metamorphosed over time from a concept belonging to the late Enlightenment to, subsequently, a legitimation of the Counter-Revolution, the Napoleonic Empire and, to a lesser extent, the Vienna order[3]. Vogt was not the only author who used this idea of the 'European republic' for counter-revolutionary purposes. It could, for instance, also be found in the writings of Gentz, Müller, and d'Ivernois.[4] In contrast to the authors discussed in the preceding chapter, however, Vogt's pluralist narrative of European history resulted in his support, rather than his criticism, of the Napoleonic imperial project. The 'European republic' was the prism through which Vogt solved the problem of how to construct a new international order in a world where old certainties had been lost and ancient institutions, such as the Holy Roman Empire, disintegrated and finally collapsed. Via this concept of the European republic, Vogt could effortlessly link the local (Mainz), to the regional (the Rhineland), the 'national' (the Holy Roman Empire

---

[1] Vogt, *Republik* (5 vol.). On Vogt: Berg, *Vogt*; Duchhardt, 'Niklas Vogt'.
[2] Vogt definitively fitted into Kleingeld's definition of German 'cultural cosmopolitanism' as 'the view that humanity expresses itself in a rich variety of cultural forms, that we should recognize different cultures in their particularity, and that attempts to achieve cultural uniformity lead to cultural impoverishment'. Kleingeld, 'Six Varieties', 515. Kleingeld here discusses the revolutionary pluralist cultural cosmopolitanism of the (Mainz clubbist) Georg Forster (1754–94), ignoring counter-revolutionary pluralist cosmopolitans such as Niklas Vogt.
[3] Parts of this chapter have been published as Lok, 'European Republic'.
[4] Lok, 'European Republic'.

of the German Nation), and the international (European and global) perspectives in a cosmopolitan vision of past, present, and future.

Studying the conceptual history of the 'European republic' in this period gives us insight into at least three important scholarly debates in the field of eighteenth-century political thought. Firstly, it will allow us to trace in a detailed manner the seemingly effortless metamorphosis of an enlightened notion, associated with reform and modernization, into a key counter-revolutionary concept. Secondly, it will demonstrate the importance of ancient history and classical models for understanding the idea of 'modern Europe' and the concept of the modern state system. The European republic was conceptualized through the prism of the ancient world, but increasingly also by distancing 'new' from 'old' Europeans.[5] Studying the conceptual history of the 'European republic' between ancients and moderns will teach us more about the transition, or its absence, from cyclical to linear historical thinking.[6]

Thirdly, conceptual histories of the 'European republic' are often missing from studies on the history of republicanism.[7] Pre-revolutionary historical republicanism is usually studied from the perspective of the state, not through the prism of the state system and the international order.[8] As we could observe from the synopsis of Vogt's multivolume work, his concept of a European republic differed fundamentally from the interpretation of the 'republic' in the tradition of classical republicanism. For Vogt and other counter-revolutionaries, however, 'freedom' was not, in the first instance, guaranteed by the political participation of virtuous citizens or by the precise form of the sovereign. Instead, he believed liberty was best guaranteed by institutional pluralism, in the sense of the absence of a centralized political, economic, religious, or cultural power, combined with ideas of moderation, balance, the rule of law, and cultural diversity. These differences notwithstanding, Vogt shared with classical republicans the Polybian preoccupation with political freedom and the threat of losing this liberty through moral corruption and self-interest, resulting in a decline and fall of the political community.[9] By looking at this particular cosmopolitan strand of 'republicanism' beyond the state, if we can indeed call it by that name, we are able to broaden the definition of republicanism and study the concept of 'republic' in entirely

---

[5] See, for this similar mechanism of drawing upon, as well as distancing from, past models in the early nineteenth century: Lok, '"A Much Superior Situation"'.

[6] Koselleck, *Vergangene Zukunft*; Koselleck, 'Einleitung', in: *Geschichtliche Grundbegriffe*, 1, 13–27. Cf. Kuijpers and Pollmann, 'Introduction', 1–24.

[7] A chapter on the 'European republic' is, for instance, absent from the standard work on European republicanism: Skinner and van Gelderen, *Republicanism*.

[8] For cosmopolitan republicanism: Kleingeld, *Kant*. Kant's federal republicanism, however, was very different from the concept of the 'European Republic' examined in this essay. Cf. Poulsen, 'Cosmopolitan Republican'.

[9] In this sense, this kind of republicanism has similarities with the neo-Roman idea of freedom: Skinner, *Liberty before Liberalism*; see more extensively: Lok, '"Just and True Liberty"'. On Polybius and classical republicanism: Pocock, *Machiavellian Moment*, 77–85.

different political and ideological contexts.[10] We can also start examining the (dis)continuities between the eighteenth-century enlightened idea of the European republic and liberal and conservative internationalism and Europeanism in the nineteenth century.[11]

To a certain extent the notion of the 'European Republic' drew on the humanist idea of the 'Republic of Letters', as well as the even older concept of the *respublica christiana*.[12] Its eighteenth-century Enlightenment articulation differed, however, from these older concepts in the sense that it referred not, in the first instance, to an intellectual continent-wide network of learned individuals or a religious and spiritual community, but primarily to a set of institutions that had developed over time. The defining characteristic of these institutions was their pluralist and fragmented nature with a common cultural, legal, and moral framework, resulting from a long historical evolution. For Vogt, the literary and scholarly Republic of Letters continued to exist in his own time, but only as one element of the larger European republic.

In the following sections, a short biography is first provided, followed by a discussion of the sources Vogt used, underscoring the transnational and 'travelling' character of his vocabulary. Then Vogt's five-volume work *On the European Republic*, will be explored, in particular the nexus between freedom, diversity, and progress. In the post-revolutionary writings, the topic of the subsequent section, it will be shown how Vogt's enlightened discourse became merged with counter-revolutionary conservatism without disappearing entirely. The two sections that follow deal with the Napoleonic era, the trauma of the collapse of the Empire, and Vogt's disappointment over the Restoration order and his designs for a perpetual European peace. The chapter ends with a brief conclusion, in which it is argued that the predicates of 'liberal' and 'conservative' do not adequately define Vogt's historical Europeanist thought.

2. From Mainz to Frankfurt

Vogt's background, to a large extent, determined his political perspective. His family belonged to the social and cultural elite of Mainz, a medium-sized city on the river Rhine, which was also of particular relevance as the seat of the archbishop who was ex officio also the 'chancellor' of the Holy Roman Empire. From 1772 onwards, Vogt studied law and philosophy at the university of that same city, but very soon he became more interested in historical studies. In 1776, he travelled

---

[10] Cf. Hammersley, *English Republican Tradition*, 203.
[11] For instance: on the eighteenth-century roots of J.S. Mill's 'principle of systematic antagonism': cf. Varouxakis, 'Guizot's Historical Works'. See also Chapter 9.
[12] On the concept of the 'Republic of Letters': Grafton 'Sketch Map'. Cf. Solleveld, 'Afterlives'.

through Germany, visiting several Protestant universities such as Göttingen and Marburg. In 1783, Vogt was appointed a professor of universal history at his alma mater, where Clemens von Metternich, the Austrian minister and architect of the Vienna order of 1815, was one of his students.[13] Vogt took an active part in reforming the university from an old-fashioned Jesuit institution into a 'modern' university on the model of (Protestant) Göttingen. The archbishop himself was the main instigator of this project to reform the university and the electorate as a whole.[14]

Like many of his contemporaries studied in this book, Vogt's relatively uneventful life as a university professor in late eighteenth-century Mainz was thrown into turmoil as a result of the revolutionary events and wars.[15] The establishment of a revolutionary republic in Mainz on 21 October 1792, 'the first modern republic on German soil', following the invasion of a French revolutionary army, took Vogt by surprise.[16] Originally, the revolutionaries regarded Vogt as a potential leader, and his publications about freedom and reform in Mainz were used for revolutionary propaganda, much to Vogt's dismay. After a period of indecision, Vogt ended the uncertainly around his political position. He took sides against the revolutionaries and fled for the first time into exile in December 1792.[17] Vogt returned when the revolutionary republic collapsed, and electoral authority was restored. Vogt's hopes of returning to university life were dashed when the university was closed as a result of a renewed French occupation in December 1797, and he left Mainz for good this time. From 1807 onwards, Vogt occupied several important offices in the city of Frankfurt during Napoleonic rule and acted as advisor to Karl Theodor von Dalberg (1744–1817), the last elector of Mainz and imperial chancellor. In 1804, he attended the coronation of Napoleon as emperor in the Notre Dame cathedral in Paris. After the collapse of the Empire, Vogt became a senator in Frankfurt where he lived out the rest of his days.[18]

Although the quality of his works and ideas should certainly not be underestimated, Vogt was not one of the leading historians or philosophers of his age, as he himself realized very well. Nonetheless, like the other writers studied in this book,

---

[13] See also Chapters 7 and 8. Tellingly, Vogt would eventually be buried on the estate of Metternich.
[14] On Mainz and Enlightened reform under elector Friedrich Karl: Blanning, *Reform and Revolution*, 163–210.
[15] For an overview on the academic literature on Vogt (mainly as a local and regional historian), see Berg, *Vogt*, 16–17.
[16] Rowe, *Reich to State*, 10.
[17] Berg, *Vogt*, 12–13. On the revolution in Mainz: Blanning, *Reform and Revolution*, 267–302; Blanning, *Revolution in Germany*; Rowe, *Reich to State*; Molitor, *Untertan zum administré*. According to Michael Rowe, most Rhinelanders supported neither the radical revolutionaries nor the counter-revolutionaries and the émigrés, but instead believed in an idealized version of the traditional system that operated 'within the constraints imposed by imperial law, local custom and consensus'. Rowe, *Reich to State*, 83.
[18] For more details on the vagaries of Vogt in the revolutionary and Napoleonic era: Berg, *Vogt*, 12–14.

in his own time the prolific Vogt was widely read.[19] In his works, we can follow opinions on Europe and European history held by a relatively large readership.[20] He re-edited many of his texts and published them under new titles, framing them in different political contexts. He also combined different functions such as professor, journalist, administrator, and political advisor. Like Calonne and Feller, he edited a journal for several years, commenting on current developments from historical and philosophical perspectives. Like other protagonists in this book, Vogt can be considered an intermediary between the world of ideas and of practical politics, a 'thinker-agent' between the spheres of abstract philosophical ideas and practical policies.

Vogt's scholarly interests were manifold: in his works, Vogt clearly pre-dated the era of academic specialization.[21] Like other Enlightenment historians, he published on local (Mainz, Frankfurt) as well as regional (Rhineland), national (German), European, and universal history (the history of humanity). His works range from ancient and medieval to early modern and contemporary history. He published for a wide audience, not merely for scholars and specialists. Interestingly, he also wrote history books specially for mothers and female pedagogues, who had the important task of educating young citizens.[22] In this chapter, those works that dealt with European history and that had a clear European perspective will primarily be discussed, although in Vogt's eyes, as we shall see, European history was not clearly demarcated from other forms of history. As Michael Rowe put it: for most Rhinelanders 'the parochial depended upon the universal'.[23]

3. Inventing Pluralism

Like many other historians of modern Europe, such as Heeren, who will be discussed in the next chapter, Vogt conceived of modern Europe through the eyes of classical sources. He was trained in ancient history, and classical authors also figure prominently among his sources.[24] He seemed especially inspired by Tacitus (c.56–117) and his idea of the contrast between the decadent, centralized Roman Empire and the virtuous and freedom-loving Germanic tribes.[25] Another important classical source is the Hellenistic historian Polybius (c.208–c.125 BC), who wrote on the inevitable decline of states. Polybius observed with his own eyes the rise of Rome and the decline of Greek independence. He attributed the rising

---

[19] Berg, *Vogt*, 1–28. [20] Vogt published more than 10,000 pages. Berg, *Vogt*, 16.
[21] On the specialization (or lack of it) of the historical discipline in the early nineteenth century: Berger, *Past as History*, 82–95.
[22] Vogt, *Geschichte der Deutschen für Mütter*. [23] Rowe, *Reich to State*, 6.
[24] Marchand, 'Ancient History'; Akça Ataç, 'Roman Historiography'; Velema, *Omstreden Oudheid*.
[25] On the influence of Tacitus in German Thought: Leerssen, *National Thought*.

power of the Roman state to its mixed constitution, which combined monarchy, aristocracy, and democracy.[26] Often Vogt drew parallels between the ancient and modern worlds, for instance comparing the European 'republic' with the Greek world, or the decadence of the late Roman Empire with eighteenth-century *philosophie*. In Vogt's writing, linear narratives were interwoven with cyclical ones, modelled on ancient history writing.

In his work on the pluralist European Republic, Vogt drew on contemporary German as well as on foreign enlightened sources. Like the other writers studied here, Vogt often referred to Montesquieu.[27] He even opened the first volume of his *Über die Europäische Republik* with a citation from the *Spirit of the Laws*. Vogt borrowed from Montesquieu the idea that Europe's unique freedom was related to its pluralist, that is politically and institutionally fragmented and mixed, character.[28] Montesquieu contrasted the Roman Empire and the Germanic tribes, which had invaded Europe in the early Middle Ages. He was critical towards the Roman legacy: the Roman Empire had lost its freedom as a result of imperial conquests and the extension of the state, causing its decline and fall.[29] The Germanic tribes, while no doubt less developed than the Romans, had, by contrast, retained for Montesquieu their freedom and independence by experimenting with an early form of representative institutions. Montesquieu explained the absence of a unitary authoritative structure by pointing to Europe's climate and physiological circumstances. These geographical factors, however, were no guarantee that political pluralism would always prevail: Europe was not immune from despotism and the dangers of a universal monarchy.[30]

In his *Reflections on Universal Monarchy* of 1734, Montesquieu referred to Europe as a 'nation composed of several nations', but the concept of Europe itself as a 'republic' did not figure prominently in his works.[31] He praised the 'federal republic', an ideal solution for republics that were too small in scale to survive in a political world dominated by monarchies, on the model on the federations of the ancient Greek republics. This federal republic formed an 'agreement by which many political bodies consent to become citizens of the larger state that they want to form. It is a society of societies that make a new one, which can be enlarged by new associates that unite with it.'[32] Montesquieu was primarily thinking here of

---

[26] Polybius, *Histories*.   [27] On Montesquieu's idea of European history, see also Chapter 2.

[28] Already in his earlier work, *Réflexions sur la monarchie universelle en Europe*, written around 1734, Montesquieu had argued that universal empires based on military hegemony were no longer compatible with modern civilisation in Europe or with contemporary warfare. On Montesquieu's aristocratic idea of freedom: de Dijn, *Liberty*.

[29] Montesquieu, *Considérations*. In this earlier work Montesquieu explained the decline and fall of the Roman Empire as the result of the establishment of a Roman universal monarchy that destroyed Roman freedom, the foundation of Rome's rise. Volpilhac-Auger, 'Considérations'.

[30] Montesquieu, *Spirit of the Laws*, 136.

[31] 'L'Europe n'est plus qu'une nation composée des plusieurs.' Montesquieu, *Réflexions*, 105.

[32] Montesquieu, *Spirit of the Laws* II, 131. Ward, 'Montesquieu on Federalism'. Ward discussed Montesquieu's federalism on a national level. On Europe as 'federation': Lilti and Spector, *Penser*, 6.

the Republic of the United Provinces, the German Empire, and the Swiss federation as forms of modern federal republics, rather than conceiving of Europe as a federal republic, as Vogt did.

Another authority for Vogt was not, surprisingly, Voltaire. Voltaire defined Europe as a great 'republic' in his *Essay on the Customs and the Spirit of the Nations* (1756). Like Montesquieu, Voltaire in his *Century of Louis XIV* (1751) characterized the 'European republic' as, on the one hand, politically fragmented and containing a diversity of regimes, but, on the other, sharing a common culture, religion, and morals:

> For a long time, Christian Europe (with the exception of Russia) could have been viewed as a sort of large republic split into several states, some of which were monarchies, others mixed; some aristocratic, others popular; but all corresponding with each other; all having a same basis of religion, though they were divided in several sects; all having the same principles of public law and politics, unknown in the other parts of the world.[33]

The Scottish historian William Robertson (1721–93), moreover, also exerted an important influence on Vogt's historical pluralism. In his work, Vogt often referred to Robertson's book *The History of the Reign of Charles V* (1769).[34] In this influential political history of Europe, Robertson focussed on the early sixteenth-century reign of Habsburg emperor Charles V as a crucial moment in the forging of the European state system. In the first part of the book, Robertson described the development of Europe from the fall of the Roman era to the sixteenth century. Like Montesquieu, Robertson saw the Roman Empire primarily in negative terms as a despotic and unfree state. The collapse of the Empire as a result of the invading barbarian tribes is described in terms of 'destructive progress', enabling the unique development of European civilization out of tribal primitive virtue and energy.[35]

The Middle Ages were discussed by Robertson in a rather balanced manner. On the one hand, Robertson criticized the medieval lack of civilization and knowledge. On the other, the Scottish historian described the development of cities, commerce, and states, and their effect on manners.[36] Robertson condemned, for instance, the superstition that motivated the medieval crusaders. But he also concluded that the overall effects of the Crusades were positive: commerce and contact between Europe and the Arab and Byzantine worlds increased, leading to

---

[33] Voltaire, 'Century of Louis XIV'; Lilti, 'Civilisation'.
[34] Smitten, 'William Robertson'; Kontler, *Translations*. Kontler, surprisingly, does not discuss Vogt. On Robertson, see also Chapter 2.
[35] Robertson, *Charles V* I, 10.
[36] 'The progress of commerce had considerable influence in polishing the manners of the European nations.' Robertson, *Charles V* I, 76.

the expansion of knowledge, increased commerce, and the growth of states. Although Robertson conceded that the medieval Church had played an important role in spreading modern legal practices and progress in general, he, like Bonneville two decades later, simultaneously condemned the papal policies that undermined European freedom.

At the end of the fifteenth century, however, the affairs of the European kingdoms became increasingly interconnected, and they started to act in 'concert and confederacy'.[37] It was in the reign of Charles V that, Robertson believed, Europe definitively acquired its unique pluralist characteristics. During the Middle Ages, the European states had been autonomous. In the sixteenth century, the states of Europe became part of a larger European system. Europe then received its salient quality of 'unity in diversity'. On the one hand, European countries formed part of a larger whole, but, on the other hand, each state also followed its unique national development. Precisely because they formed part of a larger system, the individual European states could evolve their peculiar national path:

> It was during his [Charles V's] reign, and in consequence of the perpetual efforts to which his enterprising ambition roused him, that the different kingdoms of Europe acquired internal vigour; that they discerned the resources of which they were possessed; that they came both to feel their own strength, and to know how to render it formidable to others. It was during this reign, too, that the different kingdoms of Europe, which in former times seemed to act as if they had been single and disjoined, became so thoroughly acquainted, and so intimately connected with each other, as to form one great political system, in which each took a station, wherein it has remained ever since that time with less variation than could have been expected after the events of two active centuries.[38]

Another prominent British theorist of European pluralism was the philosopher and man of letters David Hume (1711–66).[39] In his essay 'Of the Rise and Progress of the Arts and Sciences' (1742), Hume tried to find general explanations for the development of the arts and sciences. Cultural achievements could not be explained solely through the exceptional talents of a few men, Hume argued. Instead, he tried to uncover 'general causes and principles', which could be found in a people as a collective.[40] Hume's first observation was that the arts could only flourish among people who enjoyed a free government: 'these refinements require curiosity, security and law not to be found in despotic governments'.[41] More freedom could be found in a system of smaller and medium-sized states than in large empires that tended towards despotism, and therefore these smaller and medium-sized states provided a better environment for the flourishing of the arts

---

[37] Robertson, *Charles V* I, 90.   [38] Cited in Drace-Francis, *European Identity*, 79.
[39] Harris, *Hume*.   [40] Hume, 'Rise', 114.   [41] Hume, 'Rise', 119.

THE PLURALIST REPUBLIC 173

and sciences. For Hume, however, it was not the republic but the mixed and moderate monarchy of a medium size, such as Great Britain, that was the regime most conducive to freedom.[42]

In addition, Hume wrote that a system of smaller states was more beneficial to the proliferation of the arts than one large empire, as the combination of political entities created an atmosphere of cultural competition necessary for intellectual and artistic creativity:

> The next observation, which I shall make on this head, is, *That nothing is more favourable to the rise of politeness and learning, than a number of neighbouring and independent states, connected together by commerce and policy.* The emulation, which naturally arises among those neighbouring states, is an obvious source of improvement: But what I would chiefly insist on is the stop, which such limited territories give to both *power* and to *authority*.[43]

Ancient Greece was a good example of this mechanism: 'Greece was a cluster of little principalities, which soon became republics; and being united both by their near neighbourhood, and by the ties of the same language and interest, they entered in the closest intercourse of commerce and learning.'[44] Also in ancient Greece, the relationship between the states was based on the principle of the 'balance of power', although, compared to the modern European equivalent, it was cruder and more violent.[45] The rise of the Roman Empire and the coming of Christianity brought an end to this Greek cultural pluralism by forceful imposition of political and religious uniformity. The Catholic Church in the eyes of Hume could be regarded as 'one large state' or empire.

Modern Europe was described by Hume as a restored Greece on a much larger scale: 'But mankind having at length thrown off this yoke [of the church], affairs are now returned nearly to the same situation as before, and *EUROPE* is at present a copy at large, of what *GREECE* was formerly a pattern in miniature.'[46] Competition and the lack of a central authority in, Europe resulted in increased freedom and the consequent flourishing of the arts and sciences. No philosophical system could attain a hegemonic position. Hume contrasted modern Europe with China, where the imperial administration had imposed Confucianism as the dominant philosophy, resulting in the slow development of sciences in that imperial state.[47] The fact that Europe's history had seen more ruptures and crises than had China's history had, in the end, been advantageous for the cultural and philosophical development of Europe, as religious and political authorities had

---

[42] Hume, 'Liberty of the Press', 10. Sciences generally flourished most in republics, the arts in monarchical states: Hume, 'Rise', 124.
[43] Hume, 'Rise', 119. [44] Hume, 'Rise', 120. [45] Hume, 'Balance of Power', 338.
[46] Hume, 'Rise', 121. [47] Hume, 'Rise', 122.

been challenged more fundamentally than in other parts of the world, 'dethroning the tyrannical usurpers over human reason'.[48] Although Vogt disagreed with Hume on the role of Christianity, they both shared the comparison of modern Europe with ancient Greece as pluralist and free political worlds.

4. Liberty, Diversity, and Progress

Following Montesquieu and Robertson, Vogt dated the origins of the 'European Republic' in his multi-volume work around the collapse of the Roman Empire and the rise of the Germanic tribes. These primitive, but virtuous, Germanic tribes introduced the principle of freedom in European societies. The relationship between the early or 'old' Europeans in the fifth century and those 'new' Europeans in the eighteenth century was somewhat ambiguous. On the one hand, Vogt, like Bonneville, discerned an unbroken European tradition of freedom from the fifth century onwards. For Vogt, the German lands formed the core of the European Republic: Germans had provided Europe with its defining characteristics.[49] On the other hand, he regarded Germanic societies as primitive, and the European Republic could be established in its modern form only after centuries of long stadial development of tribal societies into civilized states.

The Catholic reformer Vogt showed himself to be ambivalent about the role of the Catholic Church in his narrative of European history. He viewed the popes as the leaders of the European Republic in the Middle Ages, spreading knowledge and civilization. At the same time, Vogt accused the papacy of usurpation of power and striving for despotism. He explained the Reformation primarily as a movement against papal corruption. Special praise was given to the medieval Conciliar movement, which he regarded as the true institutional representation of the European Republic: in many ways, the later European Republic could build on these Conciliar structures. Vogt, however, was not very moderate in his description of the Crusades, which he defended as a legitimized defence of European freedom against the threat of Islamic despotism. The incompetence of the crusaders, rather than the superior intelligence and warrior spirit of the Muslims, were for Vogt the cause of the eventual failure of the Crusades to uphold a Christian state in Palestine, demonstrating the religious boundaries of his enlightened cosmopolitanism.[50]

The modern and free European Republic came into existence in the sixteenth century, when the European balance between states was truly achieved, Vogt wrote after Robertson. This unique freedom resulted from the fact that the European Republic consisted not only of an equilibrium of independent states

---

[48] Hume, 'Rise', 123.   [49] Vogt, *Republik* I, 1–10.   [50] Vogt, *Republik* I, 30–3.

but also of a balance (*Gleichgewicht*) of two contrasting principles: monarchy and democracy. Too much emphasis on monarchy would have resulted in despotism, whereas a pure democracy would have ended in the dissolution of all political order. In an ideal world, Vogt preferred a republican, that is, a non-monarchical, constitution in all European countries. However, as Europe still found itself in a state of imperfect Enlightenment, a moderate monarchy was, in his view the best possible form of government. Like Montesquieu, but also in the vein of counter-revolutionary publicists such as Feller and Calonne, Vogt believed that a moderate monarchy offered the best guarantee to preserve freedom and prevent the abuse of power.[51] Vogt gave rational arguments, derived from the principle of interest, to explain why a moderate monarch would best preserve freedom: a monarch would defend freedom as this would enhance his prestige and reputation among the next generations, Vogt wrote, perhaps somewhat naively.[52]

The European Republic was also in another way 'pluralist'. According to Vogt, Europe was unique in the sense that on this continent an endless variety of constitutions from the local, the regional, and to the national level, could be found, as part of this larger European Republic. Each local government, village, or city had its own mixture of monarchical, aristocratic, and democratic forms of government. Only God himself could grasp and see the multitude and variety of constitutions in this European Republic, and so, no human lawgiver could provide homogeneous standards and uniform constitutional prescripts. Following Montesquieu, Vogt believed that every state, but also local and regional government, should have its own constitution adapted to its unique circumstances. For instance, the city government of Hamburg in Vogt's eyes was a model of urban democracy, comparable to ancient Athens and the early Roman Republic. In terms of provincial administration, Vogt praised the constitution of Catalonia, citing Robertson's description of this Spanish province at length.[53]

Three modern national constitutions were singled out by Vogt as models of 'free' states: Britain, Prussia, and the Holy Roman Empire. The British constitution was valued by Vogt for best preserving the original Germanic freedom as well as keeping a perfect balance between the estates of the realm. Prussia was a different example of a modern state, in which a strong and rational monarchy was combined with the preservation of freedom among the subjects. Vogt interpreted the Holy Roman Empire as the 'microcosmos' of the European Republic as a whole. He defended the imperial constitution against critics who pleaded for a more centralized and uniform structure.[54] Although the structure of the Empire may well have been somewhat outdated, the Empire still functioned very well in

---

[51] Cf. Lok, '"Just and True Liberty"'.
[52] Vogt, *Republik* I, 36.   [53] Vogt, *Republik* I, 47–68.
[54] On the historiographical debate on the imperial constitution at the end of the eighteenth century, see: Rowe, *Reich to State*, 5–6, notes 16, 17.

keeping a balance between the two powerful German states of Prussia and Austria, or so Vogt thought. Also, if the imperial economy and the army were more centrally administered than was at present the case, it would provide the German territorial rulers with an opportunity to establish a universal monarchy to replace the European Republic. So, despite its somewhat old-fashioned and inefficient constitution, the *Reich* stood for the constitutional variety and balance of the European Republic as a whole and guaranteed the survival of Europe's unique culture of freedom.[55]

The main threat to this delicate European balance lay in the innate lust for power of all men, and the European kings in particular. In the older tradition of the 'mirror for princes', Vogt constructed a canon of good European rulers who had protected European freedom. He started his enumeration with the 'good' French king Henri IV and ended with the seventeenth-century Swedish ruler Gustavus Adolphus and the Prussian king Frederick IV. On the wrong side of history, he placed the Habsburg rulers Emperor Charles V, the 'fanatical' Spanish king Philip II, and the Holy Roman Emperor Ferdinand, who had all yearned for imperial domination of Europe. After the Peace of the Pyrenees, the Habsburg imperial dreams had been replaced by the universal ambitions of the French monarchs, especially Louis XIV and the ministers Richelieu and Mazarin. In Vogt's own time, the main menace to European freedom was the secret collaboration of the three monarchies of Russia, Austria, and France to resurrect the Western and the Eastern Roman Empires. The carving up of Poland was, according to Vogt, only a prequel of future developments in the rest of Europe, in particular in Italy, Germany, and the Low Countries.[56]

5. Economic and Moral Pluralism

The pluralist essence of the European Republic was, for Vogt, not confined to politics and civil administration but was also extended to the other dimensions of European society, such as the economy, morals, religion, geography, and warfare. Although Europe did not possess the natural resources of other continents, contemporary Europe was the wealthiest continent on the globe. This paradox could be explained, in the eyes of Vogt, by underscoring the importance of pluralism and freedom in the production of wealth. The freedom of economic agency resulted in a prosperous economy. State interference and trade monopolies led to socio-economic impoverishment as well as political despotism. At the same time, Vogt did not plead for a simply passive role for the state. The state played a crucial role in supporting free trade and in stimulating the economy in a

---

[55] Vogt, *Republik* I, 90–101.   [56] Vogt, *Republik* I, 176–210.

useful way by using knowledge and scientific insights in the implementation of government policies. Also, the state could play a positive role by refraining from spending public finances on 'useless' expenditures such as warfare, and luxury items such as a lavish court.[57]

Vogt made it explicitly clear that he did not claim to be formulating any new ideas. He pointed to Adam Smith (1723–90) and the other Scottish enlightened writers on political economy as his main sources for his interpretation of the European economy. Like Smith, Vogt did not regard trade and economy as a separate and autonomous part of society that warranted a separate academic discipline to study it. Economic pluralism and equilibrium formed an integral part of Vogt's interpretation of the European Republic. In his eyes, the ideal economy consisted of a balance of well-developed agriculture, manufacture, and trade. He was therefore critical of economists, such as the French physiocrats, who, in his view, only favoured one economic activity: agriculture.[58] Vogt, furthermore, underscored the close relationship between prosperity and political freedom by pointing to the economic development of the different European countries. The politically free states, England and Prussia, also turned out to be the most successful in economic terms. France and Spain were, for Vogt, examples of states that once were prosperous but had been ruined by a disastrous and despotic government policy.[59]

The diversity of the different national economies and the amount of specialization and division of labour between them made intercontinental trade possible, which, according to Vogt, was beneficial to all European countries. Economic competition between the European nations, furthermore, led to the dynamic nature of the European Republic in political and cultural terms. The European Republic was, in Vogt's eyes, also an economic system in which European countries both competed and collaborated. The lack of direct state interference was not only beneficial for continental trade, but also formed an essential guarantee of European freedom and overall balance.[60]

In his discussion of Europe's 'moral system' (*Sittliches system*), Vogt tried to give his analysis extra weight by pointing towards the similarities between the physical laws governing the universe and those determining human society, in particular the European Republic.[61] The physical and social worlds were not different in nature but formed part of the same whole in Vogt's holistic view. He argued, in a somewhat esoteric manner, that both natural and human laws were based on the principle of the 'balance' (*Gleichgewicht*) of forces, originally ordained by a creative and progressive divine will. Natural and human history were

---

[57] Vogt, *Republik* II, 9–73.   [58] Vogt, *Republik* II, 1–7.
[59] Vogt, *Republik* II, 73–234.   [60] Vogt, *Republik* II, 235–45.
[61] 'Den Grund von den Verhältnissen unserer Erde und folglich auch Europas müssen wir in den ersten Bestandteilen unsers Universums, und in derselbe bewegenden oder belebenden Kraft (der Gottheit) aufsuchen.' Vogt, *Republik* III, 1.

both determined by the evolution towards an equilibrium between contrasting forces. The general direction of human and natural history was the development from a state of simplicity towards ever-increasing complexity and diversity (*Verschiedenheit*) as a result of this balancing and attraction of opposing natural as well as social forces.[62]

Echoing once again Montesquieu, Vogt pointed to the effect of physical conditions on human societies. Near the North Pole, due to the harsh climate, societies cannot develop and so remain in a primitive state. Peoples in the warm southern parts of the earth were also determined by their passions and sensual natures, which prevented them from being truly free. A truly enlightened society, inhabited by 'beautiful' and 'healthy' people, such as Europe's, can exist only in the temperate zones of the earth, where the cold and the warm elements are in equilibrium.[63] In his discussion of the effects of physical and geographical conditions on societies, Vogt, like Montesquieu, related moderate climate zones to the political and social qualities of freedom, temperance, and, in general, a superior civilization.[64]

Balance for Vogt did not, however, imply perfect harmony and unity. Only in despotisms could perfect harmony be achieved. The civilization of the European Republic could develop because it was founded on contrasting forces instead of homogeneity. Like Hume, Vogt argued that internal European competition (*Wetteifer*) between states led to dynamism and creativity.[65] This dynamic European civilization contrasted with the passive civilizations of Eastern despotism as well as the anarchy of primitive societies. Contrasts and conflicts in political, economic, and cultural terms enabled Europe's unique development. Whereas economic competition stimulated trade and prosperity, the competition of ideas fostered scientific progress. Vogt therefore criticized the imposition of a uniform moral system such as the spread of a uniform system of Roman law in the High Middle Ages. He was also highly critical in this work of the Order of the Jesuits, his old adversaries during the reform of the University of Mainz. The Jesuits, in Vogt's view, tried to curb the free exchange of ideas in Europe in order to impose a 'despotism of the mind' out of mere lust for power and control.[66]

Like Hume, Vogt compared the diversity of the Greek world with medieval Europe, contrasting both older political worlds with the stifling uniformity of the

---

[62] Vogt, *Republik* III, 1–10.

[63] 'Unter den Welttheilen ist Europa derjenige, welcher sowohl in der alten als neuen Geschichte den Hauptton angab, und dessen Einwohner die übrigen, obwohl größern, Weltheile von jeher beherrscht haben. Nicht allein günstige Begebenheiten oder das Genie größer Menschen, sondern die Natur selbst schien es zur Königin der Welt gebildet zu haben.' Vogt, *Republik* III, 21. Cf. for the imagery of the four continents: Wintle, *Image of Europe*.

[64] Vogt, *Republik* III, 10–21.   [65] Vogt, *Republik* III, 25.

[66] The theme of the Jesuits trying to stifle Enlightenment and freedom is also discussed at length in Vogt's book on Gustavus Adolphus. In a fictitious conversation, high-ranking Jesuits discussed how to take control of Europe by any means necessary. Vogt, *Gustav Adolph*.

Roman Empire. Like Greece, Europe did not consist of one culture but was the result of the intermingling of different cultures and peoples.[67] In the eighteenth-century *Querelle des anciens et des modernes*, Vogt self-evidently took a middle position. Instead of claiming the superiority of the ancients or the moderns, Vogt wrote that the 'old Europeans' (Greeks) and the 'new Europeans' (medieval people) were on an equal footing in terms of cultural and scientific development. Medieval tournaments and the ancient Olympic games both exemplified the spirit of friendly competition and contest within a larger civilization. The battle over Troy was the Greek equivalent of the medieval Crusades: these wars, which united the entire Greek and medieval worlds in a common struggle, eventually led to an increase in trade and knowledge of the 'East'. The Peloponnesian wars were the ancient equivalent of the 'modern' Thirty Years' European religious civil war of the seventeenth century. Vogt regarded Shakespeare as a modern Homer, citing extensive quotations from the works of both men in order to demonstrate their similarity.[68]

The comparison with ancient Greece also contained a warning. Classical Greece had become decadent as a result of moral degeneration and the wrong kind of philosophy, Vogt wrote, in a vein similar to that of Rigoley de Juvigny.[69] Modern *philosophie* had likewise caused the decline and decadence in modern European culture. But the Greek example also could be read as a tale of hope. The decadent culture of the classical world had eventually been regenerated and rejuvenated by the spread of a new religion, Christianity. Like Bonneville, Vogt also prophesied a spiritual and moral regeneration of European society in the near future. Enlightened progress had created material progress and technical advances, but had also led to increasing inequality and a superficial and false happiness. Vogt ruled out a restorative return to medieval Christianity, as the Catholic Church had become corrupted as well due to the lust for power of the papacy and clergy. European history was developing towards a new balance between the old Christian religion and the new, but decadent, enlightened philosophy. True Enlightenment in the near future was not merely built on a symbiosis but consisted of a new equilibrium between man and nature, and between faith and reason, Vogt prophesied in a manner not unlike Bonneville.[70]

6. A Counter-Revolutionary Equilibrium

Vogt, like most German intellectuals, originally welcomed the French Revolution in 1789.[71] The radicalization of the Revolution and the experience of the radical

---

[67] Vogt, *Republik* III, 62.   [68] Vogt, *Republik* III, 31–81.
[69] Vogt, *Republik* III, 81–4. For Rigoley, see Chapter 2.   [70] Vogt, *Republik* III, 83–95.
[71] On the general response of literate Germans to events in France: Blanning, *Reform and Revolution*, 309–17.

Mainz republic of 1792–3, which had forced him into exile, turned him eventually into an unambiguous counter-revolutionary. By drawing historical parallels, he tried to make sense of the—for him at least—shocking events of the revolutionary era.[72] Vogt analysed, for instance, the French Revolution through the prism of a medieval revolt against the French king of 1355. In this short anonymously published book, Vogt acknowledged the differences between the fourteenth and the late eighteenth centuries, but he argued that the parallels were in the end more striking: the revolt of 1355 was, like the Revolution of 1789, a democratic struggle against aristocratic dominance.

Although Vogt believed that the people were certainly justified in some of their grievances against the authorities, Vogt overall condemned the actions of the medieval rebels. The radical demands and their destructive attitude caused their eventual downfall. The king re-established his authority, but overall acted mildly: he proclaimed a general amnesty, a model to be followed in more contemporary times, in Vogt's view. In this work, Vogt did not condemn all revolts in principle: like Edmund Burke, he supported the 1688 revolution as its supposed aim was to restore a free system instead of destroying one. Vogt's lesson for the revolutionaries was clear: their immoderate and extreme wish to destroy the entire old system would result in their own undoing.[73] However, the historical parallel turned out to be incorrect in the short run: the revolutionaries emerged victorious from the revolutionary wars in the late 1790s, rather than being defeated by a monarchical and aristocratic reaction.

Vogt's counter-revolutionary ideas were more systematically developed in his two-volume *System des Gleichgewichts und der Gerechtigkeit* (1802), the bestselling book he claimed later to be his magnum opus.[74] In comparison to his earlier work on the European Republic, Vogt was decidedly less optimistic in this treatise. In the years between the two publications, he had become more cynical about the possibility of the survival of states that are solely based on legal foundations without actual military power, such as the Polish commonwealth, the Holy Roman Empire, the Italian states, and the Dutch Republic. The European great powers had proven themselves to be Machiavellian usurpers, motivated only by power and the will to aggrandize their states. In comparison with his earlier volumes, Vogt was distinctly more positive about organized religion, and the Catholic Church in particular. In this book the Church was depicted as a necessary bulwark of social order against revolutionary chaos, reflecting a more general shift in views regarding the social role of the Church after 1800.

---

[72] In his *Unterhaltungen über die Vorzuglichsten epochen der alten geschichte in Beziehung auf die Neuern Begebenheiten* (1791), Vogt made a comparison between contemporary revolutionary events and the Classical world.
[73] [Vogt], *Geschichte der Revolution*, 78–82.
[74] [Vogt], *System des Gleichgewichts*. Cf. Vogt, *Historische Testament* II, vii.

Also, Vogt, in comparison to his earlier work, drew more on classical sources such as Tacitus, Aristoteles, and Polybius, and relatively less on contemporary enlightened authors. Nonetheless, Johann Gottfried von Herder (1744–1803) was frequently invoked as an intellectual authority.[75] Abstract philosophical ideas could have dangerous social and political consequences, and should therefore be embedded in practical sciences such as history and Christian ethics, Vogt argued here.[76] In this work, he underscored even more the role of Divine Providence in sanctioning an international system of balance. However, the notion of a pluralist European Republic, now increasingly called by him 'commonwealth' (*Gemeinwesen*), no doubt to downplay the pejorative revolutionary connotations the word 'republic' had acquired after the Terror, was still prominent.

In the first book ('*Der Mensch oder von der häuslichen Gerechtigkeit*'), Vogt described the European commonwealth as one organic whole, naturally and hierarchically structured from smaller units into larger entities. From families and local communities arose larger units: the state, the world, and finally God's Empire. Like Müller, Vogt extolled the virtues of family life, and he increasingly regarded the family as the model for all social and political organization. The father should exert authority over his household, but his power was not absolute and should be tempered by moderation, fatherly love, and justice. Men, Vogt wrote, must not withdraw to their private life, but must instead perform 'manly' active public services for the state. Vogt, however, also warned against an excess of patriotism, which, in his view, inevitably led to destructive wars. He argued here for the right balance between 'cosmopolitanism' and 'patriotism'. An excess of cosmopolitanism led to individualism, selfishness, and atheism, whereas too much patriotism resulted in bigotry and militarism.[77] The case of Vogt demonstrates that cosmopolitanism, active citizenship, and Counter-Revolution were certainly not incompatible.

In Vogt's argument that the state ought to form a perfect parallel with the family, he saw the ideal king as a 'loving father', driven by the virtues of moderation and temperance.[78] Also, the constitution ought to be a balance of the combined principles of monarchy, aristocracy, and democracy rather than based on only one principle. Furthermore, society should be ordered hierarchically. Vogt used the concept of professional specialization of the Scottish school of political economy to justify the existence of social hierarchies and inequality. This hierarchically ordered state was founded not on birth, but on education. The working

---

[75] [Vogt], *System des Gleichgewichts* II, 125. For Herder as a 'Europa-Historiker': Muhlack, 'Herder'. According to Muhlack, Herder tried in various works to minimise the importance of European history by regarding it from a larger global perspective and he regarded Europeans on several occasions as 'disturbers' of universal history. At the same, Herder admired the achievements of European civilisation and recognized that, in his own time, European and universal history had, to a large extent, become synonymous.
[76] [Vogt], *System des Gleichgewichts* I, 5–7.   [77] [Vogt], *System des Gleichgewichts* I, 277.
[78] On the monarchical representation of the 'loving father': Lok and Scholz, 'Loving Father'.

classes, who in his view ought to receive only a primary-school education, provided food and stood for the principle of democracy. The warrior class of soldiers represented the principle of monarchy. This class was to be educated in professional military schools. A third class was formed by an aristocracy of merit, consisting of professors and priests: they received the highest academic training. In contrast to this well-ordered hierarchical enlightened society stood the new Revolutionary order. By building a society on abstract ideas of freedom and equality as well as atheism, the revolutionaries disastrously destroyed the principle of the social order itself. In the end, the Revolution could therefore only lead to anarchy and despotism, as Calonne, Müller, and Feller had also predicted before him.[79]

In the last part of the book (*'Die Welt oder von der göttlichen Gerechtigkeit'*), Vogt dealt with the relationship between the human world and Divine justice. Divine Providence was the invisible hand guiding the stadial unfolding of human history, combining enlightened history with Revelation. The first stage in human development consisted of primitive infancy (*Kindheid*). Some peoples still lived in this primitive stage, such as the African peoples in the South, the 'Laps' (Sami) in Northern Europe, and the Mongolians in the East. The second stage Vogt termed the youth of humanity. Man emancipated himself from the state of nature. Religion, honour, and valour were important values. This was the era of the heroes. Civilization started to develop and arts and culture began to flourish. Asian societies were still in this age, according to Vogt. In the European context, this stage was represented by the Christian Middle Ages. Patriotic feelings first come to the fore in this era.[80]

The third stage was adulthood. This stage represented modern enlightened societies, which could only be found in Europe. Science and commerce were developed. But this stage also stood for the beginning of old age. Modern European societies had become decadent and exhausted. Dominant materialism wore out the moderns and deprived their lives of meaning. Philosophy played only a destructive and corrupting role, similar to the situation in late antiquity.[81] The French Revolution was the natural outcome of this so-called age of Enlightenment. The old decadent world was destroyed by the revolutionary wars. But the Revolution also created possibilities for a new and future fourth stage of regeneration, comparable to the rise of Christianity in late antiquity.[82] This corrupt world of antiquity had contained the seeds of renewal, carried along by the vigorous Germanic tribes.[83] Vogt believed therefore that the year 1802, the aftermath of the Peace of Amiens (27 March 1802), presented a unique opportunity for such a renewal on the continent: true Enlightenment could be achieved

---

[79] [Vogt], *System des Gleichgewichts* I, 301–82.
[81] [Vogt], *System des Gleichgewichts* II, 149–90.
[82] [Vogt], *System des Gleichgewichts* II, 233–5.
[80] [Vogt], *System des Gleichgewichts* II, 63–86.
[83] [Vogt], *System des Gleichgewichts* II, 1–225.

now.[84] Consul Bonaparte, he cautiously hoped, could become a new Henri IV or a Charlemagne, a founder of a new spiritually, culturally, and politically regenerated Christian Empire on the ruins of the old world.[85] So, in this 1802 work, the older enlightened language of progress, pluralism, and liberty, was combined with a more recent counter-revolutionary emphasis on authority, hierarchy, and religion.

7. A New Carolingian Empire

In his pamphlet *The Failed Projects of This and the Last Century* (*Die gescheiterten Projekte dieses und des vorigen Jahrhunderts*) (1803), Vogt decried all attempts in the late eighteenth century to create a new political order from scratch. All endeavours by enlightened despots, such as Joseph II and radical revolutionaries alike, to build new political systems on abstract ideals, abruptly breaking with ancient constitutions, had ended in bloodshed, war, and chaos, recent history had shown. The warnings of wise and erudite men such as Mirabeau, Mallet du Pan, Burke, Müller, Gentz, Archenholz, and others had not been heeded, Vogt lamented. In this essay of counter-factual history, Vogt described several alternative scenarios of how recent history could have developed had jealous, fanatic, and power-hungry politicians not taken control of attempts to reform the existing political system.[86]

Vogt's pamphlet clearly demonstrated that in the first decade of the nineteenth century, political history, in the eyes of contemporaries, had become open-ended and 'boundless', as Calonne had also formulated it: all kinds of political regimes had become possible, politics had become fluid, solid political forms had vanished.[87] Vogt in this pamphlet, like Calonne, did not show himself to be a staunch proponent of an unchanging historical constitution. Reform of most European constitutions certainly was necessary in Vogt's eyes. However, the reforms should have been implemented in a gradual way, rather than by a destructive revolution. Innovations should be anchored in existing institutions instead of abolishing them. He feared in 1803 that the 'catastrophic' Revolution would end in a 'warmed-up' project of the likes of Richelieu. Vogt warned ominously of a new 'Caesaric Empire', that would suffocate all love of freedom and the fatherland, as well as enlightened progress.[88]

In the next decade, however, Vogt would become increasingly enthusiastic about a 'Caesaric' solution to Europe's troubles. After 1804, he became a supporter

---

[84] [Vogt], *System des Gleichgewichts* I, xxxi; II, 222–3.
[85] [Vogt], *System des Gleichgewichts* II, 296–303.   [86] Vogt, *gescheiterten Projekte*.
[87] Perhaps a comparison can be made in this respect with the 1940s: when continent-wide wars had destroyed existing states and principles, intellectuals like Vogt, produced many pages of their ideas and plans for a new international order to replace the current vacuum. Cf. Rosenboim, *Globalism*.
[88] Vogt, *gescheiterten Projekte*, 1. This essay was also included as the first essay in volume I of the *Europäische Staats-Relationen*. In the essay, he announces the future project of a journal, named *Historisch-diplomatisches Archiv* or *politische Flugschriften*.

of the Napoleonic Empire as the ideal new European order, no doubt determined by his activities in the service of Dalberg. Vogt could perhaps be regarded as a typical 'political weathervane' or *girouette*, a much-decried personage in the public opinion of these decades, a political survivor who changed his conviction with every new political wind. However, this would imply a purely instrumental interpretation of political ideas and their social role. Vogt belonged to a large group of members of the political elite in various continental countries, who changed their political alliance in this era, but—at least in their own eyes—held onto enduring principles, such as the rule of law, freedom, and cultural and political diversity. Therefore, a simple moral condemnation of Vogt's behaviour would be an anachronism.[89]

The Napoleonic Empire, so admired by Vogt, could be interpreted as a political project in 'authoritarian cosmopolitanism'.[90] According to Michael Rowe, Napoleon 'built up an empire in which the national element was increasingly diluted with each new conquest'.[91] As the Empire grew, the French national elements diminished, to be replaced by a cosmopolitan imperial political culture, to the chagrin of many former French revolutionaries. Especially in the posthumously published *Le Mémorial de Sainte-Hélène* (1823), Napoleon's Empire was described as a European, liberal, and essentially cosmopolitan project. Fulfilling the Enlightenment ideals and making uniform laws and standards would bring progress and peace to Europe and the world.[92]

In the issues of the *Europäische Staats-relationen*, the bimonthly journal Vogt edited between 1804 and 1809, he fully supported the idea of the Napoleonic Empire as the natural fulfilment of the age of true Enlightenment.[93] Vogt praised Napoleon abundantly for re-establishing order after the anarchy and internal strife of the revolutionary decade.[94] The revolutionary leader Robespierre in Vogt's eyes had conducted an essentially monarchical administration with an emphasis on centralization and the concentration of state power.[95] Napoleon's Empire, by contrast, was not a continuation of the Revolutionary regime, but for Vogt represented a partial return to the ancient European constitution. This assessment was not without justification, as Michael Rowe has shown.[96]

---

[89] Cf. Serna, *République des girouettes*; Lok, *Windvanen*.

[90] In my view, the nexus between cosmopolitanism and authoritarianism has not been sufficiently explored by historians of cosmopolitanism and authoritarianism alike.

[91] Rowe, 'French Revolution'; Annie Jourdan, 'Napoléon et la paix universelle'.

[92] Las Casas, *Mémorial de Sainte-Hélène* (manuscrit original retrouvé); 'Le projet de l'abbé de Saint-Pierre pouvait se trouver réalisé': Jourdan, 'Napoléon et la paix', 12; Woolf, *Napoleon's Integration*; Woolf, 'Napoleon and Europe Revisited'.

[93] *Europäische Staats-Relationen*, vol. I–XIV.

[94] *Staats-Relationen* II (1804), 1–66. The journal can certainly be called 'biased' as official statements of the Napoleonic administration were published in their entirety without any critical comments.

[95] *Staats-Relationen* I (1804), 181.

[96] Michael Rowe has convincingly argued for the Rhineland that Napoleon 'allowed for reinvigoration of practices, traditions, and, more subtly, *mentalités* commonly associated with the old order'. Also: 'Napoleon provided a new institutional framework through which existing values were updated.' Rowe, *Reich to State*, 9, 284.

For Vogt, Napoleon was the new Charlemagne, a Christian-Germanic lawgiver and creator of a renewed European civilization along the lines designated by Montesquieu in *Spirit of the Laws*.[97] Whereas Napoleon himself may not have taken entirely seriously the idea of him being the new Charlemagne, Vogt certainly did.[98] Just as Charlemagne had regenerated the Germanic constitution, so would Napoleon. Vogt counselled Napoleon not to govern according to classical Roman maxims, but instead to look towards the Germanic legacy. The Germanic constitutions acknowledged hierarchy and order, without resorting to absolute or despotic power. Also, in the German ancient constitution, representative bodies formed an important element of the state constitution. Vogt countered the much-heard criticism, that Napoleon's Empire had no historical precedent, with the argument that all crowns had been established at some point in history. He had no doubt that the Napoleonic imperial dignity would gain historical respectability over time, just as the Carolingian crown had centuries earlier.

Vogt praised Napoleon above all for his restoration of the Church and the reordering of Church–state relations. For Vogt, religious affairs were always at the heart of any political order.[99] The fact that Napoleon called the pope to Paris to crown him emperor testified to his true religious feelings.[100] Ultimately, Napoleon was, for Vogt, like Charlemagne: not only a conqueror or a builder of an empire, but also, and above all, the regenerator of a civilization. His Empire was not just the result of military power; it formed the practical political realization of a higher ideal.[101] Napoleon would renew and reinvigorate the corrupt and decadent European civilization, ushering in an era of true Christian Enlightenment, Vogt predicted.[102] The revolutionaries had tried to destroy the pluralism and diversity of European states and thus also almost destroyed European culture itself. Napoleon's

---

[97] As Vogt wrote admiringly: 'Ich traue es dem großen Geiste Bonaparte's zu, daß er die schädlichen Folgen vorhersehen werde, welche ein so ungeheures Reich sowohl auf die Freiheit als die echte Kultur der Nationen haben könnte. Es wird viel mehr, wie Karl der Große zwar die oberste Würde eines Imperators als den Central Punkt der verschiedenen Staaten bestehen lassen, aber einer jeden Nation die ihr zuständige Selbstständigkeit und die ihren Charakter belebende Autonomie gestatten.' *Staats-Relationen* II, 7.

[98] 'Une étude quelque peu pointue de ses écrits et de ses propos prouve qu'il n'a jamais sérieusement envisage d'être un nouveau Charlemagne ou nouveau César. Il était bien trop un homme de son temps. Ce n'est pas qu'il n'ait rêvé d'un Empire d'Occident, mais ce rêve découle d'inspirations diverses, anciennes et modernes voire contemporaines.' Jourdan, 'Napoleon et la paix', 2. Cf. Broers, 'Napoleon, Charlemagne, and Lotharingia'; Ellis, 'Napoleonic Imperialism'.

[99] This was also true for Napoleon himself: Jourdan, 'Napoleon et la paix', 13. In his 1812 work, *Gedanken über das allerheiligste des Menschengeslechtes* [Reflections on the holiest of Humanity], Vogt praised in particular Napoleon's attempts to regenerate European civilisation by restoring the role of the Catholic Church in the Napoleonic Empire and his reconciliation with the pope. On Napoleon and the pope: Caiani, *To Kidnap a Pope*.

[100] *Staats-Relationen* III (1805), 72, 75.

[101] Cf. Vogt, *Historisches Testament* I, 5; *Staats-Relationen* XI, 128.

[102] This argument was also implicitly made by Archchancellor Karl Theodor von Dalberg in his essay on Charlemagne. Vogt wrote the foreword to the German translation. Dalberg, *Betrachtungen über den Charakter Karl des Grossen*.

ascendance, by protecting Europe's unique political diversity, would herald a new European cultural Renaissance.[103]

In the *Staats-Relationen*, Vogt devoted many pages to the German constitution and its history, seamlessly reconciling German patriotism with Napoleonic cosmopolitanism.[104] The main thrust of these writings was to prepare Germans to accept the new Napoleonic order as a given, and as in the German national interest as well. Vogt reiterated the themes of his *European Republic*: the German nation was described as consisting of a large diversity of different kinds of states and nationalities within the larger framework of the German nation.[105] In particular for the Germans, the local was connected to the national and European as in no other European country.[106] More than any other nation, therefore, the Germans formed the heart of European history, Vogt argued in a vein similar to that of Müller. The Holy Roman Emperor was the natural sovereign of Europe. The early Germanic tribes, after having defeated the despotic Roman Empire, imbued Europe with their unique characteristics of freedom, initiative, and restlessness. Also, the earliest constitutions of the European countries all have a common German origin. For Vogt, as well as for other Rhinelanders, Europeanism and patriotism are clearly not in conflict, but effortlessly complemented each other.[107]

From the late Middle Ages onwards, however, German history became a tragedy. As a result of power struggles between emperor and pope, the position of the emperor had weakened. The territorial princes prevented the development of a strong central imperial authority. Sadly, Switzerland and the Netherlands had gained independence and broken away from the Empire. The religious wars, in Vogt's terminology a 'fratricidal struggle', had torn Germany apart. The German lands were consequently divided into Catholic and Protestant blocs. The constitution of the Holy Roman Empire, although still valuable, had become obsolete and had to be reformed. In his journal articles, Vogt was decidedly more critical of the constitution of the early modern Holy Roman Empire than in his earlier *European Republic*. Whereas in his earlier work he claimed that the Holy Roman Empire still functioned, in 1804 he emphasized the weakness of the German constitution and the need for an outsider to solve this problem.

Vogt's call for German regeneration resulted in an uncompromising defence of Napoleonic imperial rule. Napoleon was, in Vogt's eyes, destined to end the long

---

[103] *Staats-Relationen* III (1805), 13.
[104] Several of these articles have been published in 1810 under the title *Die deutsche Nation*.
[105] *Staats-Relationen* I ('Die Deutsche Reichsverfassung (...)'), 98–116.
[106] 'Die Deutschen allein wußten Freiheit mit Ordnung, Individualität mit Allgemeinheit, und das Kleine mit dem Groß zu paaren. Sie wußten den Bürger mit der Gemeinde, die Gemeinde mit dem Reiche mit dem Reiche, die Reiche mit dem Ganzen zu verbinden, ohne einem jeden der verschiedenen Theile seine individuelle Freiheit und Selbständigkeit zu rauben (...).' *Staats-Relationen* III (1805), 179–80.
[107] Other Rhineland contemporaries who defended the advantages of German territorial fragmentation were Franz Wilhelm von Spiegel, curator at Bonn University, and Georg Forster. Rowe, *Reich to State*, 20–1; Hansen, *Quellen zur Geschichte des Rheinlandes*, 478–83.

internecine struggle between German Catholics and Protestants, as well as other intra-German struggles. As part of the Napoleonic Empire, Germany could once more become the core of European civilization. Napoleon's marriage to the Habsburg princess Marie-Louise stood, Vogt believed, for the fusion of French and Habsburg-German history.[108] In a symbolic way, the Holy Roman Empire had, for Vogt, metamorphosed into the pan-Napoleonic Empire. Germans ought not feel any melancholy about the disappearance of the Holy Roman emperor: in the last decade of his existence, the Holy Roman emperor had resembled an 'old war hero covered in wounds', whereas the French emperor was a 'young and strong warrior', capable of bringing peace to an exhausted and war-torn Europe.[109]

Vogt, the advisor to the pro-Napoleonic chancellor Dalberg, also emphasized Napoleon's role as the protector of the Rhineland, and the cities of Mainz and Frankfurt in particular.[110] Although the elector-chancellors of Mainz ruled over a small territory, they had, for Vogt, played an important role on the German and even European stage.[111] Vogt's great Mainz hero was the elector Johann Philipp von Schönborn (1605–73), who had tried to reconcile the warring factions during the Thirty Years' War and played an important role in the Peace of Westphalia. In Vogt's view, the electors had always been the upholders of legal order and peace in Europe, as well as the proponents of moderate enlightened reforms in Mainz. Vogt saw a similar future role for the chancellor in the Napoleonic Empire, an important *trait d'union* between Napoleon and his German subjects, and a moderator between religious and political affairs.[112]

The optimism displayed by Vogt after the Treaty of Lunéville (1801), that a general *pax napoleonica* could be achieved under the leadership of Napoleon, gave way over the course of several years to pessimism and the conviction that new continental wars had become inevitable. Vogt pointed the finger at the alleged aggressiveness of the other European monarchs, who did not understand the Napoleonic vision of bringing 'perpetual peace' to the European continent in the spirit of Henri IV, Sully, and the Abbé de Saint-Pierre.[113] Alternatively, he regarded Britain and Russia as the main threats to a pan-European peace.

---

[108] His book *Die deutsche Nation* (1810) was dedicated to the Empress Marie-Louise.
[109] *Staats-Relationen* II (1804), 183.
[110] Hömig, *Dalberg*; Färber, Klose, and Reidel, *Dalberg*; Färber, *Kaiser und Erzkanzler*.
[111] 'Der Kurfürst Erzkanzler war und ist, was den Gehalt seiner Staaten betrifft, ein nicht gar mächtiger Fürst; aber seine Würde kann ihm sowohl in geistlichen als weltlichen Dingen den größten Einfluß auf das Reich, ja ganz Europa verschaffen (...).' *Staats-Relationen* I (1804), 301.
[112] *Staats-Relationen* I (1804), 299–344.
[113] *Staats-Relationen* VII (1807), 127. In his separately published book *Historical Representation of the European Federation* of 1808, he reiterates many of his older themes. Europe is once again depicted as an organic whole, hierarchically organized from the smallest landholder via noblemen and kings to the Holy Roman Emperor. He again emphasized the variety of European constitutional arrangements and the unique development of all European nation states within the wider European whole. Published during the zenith of the Napoleonic Empire, this work depicts Napoleon as the emperor who fulfilled the centuries-old dream of European perpetual peace. Vogt, *Historische Darstellung des europäischen Völkerbundes*, vol. I (a second volume was never published).

In an article on England of 1808, Vogt painted, like Feller, a blackened image of the perfidious Albion as an amoral country of hypocrites. Although the British claimed that they stood for freedom, they cared only about money and profits. Their only *raison d'état* for achieving hegemony on the world seas was to impose a commercial monopoly on all peoples.

The Tory prime minister Pitt, in particular, was Vogt's *bête noir*. He served only the interests of the crown and high nobles, brutally suppressing the common English people. The British constitution may once have been a monument of liberty, but nowadays it only served to legitimate royal despotism.[114] Vogt also juxtaposed Napoleon's freedom-loving and enlightened Empire to an aggressive, warmongering, and despotic Russia.[115] He predicted that Europe's future would be determined by the struggle between the Western Napoleonic Empire, the heir to Charlemagne, and a Russian Empire in the East, with reconquered Constantinople as its capital and drawing on the Eastern-Christian legacy. Germany's role was that of a mediator and middleman between these two giants. The rest of Europe will increasingly become part of the sphere of influence of one of the two imperial entities.

At times, Vogt lamented the fragmentation of the European continent he had praised earlier. The pluralism that had caused its phenomenal rise and unique development could also become the main reason for Europe's downfall. In the distant future, the 'sleeping continent' of America would wake up, Vogt feared. He foresaw that revolutions would also break out in Latin America as they had done in the north. South America would develop in the same way as North America had, with Brazil as an economic and political powerhouse comparable to the United States. Migration to the New World would eventually weaken old Europe, and, finally, the New World would eclipse its former colonial overlord, Vogt prophesied pessimistically, as had Feller. Vogt did not see any role for Africa other than the virgin territory of future colonization by a Napoleonic Spain.[116] Neither did he give much thought in his journal articles to the future development of Asia.

Like a contemporary Polybius, Vogt commented in the last volume of the *Staats-Relationen* (1809) on the decline of the European states and the inevitable rise of new imperial powers that would close the circle of European history. From common Germanic origins, Europe had become a 'nation' as a result of civilizational development in the age of Enlightenment. The crisis of the French Revolution also made possible a renewal of European culture that had been corrupted by the atheistic and radical *philosophie*. Napoleon's European Empire would lead to another era of cultural flourishing as well as the end of internecine religious struggle. European history had started its circle with a Carolingian Empire and

---

[114] *Staats-Relationen* XI (1808), 81–109. [115] *Staats-Relationen* II (1802), 265–71.
[116] *Staats-Relationen* XI (1808), 81–109.

would receive its final and inevitable fulfilment under the aegis of a new and modern Carolingian emperor.[117]

8. Principles for a European Peace

The sudden and unexpected collapse of the Empire in the spring of 1814 was experienced by Vogt as a traumatic turning point in European history as well as in his own life.[118] The optimism and self-confidence that had characterized Vogt's writings in the first decennium of the nineteenth century receded in his publications of the year 1814–15.[119] Like many contemporaries in these years of regime change, he felt the need to justify himself and his past behaviour as well as the positions he had taken in his earlier writings. In his *Historisches Testament* (Historical Testament, 3 vol. 1814–15), Vogt looked, reflectively, back on his life as historian and publicist. Although he would live and write for more than another two decades, he gave here the impression of an old and disillusioned man. He wrote about himself as a man who had failed in his endeavours, and his 'testament' was meant for younger generations to complete the task Vogt had set himself but had failed in its execution as a result of the revolutionary years.[120] Whereas many contemporaries immediately downplayed their allegiance to Napoleon after his fall, Vogt in his *Testament*, remarkably, still praised the French emperor, calling him a 'genius'.[121] He also proudly testified that he had witnessed Napoleon's coronation in Paris. Tellingly, however, the work avoided explicit comments on contemporary politics.[122] Vogt presented Napoleon primarily as an apolitical supporter of the arts and as a maecenas of European civilization, echoing Napoleon's later self-representation in *Le Mémorial de Sainte-Hélène*.[123]

The cataclysmic political events of 1814–15 also led Vogt to reflect more in depth on the nature and meaning of the 'history' of humanity.[124] 'History', according to Vogt in a more religious vein, should be regarded as a theodicy:

---

[117] *Staats-Relationen* XIV (1809), 128. He also wrote that history usually took a course that differed from what contemporaries thought: 'Das ewige Schicksal wirkt anders als der Wille des vergänglichen Menschen.' *Staats-Relationen* XIV (1809), 112.
[118] On the experience of (dis)continuity in 1814–15: Fureix and Lyon-Caen, 'expériences de la discontinuité'; Pestel and Rausch, 'Post-Revolutionary Experience'; Lok, 'Un oubli total'.
[119] Lentz, *Nouvelle Histoire du Premier Empire* I, IV; Waresquiel, *Cent Jours*; Bercé, *fin de l'Europe napoléonienne*; on the Rhineland specifically: Rowe, *Reich to State*, 213–42.
[120] Vogt, *Historisches Testament* I, Vorbericht (preface); 'Zeit und Umstände verhinderten mich, wie ich schon sagte, meine Werke so vollständig auszuführen, als es ihre Gegenstände vielleicht verdient hätten.' Vogt, *Historisches Testament* II, iv–v.
[121] Vogt, *Historisches Testament* I, 32; on the self-justification of the 'political weathervanes' in the transition of 1814–15: Serna, *Republique des girouettes*; Lok, 'Un oubli total'.
[122] Lok, *Windvanen*, 247–92.
[123] For instance, see for Vogt's visit to the 'Napoleonic museum': Vogt, *Historisches Testament* I, 32–59.
[124] Cf. on the relation between loss, trauma, and history writing: Ankersmit, *Sublime Experience*.

divine will was revealed through world history. Treatises on world, and especially European, history could be compared to the holy books in the sense that they gave information about providential intentions. The historian was like a priest, whose duty was to explain the higher meaning of the world by the interpretation of history.[125] Divine Providence had changed the course of human history at certain key moments. The destruction of the ancient world was such a turning point. The French Revolution should also be seen in that light. The apocalyptic destruction caused by this Revolution, also enabled, for Vogt, the regeneration of a corrupted European civilization, an argument later also made by Joseph de Maistre.[126]

Like Feller, Vogt provided a chronology of human history in twenty-eight epochs, starting with the biblical creation and ending with the outbreak of the French Revolution. But in contrast to Feller, Vogt still explicitly tried to fuse providential and Enlightenment narratives. He did not examine the biblical story of creation uncritically but instead emphasized, in a Pyrrhonic vein, the lack of sources and the impossibility of attaining indisputable historical knowledge on the earliest human history.[127] World history for Vogt was evidently mainly European history with the addition of parts of the history of the Near East and the Arabic and Islamic worlds. In his 'human history', Vogt constantly compared the developments in the 'East' with those in the 'West'. Already in the days of the biblical patriarchs and the rise of the earliest civilizations, the East and West were diverging. Following Montesquieu's climate theory, Vogt wrote that the Eastern patriarchs were religious, passive, and used to despotism, whereas Western 'European' patriarchs were uncouth and primitive but also dynamic and freedom loving.

Interestingly though, Vogt did not claim here that liberty was an exclusively European phenomenon. The Phoenicians and the Arabs could also be considered as examples of dynamic and free people, not unlike the early Germanic tribes in the West. Mohammed was compared to Charlemagne as a builder of empires and civilizations.[128] Also, Vogt emphasized that most of Western Christian culture originally came from the East. Furthermore, he nuanced the uniqueness of Western history, by comparing the rise of the pope and the emperor in the European Middle Ages to the emergence of the Turkish and Mongolian rulers, and by underscoring the cultural exchanges between East and West and the Eastern roots of the European Renaissance.[129]

In Vogt's eyes, history was cyclical as well as linear.[130] In accordance with Polybius and other classical historians he admired, Vogt believed that human

---

[125] Vogt, *Historisches Testament* II, 288–99. Vogt already made this argument in his 1802 work *System des Gleichgewichts*.
[126] Vogt, *Gedanken über das allerheiligste des Menschengeslechtes*; for Maistre, see Chapter 8.
[127] Vogt, *Historisches Testament* I, 158–60.
[128] For a positive description of the virtuous morals of the freedom-loving Arab peoples and the enlightened and civilizing character of Islam, see also: Vogt, *Europäischen Völkerbundes*, 68.
[129] Vogt, *Historisches Testament* I, 160–85.   [130] Kuijpers and Pollmann, 'Introduction', 1–24.

nature and emotions did not change fundamentally, and that political history consisted of a continuous cycle of rise and decline. However, like Herder, he also argued that all historical periods were part of a unified larger human history.[131] Historical periods were determined by a specific dominant idea, which formed its contribution to human history. Over the long run, a divinely inspired progress could be observed in human history. After periods of decline, such as late antiquity and the eighteenth century, new eras of regeneration and progress would follow.[132] The key historical narrative for the counter-revolutionary Vogt as well as for the revolutionary Bonneville was the struggle between spiritual and political freedom and despotism, in which the 'just and true' type of freedom, with the help of providence, eventually would emerge victorious.

The *Historical Testament* certainly did not turn out to be Vogt's swansong. In the next decades, he would produce several works on the local and regional history of his native Rhineland. This 'regional turn' was caused no doubt by his disillusion over the fall of Napoleon and the end of his international order.[133] With a distinct melancholy he described the golden age of the pre-revolutionary world of the Rhineland and the electorate of Mainz before it was trampled underfoot by the great powers. His regional history was at the same time a cosmopolitan historiography, as it was very much written from a European perspective: the Rhineland, and above all his native Mainz, were depicted as the heart of European history from the early Middle Ages onwards, in particular with respect to the struggle between religious and secular powers, the key theme of European historiography. The destruction of Mainz as an independent prince-bishopric marked the inevitable fall of the Holy Roman Empire, and consequently, the European Republic as a whole, connecting local with international history.[134]

After 1815, Vogt also wrote visionary pieces on the future system of Europe. In his anonymously published *The European Principles of State and Church in Accordance with the Spirit of the Age* (1818) Vogt provided his readership with ideas on how a new European order ought to be reconstructed after Napoleon. For Vogt, as for most other protagonists of this study, political order and religious renewal were intrinsically linked. Both Napoleon and the peacemakers of the Vienna conference, led by his former pupil Metternich, had in Vogt's eyes failed in providing Europe with a durable order that would regenerate European civilization. 'Vienna' had been unable to reconcile the democratic, aristocratic, and monarchical forces and principles in a new balance.[135] In this pamphlet, Vogt presented his older ideas in a new key. Vogt once again advocated the old pluralist

---

[131] Vogt, *Historisches Testament* I, 204. [132] Vogt, *Historisches Testament* I, 200–2.
[133] Vogt, *Rheinische Geschichten*.
[134] Vogt, *Geschichte des Verfalls und Untergangs der Rheinischen Staaten*, 296. This work was also published as the fourth volume of the *Rheinische Geschichten*.
[135] [Vogt], *europäischen Staats- und Kirchengrundsätze*, 79. See Chapter 8 on the conservative disappointment regarding the results of the Vienna Congress.

Germanic and Christian constitution as a model for the reconstructed European Republic.[136] Rather than merely returning to an idealized past, Vogt fervently hoped for a synthesis of the Christian and Germanic constitutions combined with ideas of progress and Enlightenment.

If the attempts to build a new pan-European republic were to fail, Vogt warned ominously, Europe would become unstable again: violent revolutions would reoccur, new Napoleons and Attilas would rise, inaugurating new ages of despotism and anarchy.[137] In this book, Vogt designed a trajectory to finally realize the centuries-old dream of bringing 'Perpetual Peace' to Europe, placing himself in the peace tradition of Henri IV and Saint-Pierre. First, a council of scholars, theologians, lawyers, and philosophers attached to Christian universities should be convened to preliminarily discuss the principles of religion, law, and constitution. These 'learned men' did not resemble for Vogt the superficial *philosophes* of the eighteenth century, but, by contrast, combined philosophy with wisdom and morality.[138] For Vogt, a new European order should be founded on the rational judgement of an expert elite. 'Impartial scholarship' was a means for solving the age-old religious and political strife. Scientists and scholars are depicted by Vogt, not unlike in the views of the early socialist Saint Simon (1760–1825), as a new aristocracy in the post-revolutionary era.[139] Furthermore, a general church council would meet to discuss and resolve religious and doctrinal differences.[140] After the religious challenges had been dealt with, an imperial diet would meet to establish a perpetual European and Christian peace.[141] This new Christian republic would be led by two emperors—one in the East based in Constantinople, and the other the emperor of the West, with Rome as his residence—whose responsibility it was to act as constitutional mediators in disputes between states.[142]

Vogt firmly believed in an active citizenship as the foundation of the future European Republic.[143] He argued, like Charles-Alexandre de Calonne, that 'civil rights are the foundation of the freedom of individual citizens as well as that of entire states'.[144] Citizens of the European Republic had the right to equal access to the law, freedom of opinion, and religion, the right to vote as well as the right to feel secure.[145] However, he also wrote that not all inhabitants of the republic were

---

[136] 'Das Staats- und Kirchen Gebäude, was die Germanier gegen das siebente Jahrhundert nach Christi Geburt, in der Europäischen Christenheit errichtet haben, war in seinen Grundfesten so tief angelegt, in seine Verhältnissen so klug berechnet, und in seinem Streben so kühn aufgetürmt, das es alle zuvor versuchte Anstalten and Festigkeit, Weisheit und Größe übertroffen hat.' Vogt, *Staats- und Kirchengrundsätze*, Vorrede, i.
[137] Vogt, *Staats- und Kirchengrundsätze*, 83–4.   [138] Vogt, *Staats- und Kirchengrundsätze*, 10.
[139] Cf. Saint-Simon, *réorganisation de la société européenne*. See also (p. 240).
[140] Vogt, *Staats- und Kirchengrundsätze*, 63–4.   [141] Vogt, *Staats- und Kirchengrundsätze*, 43.
[142] Vogt, *Staats- und Kirchengrundsätze*, 60–1.
[143] Vogt, *Staats- und Kirchengrundsätze*, 12–22.
[144] 'Auf dem Bürgerrecht beruht sowohl die Freiheit der einzelnen Bürger, als die ganzer Staaten.' Vogt, *Staats- und Kirchengrundsätze*, 29–30.
[145] Vogt, *Staats- und Kirchengrundsätze*, 30.

entitled to citizenship: only those inhabitants descended from citizens and who were not financially dependent. Women, children, aliens, servants, and small wage earners were thus excluded. He also argued that citizens belonged to a hierarchically ordered estate which determined their position in society. Non-Christians were also excluded from active and full citizenship, although no one was forced to worship against his or her will in accordance with the principle of toleration. Without property, an inhabitant could not act as a citizen: the loss of property also implied the loss of the status of active citizen. 'Aliens' and immigrants could eventually obtain the right to citizenship based on property, economic activity, or their services to the community.

In his last major publication before his death, Vogt returned to the question of how to reconstruct a stable European order after decades of turmoil, revolution, and war, still looking towards Montesquieu for guidance. He concluded that the Revolution had failed in its attempt to build a better society.[146] However, Vogt did not advocate a reactionary return to the pre-revolutionary *ancien régime*. Neither did he fully support the status quo of the Vienna order. Instead, he, perhaps not unlike Bonneville, pleaded for, as well as prophesied, a rejuvenated and regenerated European society, which would be realized in the near future. Europe, like the mythical phoenix, would arise out of its ashes in even better shape, as it had done before in history, after the collapse of the Roman Empire in the fifth century and the medieval Church in the sixteenth century. But rather than radically breaking from its roots, this new order would be built on the foundations of the 'Christian-Germanic' institutions it inherited from its medieval predecessors. Vogt used the metaphor of the Dom in Cologne as a representation of this future European institutional order: a continuous work of construction on older foundations, but also constantly being improved upon.[147]

9. Conclusion: From Enlightenment to Counter-Revolution

In Vogt's works, to conclude, the concept of European pluralism and balance was seen through a historical and temporal framework. In his publications, different conceptions of history and time coexisted. Firstly, Vogt used history in the traditional sense, as practical experience to be learned from. His European Republic could be regarded as a mirror of princes, full of practical wisdom for governors such as the prince-bishop of Mainz. Secondly, Vogt regarded history, certainly in his nineteenth-century work, as theodicy. Historical developments and violent events, such as war, were given a deeper and providential meaning,

---

[146] Vogt, *Grund- und Aufriß*, 2–3.
[147] Vogt, *Grund- und Aufriß*, 9–14. At the end of the revised edition, he described his ideal order in the form of a fictitious and utopian 'philadelphic-columbian temple in Panama'.

and the historian fulfilled a role similar to that of a priest. Religion and history, progress and providence, as well as notions of decline and future regeneration, were closely aligned in a new synthesis. Enlightened stadial progress was reconciled with Christ-centred teleology. Thirdly and finally, we also see an older classical conception of history as a continuously ongoing cyclical process of the rise and fall of civilizations and states.

In developing his pluralist idea of Europe, Vogt drew on sources from different countries and languages, including, of course, German sources, exemplifying the transnational character of enlightened ideas of European diversity. Vogt's idea of a pluralist European Republic, representative of late-Enlightenment reformist thought, was, moreover, subsequently used to defend the cause of the Counter-Revolution, the Napoleonic Empire, and more half-heartedly, the Vienna order, demonstrating the political elasticity of this concept. Vogt was a counter-revolutionary Europeanist, but not a conservative or a reactionary in the strict sense: he abhorred the revolution but did not wish for a return to a golden past or a continuation of the status quo. Instead, he adamantly advocated a European spiritual and moral renewal, building on Christian-Germanic institutional foundations.[148] The terms 'conservative' or 'liberal' therefore do not seem to be an apt description of Vogt's historical Europeanist writings. Vogt himself, for instance, made a clear distinction between 'false liberalism', that is, the atheistic, materialistic, and revolutionary liberalism he rejected, and a 'true liberalism', based on the Christian and Germanic historical foundations he accepted.[149] Instead, Vogt was interpreted here primarily as an author who stood for a pluralist conception of European history as well as a distinct idea of freedom. For Vogt—as for Calonne, Feller, and Müller—freedom was above all the absence of arbitrary rule and despotic government.[150]

---

[148] The relationship between ideas of European history and the post-revolutionary historical legal school, such as that epitomized by the works of Friedrich Carl von Savigny (1779–1861), which lies outside the scope of the present study, would be an interesting future research project. Cf. Beiser, 'Savigny'.

[149] Vogt, *Geschichte des Verfalls*, iv–v.

[150] 'For Rhinelanders, long accustomed to the checks provided by representative estates and imperial courts, such [Napoleonic legal] institutional protection against arbitrariness was immensely important (...). Napoleonic institutions, like those of the old *Reich*, provided protection against the arbitrariness Rhinelanders experienced under occupation in the 1790s, and which most associated with Eastern monarchies.' Rowe, *Reich to State*, 283. Cf. Lok, '"Just and True Liberty"'.

7
Ancient and Modern State Systems

1. A Historian of Europe

The Göttingen historian Arnold Hermann Ludwig Heeren was another telling example of a German publicist who purposefully reconfigured and adapted enlightened historical narratives to the new political context of the Napoleonic Empire. In contrast to Vogt, however, Heeren used European history to counter the Napoleonic project and to offer alternatives for the ordering of Europe. As we have already seen in the first chapter, Heeren did not regard the Napoleonic Empire as the self-evident outcome of a pluralist European history and as the vehicle for German regeneration.[1] In his *Manual of European History* of 1809, Heeren perceived the Napoleonic system as a mortal threat to Europe's unique free and pluralist system. Although Heeren did not explicitly mention Napoleon in the foreword, it was clear that he saw the French emperor as a despotic ruler and his empire as a new 'universal monarchy'. The purpose of his history book was to make readers understand why this free system had fallen into decline and had finally collapsed.[2]

After the collapse of the empire, Heeren's handbook acquired a new political meaning. The book became a statement on how to organize the state system after Napoleon. Heeren's advice to the assembled crowned heads and their secretaries at the Congress of Vienna had been that the new order should not be built from scratch, as the revolutionaries mistakenly had done, but instead continuities with centuries-old lineages should be sought. The main lesson from his *Manual* was that the peacemakers should not strive for uniformity but for pluralism, as diversity (*Mannichfaltigkeit*) had been the cornerstone of this free system.[3] Heeren even reminded his readers that he, as the author of the *Manual*, had personally played a role in the unexpected turn of events by keeping alive 'the memory of the better age' and presenting contemporaries with an alternative to the then-dominant Napoleonic order.[4]

---

[1] Heeren, *Handbuch Europäischen Staatensystems*, henceforth abbreviated as *Handbuch*. I have used the version in the collected works: Heeren, *Historische Werke*, volumes VIII–IX. Some citations have been taken from the later English translation: Heeren, *Manual of the Political System of Europe*, henceforth *Manual*. Most Anglophone works cite only this English version. See also Chapter 1.

[2] Heeren, *Handbuch*, 'Vorrede', x.   [3] Heeren, *Handbuch*, 'Nachschrift', xiv.

[4] Heeren, *Handbuch*, 'Nachschrift', xiii.

This fortunate turn of political events turned Heeren into a widely read author. Several editions of his manual appeared, and the book was translated into, among other languages, English.[5] His other books on the classical world were even more popular among a wide audience.[6] His handbook would influence European history writing throughout the nineteenth century, including the works on European history of Leopold von Ranke.[7] Heeren's fame and that of his handbook, however, was brief. Like the writings of most protagonists in this book, Heeren's works faced severe scholarly criticism after 1830, and he received a hostile press in the nineteenth century overall. Despite his many prominent students, from Bismarck to Ranke and Schopenhauer, his enlightened and cosmopolitan views were rapidly regarded as outdated in an era of growing nationalism. New criteria for academic historical research, in particular the use of historical sources, moreover, resulted in the discrediting of his studies as not meeting modern academic standards. In the early twentieth century, however, historians started to see Heeren in a new light, regarding him as an important precursor to Ranke's history writing.[8] From the 1980s onwards, more publications have appeared on Heeren and his role in the alleged transition from eighteenth-century enlightened to nineteenth-century historicist and romantic history writing.[9]

In his autobiographical 'Letter to a Friend' (*Schreiben an einen Freund*), Heeren described himself first and foremost as a 'historian of Europe'.[10] He explicitly did not identify as a 'national' German historian, although he did also publish on German history within a European context as well. Nor was he interested primarily in the national histories of other European countries: his main fascination concerned the historical relations between European countries and the nature and historical development of the European 'state system' (*Staatensystem*). He regarded 'Europe' not as an exclusive political or institutional phenomenon, but in an enlightened vein, also as a commercial network with a common culture. In this intellectual autobiography, he, furthermore, emphasized that he considered 'European' history as part of a larger cosmopolitan 'world history'. He justified his narrower focus on European history by citing pragmatic reasons, such as the lack of a profound knowledge of non-European languages and the necessity to restrict oneself.[11]

In this chapter, I will examine Heeren's interpretation of European history in its political and intellectual context, and I will situate him in the framework of post-revolutionary 'historical Europeanism'. In the next section, I discuss Heeren's self-

---

[5] Heeren, *Manual*.   [6] Becker-Schaum, *Heeren*, 207.
[7] Muhlack, 'Europäische Staatensystem'. See also Chapter 9.
[8] On the reception of Heeren in the nineteenth and twentieth centuries: Becker-Schaum, *Heeren*, 7–11. The older biography is: Kahn, *Heeren*.
[9] Becker-Schaum, *Heeren*; Becker-Schaum, 'Heeren'; Muhlack, 'Philologie zur Kulturgeschichte'; Seier, 'Heeren'.
[10] Heeren, 'Schreiben an einen Freund', lix–lxii.
[11] Heeren, 'Schreiben an einen Freund', lix, lxii.

positioning as an 'impartial' historian of Europe and his ambivalent attitude towards contemporary political affairs, followed by sections on Heeren's academic precursors, in particular the Göttingen school of *Staatenhistorie* and international law. I will then sketch Heeren's development from a scholar of the classical world into a historian of modern Europe. Subsequently, I will analyse Heeren's account of the rise of the modern state system, and his analysis of the decline and fall of this system in his own era. The following section deals with the ambivalent and multifaceted role of extra-European colonialism in his account of the international system, a topic that will also be further examined in Chapter 9 of this study. In the conclusion I will revisit and criticize current interpretations of Heeren as the reactionary creator of the classical idea of the international system.

2. Academic Impartiality

Heeren claimed to be neither a philosopher nor a poet. He generally expressed antipathy towards abstract 'philosophical' systems. He saw himself as an 'impartial' historian whose style was characterized by 'simplicity' and 'naturalness' rather than by philosophical complexity. His intellectual *Werdegang* as a 'historian of Europe' had not been the result of a preordained plan, he explained in his autobiography. Born in 1760, he came from a well-to-do Protestant family in the Northern German commercial city of Bremen: his father was the pastor of the city's main church. He described his familial background of pastors and merchants somewhat modestly as representative of the ideal and virtuous 'middle class' that, in an Aristotelian vein, was situated between the wretched poverty of the debased working classes and the decadent and corrupted riches of the nobility. His familial background in a relatively small city state enabled him in his own view to keep an impartial stance when describing the relations between the great powers.[12] He credited the American Revolution of 1776, which started when he was sixteen, with making him politically conscious for the first time.

As a student in Göttingen, he was at first not very promising: he lacked knowledge of the ancient languages and he did not care much for the theological studies his father considered his destiny. However, the teaching of the professors Heyne and Spittler first and foremost inspired him to become a scholar, because they placed less emphasis on philological knowledge and focussed more on political and cultural history.[13] In 1784, he became a *privatdozent* in Greek philology at Göttingen. To overcome a mental crisis, he travelled for two years in Italy, France, the Holy Roman Empire, and the Dutch Republic, financed by an

---

[12] On Heeren's methodology as a historian of the 'late Enlightenment': Becker-Schaum, *Heeren*.
[13] Heeren, 'Schreiben an einen Freund', xix–xxii. On the influence of Heyne and Spittler on Heeren: Muhlack, 'Enlightenment' and Becker-Schaum, *Heeren*, 29–46.

inheritance. During his travels, he made extensive use of his network as a Freemason. After his travels, he returned to work for the University of Göttingen, where he would spend the rest of his professional life.

In 1787, Heeren, with the support of the classicist Heyne, was appointed an extra-ordinary professor in the faculty of philosophy. In this capacity, he mainly taught the history of ancient and modern literature as well as classical studies. As a result of the retirement of the older generation of history professors such as Spittler, Gatterer, and Schlözer from Göttingen between 1795 and 1799, Heeren was, from 1797 onwards, able to teach the topic that most fascinated him, universal and political history. In 1801, he was called to the Göttingen ordinary chair of history, partly due to his good contacts with the Hannover administrative elites, in particular with his 'uncle' Ernst Brandes (1758–1810), demonstrating the close connections between academic scholarship and bureaucracy.[14]

Surprisingly for a political historian, Heeren published little on the contemporary political turmoil and the impact of the French Revolution on his own life.[15] His relationship with current affairs was ambivalent. On the one hand, he believed that academic scholarship should be impartial and even serve as an 'escape' from a troubled present. On the other hand, Heeren's works clearly were impacted by the unfolding of the revolutionary events and the succession of regimes in the years around 1800, and he prided himself on his stance against Napoleon. In his early years, he had expressed sympathy for the American Revolution and reform movements in Europe. However, during the Dutch 'Patriot' Revolution of 1787, which he witnessed during his travels, he already started to question revolution as a means to achieve concrete social improvement, though he confessed support for the Patriots' overall goals. Later, in his *Manual*, Heeren would regard the Dutch Patriot Revolution, with the benefit of hindsight, regretfully as the start of a wave of 'constitutional' revolutions in Europe that would eventually destroy the old system. In the 1790s, he thus did not express immediate political opinions on the French Revolution, although in his works on the ancient world revolutionary themes would unmistakably appear. Heeren's distancing from the political turmoil turned out to be a wise strategy in uncertain times and fast-changing circumstances, when even older history writing quickly became politicized. Competitors for the Göttingen chair of modern history, such as Georg Friedrich Sartorius (1765–1828), were not appointed due to their reputation as Jacobins. Heeren, by contrast, was part of the political circles that were hostile to the Revolution. He criticized his former teacher and colleague Ludwig Thimoteus

---

[14] A perfect harmony was finally achieved in his professional life between 'duty' and 'preference', as he put it in his autobiography. Heeren, 'Schreiben an einen Freund', lviii.

[15] Heeren, for instance, criticized Leopold Ranke in the 1830s for insufficiently distinguishing between academic and journalistic work. Becker-Schaum, *Heeren*, 271.

Spittler (1752–1810) for his alleged lack of zeal in educating 'quiet citizens' by teaching them the dangers of revolutions.[16]

Heeren's reluctance to take part in contemporary political discussions was not just a career strategy. The distant past, for Heeren, was a means of escape from the turmoil of the present, and the violence and heated emotions of his own era, which he abhorred. As he wrote in a letter in 1804: 'it is hard to write about contemporary history without bitterness. I prefer to escape to the Ancient world, where the voice of passion is silent, and where we can continue our quiet research'.[17] When Heeren turned to European history as a topic of study, he began by researching the more distant past of the Middle Ages rather than contemporary history. During the collapse of the Napoleonic Empire in 1813 and 1814, Heeren turned towards writing about India in ancient times as a research topic far removed from present-day political troubles. At the same time, he believed that the main utility of history writing was to put contemporary events in a broader perspective.

In the years 1809 and 1810, Heeren's writings touched more directly upon contemporary politics. In 1810, he published a text in which he addressed the question of how nations could survive if they did not possess a constitution or an independent state. By pointing to the historical examples of the Greeks under the Roman Empire, the Chinese under Mongol dynasties, and the Hindus under the Persians, he argued that nations without a state could survive culturally and eventually dominate their conquerors. His advice to his fellow Germans in times when it seemed inevitable that Germany would be incorporated into the Napoleonic Empire and disappear as an independent political entity, was to cultivate their morals, religion, language, and scholarship as imperative for survival, following these historical examples. At a moment when the Holy Roman Empire was dissolved and the German state disintegrated, it was the poets, writers, and scholars, such as Heeren himself, rather than the statesmen, who were the true spokesmen of the German nation.[18]

After the fall of the Napoleonic Empire in 1814, Heeren, against his own conviction that academics should not participate in politics and administration, became involved in the writing of a new constitution for Bremen. He also took part in the publicity offensive in support of the German Confederation (*Deutsche Bund*), which was established after the collapse of the empire.[19] This confederation, Heeren wrote enthusiastically in 1817, would be able to function as the heart of the re-established European state system, guaranteeing Europe's freedom,

---

[16] Becker-Schaum, *Heeren*, 31–2.
[17] 'Es ist schwer, über neuere Geschichte jetzt ohne Bitterkeit zu schreiben; ich flüchtete mich lieber ins Altertum, wo die Stimme der Leidenschaften schweigt; und die Untersuchung ihren ruhigen Gang geht.' Letter, Heeren to Archenholz, 24 August 1804. Cited in Becker-Schaum, *Heeren*, 167.
[18] Heeren, 'Mittel zur Erhaltung der Nationalität besiegter Völker', 1–32.
[19] Becker-Schaum, *Heeren*, 279–82.

stability, and the rule of law, in contrast to the murderous and despotic Napoleonic Empire. The confederation would act as a bastion against future revolutions in France and beyond, and as a safeguard of moderate government on the continent. For Heeren, the purpose of the *Bund* was to represent German interests in an international setting. He hoped that at some point in the future neighbouring countries, such as the Netherlands, Switzerland, and Denmark, would join the federation. Frankfurt, in his eyes, would be the ideal site for a European senate.[20]

Heeren originally supported the Carlsbad decrees (1819) as necessary measures in the struggle against revolutionary forces but later became disillusioned with their repressive character. After 1830, he criticized the newly implemented censorship measures as a threat to academic freedom.[21] Notwithstanding these objections, Heeren never became a true liberal. Fearing a new wave of revolutions that would once again engulf Europe in a maelstrom of violence and terror, Heeren published a text in 1821 on the 'monarchical principle', defending the post-revolutionary monarchy as the true basis of order and freedom in Europe, and as in the best interests of Europe's peoples. Whereas in older works, Heeren had argued that the rule of law could thrive under republics as well as under monarchies, in 1820 he firmly supported the view that sovereignty, and both the legislative and executive functions of government, should only be in the hands of the monarch. A representative assembly could advise the monarch, but the ultimate power of decision-making lay with the king.

The notion of 'popular sovereignty', an idea he associated with the 'dangerous' works of Jean-Jacques Rousseau, was too abstract and utopian, resulting in large-scale violence and anarchy, as recent history had clearly shown.[22] Also, attempts to mingle monarchical and republican forms, as advocated by liberals, would not lead to stable government and were therefore doomed. Instead, Heeren proposed a 'monarchical principle' as an alternative to the notion of popular sovereignty. His monarchy, however, was not founded on traditional arguments such as patriarchal or divine-right theories, but followed rational and enlightened goals such as peace, prosperity, and the rule of law.[23]

Unlike many of his Göttingen colleagues, Heeren never took office himself. However, much of his teaching was on the science of government as well as political history. In his courses he examined disciplines such as statistics, constitutional law, and political economy in a manner typical of the Göttingen historians. Many of his students, including Bismarck, would later in life hold important

---

[20] Heeren, 'Deutsche Bund', *HW* II, 423–51.   [21] Becker-Schaum, *Heeren*, 282–3.
[22] See for a similar view: Haller, *Restauration* I.
[23] This ideally moderate, rational, and constitutional monarchy was not a new phenomenon, Heeren argued, but had already been theorized in the centuries before the Revolution by eminent political philosophers such as Grotius, Bodin, and Hobbes. 'Political theory' for Heeren was on the side of the monarchy. Heeren, 'monarchischen Prinzips', 365–451. Cf. Boldt, *Staatslehre im Vormärz*. On the monarchical principle in Prussia: Achtelstetter, *Prussian Conservatism 1815–1856*.

political and administrative positions. From 1820 onwards he published fewer original works, but instead devoted his time to the editing of scholarly journals and the writing of numerous reviews. After completing the edition of his *opera omnia* in 1826, Heeren also co-edited a famous collection of monographs and source editions on the history of the European states or *Staatengeschichte*.

3. Universal History and Staatenhistorie

In his *Historische Werke*, Heeren clearly positioned himself as part of a Göttingen 'school' of history.[24] In several biographical sketches of professorial careers, Heeren provided his predecessors and contemporaries at the University of Göttingen with canonical status, without writing secular hagiographies. All of these biographies more or less follow the same meritocratic narrative: the scholarly lives started in modest or even dire circumstances, but due to perseverance, character, and abilities the young male scholars were able to surmount the difficulties of their birth to become, by midlife, esteemed scholars and eminent members of society. Heeren also noted that, in contrast to statesmen and military leaders, scholars spend a large part of their lives in libraries and studies, so describing their intellectual development, rather than their activities, was the most rewarding and interesting part of their biographies.[25] The greatest amount of praise from Heeren, resulting in the largest number of pages, was reserved for his mentor and father-in-law, Christian Heyne, who played a crucial role in Heeren's career as well as in his intellectual development. But he also wrote several sketches of fellow historians. He credited the Göttingen historians with the revival of historical scholarship in Germany from the middle of the eighteenth century onwards, ending a long period of traditional scholarship Heeren deemed dreary, unimaginative, and lacking all creativity.

The rise of Göttingen in the second half of the eighteenth century as a major academic laboratory of knowledge on 'Europe' and its (political) history was not a foregone conclusion, as Heeren observed.[26] At the beginning of the eighteenth century, the German lands certainly were not at the forefront of academic study of the European state system: most new knowledge was adapted from French, Italian, Dutch, and British sources. Only Samuel Pufendorf (1632–94) stood out for Heeren as a lonely intellectual giant, but he, according to Heeren at least, had no significant intellectual offspring. This lack of German forerunners made the achievements of the Göttingen historians all the more impressive, or so Heeren

---

[24] On the writing of history at Göttingen University and German Enlightenment historiography in general: Muhlack, 'German Enlightenment historiography'; Bödeker et al., *Aufklärung und Geschichte*; Hammerstein, *Jus und Historie*. Christoph Becker-Schaum, however, is sceptical about the existence of a coherent and unified Göttingen school: Becker-Schaum, *Heeren*, 116.
[25] Heeren, 'Christian Gottlob Heyne', 7.   [26] Heeren, 'Andenken an deutsche Historiker', 442.

wrote. German histories of Europe were mostly written by diplomats, statesmen, journalists, and literary figures, rather than by academics. From the middle of the eighteenth century, however, the history of the (European) states (*Staatenhistorie*), and more generally the study of Europe, began to blossom in Germany and became primarily an academic discipline.[27] At the University of Halle, European history was taught in close connection with legal science, following the lead of Pufendorf. Other important universities in this field were Jena and Leipzig.

The most important seat of learning for the study of Europe and European history became the University of Göttingen. As we saw, this Protestant university was the model for Catholic reformers such as Vogt. This new university, founded only in 1737, formed part of the electorate of Hannover ruled by the English king.[28] From all corners of Europe, Protestants, and increasingly also Catholics, came to Göttingen to study 'Europe' and European history from the perspective of different and new disciplines.[29] The Göttingen and German so-called *Staatenhistorie* developed here in close relation to other emerging disciplines, such as political economy, geography, and ethnography, as well as the older academic specializations of 'universal history' and literary histories.[30] All of these (re-)emerging disciplines shared a historical approach towards their objects of research. In the works of these late eighteenth-century German scholars, 'Europe' transformed from a spatial category into a, first and foremost, temporal and historical concept.[31]

In particular, Heeren lauded the Göttingen 'universal historians' for their contributions to scholarship and their influence on his own work on the European state system. In the work of these eighteenth-century historians, no clear boundaries existed between global and European history, as we also saw in the cases of Robertson and Voltaire. Usually, European history was regarded explicitly or implicitly as the core of universal human history, or as it was often put, 'the main theatre of the development of mankind'. Modern Europe was regarded by 'universal historians', such as Swiss historian Isaak Iselin (1728–82), as the outcome of universal history, the highest form of human civilization.[32] For German-speaking *Staaten*-historians, including Heeren, European history had a global significance: it was the norm and highest stage of world history. Europe was described as an empire of civilization and contrasted with the less civilized and even barbaric outside world. In this way, universal history from the

---

[27] Gollwitzer, *Europabild*, 64–7.
[28] On enlightened historiography in Göttingen: Marino, *Praeceptores Germaniae*; Bödeker, Büttgen, and Espagne, *Wissenschaft vom Menschen*; Boockmann and Welleneuther, *Geschichtswissenschaft*.
[29] Gollwitzer, *Europabild*, 54–6; Muhlack, 'Enlightenment', 255–6, n. 18. Göttingen became a model even for Catholic university reformers such as Niklas Vogt in Mainz, see Chapter 6.
[30] Gollwitzer, *Europabild*, 52–4.   [31] Gollwitzer, *Europabild*, 64–7.
[32] Iselin, *Geschichte der Menschheit*.

eighteenth century onwards legitimized European colonial conquests, although eighteenth-century voices critical of colonial expansion and conquest can also be found.[33]

Heeren credited Johann Christoph Gatterer (1727–99) with bringing modern world history to Germany, and also praised his innovative uses of auxiliary sciences such as geography and diplomatic history.[34] Another universal historian honoured by Heeren was Johannes von Müller (1752–1809), also a former Göttingen student. Müller's universal history was praised for its creativity and broad appeal, within and beyond the academic world. Müller's republican leanings were explained away by monarchists such as Heeren by pointing to his Swiss background, which made him atypical.[35] The most influential German universal historian was, in Heeren's eyes, August Ludwig von Schlözer (1735–1809). Schlözer's fame rested on his two-volume world history, but he also published on Russian history and the ancient Greeks.[36] The central theme in Schlözer's work was his hatred of random violence and arbitrary power. His books were not only well received by the academic community but were also of practical use to those active in state bureaucracies and the diplomatic world. Although Heeren did not regard biblical chronology as scientific, he nonetheless used the work of universal historians Schlözer and Gatterer, who still tried to fit ancient history, such as the periodization of pharaonic reigns, into biblical chronology.[37] Schlözer and Heeren shared the view of the Great Migrations at the end of the Roman era, the Crusades, and the Reformation as important ruptures and defining moments in European history.

Schlözer originally gave a positive assessment of the French Revolution as the culmination of centuries of enlightened progress. Later he changed his mind, due to revolutionary radicalism and violence, and became a critic of the revolutionary as well as Napoleonic despotism. He eventually sided with the right side of history, Heeren wrote approvingly. Heeren, however, criticized Schlözer for insufficiently making a distinction between his involvement in politics and his academic scholarship, in the end harming the quality of his research and academic writing, in self-evident contrast to the alleged politically 'impartial' stance of Heeren himself.[38] The impact of the Napoleonic political context on Schlözer's history writing became clear in his inclusion of Russian history in his narrative of modern Europe, which formed a departure from pre-revolutionary historiography. Schlözer's renewed focus on Russian history reflected his hope that the newly

---

[33] According to Gollwitzer, German authors did not have an independent voice in the debate on European colonialism and conquest. Gollwitzer, *Europabild*, 63–4. For a different view: Muthu, *Enlightenment against Empire*; Pitts, *Turn to Empire*.
[34] Heeren, 'Gatterer'. On Gatterer: Gierl, *Geschichte als präzisierte Wissenschaft*.
[35] Heeren, 'Johann von Müller'.   [36] Schlözer, *Vorstellung seiner Universal-Historie*.
[37] Becker-Schaum, *Heeren*, 136–8.
[38] Heeren, 'Schlözer', 498–514. Cf. Peters, *Altes Reich*; Hennies, *politische Theorie Schlözers*.

crowned Tsar Alexander I would join the military struggle against France and help to end French hegemony.[39] Schlözer and Heeren were not the only Göttingen historians who adapted their enlightened European histories to the new political contexts of the Revolution and the Napoleonic Empire. The biblical scholar Johann Gottfried Eichhorn (1752–1827), for instance, published works on European history, arguing that France, in contrast to Germany, had failed to cultivate a mature bourgeoisie and, consequently, had not become a fully modern polity, resulting in the coming of the disastrous French Revolution.[40]

A further Göttingen historian who exerted a profound influence on Heeren's idea of *Staatengeschichte* was, to conclude this overview of forerunners, Ludwig Thimoteus Spittler (1752–1810). In his biography, Heeren named Spittler, along with Heyne, as his most important academic mentor, despite the fact that they had a somewhat complex personal, political, and academic relationship.[41] Spittler started his academic career as a Church historian. He taught the history of the Church, not from a traditional dogmatic, but from a new, analytical enlightened historical perspective. This irenicist approach, according to Heeren, was praised by 'enlightened' Protestant and Catholics alike. Spittler, in his capacity as Church historian, published on the history of the papacy, the Crusades, and the Jesuit Order.[42] Spittler's example demonstrated that, in addition to universal, legal, and literary histories, ecclesiastic history formed one of the main sources of the new political history of the state system. Spittler, furthermore, published on German imperial history and studied the history and constitutions of Hannover and Württemberg. In contrast to purely academic Heeren, Spittler accepted an increasing number of administrative duties, eventually becoming a minister in Württemberg.

In 1782, Spittler started to teach the political history of the European states at Göttingen, publishing in 1793 and 1794 his two-volume *Design of the History of the European States* (*Entwurf der Geschichte der Europäischen Staaten*) on the basis of his lectures.[43] In the *Entwurf*, Spittler wrote the national histories first of the Atlantic countries, followed by those of the Southern, Central, and finally of

---

[39] Golf-French, 'Limits'. Golf-French writes that the impact of Napoleon showed the 'limits' of the Enlightened narrative, whereas I would argue that the enlightened narrative became first and foremost politicized as a result of the revolutionary wars.
[40] Golf-French, 'Limits', 1204–9.
[41] Heeren, 'Spittler', 515–34. On the relationship between Spittler and Heeren: Becker-Schaum, *Heeren*, 30–5. On Spittler: Reill, 'Spittler', 42–6; Grolle, *Landesgeschichte*.
[42] Spittler, *Werke*.
[43] Spittler, *Werke*, vol. 3–4 (1827–8). In the introduction to the first edition, Spittler wrote that he was aware of the dangers of writing on the political and constitutional history of the European states with their constitutional crises as turning points in times of revolution and turmoil, but he was convinced that 'reasonable historical analysis' offered the best means to shape 'obedient' and 'law-abiding citizens' ('*pflicht mäßigere und gehorsamere Staatsbürger*'). According to Becker-Schaum, this remark was intended as a riposte aimed at his conservative critics who accused him of political untrustworthiness and sedition. Becker-Schaum, *Heeren*, 32.

the North European states. The Russian and Ottoman histories were briefly mentioned. From the German lands, only the Prussian monarchy was discussed. Heeren had attended Spittler's course on the history of the European states as a student and used Spittler's overview as an important source for his own lectures. However, there were also significant differences between the two historians, Heeren emphasized. Whereas Spittler mainly wrote a collation of different national histories, Heeren wanted to write about the state system as an integrated whole: more than summarizing different national histories, Heeren's ambition in his *Manual* was to excavate the relations between the states and the common cultural and economic frames that bound these states together. Heeren formulated his approach towards the European political past as the right 'middle way' of analysing the commonalities of the European state system without ignoring the specific and unique trajectories of the European national histories.[44]

4. History and Law

In addition to the burgeoning historical sciences, the '*Staatenhistorie*', as taught and written by Heeren, arose partly out of the historically inclined interests of international jurists in the new fields of *Europäischen Völkerrecht* (European international law) and European public law.[45] From its foundation in 1734, the Göttingen law faculty had been specifically oriented towards the historical and empirical study of the law. The main aim of the Göttingen lawyers was to combine the study of law with the science of effective government of modern states. Predominant in the early phase were the professors Johann Stephan Pütter (1725–1807) and Gottfried Achenwall (1719–72), who jointly published an influential textbook in 1750, *Elementis Juris Naturae*, where they laid out the principles of international law. In his works, Achenwall legitimized and rationalized the government of enlightened absolutist states by natural law.[46] Pütter had written in praise of the Westphalian settlement, comparing the constitution of the post-Westphalian Holy Roman Empire to other balanced and free, mixed constitutional systems such as the United States of America and the Dutch Republic.[47] Imperial law and history (*Reichshistorie*), as it was practised in Göttingen in the decades before the Revolution, formed another important source for the development of Göttingen *Staatengeschichte* and the formulation of European public law.

---

[44] Heeren, *Handbuch*, xvi.
[45] On eighteenth-century *Ius Publicum Europaeum*: Duchhardt, 'Peace Treaties'; Belissa, *Fraternité Universelle*. On the interrelation of law and historiography: Hammerstein, *Jus*; Koskenniemi, *Uttermost Parts*, 873–939. Surprisingly, Koskenniemi does not discuss Heeren and his legacy.
[46] Koskenniemi, 'Positivism', 193; Streidl, *Naturrecht*.
[47] Pütter, *Historische Entwickelung der heutigen Staatsverfassung*. Cf. Keene, *Anarchical Society*, 19.

Outside Göttingen, the most influential authority on German public and imperial law was Johann Jakob Moser (1701–85).[48]

In his biographical sketch on the Göttingen law professor Georg Friedrich von Martens (1756–1821), Pütter's successor, Heeren referred to him as an important source for his own *Staatengeschichte*, despite the fact that Martens was not a historian himself. Heeren praised, in particular, Martens' scepticism towards philosophical speculation.[49] In contrast to Martens, however, for Heeren, the legal dimension was only one aspect of the state system; equally important were the cultural, economic, and political factors. Martens, like Heeren, came from the North of Germany. He was appointed professor of jurisprudence at Göttingen in 1783 and taught in this capacity there until 1808. Unlike Heeren, Martens did not stay aloof from political affairs: he was active in several functions in the Napoleonic era in the service of the Napoleonic Kingdom of Westphalia, when Göttingen University was almost destroyed by the invading French and Prussian armies. After the collapse of the empire, he was made a privy-cabinet councillor (*Geheimer Kabinettsrat*) by the newly installed King of Hanover, whom he represented at the Congress of Vienna, and he took an active part in the diet of the German Confederation at Frankfurt in 1816.[50]

In 1785, Martens published the first version of an influential handbook on European public law, intended for future diplomats and bureaucrats, which would have a large international audience.[51] This handbook was characterized by its empirical and historical approach. Given its emphasis on systematic classifications, Martens could claim that his work met the criteria of contemporary enlightened science. His interpretation of European public law, furthermore, was based on the idea of the gradual progress of humanity, and European society in particular, largely excluding the world outside Europe. Martens' most important work was his *Receuil de Traités*, a collection of treaties, declarations, and other international acts he edited. These source editions, published from 1791 onwards, played a crucial role in the construction of a specific, European tradition of public law from Westphalia. These combined legal documents from several centuries formed a de facto empirical European constitution, or so Martens claimed.[52]

The French Revolution, as Martens saw it, presented an attempt to destroy this European legal tradition. The French revolutionaries' aim to build an international

---

[48] 'Moser was an important actor in the process of making public law an academic science, neutral in method, religious in spirit, but committed—at least in some of its vocabulary—to the Enlightenment ideal of a rule of law to replace philosophical speculation and reason of state.' Koskenniemi, 'Positivism', 194–5. Cf. Walker, *Moser and the Holy Roman Empire*. On imperial law: Ranzelzhofer, *Völkerrechtliche Aspekte*; Gross, *Empire and Sovereignty*.

[49] Heeren, 'Martens'.

[50] Habenincht, *Martens*; Figge, *Martens*; Nussbaum, *Concise History*. On the Napoleonic 'weathervanes' who became important functionaries under the Restoration monarchies: Lok, *Windvanen*; Serna, *Republique des Girouettes*.

[51] Martens, *Précis du droit*. Cf. Koskenniemi, 'Positivism', 194.

[52] Koskenniemi, 'Positivism', 195.

order on abstract ideals of perpetual peace was not only impractical but also dangerous in his eyes. The revolutionary demand that all constitutions should be based on revolutionary principles would lead to endless warfare and military interventions driven by ideology. In his foreword to the new 1796 German edition of his handbook, he decried the revolutionary concept of an international order based on naturalism, as, for instance, proposed by the Abbé Grégoire to the National Convention in April 1795.[53] Martens regarded the foundation of the Napoleonic Empire not as the victory of revolutionary ideas, but as the triumph of *realpolitik* over utopian idealism.

Martens' positivist and rational enlightened approach to international law made his work ideally suited for the post-revolutionary and post-Napoleonic political world with its aversion to all forms of abstract and utopic idealism associated with the French Revolution.[54] His works, with their emphasis on procedure and the sovereignty of independent states, provided the international legal foundation for the reconstructed monarchical states system. However, it would be incorrect to regard Martens as a mere reactionary, although his writings were used to legitimize a repressive international order after 1820. For Martens himself, his positivistic interpretation of European public law presented the right 'middle way' between, on the one hand, a utopian moral universalism he associated with the French revolutionaries, and, on the other, the brutal power politics and expansionism of the large states. The goal of European law was not to create a better world, but to avoid the worst injustices, by an emphasis on prudence, historical precedent, and the use of enlightened reason.[55]

5. Ancients and Moderns

Heeren's intellectual preparation as a historian of the European state system started, paradoxically, in classical antiquity. As his biographer Becker-Schaum noted: 'Heeren has always, and in the first instance, been a historian of the Ancient World.'[56] His works on ancient history were most widely read, as well as criticized. Heeren was trained as a classical philologist. Moreover, he lectured in ancient history and literature in his first years in Göttingen. His doctorate, furthermore,

---

[53] Koskenniemi, 'Positivism', 199–203.
[54] As Martti Koskenniemi put it: 'international law became associated with enlightened decision making by statesmen, guided by the well-educated lawyer in possession of a scientific method'. Koskenniemi, 'Positivism', 198.
[55] Koskenniemi, *Gentle Civilizer*, 19–20. According to Koskenniemi, this enlightened empirical law tradition remained dominant until the second half of the nineteenth century when it was replaced by a new liberal sensibility that regarded European public law as not founded on the principle of monarchical sovereignty but primarily as the expression of European society and its peoples.
[56] 'Heeren ist immer und hauptsächlicher Althistoriker gewesen.' Becker-Schaum, *Heeren*, 17.

consisted of a study of a topic in Greek tragedy.[57] During his travels in Italy he examined ancient sources, and he edited texts by the Greek geographer and historian Strabo. In his autobiography, he mentioned, like Vogt, the late Greek historian Polybius as an important intellectual source for this own historical work.[58]

Heeren's background in the classics and the history of the ancient world was not as unique for a historian of modern Europe as it seems at first sight. Most popular writers of modern history in the eighteenth century—including Edward Gibbon and B.G. Niebuhr—were also widely read in ancient history. As has been pointed out by Susanne Marchand, among others, many German modern historians received their training as classicists. The histories by Herodotus, Thucydides, and, in Heeren's case, Polybius, provided important models on how to write modern history. Several of the new methodologies and source criticisms were developed by ancient historians and classicists, such as Heeren's mentor Heyne, to be later applied to modern history. Only much later in the nineteenth century was modern history, with the possibility of extensive archival research, considered the most 'scientific' form of historical study.[59] At the same time, ancient history and the classical historians were losing some of their status in the late eighteenth century. As we have also seen in the case study of Bonneville, modern and contemporary history were juxtaposed to an older ancient history, and increasingly seen as outdated and no longer fit for a revolutionary world, a claim contested by *anti-philosophes*.[60]

For Heeren, as for many of his contemporaries, the ancient world was both an escape and a mirror to contemplate contemporary affairs.[61] Despite his self-professed distancing of historical scholarship from contemporary politics, Heeren drew several parallels between the ancient past and the present. In 1794, he compared the contemporary struggle between the French revolutionaries and their enemies to the struggle in ancient times between 'democratic' Athens and 'aristocratic' Sparta. A revolutionary punitive action against Lyon was seen by Heeren as a contemporary re-enactment of the destruction of moderate Mytilene by an aggressive Athens led astray by democratic demagogues.[62] In his 1795 essay on the political turmoil in the ancient Roman Republic at the time of the Gracchi brothers, he directly linked the contemporary revolutionary events to the classical past.[63] Just as in contemporary France, Rome was then plagued by the strife between an aristocratic elite and the democratic people, led by the brothers

---

[57] The title of the doctoral dissertation Heeren defended on 29 May 1784 was 'De chori graecorum tragici natura et indole, ratione argumenti habita'.

[58] Heeren, 'Schreiben an einen Freund', liii.   [59] Marchand, 'Ancient History'.

[60] Lok, 'berceau des muses', 59–74.

[61] Many late eighteenth-century writers still turned to ancient history to make sense of the revolutionary events of their own era, for example: Chateaubriand, *Essai historique, politique et moral sur les révolutions anciennes et modernes* (1797).

[62] Heeren, 'Mitylene und Lion'.

[63] Tiberius Sempronius Gracchus (c.166BC–133BC) and Gaius Sempronius Gracchus (154–121BC).

Gracchi. Although Heeren professed some sympathy for the idealism of the Gracchi brothers, he concluded that their—in principle, just—actions had led to uncontrolled popular violence and anarchy, which left the Roman population eventually worse off. The lessons for revolutionary France could not be mistaken.[64]

Heeren claimed in his autobiography that his most important publication was his multivolume study of the 'Ideas on Politics [*Politik*], Intercourse [*Verkehr*] and Trade [*Handel*] of the Principal Nations of Antiquity' (1793–1815).[65] This work would make Heeren famous among a wide audience, but also gained him notoriety among academics for his allegedly unscientific use of sources. In this research project, Heeren approached the ancient world from a combined political, economic, and cultural historical perspective. This was a fresh approach which contrasted with the older philological perspective. Later he would use this methodology for his history of modern Europe, too. He explicitly stated that his aim was to describe not only ancient Europe, but also the less-researched—by European scholars at least—parts of the world in Asia (India, Persia) and Africa (Carthage, Egypt, and Ethiopia).[66] In 1799, he published a widely used and read pedagogical handbook on the history of the ancient states, based on his findings in the *Historical Researches*.[67]

Although he did not draw explicit parallels between the ancient past and the present, echoes of contemporary events can certainly be found in this work: the volume on Africa, published in 1793, for instance, dealt with the rise of republics; the volume on Asia, published in 1796, discussed the nature of 'despotism'. The volumes on the Greeks (1812) and India (1815) examined the cultural survival of conquered nations, a resonant theme in the German lands in the Napoleonic decade. Heeren, echoing Montesquieu, made a distinction, on the one hand, between despotism, which can mainly be found in Asia, where the arbitrary power of the ruler knew no boundaries, and, on the other, the monarchical rule of law, which could be found only in Europe. For Heeren it did not matter so much whether a state had a monarchical or a republican constitution, for it to be classified as a 'free' or 'constitutional' state. If the European ruler acted in accordance with the principles of law, then individual freedom was guaranteed, despite the fact that the citizen of an absolute monarchy had no right to participate in political life.[68] In the articulation of his views on ancient constitutional history,

---

[64] Becker-Schaum, *Heeren*, 182–6.
[65] Heeren, 'Ideen über die Politik, den Verkehr und den Handel vornehmsten Völker der alten Welt'. In 1833, an English translation appeared under the title *Historical Researches into the Politics, Intercourse and Trade of the Principle Nations of Antiquity*; and in French *De la politique et du commerce des peuples de l'antiquité*, 7 vol. (1830–40). On the editorial history: Becker-Schaum, *Heeren*, 103–210.
[66] Heeren, 'Vorrede', HW X, v–xiv.
[67] Heeren, *Handbuch der Geschichte der Staaten des Alterthums*.
[68] On the counter-revolutionary idea of a free state: Lok, '"Just and True Liberty"'. Cf. for a different view: de Dijn, *Freedom*, 231–76.

Heeren responded extensively to—as well as criticized—the work of Locke, Montesquieu, and Kant, among others.[69]

Heeren's study could also be regarded a contribution to the enlightened debate on political economy. Heeren's ancient world was a 'network society' connected by long-distance commerce and travel. Although commerce played an important role in his narrative, economy did not determine Heeren's history, but was only one aspect of his analysis of ancient political and social life. Like Müller, Heeren was critical of what he regarded as the overtly economic and quantitative view on politics he discerned, for instance, in Schlözer's universal history. He also associated this economic determinism with the alleged atheism of Scottish political economists as well as with political despotism.[70] Furthermore, he did not accept the enlightened view that commerce would always lead to prosperity and peace. Instead, he demonstrated in his history that commercial relations could also be a cause of war and violence, as well as of peace and prosperity. Sometimes, it was better for some nations to put trade barriers into place to protect themselves against the pernicious influence of foreign trade. There was no single universal model of political economy that was thus ideal for Heeren: every nation should have a unique political economic system that was adapted to the specific individual needs of the nation in question.[71]

Heeren described the ancient world in terms of a pluralistic state system. Due to its geography, the Greek world, in particular, was fragmented politically. This fragmentation was also the main cause for the existence of political freedom. The Hellenic world, moreover, was, for Heeren, shaped by the coexistence of different nations and states with their own 'individuality' who together formed part of a larger cultural and economic community. Heeren was, in this respect, much influenced by Johann Gottfried von Herder, who had argued that world history was shaped by individual nations, each evolving along a unique path but together forming a world historical community.[72] This classical pluralist world was brought to an end as a result of the rise of an all-powerful Rome, the ancient equivalent of the contemporary Napoleonic Empire. The Roman Empire replaced the fragmented, but relatively free, dynamic, and creative Greek world with Rome's despotic, bleak, and stifling universal monarchy.

---

[69] I follow here mainly the interpretation of Christoph Becker-Schaum, *Heeren*, 134–51.

[70] In older historiography, Heeren is regarded as a follower of the views of Smith and Montesquieu. Later historians such as Seier have tended to emphasize the extent to which Heeren differed from eighteenth-century Scottish views on the political economy: Fueter, *Geschichte der neueren Historiographie*; Seier, 'Heeren und England'; Becker-Schaum, *Heeren*, 151–65.

[71] On the idea of the 'national economy' and the criticism of free trade in the post-revolutionary era: Nakhimovsky, *Closed Commercial State*.

[72] Becker-Schaum, *Heeren*, 105–7, 126–32. For the interpretation of Heeren as 'Herderadept': Schaumkell, *Geschichte der deutschen Kultur Geschichtsschreibung*. In his works, Herder had criticized what he regarded as the uniformity of dominant French enlightened history writing: [Herder], *Philosophie der Geschichte zur Bildung der Menschheit*.

Heeren drew explicit parallels between this Greek pluralist world and the politically fragmented European state system.[73] However, in his introduction to his history of the modern state system, Heeren also distanced both worlds and emphasized the unique nature of the European state system, which, in his view, far surpassed the ancient world in its historical importance, but also in the independence of, and the amount of freedom enjoyed by, its member states.[74] Heeren underscored, for instance, the differences between ancient and modern colonization: ancient colonization was not like modern colonization exclusively driven by commercial interests, but by other motives. The independence of colonial societies from the mother country in ancient times was primarily the result of the lack of interest of the metropole in its subsidiary, whereas in the eighteenth century, colonial independence was caused by the spread of revolutionary ideology.[75]

In 1797, the productive Heeren published a book on the reception of classical literature in European history as part of a larger history of the arts and sciences.[76] In this work he underscored the importance of the classical legacy in creating a common cultural reference for all European nations. This attempt was not a mere Eurocentric 'invention of antiquity'.[77] Heeren also included the role of the Arabs and Byzantines in the transmission of the classical texts to modern Europe, and underscored the 'global' influence of classical heritage. The description of the Middle Ages was ambiguous: the epoch was credited by Heeren with the preservation and survival of classical literature as well as its decline and general neglect. The revival of the classics in Renaissance Italy was described as a fundamental spiritual revolution in European history. By beginning to study the reception of the classical tradition rather than the ancient world itself, Heeren's scholarly interests gradually shifted from ancient to modern European history.

6. Rise of the Modern Balance

In his *Manual of the History of the European State System*, Heeren refused to give an idealized, abstract, and timeless idea of the modern state system. He considered this system above all as the result of a concrete historical development.[78] It could therefore be studied only through a historical narrative and not via an abstract and

---

[73] Heeren, *Handbuch*, 13. [74] Heeren, *Handbuch*, v–vi.
[75] Becker-Schaum, *Heeren*, 162–5.
[76] Heeren, *Geschichte des Studiums der Classischen Litteratur*: vol. IV and V in *Historische Werke*.
[77] Goody, *Theft of History*.
[78] The idea of a European 'order' or 'system' was, however, not an invention of the revolutionary decade, but already existed before the Revolution. A clear conception of a 'European system' can, for instance, already be found in Mably's *Principes de négociations* (1757), although the term 'European order' is not explicitly mentioned in this work. Belissa, *Repenser*, 42–6; Mably, *Principes des négociations*. On the eighteenth-century concept of European order: Lilti and Spector, *Penser*, 19–90.

philosophical analysis.[79] Heeren demarcated 'modern' European history, starting in the sixteenth century, from the 'medieval' and the 'ancient' periods. It was only in the sixteenth century that a true and integrated 'state system' was formed, Heeren wrote following Robertson. Although most of the European states that existed in the early modern period had their origins in the Middle Ages, from the sixteenth century onwards the relations between those states became much closer. Also, the 'newer history' of the sixteenth century marked a true caesura from the medieval period, due to a number of crucial events and new developments in that period: the conquest of Constantinople by the Ottoman Turks, the 'discovery' of the Americas and the Asian voyages of exploration by Vasco da Gama, and the 'military revolution' caused by the development of new weaponry and larger armies. Furthermore, due to its extensive colonial system and imperial possessions, Europe acquired in this era a universal and global importance it had not possessed earlier. From the sixteenth century onwards, European history became universal history.[80]

For Heeren, the European state system was, from the start, characterized by a 'monarchical' political culture. Although it also contained several republics, such as the Venetian, the Swiss, and the Dutch republics, republican constitutions were rare and peripheral in modern Europe in comparison to the world of classical Greece. As a result of the prevalence of the monarchy, the influence of common people on policies was overall limited. Heeren thus justified his exclusive historiographical focus on the cabinet politics of the different European states and the exclusion of ordinary people from political history. Despite the overall prevalence of the monarchical form of government, the European state system also showed a variety of different sorts of monarchies: absolutist, limited, and constitutional. Also, various constitutional types of republics could still be found. Heeren valued this constitutional pluralism positively: it explained the unusual dynamism of the European state system.[81] Within this pluralist system, the Holy Roman Empire formed the nucleus: this imperial entity, with its pluralist constitution, formed the key polity of the European commonwealth. In the long run, German history, more than any other national history, determined the overall course of European history, Heeren argued, as had, for instance, Müller.[82]

In accordance with eighteenth-century theories of the European balance, Heeren distinguished between an autonomous 'Northern' and a 'Southern' balance. The 'Northern' balance consisted of Sweden, Russia, Denmark, and Poland. The rest of the countries were part of the 'Southern system'. The Prussian monarchy was, according to Heeren, unique in the sense that it was part of both

---

[79] Heeren was, for instance, critical of Karl Ludwig Woltmann, whom he accused of writing his history of Europe from preconceived philosophical premises. Becker-Schaum, *Heeren*, 243.
[80] Heeren, *Handbuch* I, 6–9. 'Europa erhalt in diesem Zeitraum eine universalhistorische Wichtigkeit, wie es dieselbe noch nie vorher gehabt hatte' (7).
[81] Heeren, *Handbuch* I, 9–11.   [82] Heeren, *Handbuch* I, 11.

the Northern and Southern systems, occupying a central and mediating position. A key feature of Heeren's history was the integration of the Northern and Southern systems into one pan-European system in the Napoleonic era. The main division within Europe in Heeren's historical ordering was thus not between East and West, but between the Northern and Southern parts of the continent.[83]

The states system was buttressed by several 'supports' (*stützen*), which guaranteed the legal character of the European order. To begin with, the state system was underpinned by the law of nations as described by authorities such as Pufendorf, Vattel, and Martens. In this idea of international law, Heeren included not only the formal treaties between the powers, but also the unwritten custom and usages. For him, the core of the international law was the mutual recognition of property. The second support was the protection of the 'independence' and 'freedom' of all participating states, even those of second or third rank, in accordance with the idea of 'political equilibrium' (*Politischen Gleichgewicht*). Hegemony of one state over the others should be prevented at all times by the coalitions of the remaining countries. A crucial role in keeping the balance was played by the 'sea powers', such as Britain and the Netherlands. These sea powers could guarantee the balance when it was threatened by expanding continental nations. This balance, Heeren insisted, in agreement with the balance theorists described in earlier chapters, was not a flawless system or a utopia. In contrast to the allegedly unrealistic and dangerous revolutionary ideal of perfect freedom, the best we can hope for, in Heeren's view, is that the balance system would prevent the worst abuses and hinder the rise of a despotic hegemon.[84]

The state system, furthermore, was sustained by the familial relationships between European noble families. The European republic could be regarded as, in essence, a network of Europe's aristocratic families. These informal contacts, and in particular the role of German princesses who were married to many European crowned heads, played an important role as the lubricant in Europe's internal affairs. A further common trait that all European states shared was their Germanic origin. Most European constitutions could be traced back to their origins in Germanic societies after the collapse of the Roman Empire.[85] Historical institutions such as the privileged orders of nobility and clergy, as well as the free urban citizens and the representative assemblies, all breathed this free spirit of the early German tribes. A final support of the European system was the 'limited' and 'moderate' nature of European monarchies. Compared to other parts of the world, European kings were relatively dependent upon their subjects, for instance when raising taxes for warfare, and often asked for their consent. The example of the

---

[83] On the history of the North–South and East–West intra-European geopolitical dichotomy: Rodríguez Pérez, 'Being Eurocentric', and Drace-Francis, 'Elephant'; Mishkova and Trencsényi, *European Regions*.

[84] Heeren, *Handbuch* I, 13.   [85] See Chapter 2.

failed policies of Philip II and Louis XIV demonstrated, according to Heeren, the fate of the European monarch who acted without the consent of his people.[86]

In his *Manual*, Heeren identified three distinct periods in the stadial and progressive development of the state system. The first two periods were clearly demarcated, whereas the last period lacked a well-defined ending. The first period, the 'rise' (*Entstehung*) of the state system, started in the late fifteenth century and ended in the late seventeenth century. This period was characterized by the interrelation of religious and political strife. The starting point of Heeren's narrative was fifteenth-century Italy, the main theatre of European political life at that time. Heeren praised Italy for its cultural achievements but argued that it had lost its independence as a result of the selfishness of the Italian political class. In the ensuing struggle over dominance on the Italian peninsula between France and the Habsburg ruler Charles V, the modern European state system was formed, as other European countries such as England and the Ottoman Empire joined the fight. Also, the state system at this moment acquired its unique characteristics or supports described earlier, above all the principle of the equilibrium between the powers. Heeren's judgement of Charles V was ambivalent: referring to Robertson's history, on the one hand, he praised Charles' cosmopolitan and European ambitions, while, on the other, his policies to restore Europe's political and religious unity were deemed by Heeren a failure.[87]

The nascent state system was fundamentally transformed and further developed by the coming of the Reformation and the religious wars. As a result of the Reformation, Germany became the new Europe's political centre stage, replacing the Italian peninsula. In particular for the German lands, the religious reforms were a double-edged sword, at once a 'principle of division' (*Spaltung*) as well as a 'principle of political life'. The influence of the Reformation had already been discussed by Heeren in his earlier work, an essay on the 'political consequences of the Reformation on Europe', which he submitted to a prize contest of the French National Institute in 1802. In this essay, Heeren argued that European history was the product of three violent collisions: the Crusades, the Reformation, and the French Revolution. Although each of these historical events may have been horrific experiences for contemporaries and caused many casualties and suffering, at the same time they also had a positive impact on European society. Despite—or perhaps as a result of—their destructiveness, these events were also creative moments: Europe's dynamism was the main result of these gruesome moments of turmoil and war.[88] Periods of war and large-scale violence, regrettable as they

---

[86] Heeren, *Handbuch* I, 13–17.   [87] Heeren, *Handbuch* I, 44–57.
[88] Heeren, 'Folgen der Reformation für Europa', 5–17. On the Crusades: Heeren, 'Folgen der Kreuzzüge'.

may be for those who lived through them, were also eras of change and renewal, and thus crucial times for the shaping of European civilization.[89]

As a result of the Reformation, Heeren argued, monarchs enhanced their power, and the political role of the clergy diminished. Moreover, freedom of conscience was enlarged in Protestants countries, followed by Catholic ones that followed the Protestant example. Nonetheless, Heeren, in the tradition of eighteenth-century religious Enlightenment, nuanced the difference between an allegedly liberal Protestantism and a supposedly illiberal Catholicism: despotism and freedom could be found among both Protestant and Catholic countries.[90] Republicanism, though, no doubt was more prevalent in the Protestant world. Also, as a precursor to Max Weber, Heeren argued that the Protestant ethic stimulated the development of worldwide commerce, in particular by Protestant England, the Dutch Republic, and the cities of Northern Germany. Protestantism also provided a stimulus for colonialism and European expansion to the Americas and other parts of the world. Finally, the Reformation greatly expanded the state system as a result of smaller Protestant countries resisting the attempts of the Catholic Habsburg Empire to stamp out Protestantism.[91]

With his origins in the enlightened Protestant city of Bremen, Heeren's views on the Reformation were moderately positive. In a lecture he gave in Göttingen to commemorate the tricentennial of the Reformation in 1817, Heeren, above all, emphasized the resemblances between the Reformation and the Enlightenment. Sixteenth-century reformers practised independent research and preached the freedom of conscience, in contrast to the Catholic scholastics of the time. Eventually, and over the course of many centuries, Protestant reform led to a moderate and reasonable Christianity in the spirit of Immanuel Kant and David Hume. The true Enlightenment was thus immersed in Protestant and Christian principles. Also, the Reformation had a profound, positive influence on social life, such as through the improvement of morals and societal progress, as demonstrated by the examples of advanced countries such as England, the Netherlands, and the United States.[92]

Heeren condemned the religious fanaticism he discerned in the sixteenth century, as exemplified in his eyes by the Jesuit Order and the French Catholic League. But he reserved his praise for those leaders he regarded as 'moderates', such as the French king Henri IV, the Dutch rebel leader William of Orange, and the British queen Elizabeth I. These rulers valued peace, stability, and the interest

---

[89] This 'dynamic' view of the Reformation as the harbinger of change and renewal in European history influenced the writing about the Reformation by Charles de Villers (1765–1815), a French revolutionary exiled in Göttingen. Printy, 'Protestantism and Progress', 326. On Heeren and Villers: Marino, *Praeceptores*.
[90] On the 'religious Enlightenment': Kley, *Religious Origins*; Sorkin, *Religious Enlightenment*; Beutel and Nooke, *Religion und Aufklärung*; van der Wall and Wessels, V*eelzijdige verstandhouding*.
[91] Heeren, 'Folgen der Reformation für Europa'.   [92] Heeren, 'Anhang'.

of the state more than religious purity and could therefore be regarded as the precursors of eighteenth-century religious enlightened spirit, Heeren wrote approvingly.[93] The main theatre of European history at the end of the sixteenth century was the Low Countries. The Dutch struggle against the 'universal hegemony' of the Spanish king Philip II shaped the character of the entire European equilibrium. The rise of the Dutch Republic was crucial in Heeren's eyes, not because it was a republic, but because it was a 'sea power'. These new types of sea powers, such as the Dutch Republic and later England, played a crucial role in keeping the balance on the continent.[94]

The wars of the seventeenth century acted as a catalyst for the development of the European state system. Continuous warfare destroyed traditional constitutions and regimes, enabling the renewal of political arrangements. The German Thirty Years' War almost destroyed the imperial constitution, consequently stimulating discussion of reform of imperial authority as well as instigating demand for more popular political representation. Westphalian peace reconfirmed the foundations of the state system and partly restored the German imperial constitution. Heeren nuanced the interpretation of Westphalian peace as a radical rupture in European international history, an interpretation shared by later historians.[95] In the English civil wars of the seventeenth century, furthermore, new ideas of political freedom were crafted. These ideas spread to the United States and, ultimately, would find their way back in a 'poisoned form' to the European continent, laying the ideological foundations for the late eighteenth-century Revolutions.[96] For Heeren, the seeds of Revolution were already sown in the sixteenth-century Reformation, although he did not explicitly link Protestantism and the revolutionary legacy as did many Catholic writers such as Feller, Maistre, or Vogt.

7. Consolidation, Decline, and Restoration

The second period, the time of 'consolidation'(*Befestigung*), began with the reign of the French king Louis XIV (1643–1715) and ended with the French Revolution of 1789. In Heeren's eyes, 'military mercantilism' dominated this second phase in the evolution of the international system. The central theme for Heeren in this period was the unhindered growth of commerce and international trade, which

---

[93] Heeren, *Handbuch* I, 128.
[94] Heeren, *Handbuch* I, 115. The role of 'sea powers' in the equilibrium is more extensively discussed by Heeren in his article on British continental politics: Heeren, *Britischen Continental-Interesse*, 113–343. Heeren noted that for sea powers, in contrast to land powers, commercial interests were inseparably linked to politics and diplomacy.
[95] Heeren, *Handbuch* I, 163–4. Cf. Duchhardt, *Westfälische Friede*.
[96] Heeren, *Handbuch* I, 172.

went beyond the control of monarchical states. In contrast to Montesquieu and the Scottish political economists, Heeren was less positive about the effects of the '*doux commerce*', as we have already seen in his history of the ancient world. The development of commerce led, in Heeren's view, to an increasing inequality and intense rivalry between states. Trade became a cause for war and large-scale conflict, which dominated the late seventeenth and eighteenth centuries.[97]

Politically, the late seventeenth century was determined by the attempts of the French king Louis XIV to achieve universal monarchy and dominate the state system on the European continent. This attempt failed as the international coalition that blocked the French attempts, led by the Anglo-Dutch stadtholder-king William of Orange, possessed a more efficient financial system and, therefore, had more access to funds. Finances decided the outcome of the war in this era. Heeren observed that, although the French attempts to dominate the continent failed in a military and political sense, they were successful in cultural terms. The eighteenth century was the age of French cultural and linguistic imperialism, Heeren wote with disapproval. Heeren's analysis also foreshadowed many later studies on the absolutist monarchy, by stating that even Louis XIV's rule, despite its reputation, was not truly absolutist in real terms, as the Sun King had to share power with the French nobles and clergy.[98]

Heeren's view on Europe's eighteenth century was ambiguous. On the one hand, the early eighteenth century was characterized by an increasing interdependence of the European states and the consolidation of the state system. The states of Europe became more integrated than ever before, which Heeren saw as a positive development. Also, the arts and the sciences blossomed in this century. Wealth increased through the growth of commerce and trade. States increasingly could rely on the 'sciences of the state' (*Staatswissenschaften*) to implement successful policies and augment their powers over the lives of their subjects. In Germany, literary activities reached new heights and German nobles were placed on the thrones of Europe. Yet, the eighteenth century also had its darker sides. The increasing uniformity of the dominant Francophone cultural life threatened Europe's tradition of cultural diversity. With the rise of enlightened *philosophie*, atheism spread and started to undermine the European Christian foundations. In the new world of public opinion, writers had become more powerful than princes and ministers, a dangerous development in Heeren's eyes. Outwardly, the eighteenth century was an age of brilliance and light, but inwardly the rot had started to destroy the foundations of the European system, Heeren wrote in the tradition of the eighteenth-century *anti-philosophes*.[99]

---

[97] Heeren, *Handbuch* I, 210–12. Heeren praised, in particular, Justi's two-volume *Staatswirtschaft* (1755) as the key work to understanding this period in European history.
[98] Heeren, *Handbuch* I, 238–9.   [99] Heeren, *Handbuch* II, 5–9.

Heeren interestingly emphasized, much in the vein of the new school of international history, the close connection between culture and international relations. As a result of the spread of enlightened materialism by French *philosophes*, the state increasingly came to be regarded as a mere 'machine', to be governed on the basis of insights derived only from mathematics and statistics. The moral and spiritual dimensions of the legal and political institutions were lost in these so-called enlightened states. Also, they no longer had respect for the historical boundaries of state power. As a result, these states became solely interested in acquiring new and homogeneous territory, leading to new and unjust wars of conquest. The main victim was the Polish state, which was divided between Prussia, Russia, and Austria. But also, the German lands and Italy were threatened by power-hungry machine states.[100] Heeren did not stand alone in his criticism of the purely rational and machine-like conception of the state he associated with the enlightened *philosophie*.[101] As we have seen, the emphasis on the moral nature of the state was a common theme of most *anti-philosophe* and counter-revolutionary authors. For Heeren, the state was above all a moral entity.[102] The state was not an abstract idea, but historically grown, concrete, and unique. Heeren shared these ideas with Adam Müller, who had dedicated his *Elemente der Staatskunst* to his 'teacher and friend' Arnold Heeren.[103]

In Heeren's eyes, the case of France was representative of the eighteenth-century state system, in the sense that it presented an outwardly strong and autocratic façade, but its internal state institutions were weak and rotten. The late eighteenth-century Holy Roman Empire was also increasingly incapable of implementing crucial reforms, and it was weakened by the struggle for dominance between Austria and Germany. Heeren's take on Prussia was ambivalent. He admired Prussia's economic development and its freedom of conscience. But he also warned that Prussia's autocratic rule was an anomaly vis-à-vis the German tradition of moderate monarchical rule. Also, the functioning of the Prussian state was too dependent on the mortal person of King Frederick the Great. In the Northern state system, the Russian empress Catherine strove for hegemony and duly threatened the pluralist character of the Northern system. The expansion of Russia also posed a mortal danger to the survival of the Ottoman Empire.[104] The suppression of the Jesuit Order by the pope was an omen of the future fate of the entire European *ancien régime*. On the one hand, as a moderate Protestant, Heeren had little sympathy for this, in his eyes, intolerant and power-hungry

---

[100] Heeren, *Handbuch* II, 50–69.
[101] On the metaphor of the state as machine: Stollberg-Rilinger, *Staat als Machine*; Graaf, *Terreur*, 95–8.
[102] Heeren, 'Schreiben an einen Freund', lxv and *Handbuch* I, vi. Heeren did not elaborate on his theory of the state in theoretical publications, other than through his historical writings on the state system.
[103] On the relationship between Heeren and Müller: Becker-Schaum, *Heeren*, 107.
[104] Heeren, *Handbuch* II, 139–60.

religious order with its roots in the Catholic Counter-Reformation. On the other, he was also suspicious of the radicalism of 'atheistic sophists' and their agents in the monarchical governments. As the Jesuit Order no longer presented a real threat to political and religious freedom in the late eighteenth century, Heeren preferred reforming instead of destroying this Catholic order.[105]

The third period of Heeren's *Manual*, the 'constitutional era', was the dramatic story of the decline, fall, and restoration of the state system in recent times.[106] This part of the book was the hardest to write, Heeren confessed apologetically, in the introduction to the third edition of the *Manual* in response to criticism of the earlier editions. Recent history was the most difficult to interpret and to periodize due to the lack of temporal distance from events. Heeren argued that it would be historians in the twentieth century who would be able to make definitive periodization in this epoch of the state system. However, in contrast to those who regarded the Revolution as an absolute rupture in historical time, Heeren underscored continuities in the development of the state system from the pre-revolutionary to the post-revolutionary world, taking part in the wider historiographical attempt to fit the Revolution into the 'normal' course of European history.[107]

At the time of death of Frederick the Great in 1786, the rot of the system had thus already progressed, although outwardly it still seemed to function perfectly. The 'machine states' had become autocratic bureaucracies, ruthlessly striving for power and land, breaking with the historical traditions of moderate, moral, and wise rule. The first and second estates, as a result of the development of state power, had lost all their function in society, but still continued to hold on to their privileges. Subversive ideas such as Rousseau's dangerous concept of 'popular sovereignty' were disseminated by atheistic *philosophes* to the wider population. The increasingly equal footing of enlightened sociability stood in contrast with the unequal historical manners and traditions of the monarchical state. Secret societies such as the German *Illuminati* consequently started to plot the downfall of the existing order. The development of public opinion and the free press undermined the authority of monarch and church leaders. Notwithstanding these fundamental changes, few contemporaries accurately predicted the seismic changes that would rock the state system as a result of the French Revolution.[108]

The chain of events that would lead to the collapse of continental monarchies started, for Heeren, in the Low Countries. During his travels, Heeren had personally witnessed the rise of the Dutch 'Patriots' against the stadtholderate regime, and its violent repression by a Prussian army in 1787 was the first domino in a long sequence. The Dutch Patriot 'revolution' was followed by 'democratic' uprisings in the Southern Netherlands and Liège. When revolution also broke

---

[105] Heeren, *Handbuch* II, 56–9. [106] Heeren, *Handbuch* II, 17.
[107] Heeren, *Handbuch* II, 164–72. [108] Heeren, *Handbuch* II, 164–72.

out in France in the spring of 1789, it thus formed part of a wider European movement. Heeren noted that in 1789 few contemporaries in Europe were aware of the danger of the Revolution: in the Holy Roman Empire and elsewhere, a general enthusiasm at first erupted in favour of the revolutionaries and their aims.[109]

Those few early prophetic voices that criticized the Revolution, such as Edmund Burke, Ernst Brandes, or Wilhelm Rehberg, were not listened to in the beginning and were even mocked, Heeren wrote ruefully.[110] The European cabinets generally did not know how to respond to this new phenomenon of the revolutionary regime, as it did not fit into the traditions of the state system. The war that erupted between the revolutionary armies and the international coalition was, according to Heeren, echoing Edmund Burke, unlike all other wars of the eighteenth century. It represented a struggle over constitutional ideas (*Verfassungen*) rather than a fight over mere military dominance.[111] The allied coalition lost the war due to its 'enlightened egoism': cabinets followed only their particular interests and did not champion the common European interest. The funding of the war was provided by England with the sole motive of capturing trade from the Dutch and the French for its own commercial profit.[112]

Heeren termed the French Revolution 'the great catastrophe'.[113] Like Calonne, Heeren argued that he was not in principle opposed to the idea of a written constitution, as long as this constitution was built on historical foundations and not on abstract and radical philosophical ideas. This turned out not to be the case with the French revolutionaries. Their main flaws were from the start their radical attempt to abruptly break with the old order, their championing of the 'dangerous' concept of 'popular sovereignty', and the radical separation between legislative and executive power. The monarchy that had been created under the revolutionary constitution of 1791 was, in Heeren's eyes, no more than a sham, a monarchy in appearance only. He regarded the radical phase and the politics of the Terror, which he did not discuss at length, not as an anomaly, but as the logical outcome of the revolutionary doctrines.

Like Calonne and other counter-revolutionary authors, Heeren did not regard the Thermidor regime as an end but as a continuation of revolutionary policies, its moderate face masking a radical core. Through its military victories, the revolutionary Republic spread its ideas all over Europe under the guise of 'eternal peace', destroying the ancient foundations of the state system.[114] As the result of the revolutionary wars, the Northern and the Southern state system had become one new united international order, dominated in the West by revolutionary France and in the East by despotic tsarist Russia. Prussia was sandwiched between the two

---

[109] Heeren, *Handbuch* II, 174–80.
[110] Heeren, *Handbuch* II, 180. Cf. Tijsterman, 'Rehberg'.
[111] Heeren, *Handbuch* II, 184–5.
[112] Heeren, *Handbuch* II, 185–200.
[113] Heeren, *Handbuch* II, 180.
[114] Heeren, *Handbuch* II, 201–10.

hegemons. The Holy Roman Empire was on its last legs, its final dissolution in 1806 marking the definitive collapse of the state system, and the ancient edifice was overthrown.

The final part of the book told the dramatic story of Napoleon's attempt to achieve a 'universal monarchy' by destroying the European system, and his ultimate failure to do so.[115] For Heeren, Napoleon was essentially a new Roman emperor who demanded to be glorified and exalted by the subject populations. Napoleon had built his imperial system step by step, so he only had to change the name in 1804 to fit the new political reality. By deposing the European dynasties and filling the thrones with his own family members, Napoleon fundamentally undermined the idea of legitimacy and traditional authority. The establishment of the federation of the Rhine was only one step in Napoleon's plan to dismantle the Holy Roman Empire, and, with the Empire, the entire European system, to be replaced by a continent-wide dictatorship. In contrast to Vogt, who believed Napoleon to be saviour of the Germans, for Heeren Napoleon was their nemesis.[116] At the Peace of Tilsit, Napoleon had even subjected the last bastion of the German nation, Prussia. The paradoxical international effect of Napoleon's policies was the supremacy of British ships on the oceans. Napoleon's rule was, for Heeren, part of the tradition of neither the moderate nor the absolutist monarchy: de facto it was an oriental despotism, the third monarchical category Heeren had described. In 1809, Europe had effectively become one large prison with Napoleon as its warden.[117]

The extreme arrogance and violent character of Napoleon, however, would eventually lead to his downfall. He spoiled the opportunity that his marriage to a Habsburg princess offered him to transform himself into a moderate monarch and return to the honoured European constitutional traditions. Instead, his blind thirst for power led him to expand his military campaigns. The losses in Spain were a first sign that this emperor was not invincible. The military defeats on the Russian plains, vividly described by Heeren, finally turned all of Europe against the usurper. The defining moment was the Battle of the Nations in Leipzig (1813), where the imperial chains were finally broken by the allied European armies. In Heeren's story, it was above all a unified German nation that had defeated the French despot, supporting the myth of the 'German wars of liberation'.[118] Napoleon's unexpected and failed return in the Hundred Days War, were, in Heeren's eyes, only the destructive and final desperate acts of a madman.

In the third edition of the manual, published after the fall of Napoleon, he showed himself a rather uncritical supporter of the Vienna order that had come into being in 1814 and 1815. In his history, Heeren wholeheartedly supported the return of Europe's old dynasties from exile, providing a good example of the close

---

[115] Heeren, *Handbuch* II, 274.
[116] Heeren, *Handbuch* II, 288–9.
[117] Heeren, *Handbuch* II, 320.
[118] Heeren, *Handbuch* II, 325–60; Cf. Planert, *Mythos*.

relationship between politics and history writing at this moment. The French king Louis XVIII was portrayed by Heeren as a wise and forgiving 'moderate', in accordance with the rhetoric of that regime itself.[119] He credited the European monarchs assembled in Vienna with the restoration of the old European state system on a new footing. This reconstruction Heeren considered to be the most important event in world history. He especially praised the practical nature of the Treaty of Vienna and the fact that it was not a utopian document. The Vienna peace was, for him, based on the principles of moderation, freedom, reason, and independence.[120] The newly established German confederation would act as Europe's 'peace state', Heeren hopefully predicted, forming the cornerstone of a peaceful as well as pluralistic monarchical order.[121] A new balance had now been achieved between the great powers who, 'sadder and wiser', no longer lusted after more territory, as they had in the eighteenth century. A restored and renewed European 'aristocracy' would keep the peace and stability through diplomatic conferences and conflict resolution. The stability of this new political order was furthermore cemented by the ecumenical Christian community.

According to Heeren, the Vienna peace was not the work of reactionaries, but instead allowed for a fair amount of popular participation in the decision-making process and gave a large role to the voice of public opinion, without admitting any dangerous notions such as popular sovereignty. This reasonable post-Napoleonic system differed from the pre-revolutionary order, in the sense that the European states all had a more uniform monarchical system, founded on the 'monarchical principle'. This post-revolutionary 'modern' principle of a constitutional and rational monarchy serving the people without allowing them active citizenship was nothing new, Heeren wrote elsewhere, as the idea had already been formulated by eminent political philosophers centuries ago, such as Bodin, Grotius, and Hobbes. As these classic philosophers had argued, according to Heeren, a stable and felicitous state could be guaranteed only if undivided sovereignty was placed in the hands of a wise monarch, who wielded both executive and legislative power, with the representative assemblies consigned to the important—but restricted—role of providing advice on matters of internal affairs.[122]

Heeren's narrative of the history of the state system ended with his description of the conference of Aix-la-Chapelle in 1818, when the decision was made to end the allied occupation of France. The era of Revolution could finally be closed, politically as well as historiographically, Heeren wrote confidently in his counter-revolutionary version of the 'End of History' narrative.[123] Despite their turmoil and casualties, the horrendous revolutionary and Napoleonic wars were not

---

[119] Kroen, *Politics and Theatre*; Lok and Scholz, 'Loving Father'.
[120] Heeren, *Handbuch* II, 363–75.   [121] Heeren, *Handbuch* II, 419.
[122] Heeren, 'monarchischen Prinzips', 365–451.   [123] Cf. Jones, '1816'.

without meaning in the long-term perspective of the evolution of European history. The revolutionary wars made possible a fundamental overhaul of a state system that had been corrupted in the decades before the Revolution. The experience of the revolutionary wars made Europe's monarchs aware that the international order should not be founded on rational and opportunistic principles alone, but ought to consist of a moral and spiritual order as well. This new and regenerated state system had sound and solid supports, if only because memories of the horrific recent past still haunted his contemporaries. However, as the historian Heeren wrote, no human constitutional construction was ever without its flaws, and history would not stop running its course.[124]

8. Empire and State System

One of the most remarkable aspects of Heeren's handbook was the extensive attention given to the colonial and extra-European dimension. Heeren did not regard colonial history as separate from 'mainstream' European political history.[125] This 'global' perspective on European history was not a new phenomenon in the *Manual*. Already in his studies of ancient history, Heeren had studied the classical world from Asian (Indian) and African perspectives rather than from an exclusively European one, although it should be pointed out that he read sources only in Western languages.[126] So, for him, it was only natural to look beyond the boundaries of the geographical European continent. His argument was that extra-European developments to a large extent determined intra-European developments. The *Manual* described an ever-increasing integration of the intra- and extra-European world. Of course, colonial history had been written by eighteenth-century enlightened historians. Heeren mentioned the older works by Raynal, de Pradt, and Eichhorn among his sources.[127]

In his narrative of the first period of the development of the state system, Heeren described the Spanish and Portuguese settlements in the Americas in the sixteenth century. He examined how 'copies' of European states were formed in South America by Spanish and Portuguese *conquistadores*. His verdict is, on the whole, negative. Heeren condemned the inhumane treatment of the native inhabitants of the Americas, abundantly citing the classic source of Bartholomew de la Casas (1484–1566). He also disapproved of the unequal colonial 'caste societies', that had come into being, where social positions were assigned on the basis of race

---

[124] 'Denn was wir als Menschen bauen, bleibt nie fehlerfrei!' Heeren, *Handbuch* II, 456.
[125] As Heeren wrote in the introduction to the *Manual*: 'the history of these colonies forms an integral part of the history of the European state system'. Heeren, *Handbuch* I, 8.
[126] See the fourth section of this chapter (p. 205–7).
[127] On the debate on empire and colonialism: Israel, *Democratic Enlightenment*, 413–608.

and colour.[128] In contrast to, for instance, François-Xavier de Feller, Heeren decried the 'cruel' slave trade as a disgrace.[129]

The Protestant Dutch republic and England, who took over from Spain and Portugal in the seventeenth century as the main drivers of the European colonial project, however, did not fare much better than their predecessors and made many of the same mistakes, Heeren wrote regretfully. Notwithstanding, Heeren clearly preferred the Protestant colonial projects of the English, Dutch, and Northern Germans in North America over the Catholic ones in South America, as more in line with notions of civilization and progress. He underscored the importance of the Reformation on European colonization.[130] Heeren fits, in this respect, into the analysis of Jorge Cañizares-Esguerra of the neglect and underappreciation of Catholic and Spanish colonialism in South America by Northern European Protestant historians.[131] At the same time, Heeren also concluded that the influence of the European states on the colonial trade was limited and that private enterprises had been dominant in oceanic commerce.

The role of the colonies greatly increased, in the second period, the consolidation of the state system in the era of military mercantilism, as a result of the rise of the 'sea powers' and the increase in international commerce.[132] Also, the eighteenth century marked the entry of France as a major colonial player, establishing many plantations in the Caribbean, and the rise of new colonial powers such as Denmark. Older sea powers, such as the Netherlands, consolidated their hold over their colonial possessions. Heeren described the events in an analytical and chronological manner, without much criticism or moral indignation. He once again posed as the 'impartial' historian, who merely analysed and did not judge, and as a citizen of a country without an important colonial history itself. He observed that in this period, the large-scale continental warfare, which so characterized the seventeenth century, had become situated in extra-European colonial theatres a century later. He predicted that in the future Europe would not only export its wars, but that colonial wars would also be exported to the European continent.[133]

The Declaration of American Independence in 1776 was regarded by Heeren as a crucial event, not only in colonial, but also in world history, without explicitly endorsing or criticizing this document. The birth of the United States resulted, in the eyes of Heeren, in the rise of a strong 'European' state outside the European state system. This revolutionary new state did not abide by the rules of this state system: it was economically independent, it did not possess a standing army, and

---

[128] Heeren, *Handbuch* I, 87–90.
[129] Heeren referred here to the publications on African slavery by Schlözer's pupil Matthias Christian Sprengel (1746–1803).
[130] Heeren, 'Folgen der Reformation für Europa', 100–4.
[131] Cañizares-Esguerra, *History of the New World*.   [132] Heeren, *Handbuch* I, 209.
[133] Heeren, *Handbuch* I, 93–136.

it also did not conduct a monarchical cabinet policy. Moreover, Heeren observed a direct relationship between the type of colonial settlement and its political development. Agricultural colonies with small farmers, such as the English North American colonies, tended to develop towards independence and democracy, whereas plantations or commercial colonies, for instance in the Caribbean, did not.[134] Surprisingly, the British Empire did not suffer from the U.S. gaining its independence, Heeren wrote. The British strengthened their imperial hold over other parts of the Americas, Africa, and, in particular, over India and its Asian possessions. Also, Heeren referred to the abuses, citing Edmund Burke's role in the Hastings trial. The competitors France and the Dutch Republic increasingly lagged behind Britain in the colonial competition, the Dutch colonies in particular plagued by stagnation and decline.[135]

In this chapter, Heeren also dared to reflect in more general terms on the phenomenon of European colonial adventures. His overall judgement was ambiguous. On the one hand, he stated that the European colonial project was born out of greed. He also pointed to the inhumane treatment and oppression of the colonized peoples, citing Edmund Burke on India, among others. At the same time, in line with his view on the Crusades, this negative experience also had a positive impact on European civilization. Imperialism and colonialism created a dynamic and opened up great prospects for Europeans. Europeans brought progress and their superior civilization to other parts of the world, Heeren argued, and should do this even more in the future, foreshadowing liberal imperialist thought.[136] In a true Enlightenment vein, Heeren believed that the other continents would eventually develop along the same lines as the Europeans. Heeren clearly showed himself as part of the school of Enlightenment criticism of European colonial expansions, following Raynal, Burke, and others. At the same time, despite his criticism of early colonial policies and practices, he did not in principle oppose the idea of extra-European expansion itself.[137]

In the era of the French Revolution, colonial developments were more than ever integrated into the European state system. In general, Heeren seemed to sympathize with the yearning for independence among the peoples of the European colonies, deeming them reasonable and inevitable. He discerned a longer trend of proclaiming independence, starting with the Dutch Republic in the sixteenth century, to be followed by the American republic, and culminating in many new states in the Western hemisphere. Like Edmund Burke, Heeren saw the role of the United States overall as a positive one and applauded in principle the independence of South American countries. However, he condemned the slave revolts and

---

[134] Heeren, *Handbuch* II, 103.
[135] Heeren conformed to the overall negative view of Dutch colonies in the eighteenth century: Israel, *Democratic Enlightenment*, 535–57.
[136] Pitts, *Turn to Empire*.   [137] Heeren, *Handbuch* II, 134.

the revolution in Haiti as premature and destructive. The resulting independent state of Haiti he characterized as 'curious' and certainly not worthy of admiration. The countries of the West Indies would, as a result, come out of the revolutionary decades in worse shape. Heeren supported the abolition of the slave trade through British intervention during the Restoration, though. At the same time, he also pointed out the practical difficulties accompanying the abolition, taking—in his own eyes, at least—a relatively 'moderate' stance in this respect.[138]

Heeren also signalled that Africa had come into the view of Europeans as a result of the independence of the American states, noting that 'a new world has dawned' for European eyes, and that they now had an opportunity to bring Enlightenment and progress to this 'forgotten' continent. For Asia, the main effect of the revolutionary wars was only the enhancement of British colonial power and a further weakening and even loss of Dutch Asian colonial possessions, which Heeren did not mourn, as he deemed them backward and badly managed. Overall, the effect of the French revolutionary and Napoleonic wars, for Heeren, was a weakening of Europe's role in the world and the coming into existence of many newly independent nations outside the state system. Britain's imperial dominance, furthermore, had become almost hegemonic as a result of the revolutionary wars.[139]

Heeren's ambiguous stance vis-à-vis European colonialism was also clearly expressed in his essay on the potential colonization of Egypt. He wrote this essay in 1803, during the ascendancy of Napoleon and with the memories of his Egyptian campaign still fresh. In this text, he started out by pointing to the pernicious effects of European colonialism, such as violence and oppression. He was particularly critical of the Spanish colonial conquests, which, in his eyes, were primarily based on coercion and enslavement. Also, colonial conquest would lead to jealousy and increased competition among the members of the state system. Notwithstanding these objections, in this essay Heeren glowingly described the potential of Egypt as a European colony, perhaps foreshadowing early twentieth-century plans for pan-European African colonies.[140] Climate and soil would make Egypt ideal for a diverse colonial agriculture.

Heeren foresaw a potential hazard in the presence of Islam-inspired religious fanaticism in this region, but these risks were manageable, Heeren wrote optimistically. In particular, states from Central and Eastern Europe such as Russia and Austria, who, compared to the Atlantic powers, did not possess substantial extra-European possessions, could profit from Egypt's colonial potential. Interestingly, Heeren dreamed of Egypt as a pan-'European' colony, from which all European states could profit. Greece would gain its independence and the borders of the backward Ottoman Empire would be reduced. From Egypt, the Barbary corsairs could be expelled, and a European-controlled security regime set in place.

---

[138] Heeren, *Handbuch* II, 211–22.   [139] Heeren, *Handbuch* II, 376–98.
[140] Coudenhove-Kalergi, *Pan-Europa*.

The Mediterranean could once again function as a middle sea between Europa, Africa, and Asia, the crossroads of commerce and trade under the control of the European powers.[141]

9. Conclusion: A Counter-Revolutionary Matrix

The political scientist Edward Keene credited Heeren with the invention of the modern idea of the 'state system' and his manual as the '*Ur-text*' of the research programme of the influential twentieth-century 'English school of international relations'.[142] Keene's book forms part of a larger academic endeavour to critically examine the history of the idea of the state system, and international history and law in general. In self-proclaimed contrast to the 'orthodox theory of order in world politics', these critical historians no longer regard the state system as a self-evident and purely analytical category but underscore the prescriptive character of this narrative.[143] Also, they reject the notion that the state system originated in Europe and then spread organically to the rest of the world. Instead, historians such as Marti Koskenniemi, Jennifer Pitts, and others have argued that international law and the related field of international history were increasingly restricted to the (Western half of the) European continent around 1800, with the rest of the world excluded from international law and increasingly made the subject of imperial domination.[144]

Keene sees a crucial role for Heeren in this development. Rather than pointing to Hugo Grotius and other early modern theorists of international law, Keene looked at early nineteenth-century political historians for the origins of the idea of the state system. For Keene, Heeren was a counter-revolutionary and 'reactionary' writer who conceptualized the state system as part of the battle against the Napoleonic Empire and the French Revolution.[145] Later scholars of the state system supposedly used his handbook, unconscious of the counter-revolutionary and conservative agenda underlying Heeren's ideas. David Armitage put this argument in even stronger words, naming the Counter-Revolution, with Heeren as its key representative, as the 'matrix' of the modern conception of international

---

[141] Heeren, 'Colonisation von Ägypten', 351–420. Cf. the dissertation by de Lange, 'Menacing Tides'.
[142] Keene, *Anarchical Society*, 14–26.
[143] Keene, *Anarchical Society*, 1–14. Cf. Pitts, 'International Relations', 282–98; Koskenniemi, *Uttermost Parts*. On the history of the state system: Devetak, 'Historiographical Foundations'; Muhlack, 'Staatensystem'; on the history of international history in general: Armitage, *Foundations*; Fitzmaurice, *Sovereignty*.
[144] Pitts, *Turn to Empire*; Pitts, *Boundaries*. Pitts unfortunately does not discuss the relevant works of Heeren. Heeren is also missing from the seminal book of Koskenniemi, who mainly discusses the case of Martens: Koskenniemi, *Gentle Civilizer*. See also Chapter 9.
[145] Keene, *Anarchical Society*, 16. Pitts, in a subtler way, underscored the relations between Counter-Revolution and (pluralist) historical narratives of the international system and law: Pitts, *Boundaries*, 120–33.

law. He regarded the modern notion of international society as the product of the counter-revolutionary and counter-enlightened ardour of the 1790s.[146]

Although I agree with Keene, and other critical historians, that we should regard the state system as a historical narrative crafted in a political context rather than as a neutral and ahistorical descriptive concept, Keene's analysis of Heeren is, in my view, flawed in three ways. To begin with, Heeren, as we have seen, was not a mere 'reactionary'. He, for instance, did not, as Keene suggested, reject American independence but instead welcomed it. He therefore cannot be simply typecast as an uncritical and devout supporter of a neo-absolutist monarchy. Furthermore, Heeren's views on Europe's role in the wider world and on the impact of empire on the state system cannot be described from the perspective of domination and Eurocentrism only, as they were much more ambivalent, as has been outlined in the preceding paragraph.[147] Finally, Heeren's *Manual* was not *sui generis* but, as Heeren himself argued, could build on the older Göttingen and German *Staatengeschichte*.

Heeren explicitly did not, in principle, object to written constitutions or the reform of abuses, but like most other writers featured in this book, he rejected the radical nature of revolutionary state building and its irresponsible use of abstract and universalizing concepts. Throughout his work, he championed the idea of a plural and free state system, in antiquity and in the contemporary world. His state system consisted of independent, free, and individual nations who together formed a commercial network, as well as a cultural and political community based on historically grown institutions. European monarchies were ideally characterized by moderation, and even absolutist European monarchies were, in Heeren's eyes, not as despotic as oriental states, guaranteeing their subjects private liberties while refusing them political rights. For Heeren, it was the Revolution that brought despotism, radicalism, extreme violence, and universal monarchy to the European continent in the name of abstract ideals. The experience of revolution and empire was both destructive and creative: it allowed the Europeans to build a regenerated and re-moralized new order on the ruins of the old world.

---

[146] Armitage, *Foundations*, 40–1.   [147] See also Chapter 9.

8
Vienna as a Missed Opportunity

1. La vacance du pouvoir

The invasion of Russia in 1812 marked the beginning of the end of the Napoleonic project.[1] At different times, proposals by Tsar Alexander to negotiate were rejected by Napoleon. The Battle of the Nations (*Völkerslacht* in German) at Leipzig on 16–19 October 1813 represented a turning point. Napoleonic rule all over Europe started to collapse, and the Napoleonic armies retreated to France. Despite several setbacks for the allies, on 31 March 1814, Tsar Alexander triumphantly entered Paris at the head of the allied troops. Napoleon subsequently surrendered unconditionally on 11 April 1814. On the third of May, in the trail of the allied troops, the brother of beheaded French King Louis XVI, made his entry into Paris as 'Louis XVIII, par grâce de Dieu, roi de France et de Navarre'.[2] The king had returned to France, marking an important political as well as temporal watershed.

This moment of transition from imperial authority to the restoration of the old dynasties between 1813 and 1815 could be termed '*la vacance du pouvoir*', or a power vacuum.[3] The imperial regime in France and elsewhere on the continent was not immediately replaced by the restored monarchy. The political scene for several months was characterized by confusion and misunderstandings. Alternative political ideas and legitimations competed and coexisted. All kinds of political outcomes became thinkable. The new regimes that eventually took shape in the years 1813–15 were the result of '*la force des choses*', to cite Tsar Alexander I, determined by circumstances, events (including an in-the-eyes-of-the-French humiliating foreign occupation), and the behaviour of individuals, rather than a preordained course of history or a grand design, although many later historians, such as Heeren, later discerned the hand of providence in this 'revolution' of 1814–15.[4]

Overnight the fate of royal émigrés changed dramatically. A good example of the fast-changing dynastic fortunes was Willem Frederik of Orange (1772–1843), the son of the last stadtholder of the Dutch Republic of the United Provinces. When the Napoleonic authority collapsed in the Netherlands and a provisional government was proclaimed in the name of the Prince of Orange on 17 November

---

[1] Lieven, *Russia Against Napoleon*.
[2] Lentz, *Nouvelle Histoire* II; Waresquiel and Yvert, *Restauration*.
[3] Bercé, *fin de l'Europe napoléonienne*. [4] Cited in Bertier de Sauvigny, *Restauration*, 41.

1813, the former forgotten exile Willem Frederik mobilized his envoys at the allied headquarters and returned on a British warship to become the first 'sovereign ruler', and in 1815 subsequently 'king', of the newly created United Kingdom of the Netherlands.[5] This newly constructed United Kingdom was an amalgam of the lands of the former Dutch Republic, the Austrian Netherlands, and the prince-bishopric of Liège. Its existence was justified with historical as well as with forward-looking arguments. Willem appealed, for instance, to the memory of the sixteenth-century Habsburg ruler Charles V and to his international duty in the new international order to control and watch over unruly France. Moreover, the new kingdom was presented as a vehicle of economic and industrial modernization.[6]

All over Europe exiled dynasties, such as the French Bourbons and the Orange family, returned to their native countries, resuming the reins of government. They all tried to repair the 'chain of time' and to forget the revolutionary interlude.[7] These restored monarchs at the beginning of their reigns tried to present themselves as caring and loving fathers who brought peace and prosperity, rather than vengeful kings who legitimized their rule with an appeal to divine right.[8] In most countries, the revolutionary and Napoleonic bureaucratic legacy of centralized government was not dismantled. The returned monarchs were only too glad to be able to make use of the formidable instrument of the Napoleonic bureaucracy. Many former Napoleonic officials became loyal servants of the restored monarchies, despite being labelled political 'weathervanes' in the popular press.[9] In Vogt's Rhineland, the new Prussian overlords were not regarded as liberators but as foreign conquerors.[10]

The unexpected collapse of the Napoleonic Empire presented contemporaries with a unique opportunity to reshape the international order. Counter-revolutionary imaginings of a new Europe, such as those described in the preceding chapters, could suddenly be implemented and no longer appeared chimerical. Writers such as Vogt, who had truly believed that Napoleon was the new Charlemagne, were profoundly disoriented and disillusioned. Others such as Gentz and Müller, who from the start had considered the Napoleonic regime essentially as a revolutionary chameleon and a military despotism, recognized the new opportunities that had opened up. The political revolution of 1814–15 was the moment when counter-revolutionary European narratives and plans, which had been developed in the preceding years, became closely intertwined with the actual political and institutional reordering of Europe itself.

---

[5] Koch, *Willem I*; de Graaf, 'Second-tier Diplomacy'.
[6] De Haan, den Hoed, and te Velde, *nieuwe staat*; Aerts and Deneckere, *(on) Verenigd Koninkrijk*; Lok, 'Ambivalent Memory'; Lok, *Windvanen*.
[7] Lok, '"oubli total"'; Caiani, 'Re-inventing the Ancien Regime'.
[8] Lok and Scholz, 'Loving Father'; Kroen, *Politics and Theater*.
[9] Laven and Riall, *Napoleon's Legacy*; Lok, *Windvanen*.   [10] Rowe, *Rhineland*; Planert, *Mythos*.

This chapter deals with the years 1814–15 as a moment of great expectations, but also of tremendous disappointment. For many counter-revolutionaries, Vienna was, in hindsight, a lost opportunity to create a truly regenerated Europe and to banish the spectre of revolution once and for all. Most of the historiography of these crucial years focusses on diplomatic history in a broad sense: my aim here is to connect the diplomatic creation of a new international order with counter-revolutionary ideas of European history and the newly minted tradition of 'historical Europeanism' sketched in the preceding chapters. The attempt to renew the European system in 1814–15 has to be understood in the context of yearning for a European spiritual and moral regeneration which could already be observed in the last decades of the eighteenth century. I will demonstrate the close interrelation of politics and history writing at this particular time. As we will see, contemporaries were very conscious of living in a unique historical moment and of their role in deciding Europe's future history.[11]

This chapter consists of three parts. In the next two sections, I will first examine the attempts to create a new international order at the Congress of Vienna between 1814 and 1818, which I will interpret as an enlightened endeavour, zooming in on the figure of Clemens von Metternich. In the following two sections, I will discuss the hopes for a European regeneration in the years 1814–15 among a wide variety of publicists of different political persuasions, highlighting the role of Christianity. The final sections, the third part, consider the sense of disillusion with the results of Vienna, felt not only by liberals, but also by counter-revolutionaries and conservatives alike. In particular, I will explore the case of the Catholic Sardinian diplomat Joseph de Maistre and his work *Du Pape* (1819), in which he explored an alternative European order centred around the historical role of the papacy. In the conclusion, I revisit the 'European moment' of 1814–15, and its discontents.

2. Peace and Security

In 1813–15, a new international system took shape amid the ruins of the Napoleonic Empire, building on the plans and ideas of a new order, conceptualized in the preceding years.[12] Even before the formal surrender of Napoleon, treatises were signed among the allied powers sketching the contours of the post-Napoleonic international order. On 9 March 1814, the allied powers of Britain, Russia, Austria, and Prussia concluded the Treaty of Chaumont, according to

---

[11] As Rys Jones put it: 'the maintenance of political power had become dependent on the management of time': Jones, 'Turning the Clock Back?', 16.

[12] On the plans for a European concert before 1813: Schulz, *Normen und Praxis*, 33–71; Schroeder, *Transformation*, part I.

Wolfram Siemann, the 'moment of birth' (*Geburtsstunde*) of the new European concert of powers.[13] It was agreed that peace and 'equilibrium' in Europe should be restored by mutual assistance against French aggression. These powers decided, furthermore, that an army would be raised to control insurgent France unless it agreed to restore the boundaries of 1792. Also, the shape and borders of the post-Napoleonic states were agreed upon: the united Netherlands would be ruled by the House of Orange, the Bourbons would return to Spain and France, and the German states were to form a confederation.[14]

The first Treaty of Paris, signed on 30 May 1814, formally ended the war between France and the allied coalition. Due to the conciliatory stance of—mainly—Tsar Alexander and the British minister Castlereagh, the peace that was imposed upon the French was a moderate one.[15] A full amnesty was proclaimed for partisans of earlier political regimes. The treaty set the borders for France under the House of Bourbon and restored territories to other nations. The treaty also provided a rough draft of a final settlement, which was to be concluded within the next two months at a congress involving all belligerents.[16]

From September 1814 to June 1815, the Congress of Vienna took place.[17] The Austrian minister Clemens von Metternich (1773–1859) was the conference chair, aided by his secretary Gentz, nicknamed 'the secretary of Europe'.[18] Participants included the Russian tsar, the kings of Prussia, Bavaria, and Denmark and many other princes, noblemen, and ambassadors as well as scholars, musicians, and artists. Despite its appearance as a conference of all European states, the congress was dominated by four victorious allied powers: Russia, Britain, Austria, and Prussia. Under the guidance of the skilled diplomat and political weathervane, Charles-Maurice de Talleyrand, France was swiftly readmitted as an interlocutor.[19] States of the second and third rank, however, could influence the negotiations as clients of the major powers in the many subcommittees.[20] Absent was a representative of the Ottoman sultan, who was not acknowledged as an equal partner. The Ottoman Empire was thus explicitly kept outside this European diplomatic community.[21]

The goal of this lengthy conference was not merely to make peace, as that had been done in Paris, but to 'cement and to expand an existing one'.[22] A first ambition of the conference was to definitively settle and confirm the new borders

---

[13] Siemann, *Metternich*, 458.   [14] Graaf, *Terreur*, 48.
[15] Rey, *Alexander I*; Bew, *Castlereagh*.
[16] Graaf, *Terreur*, 55–7. The decision to hold a conference in Vienna had already been made in 1813. Vick, *Congress*, 11.
[17] The literature on the Congress of Vienna is vast; studies published around the bicentennial include Vick, *Congress*; Jarett, *Congress of Vienna*; Duchhardt, *Wiener Kongress*.
[18] Siemann, *Metternich*, 487–543.   [19] Waresquiel, *Talleyrand*.
[20] On the Dutch contribution: de Graaf, 'Second-tier Diplomacy'; van Sas, *natuurlijkste bondgenoot*; de Graaf and van Leeuwen-Canneman, 'Nederlandse inbreng'.
[21] De Graaf, *Terreur*, 62–4.   [22] Vick, *Congress*, 11.

on the continent. Other topics were included in the negotiations such as the navigation on the Rhine, the constitutional form of the states, the abolition of slavery, the threat of the Barbary corsairs, and the treatment of Jewish minorities. A statistical committee decided, on the basis of precise calculations, how many kilometres and 'souls' each country could possess. In the fall of 1814, the position of the Grand Duchy of Poland and the Kingdom of Saxony were the main topics of a complex discussion among the participants. As the attempts at expansion by Prussia and Russia in these lands were resisted by Austria and Britain, a renewed outbreak of continental war became a likely prospect.

The unexpected return of Napoleon from exile on Elba on 1 March 1815 presented a complicating factor. During the desperate 'Hundred Days', the emperor would rule from Paris again, with the distinctly unheroic Louis XVIII once again exiled, this time in Ghent.[23] The impact of the Hundred Days was mixed. The renewed threat, on the one hand, had a positive effect on the attempts to build a new collective security system. Unity and resolve among the allied powers were strengthened and the conference proceedings were accelerated. At the same time the war effort produced new tensions among allies. Furthermore, providing a constitution for a new German confederation led to renewed discussions.[24] On 25 March 1815, the allied powers reconfirmed their alliance, later to be confirmed as the 'Quadruple Alliance' (20 September), and were resolved to remove the threat of Napoleon once and for all by establishing a plan for mutual security. An allied army was again assembled to definitively defeat the French emperor. After the battles of Quatre-Bras and Waterloo (16–18 June 1815), Napoleon capitulated and abdicated for a second and last time.[25]

On 9 June 1815, the final act of the Vienna conference was signed. Although the act carried great legal force and weight, the peace was also provisional. Many of the contestations persisted after the ending of the conference, with contestants debating the interpretation and the implementation of the peace treaty.[26] Nonetheless, the signing of the treaty had symbolic significance as the inauguration of a new international order. As Matthias Schulze, Beatrice de Graaf, Wolfram Siemann, and others have pointed out, the main innovation of the Vienna order was that 'security' was deemed a common responsibility of the European great powers.[27] The functioning of this new security system was demonstrated most clearly in the second occupation of France by the allied troops following the Hundred Days (1815–18). France during these three years of

---

[23] For the *Cent Jours* from a French perspective: Lentz, *Nouvelle Histoire IV*; Waresquiel, *Cent Jours*.
[24] Vick, *Congress*, 18.
[25] Due to its large financial contributions, Britain had become the leading factor in the 'Second Restoration'. Arthur Wellesley, Duke of Wellington (1769–1852), and not Tsar Alexander, became the most important statesman in the summer of 1815. De Graaf, *Terreur*, 64–82.
[26] Vick, *Congress*, 19.
[27] De Graaf, de Haan, and Vick, 'Vienna 1815', 1–19; Siemann, *Metternich*; Schulz, *Normen und Praxis*.

occupation was under the tutelage of an 'Allied Council', consisting of the representatives of the great powers, under the presidency of the Duke of Wellington. This so-called 'allied machine' dealt with a wide range of issues, such as the oversight of the armies of occupation, internal terrorist threats, retributions, and the system of fortifications surrounding France. Its aim was to ensure that provisions of the second Treaty of Paris were implemented but also to guarantee peace and stability in Europe in general.[28]

Within the framework of this council the different opinions and interests of the great powers, such as the more vengeful attitude of Prussia versus the moderate stance, vis-à-vis France, of Russia and Britain, were more or less peacefully reconciled. Despite the acts of violence and theft committed by the allied soldiers against the French population and the lack of independence of the French, historians have termed it essentially a 'moderate' occupation.[29] The decision to end the occupation was made at the conference of Aix-la-Chapelle in 1818, when France, led by the Duc de Richelieu, a moderate conservative cosmopolitan himself, was readmitted as a great European power.[30] In the wake of this conference, new international meetings would be organized to deal with problems collectively whenever security issues arose.[31]

3. Constructing an Enlightened Order

The so-called 'Congress system' has overall not been treated kindly by historians. Liberal historians have usually emphasized the repressive and reactionary character of this security arrangement of the great powers. National conservative historians have derided the European and cosmopolitan character and the alleged lack of national patriotism by the leading statesmen, such as Metternich.[32] After the First World War, for instance, the negotiators of 1919 said that they wanted to avoid the mistakes made in 1814–1815 in their new peace treaty concluding a new continental war.[33] More recent revisionist historiography, however, has taken a more nuanced and constructive view of the peacemakers assembled at Vienna, without ignoring the darker aspects of the Concert of Europe.[34] Paul Schroeder has, for instance, argued that Vienna formed a watershed in the sense that a European diplomatic revolution took place in 1813–15 in which conflicts were no longer solved by warfare but by diplomatic negotiations.[35]

Beatrice de Graaf and others have regarded 'Vienna' and the allied occupation in France in 1815–18 as a crucial moment in the formation of a modern 'European

---

[28] De Graaf, 'Allied Machine'.   [29] De Graaf, *Terreur*; Haynes, *Our Friends*.
[30] Waresquiel, *Richelieu*.   [31] Schulz, *Normen und Praxis*.   [32] Jarett, *Congress*, xiii–xiv.
[33] Duchhardt, *Kongress*, 8–15.   [34] For a contrasting view: Zamoyski, *Phantom Terror*.
[35] 'A fundamental change occurred in the governing rules, norms and practices of international politics'. Schroeder, *Transformation*, v.

security culture', in the sense that the system not only served to mobilize and uphold alliances in wartime, or in preparation towards war, but that it would also function as a system to uphold peace, social order, and public security in postwar times.[36] By focussing on networks and sociability, Brian Vick, furthermore, has pointed out that so-called liberals and conservatives mixed in social circles and that clearly defined ideological boundaries could not be drawn at this moment. Vick also underscored the role of religion and military display for the peacemakers, nuancing the view of mere pleasure-seeking and 'dancing' diplomats. Questioning the ingrained view of the peacemakers as arch-reactionaries who did not heed the wishes of the populations, he instead discovered that public opinion was indeed a factor in the negotiations, and that national feelings did play a role at the Congress of Vienna, contrary to later descriptions of the conference by hostile, nationally inclined historians.[37]

An excellent prism through which to study the world view of the peacemakers of 1815 is Clemens von Metternich. Metternich, like the other actors at the Vienna Congress, has traditionally been viewed as the representative of a reactionary and repressive political system, even dubbed the 'system Metternich'.[38] In a recent biography, Metternich has, by contrast, been interpreted primarily as the inheritor of an enlightened and cosmopolitan vision of European peace.[39] Rather than a politician bent on restoring the Holy Roman Empire, Metternich was motivated by a desire to realize the enlightened dream of perpetual peace in a pragmatic and realistic way. His first-hand experience with the Revolution in Mainz and the large-scale warfare, exile, and expropriation he and his family experienced in two preceding decades, convinced him that the revolutionary legacy essentially consisted of anarchy, fanaticism, and violence. He also personally experienced the court of Napoleon in Paris as Austrian ambassador. He consciously rejected the Napoleonic centralization of the state apparatus under a single ruler, which he had observed first-hand, instead arguing for the reform of multiple historical institutions.[40]

In the years 1813–18, he was able to put his ideas into practice, becoming one of, if not the main, architects of the Vienna conference and subsequent order.[41] An admirer of Edmund Burke, Metternich saw himself as a man of the moderate 'middle' between the two extremes of revolution and Counter-Revolution. In the

---

[36] See the previous section.   [37] Vick, *Congress*.
[38] For instance: Srbik, *Metternich*; Schroeder, 'Metternich Studies'.
[39] Siemann, *Metternich*. This excellent and meticulously researched biography can be criticized for its defensive stance: the author hardly seems to be able to view Metternich in a negative light or point out his flaws. Also, his depiction of Metternich's influence is sometimes overdrawn. Cf. Sofka, 'Metternich's Theory'.
[40] However, as head of the Austrian *Staatskanzlei*, he tried in vain to modernize and centralize the Austrian bureaucracy. Siemann, *Metternich*, 792–829.
[41] Siemann, *Metternich*, 478–543. Siemann downplays the role of other actors such as Alexander, Castlereagh, and Gentz.

1790s, he had criticized the stance of counter-revolutionary émigrés who had aggressively campaigned for a restoration through military means. For instance, he greatly admired the British constitutional model, although he did not believe this model could easily be implemented in the context of the Habsburg Empire.[42] To prevent a new revolution from erupting, he worked to establish a new system with historical roots built on the principles of balance, gradual reform, and the rule of law.

Metternich stood from a young age in close contact with the historical Europeanists studied in this book. Born into an old imperial family with roots in the Rhineland, he studied at the University of Strasbourg and in Mainz. In Strasbourg, the fifteen-year-old Metternich was lectured by Christoph Wilhelm Koch (1737–1813), a renowned expert on European law and the history of the European state system.[43] In Mainz he was taught by none other than history professor Niklas Vogt.[44] From Koch and Vogt the young Metternich acquired the view of Europe as a pluralist republic based on balance and the gradually evolving rule of law. In Mainz Metternich also read Kant's essay 'Idea for a Universal History from a Cosmopolitan Viewpoint'.[45] In many ways, Metternich's 'vision' for the reordering of the post-Napoleonic world was thus similar to the one taught by Vogt at Mainz. Of course, Vogt's 'pluralist republic', as we have seen, was not his own invention, but an articulation of more widely circulating transnational ideas. Also, in several respects, Metternich did not follow the views of his old teacher. He did not, for instance, share Vogt's providentialism and more esoteric views. And most importantly, Metternich did not agree with Vogt's identification of Napoleon as the new Charlemagne, and later they differed on the structure of the German Confederation. Nonetheless, the professor and his stellar pupil seem to have remained on good terms, and Vogt was granted his wish to be buried on Metternich's Rhineland estate of *Johannisberg*.[46]

This more liberal interpretation of the peacemakers of 1815 has, in recent years, also been extended to that other infamous form of European international collaboration, the 'Holy Alliance'. This Holy Alliance was signed by all European monarchs at the behest of Tsar Alexander I—the Ottoman sultan and the pope were not invited, and the British government declined the invitation. The Holy Alliance for later liberal generations became the byword of reactionary obscurantism and absolutist attempts to kill off the revolutionary spirit by monarchical despots. Recent research has shown that this 'Holy Alliance', very much maligned by more pragmatic diplomats such as Metternich and Castlereagh, was not a mere

---

[42] Siemann, *Metternich*, 131–8.
[43] Koch published in 1797 with Frederic Schoell, *Abregé de l'histoire des Traités de Paix entre les Puissances de l'Europe*. According to Keene, this book formed 'a vital text in the counter-revolutionary arsenal'. Keene, *Anarchical Society*, 20. Cf. Armitage, *Foundations*, 41. This analysis needs nuancing.
[44] See also Chapter 6. [45] Sofka, 'Metternich's Theory', 120–1.
[46] Siemann, *Metternich*, 69–82.

reactionary alliance. Various researchers have emphasized that Tsar Alexander and his secretary Alexandre Stourdza were primarily motivated by an enlightened and pietist ideal of bringing peace to the European continent by a reconciliation of the Orthodox, Protestant, and Catholic Christian faiths.[47] This was very much in line with the overall spiritual, irenic climate in the years after 1814. The architects of the Alliance themselves did not regard their project as 'reactionary' at all, but instead saw it as a 'middle way' between a renewal and preservation.[48] Of course, acknowledging the idealist side of Alexander does not imply denying the power play he was also involved in and the tsar's attempts to aggrandize the Russian Empire at the same time, or the fact that the Holy Alliance later became much more reactionary in character.[49]

The protagonists who founded the international order in the years 1814–18 were, in their own views, motivated primarily by an enlightened and forward-looking agenda, rather than trying to turn back the clock to an imagined past. They believed that the European system should be more in line with—what they regarded as—the historical development of European constitutions over the past centuries. At the same time, they were adamant that their construction should be an improvement upon the past and in accordance with the progress achieved by modern society. As well as repairing the chain of time, their proposals were based on the notion of progress.[50] They unquestionably rejected the French Revolution and its legacy, but they also realized that the new system should be adapted to the needs of a new age. For them, revolutionary destruction also presented an opportunity to cure the ailments of the eighteenth-century international system.

The peacemakers of 1814–15 thus described themselves as enlightened, reasonable, and moderate, inspired by the idea of the 'middle way', balance, peace, and the monarchical rule of law, including the protection of property, and as part of a wider pan-Christian moral community. Fanatical monarchists deemed 'ultra-royalists' were regarded as equally dangerous to the fragile political stability as subversive 'liberals' and 'Bonapartists'. Even as the international system took a more repressive and violent turn after 1818, increasingly stifling press and international freedom, the international order kept many of the original traits from the time of its conception. The new order after Napoleon was thus both enlightened and counter-revolutionary. For the protagonists of Vienna, this combination was not a paradox, but a self-evident outcome of the experience of the Revolution and the ensuing continent-wide wars.

Nonetheless, the self-professed enlightened agenda of the counter-revolutionary protagonists should, of course, not blind us to the darker sides of this new European

---

[47] De Graaf: 'Holy Alliance'; Ghervas, 'Balance of Power', 102–8; Cf. Nakhimovsky, *Holy Alliance*; Ghervas, *Stourdza*.
[48] Ghervas, *Stourdza*. On Russian conservatism: Alexander, *Romantics*.   [49] Rey, *Alexander I*.
[50] On Metternich and the return to 'normal' history: Jones, '1816'.

peace. 'Moderation' can be used for all kinds of imperialist agendas and to legitimize all kinds of regimes. With the appeal to moderation and reasonability, women, servants, people without property, and colonial subjects were excluded from political participation in the post-Napoleonic world.[51] With an emphasis on stability, a long-term military occupation would be imposed upon France. Forgiveness and forgetting (*oubli*) were instrumentalized to legitimize the construction of monarchical regimes without popular consent.[52] The post-Napoleonic states also collectively acted to increase their hold over other parts of the world, often violently, at the same they were striving for peace on the European continent.[53] Generally speaking, continental Restoration regimes became more repressive and authoritarian from 1818 onwards, in response to real and imagined revolutionary plots.[54] All over Europe, leading statesmen were extremely apprehensive of a return to revolution, accompanied by renewed violence and anarchy. In autobiographical writings, it was often remarked that they had the sense that they lived on a volcano that could erupt at any moment.[55]

4. 'Now or Never'

A wide variety of authors from different nationalities, social backgrounds, religious denominations, and political convictions shared the belief of the diplomats and statesmen in the possibility of a peace that would end discord and bring unity. The eighteenth-century ideals of unity and peace were remembered in pamphlets, poems, and songs all over Europe. And, of course, all of these writers projected their own convictions and ideas onto this vision of a future European peace. In the spring of 1814, it seemed to contemporaries that a unique moment in European history had arrived to truly implement a 'perpetual peace'.[56]

Characteristic of this European moment was the pervasive idea that (re)surfaced national feelings were regarded as complementary to ideals of European collaboration in the public opinion of various European countries.[57] With the disappearance of the 'centralizing' and 'despotic' Napoleonic Empire, a new

---

[51] De Haan and Lok, *Politics of Moderation*, in particular the introduction (1–28), and the chapter by de Graaf, 'Evil Passions'.

[52] Lok, '"oubli total"'. [53] See also Chapter 9.

[54] Zamoyski, *Phantom Terror*. On the liberal plots and transnational resistance: Caron and Luis, *Rien appris*, passim; Isabella, *Risorgimento in Exile*. Cf. de Haan and van Zanten, 'International Conspiracy'; Härter, 'Security and Transnational Policing'.

[55] 'Fools, you are living at the foot of mount Vesuvius', the former French Minister of Justice Étienne-Denis de Pasquier (1767–1862) exclaimed desperately in his political testament. The original text: 'Insensés, (...) vous dormez au pied de Vésuve'. *Archives de Sassy*, Pasquier, *Testament de l'homme politique* (1 July 1862).

[56] Cf. Ghervas and Armitage, *Cultural History of Peace*; Ghervas, *Conquering Peace*; Heater, *Idea*.

[57] For the Netherlands: Jensen, *Celebrating Peace*; Jensen, *Verzet tegen Napoleon*; Jensen, *Roots of Nationalism*.

pluralist and 'diverse' Europe could be constructed in which individual nations could flourish as part of the larger European monarchical commonwealth, in line with the historical Europeanism of the past decades. Dynastic and monarchical legitimacy, national feelings, and European perpetual peace were considered the pillars of this new post-Napoleonic political order. The European nations were led by their loving 'father-monarchs', who together formed one large European monarchical 'family', biologically through blood lines but also metaphorically. The enlightened pluralist historical narratives were instrumental in the shaping and legitimizing of this post-Napoleonic order of monarchies.

Exemplary for this general public mood was a Dutch pamphlet entitled *Petition to the Allied Powers to Achieve Perpetual Peace in Europe*, published in Leiden in 1814. According to the anonymous author, a unique opportunity had presented itself to establish a 'perpetual peace' in Europe:

> Now, or never, must the design of the great Henri [The French King Henri IV] be implemented. Never before were your predecessors so united: never before did they share the same noble principles. Will your successors ever be in the same position? You [kings] will now establish the future order of the European powers based on these same principles.[58]

The writer, who defined himself with false modesty as a 'simple subject without access to the kings' thrones', gave in his work, written for a Dutch audience, a short overview of the peace plans formulated in the past centuries by Henri IV, Saint-Pierre, and, to a lesser extent, Kant.[59] Kant's text was taken less seriously by the author than the older peace designs of Saint-Pierre and Sully, as it was tainted by its association with the Revolution and considered utopian. It would, according to the author, also take ages before all Kant's conditions for a republican form of government were met, and contemporaries could not wait that long. Saint-Pierre's ideas, written in the early eighteenth century and ridiculed in his own days for being chimerical, were ironically regarded by the author as more practical.[60]

Another example of the 'European' mood in the early years of the Restoration was the pamphlet written by the former Batavian revolutionary and ardent Dutch Patriot turned Orangist, Johannes van der Palm (1763–1840), entitled *De vrede van Europa* (*The Peace of Europe*, 1814). In this pamphlet, the Leiden professor van der Palm contrasts the 'false' and bloody European peace ('sleep of death' or '*doodslaap*'), which was created by the despotic Napoleon, 'the slavery of Europe', with the 'true' and 'free' peace constructed by the victorious allies. 'Europe',

---

[58] 'Nu, of nimmer, moet het ontwerp van den Grooten Hendrik tot stand komen. Nooit waren uwen voorzaten allen te zamen zoo vereenigd: Nooit waren zij allen zoo door dezelfde edele beginselen bezield. Zullen uwe nazaten het immer zijn? Gij gaat, naar die beginselen, het toekomstig stelsel van de magten van Europa vormen.' [anonymous], *Smeekschrift* (1814), 13.
[59] [anonymous], *Smeekschrift*, 27.   [60] Saint-Pierre, *Paix perpétuelle*.

for van der Palm, was essentially an anti-Napoleonic concept. Van der Palm associated 'Europe' not with a universal monarchy but with what he called 'an equilibrium of powers', a system of independent states coexisting peacefully with each other. Within the newly found continental unity, 'unique in the history of peoples', led by Europe's monarchs, the Dutch nation could once again flourish while retaining its unique character.[61]

This European mood of optimism and hope could be found in other countries as well.[62] In the eyes of the German philosopher and one-time admirer of the Napoleonic Empire, Karl Friedrich Krause (1781–1832), the achievement of 'perpetual peace' through the establishment of a European federation in Vienna would give meaning to the many dead of the intermittent warfare of the last two decades.[63] The utopian socialist philosopher Claude Henri de Saint-Simon (1760–1825), to give another well-known example, also followed in the footsteps of enlightened cosmopolitanism. He argued in his *De la réorganisation de la société européenne* of 1814, written with Augustin Thierry, that the reconstruction of Europe after the collapse of the Empire could initiate the implementation of the age-old dream of Saint-Pierre and the Duc de Sully, starting with the merger of the British and French parliaments. The new peace would undo the legacy of the Peace of Westphalia, which had resulted in a state of permanent warfare on the continent. In his pamphlet, Saint-Simon criticized the parties at the Vienna conference for aiming at an international system based on monarchical self-interest and reason of state. Saint-Simon turned to the papacy as the European institution par excellence, however, in his case, substituting scientists and technocrats for the Catholic clergy as a new European elite.[64]

5. Christian Europeanism

Religion, meaning almost exclusively Christianity, played a key role in these imaginations of a future European order after Napoleon.[65] Religious reconciliation was overall regarded as a precondition for the establishment of an enduring political peace. As we have seen, the political struggles of the age of revolution were often regarded through the lens of the Reformation and the age of the wars of religion and related to even older events in religious and Church history. The crisis

---

[61] Van der Palm, *Vrede van Europa*. This is one of many Dutch pamphlets published in 1814–15 in the Netherlands with 'Europe' in the title. On Dutch resistance against Napoleon: Jensen, *Verzet*.

[62] A systematic comparison of the publications on peace in 1814–18 in the different European countries lies outside the scope of this study, but would certainly be a worthwhile research project. For a European approach: Broers, Caiani, and Bann, *Restorations*; Caron and Luis, *Rien appris*.

[63] Krause, 'Entwurf eines europäischen Staatenbundes'. Gollwitzer, *Europabild*, 116–17; Cahen, 'project européen'.

[64] Saint-Simon, *Réorganisation*.

[65] On the discussion on Jewish rights and the Vienna Congress: Vick, *Congress*, 166–92.

of the French Revolution and the collapse of the Napoleonic Empire was regarded by authors as an opportunity to end age-old religious schisms, not only referring to Protestantism, but also to the split between the Latin and Orthodox churches in 1054.

However, Christian-inspired Europeanism was not a homogeneous movement or idea: different strands with competing agendas can be distinguished in this period. Catholic authors, such as the Sardinian diplomat Joseph de Maistre (1753–1821) and the French priest Felicité de Lamennais (1782–1854), believed that a regenerated Europe could be led only by the pope as an impartial and pan-European spiritual leader, far superior to secular princes who cared only about their self-interest.[66] In their writings, the ideological foundation for a post-revolutionary ultramontanism could be found.[67] Others such as Louis Gabriel Ambroise de Bonald (1754–1840) articulated a more national interpretation of the new Christian and monarchical European order. Although allowing for an important role for the papacy, a Catholic France was the true cornerstone of the European system, or so Bonald argued. The writings of the Dutch Protestant Guillaume Groen van Prinsterer (1801–76), which will be discussed in the next chapter, and others, demonstrate that Protestant variations of post-revolutionary Christian Europeanism can also be found.[68] But for early liberals, such as Benjamin Constant and Madame de Staël, religious reconciliation also played a crucial role in the post-Napoleonic shaping of Europe.[69] Christian Europeanism was not confined to the right, but could be found in other nascent ideological movements as well.[70]

Healing the divisions between the Christian denominations, as well as between Christianity and its *philosophe* enemies, was generally viewed as the way to achieve a perpetual political peace. The Holy Alliance formed another example of a peace design inspired by the need for religious reconciliation. Tsar Alexander, influenced by mystical thought, temporarily at least, truly believed in the common European Christian project of Catholics, Orthodox, and Protestant churches, led by the united Christian monarchs of Europe, although this vision was not universally shared by his more Orthodox-leaning Russian officials.[71] The discovery of this common Christian historical legacy formed a crucial element of almost all post-Terror counter-revolutionary doctrines.

---

[66] Karl Ludwig von Haller also believed that the Catholic Church was the only institution capable of providing the European state system with a moral grounding. Kapossy, *Haller's Critique*, 249.
[67] On post-revolutionary ultramontanism: Ramón Solans, 'Global Power'; Caiani, *Kidnap a Pope*; Chadwick, *Popes*; Boutry, 'Ultramontanisme'; Schettini, *Invention of Catholicism*. On the meanings of the concept of 'ultramontanism': Benigni, 'Ultramontanism'. On Lamennais and Maistre: Armenteros, *French Idea*.
[68] See also: Kloes, *German Awakening*; Printy, 'Protestantism'.
[69] Ghins, 'Moderation and Religion'. See also for the liberal Europeanism of Germaine de Staël and Benjamin Constant: Fontana, 'Napoleonic Empire', 124–8; Gengembre, 'Dynamisme ou fixité'.
[70] See Chapter 9.   [71] Ghervas, *Réinventer*; Craiutu, 'Rethinking Modernity'.

The revival of political Christianity had already started well before 1815, although the events of 1814–15 gave it particular political urgency.[72] A crucial work in this continent-wide re-evaluation of Christianity was *Génie du Christianisme* (1802) by the former émigré in England, and later minister of foreign affairs during the Restoration, Francois-René de Chateaubriand (1768–1848).[73] This book was published at the best possible moment. As a result of the experiences of the Terror of 1792–4, public opinion was becoming more positive towards Catholicism and organized religion. The publication was also welcomed by Napoleon himself, who increasingly was convinced of the usefulness of the Catholic Church.[74] Chateaubriand did not merely defend (Catholic) Christianity in a traditional apologetic way, but it made use of aesthetic, natural, and utilitarian arguments instead, which he claimed were more suitable for winning the hearts of his enlightened contemporaries. In many ways Chateaubriand, conventionally seen by scholars as a literary 'romantic', also continued the cosmopolitan enlightened narrative, only now framing this European historiography in the service of the Catholic Church and the Counter-Revolution.[75] This type of argument was, of course, not entirely new. As we have seen, already in the eighteenth century, Catholic apologists, such as Feller, used enlightened arguments and literary styles to defend the Catholic Church.[76] But Chateaubriand's works fell on more fertile soil and greatly influenced European public opinion of the post-Terror years.

Chateaubriand argued that because of the Catholic tradition, 'modern Europe' was superior to the ancient world, as well as to the non-European world.[77] In contrast to many enlightened *philosophes* such as Condorcet, who accused the Catholic Church of opposing progress and Enlightenment, Chateaubriand argued that the Catholic Church had been the main motor behind the development of modern European civilization over the centuries.[78] Chateaubriand advocated a return to the Christian tradition as the solution to the contemporary crisis of European culture he had already diagnosed in his earlier work *Essai historique, politique et moral sur les révolutions anciennes et modernes* (1797). In this work he, like many other authors discussed here, blamed the alleged 'atheism' of the eighteenth-century *philosophes* for Europe's cultural 'decadence'. In this way, modern philosophy and the ancient Hellenic philosophy fulfilled a similar role:

---

[72] On the campaign to re-catholicise France during the Restoration; Kroen, *Politics and Theater*, 76–108. Cf. Brejon de Lavergnée and Tort, *union du thrône*.

[73] Berchet, *Chateaubriand*; Clément, *Chateaubriand*; Aureau, *Chateaubriand*.

[74] Clément, 'Chateaubriand et la Contre-Révolution'.

[75] The English literary historian Paul Hamilton described *Génie du Christianisme* as the result of the 'dialectic of Enlightenment, rationality and Romantic expressiveness', Hamilton, *Realpoetik*, 105.

[76] Monod, *Pascal à Chateaubriand*; Palmer, *Catholics*. See also Chapter 3.

[77] Like Vogt, Chateaubriand also provided a providentialist understanding of the past: we can learn about God's character and intentions by studying European history. Chateaubriand, *Génie*, 831–92.

[78] Chateaubriand, *Génie*, 469–70.

by destroying the religious and moral foundations of classical Greece, the Hellenic philosophers had caused its decline as a culture, as the *philosophes* had done to European civilization.[79]

Count Louis Gabriel Ambroise de Bonald (1754–1840) formulated a different kind of Christian Europeanism from a more French national perspective.[80] In his pamphlet *Réflexions sur l'intérêt générale de l'Europe* (1815), written to provide advice to the statesmen assembled at Vienna, Bonald argued that the task the negotiators faced was more than merely making peace: 'it is not only peace that Europe demands, it is above all order that she needs; without order, peace is nothing but a misleading tranquility'.[81] He was hopeful that a 'perpetual peace' could be achieved on Christian and monarchical foundations, also using the 'family' as the metaphor for the continent. 'Order', according to Bonald, 'is the supreme law of intelligent beings [...]. The order that prevents revolutions, upheavals and conquests, rests in the great European family, on the two foundations of religion and monarchy.'[82] In his pamphlet, Bonald thus joined 'security' and 'order' with culture and morality.

Bonald's reflections on a new European order were structured by the memory of an older peace conference, that of Westphalia (1648), a comparison found in many reflections on perpetual peace.[83] After 'Westphalia', the careful European balance of power, which had existed since the time of Charlemagne and above all since the reign of Charles V, was disturbed. This political fragmentation and division of Europe had been especially beneficial to Protestantism and had caused almost continuous internal European warfare. Also, as a result of the Reformation, religion and politics had become separate realms, and philosophy had been able to spread and corrupt Catholic Europe. The revolutionary and Napoleonic wars were thus, for Bonald, as for many other Catholic counter-revolutionaries, in essence a continuation of the religious wars of the Reformation era: the coming of Protestantism was the ultimate cause of Europe's troubles. Bonald regarded 'Vienna' as a potential counterpoint to 'Westphalia'. It was an opportunity to establish perpetual peace in Europe, but this time on the right moral foundations. Protestant Britain for him was a greedy and warmongering nation, as well as a hothouse of atheism, and should therefore be excluded from the new continental system. Also, the Ottoman Empire, as a non-Christian power, should be driven from Europe in a new crusade of the united European armies.[84]

---

[79] Chateaubriand, *Essai Historique* (1978), 369.
[80] On Bonald: Klinck, *Counter Revolutionary Theorist*; Alibert, *triangles d'or*; Tort, *droite française*; Bertran de Balanda, *Bonald*; Reedy, 'Historical Imaginary'.
[81] 'C'est n'est pas seulement la paix que l'Europe demande, c'est surtout et avant tout de l'*ordre* qu'elle a besoin, de cet ordre sans lequel la paix n'est qu'un calme trompeur.' Bonald, *Réflexions*, 9.
[82] Bonald, *Réflexions*, 9. Cf. Bonald, *Écrits sur l'Europe*; Gengembre, 'Contre-révolution'.
[83] Bonald formulated his criticism of the Westphalian peace also in his earlier *Traité de Westphalie*.
[84] On the counter-revolutionary uses of the language of the crusade: Schettini, 'Crusaders'.

In his unabashedly Eurocentric treatise *De la Chrétienté et du Christianisme* (1825), Bonald also combined enlightened with traditional Christian ideas. He argued that the progress of the European countries, as well as their military and economic superiority, was evidence of the theological superiority and truth of Christianity, in particular Catholicism. The underdevelopment of the Islamic world, he regarded as proof of the falsehood of Islamic doctrines and beliefs.[85] The example of Bonald demonstrates that this fusion of enlightened and Christian Europeanism in the service of the Counter-Revolution could easily lead to a reinforcing of the boundaries between Europe and the Islamic world and a reinvigorated emphasis on the moral as well as the civilizational uniqueness and superiority of the European world, which needed to be defended aggressively. However, as we have seen, other historical Europeanists took a different view on Islam and Arab civilization.[86]

Apparently not discouraged by the complete defeat of the French armies by the allies at Waterloo, the French patriot Bonald confidently argued in 1815 that perpetual peace in the tradition of the plan of Henri IV and the Duc de Sully would be able to succeed only if Europe were led by a renewed Catholic and monarchical France. If this France were returned to its natural borders, including, for instance, the Southern Netherlands and the left bank of the Rhine, the country would no doubt stabilize. Only then would France be calmed, and its aggression towards its European neighbours would disappear, transforming the country into the most important pillar of the new international system. Bonald regarded the foundation of the new United Kingdom of the Netherlands, intended as a watchman over unruly France, as 'unnatural' and, therefore, as a potential source of future conflicts and turmoil. Interestingly, the fiercely counter-revolutionary Bonald, in his writings, used a combination of the revolutionary language of the 'natural borders', the enlightened language of perpetual peace, and the rhetoric of the balance of Europe to support his vision of a Franco-centric Catholic European order.

A later monarchical echo of the more irenic Christian European spirit after the collapse of the Napoleonic Empire can, finally, be observed in the musings (written in French) of the Dutch Protestant Restoration king, Willem I. Following the successful conclusion of a concordat with Pope Leo XII (1760–1829), the Protestant Willem personally wrote an unpublished essay in 1827 on religious reconciliation in his kingdom and the possibility of a European *'paix perpétuelle'*. The Netherlands, where both Protestants and Catholics lived, could in the eyes of its king act as a laboratory and vanguard for a more overarching European regeneration and unity through its resolution of internal religious differences. For a king more known for his pragmatic, financial, and technocratic mentality than for his grand political visions, this wide-ranging sketch on the idea of

---

[85] On the interrelation of *antiphilosophie* and anti-Islamism: Bravo López, 'contrarrevolucionarios'.
[86] See also Chapter 9.

European unity was quite out of character and no doubt demonstrated the pervasive influence of Christian Europeanist ideals in this period.

The end of the Napoleonic era was, according to Willem, and echoing many contemporaries, a unique opportunity in European history to end centuries of violent political and religious struggle 'and to assure a solid European peace, uniting all Christians on the basis of sentiment, charity and reciprocal love'.[87] A general European peace would be in accordance with 'the spirit of the age, the state of civilization, and the progress of the human mind'.[88] According to Willem, 'civil' (domestic) as well as 'European' (international) peace and security could be achieved only on the basis of an enlightened religious unity. The pragmatic Willem explicitly connected the question of a European security culture thus to the contemporary problem of religious disunity.

The German confederation (*Deutsche Bund*) established at the Congress of Vienna was, for Willem, an example of how states could unite without losing their independence. Also, the young United States of America, still under construction, presented a model for—in his terms—'*vieille Europe*'. By adopting the American federal constitution, Europe could prevent or at least postpone the moment the young states would overtake the old continent.[89] The Congress of Vienna had already prepared the way towards a more enduring European peace by breaking with the old habits of warfare that had been the usual European solution when differences arose. The Holy Alliance was also an important step towards a European peace, but Willem believed that Alexander I's project had only a short-lived effect and would not survive a change of political leadership.[90]

To ensure an enduring peace Willem therefore proposed the establishment of an '*Aréopage Européen*' based on the combined principles of Vienna and the spirit of the Holy Alliance. The contemporary equivalent of the hill in ancient Athens, where elders met and law was administered, would be a permanent meeting place of the representatives of the European states presided over by a deputy of the pope as moderator. In this European 'Diet', conflicts would be peacefully resolved, and the principles of European law formulated. The security of individual states would be guaranteed without their having to compromise their sovereignty or independence. Typical for the financially inclined king, this European cooperation would enable individual states to lower the costs of furnishing expensive armies and to focus exclusively on internal tranquillity and policing and the development of industry and commerce. Finally, the European Areopagus would ensure and expand European dominance over other parts of the world, Willem wrote optimistically, demonstrating the increased sense of European superiority and imperial mindset that accompanied the post-Napoleonic moment.[91]

---

[87] [Willem I], 'Opstel', 319; Koch, *Willem I*, 426–9; Bornewasser, '"credo"'.
[88] [Willem I], 'Opstel', 322.   [89] [Willem I], 'Opstel', 320.
[90] [Willem I], 'Opstel', 320–1.   [91] Cf. Woolf, 'European World-View'.

6. Dying with Europe

Notwithstanding the overall positive judgement of King Willem—and some later historians—inevitably the high hopes of the creation of a new European order at the Congress of Vienna were to be disappointed. Contrary to what one might expect considering the conservative and reactionary reputation of Vienna, many counter-revolutionary Europeanists were highly critical of the achievements of the Vienna Congress. As we have seen, even Metternich's teacher Vogt was disappointed with the results of Vienna in providing Europe with a durable new order that would regenerate European civilization. The failure to establish a new synthesis between the ancient Christian and Germanic constitution and enlightened progress would, in his view, certainly lead to new revolutions in the foreseeable future. Heeren was more positive in his overall assessment of Vienna and the successor conferences, although he also stated that no human constitution, including the treaty of 1815, was ever without its flaws.[92] Chateaubriand, moreover, criticized the 'so-called statesmen' of Vienna for paying attention only to the physical needs of nations, neglecting the equally important moral dimension: men—in his view—were primarily motivated by freedom, glory, and religion rather than by material goods and stability.[93]

This sense of disillusion was shared by some of the main protagonists of Vienna themselves. Gentz wrote in the immediate aftermath of the Congress in the summer of 1815:

> Never have the expectations of the general public been as excited as they were before the opening of this solemn assembly. People were confident of a general reform of the political system of Europe, of a guarantee of perpetual peace, even of the return of the golden age. Yet it produced only restitutions decided beforehand by the force of arms, arrangements between the great powers unfavourable to the future balance and the maintenance of peace in Europe, and some quite arbitrary rearrangements in the possessions of the lesser states, but not one act of a more elevated character, not one great measure of public order or security which might compensate humanity for any part of its long suffering or reassure it as to the future.[94]

Even Metternich's hope was dashed that '1815' would bring an end to the tumultuous 'accelerated time' of the revolutionary and Napoleonic era and inaugurate a return to what he regarded as the 'normal history' that supposedly existed before the start of the revolutionary era.[95]

---

[92] See Chapters 6 and 7. [93] Clément, *Chateaubriand*, 283.
[94] Cited in Zamoyski, *Rites of Peace*, 550. Cf. Cahen, 'Correspondence', 101.
[95] Jones, '1816', 122; Cahen, 'Correspondence', 101, n. 35.

This counter-revolutionary disillusion with the overall results of Vienna and the sense of a missed opportunity was particularly apparent in the book *Du Pape* (1819), published by the Sardinian diplomat Joseph de Maistre. In this work, Maistre provided a vision for an alternative ordering of Europe based on his analysis of European history, and in particular the role of the papacy as the European institution par excellence. Maistre came from a noble family in the Savoy region, at that time part of the Kingdom of Piedmont-Sardinia. He was educated in Chambéry, probably by Jesuits. He was trained by them not only in the classical languages but also acquired a good knowledge of the modern European languages. He would consequently defend the cause of the Jesuits his entire life, associating the French Revolution with the traditional enemies of the Jesuits within the Catholic Church, the Jansenists. He, moreover, read many enlightened works by *philosophes* such as Mirabeau. He was, at the same time, influenced by the *anti-philosophe* mysticism of Louis-Claude de Saint Martin (1743–1803) and he read occultist works, in addition to the works of moderate *philosophes*.[96]

After completing his law training at the University of Turin in 1774, Maistre followed in his father's footsteps by becoming a senator in Chambéry in 1787. He also became a member of the Scottish Rite Masonic lodge in that city from 1774 to 1790. Unlike other *anti-philosophes* such as Barruel, who regarded Freemasonry essentially as a *philosophe* sect which aimed to overthrow the social order, Maistre took a more positive stance regarding the Freemasons. This positive attitude towards Freemasonry was one of the several ways in which Maistre differed from the mainstream of Francophone counter-revolutionary authors and followed a unique path as a counter-revolutionary.

At first, Maistre, like many of his contemporaries, believed that reform of the French monarchy was necessary, and he therefore favoured the meeting of the Estates-General in 1789. After the passing of the August Decrees on 4 August 1789, he decisively turned against the course of political events in revolutionary France. From a relatively moderate and overall positive stance, Maistre developed into one of the staunchest and most vocal opponents of the French revolutionaries and their legacy. The years 1791–2 represented a turning point in Maistre's life. After the invasion of the French revolutionary armies, Maistre went into exile in Lausanne, Switzerland, where he frequented the salon of Mme de Staël. Classified as an 'émigré', his possessions were consequently confiscated by the revolutionary authorities, the new rulers of Piedmont.

The abrupt end of his professional career and his exile turned Maistre into a prolific counter-revolutionary publicist. Among other works, in 1797 he published in Lausanne the work that would make him (in)famous all over Europe: the

---

[96] Armenteros, *French Idea*, 23–4; Lebrun, *Maistre*.

Considérations sur la France ('Considerations on France'). In this work, he developed his unique literary style, characterized by irony and sarcasm. In contrast to most other counter-revolutionary and royalist treatises, Maistre's did not interpret the French Revolution as the result of a plot of a *philosophe* and Freemason sect. Instead, he argued that the 'Satanic' French Revolution was the result of the intervention of Divine Providence in human history. By unleashing the Terror on France, the Revolution eventually worked as a catharsis of this decadent and corrupted country. The French revolutionaries unknowingly were the pawns in a larger plan to create a regenerated and spiritual Catholic French and European society.[97]

Increasingly famous as a counter-revolutionary publicist among émigrés, Maistre's star also started to rise as a servant of the Sardinian monarch, who held court in Cagliari on the island of Sardinia after the French armies had taken Turin in 1798. In 1799, he was appointed Regent of Sardinia, but he had to resign after a conflict with the viceroy, evidence of his headstrong character. In 1802, he became the Sardinian ambassador to the court of Tsar Alexander I in Saint Petersburg, where the king could keep him at arm's length. His years in Saint Petersburg would become the most fruitful years in intellectual terms. The combination of an elevated social status and an active social life, as well as having few official duties as the ambassador of a medium-sized power, Maistre could devote much of his time to writing and thinking. Increasingly, during his Saint Petersburg years, his works were informed by his reading of works on mysticism.[98]

Saint Petersburg was, without any doubt, one of the capitals of a counter-revolutionary cosmopolitanism in the post-revolutionary decades. It was one of the main centres where ideas of a counter-revolutionary international order were conceived as an alternative to the revolutionary and Napoleonic international system. Not only would Russia influence the development of West European counter-revolutionary thought, in many ways Russian conservative ideas were also developed through the contact of Russian intellectuals with West European counterparts.[99] Maistre's great ambition was to bring Russia back under the control of the Catholic Church, seeing the schism of 1054 as a mistake. He converted several of his Russian friends to Roman Catholicism. In his view, Russia could be the political as well as the spiritual cradle of a reconstructed post-revolutionary Catholic Europe, and he thus placed Russia at the heart of European civilization.[100]

Maistre's active lobbying on behalf of the Catholic Church and the Jesuits in Russia, as well as his converting of Russians, however, increasingly aroused suspicion and hostility among his Orthodox hosts. In 1817, he was asked to

---

[97] Maistre, *Considerations*.
[98] Armenteros, 'Preparing the Russian Revolution'; Verpoest, 'Ancien Régime'.
[99] Verpoest, 'Ancien Régime'.   [100] Maistre, *Soirées*.

leave the Tsarist Empire and became a royal official in Turin, where he died on 26 February 1821. In his last years he devoted most of his time to the editing and publishing of his *Du Pape* (1819) and *Les soirées de Saint-Pétersbourg* (1821). He became progressively disillusioned with the order that had taken shape after the collapse of the Napoleonic Empire.[101] He also took an increasingly pessimistic stance regarding the struggle against the 'satanic' revolution. Instead of creating a counter-revolutionary order, the 'restoration' of 1815, in his eyes, in essence consolidated the revolutionary heritage. Disappointed with the restored monarchical government, Maistre turned towards the papacy as the European institution that he saw as the least susceptible to corruption. At the end of his life, he regarded his fight against revolutionary ideals as a failure. Merging his own death with the destruction of European civilization, he wrote in a somewhat melodramatic manner: 'I am dying with Europe; I am in good company.'[102]

Maistre, like many protagonists studied in this book, suffered from a blackened reputation at the hands of contemporaries and posterity alike. In the writings of nineteenth-century national and liberal historians, Maistre became an arch-reactionary, a writer with a medieval mindset. Also, in the circles of 'pure' French royalists, he was a somewhat eccentric figure due to his emphasis on the providential aspects of the French Revolution. But also his relatively negative view of *ancien régime* France, his ultramontanism, and his positive views of Freemasonry set him apart.[103] Even the pope was ill at ease with Maistre's over-enthusiastic defence of the political role of the papacy, which interfered with papal diplomatic efforts and relations with the European monarchies.[104] After the Second World War, Maistre came to be regarded as one of the intellectual fathers of Vichy France and French fascism, similar perhaps to the fate of, for instance, Adam Müller, who came to be associated with Nazism in the twentieth century. Recent historians have nuanced the interpretation of Maistre as both as an arch-reactionary and an early fascist.[105] Revisionist historians regard Maistre as a product of a moderate enlightened tradition, notwithstanding Maistre's self-professed hostility towards the *philosophes* and their ideas.[106]

---

[101] Lovie and Chetail, 'Introduction', xiv. Maistre's disappointment concerned both the Vienna Congress and its successor congresses, as well as the Holy Alliance he deemed the 'great chimera of universal Christianity'. Useche Sandoval, 'Comte's reading', 77.
[102] Cited in Armenteros, *French Idea*, 30.   [103] Armenteros and Lebrun, *European Readers*.
[104] Armenteros and Lebrun, *Legacy of Enlightenment*, 1–16.
[105] In the post-war decades Isaiah Berlin rekindled scholarly interest in Maistre in the Anglophone world in a Cold War context by describing him as one of the key figures of what he regarded as the pluralist European Counter-Enlightenment, as well as a modern protofascist due to his alleged glorification of violence. Berlin, 'Maistre'.
[106] Armenteros and Lebrun, *Legacy of Enlightenment*, 1–16. A possible criticism against the revisionist historians is that they somewhat overdid their reinterpretation of Maistre, emphasizing only his moderate, enlightened, and liberal side: Lok, 'Vijanden', 211–28.

7. A Papal Order

In 1819, Maistre published his book *Du Pape* (*On the Pope*) in response to what he regarded as a general crisis of authority in Europe.[107] This double crisis of the state and the church did not, in his view, originate in the 'satanic' revolution of 1789: in the eighteenth century, atheistic philosophy had already mortally undermined all forms of order and hierarchy. This philosophy was itself the consequence of the Reformation, the sixteenth-century revolt against the universal Catholic Church. Maistre found the solution to this general European political, religious, and moral crisis in the institution of the papacy. No other institution represented in his eyes the principle of order as well as of freedom. The papacy for Maistre embodied the right middle way between the two 'abysses' of despotism and anarchy.[108] Although Maistre insisted on the necessity of authority due to man's corrupted nature, he did not merely advocate the rule of the executioner, as several of his detractors have argued.[109] For him, it was precisely the French Revolution that stood for the random and destructive violence that terrified him.

For Maistre, Europe's unique civilization was historically characterized by the duality of order and freedom. Restless freedom, typical of 'the daring race of Japheth', set Europe apart from the continents of Noah's other, passive sons Cham and Shem, Africa and Asia. This restlessness represented Europe's greatest strength as well as its mortal threat.[110] Europe's primal challenge was thus to rein in sovereign power without destroying it altogether.[111] The argument in *Du Pape*, mostly written during Maistre's *séjour* in Saint Petersburg, was that the papacy had demonstrated, like no other European institution throughout history, its ability to be the foundation of freedom as well as moderate government. It was therefore the papacy that should, in Maistre's eyes, be the institutional foundation and guiding spiritual principle of the new international order that was being constructed on the ruins of the Napoleonic Empire.

The book was not as well received by papal bureaucracy and Catholic royalist circles as one might expect. The book was criticized by the papal authorities for its

---

[107] Maistre, *Du Pape*. The modern edition of 1966 is based on the last version of the text edited by Maistre himself, the edition of 1821, published shortly after his death. See, for the editorial history, the introduction of their edition of *Du Pape* by Lovie and Chetail. They argue that the published version of *Du Pape* was strongly influenced by the editor Guy-Marie de Place, who adapted polemical passages to make the book more acceptable to contemporary public opinion. Cf. Latreille, *Maistre*.

[108] Maistre, *Du Pape*, 134.

[109] For instance: Berlin, 'Maistre'; Triomphe, *Maistre*; Armenteros, *French History*, 10–12. Maistre wrote: 'L'homme en sa qualité d'être à la fois moral et corrompu, juste dans son intelligence, et pervers dans sa volonté, doit nécessairement être gouverné; autrement il serait à la fois sociable et insociable, et la société serait à la fois nécessaire et impossible.' Maistre, *Du Pape*, 129.

[110] Useche Sandoval, 'Comte's Reading', 80–1. On the legend of Noah's sons and the representation of the continents: Mikkeli, *Europe*; Wintle, *Image*.

[111] 'Le plus grand problème européen est donc de savoir: comment on peut restreindre le pouvoir souverain sans le détruire.' Maistre, *Du Pape*, 131.

allegedly erroneous description of the Catholic doctrine of papal infallibility. Furthermore, its enthusiastic defence of papal claims of supreme worldly authority were not considered opportune in the post-Napoleonic diplomatic world dominated by monarchical powers. Maistre's request to dedicate the book to the pope was refused, although his good intentions were acknowledged by the pope.[112] French royalists, moreover, disapproved of his criticism of Gallicanism, which he described as a 'national exaggeration', and of Gallican icons, such as Bossuet and Fénélon. They also rejected his providential view of the revolutionary events.[113] The reception of the book in the different European countries varied across ideological as well as geographical lines. His readership ranged from staunch traditionalists to the radical anti-Christian left, and from the United States to Russia.[114] *Du Pape* was widely read in Germany and exerted an influence on the Europeanist thought of Friedrich von Gentz, who became an advocate of *Du Pape* in the German-speaking world through the intermediary role of Bonald.[115] In Turin, by contrast, the book was primarily digested by religious authors, and not by political philosophers or statesmen.

Maistre's plea for a new papal European order was based, simultaneously, on philosophical and historical argumentation.[116] In this work, Maistre made selective use of an enlightened narrative of progress and civilization to defend the papacy. Voltaire's *Essai sur les Moeurs* and other canonical historical works of the historiographical Enlightenment, such as those by Edward Gibbon and David Hume, were referred to by Maistre. He responded to them in a critical, as well as approving, vein.[117] Maistre, for instance, admired Voltaire's intellect but despised his morality.[118] In *Du Pape*, the papacy was thus not defended in traditional theological and doctrinal terms, but was seen above all as the creator of a common European and enlightened civilization.[119] As Chateaubriand had done in *Génie du Christianisme*, Maistre argued that the Catholic Church had been the fountain of Europe's superior cultural, artistic, and scientific achievements. And as in the case of *Génie du Christianisme*, Maistre's defence of the Catholic Church was not written by a member of the clergy. Maistre explained in his preliminary discourse that it was an advantage that secular writers like himself defended the Church as they could be regarded as more impartial by potential readers than priests.

---

[112] The Latin dedicatory letter to Pope Pius VII was inserted in the 1884 edition of *Du Pape*.
[113] Lovie and Chetail, 'Introduction', xiv–xviii; Maistre, *Du Pape*, 31.
[114] Armenteros and Lebrun, 'Introduction', *European Readers*, 4.
[115] Cahen, 'Correspondence'.
[116] Carolina Armenteros has, in my view, convincingly termed *Du Pape* a work of 'a Europeanist theory of history'. Armenteros, *French History*, 115–55.
[117] For instance: Maistre, *Du Pape*, 45–55, 172–3. Maistre also wrote approvingly of the Protestant Edmund Burke: Maistre, *Du Pape*, 269.
[118] 'Tel est Voltaire, le plus méprisable des écrivains lorsque' on ne le considère que sous le point de vue moral.' Maistre, *Du Pape*, 184, cf. also for praise: 191.
[119] Maistre, *Du Pape*, 293.

Also, after the havoc and destruction of the Revolution, there was a lack of clergy. The Church needed all the intellectual support it could get, Maistre explained.[120]

The Catholic Church had brought moral progress to the European continent. Unlike Feller, who defended modern slavery, Maistre disapproved of the institution as incompatible with European freedom as well as the teachings of the Catholic Church. He argued that slavery, a common feature of the ancient world, had been abolished in the European Middle Ages due to the efforts of the Catholic Church.[121] Moreover, the position of women had markedly improved over the course of European history thanks to the Church. Due to Church policy, polygamy had been replaced by monogamy, a unique European institution for Maistre, based on the principle of equality of the sexes, and contrasting with the degrading polygamy found elsewhere on the globe. Overall, levels of medieval violence had been reduced under pressure of the Church. However, as a result of the Revolution and *philosophie*, new forms of 'slavery' and modern types of oppression had been reintroduced.[122]

In his earlier political writings, Maistre had, like Calonne and other counter-revolutionaries, praised monarchy as the freest type of regime, disqualifying the republic as utopian due to the shortcomings of man.[123] In his later years, however, Maistre became more cynical about the 'Machiavellian' tendencies of the European monarchies.[124] As the Vienna Congress had once again shown, monarchies cared only about their own short-term interests and their main goal was to increase their own power and their territories at the expense of their subjects and other institutions.[125] Monarchical powers therefore needed to be controlled. Intermediary bodies such as provincial parliaments, representative institutions, and the courts, as Montesquieu had famously argued, could, for Maistre, not function as the main checks on royal powers. As the revolutionary events had demonstrated, the writing of new constitutions had been a chimera. Due to human imperfection, man is not capable of constructing a new constitution with the aid of his reason. All true and legitimate constitutions, according to Maistre, originated in Divine Providence and have gradually evolved and improved over the course of many centuries.[126]

Maistre, therefore, opted for the Catholic Church as the main bridle on monarchical power and as the cornerstone of the constitutional equilibrium of a monarchical regime.[127] In his eyes, the pope was infallible in matters of the spiritual order, and sovereign in the temporal and worldly order.[128] Over the centuries, the pope had acted as an impartial and wise arbiter (*médiateur*) of Europe's interstate relations. The pope could fulfil this role because, in contrast to

---

[120] Maistre, *Du Pape*, 15. [121] Maistre, *Du Pape*, 232–3.
[122] Maistre, *Du Pape*, 233–6. [123] Armenteros, *French Idea*, 69–71.
[124] Maistre, *Du Pape*, 207. [125] Lovie and Chetail, 'Introduction', xiv.
[126] 'La souveraineté étant pour nous une chose sacrée, une émanation de la puissance divine (...).' Maistre, *Du Pape*, 135.
[127] Maistre, *Du Pape*, 278. [128] Maistre, *Du Pape*, 27.

the monarchs, he was not subjected to the 'caprices of politics' due to his celibacy and advanced age.[129] Unlike the princes, the pope was less subject to the passions that destabilize political life. His ambition was not to augment his territory: the origin of the papal state had not been military conquest but an alleged 'gift' from the Roman emperor Constantine.[130] Moreover, the papacy was able to understand and foresee long-term political events, a capability most of the princes did not possess. The permanence of the 'sovereign pontificate' was juxtaposed to the fragility and transience of worldly princely authority.

Furthermore, the papacy was able to act in the interests of Europe and 'humanity', and not merely of those of a single state.[131] For Maistre, the papacy and the Catholic Church stood for the principle of unity and endurance in European Christian civilization, with the papacy as the core of Christianity.[132] The other Christian denominations, by contrast, stood for division and anarchy, as well as for cultural and spiritual 'sterility'.[133] All those opposing papal authority were thus not only religious heretics but also political rebels against legitimate authority. They were primarily motivated by arrogance and excessive self-esteem. Like other *anti-philosophes*, Maistre lumped together all non-Catholic Christian denominations, and even Catholic enemies such as the Jansenists and the French *parlementaires*, with the 'atheistic' 'philosophy of our age' (*philosophie de notre siècle*) as consisting of one great revolt against authority.[134] Whereas the Catholic Church was a constructive and conserving force (*force conservatrice*), bringing civilization, freedom, regeneration, and order, its enemies were bent only on destruction, despotism, and barbarism.[135]

8. A Cosmopolitan Maistre?

The unity of the Catholic Church did incidentally not preclude the development of separate national identities. Maistre was overall not an early nationalist—he was, in fact, subjected to fierce criticism by nationalist authors—nor did he devote many pages in *Du Pape* to national identities.[136] He also strongly disapproved of

---

[129] Maistre, *Du Pape*, 252–8.
[130] Maistre even spent many pages defending, in historical detail, the popes who did not enjoy a good reputation. According to him, for instance, the infamous Renaissance pope Julius II had in fact been less violent and power hungry than the secular princes of his time. Maistre, *Du Pape*, 145.
[131] Maistre, *Du Pape*, 211. 'Il reste démontré que les Papes furent les instituteurs, les tuteurs, les sauveurs, et les véritables génies constituants de l'Europe.' Maistre, *Du Pape*, 293.
[132] Maistre, *Du Pape*, 25; Maistre was outspoken in his judgement on the medieval conciliar movement he considered dangerous and disadvantageous to papal authority. Only in the beginning, when the Church was a relatively small organization, could a council fulfil a useful role. Maistre, *Du Pape*, 34.
[133] Maistre, *Du Pape*, 320. [134] Maistre, *Du Pape*, 77. [135] Maistre, *Du Pape*, 142.
[136] In his earlier works, Maistre had also been influenced by Herder's account of national development, despite his criticism of the German author: Armenteros, *French Idea*, 74–7.

'national churches' such as the Church of England and the French Gallican Church. Nonetheless, he explicitly allowed for the development of separate national identities within the wider European and universal framework of the Catholic Church. Also, in line with Montesquieu's theories, papal rule could find different articulations in various European countries, depending on their national character.[137] Thus Maistre combined the pluralist theory of European history with a Catholic universalizing order based on the principle of unity (*éternelle invariabilité*) and papal sovereignty.[138]

In contrast to the pluralist authors analysed in this study, Maistre also criticized ancient Greece for its lack of unity. Greece, for Maistre, was the ultimate source of schismatic Protestantism. High praise, on the other hand, was given to the unitary spirit of the Roman Empire. In particular, the ancient Athenian Republic, an alleged cradle of superficial and atheistic philosophy, was disliked by Maistre. European history could, in his eyes, be interpreted as a permanent struggle from antiquity onwards between the 'Roman' idea of unity, on the one hand, and the 'Greek' schismatic and divisive principles, on the other. Only when the revolutionary 'Greek' spirit submitted to eternal 'Rome', could European civilization be 'resurrected' and renewed.[139]

In addition to being members of different nations, Maistre thus underscored, like Müller, that Europeans also formed part of the wider community of the 'universal' Catholic Church.[140] United by 'religious fraternity', the Christian princes constituted a kind of 'universal republic' under papal sovereignty.[141] Latin, furthermore, functioned as the common *lingua franca* for all Europeans. The use of this language marked the 'boundary of civilisation and European fraternity' (*les bornes de la civilisation et la fraternité européenne*).[142] Moreover, classicism was Europe's preferred common artistic style and for Maistre also typical of wider European civilization. Enlightened Eurocentric cosmopolitanism and Catholic universalism thus seamlessly merged in Maistre's papal theory.

This 'cosmopolitan' reading of Maistre contrasts with the stereotype of Maistre as an enemy of universalism. This view is solely based on the often-quoted remark in the *Considérations* that 'now, there is no such thing as "man" in this world. In my life I have seen Frenchmen, Italians, Russians, and so on. I even know, thanks to Montesquieu, that one can be Persian. But as for man, I declare I've never encountered

---

[137] Maistre, *Du Pape*, 121–3, 139. 'L'essentiel pour chaque nation est de conserver sa discipline particulière, c'est à dire ces sortes d'usages qui, sans tenir au dogme, constituent cependant une partie de son droit public, et se sont amalgamés depuis longtemps avec le caractère et les lois de la nation... nulle nation ne doit redouter l'infaillibilité pontificale, qui ne s'applique qu'à des objets d'un ordre supérieur.'

[138] This synthesis between Catholic unity and national pluralism, deemed typical for European civilization, could, for instance, also be found in Chateaubriand's *Génie du Christianisme*, 842.

[139] Maistre, *Du Pape*, 324–41.

[140] 'Le catholique seul est appelé comme s'il s'appelle et n'a qu'un nom pour tous les hommes.' Maistre, *Du Pape*, 318, 47.

[141] Maistre, *Du Pape*, 194.   [142] Maistre, *Du Pape*, 125–7.

him.'[143] However, when discussing Maistre's views on cosmopolitanism, a topic rarely considered in the extensive Maistre scholarship, this particular remark in his earlier polemical work should be juxtaposed to his more mature views in *Du Pape* and his other later works. Nonetheless, as in the case of Müller, even in *Du Pape* Maistre's cosmopolitanism was strictly confined to the Latin and Catholic world.[144]

Maistre singled out one European country for special treatment: France.[145] France's destiny was to act as a protector of the Catholic Church and papal authority, which set it apart from other European countries. This unique mission had already been part of French identity from its earliest beginning as a Romanized Gallic tribe. This religious character, deemed typical of the French nation, was first expressed by Druids, later replaced in their role of spiritual guides by Christian clergymen. In the Middle Ages, France fulfilled this special role under Charlemagne, but it also came to the fore when France led Europe in its Crusades against Islam. However, as a result of human weakness and arrogance France had forsaken her holy duty from the eighteenth century onwards. So-called modern philosophy had been able to undermine the institutions of Church and monarchy, destroying the foundations of France itself.[146]

However, the cataclysmic events of the revolutionary wars had enabled a purification of this rotten polity. Louis XVI had become a martyr to save his beloved kingdom, echoing the sacrifice of Christ himself. Due to divine intervention, in 1814 a son of the House of Bourbon had returned to the throne after years of violence and war. France again could fulfil its sacred mission of protecting the papacy and the Church. However, Maistre warned against too much complacency. The revolutionary ideals were resurfacing a few years after their defeat at Waterloo, and the menace of a new revolution had appeared on the horizon once again. Maistre called on the French nobility and clergy to make amends for their pre-revolutionary betrayal, by which Maistre meant the 'monstrous alliance with the immoral [philosophical] principles of the last century', by supporting the restored monarchy wholeheartedly and without any hesitation.[147]

Maistre praised the restless and freedom-loving '*génie occidental*', and, like Bonald, he was very critical of Islam. The rise of Islam in the seventh century had been possible only due to the internal divisions of Christianity, not to the strength of the Arab armies or Islamic doctrine. Islam, and in particular the

---

[143] An example of the use of this citation out of context: Ossewaarde, 'Cosmopolitanism'.

[144] On Latinate (pre-modern) cosmopolitanism in comparison to the 'Sanskrit cosmopolis': Pollock, 'Cosmopolitanism', 59–80.

[145] As much as Maistre admired France, he disliked Britain as a country of cold and calculating Protestant atheists, whom he blamed for not having contributed to the global spread of Christianity and for selecting the pursuit of profit as the sole motive for colonialism. Maistre, *Du Pape*, 225.

[146] For Maistre, the adjective 'modern' as in '*les temps modernes*' (Maistre, *Du Pape*, 34) had a negative connotation.

[147] 'Il y a des nations privilégiées qui ont une mission dans le monde.' Maistre, *Du Pape*, 20–3.

Ottoman Empire, was, for Maistre, the eternal enemy of the Christian world. Regarding the despotic, arbitrary, and immoderate nature of state power, the Ottoman Empire was comparable in Maistre's eyes to the Revolutionary Republic, underscoring the fact that the Revolution was an oriental anomaly in the European context.[148] He ruled out any' form of reconciliation between the two religions: continuous warfare was the only possible condition between the supporters of these two faiths. And Maistre once again credited the papacy with saving Europe from Ottoman conquest, which would have resulted in complete religious oppression and political tyranny. The Crusades had no doubt been justified in the eyes of Maistre. The defeat of the Ottoman naval forces at Lepanto had been a victory over the 'mortal enemy of human dignity'.[149]

Maistre had a different and more positive view of Russia, though, as a civilization in between Christian Europe and the Islamic Ottoman world.[150] As described, he regarded the separation of the Orthodox Churches from the Church of Rome in the eleventh century as a tragedy. It had been in his eyes an unlawful 'rebellion' against the legitimate authority of the bishop of Rome.[151] The Russians had for this reason not been able to participate in the progress of European civilization, and their society had consequently stagnated. This isolation and apathy, however, turned out to be a blessing as well, as *philosophie* had been able to penetrate—and thus to corrupt—Russian society far less than in Western Europe. Russia for Maistre was a potential source of the regeneration of Catholic Europe after the Orthodox Church had pledged alliance once more to Rome.[152] His work was also a refutation of the ideas of the Russian official Alexandre Stourdza (1791–1854), a former pupil and admirer of Maistre who later fell out with him, and Stourdza's critical views of Catholicism and championing of Orthodoxy in his *Considérations sur la doctrine et l'esprit de l'église orthodoxe* (1816).[153]

Du Pape was, to conclude, a political and philosophical treatise, making extensive use of historical arguments. Although Maistre blamed the *philosophes* for applying anachronistic criteria to judge the medieval popes, he himself was clearly not a proponent of a romantic or historicist approach to history.[154] Maistre was not particularly interested in archival research and source criticism. He even feared that critical historical research could undermine papal authority,

---

[148] Maistre, *Du Pape*, 278.

[149] Maistre, *Du Pape*, 288–93. On the idea of the 'crusade' in counter-revolutionary thought: Schettini, 'Crusade'. On Stoic cosmopolitanism and human dignity: Nussbaum, *Cosmopolitan Tradition*.

[150] 'Mais la Russie devenant tous les jours plus européenne et la langue universelle se trouvant absolument naturalisée dans ce grand empire (...).' Maistre, *Du Pape*, 316.

[151] Maistre, *Du Pape*, 74–5.   [152] Maistre, *Du Pape*, 320–1.

[153] Maistre, *Du Pape*, 295, 324–2. Maistre also blamed Stourdza for his positive views towards Protestantism. He also argued that 'Protestant' is a better word than 'Orthodox' for the Russian Church, placing the two churches under the same anti-Catholic denominator. Cf. Ghervas, *Réinventer*, 297–347.

[154] Maistre, *Du Pape*, 193.

by questioning its claims.[155] He underscored that the papacy had remained fundamentally unaltered over the course of European history. His idea of history can be considered typical of the post-revolutionary attempt to reconcile 'progress' with 'providence'. Maistre's defence of the Catholic Church, and the papacy in particular, was based on an enlightened historical narrative, with the pope as the main motor behind the development of European civilization since the early Middle Ages. Although he did not, like Feller, advocate a full return to the biblical history writing of Bossuet, for Maistre history was definitely not secular.[156] European history for him was a vehicle for Divine Providence. Cataclysmic events such as the French Revolution were not random but showed the active intervention of the Supreme Being, and a deeper pattern could be discovered in the European past. Maistre tried to reconcile the narrative of historical events with Catholic doctrine and eschatological political theology, in many ways adopting the ideas of the *philosophes* he so feared and despised in his works.[157]

9. Conclusion: The European Moment and Its Discontents

The years 1814–15 formed a crucible or critical juncture, when the counter-revolutionary historical narratives and ideals of renewal, developed in the preceding decades, became closely intertwined with the practical attempts to construct a new international order after Napoleon. This order, created at the Congress of Vienna, has been characterized by later hostile historians as the heyday of reactionary conservatism. In their view, 'Vienna' essentially stood for an ultimately failed attempt to repress the revolutionary spirit and to 'turn back the clock'. The historical accuracy of this negative perspective on the 'European moment' of 1814 and 1815 has been questioned in this chapter in several ways.[158]

To begin with, it has been shown that the architects of the post-Napoleonic order were—in their own eyes at least—primarily motivated by enlightened ideals of perpetual peace, prosperity, and freedom. Rejecting a pan-European federal revolutionary republic or a centralized authoritarian empire, they were inspired by an enlightened pluralist idea of a historical Europe. National feelings and the European ideal were not seen by them as contrasting notions, but were considered complementary, as they had supposedly always been in European history. European states and nations could once again develop in their individual ways, as part of the larger historical framework of the European commonwealth.

---

[155] Maistre, *Du Pape*, 33.
[156] Bossuet is highly praised by Maistre in *Du Pape*, for instance, 239, n. 1.
[157] On Maistre's historical thought: Armenteros, *French Idea*.
[158] Martyn Thompson uses the term 'European moment' for the whole revolutionary and Napoleonic period. However, in the interests of precision, the term should be reserved for the years 1814–15. Thompson, 'Ideas'.

Notwithstanding its later more repressive evolution, the post-Napoleonic international system was originally intended by its creators as a rational cosmopolitan order, self-consciously rejecting both an abstract universalism and a patriotism, associated with the French revolutionaries, deemed excessive.

Enlightened narratives of European history, such as were formulated by Vogt and Heeren, provided inspiration for the new monarchical order of 1815. This new international system was legitimized as being in accordance with Europe's allegedly unique tradition of moderate government, rule of law, and an equilibrium between freedom and order. Instead of turning back the clock, the architects of 1814–15 also regarded their project as a proper 'middle way' between 'repairing the chain of time' and adapting to the progress and social renewal of the modern age. They rejected the French Revolution as it had, too abruptly, broken with European traditions and historical institutions, building a utopian project on abstract ideals, resulting in anarchism as well as unprecedented despotism. Instead, they situated their order in the long-term development of European history.

The debates surrounding the construction of this new European and international order after Napoleon were part of a much wider conversation about the profound cultural, spiritual, and moral crises of 'civilized' Europe since the late eighteenth century. High hopes were projected onto the Congress of Vienna. Authors from all ideological backgrounds were confident that the peace process would not only install a renewed political order but would also inaugurate the spiritual and moral regeneration of European society. All kinds of plans and dreams formulated during the revolutionary and Napoleonic years, when counter-revolutionaries felt isolated and lost, could now be realized, or so it seemed. The extent to which different authors considered religious conciliation as the key towards an enduring European peace and security is striking, although, of course, the writers and statesmen greatly differed in their ideas regarding what this religious unity should look like.

Of course, these high expectations could only be disappointed. From 1818 onwards, this enlightened order increasingly acquired a repressive character and the post-war climate of unity was replaced by ideological polarization and conflicts between and within European states. Armed forces and a well-developed transnational security apparatus were increasingly used to fight revolutionary conspiracies, real and imagined, with violent means. Rather than representing the zenith of reactionary government, the Vienna Congress and its legacy were considered a failure and a missed opportunity, at least in the eyes of self-proclaimed enemies of the Revolution, such as Maistre, but also by the main protagonists such as Metternich and Gentz themselves.

Many self-styled counter-revolutionaries regarded, not incorrectly, the Vienna order as a compromise with the Napoleonic and the revolutionary legacy. Vienna had not brought about a renewal of European civilization and a continent-wide spiritual catharsis. Instead, it had only strengthened the Machiavellian state and the forces of unbelief. Anti-revolutionaries such as Maistre turned to European history for comfort and guidance instead, although they realized that their unorthodox use of human history could play into the hands of their ideological enemies. The revolutionary century would eventually become an isolated incident from the perspective of world history, they hoped. Just as in earlier moments in the European past—the rise of Christianity, and for Protestants, the Reformation—a profound spiritual and moral revolution would take place in the near future that would forever sweep away the atheistic and rebellious 'spirit of the age'.

9
Revivals of Historical Europeanism

1. Conservative Cosmopolitans

The making of counter-revolutionary Europeanism was a transnational endeavour at a moment when state boundaries had broken down under the duress of wars, and regimes changed at a pace that baffled contemporaries. European histories and other texts were translated and adapted for different audiences, often radically altering their original meaning, as we have seen in the case of Bonneville. Feller reviewed books from different countries in his journal and entertained a wide network of international contacts, usually former Jesuits. Calonne and Burke mutually influenced each other, although they also had misunderstandings, and eventually fell out. The journal *Courier de Londres* was read by an international audience on both sides of the Channel. Montesquieu's propagation of an ideal of a moderate European civilization was a common source of inspiration for all counter-revolutionary Europeanists studied here, although they adapted his works for their own agendas, as did their revolutionary opponents like Bonneville. In this sense, this study confirms the assessment by Spector and Lilti that Montesquieu's *magnum opus* formed the 'matrix of reflection' on Europe, not only in the eighteenth century, but also in the early nineteenth century.[1] The Congress of Vienna became, for a short time, the embodiment of this late conservative variation of enlightened cosmopolitanism.

However, it would be incorrect to stress only the transnational dimensions of historical Europeanism of the turn of the century. The protagonists studied here formed also part of nascent national, regional, and local traditions. Feller clearly cannot be understood without the South Netherlandish and Luxembourg political and religious context. Calonne, first and foremost, was an official of the French state, whereas, for Burke, the British 1688 Revolution was a key reference point. For no other nation was the question of the ordering of Europe more urgent than the Germans. The German tribes were generally seen by German and non-German publicists alike as providing the seeds of European liberty. German writers regarded the imperial institutional structure of the Holy Roman Empire with its assets and its flaws as the cornerstone of the entire European

---

[1] Karl Ludwig von Haller and Guillaume Groen van Prinsterer, however, were, by contrast, much more critical of the 'revolutionary legacy' of Montesquieu. See for more on Groen the fourth section of this chapter (C9S4). Haller, *Restauration* I, 53–7. Interestingly, Haller cited Feller's lemma on Montesquieu in his historical dictionary as a source against Rousseau (56).

commonwealth. As Müller clearly expressed, the German people, unlike the French, had, in his eyes, always valued diversity over centralized rule and homogeneous cultural practices, and thus were ideally placed to regenerate an exhausted European culture, corrupted by French philosophy.

Even within 'German' Europeanism, different geopolitical traditions can be discerned. For Müller, Gentz, and Metternich, although not Austrian by birth, the Austrian Empire became the nodal point of the resurrected international order. Vogt, as we have seen, regarded the Rhineland, in particular Mainz, seat of the archbishop and the imperial chancellor, as the centre of German, European, and even universal history. Heeren's perspective was rooted in enlightened Protestant Göttingen, then part of the British monarchy. Different strands can also be observed in Francophone counter-revolutionary Europeanism. Maistre was a diplomat from the Sardinian monarchy, with Turin as its capital, but France, the 'oldest daughter' of the Catholic Church, was the country he most admired. For Bonald, a France restored to its natural boundaries, an idea also propagated by the revolutionaries, was the inevitable foundation of a post-Napoleonic European order. Thus, both historical and newly minted national and local traditions were combined with wider European and transnational models and travelling ideas. The protagonists of this study, however, have to date almost exclusively been studied from a biographical or national perspective. This book has tried to examine counter-revolutionary Europeanism from a broader transnational and multilevel perspective, without, of course, having the ambition to chart this topic comprehensively. The examination of the views of different protagonists, from a selection of different regions and languages, above all underscored the varieties that can be found in the shaping of historical Europeanism in this tumultuous era.

The authors studied here could even be labelled counter-intuitively as 'conservative cosmopolitans', as they sought to combine Counter-Revolution with a certain form of enlightened cosmopolitanism. It should be pointed out again, though, that many counter-revolutionaries did not use, or even consciously rejected, the label 'conservatism': they did not wish to preserve or restore a pre-revolutionary society, which they saw as corrupted by the French *philosophes* and their political supporters. A common denominator was the rejection of the French Revolution and all it stood for in their eyes, but the question of what 'Counter-Revolution' meant was differently answered by each author. Their aim was to build a renewed and regenerated spiritual, cultural, and moral Europe on the model of its long-term historical origins, and return to the gradual institutional progress of the preceding centuries. They usually perceived themselves as 'moderates', rejecting the reactionary views of 'ultra-royalists' as well as those of the revolutionaries. Both 'excessive' views were deemed the pernicious outcome of uncontrolled passions and lack of balance.[2]

---

[2] Also, 'conservatism' as a coherent party ideology, for the most part, came into being after 1830, as was argued in Chapter 1. Cf. Fawcett, *Conservatism*.

The counter-revolutionary publicists examined in this study could be typecast as 'cosmopolitans' on the basis of the five criteria singled out in the first chapter. First of all, authors such as Müller clearly described themselves as cosmopolitans, but they also made a distinction between the 'right' kind of cosmopolitanism embedded in morals, love of the fatherland, and religion vis-à-vis a 'wrong' cosmopolitanism. This self-proclaimed counter-revolutionary cosmopolitanism took different forms. In the case of Feller, neo-Stoic notions, through a Pauline lens, formed the basis of his Catholic anti-Jansenist articulation of cosmopolitanism, which showed itself to be often intolerant towards non-Catholics' beliefs and countries. Müller provided an ideal of a Christ-centred cosmopolis, inspired by the early Christian community. In the case of Feller, Maistre, and Bonneville, cosmopolitanism was fused with eschatological and esoteric ideas. In all the writers studied here, we can discern a heightened consciousness of living in extraordinary times with unique possibilities as well as apocalyptic catastrophes. According to some publicists such as Maistre, these political catastrophes were a necessary evil required for the catharsis of European civilization.

Second, writers like Vogt, but also, for instance, Maistre and the Dutch king Willem I, conceived of ideas of a transnational institutional architecture beyond the level of the territorial or local state in order to attain 'perpetual peace' on a continent scarred by massive warfare and intrinsic violence. Others, like Heeren, Metternich, and Gentz, emphasized increased cooperation between states on the principle of a renewed, reasonable, and less violent equilibrium. Religious reconciliation was often seen as a precondition for a more enduring political peace. Many of these blueprints now seem odd and not applicable to the contemporary era, but it should be pointed out that they were influential in their own times, and, in some cases, surprising intellectual lineages can be found. For instance, Maistre's idea of an international institution centred around the mediating role of the papacy was copied and adapted by early socialists.[3] All these publications testify to the ability of these publicists to imagine alternative European and transnational institutions and to dream about attaining the enlightened ideals of perpetual peace in their times.

Third, enlightened cosmopolitanism has been interpreted as positive, valuing—within clear boundaries—the notions of cultural difference and political pluralism. All counter-revolutionary authors extolled the value of variety within a specific political context. They decried the homogeneity they associated with the wrong kind of enlightened philosophy and above all with the French Revolution. French revolutionaries, in their view, violently imposed a universal model on the world, which would eventually lead to a despotism far worse than had been attempted earlier by those who strived for the imposition of 'universal monarchy' on the

---

[3] Armenteros, *French Idea*, 283–314.

European continent. Even Maistre argued for the development of different national and local cultures within the strict framework of the unified Catholic Church. A specific idea of concepts such as pluralism and diversity, in the early twenty-first century usually associated with progressive politics, were rhetorical weapons in the armaments of the eighteenth-century Counter-Revolution. The adaptation of eighteenth-century enlightened, or, as O'Brien termed it, 'cosmopolitan', history writing, constituted a fourth criterion to label the counter-revolutionaries as inheritors of enlightened cosmopolitanism. The publicists gave an account of an original freedom that was installed in Europe's institutions, in the beginning often overshadowed by barbarism, but slowly developing over the centuries. The pluralist character of European society, united by a common culture and legal system, guaranteed this liberty deemed unique from a global perspective.[4] Fifth and finally, pleas for an active citizenship beyond the state can also be found in the counter-revolutionary writings of, for instance, Vogt and Calonne, although this aspect needs further exploration elsewhere.[5]

In the rest of this chapter, I will briefly explore the survival and revival of the historical Europeanism dissected in this study and provide some insights into the wider ramifications of this research topic. In the next section, I will reflect on the more exclusive and 'darker' side of counter-revolutionary cosmopolitanism, as well as its relation to European colonialism and imperialism. Then, I will give some examples of the afterlives of the counter-revolutionary historical Europeanists, underscoring that historical Europeanism transcended ideological boundaries and could be found on all sides of the nineteenth-century and twentieth-century political spectrum. I will then examine some works by a new generation of counter-revolutionaries, born after the Revolution, followed by a brief overview of radical and liberal legacies in the nineteenth century. This book ends with some thoughts on the rediscovery and reconfiguration of historical Europeanism in the twentieth century and its impact on the post-war project of European integration, followed by a brief coda.

2. Counter-Revolution and Empire

The self-proclaimed enlightened 'moderation' of the counter-revolutionary Europeanists, however, had its 'darker' sides too. The concept was, paradoxically, used to legitimate the exercise of power, military conquest, social hierarchy, and political exclusion as well as warfare and political strife.[6] Most authors studied here appropriated the enlightened narrative of an unfolding civilization to defend

---

[4] See for Russian views on European historic pluralism: Pasture, *Imagining*, 36–7.
[5] Cf. Lok, 'Just and True Liberty'.
[6] For the 'dark' sides of the idea of political moderation: de Haan and Lok, *Politics of Moderation*, 2.

the property and possessions of social elites with roots in the *ancien régime* against the claims of those less fortunate.[7] For Burke and Calonne, for instance, the sacredness of the right of property was one of the foundations of the ancient constitution, to be defended against the revolutionary lawlessness and legalized 'theft' that rendered all property insecure. Both men, moreover, praised moderation and enlightened civilization, but at the same time advocated relentless warfare against the revolutionary Republic and fiercely criticized efforts to reach a truce.

'Moderation' was also the banner under which the victorious allied countries imposed a military occupation on the defeated France in 1815.[8] Peace and stability were invoked to exclude the political participation of the majority of the population—women, children, labourers, servants—deemed unable to control their passions. Moderation and *oubli* were also the rhetorical phrases under which almost-forgotten and unpopular dynasties were imposed by military victors on often unwilling and indifferent populations in the Restoration age. The success of these counter-revolutionary ideas contributed to the postponing of political democracy in Europe for a century after the French Revolution, although the precise relationship between Counter-Revolution, conservatism, and the evolution of democratic political systems in the (early) nineteenth century still needs systematic and comparative investigation.[9]

This ambivalence over the counter-revolutionary rhetoric of 'moderation' could clearly be observed in the case of Niklas Vogt. On the one hand, Vogt defended, as we have seen, the idea of a European republic, founded on the noble principles of civic freedom, diversity, balance, and moderation. On the other hand, after 1793, he increasingly supported the idea of a natural and gendered hierarchy within families and communities in response to revolutionary events. In the Napoleonic age, he even used the pluralist narrative to underpin and legitimize an authoritarian and aggressive military empire. The cultural and political 'variety' Vogt prized was limited to Christian European countries, although as we have seen, his view of, for instance, the Arab peoples was on the whole positive. He did not completely exclude the possibility of the Ottoman Empire ever taking part in the European federation, although this was, in his view, not likely in the short term.[10] Finally, Vogt advocated active participation in public life by citizens,

---

[7] The neglect of socio-economic inequality was, according to Martha Nussbaum, also the main flaw of the classical Stoic cosmopolitans, who, in their turn, inspired many counter-revolutionary authors. Nussbaum, *Cosmopolitan Tradition*.

[8] De Graaf, *Fighting Terror*; Haynes, *Friends*.

[9] Annelien de Dijn argues that the hegemony of the counter-revolutionary idea of freedom after 1800 greatly hindered the democratic development of the Western world. De Dijn, *Freedom*. Daniel Ziblatt, on the other hand, holds a more positive view of the contribution of (late) nineteenth-century conservatism to the evolution of democracy in Europe. Ziblatt, *Conservative Parties*. Ziblatt pays most attention to the latter part of the century, though. The early nineteenth century needs further analysis.

[10] Vogt, *Staats- und Kirchengrundsätze*, 56.

admittedly an exclusive group for Vogt, within these larger imperial and European federations.[11] Jews, Muslims, and atheists were accorded civil rights by him, but not the wider (political) rights, which were dependent on adhesion to the Christian religion.[12] Maistre and Bonald went even further in this respect: European unity and reconciliation was to be achieved by resurrecting a perennial foe: Islam.

This renewed sense of European uniqueness due to its alleged 'moderate' and 'diverse' character had important implications for the overseas imperial project, as well as for more general visions of Europe's role in the wider world.[13] To what extent did the counter-revolutionary cosmopolitans include other parts of the world in their historical narratives, and to what extent did their work accommodate, and perhaps even glorify, European imperial dominance in other parts of the world?[14] Important critical studies have been published on the enlightened historiography, demonstrating its often hidden 'Eurocentric' character, and its role in the legitimation and shaping of the imperial project.[15] While claiming to write a universal history of the world, enlightened historians generally were taking the Northwestern European experience as a norm for all parts of the world, thus legitimizing colonial enterprises as civilizational projects by historical means. According to Stuart Woolf, the importance of the revolutionary and Napoleonic period for the development of the idea of European history was that 'a European view of the extra-European world was consolidated which drew on earlier perceptions, but transformed them into a radically different unifying concept of European civilization and progress which allowed the classification and justified the material exploitation of the rest of the world'.[16]

In her study of liberal imperialist thought, Jennifer Pitts, moreover, argued that liberal thinkers from 1800 onwards became less critical of imperialism and more exclusively focussed on Europe in their writings than were their eighteenth-century predecessors.[17] Can we draw the same clear conclusions for

---

[11] According to Pauline Kleingeld, cosmopolitanism and elitism are not mutually exclusive; see, for instance, the case of the 'elitist cosmopolitanism' of Christoph Martin Wieland (1733-1813). Kleingeld, 'Six Varieties', 507-9.

[12] Vogt, *Staats- und Kirchengrundsätze*, 76. During the negotiations of the Vienna Congress, the rights of Jews were extensively discussed but eventually no final settlement was reached, and after 1815, Jewish rights were steadily eroded. Vick, *Congress*, 166-92.

[13] On the concept of 'empire' in intellectual history, see: Cooper, *Colonialism in Question*; Burbank and Cooper, *Empires*; Osterhammel, *Colonialism*; Bayly, *Birth of the Modern World*; Armitage, *Ideological Origins*; Fitzmaurice, *Sovereignty*; Koekkoek, Richard, and Weststeijn, *Dutch Empire*.

[14] A study that explores the interrelation of historiography and empire is: Satia, *Time's Monster*.

[15] Asbach, *Europa und die Moderne*; Bhambra, *Rethinking Modernity*; Cañizares-Esguerra, *History of the New World*; Chakrabarty, *Provincializing Europe*; Goody, *Theft of History*; Blaut, *Coloniser's Model*; Brolsma, de Bruin, and Lok, 'Introduction', in *Eurocentrism*, 11-24; Murray-Miller, 'Civilization, Modernity and Europe'. The classic study on the role of scholars in the construction of the idea of the 'Orient', and the start of an extensive literature on this topic is, of course, Said, *Orientalism*.

[16] Woolf, 'Construction', 74.   [17] Pitts, *Turn to Empire*; Pitts, *Boundaries*.

the less-studied imperial thought of counter-revolutionary and early-conservative historiography? How were the imperial projects described by the counter-revolutionary historians of Europe, if at all, and to what extent were they regarded and justified as a common European endeavour? And what about the internal 'imperial' and hierarchical borders of Europe: to what extent did counter-revolutionary historians replace the traditional North–South division with an East–West one, with the West as the core and the East as the less civilized periphery of Europe?[18] These questions have so far not been answered systematically.[19]

While it is undeniably true that all counter-revolutionary history writing was 'Eurocentric' in one way or another, the views on Europe and the world beyond differed widely among the authors studied here. François-Xavier de Feller actually defended the institution of slavery, appealing to religious as well as enlightened humanitarian arguments. Göttingen historian Heeren, by contrast, was very critical of its existence, arguing that it was against the laws of humanity. The fierce counter-revolutionary Joseph de Maistre, moreover, saw the eradication of slavery from European soil as one of the great accomplishments of medieval papacy. If we take a closer look at the counter-revolutionary authors studied in this book, the picture becomes much more complicated than the clear-cut watershed presented by Pitts and others, and the complexity and diversity of views strike the reader.

If we look, for instance, at the case of Feller, we see that he expressed in his geographical and historical dictionaries a wide interest that was not confined to Europe, but included other parts of the world. He made positive remarks about Arab scholars, although his verdict on Islam was negative on all counts. At the same time, he clearly demonstrated that the non-European and non-Christian parts of the world were less developed in moral and civilizational terms than Christian Europe. Challenging *philosophe* praise, Feller showed himself to be very critical of the—in his view—barbaric Chinese civilization. He feared the rise of a Protestant and revolutionary American republic, and ominously predicted that the Americas would dominate 'the old continent' one day. The fight against atheism, for Feller, was a global struggle, with Europe as its main theatre.

Feller was an enthusiastic defender of, in particular, the Spanish imperial conquest to spread the Catholic faith and civilization to the rest of the world, countering the pervasive critique of Raynal and others of the administration of the Spanish colonies. For Feller, fusing traditional religious with enlightened and

---

[18] On this problem: Drace-Francis, 'Elephant'; Lok and Montoya, 'Centre and Periphery'.
[19] It would also be desirable to have more transnational studies on counter-revolutionary and conservative thought, which include regions and languages outside Europe, on the model of Christopher Bayly's study of liberalism in India: *Recovering Liberties*. Cf. the Russian and the Chinese cases, which are discussed in Lok, Pestel, and Reboul, *Cosmopolitan Conservatisms*. For Egypt and Latin America, see the themed issue: Lok and van Eijnatten, *Global Counter-Enlightenment*.

rational arguments to buttress his case, the Spanish had brought both religion and civilization to the New World. He was much more critical of British and Dutch— Protestant—colonial explorations that, in his view, took place only for financial motives and pure greed. Perhaps most obnoxiously, Feller defended slavery in the New World with the—enlightened—argument that it was in the best interests of the slaves themselves. The anti-slavery movements of his time he regarded primarily as a *philosophe* plot to undermine royal authority and the Catholic Church. At the same time, he decried the 'enslavement' of the Belgians who, in his view, suffered under the tyrannical rule of Joseph II. The world outside Europe, by contrast, did not figure very much in the works of Calonne, who mainly focussed on France and Europe. It is, however, telling that he restricted his usage of the concept of the ancient constitution to the European continent. He did not refer to a 'global' ancient constitution, as Burke had done for India in the Hastings process.[20] Also, Calonne, as well as Burke, emphasized that the French revolutionaries had placed France outside of Europe, making it part of 'barbarous' African history.

The Germanic writings on the international equilibrium studied here seemed to confirm the distinctness of the European continent. The writings of Gentz and Müller were above all preoccupied with an internal European view of the international system. Müller's criticism of the imperial imposition of uniform laws and civilization by the French, and his emphasis on the German nation as a microcosmos of humanity due to its diverse character, could be read as a criticism of European expansion and attempts to enforce a single civilizational model on the rest of the world. At the same time, Müller also underscored Europe's unique position as a mediator and 'middleman' on the global stage. Whereas in his *Elements*, European history and civilization formed his self-evident frame of interpretation, he also emphasized the potential universal dimension of the Christian faith. He envisaged the possibility of all states uniting in a world federation mystically centred around the persona of Christ, and thus excluding the other religions from this world community. The Jena romantics, by contrast, looked towards Asia for the spiritual regeneration of Europe, advocating a new synthesis between Orient and Occident.

Also, Vogt, following Montesquieu, mainly advocated an internal view of the European Republic, regarding its alleged pluralist character as a unique feature compared to other civilizations, which were characterized by centralized imperial structures. His work is a good example of the Eurocentric impulse of the pluralist idea of European history. For Vogt, Islam was a despotic religion, and the fall of the crusader states could only be understood as the result of the incompetence of the crusaders themselves and was not evidence of the superior qualities of their

---

[20] Bourke, *Empire*, 573–675, 820–50.

Muslim adversaries. In his view of universal history, a distinct Eurocentrism can be found. Each continent was assigned to a different epoch in a stadial view of the development of society: Africans, Laps, and Mongolians represented the first primitive or infant stage of humanity. Asian societies were comparable to medieval Europe, in the sense that both represented the second or adolescent stage of human development, characterized by religion, honour, and valour. The adulthood of mankind could be found only in modern commercial Europe. The aggressive empires of Britain and Russia were put, by Vogt, firmly outside the borders of European civilization. Vogt was especially critical of British imperialism, which, in his view, was motivated only by greed and financial considerations. Like Feller, Vogt feared that in the future Europe would be eclipsed by a rising Western hemisphere, believing that Brazil would develop on the same path as the young United States and become equally as powerful. He accorded little agency to Africa and Asia on the stage of world history. Only the dynamic and freedom-loving Arabs were praised in his later works as the 'Germans' of the Middle East.

A more complicated counter-revolutionary treatment of Europe's place in the world can be found in the works of Arnold Heeren. Heeren analysed European state relations within a wider global context in his writings on ancient history, although he realized that he was hindered in his global historiographical ambitions by his lack of knowledge of non-European languages. He also distinguished between despotic rule in Asia and the moderate and free constitutions in Europe, underscoring the unique pluralist nature of the modern European state system. In contrast to many other contemporaries, Heeren regarded imperial history as very much part of European history. He pointed out the mutual effect between imperial cores and their colonial 'peripheries', arguing that the colonial periphery increasingly influenced the politics of the European metropolis. In his works, he showed himself ambivalent towards the imperial project. In his *Manual* he seemed to be very aware of the violence and oppression produced by Europeans in other parts of the world. In this respect, Heeren fitted the pattern of eighteenth-century (German) enlightened criticism of empire as analysed by Sankar Muthu in his *Enlightenment against Empire*.[21]

As a Protestant, Heeren, however, clearly had a more positive view of the colonies established by Protestant powers such as England, the Netherlands, and the Northern German states than of Catholic colonies in the New World. Although he concluded that greed was the main motivation behind even Protestant European colonialism, he also believed that Protestant Europeans could bring civilization to other parts of the world and improve the lives of many ordinary non-Europeans. He condemned the slave revolts of Haiti as premature, but also supported in principle the abolition of the slave trade. He

---

[21] Muthu, *Enlightenment against Empire*.

simultaneously pointed out the manifold practical difficulties that abolition would bring. While arguing that colonial rivalry had led to war among European powers, he also advocated the establishment of a jointly administered colony on Egyptian soil, which would be especially beneficial to Central and Eastern European countries, which so far did not possess any non-European colonies. The Mediterranean should be a security zone controlled through a joint effort by the European powers.

The counter-revolutionary and anti-imperial argument in favour of cultural and political pluralism against a revolutionary homogeneity and despotism could in theory result in a defence of the interests of non-European societies against European cultural and military expansion. Müller, for instance, warned against the immoral economic exploitation of colonial projects.[22] Friedemann Pestel, however, has described how the *monarchiens émigrés* dreamt of reconstructing the *ancien régime* in a purer form in the Caribbean when mainland Europe seemed to be lost to the forces of the Revolution.[23] In Heeren's works we have observed an ambivalent attitude of criticizing abuses and warning of the dangers of colonial rivalry for the European state system, while at the same time arguing that it was Europe's role to spread the light of civilization to other continents, and even designing blueprints for 'European' colonies in the Mediterranean. For Heeren, 'Europe' was not a unique continent in a cultural sense: the European continent was the first location where modern society developed. But Heeren, in true Enlightenment vein, believed that other continents would eventually develop according to a similar trajectory.[24] For Heeren, Europe's uniqueness was also only a relatively recent development from the sixteenth century onwards due to the rise of the state system. In earlier periods, in particular in the ancient world, Heeren's perspective was far less Eurocentric, emphasizing the manifold commercial, cultural, and political relations among Asia, Africa, and Europe.

The nexus between racial thought, imperialism, Eurocentrism, and nineteenth-century conservatism and Counter-Revolution is, in my view, to conclude this section, an important and urgent topic for further scholarly enquiry, which is beyond the scope of this present work.[25] My preliminary conclusion is that the clear-cut shift around 1800, from a more critical stance in the eighteenth century towards a uniformly legitimizing position vis-à-vis European colonialism in the nineteenth century, as observed in the case of liberal intellectuals, should be nuanced and problematized for counter-revolutionary and early-conservative authors. More attention should instead be given to the internal contradictions

---

[22] See Chapter 5.   [23] Pestel, *Kosmopoliten*, 255–99.
[24] Heeren, 'Schreiben an einen Freund', lxvii–lxix.
[25] Pitts discusses late, but not early, nineteenth-century conservative imperialist views in her chapter 'Ideas of Empire'.

and ambiguities of counter-revolutionary views on empire and Europe's role in the wider world.

3. Beyond Ideological Boundaries

In the rest of this final chapter, I will cursorily discuss some legacies of historical Europeanist ideas of the revolutionary age after 1830, and break some ground for future research, without claiming to provide a comprehensive overview. I will suggest that the counter-revolutionary Europeanists had long and often forgotten afterlives. Their ideas were adapted, reconfigured, and revived in later epochs in European history. Later politicians and writers continued to tap into the transnational language of historical Europeanism, originally constructed in the decades around 1800. They eventually contributed to the ideological foundations of the twentieth-century post-war European project, instead of disappearing as a result of the rise of nineteenth-century nationalism, as the cliché has it. The next sections will be devoted to historical Europeanist writings of a new post-revolutionary generation, which did not experience the revolutionary events in person but for whom the French Revolution was still the benchmark for all political thought. The counter-revolutionary tradition of historical Europeanism was adopted after 1830 by publicists from various political convictions: conservatives and reactionaries, but also by left-wing radical nationalists and liberals, and even to a certain extent by socialists and communists. Similarities can be observed along with the differences, which have often gained more attention from later historians and political scientists who projected later categories back into history.[26]

It would, moreover, be anachronistic to assume that nineteenth-century activists, statesmen, and writers consistently defended one coherent ideological position or political stance. Often they fervently supported a revolutionary cause in one context, whereas they were branded as pillars of the Counter-Revolution in another.[27] Chateaubriand, for instance, defended the return of the Bourbon monarchy in France in 1815 with arguments derived from both European history and civilization as well as peace, stability, and human rights against a despotic and murderous Napoleonic rule.[28] A decade later he used the same arguments to support the revolt of the Greeks against their overlord, the Ottoman Sultan.[29]

---

[26] As Isaiah Berlin put it: '[the student of political ideas] understands neither that time nor his own if he does not perceive the contrast between what was common to Comte and Mill, Mazzini and Michelet, Herzen and Marx, on the one hand, and to Max Weber and William James, Tawney and Beard, Lytton Strachey and Wells, on the other; the continuity of the European intellectual tradition without which no historical understanding at all would be possible is, at shorter range, a succession of specific discontinuities and dissimilarities.' Berlin, 'Political Ideas', 354.

[27] Lok, *Windvanen*; Serna, *Republique des Girouettes*.   [28] Chateaubriand, *De Buonaparte*.

[29] Chateaubriand, *Note sur la Grèce*. On the Greek Revolution and Europe: Mazower, *Greek Revolution*.

Félicité Robert de Lamennais, to give another example, was an anti-Gallican ultra-Montanist fighting the spreading of atheism and revolutionary philosophy in the 1820s.[30] In 1833, he broke with the Church, espoused the idea of popular sovereignty and, in 1848, he sided with the revolutionaries against the European monarchies. The British lawyer Travers Twiss, as so elegantly described by Andrew Fitzmaurice, was a friend of Metternich and defender of the order established by Vienna in the first fifty years of his life; by the early 1860s, by contrast, he embraced the radical liberal notion that moral action was the basis of political society.[31] These examples were not exceptions, but exemplified the difficulties of clearly demarcating liberals from conservatives, and revolutionaries from counter-revolutionaries, in this century.

Nineteenth-century Europeanist authors, like their predecessors examined in this study, usually rejected both an—in their eyes—excessive nationalism and an 'anti-patriotic' and rootless internationalism. They argued that the unique European nations and cultures could flourish and develop only as part of a wider historical European and cosmopolitan commonwealth.[32] Particularly, future research shall have to provide more insight into the survival of historical Europeanism in the decades between the 1848 European (Counter-)Revolutions and the First World War. These years, commonly described in terms of hegemonic nationalism, imperialism, and universalist ideologies, also formed a crucial bridge period in the survival of (counter-)revolutionary cosmopolitanisms and conservative Europeanism.[33]

4. Unbelief and Revolution

The writings of the Dutch intellectual and self-proclaimed 'anti-revolutionary' statesman Guillaume Groen van Prinsterer (1801–76) offer an example of Protestant Europeanism in the nineteenth century. Groen's magnum opus *Ongeloof en Revolutie* (Unbelief and Revolution), published in 1847, could be regarded as a synopsis of anti-revolutionary historical Europeanism forged in the decades around 1800.[34] Born in 1801, Groen belonged to a new generation that

---

[30] Lamennais, *Essai sur l'indifférence*.   [31] Fitzmaurice, *Leopold's Ghostwriter*.

[32] This view on European history and civilization can also be found among the nineteenth-century scholars of international law. Koskenniemi, *Gentle Civilizer*.

[33] On the post-1848 reaction from a transnational perspective: Clark, 'After 1848'; Caruso, 'In Medio Stat Virtus?'. Few studies exist on European history writing between 1870 and 1914. The period is briefly sketched in Verga, *Storie*, 47–53. Cf. d'Auria, 'Progress, Decline and Redemption'. On the late nineteenth-century notion of the Pope as peacemaker: Ramón Solans, 'utopía ultramontana'. Orlando Figes, finally, has argued that the decades before the First World War witnessed the invention of a 'European' commercial mass culture rather than the zenith of cultural nationalism: Figes, *Europeans*.

[34] Groen van Prinsterer, *Ongeloof en Revolutie*.

grew up after the revolutionary events and knew them only indirectly.[35] Coming from an upper-middle-class family of members of the Walloon Reformed Church, Groen first worked as a senior bureaucrat in Brussels, serving King Willem I, in the late 1820s. After the Belgian Revolution and the dissolution of the United Kingdom of the Netherlands in 1830, which he fiercely opposed, Groen became head of the State Archives in The Hague. In this capacity, he had ample time to do historical research and to publish his historical works and editions of source collections on the House of Orange. When writing a book on Dutch national history from a Protestant and anti-liberal perspective, Groen became interested in the French Revolution as a pan-European phenomenon. In 1837, he supported the secession of protestants from the official Dutch Reformed Church (the *Afscheiding* of 1834), deemed too liberal and worldly in the eyes of some protestants, making clear that he was not always on the side of the Dutch state.

Unbelief and Revolution was based on the fifteen lectures Groen presented to a select group of friends in his stately Hague home in the years 1845 and 1846. The publication must above all be seen in the context of Groen's anxiety over the revolutionary activities of the 1840s. His fear was that a new wave of revolutions would overwhelm the European states, in repetition of the earlier revolutionary decades, ushering in a new revolutionary Terror.[36] Like Maistre's *Du pape*, *Unbelief and Revolution* did not consist of a traditional history narrative, but was a work of political philosophy and theology supported by historical arguments. For Groen, historical events were primarily the outcome and materialization of the development of the 'spirit of the age'. Historical facts functioned in his thought as experimental evidence for the truth of theoretical insights and philosophical ideas. This predominantly philosophical perspective was remarkable for a man who, as a professional archivist, was in daily contact with archives and primary sources.

Like many other historians of Europe examined in this study, Groen had an idea of history that was neither completely secular nor based purely on Scripture[37] For Groen, divine intervention interfered in world history in several ways. He—controversially for some more traditional Protestants—was convinced that religion could be defended through the use of modern historical and philosophical scholarship, rather than exclusively by arguments drawn from Holy Writ itself, as the more orthodox Calvinists believed.[38] For Groen, the Bible was the 'lamp' without which world history could not be understood.[39] However, in contrast to Maistre, Groen never wrote that the revolutionary process was directly led by the

---

[35] A modern critical biography of Groen and his afterlives is still lacking. Older biographies were usually written from a sympathetic Protestant perspective. Schutte, *Groen*; Kuiper, *Groen*.
[36] Van Dijk, *Groen's Lectures*; Suttorp, Sneller, and Veldkamp, *Groens 'Ongeloof en revolutie'*.
[37] On Groen's idea of history: Harinck and Kuiper, *Groen van Prinsterer*; van Vliet, *historische benadering*; Smitskamp, *Groen*; Zwaan, *Groen*.
[38] Groen, *Ongeloof en Revolutie*, 11–12.   [39] Groen, *Handboek*, 1.

hand of God. He interpreted revolutionary events primarily as the outcome of human behaviour and ideas. For him divine explanations and human causality coexisted in the unfolding of European history.[40]

Traditionally Groen has been interpreted by historians as a founding father and ideological forebear of the Dutch Protestant awakening and modern Dutch political Protestantism. Since the turn of the millennium, Groen is also increasingly studied from a European and international perspective, for instance underscoring his role in the German awakening.[41] And rightly so, as his *Unbelief and Revolution* could be regarded as a compendium of European *anti-philosophe* and cosmopolitan counter-revolutionary thought from the preceding decades. Groen professed to be an 'eclectic' regarding his sources.[42] Along with the Dutch Protestant counter-revolutionaries and older Enlightenment critics, Groen made extensive use of a whole range of counter-revolutionary authors from different countries, studied in the preceding chapters. To the dismay of many of his more traditional fellow Dutch Protestants, he cited not only Protestant authors such as Burke, Pitt, and Gentz, but also many Catholic and French counter-revolutionary authorities and writers such as de Bonald, de Lamennais, and de Maistre, and even older Catholic historians such as Bossuet, Fénelon, and Moreau.

Groen did not even shy away from citing the influential history of European civilization by the French liberal—and Protestant—author and politician François Guizot, as well as other liberal French historians such as Adolphe Thiers and Benjamin Constant.[43] The historians of the Göttingen school also formed a major source of reference for Groen's interpretation of European history: Groen cited Heeren's *Manual* approvingly several times.[44] This bricolage of intellectual authorities, appropriated by Groen for his own purposes, demonstrates the continuing transnational character of counter-revolutionary thought and the fluidity of boundaries between political Catholic and Protestant and even between conservative and liberal European history writing in the first half of the nineteenth century. It also showed the cosmopolitan background of an author who has been blamed for—or credited with, depending on one's perspective—the recrafting of the nineteenth-century Dutch narrative from a Protestant, Orangist, and monarchical point of view.[45]

---

[40] Groen's precise idea on the role of Divine Providence in history and the notion of secular history as revelation is a matter for scholarly debate: Smitskamp, *Groen*, 30–3, 40–50, 87–97; Verheij, 'Groen's visie'; van Dijk, *Groen's Lectures*, 85–8, 254–69; van Vliet, *historische benadering*, 82–100, 326–557.
[41] On Groen as Europeanist: Bijl, *Europese antirevolutionair*; de Bruijn and Harinck, *Groen in Europese context*. For his role in the German awakening: Kloes, *German Awakening*; an older standard work on the Protestant *Réveil* from a Dutch as well as a European perspective, is: Kluit, *Réveil*; on the varied nature of nineteenth-century theology: Fergusson, 'History, Tradition, and Scepticism'.
[42] Groen, *Ongeloof en Revolutie*, 36.
[43] Van Vliet, 'Groen en Guizot', 37–42; Bijl, *Europese antirevolutionair*; Smitskamp, *Groen*, 56–8.
[44] Groen, *Ongeloof en Revolutie*, 31 n. 3, 262 n. 3, 274.
[45] Groen, *Handboek*. Cf. for the transnational origin of national conservatisms more generally: Lok, Pestel, and Reboul, 'Introduction'.

For Groen, as for other writers in this study, the French Revolution was not an exclusively political, but in essence also a religious and spiritual event.[46] The revolutionary events were described by him in traditional *anti-philosophe* vein as the logical outcome of the spread of an atheistic philosophy throughout Europe, and in France in particular. For Groen, French history was European history in a concentrated form. He considered the revolutionary events as the 'deadly fruit' from the 'lifeless tree' of eighteenth-century philosophy.[47] Groen therefore classified, as had many eighteenth-century *anti-philosophes*, the 'century of light' as an age of darkness, 'fireworks', and 'torch light'.[48] Once these atheists' ideas had become dominant in European society, due to the desolate state of the Catholic Church, among other factors, the political consequences were inevitable. Unlike the Catholic writers, Groen did not trace the origins of eighteenth-century philosophy to the sixteenth-century Reformation. For him, by contrast, the Reformation formed the complete antithesis of the Revolution, as it had saved Europe and the world from superstition, while the Revolution had led the 'civilized world' into the abyss of unbelief.[49] For Groen, Rousseau was the inverted 'Luther' of the Revolution, spreading the dark gospel of popular sovereignty.[50]

Like other anti-revolutionaries, Groen regarded the revolutionary constitutions as a violent rupture of the European ancient constitutions, which had been formed through gradual evolution from their Christian and Germanic origins since the collapse of the Western Roman Empire. The revolutionary project was, in his eyes, not based on law, but instead consisted of the antithesis of the rule of law. In Europe, a uniquely moderate and tempered monarchical regime, combining freedom and order, had evolved due to the benign effects of Christianity. In contrast to other parts of the world, the exercise of state power had never been absolute in Christian Europe.[51] Nations and states had been able to develop individually within a common Christian cultural and legal frame. The European state system had been founded on a balance or equilibrium (*evenwigt*) of counterweights, Groen argued in the tradition of the counter-revolutionary historical Europeanists.[52] The revolutionary abstract ideals of freedom and equality, however, had led to new forms of 'slavery' and 'despotism' never previously witnessed

---

[46] By 'revolution', Groen understood 'de geheele omkeering van denkwijs en gezindheid in de terzijdestelling en verachting van vroeger beginselen over geheel de Christenheid'. Groen, *Ongeloof en Revolutie*, 6.

[47] 'Deze Voorlezingen zijn eene proeve van historisch betoog dat er een natuurlijk en noodwendig verband is tusschen Ongeloof en Revolutie; dat de rigting welke, ten gevolge der zelfverheffing van den mensch, in Staatsregt en wetenschap, niet zonder weêrspraak evenwel, heerschappij voert, uit verwerping van het Evangelie is ontstaan. (...) Ik heb uit de doodelijkheid der vrucht, zonder gedwongenheid, meen ik, het gevolg ontleend, dat de boom waarop zij groeit, geen levensboom is (...).' Groen, *Ongeloof en Revolutie*, v; on Groen's construction of the idea of the 'enlightened eighteenth century': Lok, 'Eeuw van ongeloof'.

[48] Groen, *Ongeloof en Revolutie*, 186.   [49] Groen, *Ongeloof en Revolutie*, 14.

[50] Groen, *Handboek*, 498. On Groen's periodization of world history: Smitskamp, *Groen*, 33–40.

[51] Groen, *Ongeloof en Revolutie*, 52–6.   [52] Groen, *Ongeloof en Revolutie*, 115.

on this scale in the European context.[53] For Groen, the revolutionary state stood for unbridled and arbitrary state power in the manner of Machiavelli, as well as for a society of disconnected and lost 'atomic' individuals without a sense of community or larger purpose. Rather than a reaction to the Revolution, for Groen, the violent Napoleon and his militarily aggressive imperial regime represented the apotheosis of *philosophe* unbelief.[54]

To Groen's disappointment, the so-called restoration did not end the revolutionary epoch, but instead consolidated its legacy. For him '1814–15' had not been a break in European history: Groen interpreted the half century between the original Revolution of 1789 and his moment of writing, the 1840s, in terms of the survival of unbelief and the growth of despotic state power despite the frequent changes of political regimes.[55] Like Maistre, he castigated the peacemakers of 1815, including his former king Willem I, for compromising with the principles of the Revolution for reasons of stability, rather than inaugurating a general spiritual renewal. This was demonstrated by his discussion of Gentz, whom he otherwise admired as a counter-revolutionary ideologue. Yet, as secretary at the Vienna conference 'it seems to me, perhaps because he [Gentz] was in a too highly elevated position, he did not retain the purity of his former beliefs and he sadly ignored the revolutionary dimension of the diplomacy at that time'.[56] Instead of overturning the present era, characterized by 'unbelief and revolution', and heralding a new era of Christian spirituality, the Vienna Congress, according to Groen, had merely consolidated the revolutionary and Napoleonic legacy.

In contrast to other counter-revolutionaries in this study, Groen was not a self-professed moderate: he emphatically denied that a 'middle way' or *'juste milieu'* could ever exist between revolutionary ideals and the true Protestant Christian faith. Political and religious moderates were, for him, just inconsequential people without true convictions. He, for instance, rejected the works by Montesquieu, as they, according to Groen, had turned out to be mere preludes to the publications of Rousseau and Robespierre. He also explicitly refused the label of 'conservative', as this implied for him too much of a compromise, preferring the label of 'anti-revolutionary' instead.[57] For Groen, as for Maistre, anti-revolutionaries did not just look at the past, they were not 'reactionaries' in a strict sense. The pre-revolutionary eighteenth century had been a dynamic age that was still corrupted by philosophy and in no need of restoring. For Groen, the sixteenth century, the century of the Reformation, and not the Middle Ages, formed the main historical model to be emulated. Groen, however, did not plead for a full-scale return to Reformation Europe for a comparable spiritual revolution in the future. Over the long course of world history, the revolutionary period would be considered an

---

[53] Groen, *Ongeloof en Revolutie*, 5. [54] Groen, *Ongeloof en Revolutie*, 375.
[55] Groen, *Ongeloof en Revolutie*, 366–96. [56] Groen, *Ongeloof en Revolutie*, 33.
[57] Groen, *Ongeloof en Revolutie*, 6.

exception and an aberration. Time and history were on the side of the Counter-Revolution and religion, Groen wrote hopefully.[58]

The Dutch Protestant view of a pluralist idea of Europe, as articulated by Groen, inspired the man who claimed to be Groen's successor, the Protestant founder of the Dutch Anti-Revolutionary Party (ARP) (1879), Abraham Kuyper (1837–1920).[59] Kuyper was one of the most influential late-nineteenth-century Dutch and European politicians, who travelled widely and was, for instance, well known in the United States. Kuyper adopted Groen's criticism of the enlightened spirit of the age, but adapted his anti-revolutionary philosophy to the new political context of emerging mass democracy and mass communication. In Kuyper's writings, therefore, we can observe the adaptation of the counter-revolutionary idea of a pluralist Europe over time. In a lecture delivered in 1869, Kuyper lambasted the all-pervasive 'uniformity, that is the curse of modern life'. For him, 'diversity' (*verscheidenheid*) was a divine principle, whereas uniformity (*eenvormigheid*) formed its antithesis. European history was, for Kuyper, building on older generations of historical Europeanists, characterized from its Germanic beginning by a divinely sanctioned pluralism.

However, this historical pluralism was threatened, in Kuyper's view, by an arrogant and godless attempt to impose modern uniformity. In the Middle Ages, the Catholic Church had tried in vain to impose religious uniformity, an attempt which was halted by the Reformation that had restored European original diversity and freedom. Other attempts had since been made to impose a universal monarchy, culminating in the monstrous and despotic French Revolution. Although the Revolution had been defeated, its ideal to impose a false uniformity had become the hallmark of modern life. It could be found in the modern Caesarism of a Napoleon III or a Bismarck, but also in the 'wrong' type of an anti-national and rootless 'cosmopolitanism'. In clothing and architecture, a uniform and anti-traditional style had emerged, Kuyper wrote disapprovingly. Kuyper's remedy against this modern uniformity was a return to the national, historical, and Protestant religious values and traditions of the Netherlands, as part of a wider pluralist, and above all Christian, European community characterized by difference and variation.[60]

5. Discordia Concors

The narrative of European historical pluralism was also pervasive in the most influential of all nineteenth-century historians, Leopold von Ranke (1795–1886).

---

[58] Groen, *Ongeloof en Revolutie*, 29, 408. On Groen's increasingly pessimistic perspective of the future: Smitskamp, *Groen*, 38.
[59] Recent biographies are: Koch, *Kuyper*; Snel, *zeven levens*.
[60] Kuyper, *Eenvormigheid*. I thank Robin de Bruin for bringing this text to my attention.

Ranke has traditionally been viewed as the 'father' of modern (national) historiography. Since the late 1970s and 1980s, however, scholars have argued that that the modernist and national interpretation of Ranke was essentially a projection of a later era.[61] The German historian Ernst Schulin, furthermore, wrote that Ranke should not primarily be seen as a German or Prussian national historian, but first and foremost as a historian interested in the problem of the development of 'modern Europe'. For Schulin, the foundation of Ranke's historical framework was the idea of Europe as a 'unity in diversity' (*Einheit in der Vielvalt*), a group of various states and cultures forming a larger community.[62] As we saw earlier, Ranke had been a student of Heeren in Göttingen, and he was no doubt influenced by his works.[63]

Ranke's first major work on European history was his *Geschichte der romanischen und germanischen Völker von 1494 bis 1524* (Histories of the Latin and Teutonic Nations from 1494 to 1514), published in 1824. In this early work, Ranke explicitly defined Europe in a narrow sense as the union of the Latin and the Germanic peoples, excluding, for instance, the Slavic and Russian peoples, but also Magyars and Arabs. The Latin peoples contributed religion and culture to Europe's civilization, the Germanic tribes energy and dynamism. The years around 1500 were especially crucial in Ranke's eyes, as then the European system of the 'balance of power', or *Gleichgewicht*, came into being. This fact meant that Europe would not have an imperial political order, such as existed elsewhere on the globe, but a dynamic system consisting of several competing and collaborating political powers. The bond between the Germanic and the Latin peoples did not form a complete union but was, for Ranke, characterized by 'mutual antagonisms'. This antagonism Ranke regarded as something that should be valued positively and that it was sanctioned by Divine Providence. Echoing French, English, and German Enlightenment narratives as well as counter-revolutionary historiography, Ranke argued that it was precisely the tensions and antagonisms that drove the dynamic development of Europe: 'the life of Europe consists of the energy of significant contrasts'.[64] As he contemplated the start of the long Franco–Spanish rivalry in Italy, he sighed: 'it is the life and fortune of the Germanic-Latin nations that they never attained unity'.[65]

In 1832, Ranke edited the *Historisch-politische Zeitschrift*, a journal financed by the Prussian minister of justice in which current events were analysed from a longer historical perspective. In the journal, Ranke proposed a moderate middle

---

[61] Iggers and von Moltke, *Theory and Practice*; Iggers and Powell, *Ranke*, 14; Krieger, *Ranke*; Schulin, 'Ranke'; Beiser, *German Historicist Tradition*; Henz, *Ranke in Geschichtsdenken*; Toews, 'Historicism'.
[62] Schulin, 'Ranke', 147.   [63] Muhlack, 'Staatensystem', 318–21.
[64] 'Das Leben von Europa besteht in der Energie der großen Gegensätze'; and 'Der antagonismus bildet sich aus, welcher die Europäische Welt seitdem beherscht hat', Ranke wrote in his postscript to the edition of 1874. Ranke, 'Geschichte', 323.
[65] Krieger, *Ranke*, 111–12.

way against revolutionary liberalism, on the one hand, and royalist reaction, on the other.[66] In a contribution entitled *Politisches Gespräch* or political dialogue, Ranke presented a plea for 'moderation' to overcome the political tensions and contradictions that formed the legacy of the revolutionary era. However, he rejected what he regarded as the superficial 'French' *Juste Milieu* of the July monarchy. The true (German) 'right middle' consisted for Ranke in replacing ideology with 'impartial' science and historical scholarship. In Ranke's eyes, science itself was a mode of post-revolutionary moderation.[67]

A further illustration of this view was Ranke's famous essay *Die großen Mächte* (The Great Powers), also published in the *Historisch-Politische Zeitschrift* in 1833. In this essay Ranke tried to explain the French Revolution, not as the result of a conspiracy of *philosophes*, which was the counter-revolutionary orthodoxy, nor as a freedom struggle against despotism, the main liberal narrative. Instead, he saw the Revolution as the culmination of long-term developments within the international system since Louis XIV. He also reiterated his view that Europe's cultural as well as political diversity were the main source of her unique development from a global perspective.[68] In 1834, Ranke published a history of the papacy in which he reiterated much of the historical Europeanism of his earlier works. Freedom was brought to Europe by the Germanic tribes after the fall of the Roman Empire. Subsequently, Europe's diversity was threatened by the hegemonic ambitions of the medieval papacy, which he compared to the Roman Empire. At the same time, Ranke credited the papacy, as Chateaubriand and Maistre had done before him, with playing a crucial role in the development of European civilization and of the German nation.[69]

In the 1840s, under the influence of the revolutionary turmoil of that decade, Ranke became more conservative and critical of revolutionaries. As the official historian of Prussia after 1841, he increasingly expressed sympathy for Prussia and Prussian-German national history in his writings. Nonetheless, even in his later works, Ranke continued to uphold the view of European history as essentially a unity in diversity, and the Germans as part of this wider European world. On the one hand, he emphasized the unity of European history: 'from time immemorial there was a profound internal coherence in European life: movements of apparent local origins export their analogues to distant regions (...), everything was mutually conditioned, everything hung together; over the vast arena one idea prevailed and it embraced the world'. On the other, he explained Europe's development in his *French History* (1852-61) by pointing to its lack of unity as a salient feature: 'the European world is composed of elements of original diversity

---

[66] On the mid-nineteenth-century concept of the middle way: Caruso, 'In Medio Stat Virtus?'; Starzinger, *Middlingness*, 13; Craiutu, *Virtue*, 1-32; Broers, 'Quest for a Juste Milieu'.
[67] Ranke, 'Politisches Gespräch'. See, more extensively: Lok, '"Extremes"', 77-80.
[68] Ranke, 'Die großen Mächte'.   [69] Ranke, *Römische Päpste*.

from whose inner opposition and struggle the changes in the historical epochs develop'.[70]

A pluralist view on European history can also be found in the work of Ranke's student, the Swiss historian Jacob Burckhardt (1818–97).[71] Burckhardt, for most of his professional life, was a professor at the University of Basel. His lectures on European history, presented in the years between 1865 and 1885, were posthumously published as the 'Historical Fragments' (*Historische Fragmente*).[72] As a true historical Europeanist, he defined civilization as the ability to partake in a longer historical tradition: only barbarians and the modern 'American' man (*neuamerikanische Bildungsmensch*) lived outside history.[73] Burckhardt traced the foundation of European civilization, not as most protagonists of this study did to the Germanic tribes, but to Antiquity. Among the ancient Greeks, in particular fifth-century Athens, individuals for the first time achieved impressive cultural and intellectual achievement. As a result of the personal freedom they experienced, they were able to break away from the uniform despotism typical of, for instance, Ancient Egypt and other parts of the classical Near East. Like other historical Europeanists, Burckhardt also extensively relied on the testimony of the Greek historian Polybius, who lived in Rome.[74]

Rather than decrying the Roman Empire for its centralization, as many other protagonists in this study had done, Burckhardt regarded the Romans both as the synthesizers of the classical world and as the midwives of the new Christian religion. The Roman legacy provided the universal and common framework of the developing European civilization in the coming centuries.[75] Rather than underscoring the rupture after the Fall of the (Western) Roman Empire, Burckhardt emphasized the cultural continuity between the classical world and the West European Middle Ages. Instead of a dark intermezzo, the Middle Ages for Burckhardt provided the 'youth' of European civilization, a necessary and important phase in the development of European civilization. In the vein of Enlightened historians, Burckhardt praised the Catholic Church for its civilizing role. Thanks to the efforts of the medieval Church, Europe was not conquered by

---

[70] Cited in: Krieger, *Ranke*, 250. A contemporary overview of European history was written by the conservative moderate Friedrich von Raumer (1781–1873). Raumer's eight-volume *Geschichte Europas seit dem Ende des fünfzehnten Jahrhunderts*, published between 1832 and 1850, was essentially a narrative of the decline of a European civilization after the golden age of European unity, the Middle Ages, as a result of increased state centralization and individualism. Raumer's volumes did not receive the same favourable reception as Ranke's publications and were soon forgotten. Morawiecz, 'Raumer'.

[71] On Burckhardt as a European historian: Kreis, 'Burckhardt', 101–20; Gollwitzer, *Europabild*, 316–22; Kaegi, 'Discordia Concors'; Kaegi, *Europäische Horizonte*.

[72] Burckhardt, *Fragmente*. The work is translated as *Judgments on History and Historians*.

[73] 'Der Barbar und der neuamerikanische Bildungsmensch leben geschichtslos.' Burckhardt, *Fragmente*, 2.

[74] Burckhardt, *Beschouwingen*, 124.

[75] Burckhardt, *Fragmente*, 9–23. On Roman Empire and the coming of Christianity, Burckhardt published his *Die Zeit Constantin's des Großen* (1853).

the Islamic armies. Burckhardt overall had a negative view of Islam, a religion that, in his view, oppressed freedom, creativity, and individualism. Although he condemned the violence and destruction of the crusades, he also interpreted the Crusades as a moment of cultural mobilization and a raised consciousness of the 'West'.[76]

The years between 1450 and 1598 presented for Burckhardt the golden age of European cultural achievement. Especially in Renaissance Italy, but also elsewhere on the continent, cultural productions exploded, partly inspired by Classical Antiquity.[77] This uniquely cultural flowering went hand in hand with an increasing pluriformity and diversity (*Vielartigkeit, Vielseitigkeit*) on the European continent.[78] Whereas 'unity' had been the dominant principle of the medieval centuries, from 1450 onwards Europe became characterized by various religious, political and cultural elements that competed and struggled with each other, resulting in unique dynamism.[79] At the end of the sixteenth century, the Reformation had shattered the unity of the church and a state system replaced the dream of a new empire to replace the Roman model. Burckhardt gave European civilization at this moment the motto of '*Discordia concors*'.[80] This diversity set European civilization apart from older and contemporary despotisms in Asia, Burckhardt argued, essentially following the enlightened narrative of Montesquieu. Although this European diversity was menaced on several occasions by attempts to establish universal monarchies, heroic individuals had safeguarded the pluriform nature of European civilization at least until the coming of the French Revolution.[81]

Burckhardt's European history was not a narrative of continuous progress and the unfolding of freedom, as was expressed by the national liberal view of history, dominant in his own time. From the turn of the sixteenth and seventeenth centuries, developments started to undermine this unique pluriform, free, and creative civilization. First of all, the Catholic church of the Counter-Reformation became increasingly reactionary, opposing all things new. From a stimulator of cultural production in the Middle Ages, the Catholic church, over time, increasingly oppressed new artistic developments. Burckhardt was equally critical of Protestantism. The Protestant churches became dependent on state authority

---

[76] Burckhardt, *Fragmente*, 24–56.
[77] This is, of course, the subject of his most well-known work: Burckhardt, *Kultur der Renaissance*.
[78] Burckhardt, *Fragmente*, 91, 141–6.
[79] 'Europa als alter und neuer Herd vielartigen Lebens, als Stätte der Entstehung der reichsten Gestaltungen, als Heimat alle Gegensätze, die in der einzigen Einheit aufgehen.' Burckhardt, *Fragmente*, 142.
[80] 'Europäisch ist: das Sich aussprechen aller Kräfte, in Denkmal, Bild und Wort, Institution und Partei, bis zum Individuum—das Durchleben des Geistigen nach allen Seiten und Richtungen—das Streben des Geistes, von Allem, was in ihm ist, Kunde zu hinterlassen, sich nicht an Weltmonarchien und Theokratien, wie der Orient, lautlos hinzugeben. Von einem hohen und fernen Standpunkt aus, wie der des Historikers sein soll, klingen Glocken zusammen schön, ob sie in der Nähe disharmonieren oder nicht: Discordia concors.' Burckhardt, *Fragmente*, 142.
[81] On the role of the heroic individual: Burckhardt, *Beschouwingen*, 247–88.

for their survival. By turning into a branch of the state administration, the Protestant churches lost their religious motivation and became vulnerable to changes in the leadership of the state. The Reformation, in Burckhardt's eyes, had overall been a disaster for Germany due to the violence and destruction that followed it, rather than the moment of the birth of a German national consciousness as contemporary liberal nationalists had it.[82] The most important effect of the Reformation was, to Burckhardt, a fundamental enhancement of state powers and state centralization, which threatened to incorporate the other social institutions. The eighteenth century witnessed the balance of a few omnipotent 'great powers', to the detriment of the smaller states and other entities that existed in previous centuries.[83] Enlightened philosophical criticism led subsequently to a social and political crisis that paved the way for the French Revolution.[84]

The French Revolution, for Burckhardt, and in line with the analysis of Alexis de Tocqueville, was not a new phenomenon but in many ways accelerated older developments.[85] In the century that followed the French Revolution, Europe's unique pluriformity, freedom and culture were increasingly threatened by the rise of modern 'mechanical' politics and culture.[86] To begin with, Burckhardt feared the ever-increasing power and influence of the nation state, once again demonstrated by the regimes of Napoleon III and the national unification of Germany and Italy.[87] The authoritarian Napoleonic Empire, ruled by a charismatic dictator, had become the model for the modern European state, rather than the end of an old imperial tradition. Moreover, a mass society and culture had come into being that above all valued homogeneity and stifled creativity. The French Revolution for Burckhardt had resulted in the breakthrough of the Industrial Revolution and the capitalist economy, with profit making as its highest social value. The legal inequality of the *ancien régime* had been replaced by an even more profound social-economic inequality. The memory of the older European history and culture, in particular those of the classical age and the Renaissance, however, consoled Burckhardt living in times he deplored.

For Burckhardt, the French Revolution had made everything impermanent and fluid.[88] The social fabric of society had fallen into disrepair and families were

---

[82] Burckhardt, *Fragmente*, 93.   [83] Burckhardt, *Fragmente*, 160–93.
[84] Burckhardt, *Beschouwingen*, 168–70.
[85] Kaegi, 'Vorwort', xxi; Kahan, *Aristocratic Liberalism*. Cf. de Dijn, *Liberty*. On Burckhardt as a political conservative: Hinde, *Burckhardt*. For a critical view of his ideas of race: Mattioli, *Burckhardt*.
[86] 'Tödlich für Europa ist immer nur Eins erscheinen: Erdrückende mechanische Macht, möge sie von einem erobernde Barbarenvolk oder von angesammelten heimischen Machtmitteln im Dienst Eines Staates oder im Dienst Einer Tendenz, etwa der heutigen Massen, ausgehen.' Burckhardt, *Fragmente*, 143. In his *Weltgeschichtliche Betrachtungen*, Burckhardt also lamented the loss of cultural pluriformity as well as the accidental in the modern age. Burckhardt, *Beschouwingen*, 101.
[87] In his *Weltgeschichtliche Betrachtungen*, Burckhardt described state power in essence as violent and evil. He was also critical of religion. Culture and autonomous cultural creativity were part of the domain he clearly preferred. Burckhardt, *Beschouwingen*, 68–9.
[88] Burckhardt, *Fragmente*, 194–5.

being destroyed. Echoing older *anti-philosophe* criticism, Burckhardt feared the coming of a society of self-serving individuals. These modern individuals were basically mass consumers instead of roundly developed individuals and citizens, such as had existed in the Italian Renaissance and classical Athens. Increasing specialization, in the economy as well as in the cultural world, threatened true creativity. Despite the technical innovations and nineteenth-century self-confidence and even arrogance, real moral or cultural progress had not been made in the last hundred years, Burckhardt wrote critically. Since the French Revolution, Europeans were only seeking novelty and change, ignoring the value and beauty of European history and cultural traditions.[89] The French Revolution thus presented for Burckhardt a 'crisis', a terrible moment of accelerated historical change and renewal, that at the same time made the study of history all the more imperative and interesting.[90] Rather than ending the Revolution by a new *Juste Milieu* between old and new, the era of the Restoration between the fall of the Napoleonic Empire and the 1848 Revolutions only served as a prelude to new Revolutions, armed conflicts, and struggles and, possibly, a new continent-wide war that would put all earlier conflicts in shadow.[91]

The 'Ceasaric' rule of Napoleon III over France (1852–70) and the German unification in 1871 gave new impulses to the tradition of historical Europeanism. In the 1870s, as Emiel Lamberts has shown, a 'Black International' of catholic nobles and others loyal to the Habsburg monarchy and Vatican, fought the new 'Leviathan' of the modern nation state, personified by Bismarck's unified Germany, as well as the menace of socialist internationalism.[92] Publicists and academics, such as Burckhardt and others, were critical of the rise of an all-powerful (national) state and the coming of a mass society shaped by commerce and seeking of profit and characterized by cultural conformity. Their nineteenth century was a time of ahistoricity and mediocrity, cultural pessimists like Burckhardt lamented. For these cultural critics, conflict, struggle, and antagonism could once again lead to a cultural regeneration of a contemporary Europe, as it had done in the past. These late nineteenth-century pessimistic views on European decadence and the need for renewal, partly building on the writings of the counter-revolutionaries and *anti-philosophes* of the (pre-)revolutionary decades, but also on new social-Darwinists' pseudo-science, prepared the ground for the revival of historical Europeanism after the two world wars of the twentieth century.[93]

---

[89] Burckhardt, *Geschichte des Revolutionzeitalters*.   [90] Burckhardt, *Beschouwingen*, 229–32.
[91] Burckhardt, *Beschouwingen*, 51.   [92] Lamberts, *Black International*.
[93] Auria, 'Progress'; Nurdin, 'idée de l'Europe'; Verga, *Storie*, 47–55; Burrow, *Crisis of Reason*; Lok, 'IJzer en bloed'. A different and more pacific variation of conservative Europeanism of the *fin-de-siècle* can be found in the Peace Movement, personified by the Austrian pacificist baroness Bertha von Suttner: Somsen, 'Princess at the Conference'. See for a legally informed liberal Europeanism in the late nineteenth century: Koskenniemi, *Gentle Civilizer*.

6. Hegel and Guizot

Historical Europeanism in the post-revolutionary decades was certainly not the exclusive domain of writers hostile to the French Revolution. Also, on the other side of the political spectrum, among those publicists and activists who, in principle, supported the revolutionary legacy in one way or another, historical Europeanist and cosmopolitan ideas and networks can be found. In opposition to the increasingly repressive internal and domestic Restoration order, from the 1820s onwards transnational networks were formed by exiles who opposed the Restoration monarchies and their security policies.[94] As we saw, no hard boundaries can be drawn between these forms of revolutionary and counter-revolutionary cosmopolitanism: actors supported revolution in one context and offered their services to Restoration kings and the Counter-Revolution in another.[95]

Like the counter-revolutionary Europeanists, these revolutionary cosmopolitans did not see Europeanism and nationalism as contradictory ideals. They believed in the creation of a new European (con)federation, consisting of states with republican constitutions that were able to develop their national identities within a larger cosmopolitan entity.[96] A prominent example of this left-wing, democratic, national cosmopolitanism was, for instance, Giuseppe Mazzini (1805–72). For Mazzini, Italy's destiny was to lead Europe in a revolutionary attempt to create a new revolutionary world, fusing progressive nationalism with a cosmopolitan and an internationalist world view.[97] However, this study has primarily focussed on the survival and adaptation of historical Europeanism among the less-studied counter-revolutionary opponents, without claiming that they were the unique inheritors of enlightened cosmopolitan legacy. Precisely these exciting, but less-explored, intellectual crosslinks between revolutionary, middle-way, and counter-revolutionary cosmopolitanism forms a promising topic for further scholarly research.[98]

In the 1820s, liberals in various European countries who overall were sympathetic to the Revolution and its legacy, also began to write European histories to counter the monopoly the counter-revolutionaries claimed over the European past.[99] These Restoration liberals responded to works published by royalists as

---

[94] Caron and Luis, *Rien appris*, 7–17, 355–460, 461–6; Isabella, *Risorgimento in Exile*; Isabella and Zanou, *Mediterranean Diasporas*; Creyghton, *Revolutionary Cosmopolitanism*. Cf. Scrivener, *Cosmopolitan Ideal*. On 1848, from a transnational perspective: Moggach and Stedman Jones, *1848 Revolutions*.
[95] Isabella, 'Crossing the Mediterranean'. [96] Pasture, *Imagining*, 55–61.
[97] Recchia and Urbinati, *Cosmopolitanism of Nations*; Bayly and Biagini, *Giuseppe Mazzini*.
[98] For example: Arcangelis, 'Cosmopolitan Morphology'.
[99] On the nineteenth-century liberal tradition: Fawcett, *Liberalism*, 33–138; de Dijn, *Liberty*; Rosenblatt, *Lost History*; Leonhard, *Liberalismus*; Seigel, 'European Liberalism'. For a critical view: Bell, 'What is Liberalism?'. On liberal historiography: Berger, *Past as History*, 80–139. The topic of 'liberal Europeanism' is understudied in these works, as well as the connection to the Counter-Revolution.

well as critiquing them.[100] They could also build on older works published at the beginning of the nineteenth century. The French Kantian philosopher and moderate revolutionary Charles de Villers (1765–1815), for instance, in 1804 wrote a study on the impact of the Reformation on European history, underscoring the importance of Europe's political and religious pluralism. In this work, the cosmopolitan Villers, who had migrated to Göttingen in 1794 to escape the revolutionary reign of Terror to become a professor of philosophy at that university, was much influenced by the publications of Heeren.[101]

At the start of the new century, moreover, the moderate Swiss revolutionaries Madame de Staël and Benjamin Constant began to propagate a pluralist idea of Europe as an association of nations, bound by mutual commercial interests and a common need for freedom and peace, to counter the—in their view—hegemonic and despotic Napoleonic Empire. Staël envisioned a Europe of nations in which the genius of the Northern and Southern peoples would be reconciled in peaceful cooperation. For her as well, the diversity and variety of (national and local) traditions and cultures was the 'winning feature' of European civilization. Both Staël and Constant drew, like their moderate counter-revolutionary counterparts, on the works of Montesquieu.[102] The pluralist idea of Europe was thus a notion entertained and developed by democratic revolutionaries, early liberals, conservatives, and counter-revolutionaries alike for their own purposes.

The lectures on 'world history' given by the protestant German philosopher Friedrich Hegel (1770–1831) were another telling example of post-revolutionary historical Europeanism, and were appropriated by liberals and their adversaries alike.[103] These lectures, given in the 1820s at the University of Berlin, were posthumously published on the basis of the notes of his students as the *Philosophy of History* (*Vorlesungen über die Philosophie der Geschichte*).[104] In this influential work, Hegel gave a stadial account of a rational development of the 'world spirit' (*vernünftige Gang des Weltgeistes*) through history, in accordance with a providential plan. He presented a pluralist Germanic Europe as the end and fulfilment of this evolution.[105] Hegel, moreover, made a distinction between the civilizations and states that took part in this specific philosophical account of world historical development, and those regions such as the Americas, Africa, and

---

[100] For France: Mellon, *Political Uses*.   [101] Villers, *Essai*. Cf. Printy, 'Protestantism'.
[102] Fontana, 'Napoleonic Empire'; Craiutu, *Virtue*; Sluga, 'Madame de Staël'.
[103] On Hegel's historical and political thought: Beiser, *Hegel*, 259–81. Beiser situates Hegel in the political milieu of the Prussian and German Reform movement. Although Hegel's original enthusiasm for the French Revolution waned due to its radicalization, he did not, according to Beiser, become a counter-revolutionary. Hegel was critical about certain aspects of the Enlightenment legacy, but he never abandoned enlightened ideas altogether. His ambition was to synthesize Enlightenment with some elements of romanticism, essentially a thinker of the middle way, or *Juste Milieu*, typical of the Restoration era. Beiser, *Hegel*, 22.
[104] Hegel, *Vorlesungen*, 561–8 for the editorial history of the text.   [105] Hegel, *Vorlesungen*, 22.

the Slavic world, that were considered by him outside 'world history', although he did not altogether exclude a future role for them.[106]

The various civilizations and peoples in world history served as stepping stones (*Stufen*) for the World Spirit to develop and perfect itself via a dialectical process of overcoming contradictions and permanent historical change. Hegel's narrative of an unfolding freedom and self-reflexion started in Asia (*Morgenland*).[107] The first stirrings or infancy of the Spirit could, according to Hegel, be found in the ancient civilizations of China, India and, especially, Persia. But these Asian civilizations were, in his view, purely despotic in nature, only the person of the ruler was truly free, all his subjects were slaves. Their unconscious homogeneity and lack of internal contradictions (*Gegensätze*) and variety consequently led to the stagnation of these ancient cultures (China, India) and their decline and fall in the case of Persia.[108]

True individual freedom could, for the first time in world history, be found among the ancient Greeks who, in Hegel's view, assimilated many cultural elements from its Asian predecessors and neighbours. Similar to other historical Europeanists, Hegel compared ancient Greece to modern Europe. The unique diverse (*verschiedenachtig*) geography led to a system of smaller states rather than one large centralized empire. Democracy was the political form pioneered by the Greeks, in particular by the Athenians, the age of adolescence of the Spirit. The strength of classical civilization, the diversity and individualism, would eventually also be its undoing.[109]

For Hegel, the Roman Empire was not a new Asian-style despotic state, but the next step in the development of the World Spirit, the maturity of the World Spirit, absorbing all earlier cultural achievements. Whereas classical Greece was characterized by (an excess of) subjective individualism, in Rome, abstract and 'general' ideas dominated over freedom, in particular in the system of law. At the same time, Rome was defined by dualisms, such as the struggle between patricians and plebians, which explained its dynamism. Similar to other historical Europeanists in this study, Hegel relied extensively on the authority of the Greek exile historian in Rome, Polybius. Both classical Greece and Rome lacked balance and were in their own way unhinged, necessitating further world historical evolution. The universal Rome Empire, moreover, functioned as the cradle of Christianity, the next step in the gradual self-awareness of the World Spirit.[110]

Christianity could not fully develop within the structure of the empire, as the Byzantine Empire demonstrated, but needed the barbaric but vigorous Germanic tribes for this purpose. In these Christianized Germanic tribes, the seeds could

---

[106] Hegel, *Vorlesungen*, 109–33.
[107] 'Die Weltgeschichte ist der Fortschritt im Bewußtsein der Freiheit.' Hegel, *Vorlesungen*, 32.
[108] Hegel, *Vorlesungen*, 142–274.   [109] Hegel, *Vorlesungen*, 335–8.
[110] Hegel, *Vorlesungen*, 385–406.

be found from which a moderate, pluralist, and mildly mannered Germanic European civilization could later develop that would unite the older elements of the world's historical development, the spirit's wise old age or *Greisenalter*. The crucial step in this final phase was, for the Protestant Hegel, the coming of the sixteenth-century Reformation. The Reformation was an inevitable and desirable response to the corruption and lack of inner spirituality of the late medieval Catholic Church. The Reformation ushered in a new 'inwardness' (*Innerlichkeit*), that allowed for the full development of the consciousness of the World Spirit.[111] The Catholic tradition for Hegel formed the main explanation for the fact that the Revolution in France, a necessary next step in the unfolding of freedom in world history in his view, had derailed into utopianism, anarchism, and terror. The definitive synthesis of individual freedom and objective general order, the fulfilment of the World Spirit and Reason (*Vernunft*), and the solution to the conundrum posed by the legacy of the French Revolution, would subsequently be achieved in a Prussian-led monarchical and Protestant Germany.[112]

Hegel's historical ideas decisively influenced French protestant historian and statesman François Guizot, who wrote the most influential of all nineteenth-century histories of Europe: the *General History of Civilization in Europe* (*Histoire de la civilization en Europe*), first published in 1828.[113] Guizot, born during the Terror in 1794 and exiled in Geneva in his youth, belonged—like Groen and Ranke—to a new post-revolutionary generation of historians of Europe. To a certain extent, Guizot too echoed the eighteenth-century enlightened narratives of Montesquieu, Robertson, and Gibbon, whom he translated. He, however, also added new elements, partly derived from German idealist philosophy.[114] According to his publisher, Guizot's history ought to be seen in the tradition of classic French universal histories, such as those written by Bossuet and Voltaire. Guizot supposedly even surpassed his predecessors by focussing on the development of 'civilization' rather than merely on religious beliefs or political institutions.[115]

At the age of twenty-five, Guizot was appointed as a professor at the Sorbonne, assisted by his excellent contacts in Parisian intellectual circles. In 1814, after the collapse of the Empire, he became secretary-general of the ministry of the interior under the First Restoration regime, followed by the position of secretary-general

---

[111] Hegel, *Vorlesungen*, 491–505.

[112] Hegel, *Vorlesungen*, 532–40. Hegel's idea of a new synthesis of freedom and order as the outcome of European history was also central in his political thought, see Pinkard, *Hegel*, 351.

[113] Guizot, *Histoire*; on the editorial history, see the 'preface' by Rosanvallon. On the global influence of Guizot's history of Europe: Hill, 'Conceptual Universalization'. Rosanvallon writes regarding Hegel's influence on Guizot: 'la dette de Guizot vis-à-vis de la philosophie allemande doit ainsi être soulignée'. Rosanvallon, 'présentation', 31. Rosanvallon does not elaborate upon this influence.

[114] Lilti, *Écrire*, 165–6. On the influence of Montesquieu on Guizot: Goldzink, *solitude de Montesquieu*; Marcello Verga has also argued that Guizot revived the enlightened tradition of the 'pluralist' history writing of Europe, but he ignores the crucial role of counter-revolutionary historians: Verga, 'European Civilisation'. See more extensively: Verga, *Storie*.

[115] Guizot, *Histoire*, 41–2.

of the ministry of justice in the Second Restoration, illustrating his intermediary role between the world of European historical ideas and of practical politics and administration. Under pressure from the ultra-royalist reaction after the assassination of the Duc de Berry in 1820, he was deprived of his state offices. From 1822 onwards his successful and popular courses on European history at the University of Paris were interrupted. He was able to resume them only in 1828, demonstrating the political sensitivity of the teaching of European history in France in the 1820s. Guizot, in the meantime, became an oppositional figure, critical of the government of King Charles X, and a liberal publicist. He was reinstated as a minister after the 1830 revolution and the establishment of the so-called July Monarchy. During the Revolution of 1848, Guizot ended up on the counter-revolutionary side, resulting in his exile after the Fall of the Orléanist regime. After his return to France in 1850, he did not occupy any offices, leading the life of a protestant scholar.[116]

In his *General History*, Guizot countered the counter-revolutionary and royalist narrative that the French Revolution had represented a rupture with French and European history. Instead Guizot, like Bonneville, argued that liberty had already been present in European history from the start when the Germanic peoples caused the fall of the (Western) Roman Empire. For the self-proclaimed 'moderate' or doctrinaire liberal Guizot, it was exactly royal absolutism and clerical despotism that had, in his view, become once again dominant in French political life in the 1820s and had formed a break with the ancient European traditions.[117] The French Revolution for him meant a return to, even a restoration of, the original historical development of European civilization, rather than a departure.

Although Guizot's book was entitled a 'history of Europe', France was considered the 'foyer' of Europe. European history, in Guizot's view, was thus to a large extent an extension of French national history. But the *General History of European Civilization*, however, was more than just another French national history: it also contained a vision of what Europe was and ought to be. Guizot, too, stated that pluralism was the essential hallmark of European civilization: the lack of a single 'dominant principle' set it apart from other civilizations, ancient and contemporary, and formed the main explanation for its extraordinary development and progress.

> When we regard the civilisations which have preceded that of modern Europe, whether in Asia or elsewhere, including even Greek and Roman civilisation, it is impossible to help being struck with the unity which pervades them. They seem

---

[116] Theis, *Guizot*; Theis, *traversée d'un siècle*. On Guizot and the doctrinaires: Rosanvallon, *moment Guizot*; Craiutu, *Liberalism under Siege*; Johnson, *Guizot*; Caruso, 'In Medio'.

[117] On history writing and the French Restoration: Mellon, *Political Uses*; Crossly, 'History as Principle'; Tollebeek, *illusionisten*. On the political culture of the French Restoration and the Catholic cultural offensive: Kroen, *Politics and Theater*.

to have emanated from a single fact, from a single idea; one might say that society has attached itself to a solitary dominant principle, which has determined its institutions, its customs, its creeds, in one word, all of its developments. (...) It has been wholly otherwise with the civilisation of modern Europe. Without entering into details, look upon it, gather together your recollections; it will immediately appear to you varied, confused, stormy.[118]

In the prefaces of later editions, Guizot described himself as a proponent of the idea of a *juste milieu* or 'middle way' between reckless (revolutionary) progress and reactionary stagnation. In the preface of the 1855 edition, he responded to Catholic and anti-liberal reviewers who fervently disagreed with his critical analysis of the Catholic Church in his work. For Guizot, 'European civilisation' in essence consisted of finding the right balance between freedom and authority. Guizot mentioned among his critics Abbé Balmès, Donoso Cortés, and Abbé Gorini, all of whom defended a Catholic and anti-liberal reading of European civilization in their writings.[119] These Catholic publicists, in Guizot's view, only defended the principle of authority and ignored the ideal of freedom, and thus were not on the side of a traditionally balanced European civilization. The transnational debate on Guizot's work became thus also a pan-continental controversy regarding the nineteenth-century interpretation of European history itself.[120]

Guizot's interpretations of European history and civilization were adopted by many influential nineteenth-century authors from various countries, forming a matrix for the liberal as well as the anti-liberal imagining of Europe. Guizot's history influenced notable liberals such as John Stuart Mill and Alexis de Tocqueville, but also anti-revolutionaries, such as Groen van Prinsterer, and even socialist and communist authors, Karl Marx among them. Mill, partly building on Guizot's insights, further developed the idea of the 'principle of systematic antagonism', allegedly unique for the European experience.[121] Pluralism was equated by liberal historians with modernity as well as the idea of European freedom.[122] What is often not noted by students of liberal internationalism is that this pluralist idea of European history was formulated earlier by

---

[118] The citation continues 'all forms, all principles of social organisation co-exist therein; powers spiritual and temporal; elements theocratic, monarchical, aristocratic, democratic; all orders, all social arrangements mingle and press upon one another; there are infinite degrees of liberty, wealth, and influence. These various forces are in a state of continual struggle among themselves, yet no one succeeds in stifling the others, and taking possession of society.' Guizot, *Histoire*, 28–30.

[119] On Balmès and Donoso Cortés: Menczer, *Tensions*, 157–91. Donoso Cortés was strongly influenced by French counter-revolutionaries such as Bonald and Maistre, and in his turn inspired other European anti-liberals such as Schmitt. The uses of the European past by these mid-century catholic authors deserves further scholarly investigation without an explicit ideological perspective. On the links between the French and Spanish counter-revolutions: Luis, 'France and Spain'.

[120] Guizot, *Histoire*, 'préface de la sixième édition (1855)', 51–3.

[121] Varouxakis, 'Guizot's Historical Works'.

[122] Delanty, *Formations*; Asbach, *Europa*; Lok, 'Construction', 179–92.

counter-revolutionary historians. In many ways, these liberal historians responded to and adopted the counter-revolutionary narratives of European history for their own agendas.

7. Hallam and Thorbecke

Mill was not the only English intellectual interested in European history in the vein of Guizot. The works of the historian Henry Hallam (1777–1859), for instance, can be seen as evidence that European or cosmopolitan history writing on the British Isles did not end with the death of Edmund Burke, as John Pocock suggested, but has a nineteenth-century afterlife which merits further systematic examination.[123] The independently wealthy and pragmatic gentleman Hallam, educated as a lawyer, was not an active politician. He frequented and sympathized with the leadership of the Whig party, although he also moved in Tory circles, once again demonstrating the porosity of nineteenth-century ideological boundaries.[124] Traditionally interpreted as an 'insular' English constitutional historian and propagandist of the Whig party, mainly due to the reception of his *Constitutional History of England* published in 1827, recent historiography has given more attention to the European dimensions of his work.[125] In 1818, Hallam published his main work on European history: a two-volume *View of the State of Europe during the Middle Ages*.[126] Almost two decades later, in 1837, he would publish a history of European literature from the fifteenth to the seventeenth century, as well as other writings on the European past.[127]

Hallam was a cosmopolitan intellectual, too. He made long journeys on the European continent and entertained an extensive network of contacts and correspondents on the other side of the Channel. He avidly read foreign works, although he had difficulty mastering the German language. His publications were digested by continental readers, among them none other than Leopold von Ranke. He was also actively involved with the many exiles and refugees living in London during the Napoleonic years and later. Hallam was, furthermore, an intimate friend of Guizot for many years, with whom he corresponded regularly. Hallam even visited his country house in Val Richer. During his exile in London,

---

[123] 'Because of its sea-borne division between insular and peninsular Europe, however, there can be said to have arisen a division between histories, one of which has been allowed to represent itself as the history of the whole: while that of England, not explained by the histories of the peninsular subcontinent, did not in the nineteenth or twentieth centuries discover a larger context in which to include itself (. . .).' Pocock, 'Enlightenment and Counter-Enlightenment', 137. John Burrow has, by contrast, underscored the continuities between Europeanist Enlightenment historiography and early nineteenth-century British history writing: Burrow, *Liberal Descent*, 28. On the relationship between British and European historiography in the mid-nineteenth century: Stuchtey, 'Literature'.
[124] Bentley, 'Hallam', 453–73.   [125] Bentley, 'Hallam', 455–8.
[126] Hallam, *View of the State*.   [127] Hallam, *Introduction*; Hallam, *Supplement*.

after having fled France in the revolutions of 1848, Guizot, bereft of his library, borrowed many books from Hallam in order to be able to continue his scholarly work. Hallam shared with Guizot the idea that European civilization rested on a fine balance of freedom and order. Both agreed that unbridled freedom in the form of democratic government would inevitably lead to anarchy and chaos, but they also abhorred reactionary royalism.[128]

In his *View of the State of Europe*, Hallam too gave an account of European history, starting with the fall of the Roman Empire in the West and culminating in the pluralist European state system in the sixteenth century. His narrative was also one of original freedom, which was threatened and eventually emerged victorious. In his history, he showed himself to be as critical of the despotism of the Church as of that of the kings. His history was negatively reviewed by Tory critics, who believed he had been too harsh on the historical role of the clergy. The origin of English freedom for Hallam was not to be found in the 'Glorious Revolution' of 1688. This revolution had formed the mere capstone of the gradual development towards more freedom from the Middle Ages onward. For Hallam, English medieval history was very much part of the wider European experience of feudalism, the English case being unique only due to the early unification of the English state following the invasion of William the Conqueror in 1066.[129]

In the Low Countries, the 'doctrinaire' strand of the pluralist narrative of European history was put forward by Johan Rudolf Thorbecke (1798–1872). Thorbecke would become the main author of the successful Dutch liberal constitution of 1848 and the first Dutch liberal prime minister.[130] In many ways, Thorbecke's liberal ideas were similar to Guizot's: Thorbecke admired the historical scholarship and political insights of the French intellectual, as well as those of other French doctrinarians.[131] In the late 1820s, the young Thorbecke was appointed a professor *extraordinarius* in political and diplomatic history and statistics at the University of Ghent, a recently founded university in Willem I's new Kingdom of the United Netherlands. In his courses on the political history of Europe, Thorbecke, whose family had German roots and who had studied in Germany on a government scholarship, relied mainly on the work of his former teacher Arnold Heeren and other Göttingen historians. Heeren's *Manual* formed the basis for much of Thorbecke's teaching.[132] Also in other ways, Thorbecke was influenced by the Europeanist intellectual climate of the 1820s.[133] Thorbecke, for

---

[128] Bentley, 'Hallam', 461–2, 468–70.   [129] Bentley, 'Hallam', 463–5.
[130] Aerts, *Thorbecke*.   [131] Drentje, *Thorbecke*, 228–31.
[132] Drentje, *Thorbecke*, 216–28; Drentje, 'Europese statensysteem'.
[133] On Thorbecke and German early nineteenth-century Europeanism: Drentje, *Thorbecke*, 198–202. Drentje mentioned the Göttingen philosopher Bouterwek as an influential German proponent of the 'new Europeanism', which regarded Europe essentially as a 'cultural space', with Germany at its core.

instance, also read Ranke's articles in the *Historisch-politische Zeitschrift* and shared many of the ideas put forward in them.[134]

In his inaugural lecture of 1825, Thorbecke, like Heeren, interpreted European history as the development of autonomous and unique nations and states that jointly formed a cultural and legal community. Freedom was, once again, introduced in Europe by the Germanic tribes after the fall of the centralized Roman Empire. Feudalism was a primitive system, but it allowed for a certain autonomy of its constituent parts, while at the same time enabling the foundation of a new order and political development. The Catholic Church played a civilizing role for the Lutheran Thorbecke. Over the centuries, 'Europe' developed into a true Christian commonwealth (*gemeenschap*) and a diplomatic community. The sixteenth century, and the Reformation in particular, formed a watershed in this respect, Thorbecke agreed with Heeren. From this century onwards, Europe consisted of an equilibrium (*evenwicht*), which was often threatened, but also preserved thanks to smaller states such as the Dutch Republic. Thorbecke, wisely for a younger and not yet established academic, did not offer pronouncements on the historical events of the French Revolution, a politically sensitive topic in the 1820s, but argued that the present situation of the European continent could be understood only from the perspective of long-term political—as well as social—development and progress through the ages. Europe was, by definition, a historical continent.[135]

When the revolutions of 1830 erupted, and the Southern Netherlands broke away from the United Kingdom of the Netherlands to form the kingdom of Belgium, Thorbecke—like his erstwhile friend Groen—was at first highly critical of these revolutionaries. He rejected the Belgian claims, not out of political conservatism, but because he believed them to be too radical in their attempts to build a new state. He also feared that the collapse of the United Kingdom of the Netherlands would lead to the resurgence of France as a threat to the renewed equilibrium of the state system as established in 1814–15. New European wars and new Napoleons would result from this collapse, Thorbecke feared. Following the 1830 Revolution, Thorbecke had to leave Ghent, and consequently took up a professorship in the law faculty of Leiden University. In Leiden, he increasingly became interested in Dutch constitutional law, an interest that would eventually lead to the liberal constitutional revision of 1848. However, Thorbecke, in contrast to most of his more provincially and nationally oriented countrymen, continued to regard the Dutch constitution and its history from a wider European comparative legal and historical perspective.[136]

The German historian Georg Gottfried Gervinus can be considered as a final example of mid-nineteenth-century historical Europeanism. His *History of the*

---

[134] Drentje, *Thorbecke*, 292.   [135] Thorbecke, 'Inaugurale rede'.
[136] Thorbecke, *staten-stelsel van Europa*. Cf. Drentje, *Thorbecke*, 267–326.

Nineteenth Century from the Vienna Treaties on (*Geschichte des Neunzehnten Jahrhunderts seit den Wiener Verträgen*) of 1855–66 formed a European 'counterblast' to the Prussian-inspired nationalism prevailing among North German historians at the time.[137] No doubt many more examples of liberal historical Europeanism can be found in other countries such as Spain, Italy, Portugal, the Nordic countries, and Central or Eastern Europe.[138] As these examples amply demonstrate, future historians need to study the writing of European histories and historically informed European ideals from a transnational and comparative perspective, crossing the porous lines between so-called anti-revolutionary, conservative, and liberal authors.

European historical narratives can, finally, even be found among nineteenth-century communists and socialists, and other thinkers for whom social justice was a primary concern. Western Europe was regarded by authors such as Auguste Comte and Moses Hess, in particular in his Hegelian idea of a 'European triarchy' (1841), as the vanguard of a new communist and socialist utopian society.[139] Even Marx and Engels articulated the idea of a triple alliance of France, England, and a unified Germany as the historical European nucleus of a new world order, making them much more Eurocentric than is often realized.[140] Marx and Engels believed that the world revolution would be inaugurated by a vanguard of 'civilized nations', in particular a federation of France and Germany, which would defeat the two main antagonists: the capitalist power par excellence, Great Britain, and the backward Russian Empire, the guardian of the reactionary Vienna order.

Far from only preaching the disappearance of all nation states, the communist authors saw a special role for a limited number of federated European nations in the coming of the communist revolution, as the culmination of the unique trajectory of European history. This often-neglected tradition of nineteenth-century 'socialist Europeanism', which needs to be analysed in full elsewhere, also contained a historical component. Moreover, it can be traced back at least to Mazzini and to Saint-Simon's European peace ideals based on the fusion of the French and English parliaments formulated during the Vienna peace congress.[141] Saint-Simon, in his turn, drew heavily upon the European ideals of the counter-revolutionary author Maistre, demonstrating the circulation of historical Europeanist ideas among writers from radically different political persuasions, classified by later generations of academics in terms of diametrically opposing ideologies.[142]

---

[137] Berger, 'Past and Present', 29.
[138] For the relationship between national and European history in central and Eastern Europe, see Baar, *Historians and Nationalism*. For Italy see, for instance: Isabella, 'Aristocratic Liberalism'.
[139] Hess, *Europäische Triarchie*.
[140] Van Ree, *Boundaries*, 53–61. Cf. Claeys, 'Early Socialism'.   [141] Van Ree, *Boundaries*, 79.
[142] On Maistre's influence on the historical thought of socialist historians: Armenteros, *French Idea*, 283–14.

8. Post-war Revivals

The catastrophe of the First World War led to the development of a renewed internationalism that often took the form of historical Europeanism. This post-war Europeanism partly drew on ideas of European decline and regeneration expressed at the middle and end of the nineteenth century.[143] European and cosmopolitan ideals were regarded by many intellectuals in the Interbellum as an alternative to the—in their view—unbounded nationalism that, in this reading, had led to the horrendous trench warfare of 1914-18. This post-war Europeanism has been studied in depth.[144] However, existing studies usually do not often explore to what extent this twentieth-century Europeanism drew on the older historical narratives developed in the age of (Counter-)Revolution. Europeanism is therefore mistakenly interpreted in these studies as an exclusively twentieth-century phenomenon, which can be understood only in the context of the supposedly uniquely violent and morally reprehensible nature of the world wars of that age.[145]

In many ways, however, the older historical narratives, constructed around 1800, were reactivated, reinvented, and adapted to new contexts in the twentieth century. When studying the history of the idea of Europe in the twentieth century, including the process of European integration and its discontents, new insights could be gained by looking at the echoes and longer memories of the earlier 'European moment' around 1800 in more detail. In particular, the twentieth-century appropriation of the older historical narratives, put forward by the (counter-)revolutionary authors in the age of revolutions, should be investigated more extensively.[146] The pluralist theme of a uniquely European 'unity in variety', so pervasive in (post-)revolutionary historical Europeanism, could also be found in a new key in the writings of a wide variety of writers and novelists of different political persuasions in the Interbellum, along with other formulations of the European ideal.[147]

---

[143] At the same time, the First World War, paradoxically, ushered in a climate of new forms of radical nationalism and state intervention as well: 'The First World War and its aftermath at once promoted such processes of nationalisation, increasing state intervention and engendering radical nationalist movements and autarkic dictatorships, at the same time as highlighting the necessity of international cooperation and institutions (. . .).' Hewitson, 'Conclusion', 326; d'Auria and Vermeiren, *Visions*.

[144] Rößner, *Geschichte Europas*; Spiering and Wintle, *European Identity*; Reijnen and Rensen, *European Encounters*; Hewitson and d'Auria, *Europe in Crisis*; Muet, *débat européen*; Schulz, *Europa-Netzwerke*. On the European dichotomy of progress and decline before the First World War: d'Auria, 'Progress', 686-704.

[145] A few literary studies actually focus on the reception of eighteenth- and nineteenth-century writers: Kraume, *Europa der Literatur*; Lützeler, *Kontinentalisierung*; Verga, *Storie*.

[146] Unmistakable continuities and reinventions between counter-revolutionary cosmopolitanism and the 'aristocratic Europeanism' of the Interbellum can, for instance, be observed. Gusejnova, 'Noble Continent?'; Gusejnova, *European Elites*.

[147] Valéry, 'European Man' (1922). Ifversen, 'Crisis', 14-31. For the (dis)continuities of Valéry's post-war European ideas with his notion of decline and pluralism in the decades before the First World War: d'Auria, 'Progress', 694-7; José Ortega y Gasset argued, echoing post-revolutionary writers, that

A flood of new 'histories of Europe' were published after 1914 to make sense of the recent transcontinental war and a general perception of a crisis of European civilization. These histories, by putting recent troubling events in a larger temporal perspective, fulfilled a role not unlike the histories published during and after the revolutionary and Napoleonic wars.[148] Both after 1914 and after 1792, a historically grown European 'civilization' was contrasted with the rising forces of 'barbarism' that broke with the traditions, usually associated with the ideological opponent. Moreover, as in the post-revolutionary decades, the histories of Europe were meant to provide inspiration and guidelines for the present and future regeneration of 'Europe'.[149] These new histories of Europe abundantly demonstrated the intimate connections between post-war European history writing and the political ordering of Europe itself, echoing the situation in the decades around 1800.[150]

Interbellum Historians of Europe too emphasized variety, fragmentation, competition, struggle, and even war, as reasons for the allegedly extraordinary development of European civilization.[151] In his five-volume *World History*, or *Weltgeschichte*, published between 1923 and 1928, the liberal-conservative historian Hans Delbrück, for instance, explained the superiority of the West and Europe over the Orthodox and Islamic worlds by pointing to the creative opposition of different nationalities. Like Ranke, Delbrück regarded the relationship between Latin and Germanic peoples as the core of European history. The rivalry between Latin and Germanic elements had resulted in centuries of warfare. At the same time, the dichotomy and contradictions between Latin and German elements had also created the unique and dynamic features of European civilization.[152]

Moreover, the Catholic English historian Christopher Dawson argued in his influential book *The Making of Europe* (1932) that the Dark Ages were critical to the formation of European unity as a synthesis between the Germanic North and the spiritual order of the Church and the traditions of the Latin culture.[153] Dawson's view of a historically grown and moral European civilization, framed as an alternative to both modern radical nationalism and a rootless internationalism, formed a reformulation of the narratives of the historical Europeanists of the revolutionary era in a new key. Conservative historians in Germany, the

---

'the swarm of Western peoples, which has started its flight over history since the collapse of the Ancient World, has been characterised by a twofold lifeform. It so happened that when [these peoples] developed their unique character, at the same time between and above them a common culture of thoughts, practices and beliefs arose (...) The homogeneity of the [Western] peoples never impaired their diversity. On the contrary, every new uniform principle stimulated the diversification.' Ortega y Gasset, *De opstand der horden*, 13. The translation is my own.

[148] Woolf, 'Europe and Its Historians'. [149] Woolf, 'Europe and Its Historians', 325–7.
[150] Pirenne, *Histoire de l'Europe*; Croce, *Storia dell'Europa*; Hazard, *crise*. Cf. Verga, *Storie*, 55–116.
[151] For instance, Oswald Spengler in his universal history: Spengler, *Untergang des Abendlandes*.
[152] Delbrück, *Weltgeschichte* II, 436, 399; III, 562.
[153] Dawson, *Making of Europe*. Dawson's European ideals were restated in his later work *Understanding Europe*. On Dawson as a European historian: Leucht, 'Dawson'.

Netherlands, and Britain in this period, defended, like Dawson, a fundamentally Christian vision of Europe, often glorifying a medieval 'golden era' as an alternative to present ungodly and violent modern times. The eighteenth-century Enlightenment and the French Revolution were described by these self-styled anti-modern historians as paving the way for the horrific events of the twentieth century, echoing older *anti-philosophe* sentiments critical of modernity. These so-called enlightened epochs, according to these Christian and conservative historians, had inaugurated a Machiavellian all-powerful state and a democratic society consisting of selfish and atheistic individuals, as the counter-revolutionaries had also argued more than a century before. Along with the idea of a historically grown Christian institutional commonwealth, a revived language of European pluralist exceptionalism can thus also be discerned, which partly drew on the older traditions of counter-revolutionary history writing.[154]

The Catholic authoritarian, fascist, and national-socialist regimes that replaced in many countries the liberal democracies in the 1920s and 1930s also appropriated the counter-revolutionary European narratives for their own cultural agendas.[155] Often the national elements in counter-revolutionary thought were stressed, while downplaying their cosmopolitanism.[156] In 1943, for instance, Ranke's *Politisches Gespräch* was re-edited by the Austrian national-socialist historian Heinrich Ritter von Srbik (1878–1951). Srbik was a Metternich specialist, and during the war he was the president of the Austrian Academy of Sciences. In the preface, Srbik drew a comparison between his own fascist time and the Restoration era, in his eyes both periods of 'large-scale reordering of Europe and Germany'. He extensively elaborated on the lessons that could be learned from Ranke, in his eyes 'the national educator and *"Schicksalsgestalters"* of the German nation'.

Srbik, furthermore, made comparisons between Ranke's attempt to use the impartial writing of (European) history to find a 'middle way' between the ideological extremes of the national principle and the Prussian state, on the one hand, and the contemporary national-socialist project for a new German order, on the other. This use of Ranke for national-socialist purposes perfectly demonstrated the malleability of the idea of the *juste milieu* in different political contexts in different periods in modern European history.[157] It was the adoption of these

---

[154] Rößner, *Geschichte Europas*, 82–99, 218–34. Although Rößner's book on post-war European history writing is valuable, it also presents problems. By selecting Dutch, German, and British sources, she omits, for instance, important historiographical traditions such as those of France and Italy, which may be entirely different from their Germanic counterparts. The re-use of older eighteenth- and nineteenth-century European notions, moreover, does not receive a prominent role in this study.

[155] On national-socialist Europeanism, see: Martin, *Nazi-Fascist New Order*; Griffin, 'Europe for the Europeans'. Of course, ideas of historical pluralism were also used to counter Nazism and fascism during the Second World War, a potential topic for further research.

[156] French fascist intellectuals articulated their own version of the European ideals as well: Rensen, *Lijden aan de tijd*; Knegt, *Fascism*.

[157] Srbik, 'Geleitwort'. The 'Politisches Gespräch' was also edited by Friedrich Meinecke in the aftermath of the First World War (in 1924).

counter-revolutionary writers and their European narratives for a fascist and national-socialist agenda in the middle of the twentieth century that would consequently lead to their discrediting after the defeat of the Axis powers of Germany and Italy in 1945.[158] In the post-war years the memory of authors such as Maistre and Müller was tainted by the association with a much later fascist past, which distorted their ideas in fundamental ways.

During and after the Second World War, the historical language of European pluralism was once again reactivated in the attempt to build a new European institutional order and identity on the ruins of the Third Reich.[159] Intellectuals and politicians in the post-war years drew, in this respect, on European ideas formulated in the Interbellum, but also on older late eighteenth-century and nineteenth-century ideas. The pluralist 'unity in diversity' theme was reinvented by conservative and liberal Europeanists in a new context: European diversity and freedom, now exclusively defined as a feature of only the Western half of the continent, was explicitly contrasted with the supposedly 'totalitarian' nature of the collapsed Nazi empire as well as of the Soviet Union. The Soviet Union was framed in these post-war narratives as the twentieth-century equivalent of the older universal empires and Asian despotism so much decried in the eighteenth century.

To a lesser extent European cultural pluralism was propagated by continental intellectuals as an alternative to a homogeneous American capitalist mass culture, the outgrowth of the 'wrong' type of Enlightenment, as well.[160] Whereas both the US and the USSR, according to this post-war narrative, represented political and cultural monolithic systems, and thus stood in a tradition of universal monarchy as well as revolutionary centralism, 'Europe'—by contrast—embodied (con)federation, civilization, Christian morality, individual freedom, and pluriformity, in the manner of the histories by writers like Vogt, Heeren, or Müller.[161] And perhaps also similar to 1815, a renewed emphasis on European narratives and the fortunes of the European continent resulted in a relative neglect of the world outside Europe, in particular decolonizing Africa and Asia.[162]

Especially for German post-war historians, the idea of a unique European historical pluralism provided a way to reintegrate a defeated Germany into a larger European historical context.[163] Catholic historians redeveloped after 1945

---

[158] For the appropriation of the concept of the 'third way' by French fascists: Knegt, 'French Fascism'. Jan-Werner Müller extensively discusses the use of nineteenth-century counter-revolutionaries such as Adam Müller, Maistre, and Donoso Cortés in the writing of Carl Schmitt: Müller, *Dangerous Mind*, 23, 53, 105, and 163 on Schmitt's historically informed Europeanism: McCormick, 'Carl Schmitt's Europe'.

[159] Woolf, 'Europe and Its Historians', 330–5; Verga, *Storie*, 117–65. An example was Burckhardt's biographer and successor in Basel, Werner Kaegi (1901–79). Verga, *Storie*, 126–7.

[160] Rößner, *Geschichte Europas*.   [161] Woolf, 'Europe and Its Historians', 327–30.

[162] Gildea, *Empires of the Mind*; Buettner, *Europe after Empire*; Stoler, 'Colonial Aphasia'.

[163] See, for instance: Gollwitzer, *Europabild*. On post-war German ideas of Europe and the West: Conze, *Europa der Deutschen*; Schildt, *Abendland und Amerika*; Bavaj and Steber, *Germany and 'the West'*. For an Italian example: Delzell, 'Omodeo'. Cf. Hewitson and d'Auria, *Europe in Crisis*, 62–81.

the notion of Germany as part of a wider occidental historical tradition, blaming Prussian Protestantism and the modern emancipation of the masses for the rise of the Nazis and the catastrophe of the Second World War.[164] By contrast, conservative Protestant historians, such as Gerhard Ritter (1888–1967) and Hans Rothfels (1891–1976), tried to salvage the national historiographical tradition by portraying national-socialism as the exception in German history.[165] In his *Die Neugestaltung Europas in 16. Jahrhundert*, first published in 1950, Ritter, citing Ranke, praised Europe's unique duality, contrasting it with the monolithic character of Asian and Islamic civilizations, in a typical historical Europeanist vein.[166]

In his essay in the *Schweizer Monatsheft* of 1947 on the unity of the *Abendland*, Walter Goetz (1867–1958) argued optimistically that Europe consisted of a tradition that was capable of eternally renewing itself. Even the Reformation and the rise of nation states had not been able to fundamentally undermine European unity. It was precisely this lack of unity and the national diversity, evidence of European 'individualism', that made the continent unique in the world, according to Goetz, following an enlightened cosmopolitan narrative. The bipolarity of European culture, at once national as well as universal, prevented the dominance of a one-sided intellectual sphere (*einseitigen Gedankenwelt*).[167] In this essay, he explicitly referred to his nineteenth-century predecessor Ranke as a source of inspiration.

Friedrich Meinecke (1862–1954) famously made use of the concept of European dialectic in his post-war book *The German Catastrophe* (*Die Deutsche Katastrophe*) of 1946.[168] In this essay he, in many ways, continued the argument of his earlier famous work of 1908, *Cosmopolitanism and the National State* (*Weltbürgertum und Nationalstaat*), adapting the argument to the new context of the post-war years. In his earlier work, Meinecke maintained that the German national state was the result of a tension between universal and national ideas in a 'complex process of confrontation and union'.[169] The German national idea was, in his view, the product of both a liberal-democratic strand and—in his eyes—a far-less-studied 'romantic-conservative strand'.[170] Meinecke argued in *The German Catastrophe* that the German nation, after its defeat, did not need to accept a bland cosmopolitanism and universalism from the American capitalist and the Russian communist conquerors. Instead, Germany should return to its

---

[164] For Catholic historiography: Schulze, *Geschichtswissenshaft*, 266–80.
[165] Berger, *Past as History*, 288; on Ritter: Cornelißen, *Gerhard Ritter*.
[166] Ritter, *Neugestaltung Europas*, 14.   [167] Goetz, 'Einheit des Abendlandes'.
[168] Frey and Jordan, 'National History', 282–97.   [169] Meinecke, *Cosmopolitanism*, 21.
[170] Meinecke, *Cosmopolitanism*, 22. In the end, however, Meinecke believed that the final goal of history was the national state. He praised Bismarck for destroying the 'poison' of universalism that the Holy Alliance had administered to Germany as a medicine. Meinecke, *Cosmopolitanism*, 229.

early nineteenth-century tradition of combining the contrasting forces of the cosmopolitan and the national, the individual and the universal.[171]

Meinecke's use of the post-revolutionary past for contemporary political purposes was not unique.[172] In his classic study *Europabild und Europagedanke* of 1951, the Münster historian Heinz Gollwitzer, as we have seen, traced German European ideals in the eighteenth and nineteenth centuries, situating German history in an older tradition of enlightened and pluralist Europeanism.[173] Another salient example of the post-war uses of early nineteenth-century political history was the work of Fritz Valjavec (1909–60), a historian tainted by his Nazi past, who reinvented himself after 1945 as a Cold War historian. In his *Die Entstehung der politischen Strömungen in Deutschland: 1770–1815*, like Gollwitzer's *Europabild* originally published in 1951, Valjavec also provided an implicit historical legitimation of the post-war integration of Germany into Western Europe by a description of German liberalism and conservatism in the late eighteenth and nineteenth centuries. He argued that liberalism and conservatism were not foreign Western imports but had grown on German native soil. He also stated that the roots of German conservativism and, above all, liberalism could be found in the eighteenth-century German Enlightenment. German political history therefore, according to Valjavec, did not follow a trajectory different from that of other Western European countries.[174]

Even the dissertation of German historian Reinhart Koselleck, *Critique and Crisis*, defended in 1954 at Heidelberg University, could be considered part of a conservative historical Europeanist tradition. In his thesis, Koselleck gave an analysis of the 'pathogenesis' or disease of 'modern' society, attacking the alleged hypocrisy and utopianism of the eighteenth-century *philosophes*, resulting from their exclusion from political power-sharing by the French *ancien régime* monarchy. This alleged enlightened utopianism, according to Koselleck, in the vein of the tradition of Enlightenment criticism, lay at the roots of the ordeals of modern Europe, including the rise of national-socialism, communism, and unbounded capitalism.[175]

Most continental historians of Europe writing in the post-war decades, such as the Swiss historian Denis de Rougemont (1906–85) or the French Jean-Baptiste Duroselle (1917–94), implicitly or explicitly supported the project of federal

---

[171] Meinecke, *deutsche Katastrophe*, 172. Cf. Schulze, *Geschichtswissenschaft*, 46–76; Krol, *geweten van Duitsland*, 35–63. 'Weltbürgertum und Nationalgeister sind auch hier [das abendländische Kulturleben] keine starren Gegensätze, sonder ineinander verflochten. (...) Das Universellste und das Individuellste vermögen sich hier einander zu begatten.' Meinecke, *deutsche Katastrophe*, 172–3.

[172] Rößner, *Geschichte Europas*; Bailey, *Yesterday and Tomorrow*; Berger, *Past as History*, 287–8; Schulze, *Geschichtswissenschaft*, 16–30; Brockmann, 'Germany as Occident'.

[173] The German idea of 'Europe' in this period was characterized by pluralism and '*Vielheit in der Einheit*': Gollwitzer, *Europabild*, 43. Cf. Kraus, 'Gollwitzer', 304–5. However, Gollwitzer himself denied any link between contemporary political developments and his scholarly work: Kraus, 'Gollwitzer', 319–20. See also Chapter 5.

[174] Valjavec, *politischen Strömungen*. See also Chapter 5.   [175] Koselleck, *Critique and Crisis*.

European integration by presenting it as the natural and benevolent ending of a long continental history marred by violence and internal strife.[176] However, not all intellectuals, who after 1945 extolled the virtues of a common pluralist European civilization, supported the project of the post-war political integration of Europe. The Christian poet and American-English literary critic T.S. Eliot (1888–1965) offers a good example. In his *Notes towards the Definition of a Culture* (1948), Eliot enthusiastically emphasized the 'unity in diversity' theme of European civilization: 'I have already affirmed that there can be no European culture if the several countries are isolated from each other: I add now that there can be no European culture if these countries are reduced to [one] identity. We need variety in unity and not the unity of organisation, but the unity of nature.'[177] Eliot, however, saw this narrative of 'cultural unity in diversity' as an alternative to political and institutional unification of Europe, which he opposed.[178]

Newly established Christian-democratic parties were the dominant political forces in most West European countries and Christian democracy was the most important ideology in post-war Europe. In opposition to the blood-stained earthly utopias of the fascist, national-socialist, and communist regimes, post-war Europe was, perhaps not unlike the Restoration era, characterized by an ideological emphasis on stability, family life, and prosperity within a developing Cold War setting as well as by a dislike of political experiments and ideals.[179] Conservative and Christian intellectuals and politicians were also a major driving force in the formulation of the new doctrine of human rights as the moral basis for the post-war order.[180] As in the post-revolutionary era, the post-war Christian democracy, extolling concepts such as moderation, morality, and stability, possessed strong European and even Eurocentric overtones, and was the main ideological driver of the project of European integration.[181]

The extent to which this revived post-war Christian democracy and conservatism in continental Europe situated itself in the older tradition of counter-revolutionary

---

[176] See extensively: Verga, *Storie*, 117–80; also: Woolf, 'Europe and Its Historians', 330–5; Berger, 'Past and Present', 33–5. Examples of post-war pro-European history writing are: Rougement, *Vingt-huit siècles de l'Europe*; Duroselle, *idée d'Europe*. See also the Prologue.
[177] Eliot, 'Unity of European Culture', 120.
[178] Echoes of this view can also be found in the British discussion on Brexit since 2016: The British Prime minister Theresa May, in a speech on post-Brexit Britain delivered on 17 January 2017, argued that: '(...) our continent's great strength has always been its diversity. And there are two ways of dealing with different interests. You can respond by trying to hold things together by force, tightening a vice-like grip that ends up crushing into tiny pieces the very things you want to protect. Or you can respect difference, cherish it even, and reform the EU so that it deals better with the wonderful diversity of its member states.' 'The government's negotiating objectives for exiting the EU', Speech, Theresa May, 17 January 2017. See https://www.gov.uk/government/speeches/the-governments-negotiating-objectives-for-exiting-the-eu-pm-speech (accessed 17 June 2020).
[179] Müller, *Contesting Democracy*, 125–70; Stone, *Goodbye to All That?*, 56–66.
[180] Duranti, *Conservative Human Rights Revolution*; Moyn, *Christian Human Rights*.
[181] Kaiser, *Christian Democracy*; Berthezène and Vinel, *Post-war Conservatism*; Steber, *Hüter der Begriffe*; Smith, 'Conservatism and Its Discontents'; Großmann, *Internationale der Konservativen*; Patel, *Project Europe*. For the Netherlands: de Bruin, *Elastisch Europa*, 147–91.

Europeanism and, in what way, needs to be examined further elsewhere. That is also true of the question of why and when the European ideal came to be associated, in the post-war decades, almost exclusively with a politically progressive and liberal tradition, obscuring its counter-revolutionary roots, opposed by right-wing and self-proclaimed conservative critics who extolled the virtues of the purified nation state, as described in the prologue.[182] Suffice it to say, in concluding this section, that both the moderate conservative and Christian-democrat tradition, which strongly supported European integration in the post-war decades, and the more recent Eurosceptic 'conservative nationalists', generally hostile to the 'European project', drew in their own way on the longer legacies of counter-revolutionary historical Europeanism, demonstrating its fundamental political malleability over the centuries.

9. Coda: The Making of a Tradition

The tentative conclusion of this final chapter is that ideas of Europe and European history were evidently not created *ex nihilo* in the aftermath of the cataclysmic events of the twentieth-century world wars. Instead, due to the political circumstances surrounding the urgent need to build a new international political order, older narratives such as the view of Europe as a continent uniquely characterized by a combination of variety and unity were revived and adapted to new circumstances. This book has argued that the revolutionary age was a critical junction in the reconfiguration and transformation of these older (counter-)enlightened narratives of the European past, at a moment when European civilization was perceived to be in crisis and in urgent need of regeneration in the eyes of contemporaries. It has pointed, in particular, to the key, but often ignored, role played by counter-revolutionary writers in (re)constructing a European past, in order to make sense of current predicaments, as well as to provide inspiration for a renewed and regenerated political and spiritual order. Far from the rise of a secular idea of Europe, this study demonstrated the esoteric and providential meaning of the post-revolutionary writing of European history, jointly with the uses of the Enlightened legacies. By studying the European past, insights could be gained in the providential plan, as well as being a theodicy, providing reasons for the existence of evil.

---

[182] (Radical) Right wing Europeanism did not disappear altogether in the post-war decades. In the 1960s and 1970s, French journalist Alain de Benoist, partly building on elements of the European counter-revolutionary tradition, for instance developed an anti-liberal and anti-christian Europeanist ideology under the label of the New Right or *Nouvelle Droite*, based on notions of 'ethnopluralism', ethnonationalism, anti-Americanism, and regionalism. De Benoist's works form a source of inspiration for twenty-first-century European 'identitarian' and 'alt-right' movements. Bar-On, 'Nouvelle droite'; Hawley, *Alt-right*; Müller, *Contesting Democracy*, 171–202.

In the violent and tumultuous decades around 1800, the intellectual tradition of 'historical Europeanism' was crafted by a wide variety of self-proclaimed opponents of the Revolution and its ideals. The Europeanists defined Europe in terms of a centuries-long historical continuity of institutions, laws, customs, culture, and ideas. Although the articulation of these Europeanist ideas varied greatly among the authors, four key elements can be found in their writings. These elements were both descriptive, in the sense that they described an actual situation according to the authors, and prescriptive, an ideal for the future. Firstly, a pluriform and diverse Europe was contrasted with a homogeneous and despotic empire, be it in Antiquity, Asia, or within Europe itself, as exemplified by the subsequent attempt to establish a new 'universal monarchy', or the Revolutionary and Napoleonic attempts to uniformly impose its system in all countries of the continent. Secondly, from its beginning Europe was characterized by a unique form of 'freedom' that could not be found elsewhere in the world, and that also fundamentally differed from the individualist concept of freedom as articulated by the revolutionaries. The superficial and dangerous revolutionary freedom was usually juxtaposed to the historical freedoms introduced by the Germanic tribes, if not the ancient Greeks or Hebrews, at the beginning of European history. Thirdly, the historical Europeanists underscored the alleged 'moderate' exercise of power and customs, contrasting this moderation with the radicalism of oriental despotism or the violent terror regime of the French Revolution. The new and supposedly all-powerful national state forged in the Revolution, was regarded by the historical Europeanists as the product of a new and 'excessive' revolutionary patriotism, and not fitting in European traditions.

Fourthly and finally, they believed in the gradual progress of European society and culture, where new elements could be added to 'the ancient edifice' to correct its flaws, but its essence remained intact. Historical Europeanists were horrified by the revolutionary attempt to build a new political system based on abstract and universal ideas instead of on historical precedents. These four elements could, in their eyes, only be found on the European continent, and were usually related to the Christian religion and Church. Different views existed on the specific role of Catholic, Protestant, and Orthodox churches. Islam was usually excluded from the European world. Judaism, in some cases, was seen as one source of European institutions and law. And even in Europe, this unique civilization was not secure but had to be constantly defended against threats from within and without. The contemporary revolutionaries instigated the latest, and most deadly, attempt to destroy this historically grown Europe.

This study has shown the crucial role of counter-revolutionary writers in the making of historical Europeanism. But historical Europeanism was not confined to counter-revolutionary and conservative ideologies only. Historical Europeanist ideas could be found among politicians and intellectuals from different political persuasions from the late eighteenth century onwards. The perspective of historical Europeanism, moreover, allows us to study the renewal and adaptation of political traditions beyond the traditional ideological dividing lines of nineteenth-century conservatism, liberalism, and socialism, as well as cosmopolitanism and nationalism. This chapter argued that enlightened notions of historical Europeanism and cosmopolitanism survived in the age of romantic nationalism in unsuspected and surprising ways. Throughout the nineteenth and twentieth centuries, these ideas of European history and civilization were rediscovered and adapted to new political contexts. The watersheds of the 'revolutions' of 1830, 1848, 1871, 1918, and 1945 were important turning points in the remaking of the historical Europeanist tradition. Although the exact form and articulation of this historical Europeanism was shaped by the specific political circumstances of the reordering of Europe in the (post-)revolutionary age, the narratives forged at this moment enjoyed long afterlives, shaping in manifold ways our contested idea of European history and memory to this day.[183]

---

[183] See the Prologue. For examples of late twentieth- and early twenty-first-century history writings in which Europe's unique pluralist character is underscored, see Lok, 'Fragmented Continent', 43–6.

Bibliography

Archival sources

Archives Nationales (Paris, Pierrefitte-sur-Seine): Fonds Calonne, 297 AP/3, no. 124–38.
Archives de Sassy (Normandy, France): Etienne-Denis Pasquier, *Testament de l'homme politique* (1 July 1862).
National Archives (London, Kew): PRO PC1/123–31 Calonne papers.

Printed primary sources (until 1950)

Apologie du Décret du Gouvernement-Général des Pays-Bas, du 18 Mai 1789, contre la nouvelle édition du Dictionnaire Historique de l'abbé de Feller (St. Tron: libraires associés, 1789).
Auckland, William Eden, baron of, *Some Remarks on the Apparent Circumstances of the War, in the Fourth Week of October 1795* (London: J. Walter, 1795).
Barruel, Augustin, *Mémoires pour servir à l'Histoire du Jacobinisme*, 5 vol. (Hamburg: P. Fauche, 1797–9, first edition; 1803, second edition).
Bayle, Pierre, *Dictionnaire historique et critique* (Rotterdam: Reinier Leers, 1697).
Bonald, Louis de, *Traité de Westphalie et celui de Campo Formio et de leur rapport avec le système politique des puissances européennes, et particulièrement de la France* (Paris: Le Normant, 1801).
Bonald, Louis de, *Réflexions sur l'intérêt général de l'Europe, suivies de quelques considérations sur la noblesse* (Paris: Le Normant, 1815).
Bonald, Louis de, *Écrits sur l'Europe: textes présentés et annotés par Michel Toda* (Versailles: éditions de Paris, 2006).
Bonneville, Nicolas de, *Le nouveau Théâtre allemand*, traduit par Mrs. Friedel et de Bonneville, 12 vol. (Paris: no publisher, 1784–85–86).
Bonneville, Nicolas de, *Essais: Choix des petits romans imités de l'Allemand*, suivis de quelques essais de poésies lyriques (Paris: Barrois and Royer, 1786).
Bonneville, Nicolas de, *Lettre de Nicolas de Bonneville, avocat au parlement de Paris, à Mr. Le Marquis de Condorcet* (London: G.G.J. & J. Robinson, 1787).
Bonneville, Nicolas de, *Histoire de l'Europe moderne depuis l'irruption des peuples du Nord dans l'Empire Romain, jusqu'à la paix de 1783, vol. I–II* (Geneva: no publisher, 1789).
Bonneville, Nicolas de, *De l'esprit des religions. Ouvrage promis et nécessaire à la confédération universelle des amis de la vérité* (Paris: L'imprimerie du cercle social, 1791).
Bonneville, Nicolas de, *Histoire de l'Europe moderne depuis l'irruption des peuples du Nord dans l'Empire Romain, jusqu'à la paix de 1783, vol. III* (Paris: L'imprimerie du Cercle social, 1792).
Bonneville, Nicolas de, 'Notice sur les principaux historiens qui ont écrit des affaires de l'Europe'. In de Bonneville, *Histoire de l'Europe moderne* [Prospectus] (Geneva: no publisher, no date).

Bossuet, Jean-Bénigne, *Discours sur l'histoire universelle à Monseigneur le Dauphin: pour expliquer la suite de la religion et les changemens des empires: depuis le commencement du monde jusqu'à l'empire de Charlemagne* (Paris: I. Roulland, 1681).

Burckhardt, Jacob, *Die Zeit Constantin's des Großen* (Basel: Schweighauer'sche Verlagsbuchhandlung, 1853).

Burckhardt, Jacob, *Die Kultur der Renaissance in Italien* (Cologne: Phaidon, 1956; first published 1860).

Burckhardt, Jacob, *Historische Fragmente: Mit ein vorwort von Werner Kaegi* (Stuttgart and Berlin: Deutsche Verlag, 1942).

Burckhardt, Jacob, *Geschichte des Revolutionzeitalters*. Kritische Gesamtausgabe band 28, edited by Wolfgang Hardtwig, Simon Kießling, Bernd Klesmann, Philipp Müller, and Ernst Ziegler (Munich: C.H. Beck, 2009).

Burckhardt, Jacob, *Wereldhistorische Beschouwingen* (Amsterdam: Boom, 2020; Dutch translation of *Weltgeschichtliche Betrachtungen*, 1905.

Burke, Edmund, *The Correspondence of Edmund Burke*, vol. VI (July 1789–December 1791), edited by Alfred Cobban and Robert Smith (Cambridge: Cambridge University Press, 1967).

Burke, Edmund, *Reflections on the Revolution in France: A Critical Edition*, edited by Jonathan Clarke (Stanford, CA: Stanford University Press, 2002).

Burke, Edmund, 'Reflections on the Revolution in France'. In Burke, *Revolutionary Writings*, edited by Iain Hampsher-Monk (Cambridge: Cambridge University Press 2014), 1–250.

Burke, Edmund, 'The First Letter on a Regicide Peace'. In Burke, *Revolutionary Writings*, edited by Iain Hampsher-Monk (Cambridge: Cambridge University Press, 2014), 251–334.

Burke, Edmund, *The Writings and Speeches of Edmund Burke, vol. I–IX*, edited by Paul Langford and William Burton Todd (Oxford: Clarendon Press, 1981–2015).

[Calonne, Charles-Alexandre de], *Discours prononcé de l'ordre du Roi et sa présence, par M. de Calonne contrôleur général des finances, dans l'assemblée des notables, tenue à Versailles le 22 Février 1787* (Versailles: Ph.-D. Pierres, 1787).

Calonne, Charles-Alexandre de, *Lettre adressée au Roi* (London: Spilsbury, 9 February 1789).

Calonne, Charles-Alexandre de, *Seconde lettre adressée au Roi* (London: Spilsbury, 5 April 1789).

Calonne, Charles-Alexandre de, *De l'état de la France. Présent et à venir* (London: no publisher, October 1790).

Calonne, Charles-Alexandre de, *De l'etat de la France, Tel qu'il peut et qu'il doit être* (London: no publisher, November 1790).

Calonne, Charles-Alexandre de, *Considerations on the Present and Future State of France*. Translated from the French (London: J. Evans, 1791).

Calonne, Charles-Alexandre de, *Esquisse de l'Etat de la France* (London: no publisher, 1791).

Calonne, Charles-Alexandre de, *Tableau de l'Europe jusqu'au commencement de 1796 et pensées sur ce qui peut procurer promptement une paix solide* (London: no publisher, March 1796).

Calonne, Charles-Alexandre de, *The Political State of Europe at the Beginning of 1796: Or Considerations on the Most Effectual Means of Procuring a Solid and Permanent Peace*. Translated from the French by D. St. Quentin (London: Debrett, Murray, Highley, and Richardson, 1796).

[Calonne, Charles-Alexandre de], *Tableau de l'Europe en novembre 1795, et pensées sur ce qu'on a fait & qu'on n'auroit pas dû faire (...)* (London: J. de Boffe, no date).

Casas, Comte de las, *Le Mémorial de Saint Hélène*, 2 vol. (Paris: Flammarion, 1951).

Casas, Emmanuel de las, *Le Mémorial de Sainte-Hélène. Le manuscrit original retrouvé*, edited by Thierry Lenz, Peter Hicks, François Houdecek, and Chantal Prévot (Paris: Perrin, 2017).

Chateaubriand, François-René de, *Essai historique, politique et moral sur les révolutions anciennes et modernes, considérées dans leurs rapports avec la Révolution française* (London: J. Deboffe, 1797).

Chateaubriand, François-René de, *De Buonaparte, des Bourbons, et de la nécessité de se rallier à nos princes légitimes, pour la bonheur de la France, et celui de l'Europe* (Paris: Mame Frères, 1814).

Chateaubriand, François-René de, *Note sur la Grèce* (Paris: Le Normant, 1825).

Chateaubriand, François-René de, *Essai Historique, politique et moral sur les révolutions anciennes et modernes, considérées dans leurs rapports avec la révolution française (1797)*. Texte établi, présenté et annoté par Maurice Regard (Paris: Gallimard, 1978).

Chateaubriand, François-René de, *Génie du Christianisme (1802)*. Texte établi, presenté et annoté par Maurice Regard (Paris: Gallimard, 1978).

Chateaubriand, François-René de, *Memoirs from beyond the Tomb*. Translated by Robert Baldick (London: Penguin, 1961, first edition; 2014, new edition).

Condorcet, Nicolas de, *Esquisse d'un tableau historique des progrès de l'esprit humain* (Paris: Agasse, 1795—the year III of the revolutionary calandar).

Copeland, Thomas, and Milton Shunway Smith, *A Checklist of the Correspondence of Edmund Burke*. Arranged in chronological order and indexed under the names of 1200 correspondents (Cambridge: Cambridge University Press, 1955).

Coudenhove-Kalergi, Richard, *Pan-Europa* (Vienna: Pan-Europa-Verlag, 1923).

Courier de Londres (1776 to 1820).

Croce, Benedetto, *Storia dell'Europa* (Bari: Laterza, 1932).

Dalberg, Karl Theodor von, *Betrachtungen über den Charakter Karl des Großen*. Translated from the French, with a preface by Niklas Vogt (Frankfurt: Andreäischen Buchhandlung, 1806).

Dawson, Christopher, *The Making of Europe: An Introduction to the History of European Unity* (London: Sheed and Ward, 1932).

Dawson, Christopher, *Understanding Europe* (London: Sheed and Ward, 1952).

Delbrück, Hans, *Weltgeschichte: Vorlesungen, gehalten an der Universität Berlin 1896–1920*, 5 vol. (Berlin: Otto Stollberg, 1924–8).

Dictionnaire de l'Académie française of 1842. Complément (1842).

D'Ivernois, François (Francis), *Réflexions sur la guerre, en réponse aux réflexions sur la paix, adressées au Mr. Pitt et aux Français* (London: P. Elmsley, 1795).

D'Ivernois, François (Francis), *État des Finances et des Resources de la République Française, au 1er Janvier 1796* (London: W. & C. Spilsbury, 1796).

Electronic Enlightenment Scholarly Edition of Correspondence, Version 3.0 (University of Oxford, 2017), edited by Robert McNamee et al. Available at: https://doi.org/10.13051/ee:doc/burkedOU0010291a1c (accessed 16 July 2018).

Eliot, Thomas (T.S.), 'The Unity of European Culture'. In Eliot, *Notes towards a Definition of Culture* (London: Faber, 1948).

Europa. Eine Zeitschrift, vol. I, edited by Friedrich Schlegel (Frankfurt a.M.: Wilmans, 1803). Re-edition by Ernst Behler (Stuttgart: J.G. Cotta, 1963).

Europäische Staats-Relationen, vol. I–XIV, edited by Niklas Vogt (Frankfurt a.M.: Andreäischen Buchhandlung, 1804–9).

Feller, Francois-Xavier de, *Dictionnaire historique ou histoire abrégée des hommes qui se sont fait un nom par le génie, les talens, les vertus, les erreurs, depuis le commencement du monde jusqu'á nos jours* (Liège: Fr. Lemaire; Augsburg: Mathieu Rieger, 1781-4; in six volumes; 1789-94 and 1797, second edition (Liège and Augsburg, 8 volumes with supplement).

Feller, François-Xavier de, *Dictionnaire géographique*, vol. I (Liège: Bassompierre, 1791-2).

Feller, François-Xavier de, 'Chronologie de l'histoire universelle'. In Feller, *Dictionnaire historique* I (1797), 1-134.

Feller, François-Xavier de, *Itinéraire ou voyages de Mr. L'abbé Defeller en diverses parties de l'Europe*. Ouvrage posthume, vol. I–II (Paris: Auguste Delalain; Liège: Fr. Lemarié, 1820).

[Feller, François-Xavier de], *Mélanges de politique, de morale et de littérature, extraits des journaux de M. l'abbé de Feller*, vol. I (Louvain: Vanlinthout and Vandenzande, 1822).

Feller, François-Xavier de, *Geschiedkundig Woordenboek: of beknopte levensbeschrijvingen van mannen, die, van het begin der wereld tot op onzen tijd, zich door vernuft, begaafdheden, deugden, dwalingen of misdaden hebben beroemd of berucht gemaakt* ('s-Hertogenbosch: J.J. Arkesteyn, 1828-48).

Feller, François-Xavier de, *Dizionario Storico ossia Storia Compendiata degli uomini memorabili per ingegno, dottrina, virtù, errori, delitti, dal principio del mondo fino ai nostri giorni dell'abbate Francesco Saverio de Feller*. Prima traduzione Italiana, sulla settima edizione Francese, con notabili correzioni ed aggiunte, tratte dai migliori biografi (Venezia: Girolamo Tasso, 1830).

Flexier de Réval, L'abbé [François-Xavier de Feller], *Catéchisme philosophique ou recueil d'observations propres à défendre la religion chrétienne contre ses ennemis* (Liege: J.F. Bassompierre, 1773, first edition); (Paris: Berton, 1777, second edition); (Tournay: J. Casterman, 1828 edition also used).

Gentz, Friedrich, 'Über den Ewigen Frieden', *Historisches Journal, herausgegeben von Friedrich Gentz* (December 1800), 711-90.

Gentz, Friedrich, *Über den Ursprung und Charakter des Krieges gegen die Französische Revolution* (Berlin: Fröhlich, 1801).

Gentz, Friedrich, *Von dem politischen Zustande von Europa vor und nach der Französischen Revolution* (Berlin: Frölich, 1801).

Gentz, Friedrich, *Fragmente aus der neusten Geschichte des Politischen Gleichgewichts in Europa* (St Petersburg: J.H. Hartnoch, 1806, second edition).

Gentz, Friedrich, *Fragments upon the Balance of Power in Europe*. English translation (London: Peltier, 1806).

Goethe, Johann von, 'Der Zauberlehrling'. In Friedrich Schiller (ed.), *Musen-Almanach für das Jahr 1798* (Tübingen: J.G. Cotta, 1798), 32-7.

Goetz, Walter, 'Die Einheit des Abendlandes', *Schweizer Monatshefte: Zeitschrift für Politik, Wirtschaft Kultur* 29, no. 7 (1949-50), 393-404.

Groen van Prinsterer, Guillaume, *Ongeloof en Revolutie: Eene reeks van historische voorlezingen* (Leiden: Luchtmans, 1847).

Groen van Prinsterer, Guillaume, *Handboek der geschiedenis van het vaderland* (Amsterdam: Höveker, 1875).

Guizot, François, *Histoire de la civilisation en Europe*, edited by Pierre Rosanvallon (Paris: Hachette, 1985).

Hallam, Henry, *View of the State of Europe during the Middle Ages*, 2 vol. (London: John Murray, 1818).

Hallam, Henry, *Introduction to the Literature of Europe in the Fifteenth, Sixteenth and Seventeenth Centuries*, 4 vol. (London: John Murray, 1837-9).

Hallam, Henry, *Supplement Notes to the View of the State of Europe during the Middle Ages*, 4 vol. (London: John Murray, 1848).

Haller, Karl Ludwig von, *Handbuch der allgemeinen Staatenkunde, des darauf gegründeten allgemeinen Staatsrechts und der allgemeinen Staatsklugheit nach den Gesetzen der Natur* (Winterthur: Steiner, 1808).
Haller, Karl Ludwig von, *Restauration der Staats-Wissenschaft oder Theorie des natürlich-geselligen Zustandes, der Chimäre des künstlich-bürgerlichen entgegengesetzt*, vol. I (Winterthur: Steiner, 1816).
Hansen, Joseph (ed.), *Quellen zur Geschichte des Rheinlandes im Zeitalter der französischen Revolution 1780–1801*, vol. I (Bonn: Hanstein, 1931).
[Hardenberg, Friedrich von], *Novalis Schriften. Die Werken Friedrich von Hardenbergs*, edited by Richard Samuel, Hans-Joachim Mähl, and Gerhard Schulz (Stuttgart: Kohlhammer, 1960–2008).
Harpe, Jean-François de la, *De l'état des lettres en Europe: Depuis la fin du siècle qui a suivi celui d'Auguste, jusqu'au règne de Louis XIV* (Paris: Migneret, 1797).
[Hauterive, Alexandre Maurice comte d'], *De l'état de la France, à la fin de l'an VIII* (Paris: Henrics, 1800).
Hazard, Paul, *La crise de la conscience européenne (1680–1715)*, 2 vol. (Paris: Furne Bovin, 1935).
Heeren, Arnold, 'Mitylene und Lion', *Politische Annalen* 5 (February 1794), edited by Christoph Girtanner.
Heeren, Arnold, *Handbuch der Geschichte der Staaten des Alterthums, mit besonderer Rücksicht auf ihre Verfassungen, ihren Handel und ihre Colonieen*, zum Gebrauch öffentlicher Vorlesungen (Göttingen: Röwer, 1799).
Heeren, Arnold, *Geschichte des Studiums der Classischen Litteratur seit dem Wiederaufleben der Wissenschaften: mit einer Einleitung, welche die Geschichte der Werke der Classiker im Mittelalter enthält*, 2 vol. (Göttingen: Röwer, 1797–1801).
Heeren, Arnold Hermann Ludwig, *Handbuch der Geschichte des Europäischen Staatensystems und Seiner Kolonien, von der Entdeckung beider Indien bis zur Errichtung des französischen Kayser Throns* (Göttingen: Röwer, 1809, first edition; 1819, third edition). I have used here the edition in the *Historische Werke* vol. VIII–IX (Göttingen: Röwer, 1822).
Heeren, Arnold Herman Ludwig, *Manuel Historique du système des états de l'Europe (...)* (Paris: Barrois, 1821).
Heeren, Arnold Herman Ludwig, *Handboek der geschiedenis van de staatsgesteldheid van Europa en deszelfs volkplantingen (...)* (Zutphen: H.C.A. Thieme, 1822).
Heeren, Arnold Hermann Ludwig, *Historische Werke* (*HW*), 15 vol. (Göttingen: Röwer, 1821–6).
Heeren, Arnold, 'Schreiben an einen Freund, Biographische Nachrichten enthaltend'. In *HW* I, xi–lxxviii.
Heeren, Arnold, 'Entwickelung der politischen Folgen der Reformation für Europa'. In *HW* I, 1–104.
Heeren, Arnold, 'Anhang: Etwas über die Folgen der Reformation für die Philosophie: eine am Reformationsjubileo gehaltene Rede'. In *HW* I, 105–12.
Heeren, Arnold, 'Versuch einer historische Entwicklung des Ursprungs und des Fortgangs des Britischen Continental-Interesse'. In *HW* I, 113–343.
Heeren, Arnold, 'Über die Entstehung, die Ausbildung und den praktische Einfluß der politische theorien und die Erhaltung des monarchischen Prinzips in dem neuern Europa'. In *HW* I, 365–451.
Heeren, Arnold, 'Über die Mittel zur Erhaltung der Nationalität besiegter Völker'. In *HW* II, 1–32.

Heeren, 'Versuch einer Entwicklung der Folgen der Kreuzzüge für Europa' (1807). In *HW* II, 33–349.
Heeren, Arnold, 'Über die Colonisation von Ägypten, und ihre Wirkungen auf das Europäische Staatensystem'. In *HW* II, 351–420.
Heeren, Arnold, 'Der Deutsche Bund in seinen Verhältnisse zu dem Europäischen Staatensystem bei Eröffnung des Bundestags 5 nov. 1816'. In *HW* II, 423–51.
Heeren, Arnold, 'Christian Gottlob Heyne, biographisch dargestellt'. In *HW* VI, 1–429.
Heeren, Arnold, 'Andenken an deutsche Historiker aus den letzten fünfzig Jahren'. In *HW* VI, 430–49.
Heeren, Arnold, 'Johann Christop Gatterer'. In *HW* VI, 450–68.
Heeren, Arnold, 'Johann von Müller'. In *HW* VI, 469–97.
Heeren, Arnold, 'August Ludwig von Schlözer'. In *HW* VI, 498–514.
Heeren, Arnold, 'Ludwig Timotheus von Spittler'. In *HW* VI, 515–34.
Heeren, Arnold, 'Georg Friedrich von Martens'. In *HW* VI, 535–44.
Heeren, Arnold, 'Ideen über die Politik, den Verkehr und den Handel vornehmsten Völker der alten Welt'. In *HW* X–XV (1824–6).
Heeren, Arnold, *Historical Researches into the Politics, Intercourse and Trade of the Principle Nations of Antiquity*, 3 vol. (Oxford: D.A. Talboys, 1833).
Heeren, Arnold, *Manual of the Political System of Europe and its Colonies, from its Formation at the Close of the Fifteenth Century to its Re-establishment upon the Fall of Napoleon*. Translated from the fifth German edition, 2 vol. (Oxford: D.A. Talboys, 1834).
Heeren, Arnold, *De la politique et du commerce des peuples de l'antiquité*, 7 vol. (Paris: Firmin Didot, 1830–40).
Heeren, Arnold Herman Ludwig, *A Manual of the History of the Political System of Europe and Its Colonies* (London: H.G. Bohn, 1846).
Hegel, Georg, *Vorlesungen über die Philosophie der Geschichte* (Frankfurt a.M.: Suhrkamp, 1986).
[Herder, Johann Gottfried von], *Auch eine Philosophie der Geschichte zur Bildung der Menschheit* (Riga: Hartknoch, 1774).
Hess, Moses, *Die Europäische Triarchie* (Leipzig: Otto Wigand, 1841).
Hume, David, *Essays: Moral, Political and Literary*, edited by Eugene Miller (Carmel, IN: Liberty Fund, 1985).
Hume, David, 'Of the Liberty of the Press'. In Hume, *Essays*, 9–13.
Hume, David, 'Of the Rise and Progress of the Arts and Sciences'. In Hume, *Essays*, 111–37.
Hume, David, 'Of the Balance of Power'. In Hume, *Essays*, 332–41.
Iselin, Isaak, *Über die Geschichte der Menschheit* (Karlsruhe: Schmieder, 1791).
Journal Historique et Littéraire (1773–94), edited by François-Xavier de Feller.
Justi, Johann Heinrich Gottlob von, *Staatswirtschaft oder systematische Abhandlung aller ökonomischen und Cameralwissenschaft*, 2 vol. (Leipzig: Breitkopf, 1755).
Justi, Johann Heinrich Gottlob von, *Die Chimäre des Gleichgewichts von Europa. Eine Abhandlung worinnen die Nichtigkeit und Ungerechtigkeit dieses zeitherige Lehrgebäude der Staatskunst deutlich vor Augen gelegt* (...) (Altona: D. Iverson, 1758).
Kahle, Ludwig Martin, *La bilance de l'Europe considerée comme règle de la paix et la guerre* (Berlin: Gottingae, 1744).
Kant, Immanuel, 'Zum ewigen Frieden'. In *Kants Gesammelte Schriften*, vol. VIII (Berlin: Walter de Gruyter, 1902), 341–86.
Kant, Immanuel, *Towards Perpetual Peace and other Writings on Politics, Peace, and History (Rethinking the Western Tradition)*, edited by Pauline Kleingeld (New Haven, CT: Yale University Press, 2016).

Koch, Christoph Wilhelm, and Frederic Schoell, *Abregé de l'histoire des Traités de Paix entre les Puissances de l'Europe, depuis la paix de Westphalie* (Paris: Gide, 1817, third edition).
Krause, Karl Friedrich, 'Entwurf eines europäischen Staatenbundes als Basis des allgemeinen Friedens und als rechtlichen Mittels gegen jeden Angriff wider die innere und äußere Freiheit Europas'. In Brockhaus (ed.), *Deutschen Blättern, vol. IV*; new edition by Hans Reichel (Leipzig: Félix Meiner, 1920).
Kuyper, Abraham, *Eenvormigheid, de vloek van het moderne leven. Lezing, gehouden in het Odéon te Amsterdam, 22 april 1869* (Amsterdam: H. de Hoogh & Co, 1870, second edition).
Lamennais, Félicité de, *Essai sur l'indifférence en matière de religion*, 4 vol. (Paris: Librairie Classique, 1817–24).
Mably, Gabriel Bonnot de, *Observations sur l'histoire de France*, 2 vol. (Geneva: Compagnie des Libraries, 1765).
Mably, Gabriel Bonnot de, *Principes des négociations pour servir d'introduction au droit public de l'Europe*. Introduction et notes par Marc Belissa (Paris: Kimé, 2001).
Mackintosh, James, *Vindicae Gallicae: Defense of the French Revolution and Its English Admirers, against the Accusations of the Right Hon. Edmund Burke, Including some Strictures on the Late Production of Mons. Calonne* (London: G.G.J. & J. Robinson, 1791, first edition; 1794, fourth edition).
[Maisonfort, Antoine du Bois des Cours, marquis de la], *De l'état réel de la France à la fin de l'année 1795 et de la situation politique des puissances de l'Europe à la même époque*, 2 vol. (Hamburg: P.F. Fauche, 1796).
Maistre, Joseph de, *Les Soirées de Saint-Pétersbourg, ou Entretiens sur le gouvernement temporel de la Providence* (Paris: Rusand, 1821).
Maistre, Joseph de, *Du Pape*, edited by Jacques Lovie and Joannès Chetail (Geneva: Droz, 1966).
Maistre, Joseph de, *Considerations on France*, edited by Richard Lebrun (Cambridge: Cambridge University Press, 1994).
Mallet du Pan, Jacques, *Considérations sur la nature de la Révolution de la France, et sur les causes qui en prolongent la durée* (London and Brussels: Flon, 1793).
Mallet du Pan, Jacques, *The Dangers which Threaten Europe: The Chief Causes of the Ill-Success of the Last Campaign; What Errors to Be Adopted in Order to Render the Present One Decisive in Favour of the Real Friends of Good Order and Peace*. From the French (New York: Rivington, 1795).
Martens, Georg Friedrich von, *Précis du droit des gens moderne de l'Europe fondé sur les traités et l'usage* (Göttingen: Dieterich, 1785).
Meinecke, Friedrich, *Die deutsche Katastrophe: Betrachtungen und Erinnerungen* (Wiesbaden: E. Brockhaus; Zürich: Aero, 1946).
Meinecke, Friedrich, *Die Idee der Staatsräson in der neueren Geschichte*. In Meinecke, *Werke* I, edited by Walther Hofer (Munich: De Gruyter, 1960).
Meinecke, Friedrich, *Weltbürgertum und Nationalstaat* (Munich: Oldenbourg, 1962).
Meinecke, Friedrich, *Cosmopolitanism and the National State*. Translated by Robert Kimber (Princeton, NJ: Princeton University 1970).
Montesquieu, Charles Louis (baron) de, *The Spirit of the Laws*, edited by Anne Cohler, Basia Miller, and Harold Stone (Cambridge: Cambridge University Press, 1989).
Montesquieu, Charles Louis de, *Réflexions sur la monarchie universelle en Europe (1734)*. Introduction et notes de Michel Porret (Geneva: Droz, 2000).

Montesquieu, Charles Louis de, *Considérations sur les causes de la grandeur des Romains et de leur décadence*, edited by Catherine Volpilhac-Auger (Paris: Gallimard, 2008).
Montgaillard, Maurice de, *Nécessité de la Guerre et dangers de la paix* (The Hague: F. Bool; London: E. Harlow, October 1794).
Montlosier, François-Dominique de, *De la nécessité d'une contre-révolution en France, pour rétablir les finances, la religion, les mœurs, la monarchie et la liberté* (no place: no publisher, 1791).
Montlosier, Maurice de, *Des effets de la violence et de la modération dans les affaires de la France* (London: Baylis, 1796).
Montlosier, Maurice de, *Vue sommaire sur les moyens de paix pour la France, pour l'Europe, pour les émigrés* (London: Baylis, 1796).
Müller, Adam Heinrich, *Die Lehre vom Gegensatze* (Berlin: Verlag der Realschulbuchhandlung, 1804).
Müller, Adam Heinrich, *Vorlesungen über die deutsche Wissenschaft und Literatur* (Dresden: Arnoldischen Buchhandlung, 1807, second edition).
Müller, Adam Heinrich, *Die Elemente der Staatskunst: oeffentliche Vorlesungen, vor Sr. Durchlaucht dem Prinzen Bernhard von Sachsen-Weimar und einer Versammlung von Staatsmännern und Diplomaten, im Winter von 1808 auf 1809, zu Dresden, 3 vol.* (Berlin: J.D. Sander, 1809).
Müller, Adam Heinrich, *Die Elemente der Staatskunst. Sechsunddreißig Vorlesungen* (Meersburg & Leipzig: F.W. Hendel, 1936).
Ortega y Gasset, José, *De opstand der horden*. Translation of the 1933 edition by Johan Brouwer (The Hague: H.P. Leopold, 1958).
Palm, Johannes van der, *De vrede van Europa* (Leiden: Du Mortier en Zoon, 1814).
Parrel, Christian de (ed.), *Les papiers de Calonne, documents pour servir à l'histoire de la contre-révolution. Première série: les finances des Princes en 1790, 1791, 1792* (Cavaillon: Mistral, 1932).
Pirenne, Henri, *Histoire de l'Europe* (Paris: Alcan, 1936).
Polybius, *The Histories*. Translated by R. Waterfield (Oxford: Oxford University Press, 2010).
Pradt, Dominique Frédéric Dufour de, *Antidote au Congrès de Rastadt ou plan d'un nouvel équilibre politique en Europe* (London: no publisher, 1798).
Pufendorf, Samuel, *Einleitung zu der Historie der vornehmsten Reiche und Staaten, so itziger Zeit in Europa sich befinden* (Frankfurt am Main: Knoch, 1682).
Pütter, Johann Stephan, *Historische Entwickelung der heutigen Staatsverfassung des Deutschen Reichs*, 3 vol. (Göttingen: Vandenhoeck, 1786–7).
Ranke, Leopold von, 'Die großen Mächte', *Historisch-Politische Zeitschrift* II (1833), 1–52.
Ranke, Leopold von, *Die Römische Päpste in den letzten vier Jahrhunderten* (Cologne: Agrippina Verlag, 1834).
Ranke, Leopold von, 'Politisches Gespräch', *Historisch-Politische Zeitschrift* II (1836), 775–86.
Ranke, Leopold von, 'Geschichte der romanischen und germanischen Völker von 1494 bis 1524'. In von Ranke, *Sämtliche Werke*, vol. 33-4 (Leipzig: Duncker und Humblot 1874).
Ranke, Leopold von, *Politisches Gespräch*, herausgegeben von H. Ritter von Srbik (Leipzig: Insel, 1943).
Raynal, Guillaume Thomas, *L'Histoire philosophique et politique des établissements et du commerce des Européens dans les deux Indes*, 4 vols. (Amsterdam: no publisher, 1770).
Rigoley de Juvigny, Jean-Antoine, *De la décadence des lettres et des mœurs, depuis les Grecs et le Romains jusqu'à nos jours* (Paris: Merigot, 1786, first edition; 1787, second edition).

Ritter, Gerard, *Die Neugestaltung Europas in 16. Jahrhundert. Die Kirchlichen und Staatlichen Wandlungen im Zeitalter der Reformation und der Glaubenskämpfe* (Berlin: Tempelhof, 1950).
Robert de Lézardière, Marie-Charlotte-Pauline, *Théorie des lois politiques de la monarchie française*, 4 vol. (Paris: comptoir des imprimeurs, 1844, second edition).
Robertson, William, *The History of the Reign of the Emperor Charles V with a View of the Progress of Society in Europe, from the Subversion of the Roman Empire, to the Beginning of the Sixteenth Century*, 3 vol. (London: W. Strahan, 1769).
Robertson, William, 'History of the Reign of Charles V' (1769). In Robertson, *Works*, 6 vol. (London: T. Cadell, 1826), vol. 4.
[Russell, William], *The History of Modern Europe: With an Account of the Decline and Fall of the Roman Empire, and a View of the Progress of Society, from the Fifth to the Eighteenth century. In a Series of Letters from a Nobleman to His Son*, vol. I–II (London: G. Robinson, 1779).
Saint-Pierre, Abbé de, *Projet pour rendre la paix perpétuelle en Europe*, 2 vol. (Utrecht: Antoine Schouten, 1713).
Saint-Simon, Comte de, *De la réorganisation de la société européenne*, edited by Dimitris Foufoulas (Paris: Éditions Payot et Rivages, 2014).
Schiller, Johann Christoph Friedrich, 'Der Antritt des neuen Jahrhunderts'. In Schiller, *Sämtliche Werke, vol. I, Gedichte*, edited by Jochen Golz (Berlin: Aufbau-Verlag, 1980), 497.
Schlegel, August, 'Über Litteratur, Kunst und Geist des Zeitalters'. In *Europa. Eine Zeitschrift*. Edited by Friedrich Schlegel, vol. II (Frankfurt a.M.: Wilmans, 1803), 1–95.
Schlegel, Friedrich, '*Reise nach Frankreich*'. In *Europa. Eine Zeitschrift*. Edited by Friedrich Schlegel. Vol. I (Frankfurt a. M.: Wilmans, 1803), 5–40.
Schlözer, August Ludwig von, *Vorstellung seiner Universal-Historie (1772/73)*. Nachdruck der Ausgabe Göttingen (Gotha: Dieterich, 1772), edited by H.W. Blanke (Waltrop: Spenner, 1997).
Schmitt, Carl, *Politische Romantik* (Munich: Duncker & Humblot, 1919).
[anonymous], *Smeekschrift aan de Vereenigde Mogendheden, om den vrede in Europa voor altijd onverbreekbaar te maken en berigt wegens ontwerpen daartoe* (Leiden: D. du Mortier en zoon, 1814).
Schroekh, Johann, *Allgemeine Welt-Geschichte für Kinder*, 6 vol. (no place: no publisher, 1786).
Spengler, Oswald, *Der Untergang des Abendlandes: Umrisse einer morphologie der Weltgeschichte*, 2 vol. (Munich: C.H. Beck, 1923).
Spittler, Ludwig Timotheus von, *Sämmtliche Werke*, 15 vol., edited by Karl Wächter (Stuttgart: J.G. Cotta, 1827–37).
Srbik, Heinrich von, 'Geleitwort'. In Leopold von Ranke (ed.), *Politisches Gespräch* (Leipzig 1943), 1–18.
Srbik, Heinrich von, *Metternich. Der Staatsmann und der Mensch*, 2 vol. (Munich: Bruckmann, 1925, first edition; 1956, new edition).
Thorbecke, Johan, 'Inaugurale rede over de inhoud van de historisch-politieke wetenschap' (Inaugural lecture Ghent, 1825). Translated from the Latin.
Thorbecke, Johan, *Over de verandering van het algemeen staten-stelsel van Europa sedert de Fransche omwenteling* (Leiden: S. & J. Luchtmans, 1831).
Valéry, Paul, 'European Man' (1922). Cited in Drace-Francis, *Identity*, 185–6.
Villers, Charles de, *Essai sur l'esprit et l'influence de la réformation de Luther, ouvrage qui a remporté le prix sur cette question proposée dans la séance publique du 15 germinal an X, par l'Institut national de France* (Paris: no publisher, 1804).

Vogt, Niklas, *Gustav Adolph König in Schweden. Als Nachtrag zur Europäischen Republik*, 2 vol. (Frankfurta.M.: Varrentrap, 1790).

Vogt, Niklas, *Unterhaltungen über die Vorzuglichsten epochen der alten geschichte in Beziehung auf die Neuern Begebenheiten* (Frankfurt a.M: Varrentrapp, 1791).

Vogt, Niklas, *Über die Europäische Republik* (Frankfurt a.M.: Varrentrapp, 1787–92).

[Vogt, Niklas], *Geschichte der französischen Revolution vom Jahre 1355* (Frankfurt & Leipzig: publisher unknown, 1792).

[Vogt, Niklas], *System des Gleichgewichts und der Gerechtigkeit*, 2 vol. (Frankfurt a.M.: Andreäischen Buchhandlung, 1802).

Vogt, Niklas, *Die gescheiterten Projekte dieses und des vorigen Jahrhunderts, Nach öffentliche und geheimen Nachrichten* (Frankfurt a.M.: Andreäischen Buchhandlung, 1803).

Vogt, Niklas, *Historische Darstellung des europäischen Völkerbundes* (Frankfurt a.M.: Andreäischen Buchhandlung, 1808).

Vogt, Niklas, *Abriß einer Geschichte der Deutschen für Mütter und Lehrerinnen* (Frankfurt a.M.: Andreäischen Buchhandlung, 1810).

Vogt, Niklas, *Die deutsche Nation und ihre Schicksale* (Frankfurt a.M.: Andreäischen Buchhandlung, 1810).

Vogt, Niklas, *Gedanken über das allerheiligste des Menschengeschlechtes* (Bamberg: Joseph Anton Goebhardt, 1812).

Vogt, Niklas, *Historische Testament*, 2 vol. (Mainz: Florian Kupferberg, 1814–15).

Vogt, Niklas, *Rheinische Geschichten und Sagen*, 3 vol. (Frankfurt a.M.: Hermannschen Buchhandlung, 1817).

[Vogt, Niklas], *Die europäischen Staats- und Kirchengrundsätze in dem Geiste unsrer Zeit dargestellt* (Mainz: Florian Kupferberg, 1818).

Vogt, Niklas, *Geschichte des Verfalls und Untergangs der Rheinischen Staaten des alten deutschen Reiches* (Frankfurt a.M.: Hermannschen Buchhandlung, 1833).

Vogt, Niklas, *Grund- und Aufriß des christlich-Germanischen Kirchen- und Staatsgebäudes im Mittelalter nach unverwerflichen Urkunden und Zeugnissen* (Bonn: Adolph Marcus, 1836, second edition).

Voltaire, 'The Century of Louis XIV (1751)'. In Seth and Von Kulessa (eds.), *Idea of Europe*.

Voltaire, *Essai sur les Moeurs et l'Esprit des Nations*. In *Complete Works of Voltaire*, vol. 21–27, edited by Bruno Bernard, John Renwick, Nicholas Cronk, and Janet Godden (Oxford: Voltaire Foundation, 2009–2019).

[Willem I, koning], 'Opstel des konings, Juli 1827'. In Herman Theodor Colenbrander (ed.), *Gedenkstukken der Algemeene Geschiedenis van Nederland van 1795 tot 1840*, vol. IX–(2) (Den Haag: Martinus Nijhoff, 1917), 319–24.

Secondary sources

Achtelstetter, Laura, *Prussian Conservatism 1815–1856: Ecclesiastical Origins and Political Strategies* (Wiesbaden: Springer, 2021).

Aerts, Remieg, *Thorbecke wil het: Biografie van een staatsman* (Amsterdam: Prometheus, 2018).

Aerts, Remieg, and Gita Deneckere (eds.), *Het (on) Verenigd Koninkrijk 1815–1830–2015: Een politiek experiment in de Lage Landen* (Rekkem: Ons Erfdeel, 2015).

Akça Ataç, Cemile, 'Roman Historiography of Eighteenth-century Britain beyond Gibbon: Ancient Norms of Empire for Moderns'. In Bourgault and Sparling (eds.), *Companion*, 469–504.

Albrecht, Andrea, *Kosmopolitismus: Weltbürgerdiskurse in Literatur, Philosophie und Publizistik um 1800* (Berlin: Walter de Gruyter, 2005).

Albrecht, Wolfgang, and Christoph Weiß, 'Einleitende Bemerkungen zur Beantwortung der Frage: Was heißt Gegenaufklärung'. In Weiß and Albrecht (eds.), *'Obscuranten'*, 16–35.

Alexander, Martin, *Romantics, Reformers, Reactionaries: Russian Conservative Thought and Politics in the Reign of Alexander I* (Dekalb, IL: Northern Illinois University Press, 1997).

Alibert, Jacques, *Les triangles d'or d'une société Catholique: Louis de Bonald, théoricien de la contre-révolution* (Paris: Pierre Téqui, 2002).

Alimento, Antonella, and Koen Stapelbroek (eds.), *The Politics of Commercial Treaties in the Eighteenth Century: Balance of Power, Balance of Trade* (Cham: Palgrave Macmillan, 2017).

Allan, David, 'Identity and Innovation: Historiography in the Scottish Enlightenment'. In Bourgault and Sparling (eds.), *Companion*, 307–41.

Anderson, Matthew, 'Eighteenth Century Theories of Balance of Power'. In Ragnhild Hatton and Matthew Anderson (eds.), *Studies in Diplomatic History: Essays in Memory of David Bayne Horn* (London: Shoe String, 1970), 183–98.

Ankersmit, Frank, *Sublime Historical Experience* (Stanford, CA: Stanford University Press, 2005).

Appiah, Kwame Anthony, *Cosmopolitanism: Ethics in a World of Strangers* (New York: Norton, 2006).

Applebaum, Anne, *Twilight of Democracy: The Seductive Lure of Authoritarianism* (New York: Doubleday, 2020).

Aprile, Sylvie *Le Siècle des exilés, bannis et proscrits, de 1789 à la Commune* (Paris: CNRS, 2010).

Arcangelis, Alessandro de, 'The Cosmopolitan Morphology of the National Discourse: Italy as a European Centre of Intellectual Modernity'. In Axel Körner, Tessa Hauswedell, and Ülrich Tiedau (eds.), *Re-Mapping Centres and Periphery: Asymmetrical Encounters in European and Global Contexts* (London: University College London Press, 2019), 135–54.

Arendt, Hannah, *Rahel Varnhagen: Lebensgeschichte einer Deutsche Jüdin aus der Romantik* (Munich: Piper, 1959, first edition; 2021, new edition).

Arjakovsky, Antoine (ed.), *Histoire de la conscience européenne* (Paris: Salvator, 2016).

Armenteros, Carolina, *The French Idea of History: Joseph de Maistre and His Heirs, 1794–1854* (Ithaca, NY: Cornell University Press, 2011).

Armenteros, Carolina, 'Preparing the Russian Revolution: Maistre and Uvarov on the History of Knowledge'. In Armenteros and Lebrun (eds.), *European Readers*, 213–48.

Armenteros, Carolina, 'From Centre to Periphery: Monarchism in France, 1791–1831', *De achttiende eeuw* 45, no. 2 (2012), 192–226.

Armenteros, Carolina, 'Royalist Medievalisms in the Age of Revolution: From Robert de Lézardière to Chateaubriand, 1792–1831', *Relief* 8, no. 1 (2014), 20–47.

Armenteros, Carolina, and Richard Lebrun (eds.), *Joseph de Maistre and the Legacy of Enlightenment* (Oxford: Voltaire Foundation, 2011).

Armenteros, Carolina, and Richard Lebrun (eds.), *Maistre and His European Readers. From Friedrich von Gentz to Isaiah Berlin* (Leiden: Brill, 2011).

Armitage, David, 'Edmund Burke and Reason of State', *Journal of the History of Ideas* 61, no. 4 (2000), 617–34.

Armitage, David, *The Ideological Origins of the British Empire* (Cambridge: Cambridge University Press, 2000).

Armitage, David, *Foundations of Modern International Thought* (Cambridge: Cambridge University Press, 2013).

Armitage, David, 'Foreword'. In Palmer (ed.), *Age of Democratic Revolution*, xv–xxii.
Armitage, David, and Sanjay Subrahmanyam (eds.), *The Age of Global Revolutions in Global Context, ca.1760–1840* (Basingstoke: Palgrave Macmillan, 2010).
Artola Renedo, Andoni, and Antonio Calvo Maturana, 'Declinaciones de la reacción eclesiástica contra la Revolución francesa en España (1789–1808)', *Hispania* 77, no. 256 (2017), 437–69.
Artola Renedo, Andoni, and Jean-Philippe Luis, 'Introduction: La contre-révolution dans le processus de sortie de l'Ancien Régime (de 1789 aux années 1830)', *Siècles* 43, Transferts culturels et politiques entre révolution et contre-révolution en Europe (1789–1840) (2016).
Asal, Sonja, 'The Contemporaneity of "Counter-Enlightenment": From the French Revolution to German Post-War Sociology', *HCM* 7 (2019), 940–70.
Asbach, Olaf (ed.), *Europa und die Moderne im langen 18. Jahrhundert (Europa und Moderne, vol. 2)* (Hannover: Wehrhahn, 2014).
Aston, Nigel, *The End of an Élite: The French Bishops and the Coming of the French Revolution* (Oxford: Oxford University Press, 1992).
Aureau, Bertrand, *Chateaubriand penseur de la Révolution* (Paris: Éditions Honoré Champion, 2001).
Auria, Matthew d', 'Progress, Decline and Redemption: Understanding War and Imagining Europe, 1870s–1890s', *European Review of History* 25, no. 2 (2018), 686–704.
Auria, Matthew d', *The Shaping of French National Identity: Narrating the Nation's Past, 1713–1830* (Cambridge: Cambridge University Press, 2020).
Auria, Matthew d', and Jan Vermeiren, 'Narrating Europe: Conceptions of European History and Identity in Historiography and Intellectual Thought', *Special Issue: History 356* 103, no. 3 (July 2018).
Auria, Matthew d', and Jan Vermeiren, 'Narrating Europe: (Re)Thinking Europe and Its Many Pasts', *History 356* 103, no. 3 (July 2018), 385–400.
Auria, Matthew d', and Jan Vermeiren (eds.), *Visions and Ideas of Europe during the First World War* (London: Routledge, 2019).
Baár, Monika, *Historians and Nationalism: East-Central Europe in the Nineteenth Century* (Oxford: Oxford University Press, 2010).
Baczko, Bronislaw, *Comment sortir de la Terreur: Thermidor et la Révolution* (Paris: Gallimard, 1989).
Bailey, Christian, *Between Yesterday and Tomorrow: German Visions of Europe, 1926–1950* (New York and Oxford: Berghahn, 2013).
Baker, Keith, *Inventing the French Revolution: Essays on French Political Culture in the Eighteenth Century* (Cambridge: Cambridge University Press, 2012).
Baldensperger, Fernand, *Le mouvement des idées dans l'émigration française (1789–1815)*, 2 vol. (Paris: Plon, 1924).
Bann, Stephen, *The Clothing of Clio: A Study of the Representation of History in Nineteenth Century Britain and France* (Cambridge: Cambridge University Press, 1984).
Bar-On, Tamir, 'Fascism to the Nouvelle Droite: The Dream of Pan-European Empire', *Journal of Contemporary European Studies* 16, no. 3 (2008), 327–45.
Baudet, Thierry, *Oikofobie. De angst voor het eigene* (Amsterdam: Prometheus, 2013).
Baudet, Thierry, and Michiel Visser (eds.), *Conservatieve Vooruitgang: De grootste denkers van de 20ste eeuw* (Amsterdam: Bert Bakker, 2010).
Baudet, Thierry, and Michiel Visser (eds.), *Revolutionair Verval en de conservatieve vooruitgang in de 18de en 19de eeuw* (Amsterdam: Bert Bakker, 2011).

Bavaj, Riccardo, and Martina Steber (eds.), *Germany and 'the West': The History of a Modern Concept* (New York: Berghahn, 2015).
Baxa, Jacob, *Adam Müllers Philosophie, Ästhetik und Staatswissenschaft* (Berlin: Junker & Dünhaupt, 1929).
Bayly, Christopher, *The Birth of the Modern World, 1780–1914: Global Connections and Comparisons* (Oxford: Oxford University Press, 2004).
Bayly, Christopher, *Recovering Liberties: Indian Thought in the Age of Liberalism and Empire* (Cambridge: Cambridge University Press, 2012).
Bayly, Christopher, and Eugenio Biagini, *Giuseppe Mazzini and the Globalization of Democratic Nationalism, 1830–1920* (Oxford: Oxford University Press, 2008).
Bayne, T.W., revised by Alexander Du Toit, 'William Russell (1746-1793)', *Oxford Dictionary of National Biography*, Available at: https://doi.org/10.1093/ref:odnb/24347.
Beck, Ulrich, and Edgar Grande, *Cosmopolitan Europe* (Malden: Polity Press, 2004/7).
Becker-Schaum, Christoph, *Arnold Hermann Ludwig Heeren: ein Beitrag zur Geschichte der Geschichtswissenschaft zwischen Aufklärung und Historismus* (Frankfurt a.M.: Peter Lang, 1993).
Becker-Schaum, Christoph, 'Arnold Hermann Ludwig Heeren (1760–1842)'. In Duchhardt et al. (eds.), *Europa-Historiker* III, 63–88.
Behler, Ernst, *Die Zeitschriften der Brüder Schlegel: Ein Beitrag zur Geschichte der deutschen Romantik* (Darmstadt: Wissenschaftliche Buchgesellschaft, 1983).
Beik, Paul, *The French Revolution Seen from the Right: Social Theories in Motion, 1789–1799* (New York: Howard Fertig, 1970).
Beiser, Frederick, *Enlightenment, Revolution and Romanticism* (Cambridge, MA: Harvard University Press, 1992).
Beiser, Frederick, *Hegel* (New York: Routledge, 2005).
Beiser, Frederick, *The German Historicist Tradition* (Oxford: Oxford University Press, 2011).
Beiser, Frederick, 'Savigny and the Historical School of Law'. In Beiser, *German Historicist Tradition*, 214–52.
Belissa, Marc, *Fraternité Universelle et Intérêt National (1713–1795). Les cosmopolitiques du droit des gens* (Paris: Éditions Kimé, January 1998).
Belissa, Marc, *Repenser l'ordre Européen (1795–1802). De la société des rois aux droits des Nations* (Paris: éditions Kimé, 2006).
Belissa, Marc, and Bernard Cottret (eds.), *Cosmopolitismes, patriotismes: Europe et Amériques 1773–1802* (Rennes: Les Perséides, 2005).
Bell, Duncan, 'What Is Liberalism?', *Political Theory* 42, no. 6 (2014), 682–715.
Benigni, Umberto, 'Ultramontanism'. In *The Catholic Encyclopedia, vol. 15* (New York: Robert Appleton Company, 1912).
Bentley, Michael, 'Henry Hallam Revisited', *The Historical Journal* 55, no. 2 (2012), 453–73.
Bercé, Yves-Marie, *La fin de l'Europe napoléonienne 1814: La vacance du pouvoir* (Paris: H. Veyrier, 1990).
Berchet, Jean-Claude, *Chateaubriand* (Paris: Gallimard, 2012).
Berg, Ursula, *Niklas Vogt (1756–1836): Weltsicht und politische Ordnungsvorstellungen zwischen Aufklärung und Romantik* (Stuttgart: Franz Steiner, 1992).
Berger, Stefan (with C. Conrad), *The Past as History: National Identity and Historical Consciousness in Modern Europe* (Basingstoke: Palgrave, 2015).
Berger, Stefan, 'Building the Nation among Visions of Empire'. In Stefan Berger and Alexei Miller (eds.), *Nationalising Empires* (Budapest: Central European Press, 2015), 247–308.

Berger, Stefan, 'The Past and Present of European Historiography: Between Marginalisation and Functionalisation'. In Brolsma, de Bruin, and Lok (eds.), *Eurocentrism*, 25–42.
Berger, Stefan, *History and Identity: How Historical Theory Shapes Historical Practice* (Cambridge: Cambridge University Press, 2021).
Berger, Stefan, and Eric Storm (eds.), *Writing the History of Nationalism* (London: Bloomsbury, 2019).
Berger, Stefan, Mark Donovan, and Kevin Passmore (eds.), *Writing National Histories: Western Europe since 1800* (London: Routledge, 1999).
Berlin, Isaiah, 'Political Ideas in the Twentieth Century', *Foreign Affairs* 28, no. 3 (April 1950), 351–85.
Berlin, Isaiah, 'The Counter-Enlightenment'. In Berlin, *Against the Current. Essays in the History of Ideas*, edited by Henry Hardy (London: Pimlico, 1979), 1–32.
Berlin, Isaiah, 'Alleged Relativism in Eighteenth Century European Thought'. In Berlin, *The Crooked Timber of Humanity: Chapters in the History of Ideas*, ed. Henry Hardy (New York: Knopf, 1990), 70–90.
Berlin, Isaiah, 'Joseph de Maistre and the Origins of Fascism'. In Berlin, *The Crooked Timber of Humanity: Chapters in the History of Ideas*, edited by Henry Hardy (London: John Murray, 1990), 91–174.
Bernardi, Bruno, 'L'idée d'équilibre européen dans le jus gentium des modernes: esquisse d'histoire conceptuelle'. In Lilti and Spector (eds.), *Penser l'Europe*, 19–46.
Berthezène, Clarisse, and Jean-Christian Vinel (eds.), *Post-war Conservatism: A Transnational Investigation. Britain, France and the United States* (Cham: Palgrave Macmillan/Springer, 2017).
Bertier de Sauvigny, Guillaume, *La Restauration* (Paris: Champs histoire, 1993).
Bertran de Balanda, Flavien-Alexandre, *Bonald, la Réaction en action* (Paris: Réédition Champ d'Azur, 2010).
Beutel, Albrecht, and Martha Nooke (eds.), *Religion und Aufklärung: Akten des Ersten Internationalen Kongresses zur Erforschung der Aufklärungstheologie* (Münster, 30. März bis 2. April 2014), no. 2 (Tübingen: Mohr Siebeck, 2016).
Bew, John, *Castlereagh: A Life* (Oxford: Oxford University Press, 2012).
Bhambra, Gurminder, *Rethinking Modernity: Postcolonialism and the Sociological Imagination* (London: Palgrave, 2007).
Bialasiewicz, Luiza, 'Spectres of Europe: Europe's Past, Present, and Future'. In Dan Stone (ed.), *The Oxford Handbook of Post-War European History* (Oxford: Oxford University Press, 2012), 98–119.
Bijl, Jelle, *Een Europese antirevolutionair: Het Europabeeld van Groen van Prinsterer in tekst en contekst* (Amsterdam: VU University Press, 2011).
Bireley, Robert, *The Counter-Reformation Prince: Anti-Machiavellianism or Catholic Statecraft in Early Modern Europe* (Chapel Hill, NC: University of North Carolina Press, 1990).
Blanning, Tim, *Reform and Revolution in Mainz, 1743–1803* (Cambridge: Cambridge University Press, 1974).
Blanning, Tim, *The French Revolution in Germany: Occupation and Resistance in the Rhineland 1792–1802* (Oxford: Clarendon Press, 1983).
Blanning, Tim, *The French Revolutionary Wars, 1787–1802* (London: Arnold, 1996).
Blanning, Tim, *The Pursuit of Glory: Europe 1648–1815* (London: Penguin, 2008).
Blaufarb, Rafe, Alan Forrest, and Karen Hagemann (eds.), *The Palgrave Macmillan Series on "War, Culture and Society, 1750–1850"* (Cham: Palgrave Macmillan, 2009–).
Blaut, James, *The Coloniser's Model of the World: Geographical Diffusionism and Eurocentric Theory* (London: Guilford Press, 1993).

Bödeker, Hans, Philippe Büttgen, and Michel Espagne (eds.), *Die Wissenschaft vom Menschen im Göttingen um 1800: Wissenschaftliche Praktiken, institutionelle Geographie, europäische Netzwerke* (Göttingen: Vandenhoeck & Ruprecht, 2008).
Bödeker, Hans, Georg Iggers, Jonathan Knudsen, and Peter Reill (eds.), *Aufklärung und Geschichte. Studien zur deutschen Geschichtswissenschaft im 18. Jahrhundert* (Göttingen: Vandenhoeck und Ruprecht, 1986).
Boer, Pim den, 'Towards a Comparative History of Concepts: Civilisation and *beschaving*', *Contributions on the History of Concepts* 3 (2007), 207–33.
Boldt, Hans, *Staatslehre im Vormärz* (Düsseldorf: Droste, 1970).
Boockmann, Hartmut, and Hermann Welleneuther (eds.), *Geschichtswissenschaft in Göttingen: Eine Vorlesungsreihe* (Göttingen: Vandenhoeck & Ruprecht, 1987).
Boom, Mathijs, 'Against Enlightened Abstraction: The Historical Thought of Adriaan Kluit', *De achttiende eeuw* 46, no. 2 (2014), 128–54.
Bornewasser, Johannes, '"Het credo ... geen rede van twist": Ter verklaring van een koninklijk falen (1826–1829)'. In Bornewasser, *Kerkelijk verleden in een wereldlijke context: Historische opstellen, gebundeld en aangeboden aan de schrijver bij zijn aftreden als hoogleraar aan de Theologische Faculteit Tilburg* (Amsterdam: Van Soeren, 1989), 113–48.
Bos, Jacques, 'Historical Thought from the Renaissance to the Enlightenment', *De Achttiende eeuw* 46, no. 2 (2014), 27–49.
Bossche, Geert van den, *Enlightened Innovation and the Ancient Constitution: The Intellectual Justifications of Revolution in Brabant (1787–1790)* (Brussels: Koninklijke Vlaamse Academie van België voor Wetenschappen en Kunsten, 2001).
Boucher, François-Emmanuel, '*Philosophes*, Anticlericalism, Reactionaries and Progress in the French Enlightenment Historiography'. In Bourgault and Sparling (eds.), *Companion*, 373–400.
Bourgault, Sophie, and Robert Sparling (eds.), *A Companion to Enlightenment Historiography* (Leiden: Brill, 2013).
Bourgault, Sophie, and Robert Sparling, 'Introduction'. In Bourgault and Sparling (eds.), *Companion*, 1–22.
Bourke, Richard, *Empire and Revolution: The Political Life of Edmund Burke* (Princeton, NJ: Princeton University Press, 2017).
Bourke, Richard, 'What Is Conservatism? History, Ideology and Party', *European Journal of Political Theory* 17, no. 4 (2018), 449–75.
Boutellier, Hans, *Het nieuwe westen: De identitaire strijd om de sociale verbeelding* (Amsterdam: Van Gennep, 2021).
Boutry, Philippe, 'Ultramontanisme'. In Philippe Levillain (ed.), *Dictionnaire historique de la papauté* (Paris: Fayard, 1994), 1651–3.
Brasart, Patrick, 'Bonneville et le cercle social, ou le bizarre en révolution', *Littérature* 169, no. 1 (2013), 67–86.
Braune, Frieda, *Edmund Burke in Deutschland: Ein Beitrag zur Geschichte des historisch-politischen Denkens* (Heidelberg: Winters, 1917).
Bravo López, Fernando, 'Los contrarrevolutionarios y el Islam: un análisis del pensamiento antiislámico de Louis de Bonald', *Historia Contemporánea* 53 (2016), 427–59.
Breckmann, Warren, and Peter Gordon (eds.), *The Cambridge History of Modern European Thought, vol. I: The Nineteenth Century, vol. II: The Twentieth Century* (Cambridge: Cambridge University Press, 2019).
Brejon de Lavergnée, Matthieu, and Olivier Tort (eds.), *L'union du trône et de l'autel? Politique et religion sous la Restauration* (Paris: Presses de l'université Paris-Sorbonne, 2012).

Brockmann, Stephen, 'Germany as Occident at the Zero Hour', *German Studies Review* 25, no. 3 (2002), 477-96.

Broers, Michael, *Europe after Napoleon: Revolution, Reaction and Romanticism, 1814-48* (Manchester: Manchester University Press, 1996).

Broers, Michael, 'Napoleon, Charlemagne, and Lotharingia: Acculturation and the Boundaries of Napoleonic Europe', *The Historical Journal* 44 (2001), 135-54.

Broers, Michael, 'The Quest for a Juste Milieu: The Restoration as a Silver Age?'. In Reinhard Stauber (ed.), *Mächtepolitik und Friedenssicherung: Zur politischen Kultur Europas im Zeichen des Wiener Kongresses* (Berlin & Münster: Lit Verlag, 2014), 33-46.

Broers, Michael, *Napoleon, vol. I: Soldier of Destiny; vol. II: The Spirit of the Age* (London: Faber & Faber, 2014 and 2018).

Broers, Michael, Ambrogio Caiani, and Stephen Bann (eds.), *A History of the European Restorations, vol. II: Culture, Society and Religion* (London: Bloomsbury, 2019).

Broers, Michael, Peter Hicks, and Agustín Guiméra (eds.), *The Napoleonic Empire and the New European Culture* (Basingstoke: Palgrave Macmillan, 2012).

Brolsma, Marjet, Robin de Bruin, and Matthijs Lok (eds.), *Eurocentrism in European History and Memory* (Amsterdam: Amsterdam University Press, 2019).

Bromwich, David, *The Intellectual Life of Edmund Burke: From the Sublime and Beautiful to American Independence* (Cambridge, MA: Belknap Press, 2014).

Bruijn, Jan de, and George Harinck (eds.), *Groen van Prinster in Europese context* (Hilversum: Verloren, 2004).

Bruin, Robin de, *Elastisch Europa. De integratie van Europa en de Nederlandse politiek, 1947-1968* (Amsterdam: Wereldbibliotheek, 2014).

Buettner, Elizabeth, *Europe after Empire: Decolonization, Society, and Culture* (Cambridge: Cambridge University Press: 2016).

Burbank, Jane, and Frederick Cooper, *Empires in World History: Power and the Politics of Difference* (Princeton, NJ: Princeton University Press, 2010).

Burgdorf, Wolfgang, 'Imperial Reform and Visions of a European Constitution in Germany around 1800', *History of European Ideas* 19 (1994), 401-8.

Burgdorf, Wolfgang, 'Johann Heinrich Gottlob von Justi (1720-1771)'. In Duchhardt et al. (eds.), *Europa-Historiker* I, 51-78.

Burgess, Glenn, *The Politics of the Ancient Constitution: An Introduction to English Political Thought, 1603-1642* (University Park, PA: Pennsylvania State University Press, 1993).

Burke, Peter, 'Did Europe Exist before 1700?', *History of European Ideas* 1 (1980), 21-9.

Burrow, John, *The Crisis of Reason: European Thought, 1848-1914* (New Haven, CT: Yale University Press, 2002).

Burrow, John, *A Liberal Descent: Victorian Historians and the English Past* (Cambridge: Cambridge University Press, 2009).

Burrows, Simon, *French Exile Journalism and European Politics, 1792-1814* (London: Royal Historical Society Studies in History New Series, 2000).

Burrows, Simon, 'Counter-revolution, Conservatism and Conspiracy in the Cosmopolitan Public Sphere from 1770s to 1790s: Mallet du Pan, Barruel and the Philosophes'. In Lok, Pestel, and Reboul (eds.), *Cosmopolitan Conservatisms*, 86-107.

Burrows, Simon, Edmond Dziembowski, and Ann Thomson (eds.), *Cultural Transfers: Studies on Franco-British Intellectual and Cultural Exchange in the Long Eighteenth Century*. Studies on Voltaire and the Eighteenth Century (Oxford: Oxford University Press, 2010).

Burson, Jeffrey, *The Rise and Fall of Theological Enlightenment: Jean-Martin de Prades and Ideological Polarization in Eighteenth-century France* (Notre Dame: Notre Dame University Press, 2010).

Burson, Jeffrey and Ulrich Lehner (eds.), *Enlightenment and Catholicism in Europe: A Transnational History* (Notre Dame: University of Notre Dame Press, 2014).
Burson, Jeffrey, and Jonathan Wright (eds.), *The Jesuit Suppression in Global Context: Causes, Events, and Consequences* (Cambridge: Cambridge University Press, 2015).
Busse, Gisela von der, *Die Lehre vom Staat als Organismus: Kritische Untersuchungen zur Staatsphilosophie Adam Müllers* (Berlin: Junker & Dünnhaupt, 1928).
Cahen, Raphael, 'The Correspondence of Friedrich von Gentz: The Reception of Du Pape in the German-speaking World'. In Armenteros and Lebrun (eds.), *European Readers*, 95–121.
Cahen, Raphael, *Friedrich Gentz 1764–1832 Penseur post-Lumières et acteur du nouvel ordre européen* (Berlin and Munich: De Gruyter Oldenbourg, 2017).
Cahen, Raphael, 'Le project européen de Krause'. In Oscar Ferreira (ed.), *Krausisme juridique et politique en Europe* (Paris: Garnier, 2021), 267–87.
Caiani, Ambrogio, 'Re-inventing the Ancien Régime in Post-Napoleonic Europe', *European History Quarterly* 47, no. 3 (2017), 437–60.
Caiani, Ambrogio, *To Kidnap a Pope: Napoleon and Pius VII* (New Haven, CT: Yale University Press, 2021).
Caiani, Manuela, 'Radical Right Cross-National Links and International Cooperation'. In Jens Rydgren (ed.), *The Oxford Handbook of the Radical Right* (Oxford: Oxford University Press, 2018), 394–411.
Calderon Argelich, Alfonso, *Olvido y Memoria del siglo XVIII español* (Madrid: Cátedra, 2022).
Cameron, Euan, 'The Turmoil of Faith'. In Cameron (ed.), *The Sixteenth Century* (Oxford: Oxford University Press, 2006), 145–73.
Cañizares-Esguerra, Jorge, *How to Write the History of the New World: Histories, Epistemologies, and Identities in the Eighteenth-Century Atlantic World* (Stanford, CA: Stanford University Press, 2002).
Caradonna, Jeremy, 'There Was No Counter-Enlightenment', *Eighteenth Century Studies* 49, no. 1 (2015), 51–69.
Carcassonne, Elie, *Montesquieu et le problème de la Constitution Française au XVIIIe Siècle* (Paris: Presses universitaires de France, 1927).
Caron, Jean-Claude, and Jean-Philippe Luis (eds.), *Rien appris, rien oublié? Les Restaurations dans l'Europe postnapoléonienne (1814–1830)* (Rennes: PUR, 2015).
Carpenter, Kristy, *Refugees of the French Revolution: Émigrés in London, 1789–1802* (Basingstoke: Macmillan, 1999).
Carpenter, Kristy, and Philip Mansel (ed.), *The French Émigrés in Europe and the Struggle against Revolution, 1789–1814* (Basingstoke: Macmillan, 1999).
Caruso, Amerigo, *Nationalstaat als Telos? Der konservative Diskurs in Preußen und Sardinien-Piemont 1840–1870* (Berlin and Boston, MA: De Gruyter, 2017).
Caruso, Amerigo, 'In Medio Stat Virtus? The Adaptability of the Moderate Project of Politics in Mid-Nineteenth-Century Europe (1830–1870)'. In de Haan and Lok, *Politics of Moderation*, 109–30.
Cesari, Chiara de, and Ayhan Kaya (eds.), *European Memory in Populism: Representations of Self and Other* (London: Routledge, 2019).
Chadwick, Owen, *The Popes and European Revolution* (Oxford: Clarendon, 1981).
Chadwick, Owen, *From Bossuet to Newman* (Cambridge: Cambridge University Press, 1957, first edition; 1987, new edition).
Chakrabarty, Dipesh, *Provincializing Europe: Postcolonial Thought and Historical Difference* (Princeton, NJ: Princeton University Press, 2000).

Chappey, Jean-Luc, 'Les anti-lumières et les oppositions intellectuelles à la Révolution'. In Martin (ed.), *Révolution*, 165–80.

Chélin, Henri, *Friedrich Schlegel's Europa* (Frankfurt a.M.: Lang, 1981).

Claeys, Gregory, 'Early Socialism as Intellectual History', *History of European Ideas* 40, no. 7 (2014), 893–904.

Claeys, Gregory, 'Some Nineteenth Century Appraisals of Burke's Reflections: From Sir James Mackintosh to John Morley'. In Fitzpatrick and Jones (eds.), *Reception of Edmund Burke*, 75–90.

Clark, Christopher, 'After 1848: The European Revolution in Government', *Transactions of the Royal Historical Society* No. 22 (Cambridge: Cambridge University Press, 1997), 171–97.

Clark, Frederick, 'Dividing Time: The Making of Historical Periodization in Early Modern Europe'. Dissertation, Princeton University, 2014.

Clarke, Jonathan, *English Society 1660–1832: Religion, Ideology and Politics during the Ancien Regime* (Cambridge: Cambridge University Press, 2000).

Clément, Jean-Paul, 'Chateaubriand et la Contre-Révolution, ou la liberté sur le pavois'. In Jean Tulard (ed.), *La Contre-Révolution en France* (Paris: Perrin, 1990).

Clément, Jean-Paul, *Chateaubriand* (Paris: Flammarion, 1998).

Compagnon, Antoine, *Les antimodernes de Joseph de Maistre à Roland Barthes* (Paris: Gallimard, 2005).

Confino, Alan, *Foundational Pasts: The Holocaust as Historical Understanding* (Cambridge: Cambridge University Press, 2011).

Conrad, Sebastian, *What Is Global History?* (Princeton, NJ: Princeton University Press, 2017).'

Conze, Vanessa, *Das Europa der Deutschen: Ideen von Europa in Deutschland zwischen Reichstradition und Westorientierung (1920–1970)* (Munich: De Gruyter Oldenbourg, 2005).

Cooper, Frederick, *Colonialism in Question: Theory, Knowledge, History* (Los Angeles, CA: University of California Press, 2005).

Cooper, Frederick, *Citizenship, Inequality and Difference: Historical Perspectives* (Princeton, NJ: Princeton University Press, 2018).

Cornelißen, Christoph, *Gerhard Ritter: Geschichtswissenschaft und Politik im 20. Jahrhundert* (Düsseldorf: Droste Verlag, 2001).

Craiutu, Aurelian, *Liberalism under Siege: The Political Thought of the French Doctrinaires* (Lanham, MD: Lexington Books, 2003).

Craiutu, Aurelian, *A Virtue for Courageous Minds: Moderation in French Political Thought, 1748–1830* (Princeton, NJ: Princeton University Press, 2012).

Craiutu, Aurelian, 'Rethinking Modernity, Religion and Tradition: The Intellectual Dialogue between Alexandre Stourdza and Joseph de Maistre', *History of European Ideas* 40, no. 1 (2013), 277–89.

Creyghton, Camille, *Résurrections de Michelet: Politique et Historiographie en France depuis 1870* (Paris: Editions EHESS, 2019).

Creyghton, Camille (ed.), *Revolutionary Cosmopolitanism: Transnational Migration and Political Activism, 1815–1848* (Utrecht University: forthcoming).

Crossly, Ceri, 'History as Principle of Legitimation in France (1820–1848)'. In Berger, Donovan, and Passmore (eds.), *Writing National Histories*, 49–56.

Dam, Michiel van, 'Een spirituele revolutie? Geloof en zelf-representatie tijdens de Brabantse omwenteling (1787–1790)', 'De Zuidelijke Nederlanden in Revolutie', *Special Issue: De Achttiende eeuw* 1, no. 49 (2017), 11–22.

Dam, Michiel van, 'Between Enlightened Reform and Spiritual Revolt: Religious Self-Historization and- Governance in the Southern Netherlands during the Catholic Enlightenment (1760-1790)'. Dissertation, University of Ghent, 2019.
Dam, Michiel van, 'A Christian Cosmopolitanism: Pauline Universalism and Cynic Apostolicism during the Brabant Revolt (1787-1790)'. In Lok, Pestel, and Reboul (eds.), *Cosmopolitan Conservatisms*, 131-51.
Daudet, Ernest, *Histoire de l'émigration pendant la Révolution française* (Paris: Hachette, 1904-7).
Dawson, Hannah, and Annelien de Dijn (eds.), *Rethinking Liberty before Liberalism* (Cambridge: Cambridge University Press, 2022).
Dehio, Ludwig, *Gleichgewicht oder Hegemonie: Betrachtungen über ein Grundproblem der neueren Staatengeschichte* (Krefeld: Scherpe, 1948).
Delanty, Gerard, *Inventing Europe: Idea, Identity, Reality* (Basingstoke: Palgrave Macmillan, 1995).
Delanty, Gerard, 'Europe and the Idea of "Unity in Diversity"'. In Lindhal (ed.), *Wither Europe?*, 25-42.
Delanty, Gerard, *The Cosmopolitan Imagination: The Renewal of Critical Social Theory* (Cambridge: Cambridge University Press, 2009).
Delanty, Gerard, *Formations of European Modernity. A historical and political sociology of Europe* (Cham: Palgrave Macmillan, 2018).
Delzell, Charles, 'Adolfo Omodeo: Historian of the "Religion of Freedom"'. In H.A. Schmitt (ed.), *Historians of Modern Europe* (Baton Rouge, LA: Louisiana State University Press, 1971), 123-50.
Deseure, Brecht, *Onhoudbaar Verleden: Geschiedenis als politiek instrument tijdens de Franse periode in België* (Leuven: Universitaire Pers Leuven, 2014).
Deseure, Brecht, 'De lange schaduw van de Blijde Inkomst: revolutionair discours over de oude grondwetten in België'. In Dave de Ruysscher (ed.), *Rechtsgeschiedenis op nieuwe wegen* (Antwerpen: Maklu, 2015), 35-58.
Devetak, Richard, 'Historiographical Foundations of Modern International Thought: Histories of the European States-System from Florence to Göttingen', *History of European Ideas* 41, no. 1 (2015), 62-77.
Dijk, A.J. van, *Groen van Prinsterer's Lectures on 'Unbelief and Revolution'* (Jordan State, Ontario: Wedge Publishing Foundation, 1989).
Dijn, Annelien de, *Liberty in a Levelled Society? French Political Thought from Montesquieu to Tocqueville* (Cambridge: Cambridge University Press, 2008).
Dijn, Annelien de, 'The Politics of Enlightenment: From Peter Gay to Jonathan Israel', *The Historical Journal* 55, no. 3 (September 2012), 785-805.
Dijn, Annelien de, 'Montesquieu's Controversial Context: The Spirit of the Laws as a Monarchist Tract', *History of Political Thought* 34, no. 1 (2013), 66-88.
Dijn, Annelien de, 'Was Montesquieu a Liberal Republican?', *The Review of Politics* 76, no. 1 (2014), 21-42.
Dijn, Annelien de, *Freedom: An Unruly History* (Cambridge, MA: Harvard University Press, 2020).
Dinan, Desmond, *Ever Closer Union: An Introduction to European Integration* (Basingstoke: Palgrave Macmillan, 2005).
Dionisotti, Carlo, *Europe in Sixteenth Century Literature* (Oxford: Clarendon Press, 1971).
Drace-Francis, Alex, *European Identity: A Historical Reader* (Basingstoke: Palgrave, 2013).
Drace-Francis, Alex, 'The Elephant on the Doorstep? East European Perspectives on Eurocentrism'. In Brolsma, de Bruin, and Lok (eds.), *Eurocentrism*, 157-94.

Drentje, Jan, 'Thorbecke en het Europese statensysteem van Alexander Heeren', *Tijdschrift voor Geschiedenis* 111 (1998), 377-410.
Drentje, Jan, *Thorbecke: Een filosoof in de politiek* (Amsterdam: Boom, 2004).
Duchhardt, Heinz, *Gleichgewicht der Kräfte: Convenance, Europäisches Konzert. Friedenskongress und Friedensschlüsse vom Zeitalter Ludwig XIV. bis zum Wiener Kongreß* (Darmstadt: Wissenschaftliche Buchgesellschaft, 1976).
Duchhardt, Heinz, *Altes Reich und europäische Staatenwelt 1648-1806* (Munich: Oldenbourg, 1990).
Duchhardt, Heinz, *Der Westfälische Friede: Diplomatie—politische Zäsur—kulturelles Umfeld—Rezeptionsgeschichte* (Munich: Oldenbourg, 1998).
Duchhardt, Heinz, 'Peace Treaties from Westphalia to the Revolutionary Era'. In Randall Lesaffer (ed.), *Peace Treaties and International Law in European History: From the Late Middle-Ages to World War I* (Cambridge: Cambridge University Press, 2004).
Duchhardt, Heinz, 'Niklas Vogt (1756-1803)'. In Duchhardt et al. (eds.), *Europa-Historiker* III, 43-62.
Duchhardt, Heinz, *Der Wiener Kongress: Die Neugestaltung Europas 1814/15* (Munich: C.H. Beck, 2013).
Duchhardt, Heinz, and Andreas Kunz (eds.), *Europäische Geschichte als historiographisches Problem* (Mainz: Phillip von Zabern, 1997).
Duchhardt, Heinz, Malgorzata Morawiec, Wolfgang Schmale, and Winfried Schulze (eds.), *Europa-Historiker: Ein biographisches Handbuch*, 3 vol. (Göttingen: Vandenhoeck & Ruprecht, 2006-7).
Duranti, Marco, *The Conservative Human Rights Revolution: European Identity, Transnational Politics, and the Origins of the European Convention* (Oxford: Oxford University Press, 2017).
Duroselle, Jean-Baptiste, *L'idée d'Europe dans l'histoire* (Paris: Denoël, 1965).
Duroselle, Jean-Baptiste, *Europe: A History of Its Peoples* (New York: Viking, 1990).
Dussen, Jan van der, and Kevin Wilson (eds.), *The History of the Idea of Europe* (London: Routledge, 1995).
Dwan, David, and Christopher Insole (eds.), *The Cambridge Companion to Edmund Burke* (Cambridge: Cambridge University Press, 2012).
Edelstein, Dan, *The Terror of Natural Right: Republicanism, the Cult of Nature, and the French Revolution* (Chicago, IL: University of Chicago Press, 2009).
Edelstein, Dan, *The Enlightenment: A Genealogy* (Chicago, IL: University of Chicago, 2010).
Edelstein, Dan (ed.), *The Super-Enlightenment: Daring to Know Too Much* (Oxford: Studies on Voltaire & the Eighteenth Century, 2010), 137-66.
Ellis, Geoffrey, 'The Nature of Napoleonic Imperialism'. In Philip Dwyer (ed.), *Napoleon and Europe* (London: Longman, 2001), 1-21, 97-117.
Epstein, Klaus, *The Genesis of German Conservatism* (Princeton, NJ: Princeton University Press, 1966).
Escrig Rosa, Josep, 'Pasión racional, razón apasionada: El primer antiliberalismo reaccionario en España', *Ayer* 111 (2018), 135-61.
Espagne, Michel, *Les transferts culturels franco-allemands* (Paris: PUF, 1999).
Espagne, Michel, and Michael Werner (eds.), *Transferts: Les relations interculturelles dans l'espace franco-allemand* (Paris: Ed. Recherche sur les civilisations, 1988).
Everdell, William, *Christian Apologetics in France, 1730-1790: The Roots of Romantic Religion* (Lewiston: Edwin Mellen, 1987).

Färber, Konrad, *Kaiser und Erzkanzler: Carl von Dalberg und Napoleon am Ende des Alten Reiches; die Biographie des letzten geistlichen Fürsten in Deutschland* (Regensburg: Mittelbayer, 1988).

Färber, Konrad, Albrecht Klose, and Hermann Reidel, (eds.), *Carl von Dalberg: Erzbischof und Staatsmann (1744–1817)* (Regensburg: Mittelbayer, 1994).

Fawcett, Edmund, *Liberalism: The Life of an Idea* (Princeton, NJ: Princeton University Press, 2018).

Fawcett, Edmund, *Conservatism: The Fight for a Tradition* (Princeton, NJ: Princeton University Press, 2020).

Feindt, Gegor, Félix Krawatzek, Friedemann Pestel, and Rieke Trimçev (eds.), 'European Memory: Universalising the Past?', *Special Issue: European Review of History* 24, no. 4 (2017).

Fergusson, David, 'History, Tradition, and Scepticism: The Patterns of Nineteenth-century Theology'. In Breckmann and Gordon (eds.), *European Thought* I, 65–87.

Figes, Orlando, *The Europeans: Three Lives and the Making of a Cosmopolitan Culture* (London: Penguin, 2020).

Figge, Robert, *Georg Friedrich von Martens: sein Leben und seine Werke. Ein Beitrag zur Geschichte der Völkerrechtswissenschaft* (Gleiwitz: Hill, 1914).

Fillafer, Franz, and Jürgen Osterhammel, 'Cosmopolitanism and the German Enlightenment'. In Helmut Walser Smith (ed.), *The Oxford Handbook of Modern German History* (Oxford: Oxford University Press, 2011).

Fitzmaurice, Andrew, *Sovereignty, Property and Empire, 1500–2000* (Cambridge: Cambridge University Press, 2017).

Fitzmaurice, Andrew, *King Leopold's Ghostwriter: The Creation of Persons and States in the Nineteenth Century* (Princeton, NJ: Princeton University Press, 2021).

Fitzpatrick, Martin, and Peter Jones (eds.), *The Reception of Edmund Burke in Europe* (London: Bloomsbury Academic, 2017).

Fontana, Biancamaria, 'The Napoleonic Empire and the Europe of Nations'. In Anthony Pagden (ed.), *The Idea of Europe: From Antiquity to the European Union* (Cambridge: Cambridge University Press, 2002), 116–28.

Force, Pierre, 'Voltaire and the Necessity of Modern History', *Modern Intellectual History* 6, no. 3 (2009), 457–84.

Forsyth, Murray, 'The Old European States-System: Gentz vs. Hauterive', *The Historical Journal* 23 (1980), 521–38.

Freeden, Michael, *Ideologies and Political Theory: A Conceptual Approach* (Oxford: Oxford University Press, 1998, first edition; 2003, new edition).

Freeden, Michael, Javier Fernández Sebastián, and Jörn Leonhard (eds.), *In Search of European Liberalisms: Concepts, Languages, Ideologies* (New York: Berghahn, 2019).

Frey, Hugo, and Stefan Jordan, 'Re-assessing National History after the End of the Second World War: Friedrich Meinecke and Raymond Aron Compared'. In Stefan Berger and Chris Lorenz (eds.), *Nationalising the Past: Historians as Nation-Builders in Modern Europe* (Basingstoke: Palgrave, 2010), 282–97.

Fritzsche, Peter, *Stranded in the Present: Modern Time and the Melancholy of History* (Cambridge, MA: Harvard University Press, 2010).

Fueter, Eduard, *Geschichte der neueren Historiographie* (Munich and Berlin: Oldenbourg, 1936).

Fureix, Emmanuel, and Judith Lyon-Caen (eds.), '1814–1815: Expérience de discontinuités', *Special Issue: Revue d'histoire du XIX siècle* 49, no. 2 (2014).

Furet, François, *Nicolas de Bonneville and the Social Circle, 1787–1800* (Paris: Hachette, 1976).
Furet, François, *La Révolution* I (1770–1814) (Paris: Hachette, 1988).
Furet, François, and Mona Ozouf (eds.), *The French Revolution and the Creation of Modern Political Culture, vol. III: The Transformation of Political Culture: 1789–1848* (Oxford: Pergamon, 1989).
Garrard, Graeme, *Rousseau's Counter-Enlightenment: A Republican Critique of the Philosophes* (New York: SUNY Press, 2003).
Gaspar, Renaat, *Op de vlucht voor de guillotine: herinneringen van émigrés aan hun verblijf in de Republiek der Verenigde Nederlanden, 1793–1795* (Zutphen: Walburg Pers, 2010).
Gay, Peter, *The Enlightenment: An Interpretation*, 2 vol. (New York: Knopf, 1966–9).
Gengembre, Gérard, 'Burke'. In François Furet and Mona Ozouf (eds.), *A Critical Dictionary of the French Revolution* (Cambridge, MA: Harvard University Press, 1989), 916–23.
Gengembre, Gérard, 'La Contre-révolution: Europe française ou Europe papale?', *L'idée de l'Europe au fil de deux millénaires* (Beauchesne: Michel Perrin éd., 1994), 161–74.
Gengembre, Gérard, 'Dynamisme ou fixité: l'Europe chez les penseurs libéraux et contre-révolutionaires après 1800', *Tumultes* 7 (1996), 29–38.
Ghervas, Stella, *Réinventer la tradition: Alexandre Stourdza et l'Europe de la Sainte Alliance* (Paris: Honoré Champion, 2008).
Ghervas, Stella, 'La Paix par le droit, ciment de la civilisation en Europe? La perspective du siècle des Lumières'. In Lilti and Spector (eds.), *Penser l'Europe*, 47–70.
Ghervas, Stella, 'From the Balance of Power to a Balance of Diplomacy'. In de Graaf, de Haan, and Vick (eds.), *Securing Europe*, 95–113.
Ghervas, Stella, *Conquering Peace: From the Enlightenment to the European Union* (Cambridge, MA: Harvard University Press, 2021).
Ghervas, Stella, and David Armitage (eds.), *A Cultural History of Peace in the Age of Enlightenment, 1648–1815* (London: Bloomsbury 2019).
Ghins, Arthur, 'Moderation and Religion in France after the Revolution: Germaine de Staël and Benjamin Constant'. In de Haan and Lok (eds.), *Politics of Moderation*, 49–66.
Gierl, Martin, *Geschichte als präzisierte Wissenschaft: Johann Christoph Gatterer und die Historiographie des 18. Jahrhunderts im ganzen Umfang* (Stuttgart: Frommann-Holzboog, 2012).
Gildea, Robert, *Empires of the Mind: The Colonial Past and the Politics of the Present* (Cambridge: Cambridge University Press, 2019).
Godechot, Jacques, *The Counter-Revolution: Doctrine and Action, 1789–1804*. English translation of the French original version of 1961 (New York: Howard Fertig, 1971).
Goldzink, Jean, *La solitude de Montesquieu: le chef-d'œuvre introuvable du libéralisme* (Paris: Fayard, 2011).
Golf-French, Morgan, 'The Limits of the Enlightened Narrative: Rethinking Europe in Napoleonic Germany', *History of European Ideas* 46, no. 8 (2020), 1197–213.
Gollwitzer, Heinz, *Europabild und Europagedanke: Beiträge zur deutschen Geistesgeschichte des 18. und 19. Jahrhundert* (Munich: C.H. Beck, 1951, first edition; 1964 new edition).
Goodwin, Albert, 'Calonne, the Assembly of French Notables of 1787 and the Origins of the "Révolte nobiliaire"', *English Historical Review* 61 no. 240 (May 1946) and no. 241 (September 1946), 329–77, 202–34.
Goody, Jack, *The Theft of History* (Cambridge: Cambridge University Press, 2006).
Gosewinkel, Dieter, *Anti-liberal Europe: A Neglected Story of Europeanisation* (New York: Berghahn, 2014).

Gossmann, Lionel, *Between History and Literature* (Cambridge, MA: Harvard University Press, 1990).
Goulemot, Jean, *Le règne de l'Histoire: Discours historiques et révolutions.* XVIIe–XVIIIe siècles (Paris: Albin Michel, 1996).
Graaf, Beatrice de, 'Second-tier Diplomacy: Hans von Gagern and William I in Their Quest for an Alternative European Order, 1813–1818', *Journal of Modern European History* 12, no. 4 (2014), 546–66.
Graaf, Beatrice de, *Tegen de terreur: Hoe Europa veilig werd na Napoleon* (Amsterdam: Bert Bakker, 2018).
Graaf, Beatrice de, 'The Allied Machine: The Conference of Ministers in Paris and the Management of Security, 1815-18'. In de Graaf, de Haan, and Vick (eds.), *Securing Europe*, 130–49.
Graaf, Beatrice de, 'Taming the Evil Passions: Moderation in the International Relations'. In de Haan and Lok (eds.), *Politics of Moderation*, 89–107.
Graaf, Beatrice de, *Fighting Terror after Napoleon: How Europe Became Secure after 1815* (Cambridge: Cambridge University Press, 2020).
Graaf, Beatrice de, 'How Conservative Was the Holy Alliance Really? Tsar Alexander's Offer of Radical Redemption to the Western World'. In Lok, Pestel, and Reboul (eds.), *Cosmopolitan Conservatisms*, 241–60.
Graaf, Beatrice de, and Mieke van Leeuwen-Canneman, 'De Nederlandse inbreng in het Europees concert, 1815–18', *BMGN* 133, no. 1 (2018), 22–52.
Graaf, Beatrice de, Ido de Haan, and Brian Vick (eds.), *Securing Europe after Napoleon: 1815 and the New European Security Culture* (Cambridge: Cambridge University Press, 2019).
Graaf, Beatrice de, Ido de Haan, and Brian Vick, 'Vienna 1815: Introducing a European Security Culture'. In de Graaf, de Haan, and Vick (eds.), *Securing Europe*, 1–19.
Graeber, David, and David Wengrow, *The Dawn of Everything: A New History of Humanity* (London: Penguin, 2021).
Grafton, Anthony, *The Footnote: A Curious History* (Cambridge, MA: Harvard University Press, 1999).
Grafton, Anthony, *What Was History? The Art of History in Early Modern Europe* (Cambridge: Cambridge University Press, 2007).
Grafton, Anthony, 'A Sketch Map of a Lost Continent: The Republic of Letters'. Available at: https://arcade.stanford.edu/rofl/sketch-map-lost-continent-republic-letters (accessed 23 June 2020).
Green, Jonathan, 'Friedrich Gentz's Translation of Burke's *Reflections*', *The Historical Journal* 57, no. 3 (2014), 639–59.
Green, Jonathan, '"Fiat Justitia, pereat mundus, pereat mundus": Immanuel Kant, Friedrich Gentz and the Possibility of Prudential Enlightenment', *Modern Intellectual History* 14, no. 1 (2017), 35–65.
Green, Jonathan, Edmund Burke's German Readers at the End of Enlightenment, 1790–1815 (PhD dissertation, University of Cambridge, 2018). Available at: https://doi.org/10.17863/CAM.21203.
Greiffenhagen, Martin, *Das Dilemma des Konservatismus in Deutschland* (Munich: Piper, 1971).
Grell, Chantal, *Le dix-huitième siècle et l'Antiquité en France, 1680–1789* (Paris: Studies on Voltaire, 1961).
Grell, Chantal, *L'histoire entre érudition et philosophie: étude sur la connaissance historique à l'âge des Lumières* (Paris: Presses universitaires de France, 1993).

Griffin, Roger, 'Europe for the Europeans: Fascist Myths of the European New Order 1922-1992'. In Mathew Feldman (ed.), *A Fascist Century: Essays by Roger Griffin* (London: Palgrave Macmillan, 2008), 132-80.

Griggs, Tamara, 'Universal History from Counter-Reformation to Enlightenment', *Modern Intellectual History* 4, no. 2 (2007), 219-47.

Grolle, Joist, *Landesgeschichte in der Zeit der deutschen Spätaufklärung: Ludwig Timotheus Spittler (1752-1810)* (Göttingen: Musterschmidt, 1963).

Großmann, Johannes, *Die Internationale der Konservativen: Transnationale Elitenzirkel und private Außenpolitik in Westeuropa seit 1945* (Munich: Oldenbourg: 2014).

Gross, Hans, *Empire and Sovereignty: A History of the Public Law Literature in the Holy Roman Empire* (Chicago, IL: University of Chicago Press, 1973).

Gruner, Wolfgang, *Gleichgewicht in Geschichte und Gegenwart* (Hamburg: Krämer, 1989).

Gusejnova, Dina, 'Noble Continent? German-speaking Nobles as Theorists of European Identity in the Interwar Period'. In Hewitson and d'Auria (eds.), *Europe in Crisis*, 111-34.

Gusejnova, Dina, *European Elites and Ideas of Empire, 1917-1957* (Cambridge: Cambridge University Press, 2016).

Haan, Ido de, *Politieke reconstructie: Een nieuw begin in de politieke geschiedenis* (Inaugural lecture Utrecht University, 2004).

Haan, Ido de, and Matthijs Lok (eds.), *The Politics of Moderation in Modern European History* (Basingstoke and Cham: Palgrave, 2019).

Haan, Ido de, and Matthijs Lok, 'Introduction: The Politics of Moderation'. In de Haan and Lok (eds.), *Politics of Moderation*, 1-28.

Haan, Ido de, and Jeroen van Zanten, 'Constructing an International Conspiracy: Revolutionary Concertation and Police Networks in the European Restoration'. In de Graaf, de Haan, and Vick (eds.), *Securing Europe*, 171-92.

Haan, Ido de, Paul den Hoed, and Henk te Velde (eds.), *Een nieuwe staat: Het begin van het koninkrijk der Nederlanden* (Amsterdam: Bert Bakker, 2013).

Haas, Ernst, 'The Balance of Power: Prescription, Concept or Propaganda', *World Politics* 5, no. 4 (1953), 442-77.

Habenincht, Walter, *Georg Friedrich von Martens: Eine biografische und Völkerrechtlichte Studie* (Göttingen: Vandenhoeck & Ruprecht, 1934).

Hale, John, *The Civilisation of Europe in the Renaissance* (London: Fontana Press, 1994).

Hamilton, Paul, *Realpoetik: European Romanticism and Literary Politics* (Oxford: Oxford University Press, 2013).

Hammersley, Rachel, *The English Republican Tradition and Eighteenth-century France: Between the Ancients and the Moderns* (Manchester: Manchester University Press, 2010).

Hammerstein, Notker, *Jus und Historie: Ein Beitrag zur Geschichte des historischen Denken an deutschen Universitäten im späten 17. Und im 18. Jahrhundert* (Göttingen: Vandenhoeck & Ruprecht, 1973).

Hampsher-Monk, Iain, *The Political Philosophy of Edmund Burke* (London: Longman, 1987).

Hampsher-Monk, Iain, *The Impact of the French Revolution: Texts from Britain in the 1790s* (Cambridge: Cambridge University Press, 2005).

Hampsher-Monk, Iain, 'Editor's Introduction'. In Burke, *Revolutionary Writings*, xi-xxxvi.

Hampsher-Monk, 'A Note on the Texts of Reflections and the Letter on a Regicide Peace'. In Burke, *Revolutionary Writings*, lviii-lxi.

Hampsher-Monk, Iain, 'Reflections on the Revolution in France'. In Dwan and Insole (eds.), *Companion*, 195-208.

Hampsher-Monk, Iain, 'Burke's Counter-Revolutionary Writings'. In Dwan and Insole (eds.), *Companion*, 209–20.
Harinck, George, and Roel Kuiper (eds.), *Groen van Prinsterer en de geschiedenis: historische opstellen* (Kampen: Van den Berg, 1994).
Harivel, Philippe Le, *Nicolas de Bonneville: Pré-romantique et révolutionaire, 1760–1828* (Strasbourg: Istra, 1923).
Harris, James, *Hume: An Intellectual Biography* (Cambridge: Cambridge University Press, 2015).
Härter, Karl, 'Security and Transnational Policing of Political Subversion and International Crime in the German Confederation after 1815'. In de Graaf, de Haan, and Vick (eds.), *Securing Europe*, 171–213.
Hartmann, Peter-Claus, *Das Heilige Römische Reich deutscher Nation in der Neuzeit, 1486–1806* (Stuttgart: Reclam, 2005).
Hartog, François, *Régimes d'historicité: présentisme et expériences du temps* (Paris: Seuil, 2003).
Hawley, George, *Making Sense of the Alt-Right* (New York: Columbia University Press, 2017).
Hay, Dennis, *Europe: The Emergence of an Idea* (Edinburgh: Edinburgh University Press, 1957).
Haynes, Christine, *Our Friends the Enemies: The Occupation of France after Napoleon* (Cambridge, MA: Harvard University Press, 2018).
Heater, Derek, *The Idea of European Unity* (London: Palgrave Macmillan, 1992).
Henke, Christian, *Coblenz: Symbol für die Gegenrevolution* (Stuttgart: Jan Thorbecke, 2000).
Hennies, Werner, *Die politische Theorie Schlözers zwischen Aufklärung und Liberalismus* (Munich: Tuduv, 1985).
Henz, Günter, *Leopold von Ranke in Geschichtsdenken und Forschung, Band I: Persönlichkeit, Werkentstehung, Wirkungsgeschichte* (Berlin: Duncker & Humblot, 2014).
Herrera, Julio, *Serviles! El grupo reaccionario de las Cortes de Cádiz* (Málaga: Fundación Unicaja, 2007).
Herrero, Javier, *Los orígenes del pensamiento reaccionario español* (Madrid: ITS, 1973).
Heuvel, Gerd van den, 'Cosmopolite, Cosmoli(ti)sme'. In Rolf Reichhardt and Eberhart Schmitt (eds.), *Handbuch politisch-sozialer Grundbegriffe in Frankreich, 1680–1820*, vol. 6 (Munich: De Gruyter, 1986), 41–55.
Hewitson, Mark, 'Conclusion'. In Hewitson and d'Auria (eds.), *Europe in Crisis*, 323–32.
Hewitson, Mark, and Matthew d'Auria (eds.), *Europe in Crisis: Intellectuals and the European Idea, 1917–1957* (New York: Berghahn, 2012).
Hill, Christopher, 'Conceptual Universalization in the Transnational Nineteenth Century'. In Moyn and Sartori (eds.), *Global Intellectual History*, 134–58.
Hinde, John, *Jacob Burckhardt and the Crisis of Modernity* (Montreal: McGill-Queen's University Press, 2000).
Hirschman, Albert, *The Rhetoric of Reaction: Perversity, Futility, Jeopardy* (Cambridge, MA: Harvard University Press, 1991).
Hobsbawm, Eric, *The Age of Revolution, Europe 1789–1848* (London: Weidenfeld & Nicolson, 1962).
Holmes, Stephen, *The Anatomy of Antiliberalism* (Cambridge, MA: Harvard University Press, 1996).
Hömig, Herbert, *Carl Theodor von Dalberg: Staatsmann und Kirchenfürst im Schatten Napoleons* (Paderborn: Schöningh, 2011).

Hont, István, *Jealousy of Trade: International Competition and the Nation-State in Historical Perspective* (Boston, MA: Harvard University Press, 2005).
Höpel, Thomas, *Emigranten der Französischen Revolution in Preußen (1789–1806): Eine Studie in vergleichender Perspektive* (Leipzig: Leipziger Universitätsverlag, 2000).
Horstmann, Axel, 'Kosmopolit, Kosmopolitismus'. In Joachim Ritter and Karlfried Gründer (eds.), *Historisches Wörterbuch der Philosophie*, vol. IV (Basel: Schwabe, 1976), 1115–67.
Hunt, Lynn, *Writing History in the Global Era* (New York: Norton, 2014).
Huntington, Samuel, 'Conservatism as an Ideology', *The American Political Science Review* 51, no. 2 (1957), 454–73.
Ifversen, Jan, 'The Crisis of European Civilization after 1918'. In Menno Spiering and Michael Wintle (eds.), *Ideas of Europe since 1914: The Legacy of the First World War* (Basingstoke: Palgrave Macmillan, 2002), 14–31.
Ifversen, Jan, 'Myth and History in European Post-War History Writing'. In Spiering and Wintle (eds.), *European Identity*, 75–91.
Iggers, George, and Konrad von Moltke (eds.), *The Theory and Practice of History: Leopold von Ranke* (New York: Routledge, 1993).
Iggers, Georg, and James Powell (eds.), *Leopold von Ranke and the Shaping of the Historical Discipline* (Syracuse, NY: Syracuse University Press, 1990).
Ikenberry, Gilford John, *After Victory: Institutions, Strategic Restraint, and the Rebuilding of Order after Major Wars* (Princeton, NJ: Princeton University Press, 2001).
Isabella, Maurizio, *Risorgimento in Exile: Italian émigrés and the liberal international in the post-Napoleonic Era* (Oxford: Oxford University Press, 2009).
Isabella, Maurizio, 'Aristocratic Liberalism and Risorgimento: Cesare Balbo and Piedmontese Political Thought after 1848', *History of European Ideas* 39, no. 6 (2013), 835–57.
Isabella, Maurizio, 'Crossing the Mediterranean in the Age of Revolutions: The Multiple Mobilities of the 1820s'. Keynote address, conference *Revolutionary Cosmopolitanism. Transnational Migration and Political Activism, 1815–1848*, organised by Camille Creyghton (Utrecht, 22 January 2021).
Isabella, Maurizio, with Konstantina Zanou (eds.), *Mediterranean Diasporas: Politics and Ideas in the Long Nineteenth Century* (London: Bloomsbury, 2016).
Israel, Jonathan, *Democratic Enlightenment: Philosophy, Revolution, and Human Rights 1750–1790* (Oxford: Oxford University Press, 2011).
Israel, Jonathan, *The Enlightenment that Failed: Ideas, Revolution, and Democratic Defeat, 1748–1830* (Oxford: Oxford University Press, 2019).
Jacob, Margaret, *The Radical Enlightenment: Pantheists, Freemasons and Republicans* (London: Allen & Unwin, 1981).
Jacob, Margaret, *Strangers Nowhere in the World: The Rise of Cosmopolitanism in Early Modern Europe* (Philadelphia, PA: University of Pennsylvania Press, 2006).
Jacob, Margaret, *The Secular Enlightenment* (Princeton, NJ: Princeton University Press, 2019).
Jainchill, Andrew, *Reimagining Politics after the Terror: The Republican Origins of French Liberalism* (Ithaca, NY and London: Cornell University Press, 2008).
Jarett, Mark, *The Congress of Vienna and Its Legacy: War and Great Power Diplomacy after Napoleon* (London: I.B. Tauris, 2014).
Jasanoff, Maya, 'Revolutionary Exiles: The American Loyalist and French Emigré Diasporas'. In Armitage and Subrahmanyam (eds.), *Age of Revolutions*, 37–58.
Jennings, Jeremy, 'Edmund Burke, the French Revolution and His Critics'. In Fitzpatrick and Jones (eds.), *Reception of Edmund Burke*, 91–104.
Jensen, Lotte, *Verzet tegen Napoleon* (Nijmegen: Vantilt, 2013).

Jensen, Lotte (ed.), *The Roots of Nationalism: National Identity Formation in Early Modern Europe, 1600-1815* (Amsterdam: Amsterdam University Press, 2016).
Jensen, Lotte, *Celebrating Peace: The Emergence of Dutch Identity, 1648-1815* (Nijmegen: Vantilt, 2017).
Johnson, Douglas, *Guizot: Aspects of French History, 1787-1874* (London: Routledge, 1963).
Jolly, Pierre, *Calonne 1734-1802* (Paris: Plon, 1949).
Jones, Emily, *Edmund Burke and the Invention of Modern Conservatism, 1830-1914: An Intellectual History* (Oxford: Oxford University Press, 2017).
Jones, Rhys, '1816 and the Resumption of "Ordinary History"', *Journal for Modern European History* 14, no. 1 (2016), 119-42.
Jones, Rhys, 'Turning the Clock Back? The Politics of Time in Restoration Europe, 1815-30'. In Broers, Caiani, and Bann (eds.), *European Restorations*, vol. II, 15-27.
Jorink, Eric, *Reading the Book of Nature in the Dutch Golden Age, 1575-1715*. Translated by Peter Mason (Leiden: Brill, 2010).
Jourdan, Annie, 'Napoléon et la paix universelle: Utopie et réalité'. In Jean-Clément Martin (ed.), *Napoléon et l'Europe* (Rennes: Presses Universitaires de Rennes, 2002), 55-70.
Jourdan, Annie, *La Révolution. Une exception française* (Paris: Flammarion, 2006).
Jourdan, Annie, *La révolution batave entre la France et l'Amérique: 1795-1806* (Rennes: Presses universitaires de Rennes, 2015).
Jourdan, Annie, *Nouvelle histoire de la Révolution* (Paris: Flammarion, 2018).
Judge, Jane, '"Qu'allons-nous devenir?": Belgian National Identity in the Age of Revolution'. In Jensen (ed.), *Roots of Nationalism*, 291-307.
Judt, Tony, 'The Past Is Another Country: Myth and Memory in Postwar Europe', *Daedalus* 121, no. 4 (Fall 1992), 83-118.
Judt, Tony, *Postwar. A history of Europe since 1945* (London: Pimlico, 2007).
Jung, Theo, *Zeichen des Verfalls: Semantische Studien zur Entstehung der Kulturkritik im 18. und frühen 19. Jahrhundert* (Göttingen: Vandenhoeck & Ruprecht, 2012).
Kaeber, Ernst, *Die Idee des europäischen Gleichgewichts in die publizistischen literatur vom 16: Bis zur Mitte des 18. Jahrhunderts* (Berlin: Duncker, 1907).
Kaegi, Werner, 'Vorwort'. In Burckhardt (ed.), *Fragmente*.
Kaegi, Werner, *Europäische Horizonte im Denken Jacob Burckhardts* (Basel: Benno Schwabe, 1962).
Kaegi, Werner 'Discordia Concors: Vom mythus Basels and der Europa-Idee Jacob Burckhardts'. In M. Sieber (ed.), *Discordia Concors: Festgabe für Edgar Bonjour* (Basel: Helbing und Lichtenhahn, 1968), 133-52.
Kahan, Alan, *Aristocratic Liberalism: The Social and Political Thought of Jacob Burckhardt, John Stuart Mill, and Alexis de Tocqueville* (Oxford: Oxford University Press, 1992).
Kahn, Irene Jetta, *Der historiker Arnold Hermann Ludwig Heeren: Ein Beitrag zur Geschichte der Göttinger Schule* (Ludwigshafen: Neubauer, 1939).
Kaiser, Wolfram, *Christian Democracy and the Origins of European Union* (Cambridge: Cambridge University Press, 2007).
Kapossy, Béla, 'Karl Ludwig von Haller's Critique of Liberal Peace'. In Kapossy, Nakhimovsky, and Whatmore (eds.), *Commerce and Peace*, 244-71.
Kapossy, Béla, 'Words and Things: Languages of Reform in Wilhelm Traugott Krug and Karl Ludwig von Haller'. In Béla Kapossy, Susan Richter, Thomas Maissen, and Manuela Albertone (eds.), *Languages of Reform in the Eighteenth Century* (London: Routledge, 2019), 383-404.
Kapossy, Béla, and Michael Sonenscher (eds.), *Politics in Commercial Society: Jean-Jacques Rousseau and Adam Smith* (Boston, MA: Harvard University Press, 2015).

Kapossy, Béla, Isaac Nakhimovsky, and Richard Whatmore (eds.), *Commerce and Peace in the Enlightenment* (Cambridge: Cambridge University Press, 2017).

Karmin, Otto, *Sir Francis d'Ivernois: sa vie, son œuvre et son temps* (Geneva: Revue historique de la révolution française et de l'empire, 1920).

Kates, Gary, *The 'Cercle Social', the Girondins, and the French Revolution* (Princeton, NJ: Princeton University Press, 1985).

Kattenberg, Lisa, 'The Power of Necessity: Reason of State in the Spanish Monarchy, ca. 1590–1650'. Dissertation, University of Amsterdam, 2018.

Kaye, Joel, *A History of Balance, c. 1250–1375: The Emergence of a New Model of Equilibrium and Its Impact on Thought* (Cambridge: Cambridge University Press, 2014).

Keene, Edward, *Beyond the Anarchical Society: Grotius, Colonialism and Order in World Politics* (Cambridge: Cambridge University Press, 2002).

Kidd, Colin, *The Forging of Races: Race and Scripture in the Forging of the Atlantic World, 1600–2000* (Cambridge: Cambridge University Press, 2006).

Kleinert, Susanne, *Nicolas de Bonneville: Studien zur ideengeschichtlichen und Literaturtheoretischen Position eines Schriftstellers der Französischen Revolution* (Heidelberg: Carl Winter, 1981).

Kleingeld, Pauline, 'Kant's Cosmopolitan Law: World Citizenship for a Global Order', *Kantian Review* 2 (1980), 72–90.

Kleingeld, Pauline, 'Six Varieties of Cosmopolitanism in Late Eighteenth-Century Germany', *Journal of the History of Ideas* 60, no. 3 (July 1999), 505–24.

Kleingeld, Pauline, 'Romantic Cosmopolitanism: Novalis's "Christianity or Europe"', *Journal of the History of Philosophy* 46, no. 2 (2008), 269–84.

Kleingeld, Pauline, *Kant and Cosmopolitanism: The Philosophical Ideal of World Citizenship* (Cambridge: Cambridge University Press, 2011).

Kleingeld, Pauline, 'Cosmopolitanism', *Stanford Encyclopaedia of Philosophy* (first published 2002, substantive revision 2019). Available at: https://plato.stanford.edu/entries/cosmopolitanism/ (accessed 24 June 2020).

Klesmann, Bernd, *Die Notabelnversammlung 1787 in Versailles: Rahmenbedingungen und Gestaltungsoptionen eines nationalen Reformprojekts* (Ostfildern: Jan Thorbecke Verlag, 2019).

Kley, Dale van, *The Religious Origins of the French Revolution from Calvin to the Civil Constitution, 1560–1791* (New Haven, CT: Yale University Press, 1996).

Klinck, David, *The French Counter Revolutionary Theorist Louis de Bonald (1754–1840)* (Berlin: Peter Lang, 1996).

Klinger, Andreas, and Hans-Werner Hahn (eds.), *Das Jahr 1806 im europäischen Kontext: Balance, Hegemonie und Politische Kulturen* (Cologne: Böhlau, 2008).

Kloes, Andrew, *The German Awakening: Protestant Renewal after the Enlightenment, 1815–1848* (Oxford: Oxford University Press, 2019).

Kluit, M. Elisabeth, *Het protestantse Réveil in Nederland en daarbuiten 1815–1865* (Amsterdam: H.J. Paris, 1970).

Knegt, Daniel, *Fascism, Liberalism and Europeanism in the Political Thought of Betrand de Jouvenel and Alfred Fabre-Luce* (Amsterdam: Amsterdam University Press, 2017).

Knegt, Daniel, 'French Fascism as a "Revolution of the Centre": Intellectuals between Revolution and Conservation'. In de Haan and Lok (eds.), *Politics of Moderation*, 151–62.

Koch, Jeroen, *Abraham Kuyper: Een biografie* (Amsterdam: Boom, 2006).

Koch, Jeroen, *Koning Willem I, 1772–1843* (Amsterdam: Boom, 2013).

Koehler, Benedikt, *Aesthetik der Politik: Adam Müller und die politische Romantik* (Stuttgart: Klett-Cota, 1980).

Koekkoek, René, *The Citizenship Experiment: Contesting the Limits of Civic Equality and Participation in the Age of Revolutions* (Leiden: Brill, 2019).
Koekkoek, René, Anne-Isabelle Richard, and Arthur Weststeijn (eds.), *The Dutch Empire between Ideas and Practice* (Cham: Palgrave Macmillan, 2019).
Koll, Johannes, *'Die belgische Nation': Patriotismus und Nationalbewusstsein in den Südlichen Niederlanden in späten 18. Jahrhundert* (Münster: Waxmann, 2003).
Kondylis, Panajotis, *Konservatismus: Geschichtlicher Gehalt und Untergang* (Stuttgart: Ernst Klett Verlag, 1986).
Kontler, László, *Translations, Histories, Enlightenments: William Robertson in Germany, 1760–1795* (Basingstoke: Palgrave, 2014).
Kontler, László, 'Varieties of Old Regime Europe: Thoughts and Details on the Reception of Burke's Reflections in Germany', Fitzpatrick and Jones, *Reception of Edmund Burke*, 313–30.
Koselleck, Reinhart, *Vergangene Zukunft: Zur Semantik geschichtlicher Zeiten* (Frankfurt a. M.: Suhrkamp, 1979).
Koselleck, Reinhart, 'Einleitung'. In Otto Brunner, Werner Conze, and Reinhardt Koselleck (eds.), *Geschichtliche Grundbegriffe: Historisches Lexikon zur politisch-sozialen Sprache in Deutschland*, vol. I (Stuttgart: Klett-Cota, 1979), 13–27.
Koselleck, Reinhart, *Critique and Crisis: Enlightenment and the Pathogenesis of Modern Society* (Boston, MA: MIT Press, 1988). Translation from the German original version of 1959.
Koselleck, Reinhart, 'Begriffsgeschichte and Social History'. In Koselleck, *Futures Past: On the Semantics of Historical Time*. Translated and with an introduction by Keith Tribe (New York: Columbia University Press, 2004).
Koskenniemi, Martti, *The Gentle Civilizer of Nations: The Rise and Fall of International Law, 1870–1960* (Cambridge: Cambridge University Press, 2001).
Koskenniemi, Martti, 'Into Positivism: Georg Friedrich von Martens (1756–1821) and Modern International Law', *Constellations* 15, no. 2 (2008), 189–207.
Koskenniemi, Martti, *To the Uttermost Parts of the Earth: Legal Imagination and International Power, 1300–1870* (Cambridge: Cambridge University Press, 2021).
Kossmann, Ernst, *Verlicht conservatisme: over Elie Luzac* (Groningen: inaugural lecture, 1966).
Kossmann, Ernst, 'Over Conservatisme. Johan Huizinga-Lezing 1980'. In Ernst Kossmann, *Politieke theorie en geschiedenis: Verspreide opstellen en voordrachten* (Amsterdam: Bert Bakker, 1987), 9–25.
Krastev, Ivan, and Stephen Holmes, *The Light That Failed: Why the West Is Losing the Fight for Democracy* (New York: Pegasus, 2019).
Kraume, Anne, *Das Europa der Literatur: Schriftsteller blicken auf den Kontinent, 1815–1945* (Berlin: De Gruyter, 2010).
Kraus, Hans-Christof, 'Heinz Gollwitzer (1917–1999)'. In Duchhardt et al. (eds.), *Europa-Historiker* II, 295–322.
Krebs, Christopher, *A Most Dangerous Book: Tacitus' Germania from the Roman Empire to the Third Reich* (New York: W.W. Norton, 2012).
Kreis, Georg, 'Jacob Burckhardt (1818–1897)'. In Duchhardt et al. (eds.), *Europa-Historiker* II, 101–20.
Krieger, Leonard, *The German Idea of Freedom: History of a Political Tradition* (Chicago, IL: University of Chicago Press, 1957, first edition; 1972, new edition).
Krieger, Leonard, *Ranke: The Meaning of History* (Chicago, IL: University of Chicago Press, 1977).

Kroen, Sheryl, *Politics and Theater: The Crisis of Legitimacy in Restoration France, 1815-1830* (Berkeley and Los Angeles, CA: University of California Press, 2000).

Krol, Reinbert, 'Het geweten van Duitsland: Friedrich Meinecke als pleitbezorger van het Duitse historisme'. Dissertation, Rijksuniversiteit Groningen, 2013.

Kuijpers, Erika, and Judith Pollmann, 'Introduction: On the Early Modernity of Modern Memory'. In Kuijpers et al. (eds.), *Memory before Modernity*, 1-24.

Kuijpers, Erika, Judith Pollmann, Johannes Müller, and Jasper van der Steen (eds.), *Memory before Modernity: Practices of Memory in Early Modern Europe* (Leiden: Brill 2013).

Kuiper, Roel, *'Tot een voorbeeld zult gij blijven' Mr. G. Groen van Prinsterer (1801-1876)* (Amsterdam: Buijten & Schipperheijn, 2001).

Kulessa, Rotraud, and Catriona Seth (eds.), *Die Europaidee im Zeitalter der Aufklärung* (Cambridge: Open Book Publishers, 2017).

Lacour-Gayet, Robert, *Calonne: Financier, Réformateur, Contre-révolutionnaire, 1734-1802* (Paris: Hachette, 1963).

Lagenbacher, Nora, and Britta Schellenberg, *Is Europe on the Right Path? Right-Wing Extremism and Right-Wing Populism in Europe* (Berlin: Friedrich Ebert Stiftung, 2011).

Lamberts, Emiel, *The Black International: L'Internationale noire (1870-1878)* (Leuven: Leuven University Press, 2002).

Lange, Erik de, 'Menacing Tides: Security, Piracy and Empire in the Nineteenth-Century Mediterranean'. Dissertation, Utrecht University, 2020.

Latreille, Camille, *Joseph de Maistre et la papauté* (Paris: Hachette, 1906).

Laven, David, and Lucy Riall (eds.), *Napoleon's Legacy: Problems of Government in Restoration Europe* (Oxford & New York: Berg, 2000).

Lebrun, Richard, *Joseph de Maistre: An Intellectual Militant* (Kingston and Montreal: McGill-Queen's University Press, 1988).

Lecoq, Anne-Marie (ed.), *La querelle des anciens et des modernes, précédée d'un essai de Marc Fumaroli* (Paris: Gallimard, 2001).

Leerssen, Joep, *Nationaal denken in Europa: Een cultuurhistorische schets* (Amsterdam: Amsterdam University Press, 1999).

Leerssen, Joep, *National Thought in Europe: A Cultural History* (Amsterdam: Amsterdam University Press, 2006).

Leerssen, Joep (ed.), *Encyclopedia of Romantic Nationalism in Europe*, 2 vol. (Amsterdam: Amsterdam University Press, 2018).

Leerssen, Joep, 'Romancing the Monarchy: Romantic Queens and Soft Power'. In Lok, Pestel, and Reboul (eds.), *Cosmopolitan Conservatisms*, 283-306.

Lehner, Ulrich, *Enlightened Monks: German Benedictines, 1740-1803* (Oxford: Oxford University Press, 2011).

Lehner, Ulrich, *The Catholic Enlightenment: The Forgotten History of a Global Movement* (Oxford: Oxford University Press, 2016).

Lehner, Ulrich, and Michael Printy (eds.), *The Companion to the Catholic Enlightenment in Europe* (Leiden: Brill, 2010).

Lentz, Thierry, *Le Grand Consulat, 1799-1804* (Paris: Fayard, 1999).

Lentz, Thierry, *Nouvelle Histoire du premier Empire*, 4 vol.: *vol. I: Napoléon et la conquête de l'Europe, 1804-1810* (Paris: Fayard, 2002), *vol. II: L'enfondrement du système napoléonien, 1810-1814* (Paris: Fayard, 2004), *vol. III: La France et l'Europe de Napoléon* (Paris: Fayard, 2007), *vol. IV: Les Cent Jours: l'empire sans le système 1815* (Paris: Fayard, 2010).

Leonhard, Jörn, *Liberalismus: Zur historischen Semantik eines europäischen Deutungsmusters* (Munich: Oldenbourg, 2001).

Leucht, Brigitte, 'Christopher Dawson (1889–1970)'. In Duchhardt et al. (eds.), *Europa-Historiker* II, 211–30.
Lieven, Dominic, *Russia Against Napoleon: The Battle for Europe, 1807 to 1814* (London: Allen Lane/Penguin, 2009).
Lievisse Adriaanse, Mark, 'Een culturele wapenstilstand zit er niet in', *NRC Handelsblad* no. 7 February 2020.
Lilla, Mark, *G.B. Vico: The Making of an Anti-Modern* (Cambridge, MA: Harvard University Press, 2003).
Lilti, Antoine, 'Does Intellectual History Exist in France? The Chronicle of a Renaissance Foretold'. In Darrin McMahon and Sam Moyn (eds.), *Rethinking Modern Intellectual History* (Oxford: Oxford University Press, 2014), 56–73.
Lilti, Antoine, 'La civilisation est-elle européenne? Écrire l'histoire de l'Europe au XVIIIe siècle', Lilti and Spector (eds.), *Penser l'Europe*, 139–66.
Lilti, Antoine, *The World of the Salons: Sociability and Worldliness in Eighteenth-Century Paris* (Oxford: Oxford University Press, 2015).
Lilti, Antoine, and Céline Spector (eds.), *Penser l'Europe au XVIIIe siècle: Commerce, Civilisation, Empire* (Oxford: Voltaire Foundation, 2014).
Lilti, Antoine, and Céline Spector (eds.), 'Introduction: l'Europe des Lumières, généalogie d'un concept'. In Lilti and Spector (eds.), *Penser l'Europe*, 1–9.
Lindhal, Rutger (ed.), *Wither Europe? Borders, Boundaries, Frontiers in a Changing World* (Gothenburg: CERGU, 2003).
Linton, Marisa, *Choosing Terror: Virtue, Friendship, and Authenticity in the French Revolution* (Oxford: Oxford University Press, 2013).
Lock, Frederick, *Edmund Burke*, vol. I: *1730–1784* (Oxford: Clarendon Press, 1998); vol. II: *1784–1797* (Oxford: Clarendon Press, 2006).
Lok, Matthijs, *Windvanen: Napoleontische bestuurders in de Nederlandse en de Franse Restauratie, 1813–1820* (Amsterdam: Bert Bakker, 2009).
Lok, Matthijs '"Le véritable berceau des muses": De Oudheid in het Franse contrarevolutionaire denken (1786–1800)'. In Raat, Velema, and Baar-de Weerdt (eds.), *Oudheid*, 59–74.
Lok, Matthijs, 'IJzer en bloed: staatsvorming en nationalisme, 1848–1914'. In Leo Wessels and Toon Bosch (eds.), *Nationalisme, Naties en Staten: Europa vanaf circa 1800 tot heden* (Nijmegen: Vantilt, 2012), 282–410.
Lok, Matthijs, 'De eeuw van ongeloof: De constructie van de "achttiende eeuw" in Groen's *Ongeloof en Revolutie* (1847)', *De Negentiende eeuw* 37, no. 1 (2013), 17–35.
Lok, Matthijs (ed.), 'The Enlightenment and the Past', *Special Issue: De achttiende eeuw (Dutch-Flemish Journal for Eighteenth-Century Studies)* 46, no. 2 (2014).
Lok, Matthijs, '"Un oubli total du passé"?: The Political and Social Construction of Silence in Restoration Europe (1813–1830)', *History & Memory* 26, no. 2 (2014), 40–75.
Lok, Matthijs, 'Vijanden van de Verlichting: Antiverlichting en Verlichting in de Europese intellectuele geschiedenis', *Tijdschrift voor Geschiedenis* 127, no. 2 (2014), 211–28.
Lok, Matthijs, 'A Revolutionary Narrative of European History: Bonneville's History of Modern Europe (1789–1792)', *History* 103, no. 3 (July 2018), 434–50.
Lok, Matthijs, 'François-Xavier de Feller (1735–1802) et l'élaboration des Contre-Lumières européennes: Une reconnaissance'. In Sophie Letterier and Olivier Tort (eds.), *Rhétorique et politisation, de la fin des Lumières au printemps des peuples* (Artois: Artois Presses Université, 2021), 119–28.
Lok, Matthijs, 'Vuursalamanders tegen de Verlichting: Wetenschappelijke kennis en verlichtingskritiek in Fellers *Journal Historique et Litteraire*', *Jaarboek De Achttiende eeuw* no. 54 (Amsterdam: Amsterdam University Press, 2022), 166–82.

Lok, Matthijs, 'La construction de l'Europe moderne, entre esprit des Lumières et des Contre-Lumières'. In Arjakovsky (ed.), *Histoire de la conscience européenne*, 179-92.
Lok, Matthijs, 'The Fragmented Continent: The Invention of European Pluralism in History Writing from the Eighteenth to the Twenty-first Century'. In Brolsma, de Bruin, and Lok (eds.), *Eurocentrism* (eds.), 43-64.
Lok, Matthijs, '"The Extremes Set the Tone": Counter-Revolutionary Moderation in Continental Conservatism (ca. 1795-1835)'. In de Haan and Lok (eds.), *Politics of Moderation*, 67-88.
Lok, Matthijs, 'The Congress of Vienna as a Missed Opportunity: Conservative Visions of a New European Order after Napoleon'. In de Graaf, de Haan, and Vick (eds.), *Securing Europe*, 56-72.
Lok, Matthijs, '"A Much Superior Situation": The Ambivalent Memory of the Dutch Revolt and the Construction of the Dutch Restoration Regime'. In Broers, Caiani, and Bann (eds.), *European Restorations II*, 28-37.
Lok, Matthijs, '"A Just and True Liberty": The Idea of (Neo-Roman) Freedom in Francophone Counter-Revolutionary Thought (ca. 1780-1800)'. In Dawson and de Dijn (eds.), *Rethinking Liberty*, 178-93.
Lok, Matthijs, 'The European Republic from the Enlightenment to the Counter-Revolution'. In Oddens, Rutjes, and Weststeijn (eds.), *Discourses of Decline*, 200-15.
Lok, Matthijs, and Joris van Eijnatten, 'Global Counter-Enlightenment: Introductory Remarks', *HCM* 7 (2019), 406-22.
Lok, Matthijs, and Joris van Eijnatten (eds.), themed issue on the 'Global Counter-Enlightenment' in the *International Journal for History, Culture and Modernity* (HCM) (Brill Journals, 2019).
Lok, Matthijs, and Alicia Montoya (eds.), 'Centre and Periphery in the Enlightenment: Introduction', *Special Issue: De Achttiende eeuw (The Eighteenth Century)* 2, no. 45 (2012), 131-5.
Lok, Matthijs, and Natalie Scholz, 'The Return of the Loving Father: Masculinity, Legitimacy and the French and Dutch Restoration Monarchies (1813-1815)', *Bijdragen en Mededelingen betreffende de Geschiedenis der Nederlanden 127*, no. 1 (2012), 19-44.
Lok, Matthijs, Friedemann Pestel, and Juliette Reboul, 'Cosmopolitan Conservatisms: Introduction'. In Matthijs Lok, Friedemann Pestel, and Juliette Reboul (eds.), *Cosmopolitan Conservatisms: Countering Revolution in Transnational Networks, Ideas and Movements c.1700-1930* (Leiden: Brill, 2021), 1-37.
Lovie, Jacques, and Joannès Chetail, 'Introduction'. In Joseph de Maistre, *Du Pape*, edited by Jacques Lovie and Joannès Chetail (Geneva: Droz, 1966).
Lucas, Colin, 'Edmund Burke and the *Émigrés*'. In Furet and Ozouf (eds.), *French Revolution*, 101-14.
Luis, Jean-Philippe, *L'utopie réactionnaire: Épuration et modernisation de l'état dans l'Espagne de la fin de l'Ancien Régime (1823-1834)* (Madrid: Casa de Velásquez, 2002).
Luis, Jean-Philippe, 'France and Spain: A Common Territory of Anti-Revolution (End of the 18th Century-1880). In Lok, Pestel, and Reboul (eds.), *Cosmopolitan Conservatisms*, 261-82.
Lützeler, Paul, *Kontinentalisierung: das Europa der Schriftsteller* (Bielefeld: Aisthesis Verlag, 2007).
Macmillan, Margaret, *Peacemakers: The Paris Peace Conference of 1919 and Its Attempt to End War* (London: John Murray, 2003).

Maire, Catherine, *De la cause de Dieu à la cause de la Nation: Le jansénisme au XVIIIe siècle* (Paris: Gallimard, 1998).
Mali, Joseph, and Robert Wokler (eds.), *Isaiah Berlin's Counter-Enlightenment* (Philadelphia, PA: American Philosophical Society, 2003).
Maliks, Reidar, 'The State of Freedom: Kant and His Conservative Critics'. In Quentin Skinner and Martin van Gelderen (eds.), *Freedom and the Construction of Europe, vol. 2* (Cambridge: Cambridge University Press, 2013), 190–8.
Mannheim, Karl, 'Conservative Thought'. In Kurt Wolff (ed.), *From Karl Mannheim* (New Brunswick, NJ: Transaction Publishers, 1993), 260–350.
Mansel, Philip, *Louis XVIII* (London: Sutton, 1999).
Marchand, Suzanne, 'Ancient History in the Age of Archival Research'. In Loraine Daston (ed.), *Science in the Archives: Pasts, Presents, Futures* (Chicago, IL: Chicago University Press, 2017).
Marino, Luigi, *Praeceptores Germaniae: Göttingen 1770–1820* (Göttingen: Vandenhoeck & Ruprecht, 1995).
Martin, Benjamin, *The Nazi-Fascist New Order for European Culture* (Cambridge, MA: Harvard University Press, 2016).
Martin, Jean-Clément, *Contre-Révolution, Révolution et Nation en France 1789–1799* (Paris: Seuil, 1998).
Martin, Jean-Clément (ed.), *La Contre-Révolution en Europe. XVIIIe–XIX siècles. Réalités politiques et sociales, résonances culturelles et idéologiques* (Rennes: PUR, 2001).
Martin, Jean-Clément (ed.), *La Révolution à l'œuvre: Perspectives actuelles dans l'histoire de la révolution française* (Rennes: PUR, 2005).
Masseau, Didier, *Les Ennemis des philosophes: L'antiphilosophie au temps des Lumières* (Paris: Albin Michel 2000).
Masseau, Didier, *Dictionnaire des anti-lumières et antiphilosophes (France, 1715–1815)* (Paris: Champion, 2017).
Mattioli, Aram, *Jacob Burckhardt und die Grenzen der Humanität* (Weitra: Bibliothek der Provinz, 2001).
Mazower, Mark, *Dark Continent: Europe's Twentieth Century* (New York: Knopf, 1998).
Mazower, Mark, *The Greek Revolution and the Making of Modern Europe* (London: Allan Lane, 2021).
McCormick, John, 'Carl Schmitt's Europe: Cultural, Imperial and Spatial Proposals for European Integration, 1923–1955'. In Christian Joerges and Navraj Singh Galeigh (eds.), *Darker Legacies of Law in Europe: The Shadow of National Socialism and Fascism over Europe and its Legal Traditions* (Oxford: Hart, 2003), 133–41.
McCormick, John, *Europeanism* (Oxford: Oxford University Press, 2010).
McMahon, Darrin, *Enemies of the Enlightenment: The French Counter-Enlightenment and the Making of Modernity* (Oxford: Oxford University Press, 2001).
McMahon, Darrin, 'Seeing the Century of Lights as a Time of Darkness'. In Florence Lotterie and Darrin McMahon (eds.), *Les Lumières européennes dans leur relations avec autres grandes cultures et religions* (Paris: Champion, 2002), 81–104.
McMahon, Darrin, *Happiness: A History* (New York: Grove Press, 2006).
McMahon, Darrin, *Divine Fury: A History of Genius* (New York: Basic Books, 2013).
McMahon, Darrin, 'What is Counter-Enlightenment?'. In Lok and Eijnatten (eds.), *Global Counter-Enlightenment*, 33–46.
McMahon, Darrin, and Sam Moyn (eds.), *Rethinking Modern Intellectual History* (Oxford: Oxford University Press, 2014).

McManners, John, *Church and Society in Eighteenth-century France*, 2 vol. (Oxford: Oxford University Press, 1998).
Mellon, Stanley, *The Political Uses of History: A Study of Historians in the French Restoration* (Stanford, CA: Stanford University Press, 1958).
Menczer, Béla, *Tensions of Order and Freedom: Catholic Political Thought, 1789–1848* (New Brunswick, NJ: Transaction Publishers, 1994).
Middell, Matthias (ed.), *Widerstände gegen Revolution, 1789 bis 1989* (Leipzig: Leipziger Universitätsverlag, 1994).
Middell, Matthias, and Lluís Roura Aulinas (eds.), *Transnational Challenges to National History Writing* (Basingstoke: Palgrave, 2013).
Mikkeli, Heikki, *Europe as an Idea and an Identity* (Basingstoke: Palgrave, 1998).
Mishkova, Diana, and Balácz Trencsényi, *European Regions and Boundaries: A Conceptual History* (New York: Berghahn, 2017).
Mitchell, Leslie, 'Introduction'. In Edmund Burke, *The Writings and Speeches of Edmund Burke, vol. VIII, The French Revolution 1790–1794*, edited by Leslie Mitchell (Oxford: Clarendon Press, 1989).
Mix, York-Gothard, and Jochen Strobel (eds.), *Der Europäer August Wilhelm Schlegel: Romantische Kulturtransfer—romantische Wissenswelten* (Berlin: De Gruyter, 2010).
Moggach, Douglas, and Gareth Stedman Jones (eds.), *The 1848 Revolutions and European Political Thought* (Cambridge: Cambridge University Press, 2020).
Molitor, Hans-Georg, *Vom Untertan zum administré: Studien zur französischen Herrschaft und zum Verhalten der Bevölkerung im Rhein-Mosel-Raum von den Revolutionskriegen bis zum Ende der Napoleonische Zeit* (Wiesbaden: F. Steiner, 1980).
Monod, Albert, *De Pascal à Chateaubriand: Les défenseurs français du Christianisme de 1670 à 1820* (Paris: Alcan, 1916).
Montoya, Alicia, 'Introduction: Madame de Genlis and Enlightenment Thought', *Relief* 7, no. 1 (2013), 1–3.
Montoya, Alicia, *Medievalist Enlightenment: From Charles Perrault to Jean-Jacques Rousseau* (Cambridge: Boydell & Brewer, 2013).
Montoya, Alicia, 'Middlebrow, Religion, and the European Enlightenment: A New Bibliometric Project, *MEDIATE* (1665–1820)', *French History and Civilization* 7 (2017), 66–79.
Montoya, Alicia, 'Marie Leprince de Beaumont (1711–1780): A Popular Religious Pedagogue'. In Ulrich Lehner (ed.), *Women, Enlightenment and Catholicism: A Transnational Biographical History* (London: Routledge, 2018), 22–34.
Moore, Fabienne, 'The Poetry of the Super-Enlightenment: The Theories and Practices of Cazotte, Chassaignon, Mercier, Saint-Martin and Bonneville'. In Dan Edelstein (ed.), *The Super-Enlightenment: Daring to Know Too Much* (Oxford: Studies on Voltaire and the Eighteenth Century, 2010), 137–66.
Morawiecz, Malgorzata, 'Friedrich Ludwig Georg von Raumer (1781–1873)'. In Duchhardt et al. (eds.), *Europa-Historiker* II, 77–100.
Mori, Jennifer, *William Pitt and the French Revolution, 1785–1795* (New York: St. Martin's Press, 1997).
Mortier, Roland, 'L'idée de la décadence littéraire au XVIIIe siècle', *Studies on Voltaire and the Eighteenth Century* 57 (1967), 1013–29.
Mossé, Claude, *L'antiquité dans la Révolution française* (Paris: Albin Michel, 1989).
Moyn, Sam, *Christian Human Rights* (Philadelphia, PA: University of Pennsylvania Press, 2015).
Moyn, Sam, and Andrew Sartori (eds.), *Global Intellectual History* (New York: Columbia University Press, 2013).

Moyn, Sam, and Andrew Sartori, 'Approaches to Global Intellectual History'. In Moyn and Sartori (eds.), *Global Intellectual History*, 3–30.
Mudde, Cas, *Populist Radical Right Parties in Europe* (Cambridge: Cambridge University Press, 2007).
Muet, Yannick *Le débat européen dans l'entre-deux-guerres* (Paris: Presses universitaires de France, 1997).
Muhlack, Ulrich, 'Das Europäische Staatensystem in der Deutschen Geschichtsschreibung des 19. Jahrhunderts'. In Notker Hammerstein and Gerrit Walther (eds.), *Staatensystem und Geschichtsschreibung: Ausgewählte Aufsätze zu Humanismus und Historismus, Absolutismus und Aufklärung* (Berlin: Duncker & Humblot, 2006), 313–53.
Muhlack, Ulrich, 'Johann Gottfried Herder (1744–1803)'. In Duchhardt et al. (eds.), *Europa-Historiker* II, 49–76.
Muhlack, Ulrich, 'Von der Philologie zur politischen Kulturgeschichte: Arnold Hermann Ludwig Heerens Weg zu einer historischen, Wissenschaft vom Menschen'. In Hans Bödeker, Philippe Büttgen, and Michel Espagne (eds.), *Die Wissenschaft vom Menschen in Göttingen um 1800: Wissenschaftliche Praktiken, institutionelle Geographie, europäischen Netzwerke* (Göttingen: Vandenhoeck & Ruprecht, 2008).
Muhlack, Ulrich, 'German Enlightenment Historiography and the Rise of Historicism'. In Bourgault and Sparling (eds.), *Companion*, 249–306.
Muhs, Rudolf, Johannes Paulmann, and Willibald Steinmetz (eds.), *Aneignung und Abwehr: Interkultureller Transfer zwischen Deutschland und Großbritannien im 19. Jahrhundert* (Bodenheim: Philo, 1998).
Müller, Jan-Werner, *Memory and Power in Post-War Europe: Studies in the Presence of the Past* (Cambridge: Cambridge University Press, 2002).
Müller, Jan-Werner, *A Dangerous Mind: Carl Schmitt in Post-War European Thought* (New Haven, CT: Yale University Press, 2003).
Müller, Jan-Werner, 'Comprehending Conservatism: A New Framework for Analysis', *Journal of Political Ideologies* 11, no. 3 (2006), 359–65.
Müller, Jan-Werner, *Contesting Democracy: Political Ideas in Twentieth-century Europe* (New Haven, CT: Yale University Press, 2011).
Müller, Jan-Werner, 'On Conceptual History'. In McMahon and Moyn (eds.), *Rethinking Modern European Intellectual History*, 74–93.
Müller, Jan-Werner, *What Is Populism?* (Philadelphia, PA: University of Pennsylvania Press, 2016).
Muller, Jerry, 'Introduction: What Is Conservative Social and Political Thought?'. In Muller, *Conservatism: An Anthology of Social and Political Thought from David Hume to the Present* (Princeton, NJ: Princeton University Press, 1997).
Muller, Jerry, 'Conservatism: The Utility of History and the Case against Rationalist Radicalism'. In Breckmann and Gordon (eds.), *European Thought* I, 232–54.
Murray-Miller, Gavin, 'Civilization, Modernity and Europe: The Making and Unmaking of a Conceptual Unity', *History* 103, no. 3 (July 2018), 418–33.
Muthu, Sankar, *Enlightenment against Empire* (Princeton, NJ: Princeton University Press, 2003).
Nakhimovsky, Isaac, *The Closed Commercial State: Perpetual Peace and Commercial Society from Rousseau to Fichte* (Princeton, NJ: Princeton University Press, 2011).
Nakhimovsky, Isaac, 'The "Ignominious Fall of the European Commonwealth": Gentz, Hauterive, and the Armed Neutrality of 1800'. In Koen Stapelbroek (ed.), *Trade and War: The Neutrality of Commerce in the Interstate System* (Helsinki: Helsinki Collegium for Advanced Studies, 2011), 177–90.

Nakhimovsky, Isaac, *The Most Liberal of All Ideas: The Political Thought of the Holy Alliance* (Princeton, NJ: Princeton University Press, forthcoming).
Neuheiser, Jörg, *Crown, Church and Constitution: Popular Conservatism in England, 1815–1867* (New York: Berghahn, 2016).
Nippel, Wilfried, 'Images of Antiquity in the French Revolution'. In Raat, Velema, and Baar-de Weerdt (eds.), *Oudheid*, 31–46.
Norman, Larry, *The Shock of the Ancient: Literature and History in Early Modern France* (Chicago, IL: University of Chicago Press, 2011).
Norton, Robert, 'The Myth of the Counter-Enlightenment', *Journal of the History of Ideas* 68, no. 4 (2007), 635–58.
Nurdin, Jean, 'L'idée de l'Europe dans la pensée allemande à l'époque Bismarckienne'. Dissertation, Université Paul Verlaine, Metz, 1977.
Nussbaum, Arthur, *A Concise History of International Law* (New York: Macmillan, 1954).
Nussbaum, Martha, *The Cosmopolitan Tradition: A Noble but Flawed Idea* (Cambridge, MA: Belknap, 2019).
O'Brien, Karen, *Narratives of the Enlightenment: Cosmopolitan History from Voltaire to Gibbon* (Cambridge: Cambridge University Press, 1997).
Oddens, Joris, Mart Rutjes, Arthur Weststeijn (eds.), *Discourses of Decline: Essays in Honour of Wyger R.E. Velema* (Leiden: Brill, 2022).
Ossewaarde, Marinus, 'Cosmopolitanism and the Society of Strangers', *Current Sociology* 55, no. 3 (2007), 367–88.
Osterhammel, Jürgen, *Colonialism: A Theoretical Overview* (Princeton, NJ: Princeton University Press, 1999).
Oudenampsen, Merijn, *De conservatieve revolte: Een ideeëngeschiedenis van de Fortuyn* (Nijmegen: Vantilt, 2018).
Outram, Dorinda, *The Enlightenment* (Cambridge: Cambridge University Press, 2013).
Owens, Patricia, and Katharina Rietzler (eds.), *Women's International Thought: A New History* (Cambridge: Cambridge University Press, 2021).
Pagden, Antony (ed.), *The Idea of Europe: From Antiquity to the European Union* (Cambridge: Cambridge University Press, 2002).
Pagden, Anthony, 'Stoicism, Cosmopolitanism and the Legacy of European Imperialism', *Constellations* 7, no. 1 (2008), 3–22.
Pagden, Anthony, *The Pursuit of Europe: A History* (Oxford: Oxford University Press, 2022).
Pakier, Malgorzata, and Bo Stråth (eds.), *A European Memory? Contested Histories and Politics of Remembrance* (New York: Berghahn, 2010).
Palmer, Robert, *Catholics and Unbelievers in Eighteenth Century France* (Princeton, NJ: Princeton University Press, 1939).
Palmer, Robert, *The Age of Democratic Revolution: A Political History of Europe and America, 1760–1800* (Princeton, NJ: Princeton University Press, 2014, new edition).
Parker, Harold, *The Cult of Antiquity and the French Revolutionaries: A Study in the Development of the Revolutionary Spirit* (Chicago, IL: University of Chicago Press, 1937).
Pasture, Patrick, *Imagining European Unity since 1000 AD* (Basingstoke: Palgrave Macmillan, 2015).
Patel, Klaus, *Project Europe: A History* (Cambridge: Cambridge University Press, 2018).
Peardon, Thomas, *The Transition in English Historical Writing, 1760–1830* (New York: AMS, 1966).
Pernau, Margrit, and Dominic Sachsenmaier (eds.), *Global Conceptual History: A Reader* (London: Bloomsbury, 2016).

Pestel, Friedemann, *Kosmopoliten wider Willen: Die 'monarchiens' als Revolutionsemigranten* (Berlin: Walter de Gruyter, 2015).

Pestel, Friedemann, 'On Counter-revolution: Semantic Investigations of a Counter Concept during the French Revolution', *Contributions to the History of Concepts* 12 (2017), 50–75.

Pestel, Friedemann, 'The Age of Emigrations: French Emigrés and Global Entanglements of Political Exile'. In Laure Philip and Juliette Reboul (eds.), *French Emigrants in Revolutionised Europe: Connected Histories and Memories* (Basingstoke: Palgrave, 2019), 205–31.

Pestel, Friedemann, 'Contre-révolution'. In Jörn Leonhard and Hans-Jürgen Lüsebrink (eds.), *Handbuch politisch-sozialer Grundbegriffe in Frankreich 1680–1820* (Berlin: De Gruyter Oldenbourg, 2021), 163–230.

Pestel, Friedemann, and Pasi Ihalainen, 'Revolution beyond Borders: The Universal and Cosmopolitan in the French Revolution, 1789–1815'. In Pasi Ihalainen and Antero Holmila (eds.), *Nationalism and Internationalism Intertwined: A European History of Concepts beyond the Nation State* (New York: Berghahn, 2022), 35–59.

Pestel, Friedemann, and Fabian Rausch (eds.), 'The Post-Revolutionary Experience of 1814/15', Special Issue: *Journal of Modern European History* 15, no. 2 (2017).

Peters, Martin, *Altes Reich und Europa: Der Historiker, Statistiker und Publizist August Ludwig (v.) Schlözer (1735–1809)* (Münster: LIT Verlag, 2003).

Philip, Laure, and Juliette Reboul (eds.), *French Emigrants in Revolutionised Europe Connected Histories and Memories* (Cham: Palgrave, 2019).

Phillips, Mark, *Society and Sentiment: Genres of Historical Writing in Britain, 1740–1820* (Princeton, NJ: Princeton University Press, 2000).

Philp, Mark, 'Vulgar Conservatism, 1792–3', *The English Historical Review* vol. 110, no. 435 (February, 1995), 42–69.

Pieper, Josef, *Tradition: Concept and Claims*. Trans. E. Christian Kopff (Wilmington: ISI, 2008).

Pierse, Síofra, 'Voltaire: Polemical Possibilities of History'. In Bourgault and Sparling (eds.), *Companion*, 153–87.

Piguet, Marie-France, '"Contre-révolution", "guerre civile", "lutte entre deux classes": Montlosier (1755–1838) penseur du conflit politique moderne', *Asterion* 6 (2009). Available at: http://journals.openedition.org/asterion/1485.

Pinkard, Terry, *Hegel: A Biography* (Cambridge: University Press, 2000).

Pitts, Jennifer, *A Turn to Empire: The Rise of Imperial Liberalism in Britain and France* (Princeton, NJ: Princeton University Press, 2005).

Pitts, Jennifer, 'International Relations and the Critical History of International Law', *International Relations* 31, no. 3 (2017), 282–98.

Pitts, Jennifer, *Boundaries of the International: Law and Empire* (Cambridge, MA: Harvard University Press, 2018).

Pitts, Jennifer, 'Ideas of Empire: Civilisation, Race and Global Hierarchy'. In Breckmann and Gordon (eds.), *European Thought* I, 447–69.

Planert, Ute, *Der Mythos vom Befreiungskrieg. Frankreichs Kriege und der deutsche Süden. Alltag—Wahrnehmung—Deutung 1792–1841* (Paderborn: Schöningh, 2007).

Plongeron, Bernard, *Théologie et politique au siècle des lumières (1770–1820)* (Geneva: Droz, 1973).

Po-Chia Hsia, Ronnie, *The World of Catholic Renewal 1540–1770* (Cambridge: Cambridge University Press, 1998).

Pocock, John, 'Burke and the Ancient Constitution—A Problem in the History of Ideas', *The Historical Journal* 3, no. 2 (1960), 125–43.

Pocock, John, *The Machiavellian Moment: Florentine Political Thought and the Atlantic Republican Tradition* (Princeton, NJ: Princeton University Press, 1975).
Pocock, John, 'Clergy and Commerce: The Conservative Enlightenment in England'. In *L'Età dei Lumi: Studi storici sul settecento Europeo in onore di Franco Venturi*, 2 vols. (Naples: Jovene, 1985), vol. 1: 524–62.
Pocock, John, 'Josiah Tucker on Burke, Locke, and Price: A Study in the Varieties of Eighteenth-century Conservatism'. In Pocock, *Virtue, Commerce, and History: Essays on Political Thought and History, Chiefly in the Eighteenth Century* (Cambridge: Cambridge University Press, 1985), 157–91.
Pocock, John, *The Ancient Constitution and the Feudal Law: A Study of English Historical Thought in the Seventeenth Century*. A reissue with a retrospect (Cambridge: Cambridge University Press, 1987).
Pocock, John, 'Conservative Enlightenment and Democratic Revolutions: The American and French Cases in British Perspective', *Government and Opposition* 24 (1989), 81–105.
Pocock, John, *Barbarism and Religion, vol. II: Narratives of Civil Government* (Cambridge: Cambridge University Press, 1999).
Pocock, John, 'Enlightenment and Counter-Enlightenment, Revolution and Counter-Revolution: A Eurosceptical Inquiry', *History of Political Thought* XX, no. 1 (1999).
Pocock, John, *Political Thought and History: Essays on Theory and Method* (Cambridge: Cambridge University Press, 2009).
Pocock, John, 'Time, Institutions and Action: An Essay on Traditions and Their Understanding (1968)'. In Pocock, *Political Thought*, 187–216.
Polasky, Janet, 'Providential History in Belgium at the End of the Eighteenth Century', *Revue belge de philologie et d'histoire* 55, no. 2 (1977), 416–24.
Polasky, Janet, *Revolution in Brussels* (Brussels: Académie Royale de Belgique and University Press of New England, 1985).
Polasky, Janet, *Revolutions without Borders. The Call to Liberty in the Atlantic World* (New Haven: Yale University Press, 2015).
Pollock, Sheldon, 'Cosmopolitanism, Vernacularism, and Premodernity'. In Moyn and Sartori (eds.), *Global Intellectual History*, 59–80.
Popkin, Jeremy, *The Right-Wing Press in France, 1792–1800* (Chapel Hill, NC: University of North Carolina Press, 1980).
Porte, Eleá de la, 'History beyond the Nation: Dutch World Histories in the Enlightenment', *De Achttiende eeuw* 46, no. 2 (2014), 50–79.
Porte, Eleá de la, 'Verlichte verhalen: De omgang met het verleden in de Nederlandse Verlichting'. Dissertation, University of Amsterdam, 2019.
Porter, Roy, *The Enlightenment* (Basingstoke: Palgrave, 2001).
Poulsen, Frank, 'A Cosmopolitan Republican in the French Revolution: The Political Thought of Anacharsis Cloots'. Dissertation, European University Institute, 2018.
Prandi, Alfonso, *Cristianesimo offeso e difeso, Deismo e apologetica cristiana nel secondo Settecento* (Bologna: Il Mulino, 1975).
Printy, Michael, 'Protestantism and Progress in the Year XII: Charles Villers' Essay on the Spirit and Influence of Luther's Reformation (1804)', *Modern Intellectual History* 9, vol. 2 (2012), 303–29.
Proschwitz, Gunnar, and Mavis von Proschwitz, *Beaumarchais et le Courier de l'Europe: documents inédits ou peu connus* (Oxford: Oxford University Press, 1990).
Raat, Alexander, Wyger Velema, and Claudette Baar-de Weerdt (eds.), *De Oudheid in de Achttiende eeuw; Classical Antiquity in the Eighteenth century* (Utrecht & Valkenswaard: Werkgroep 18e eeuw & Hola Press, 2012).

Raedts, Peter, *De ontdekking van de Middeleeuwen: Geschiedenis van een illusie* (Amsterdam: Wereldbibliotheek, 2012).
Ramón Solans, Francisco Javier, 'A Renewed Global Power: The Restoration of the Holy See and the Triumph of Ultramontanism, 1814–1848'. In Broers, Caiani, and Bann (eds.), *Restorations* II, 72–84.
Ramón Solans, Francisco Javier, 'Una utopía ultramontana: El papa como árbitro internacional de la paz en el siglo XIX', *Pasado y Memoria. Revista de Historia Contemporánea* 23 (2021), 117–38.
Rance, Karine, 'L'émigration nobiliaire Français en Allemagne: Une "migration de maintain" (1789–1815)', *Génèses* 30 (1998), 5–29.
Rance, Karine, 'La Contre-revolution à l'œuvre en Europe'. In Martin (ed.), *Révolution*, 182–92.
Ranzelzhofer, Albrecht, *Völkerrechtliche Aspekte des Heiligen Römischen Reiches nach 1648* (Berlin: Duncker & Humblot, 1967).
Rapport, Michael, *Nationality and Citizenship in Revolutionary France: The Treatment of Foreigners, 1789–1799* (Oxford: Clarendon Press, 2000).
Raskolnikoff, Mouza, 'L'adoration des Romains sous la Révolution française et la réaction de Volney et des idéologues'. In Raskolnikoff, *Des Anciens et les Modernes* (Paris: Éditions de la Sorbonne, 1990).
Reboul, Juliette, *French Emigration to Great Britain in Response to the French Revolution* (Cham: Palgrave Macmillan, 2017).
Recchia, Stefano, and Nadia Urbinati (eds.), *A Cosmopolitanism of Nations: Giuseppe Mazzini's Writings on Democracy, Nation Building, and International Relations* (Princeton, NJ: Princeton University Press, 2009).
Ree, Erik van, *Boundaries of Utopia: Imagining Communism from Plato to Stalin* (London: Routledge, 2015).
Reedy, Jay, 'The Historical Imaginary of Social Science in Post-Revolutionary France: Bonald, Saint-Simon, Comte', *History of the Human Sciences* 7, no. 1 (1994), 1–26.
Reijnen, Carlos, and Marleen Rensen (eds.), *European Encounters: Intellectual Exchange and the Rethinking of Europe (1914–1945)*. European Studies 32 (Amsterdam: Amsterdam University Press, 2014).
Reill, Peter Hanns, 'Ludwig Timotheus Spittler'. In Hans-Ulrich Wehler (ed.), *Deutsche Historiker, vol. IX* (Göttingen: Vandenhoeck & Ruprecht, 1982), 42–6.
Reill, Peter Hanns, *The German Enlightenment and the Rise of Historicism* (Los Angeles, CA: University of California Press, 1975, new edition; 2018, re-edition).
Reinhold, Aris, *Die Staatslehre Adam Müllers in ihrem Verhältnis zur Deutschen Romantik* (Tübingen: Mohr, 1929).
Rensen, Marleen, *Lijden aan de tijd: Franse intellectuelen in het interbellum* (Soesterberg: Aspekt, 2009).
Rétat, Pierre, 'L'âge des dictionnaires'. In Roger Chartier, Henri-Jean Martin, and Jean-Pierre Vivet (eds.), *Histoire de l'Edition française* (Paris: Promodis, 1984) vol. II, 186–94.
Rey, Marie-Pierre, *Alexander I: The Tsar Who Defeated Napoleon* (Dekalb, IL: Northern Illinois University Press, 2012).
Richter, Melvin, 'Reconstructing the History of Political Languages: Pocock, Skinner and the *Geschichtliche Grundbegriffe*'. *History and Theory* 29, no. 1 (1990), 38–70.
Rigney, Ann, *Imperfect Histories: The Elusive Past and the Legacy of Romantic Historicism* (Ithaca, NY: Cornell University Press, 2001).
Rigney, Ann, *The Afterlives of Walter Scott: Memory on the Move* (Oxford: Oxford University Press, 2012).

Rigney, Ann, 'Transforming Memory and the European Project', *New Literary History* 43, no. 4 (2012), 607–28.
Riquet, Michel, *Augustin de Barruel: Un Jésuite face aux Jacobins francs-maçons 1741–1820* (Paris: Beauchesne, 1989).
Roberts, James, *The Counter-Revolution in France* (Basingstoke: Macmillan, 1990).
Robertson, John, *The Case for the Enlightenment: Scotland and Naples 1680–1760* (Cambridge: Cambridge University Press, 2005).
Robertson, Ritchie, *The Enlightenment: The Pursuit of Happiness, 1680–1790* (London: Allen Lane, 2020).
Robin, Corey, *The Reactionary Mind: Conservatism from Edmund Burke to Sarah Palin* (Oxford: Oxford University Press, 2011).
Rodríguez Pérez, Yolanda, 'Being Eurocentric within Europe: Nineteenth-century English and Dutch Literary Historiography and Oriental Spain'. In Brolsma, de Bruin, and Lok (eds.), *Eurocentrism*, 157–78.
Roegiers, Jan, 'De Brabantse omwenteling in haar politieke, religieuze en culturele context'. In Jean Lorette, Patrick Lefevre, and Piet de Gryse (eds.), *Handelingen van het Colloquium over de Brabantse omwenteling 13–14 oktober 1983* (Brussels: Koninklijk Legermuseum, 1984), 75–91.
Roegiers, Jan, 'At the Origin of Revolution: Printing in Exile', *Quaerendo* 38, no. 4 (2008), 322–32.
Roggen, Ronald, *'Restauration' Kampfruf und Schimpfwort: Eine Kommunikationsanalyse zum Hauptwerk des Staatstheoretikers Karl Ludwig von Haller (1768–1854)* (Freiburg: Universitätsverlag Freiburg Schweiz, 1999).
Rosanvallon, Pierre, *Le moment Guizot* (Paris: Gallimard, 1985).
Rosanvallon, Pierre, 'présentation'. In François Guizot (ed.), *Histoire de la civilisation en Europe*, edited by Pierre Rosanvallon (Paris: Hachette, 1985).
Rosenblatt, Helena, *The Lost History of Liberalism: From Ancient Rome to the Twenty-First Century* (Princeton, NJ: Princeton University Press, 2018).
Rosenboim, Or, *The Emergence of Globalism: Visions of World Order in Britain and the United States, 1939–1950* (Princeton, NJ: Princeton University Press, 2017).
Rößner, Susan, *Die Geschichte Europas schreiben: Europäische Historiker und ihr Europabild im 20. Jahrhundert* (Frankfurt: Campus, 2009).
Rothschild, Emma, *Economic Sentiments: Adam Smith, Condorcet, and the Enlightenment* (Cambridge, MA: Harvard University Press, 2002).
Rotmans, Jan, 'Circles of Desire and the Corruption of Virtue: The Historical Thought of Cornelis Zillessen (1736–1828)', *De Achttiende eeuw/The Eighteenth Century* 46, no. 2 (2014), 79–106.
Rotmans, Jan, 'Enlightened Pessimism: Republican Decline in Dutch Revolutionary Thought, 1780–1800'. Dissertation, University of Amsterdam, 2020.
Rougement, Denis de, *Vingt-huit siècles de l'Europe: la conscience européenne à travers les textes d'Hesiode à nos jours* (Paris: Payot, 1961).
Rowe, Michael, *From Reich to State: The Rhineland in the Revolutionary Age, 1780–1830* (Cambridge: Cambridge University Press, 2003).
Rowe, Michael, 'The French Revolution, Napoleon, and Nationalism in Europe'. In John Breuilly (ed.), *The Oxford Handbook of the History of Nationalism* (Oxford: Oxford University Press, 2013).
Roy, Olivier, *Is Europe Christian?* (Oxford: Oxford University Press, 2020).
Sachsenmaier, Dominic, *Global Perspectives on Global History: Theories and Approaches in a Connected World* (Cambridge: Cambridge University Press, 2011).

Said, Edward, *Orientalism: Western Conceptions of the Orient* (New York: Pantheon Books, 1978)
Salber Phillips, Mark, *On Historical Distance* (New Haven, CT: Yale University Press, 2013).
Sas, Niek van, *Onze natuurlijkste bondgenoot: Nederland, Engeland en Europa, 1813-1831* (Groningen: Wolters Noordhoff, 1985).
Sassatelli, Monica, *Becoming Europeans: Cultural Identity and Cultural Policies* (Basingstoke: Palgrave, 2009).
Satia, Priya, *Time's Monster: How History Makes History* (Cambridge, MA: Harvard University Press, 2020).
Schaumkell, Ernst, *Geschichte der deutschen Kultur Geschichtsschreibung von der Mitte des 18. Jahrhunderts bis zur Romantik im Zusammenhang mit der allgemeinen geistigen Entwicklung* (Leipzig: B.G. Teubner, 1905).
Schettini, Glauco, '18th-Century Crusaders: The War against Revolutionary France and the Birth of Catholic Conservatism'. In Lok, Pestel, and Reboul (eds.), *Cosmopolitan Conservatisms*, 152-74.
Schettini, Glauco, 'The Invention of Catholicism: A Global Intellectual History of the Catholic Counterrevolution, 1780-1849' (Doctoral dissertation, Fordham University, 2022).
Schiffmann, Zachary, *The Birth of the Past* (Baltimore, MD: John Hopkins University Press, 2017).
Schildt, Axel, *Zwischen Abendland und Amerika: Studien zur westdeutschen Ideeenlandschaft der 50er Jahre* (Munich: De Gruyter Oldenbourg, 1999).
Schlereth, Thomas, *The Cosmopolitan Ideal in Enlightenment Thought: Its Form and Function in the Ideas of Franklin, Hume, and Voltaire, 1694-1790* (Notre Dame: University of Notre Dame Press, 1977).
Schmidt, James, 'Inventing the Enlightenment: Anti-Jacobins, British Hegelians and the Oxford English Dictionary', *Journal of the History of Ideas* 64 (2003), 421-3.
Schmidt, James, 'The Counter-Enlightenment: Historical Notes on a Concept Historians Should Avoid', *Eighteenth-century Studies* 49, no. 1 (2015), 83-6.
Schmidt, James, 'Light, Truth and Counter-Enlightenment'. In Anton Matystsin and Dan Edelstein (eds.), *Let There Be Enlightenment: The Religious and Mystical Sources of Rationality* (Baltimore, MD: Johns Hopkins University Press, 2018), 268-90.
Schmidt, Peer, 'Contra "la falsa filosofía": La Contra Ilustración y la crítica al reformismo borbónico en Nueva España'. In Karl Kohut and Sonia Rose (eds.), *La formación de la cultura virreinal, vol. 3. El siglo XVIII* (Madrid, Frankfurt: Vervuert, 2006), 231-54.
Schofield, Philip, 'Conservative Political Thought in Britain in Response to the French Revolution', *The Historical Journal* 29, no. 3 (September 1986), 601-22.
Schroeder, Paul, 'Metternich Studies since 1925', *Journal of Modern History* 33 (1961), 237-60.
Schroeder, Paul, *The Transformation of European Politics, 1763-1848* (Oxford: Oxford University Press, 1996).
Schulin, Ernst, 'Leopold von Ranke'. In Duchhardt et al. (eds.), *Europa-Historiker* I, 129-52.
Schulz, Karl-Heinz, 'Kosmopolitismus und Nationalismus bei den Brüdern Schlegel', *Recherches germaniques* 19 (1989), 31-67.
Schulz, Matthias, *Normen und Praxis: Das Europäische Konzert der Großmächte als Sicherheitsrat, 1815-1860* (Munich: Oldenbourg, 2009).
Schulz, Matthias, *Europa-Netzwerke und Europagedanke in der Zwischenkriegszeit* (Mainz: Institut für Europäische Geschichte, 2010).

Schulze, Winfried, *Deutsche Geschichtswissenschaft nach 1945* (Munich: Oldenbourg, 1989).
Schutte, Gerrit Jan, *Mr. G. Groen van Prinsterer* (Goes: Oosterbaan & Lecointre, 1977).
Scrivener, Michael, *The Cosmopolitan Ideal in the Age of Revolution and Reaction, 1776-1832* (London: Pickering & Chatto, 2007).
Sebastiani, Silvia, *The Scottish Enlightenment: Race, Gender and the Limits of Progress* (New York: Palgrave Macmillan, 2013).
Seier, Hellmut, 'Heeren und England'. In Lothar Kettenacker, Manfred Schlenke, and Hellmut Seier (eds.), *Studien zur Geschichte Englands und der deutsch-britischen Beziehungen* (Munich: Oldenbourg, 1981).
Seier, Hellmut, 'Arnold Hermann Ludwig Heeren'. In Hans-Ulrich Wehler (ed.), *Deutsche historiker, vol. 9* (Göttingen: Vandenhoeck & Ruprecht, 1982), 61-80.
Seigel, Jerrold, 'European Liberalism in the Nineteenth Century'. In Breckmann and Gordon (eds.), *European Thought* I, 172-95.
Serna, Pierre, *La République des girouettes. 1789-1815 et au-delà: une anomalie politique. La France de l'extrême centre* (Seyssel: Champ Vallon, 2005).
Serna, Pierre, 'Introduction: l'Europe, une idée nouvelle à la fin du XVIIIe siècle?', *La Révolution française* 'Dire et faire l'Europe à la fin du XVIIIe siècle' (online publication, 14 June 2011), 1-16.
Shea, Louisa, *The Cynic Enlightenment: Diogenes in the Salon* (Baltimore, MD: Johns Hopkins Press, 2010).
Siemann, Wolfram, *Metternich: Stratege und Visionär. Eine Biographie* (Munich: C.H. Beck, 2016).
Signoret-Serrano, Georgette, *Les idées politiques de Pauline de Lézardière* (Paris: Thèse Droit, 1969).
Simon Schuhmacher, Lioba, 'Burke's Political and Aesthetic Ideas in Spain: A View from the Right?' In Fitzpatrick and Jones (eds.), *Reception of Edmund Burke*, 229-52.
Skinner, Quentin, 'Meaning and Understanding in the History of Ideas', *History and Theory* 8, no. 1 (1969), 3-53.
Skinner, Quentin, *The Foundations of Modern Political Thought*, 2 vol. (Cambridge: Cambridge University Press, 1978).
Skinner, Quentin, *Liberty before Liberalism* (Cambridge: Cambridge University Press, 1998).
Skinner, Quentin, and Martin van Gelderen (eds.), *Republicanism: A Shared European Heritage*, 2 vol. (Cambridge: Cambridge University Press, 2005).
Sluga, Glenda, 'Madame de Staël and the Transformation of European Politics, 1812-17', *The International History Review* 37, no. 1 (2015), 142-66.
Sluga, Glenda, *The Invention of International Order: Remaking Europe after Napoleon* (Princeton, NJ: Princeton University Press, 2021).
Sluga, Glenda, 'Women and the History of International Thinking' (online lecture Amsterdam-Utrecht Seminar for Global Intellectual History, 2 February 2021).
Sluga, Glenda, and Julia Horne, 'Cosmopolitanism: Its Pasts and Practices', *Journal of World History* 21, no. 3 (2010), 369-73.
Smith, Steven, 'Conservatism and Its Discontents'. In Gordon and Breckman (eds.), *Modern European Thought*, vol. 2, 391-416.
Smitskamp, Hendrik, *Groen van Prinsterer als historicus* (Amsterdam: H.J. Paris, 1940).
Smitten, Jeffrey, 'William Robertson: The Minister as Historian'. In Bourgault and Sparling (eds.), *Companion*, 101-31.
Snel, Johan, *De zeven levens van Abraham Kuyper* (Amsterdam: Prometheus, 2020).

Sofka, James, 'Metternich's Theory of European Order: A Political Agenda for "Perpetual Peace"', *The Review of Politics* 60, no. 1 (Winter 1998), 115–49.

Solleveld, Floris, 'Afterlives of the Republic of Letters: Learned Journals and Scholarly Community in the Early Nineteenth Century', *Erudition and the Republic of Letters* 5 (2020), 82–116.

Somsen, Geert, 'The Princess at the Conference: Science, Pacifism, and Habsburg Society', *History of Science* 59, no. 4 (2021), 434–60.

Sorkin, David, *The Religious Enlightenment: Protestants, Jews and Catholics from London to Vienna* (Princeton, NJ: Princeton University Press 2008).

Spector, Céline, *Montesquieu: Liberté, droit et histoire* (Paris: Michalon, 2010).

Sperber, Jonathan, *Europe, 1850–1870: Progress, Participation and Apprehension* (London: New York, 2013).

Spiering, Menno, and Michael Wintle (eds.), *European Identity and the Second World War* (Basingstoke: Palgrave, 2011).

Sprunck, Alphonse, 'François-Xavier de Feller, 1735–1802'. In Jules Mersch (ed.), *Biographie nationale du Pays de Luxembourg depuis ses origines jusqu'à nos jours* (Luxembourg: Victor Buck, 1947), 123–254.

Starobinski, Jean, *Action et réaction: Vie et aventures d'un couple* (Paris: Seuil, 2003).

Starzinger, Vincent, *Middlingness: Juste Milieu Political Theory in France and England, 1815–1848* (Charlottesville, VA: University Press of Virginia, 1965).

Steber, Martina, *Die Hüter der Begriffe: Politische Sprachen des Konservativen in Großbritannien und der Bundesrepublik Deutschland, 1945–1980* (Berlin: De Gruyter Oldenbourg, 2017).

Steinberg, Ronen, *The Afterlives of the Terror: Facing the Legacies of Mass Violence in Post-revolutionary France* (Ithaca, NY: Cornell University Press, 2019).

Sternhell, Zeev, *The Anti-Enlightenment Tradition*, translated by David Maisel (New Haven, CT and London: Yale University Press, 2010).

Stoler, Ann, 'Colonial Aphasia: Race and Disabled Histories in France', *Public Culture* 23, no. 1 (2011), 121–56.

Stollberg-Rilinger, Barbara, *Der Staat als Maschine: Zur politischen Metaphorik des absoluten Fürstenstaats* (Berlin: Duncker & Humblot, 1986).

Stollberg-Rilinger, Barbara, *Das Heilige Römische Reich Deutscher Nation: Vom Ende des Mittelalters bis 1806* (Munich: C. H. Beck, 2009).

Stone, Dan, *Goodbye to All That? The Story of Europe since 1945* (Oxford: Oxford University Press, 2014).

Stovall, Tyler, *White Freedom: The Racial History of an Idea* (Princeton, NJ: Princeton University Press, 2021).

Stråth, Bo, *Europe's Utopia's of Peace 1815, 1919, 1951* (London: Bloomsbury, 2016).

Streidl, Paul, *Naturrecht, Staatswissenschaften und Politisierung bei Gottfried Achenwall (1719–1772)* (Münster: Utz, 2003).

Stuchtey, Benedikt, 'Literature, Liberty and Life of the Nation: British Historiography from Macauley to Trevelyan'. In Berger, Donovan, and Passmore (eds.), *Writing National Histories*, 30–46.

Stuurman, Siep, *The Invention of Humanity: Equality and Cultural Difference in World History* (Cambridge, MA: Harvard University Press, 2017).

Susane, G., *La tactique financière de Calonne* (Paris: Rousseau, 1901).

Sutherland, Donald, *France 1789–1815: Revolution and Counter-Revolution* (Oxford: Oxford University Press, 1985).

Suttorp, Leendert Christiaan, Zeger Willem Sneller, and J. Veldkamp (eds.), *Groens 'Ongeloof en revolutie': een bundel studiën* (Wageningen: Zomer & Keuning, 1949).

Tackett, Timothy, *The Coming of the Terror in the French Revolution* (Cambridge, MA: Harvard University Press, 2017).

Theis, Laurent, *François Guizot* (Paris; Fayard, 2008).

Theis, Laurent, *Guizot: La traversée d'un siècle* (Paris: CNRS éditions, 2014)

Thiesse, Anne-Marie, *La Création des identités nationales: Europe, XVIIIe-XXe siècle* (Paris: Seuil, 2014).

Thom, Martin, *Republics, Nations and Tribes* (London: Penguin, 1995).

Thompson, Edward, 'Britain and the French Revolution', *History Workshop Journal* 39 (1995), 79-88.

Thompson, Martyn, 'Ideas of Europe during the French Revolution and Napoleonic Wars', *Journal of the History of Ideas* 55, no. 1 (2014), 37-58.

Tijsterman, Sebastiaan, 'August Wilhelm Rehberg (1757-1836)'. In Baudet and Visser (eds.), *Revolutionair Verval*, 165-84.

Toews, John, 'Historicism from Ranke to Nietzsche', Breckmann and Gordon, *European Thought* I, 301-29.

Tollebeek, Jo, *De illusionisten: Geschiedenis en cultuur in de Franse romantiek* (Leuven: Leuven University Press, 2000).

Tort, Olivier, *La droite française: Aux origines de ses divisions, 1814-1830* (Paris: Éditions du CTHS, 2013).

Trencsenyi, Balázs, Michal Kopeček, Luka Lisjak Gabrijelčič, Maria Falina, and Mónika Baár (eds.), *A History of Modern Political Thought in East Central Europe* (Oxford: Oxford University Press, 2018).

Triomphe, Robert, *Joseph de Maistre: Étude sur la vie et sur la doctrine d'un matérialiste mystique* (Geneva: Droz, 1963).

Trousson, Raymond, 'L'abbé F.-X. de Feller et les "philosophes"', *Études sur le XVIIIe siècle* 6 (1979), 103-15.

Tuck, Richard, *Philosophy and Government 1572-1651* (Cambridge: Cambridge University Press, 1999).

Uerlings, Herbert, 'Das Europa der Romantik'. In Silvio Vietta, Dirk Kemper, and Eugenio Spedicato (eds.), *Das Europa-projekt der Romantik und die Moderne* (Tübingen: Max Niemeyer Verlag, 2005).

Useche Sandoval, Tonatiuh, 'August Comte's Reading of Maistre's Du Pape: Two Theories of Spiritual Authority'. In Armenteros and Lebrun (eds.), *European Readers*, 75-94.

Valjavec, Fritz, *Die Entstehung der politischen Strömungen in Deutschland 1770-1815* (Munich: Oldenbourg, 1951).

Valjavec, Fritz, 'Die Entstehung des europäischen Konservatismus'. In Hans-Gerd Schumann (ed.), *Konservatismus* (Cologne: Kiepenheuer & Witsch, 1974), 138-55.

Vanysacker, Dries, *The Erudite Activities and Contacts of Papal Nuncio Giuseppe Garampi in Warsaw and Vienna, 1772-1785* (Leuven: K.U.L. Departement Geschiedenis, 1994).

Vanysacker, Dries, *Cardinal Giuseppe Garampi (1725-1792): An Enlightened Ultramontane* (Brussels: Institut historique belge de Rome, 1995).

Varouxakis, Georgios, 'Guizot's Historical Works and J.S. Mill's Reception of Tocqueville', *History of Political Thought* 20, no. 2 (1999), 292-312.

Vartija, Devin, 'The Colour of Equality, Racial Classification and Natural Equality in Enlightenment Encyclopaedias'. Dissertation, University of Utrecht, 2018.

Velde, Henk te, and Donald Haks (eds.), *Oranje onder: Populair Orangisme van Willem van Oranje tot nu* (Amsterdam: Bert Bakker, 2014).

Velema, Wyger, *Enlightenment and Conservatism in the Dutch Republic: The Political Thought of Elie Luzac (1721-1796)* (Assen and Maastricht: Speculum historiale, 1993).

Velema, Wyger, *Omstreden Oudheid: De Nederlandse achttiende eeuw en de klassieke politiek* (Amsterdam: Vossiuspers, 2010).

Velema, Wyger, 'Introduction: The Enlightenment and the Past: Old Controversies and New Perspectives', *The Enlightenment and the Past. Special Issue: De achttiende eeuw (Dutch-Flemish Journal for Eighteenth-Century Studies)* 46, no. 2 (2014), 7-26.

Velema, Wyger, 'Enlightenment against Revolution: The Genesis of Dutch Conservatism'. In Lok, Pestel, and Reboul (eds.), *Cosmopolitan Conservatisms*, 108-30.

Verga, Marcello, 'European Civilisation and the "Emulation of the Nations": Histories of Europe from the Enlightenment to Guizot', *History of European Ideas* 34 (2008), 353-60.

Verga, Marcello, *Storie d'Europa Secoli XVIII-XXI* (Rome: Carocci editore, 2017).

Verheij, Cees, 'Groen's visie op de presentatie van God in schepping en geschiedenis'. In Harinck and Kuiper (eds.), *Groen*, 93-106.

Verpoest, Lien, 'The Ancien Régime and the Jeune Premier: The Birth of Russian Conservatism in Vienna (1803-1812)'. In Lok, Pestel, and Reboul (eds.), *Conservatisms*, 219-40.

Vick, Brian, *The Congress of Vienna: Power and Politics after Napoleon* (Cambridge, MA: Harvard University Press, 2014).

Vick, Brian, 'Transnational Networks, Salon Sociability, and Multilateral Exchanges in the Study of Conservatism during and after the Revolutionary Era'. In Lok, Pestel, and Reboul (eds.), *Cosmopolitan Conservatisms*, 197-218.

Vierhaus, Rudolf, 'Konservativ, konservatismus'. In Otto Brunner, Werner Konze, and Reinhart Koselleck (eds.), *Geschichtliche Grundbegriffe: Historisches Lexicon zur politisch-sozialen Sprache in Deutschland*, vol. 3 (Stuttgart: Klett-Cotta, 1982).

Vincent, John, 'Edmund Burke and the Theory of International Relations', *Review of International Studies* 10, no. 3 (July 1984), 205-18.

Vliet, W.G.F. van, *Groen van Prinsterers historische benadering van de politiek* (Hilversum: Verloren, 2008).

Vliet, W.G.F. van, 'Groen van Prinsterer en Guizot'. In de Bruijn and Harinck (eds.), *Groen*, 37-42.

Volpilhac-Auger, Catherine, 'Considérations sur les causes de la grandeur des Romains et de leur décadence'. In *A Montesquieu Dictionary*. Available at: http://dictionnaire-montesquieu.ens-lyon.fr/en/article/1376399421/fr/.

Vovk van Gaal, Taja, 'Comment forger un récit européen? La Maison de l'histoire européenne: travaux en cours'. In Arjakovsky (ed.), *Histoire de la conscience européenne*, 57-68.

Wagner, Jacques, 'Feller, François-Xavier de'. In Didier Masseau (ed.), *Dictionnaire des anti-Lumières et des antiphilosophes (France, 1715-1815)*, Vol. I (A-I) (Paris: Champion, 2017), 550-8.

Wahnich, Sophie, 'L'Europe dans le discours révolutionnaire', *Tumultes* 7 (1996), 11-28.

Wahnich, Sophie, *L'impossible citoyen: L'étranger dans le discours de la Révolution française* (Paris: Albin Michel 1997).

Walker, Mack, *Johann Jakob Moser and the Holy Roman Empire of the German Nation* (Chapel Hill, NC: University of North Carolina Press, 1981).

Wall, Ernestine van der, and Leo Wessels (eds.), *Een veelzijdige verstandhouding: Religie en Verlichting in Nederland 1650-1850* (Nijmegen: Vantilt, 2008).
Ward, Lee, 'Montesquieu on Federalism and Anglo-Gothic Constitutionalism', *Publius: The Journal of Federalism* 37, no. 4 (2007), 551-77.
Waresquiel, Emmanuel de, *Talleyrand: Le prince immobile* (Paris: Fayard, 2006).
Waresquiel, Emmanuel de, *Cent Jours: La Tentation de l'impossible, mars-juillet 1815* (Paris: Fayard, 2008).
Waresquiel, Emmanuel de, *Le Duc de Richelieu* (Paris: Perrin, 1990, first edition; 2009, second edition).
Waresquiel, Emmanuel and Benoît Yvert, *Histoire de la Restauration, 1814-1830: Naissance de la France moderne* (Paris: Éditions Perrin, 2002).
Weichlein, Siegfried, 'Cosmopolitism, Patriotism, Nationalism'. In Tim Blanning and Hagen Schulze (eds.), *Unity in Diversity in European Culture* (Oxford: Oxford University Press, 2006).
Weiß, Volker, *Die autoritäre Revolte: Die Neue Rechte und der Untergang des Abendlandes* (Stuttgart: Klett-Cotta, 2018).
Weiß, Christoph, with Wolfgang Albrecht (eds.), *Von 'Obscuranten' und 'Eudämonisten': Gegen-aufklärerische, konservative und antirevolutionäre Publizisten im späten 18. Jahrhundert* (St. Ingbert: Röhrig, 1997).
Werner, C., 'Zu Geschichtsauffassung Nicolas de Bonnevilles'. In Werner Krauss and Walter Dietze (eds.), *Neue Beiträge zur Literatur der Aufklärung* (Berlin: Rütten & Loening, 1964).
Whatmore, Richard, *What Is Intellectual History?* (Cambridge: Polity Press, 2016).
Whatmore, Richard, *Terrorists, Anarchists, and Republicans: The Genevans and the Irish in Time of Revolution* (Princeton, NJ: Princeton University Press, 2019).
Wintle, Michael, 'Introduction: Cultural Diversity and Identity in Europe'. In Wintle (ed.), *Culture and Identity in Europe* (Aldershot: Avebury, 1996), 1-8.
Wintle, Michael, *The Image of Europe: Visualizing Europe in Cartography and Iconography throughout the Ages* (Cambridge: Cambridge University Press, 2009).
Withers, Charles, *Placing the Enlightenment: Thinking Geographically about the Age of Reason* (Chicago, IL: University of Chicago Press, 2007).
Wolff, Larry, *Inventing Eastern Europe: The Map of Civilisation on the Mind of the Enlightenment* (Stanford, CA: Stanford University Press, 1994).
Woloch, Isser, *Napoleon and His Collaborators: The Making of a Dictatorship* (New York: W.W. Norton, 2002).
Woolf, Stuart, 'French Civilisation and Ethnicity in the Napoleonic Empire', *Past & Present* 124 (August 1989), 96-120.
Woolf, Stuart, *Napoleon's Integration of Europe* (London: Routledge, 1991).
Woolf, Stuart, 'The Construction of a European World-View in the Revolutionary-Napoleonic Years', *Past & Present* 137 (November 1992), 72-101.
Woolf, Stuart, 'Napoleon and Europe Revisited', *Modern and Contemporary France* 8, no. 4 (2000), 469-78.
Woolf, Stuart, 'Europe and Its Historians', *Contemporary European History* 12, no. 3 (2003), 323-37.
Wright, Johnson Kent, *A Classical Republican in Eighteenth-century France: The Political Thought of Mably* (Stanford, CA: Stanford University Press, 1997).
Zamoyski, Adam, *Rites of Peace: The Fall of Napoleon and the Congress of Vienna* (London, Harper Collins, 2007).

Zamoyski, Adam, *Phantom Terror: The Threat of Revolution and the Repression of Liberty 1789-1848* (London: Harper Collins, 2015).

Ziblatt, Daniel, *Conservative Parties and the Birth of Democracy* (Cambridge: Cambridge University Press, 2017).

Ziblatt, Daniel, and Steven Levitsky, *How Democracies Die* (New York: Penguin, 2018).

Zielonka, Jan, *Counter-Revolution: Liberal Europe in Retreat* (Oxford: Oxford University Press, 2018).

Zwaan, Johan, *Groen van Prinsterer en de klassieke oudheid* (Amsterdam: A.M. Hakkert, 1973).

Index

For the benefit of digital users, indexed terms that span two pages (e.g., 52–53) may, on occasion, appear on only one of those pages.

Abendland 2, 297, 298n.171
Abuses 6, 8–9, 90–1, 105, 109, 111, 116–17, 122–3, 174–5, 213, 224–5, 228, 269
Absolutism, absolutist 11, 27n.92, 46, 58–9, 80–1, 93, 98, 103–4, 205–6, 212, 217, 221, 228, 236–7, 287
Abstraction (criticism of), abstract 2n.11, 19–20, 33, 73–4, 92–5, 130, 132, 141–3, 148–9, 151, 153–4, 157, 159–61, 168–9, 181–3, 197, 200, 206–7, 211–12, 218, 220, 228, 257–8, 274–5, 285, 301
Achenwall, Gottfried 205–6
Administration, *see also* Bureaucracy 25, 33–4, 106–7, 114, 137–8, 173–7, 184, 199–200, 266–7, 280–1, 286–7
Areopagus 245
Aesthetics 89, 116, 151, 242
Aix-la-Chapelle, Conference of 222–3
Africa, Africans 51, 77–8, 84–5, 88–9, 97–8, 117–18, 182, 188, 209–10, 223–7, 250, 266–9, 284–5, 296
Agriculture 177, 224–6
Albrecht, Andrea 139–40
Alembert, Jean d' 37–8, 51, 80
Alexander I (tsar) 203–4, 229, 232, 236–7, 241, 245, 248
Alfred the Great (king of the Anglo-Saxons) 61
Aliens, *see also* immigrants 192–3
Alliance (military), *see also* Holy Alliance 96, 99–100, 107, 125–6, 183–4, 233–7, 255–6, 292
Alternative für Deutschland (AfD) 2
America
    America (North, *see also* American Republic) 86, 188
    America (South, Latin) 188, 223–4, 266n.19
    America (United States of) 31, 38–9, 92–3, 131, 188, 205–6, 238, 245, 250–1, 267–8, 276
American Revolution, Independence 88, 103, 116–17, 197–9, 224–5, 228
Amiens, Peace of 100–1, 182–3

Anarchy (fear of) 3–5, 8–9, 19–20, 29, 88–9, 102, 109–10, 125, 128, 178, 181–2, 184, 192, 200, 208–9, 235, 237–8, 250, 253, 289–90
Ancien Régime 8–9, 24, 56–7, 65, 73, 89–91, 99–100, 107–8, 121, 127–8, 132–3, 137, 141–2, 145–6, 163–4, 193, 218–19, 249, 263–4, 269, 281, 298
Ancient Constitution, *see* Constitution
Ancients, *see* Querelle
Ancillon, Friedrich 148
Anglo-Saxons 61
Antagonism, *see also* Contradictions 13–14, 167n.11, 277, 282, 288–9
Anticlericalism 47, 50–1, 79
Anti-democracy, antidemocratic 32
Anti-liberalism, antiliberal 10, 23
Anti-philosophy, anti-philosophes 1, 5, 16–20, 30, 41, 67, 101–2, 112–13, 115–16, 132–3, 154–60, 195, 208, 217–18, 247, 273–4, 281–2, 294–5
Anti-Revolution 35, 106, 108, 114, 258–9, 271–6, 288–9, 291–2
Anti-Revolutionary Party (ARP) 276
Antiquity 13–15, 56, 95, 95n.156, 96n.160, 159–60, 162, 182–3, 207–11, 228, 254, 279–80, 301
Apocalypse, apocalyptic, *see also* Eschatology 87, 89–90, 92, 97–8, 189–90, 262
Apologist (Catholic), Apologetic 18, 18n.47, 47, 68–9, 74, 79, 84, 86, 98, 242
Arabs, Arabian 60, 80, 80n.72, 84–5, 97, 161–2, 171–2, 190, 190n.128, 211, 244, 255–6, 264–8, 277
Archenholz, Johann von 183
Aristocracy, *see also* nobility 21, 24, 33–5, 110–13, 121, 169–71, 175, 179–82, 191–2, 208–9, 213–14, 221–2, 293n.146
Aristoteles 181
Armitage, David 32, 227–8
Arrogance (human, criticism of), *see also* Hubris 73–4, 94–6, 221, 253, 255, 276, 281–2
Artois, count of, *see also* Charles X 133–4

Arts 15, 44, 48, 52, 56, 61, 79, 93–8, 172–3, 182, 189, 211, 217
Asia 13–14, 60–1, 71–2, 77, 84–5, 97–8, 117–18, 139, 156–7, 162, 182, 188, 209–12, 223–7, 250, 267–9, 280, 285, 287–8, 296–7, 301
Assemblée Nationale, *see* National Assembly
Assembly of Notables (Assemblée des Notables) 103–5, 109, 135
Atheism, atheists 18–20, 51, 74–6, 79, 86–9, 119, 122, 125, 132–3, 152–3, 181–2, 210, 217, 242–3, 255n.145, 264–6, 270–1, 274
Athens 175, 208–9, 245, 254, 279, 281–2
Atlantic 23n.74, 69, 204–5, 226–7
Auckland, Lord 125–6
Augustus (emperor), Augustan 83, 94–6
Aurelius, Marcus (emperor) 95
Austria (*see also* Habsburg dynasty, Austrian Netherlands) 12–13, 33, 99–101, 133, 146–50, 167–8, 175–6, 218–19, 226–7, 231–3, 235, 261, 295
Austrian Netherlands (*see also* Belgium, Southern Netherlands) 67, 229–30
Authoritarianism, authoritarian 1n.1, 10, 151, 184, 184n.90, 237–8, 257–8, 264–5, 281, 295
Averroes 80
Awakening 273

Babylonia 78
Balance, *see also* equilibrium and Gleichgewicht
Balance (general) 7, 13–16, 29, 34–5, 127–8, 133, 138–9, 141, 145, 155–8, 165–7, 174–83, 191–4, 211–16, 221–2, 235–7, 244, 246, 261, 264–5, 274–5, 280–1, 285, 288–90
Balance of Power 44, 56, 110, 127–8, 141–3, 145–9, 151, 173, 243, 277
Baldensperger, Fernand 112–13, 113n.72
Balmès, Abbé 288
Barbarism, barbarian, barbaric 29, 42, 83–4, 85n.101, 95–7, 127, 143, 171, 202–3, 253, 262–3, 266, 279, 285–6, 294
Barbary Corsairs 226–7, 232–3
Barruel, Augustin de 85n.102, 86, 86n.104, 87, 91, 95, 95n.157, 98, 115–16, 247
Bartholomew's Day Massacre, Saint 161–2
Basel 100–1, 279
Batavian Republic, *see also* Dutch Republic 31n.115, 100–1, 115, 239–40
Battle of the Nations (Völkerslacht) 221, 229
Baudet, Thierry 1–2, 2n.11
Bavaria 232
Bayle, Pierre 68, 78–9
Becker-Schaum, Christoph 207–8
Begriffsgeschichte 31–2
Belissa, Marc 99–100, 145

Bengal 71–2, 116
Belgian revolt, *see also* Brabant revolt 92
Belgian Revolution 271–2
Belgium, *see also* Austrian Netherlands, Liege, Southern Netherlands, United Kingdom of the Netherlands 31, 70–1, 72, 139, 291
Berlin, *see also* Prussia 150, 284–5
Berlin, Isaiah 18–19
Berger, Stefan 12, 33–4, 45
Bergier, Nicolas-Sylvestre 79
Berruyer, Isaac 68
Berry, Duc de 286–7
Bible, biblical, *see also* Writ, Scripture 44, 68–9, 76, 78, 80–3, 89–90, 92, 190, 203–4, 256–7, 272–3
Bismarck, Otto von 196, 200–1, 276, 282, 297n.170
Blockade, Continental 137–8
Bonaparte, General, Consul, *see also* Napoleon I 100–1, 137, 183
Boulainvilliers, Henri de 57–8, 58n.126
Bonald, Louis de 18–19, 240–6, 250–1, 255–6, 261, 264–5, 273
Bonapartism, Bonapartists 237
Bonneville, Nicolas de 21, 35, 37, 67, 76–7, 82, 84–6, 95–6, 110, 136, 171–2, 174, 179, 190–1, 193, 208, 260, 262, 287
Bossuet, Jacques-Bénigne de 41, 44, 46–7, 53, 69, 80–3, 86, 97–8, 250–1, 256–7, 273, 286
Bourbon (dynasty, *see also* monarchy) 25–6, 38–9, 111, 128, 133–4, 230–2, 255, 270–1
Bourke, Richard 28, 116–17
Brabant Revolt, *see also* Belgian Revolt 92–3
Brandes, Ernst 198, 220
Brazil 188, 267–8
Bremen 197, 199–200, 215
Brien, Karen O' 43n.35, 45, 262–3
Britain, Great, *see also* England and Scotland 24, 31, 35, 48, 63–4, 99–101, 106, 113, 116, 118, 125–7, 131, 142, 147, 155, 172–3, 175–6, 187–8, 213, 224–5, 231–4, 243, 267–8, 292, 294–5
Brumaire, Coup of 137
Brunner, Otto 31–2
Brussels 1–2, 70, 271–2
Buffon, Georges-Louis de 86
Burckhardt, Jacob 24n.77, 279–82
Bureaucracy, bureaucrats, *see also* administration 32–3, 153–4, 198, 203, 206, 219, 230, 235n.40, 250–1
Burke, Edmund 28, 35, 92–3, 101–2, 116–36, 146–9, 151–4, 183, 220, 224–6, 235–6, 260–1, 263–4, 266–7, 273, 289
Burke, Richard 123–4
Byzantium, Byzantine 59–61, 84, 171–2, 211, 285–6

Caesar, Caesarism 183–4, 276
Cahen, Raphaël 145–6
Calonne, Alexandre de 33, 35, 99, 137, 139, 146–9, 153, 168–9, 174–5, 181–3, 192–4, 220–1, 252, 260–4, 266–7
Calonne, Jacques-Ladislas-Joseph de 107
Cannibalism 92
Cambridge School 40–1
Cañizares-Esguerra, Jorge 224
Canon (of European Historians) 13, 39–41, 45–50, 65
Capet, Hugo (king of France) 63
Capitalism, capitalist 1, 281, 292, 296–8
Caribbean 224–5, 269
Carlsbad, Decrees of 150, 200
Carolingians (dynasty), Carolingian empire 59, 183–9
Carolus Magnus, see Charlemagne
Carthage 209
Casas, Bartholomew de las 223–4
Castlereagh, Viscount 232, 236–7
Catalonia 175
Catechism 76, 78
Catharsis 247–8, 258–9, 262
Catherine the Great (Empress of Russia) 87, 218–19
Catholic Church (see also Papacy and Catholic clergy) 18n.47, 43–4, 46, 50, 59–60, 62, 67, 160–3, 173–4, 179–80, 240–57, 261–3, 266–7, 274, 276, 279–81, 285–6, 288, 291
Celibacy 59, 252–3
Celtic 64
Cercle social 38, 52–3
Chaos (fear of) 56, 59, 69–70, 90–3, 106, 117–18, 180, 183, 289–90
Charlemagne 14, 59, 85, 95–6, 137–8, 182–3, 185–6, 188, 190, 231–2, 236, 243, 255
Charles I (king of England) 62–3
Charles V (Holy Roman emperor) 45, 86, 171–2, 176, 214, 229–30, 243
Charles X (king of France) 133–4, 286–7
Charte, La (1814) 25–6
Chateaubriand, François-René de 25–6, 28–9, 77–8, 112–13, 137, 242–3, 246, 251–2, 270–1, 278
Chaumont, Treaty of 231–2
China, Chinese 44, 68–9, 78, 78n.64, 82, 142, 173–4, 199, 266, 266n.19, 285
Chivalry, see also Valour 95–6, 117–18
Church, see Catholic Church
Church Council, see also Conciliar Movement 84, 192
Christ, Jesus, see also Saviour 52–3, 154–60, 193–4, 255, 262, 267

Christian Democracy 299–300
Christianity 5, 11, 15, 60, 76n.53, 77–9, 95–6, 142, 157, 159–62, 173–4, 179, 182–3, 215, 231, 240–6, 253, 255–6, 258–9, 274–5, 285–6
Chronology 80–6, 190, 203
Citizenship 20–3, 181, 192–3, 222, 262–3
Civil society 41–2, 132
Civil war 3, 58–9, 61, 108, 178–9, 216
Civilization 1–3, 5, 9, 13–16, 22–3, 29, 35–6, 42, 44, 48, 56, 59–60, 69, 72–3, 78, 82–6, 95–7, 112–13, 117–18, 124, 126–9, 136, 139, 151–2, 155–7, 159–60, 162–3, 165, 202–3, 214–15, 224–5, 242–6, 248–71, 273, 276–90, 294–6, 298–302
Class 34–5, 52, 59–60, 181–2, 197, 214, 271–2
Classics 96, 208, 211
Classicism, classicist 8–9, 208, 254
Clergy, Clergymen
    Clergy (general) 33–4, 50, 105, 157, 179, 213–15, 217, 240, 251–2, 255, 290
    Catholic clergy, see also Catholic Church 15, 46–7, 50–1, 54, 57–60, 63, 74–5, 79–80,
Climate 77–8, 165, 170, 178, 190, 226
Cloots, Anarchis 21
Clovis I, king of the Franks 135
Coblenz 106–7, 112–13, 123–4
Cold War 18–19, 249n.105, 298–9
Cologne 193
Colonialism, see also empire 196–7, 203n.33, 215, 223–7, 263, 268–70
Colonies, Colony
    Colonies (general) 7, 224–7, 268–9
    British colonies 119, 224–5
    Dutch colonies 291
    Spanish colonies 88–9, 266–7
Commerce, see also Trade and Market 43–4, 52, 61, 103–4, 147, 171–3, 182–3, 210, 215–17, 224, 226–7, 245, 282
Commons, House of 116
Commonwealth
    Commonwealth (Christian) 11, 156–7, 291, 294–5
    Commonwealth (European) 7–8, 22–3, 102, 116–21, 134–6, 148–9, 154–6, 158, 181, 212, 238–9, 257–8, 260–1, 271
    Commonwealth (Poland) 180
Communism, communist 270, 288–9, 292, 297–9
Competition 15, 173–4, 177–9, 224–6, 294
Comte, Auguste 270n.26, 292
Condillac, Abbé de 46–7
Concert (of Europe) 231–2, 234–5

Conciliar movement, *see also* Church Council 174, 253n.132
Condorcet, Nicolas de 45–6, 50–1, 55, 59–60, 242–3
Congress of Vienna, *see* Vienna
Conquistadores 223–4
Conservateur, Le (journal) 25–6
Conspiracy, *see also* Plot 87n.112, 258, 278
Constant, Benjamin 28–9, 241, 273, 284
Constantine (emperor) 59, 84n.96, 252–3
Constantinople 83, 188, 192, 211–12
Constitution
  American Constitution 245
  Ancient Constitution 102, 263–4, 266–7
  Constitution (general) 146–7, 155–6, 175, 183, 192, 199, 220, 246, 252
  Dutch Constitution 290–1
  English (British) Constitution 99, 158, 175–6, 188
  European Constitution, (*see also* Ius Publicam Europaeum) 184, 206
  French Constitution 25–6, 57–8, 90–1, 99
  German Constitution 137–164, 137–228
  Mixed Constitution 155, 169–70, 181–2, 205–6
  Republican Constitution 144, 172–5, 209–10, 212, 283
Consulate (France), Consul 106–7, 137, 161, 182–3
Conqueror, William The 61, 290
Contradictions, Doctrine of, *see also* antagonism 151, 155–7, 285, 294
Convention, *see also* National Assembly 105, 206–7
Conze, Werner 31–2
Corruption (criticism of) 18, 35–6, 61, 65–7, 69, 94, 116, 126–8, 166–7, 174, 248–9, 285–6
Corsica 137
Cosmopolitanism, Cosmopolitan 2, 16, 20–3, 29, 37–40, 45, 49–51, 64–6, 69–73, 83, 97, 101, 136, 139–41, 145–9, 156–7, 161, 163–7, 184, 191, 196, 214, 234–8, 242, 253–9, 262–3, 271, 273, 283–300
Counter-Enlightenment, *see also* Anti-philosophy 4, 16–20, 23–4, 30, 32, 67, 69, 246–50
Counter-Reformation 75, 84–5, 218–19, 280–1
Counter-Revolution (concept) 23–5, 107–12
Courier de Londres 102, 112–16, 125, 129, 133–4, 260
Courier de l'Europe, Le, *see* Courier de Londres
Crimea 106–7
Cromwell, Oliver 38–9, 62–3
Crusades, crusaders 60–1, 63, 121, 135–6, 162, 171–2, 174, 178–9, 203–4, 214–15, 225, 243, 255–6, 267–8, 279–80

Cultural transfer 31n.115, 32
Customs, Custom, *see also* Manners 3, 58–60, 80, 103–4, 130–2, 154–5, 168n.17, 171, 213, 287–8, 301
Cynic 21, 69, 71

Dalberg, Karl 168, 183–4, 187
Dark Ages, *see also* Middle Ages 84, 93–7, 294–5
Darkness, *see also* Lights 60, 89, 274
Darwinism 282
Dawson, Christopher 294–5
Decadence 5, 83, 93–8, 152, 169–70, 179, 242–3, 282
Decline 2, 7–8, 35–6, 44, 65–6, 69, 83, 94, 96, 152, 157, 159–62, 166–7, 169–70, 179, 188–91, 193–7, 211, 216–25, 242–3, 285, 293
Deism, deist 60
Delanty, Gerard 10–11
Delbrück, Hans 294
Democracy 1–2, 15, 38, 58–9, 169–70, 174–5, 181–2, 224–5, 264, 265n.11, 276, 285, 299–300
Denmark 199–200, 212–13, 224, 232
Despotism, *see also* tyranny
  Asian (Oriental), Despotism 77–8, 84–5, 117–18, 149, 178, 209–10, 221, 279, 296, 301
  Despotism (general) 57–8, 64, 77–8, 88, 156, 170, 172–4, 176–8, 190–1, 210, 215, 250, 253, 278, 287
  Napoleonic Despotism 163–4, 203–4, 230
  Revolutionary Despotism 3–5, 8–9, 19–20, 29, 65, 91–3, 98, 102, 106, 111, 125, 134, 137, 148–9, 181–2, 192, 228, 258, 262–3, 269, 274–5
  Roman Despotism 56–7, 157
  Royal Despotism 104, 110–11, 174–5, 188, 287
Dictionary (historical) 68–9, 78–82, 84–6, 88n.117
Diderot, Denis 88–9, 115–16, 116n.88
Diet 192, 206, 245
Dignity 21, 255–6, 256n.149
Dijon 94–6
Diplomacy, diplomats 99–100, 147–8, 201–2, 206, 231–8, 275
Directory (regime), *see also* Thermidor 100–2, 124–5, 128, 130, 135–6, 144–5
Discordia concors, *see also* unity in diversity 276–83
Diversity, *see also* pluralism 1–4, 13–16, 22–3, 138–9, 148–9, 151, 155, 163, 165–7, 172, 174–89, 194–5, 217, 260–70, 276–300
Divine right, droit divin 111, 200, 230
Doctrine, Catholic 67–8, 73–6, 80–1, 250–1, 256–7

INDEX

Donoso Cortés, Juan 35, 288, 288n.119
Dresden 150
Druids 52–3, 59–60, 65–6, 255
Duroselle, Jean-Baptiste 298–9
Dutch Revolt, *see also* Dutch Republic and Philip II 88

Eastern Europe 35, 60, 71–2, 72n.28, 226–7, 268–9, 291–2, 292n.138
Economy, *see also* commerce, market, political economy, and trade 15n.32, 26–7, 103, 153n.92, 165, 175–9, 181–2, 200–2, 210, 281–2
Edmund Burke Foundation 1
Education, educators 33–5, 37, 43–4, 91–2, 94n.152, 96, 98, 181–2
Effeminate, *see also* masculinity 34–5, 58
Egypt 78, 83, 209, 226–7, 268–9, 279
Eichhorn, Johann 203–4, 223
Elba 233
Eliot, T.S. 298–9
Elizabeth I (Queen of England) 215–16
Émigrés, *see also* exiles, refugees 35, 104, 106–9, 112–16, 120–4, 129–34, 229–30, 235–6, 242, 247–8, 269
Empire, *see* Colonialism
Emulation 162, 173, 275–6
Encyclopédie, Encyclopédistes 79, 93–4
Enemies (of Humanity) 51–3, 108–9
England, *see also* Britain 37–8, 48, 61, 63–4, 88, 92–3, 99, 155–6, 177, 187–8, 214–16, 220, 224, 242, 253–4, 268–9, 289, 292
Epstein, Klaus 27–30, 30n.109
Eschatology, *see also* Apocalypse 83, 98, 256–7, 262
Esoterism, Esoteric, *see also* mysticism 11, 39, 50–3, 65–6, 177–8, 236, 262, 300
Estates-General (France) 89–91, 105–8, 111, 135, 247
Ethiopia 77–8, 209
Equality 51, 63–4, 90–1, 106, 132, 148, 157, 181–2, 252, 274–5
Equilibrium, *see also* balance and Gleichgewicht 7, 15, 110–11, 137, 165, 213–16, 231–2, 239–40, 252–3, 258, 262, 267, 274–5, 291
Eurocentrism, Eurocentrist 9, 44, 54, 71–2, 80, 137–8, 211, 228, 244, 254, 265–70, 292, 299
Europa (Journal) 161–2
Europäische Staats-Relationen 184, 186, 188–9
European Integration 1–2, 10–11, 137–8, 263, 293, 298–300
European Union 1–2
European Parliament 1–2
Euroscepticism, Eurosceptic 299–300

Excess (criticism of), excessive 4, 20, 61, 83, 132–3, 163–4, 181, 253, 257–8, 261, 271, 285, 301
Exiles, *see also* refugees and émigrés 5, 101, 112, 283, 289–90

Fall (of Man) 82
Family (concept) 155, 160, 181–2, 238–9, 243, 299
Fanaticism, fanatic 4, 20, 46, 50, 60–1, 63–4, 75, 79, 85, 88, 90–1, 111, 121–2, 130, 134, 153–4, 176, 183, 215–16, 226–7, 235, 237
Fascism, fascist 1–2, 10, 28, 249, 295, 296n.158
Father (concept) 181–2, 238–9
Federation, *see also* German Confederation, Switzerland 52–3, 53n.99, 101–2, 141–6, 148, 158–60, 170–1, 199–200, 206, 221, 240, 264–5, 267, 283, 292, 296
Feller, François-Xavier de 19, 35, 41, 67, 99, 110–13, 116–17, 139, 155, 158, 168–9, 174–5, 181–2, 187–8, 190, 194, 216, 223–4, 242, 252, 256–7, 260–3, 266–8
Fénelon, François 250–1, 273
Ferguson, Adam 42, 48–9
Feudalism, feudal 43–4, 58–9, 117, 156–7, 157n.113, 158, 160, 290–1
Fichte, Johann 144–5, 160
Fitzmaurice, Andrew 270–1
Fleurus, Battle of 125–6
Forgetting (oubli) 3, 94, 134, 237–8, 264
Fragmentation 14, 61, 138, 188, 210, 243, 294
Francis I (king of France) 93
Frankfurt 168–9, 187, 199–200, 206
Franks 52–3, 57–8, 63, 111n.60
Frederick the Great (king of Prussia) 87, 218–19
Freeden, Michael 27–8
Freedom, *see also* liberty 4, 8–9, 13–14, 29–30, 37, 73, 77, 84–5, 89–93, 92n.141, 95–6, 98, 106, 110–11, 116–17, 135–6, 138, 143–4, 147–8, 152–4, 157, 165, 195, 237, 246, 250–3, 255–9, 262–5, 274–6, 278–81, 283–93, 296, 301
Freemasonry, Freemasons 27, 37–8, 52, 197–8, 247–9

Gallicanism, gallican 250–1, 253–4, 270–1
Gama, Vasco da 211–12
Gatterer, Johann 45, 198, 203
Gauchat, Abbé 68–9
Gauls (ancient), gallic 54, 95–6, 255
Gender 23n.72, 34–5, 34, 155, 264–5
Geneva 127–9, 286
Genius 48–9, 51–3, 60, 78–9, 90–1, 189, 284
Genlis, Madame de 34, 74–5
Gentleness, gentle 76–8

Gentz, Friedrich (von) 28–9, 128–9, 141, 144–54, 163–6, 183, 230, 232, 246–7, 258, 261–2, 267, 273, 275
Geography 77–8, 87, 176–7, 202–3, 210, 285
George III (king of England) 88
German Confederation (*Deutscher Bund*) 41–2, 146–7, 199–200, 206, 221–2, 231–3, 236, 245
Germans (ancient)
  Germanic tribes 15, 46–7, 52–4, 57–64, 84, 95–6, 135, 152, 156, 169–70, 174, 182–3, 186, 188–90, 213–14, 277–9, 285–7, 291, 294, 301
  Germanic constitution (institutions) 15, 185, 191–4, 213–14, 246, 274–6, 284–5
  Germanic druids 59–60, 65–6
  Germanic liberty (freedom) 57–63, 65, 169–70, 175–6
  Germanic invasions 14
Germany, see also Holy Roman Empire 27, 31, 120, 137–228, 250–1, 280–2, 285–6, 290–300
Gervinus, Georg 291–2
Ghent 233, 290–1
Giambullari, Pier 43
Gibbon, Edward 48–9, 67n.2, 208, 251–2, 286
Girondins 38–9, 62–3
Gleichgewicht, *see also* balance and equilibrium 7, 138, 142, 145, 147–8, 151, 155, 165, 174–5, 177–8, 180, 213, 277
Global intellectual history 32
Glorious Revolution (Britain) 24, 116–17, 122, 290
Goethe, Johann (von) 37–8, 69–70
Goetz, Walter 297
Gollwitzer, Heinz 12, 140–2, 298
Gorini, Abbé 288
Görres, Joseph 144–5
Göttingen 7–9, 35, 45, 142, 150, 167–8, 195, 261, 266, 273, 276–7, 283–4, 290–1
Graaf, Beatrice de 233–5
Gracchus, Gracchi 208–9
Greeks (ancient)
  Greeks (general) 21, 80, 156, 169–70, 173, 178–9, 207–11, 279, 285, 287–8
  Greek (byzantine) 61
  Greek laws 156–7
  Greek philosophers 7
  Greek republics 170–1
Greece (modern), Greeks 226–7, 270–1
Green, Jonathan 145–6
Grégoire, Abbé 207
Groen van Prinsterer, Guillaume 26, 35, 241, 260n.1, 271–6, 286, 288–9, 291
Grotius, Hugo 153–4, 222, 227–8

Guicciardini, Francesco 42–3
Guicciardini, Lodovico 43
Guizot, François 62, 273, 283–91
Gustavus Adolphus (king of Sweden) 176

Habsburg (dynasty) (*see also* Holy Roman Empire, Austria) 64, 70–2, 81, 91–2, 98, 100–1, 116–17, 133, 148–9, 171, 176, 186–7, 214–15, 221, 229–30, 235–6, 282
Hague, The 271–2
The Hague, Treaty of 100–1
Haiti 225–6, 268–9
Hallam, Henry 289–93
Haller, Karl von 35–6, 154n.98, 200n.22, 241n.66, 260n.1
Hamburg 127–8, 175
Hannover 198, 202, 204
Hanseatic League 63
Happiness, happy 76, 87–9, 91, 139, 179
Hardouin, Jean 68
Harivel, Philippe l' 39
Harpe, Jean-François de la 96–8
Hastings, Warren 116, 224–5, 266–7
Hauterive, Alexandre d' 147
Hebrews (ancient), *see also* Israel, Jews 14, 68–9, 301
Heeren, Arnold Hermann Ludwig 7–10, 14, 16, 18, 20, 22–3, 25, 33, 35, 138, 143, 150, 164, 169–70, 195, 229, 246, 258, 261–70, 273, 276–7, 283–4, 290–1, 296
Hegel, Friedrich 283–9
Hegemony, hegemon 7, 133, 139, 147, 170n.28, 187–8, 203–4, 213, 215–16, 218–19
Hellenism, Hellenic 169–70, 210, 242–3
Henri IV (king of France) 76, 103–4, 125, 176, 182–3, 187–8, 192, 215–16, 239, 244
Henry VIII (king of England) 90–1
Herder, Johann Gottfried (von) 18–19, 73–4, 181, 181n.75, 190–1, 210, 210n.72, 253n.136
Heretic, heretics 80–1, 253
Herodotus 94–5, 208
Hess, Moses 292
Heyne, Christian 197–8, 201, 204, 208
Historicism, historicist 40–1, 196, 256–7
Historisch-politische Zeitschrift 277–8, 290–1
Hobsbawn, Eric 24
Holocaust 2–3
Holy Alliance 236–7, 241, 245, 249n.101, 297n.170
Holy Roman Empire 4, 12–13, 27–8, 64, 70–2, 100–1, 127–8, 138–9, 147–8, 165–8, 175–6, 180, 186–7, 191, 197–9, 205–6, 212, 218–21, 235, 260–1
Homer 94–5, 178–9

Honour, *see also* Valour and Chivalry 182, 267–8
House of European History 1–2
Household, *see also* Family 34–5, 181
Hubris, *see also* Arrogance 2n.11, 69–70, 83, 94–5
Huguenot 112
Humanism, humanist 16, 21, 41–3, 47, 55–6, 68, 73, 84, 94, 142, 153–4, 167
Humanity 46, 51–4, 63, 70, 108–9, 144, 158–9, 165n.3, 169, 182, 189–90, 206, 246, 253, 266–8
Hume, David 40, 48–9, 73–4, 84, 86, 148, 172–4, 178–9, 215, 251–2
Hundred Days, The 221, 233–4
Hungary, Hungarian 1, 60, 71–2
Huntington, Samuel 28

Iberian peninsula, *see also* Spain 35
Idéologues 144–5
Ignorance 50–3, 57–8, 60, 62, 65, 70, 127–8
Illuminati 27, 75n.45, 219
Impartiality 21, 115, 197–201
Incredulity (*see also* atheism) 80, 87, 95
India, Indian 68–9, 78, 116–17, 142, 162, 199, 209–10, 223–5, 266–7, 266n.19, 285
Individualism (criticism of) 20, 23n.70, 157–60, 181, 279–80, 285, 297, 301
Infancy 182
Interbellum 293–300
Intermediary power 17, 33, 114, 138, 143, 168–9, 250–2, 286–7
Internationalism 5–6, 22, 23n.72, 29–30, 115–16, 166–7, 271, 282, 288–9, 293–5
Intolerance, *see also* toleration 61, 63–4, 75, 97, 218–19, 262
Inwardness 285–6
Iselin, Isaak 202–3
Islam 59–60, 63, 84–5, 226–7, 244, 255–6, 264–8, 279–80, 301
Islamic migrants 2
Israel (ancient), *see also* Hebrews 82, 156, 159
Italy 31, 35, 42–3, 48, 71–2, 100–1, 106–7, 155–6, 176, 197–8, 207–8, 211, 214, 218, 277, 280–1, 283, 291–2, 295–6, 295n.154
Ius Publicum Europaeum, *see* Law
Ivernois, Francis d' 37, 127–9, 131, 133–4, 139, 146

Jacobinism, Jacobins 38, 87, 114–16, 119, 130, 198–9
Jansenism, Jansenists 67, 72, 74–5, 74n.38, 79, 80n.75, 86, 92, 247, 253, 262
Jena 160, 201–2
Jena Romantics 160, 267
Jerusalem 88–9

Jesuits, Jesuit order 35, 37–8, 67, 167–8, 178, 178n.66, 204, 215–16, 218–19, 247–9, 260
Jews, *see also* Israel, Hebrews and Mosaic Law 61, 64, 97–8, 156–7, 159, 232–3, 264–5
John Lackland (King of England) 62–3
Jones, Emily 28
Joseph II (Holy Roman Emperor) 70–1, 91–2, 183, 266–7
Journalism, Journalist 33–4, 70, 114, 116, 168–9, 201–2
Juste Milieu (*see also* Middle way) 275–8, 281–2, 286–8, 295–6
Justi, Johann von 143

Kahle, Ludwig 142
Kant, Immanuel 21, 143–6, 148, 156, 160, 163, 209–10, 215, 236, 239, 283–4
Keene, Edward 227–8
Kleinert, Susanne 39
Kleingeld, Pauline 139–40, 160–1
Koch, Christoph 236
Koselleck, Reinhard 11, 31–2, 298
Koskenniemi, Marti 227
Kossmann, Ernst 17
Krause, Karl 240
Krieger, Leonard 154–5
Kuyper, Abraham 276

Lamberts, Emiel 282
Lamennais, Félicité de 241, 270–1, 273
Laps (Sami) 182
Latin 1–2, 42–3, 80, 254, 277, 294–5
Latin America, *see* America
Latin Christianity (*see also* Catholic church) 60, 254–5
Lausanne 247–8
Law
 Common law (English) 123
 Customary law (general) 58–9
 Feudal law 156–8
 International law, Law of Nations, European Law 42, 126–7, 142, 196–7, 205–7, 213, 227–8, 235–6, 245, 301
 Law (general) 62, 109, 119, 150, 153, 167–8, 172–3, 192–3, 243
 Mosaic law, Jewish law 156–7
 Natural law 21, 37, 53–4, 58–9, 61, 90–1, 108–9, 119, 142, 146n.49, 205–7
 Penal law 72
 Positive law 205–7
 Private law, property law 119, 132, 154–5, 157
 Public law, constitutional law, *see also* Constitution 132, 157–8, 171, 200–1, 205–7, 291

Law (*cont.*)
   Roman law (criticism of) 119, 154n.98, 157–8, 178, 285
   Rule of Law 29, 89–90, 102, 110–11, 117, 135–6, 142, 148, 155, 166–7, 183–4, 199–200, 209–10, 235–7, 258, 274–5
Legislative Assembly, *see also* National Assembly 110–11
Legislative power 110–11, 200, 220, 222
Leibniz, Gottfried 142
Leiden 239–40, 291
Leipzig 201–2, 221, 229
Leo X (pope) 93
Leo XII (pope) 244–5
Lepanto, Naval battle of 255–6
Liberalism (*see also* anti-liberalism) 28n.103, 30, 140–1, 194, 266n.19, 277–8, 298, 301–2
Liberals 25–6, 28–9, 120, 200, 231, 234–5, 237, 241, 270–1, 283–93
Liberties, ancient 70–1, 85, 91–2
Libertinage 89–90
Liberty, *see also* freedom and Germanic liberty
   Liberty (general) 7, 30, 54, 57–63, 88, 92–3, 102, 110–11, 116–17, 125, 131–2, 136, 144, 166–7, 174–6, 182–3, 188, 190
   European liberty 15, 51, 54, 59–60, 65, 166–7, 260–3, 287
   Revolutionary liberty 37, 91–3, 132, 154, 157
   Roman liberty 56
Liège 35, 70–2, 75, 78–9, 127–8, 219–20, 229–30
Lights, Lumières, *see also* Darkness 17–19, 37, 60, 62, 73–4, 84, 94n.152, 96, 217, 274
Lille 103
Lilti, Antoine 41–3, 260
Limited government, *see also* Temperance 212–14
Literature, *see also* Novel 31, 33–4, 50, 71–2, 93–4, 151, 198, 207–8, 211, 289
Locke, John 209–10
London 37–8, 45–6, 48, 99, 105–7, 112–14, 289–90
Lords, House of 105, 155
Louis IX 'Saint Louis' (king of France) 63
Louis XIV (king of France) 45–7, 80–1, 89, 89n.119, 93, 96, 103, 126, 135, 171, 176, 213–14, 216–17, 278
Louis XVI (king of France) 61–3, 99, 103–6, 108, 229, 255
Louis XVII (king of France) 62–3, 125
Louis XVIII (king of France) 103–4, 115, 125, 125n.139, 221–2, 229, 233
Love 46–7, 83, 95–6, 181, 183, 245, 262
Lucas, Colin 120–1
Lunéville, Peace of 145, 147–8, 187–8
Luther, Lutheran 274, 291

Luxe, Luxury 58, 60, 176–7
Luxemburg, Luxembourg 31, 70, 72, 260–1
Lyon 208–9

Maastricht 71
Mably, Abbé de 48–9, 57–8, 211n.78
Machiavelli, Niccolò 92n.142, 274–5
Machiavellianism, Machiavellian 81, 92n.142, 180, 252, 258–9, 294–5
Machine (states) 151, 218–19, 233–4
Mackintosh, James 118, 121–3
Madrid 106–7
Magna Carta 61
Mainz 8–9, 35, 55, 165, 235–6, 261
Mainz Republic, *see* republic
Maistre, Joseph de 18–19, 25, 28–9, 35, 63, 77–8, 84, 98, 112–13, 189–90, 216, 231, 241, 246–59, 261–6, 272–3, 275–6, 278, 292, 295–6
Mallet du Pan, Jacques 87n.112, 112–13, 128–9, 183
Manners, *see also* Customs 14, 43–4, 60, 77–8, 117, 119, 127–8, 171–2, 219
Mannheim, Karl 26–7, 92n.141
Marchand, Susanne 208
Maréchal-Le Pen, Marion 1
Marie-Louise (empress) 186–7
Market, *see also* (political) economy, trade and commerce 15, 133
Martens, Georg von 206–7
Martin, Jean-Clément 107, 112
Martyr, Martyrdom 62, 255
Marx, Karl 288–9, 292
Masculinity, *see also* Effeminate and Gender 34–5
Masseau, Didier 18–19, 73, 90n.126
Materialism (criticism of), materialist 18, 157–8, 163, 182–3, 194, 218
Mazarin, Cardinal 103, 176
Mazzini, Giuseppe 283, 292
McMahon, Darrin 18–19, 72n.26, 75
Mecca 59–60
Medium-size (state, power) 77, 172–3, 248
Mediterranean 226–7, 268–9
Méhégan, Chevalier de 46–7
Meinecke, Friedrich 139–40, 149–50, 297–8
Merriam Webster Dictionary 9
Metternich, Clemens von 12–13, 33, 149–50, 167–8, 191–2, 231–2, 234–8, 258, 261–2, 270–1
Middle Ages
   Middle Ages (general) 14, 43–4, 52–4, 60, 64, 84, 95–6, 156, 158, 171–2, 174, 182, 190, 199, 211–12, 252, 255, 275–6, 279–81, 289–90
   Early Middle Ages 42–4, 54, 61, 170, 191, 256–7

High Middle Ages 14, 43–4, 60, 178
Late Middle Ages 14, 186
Middlebrow (Enlightenment) 34
Middle way, *see also* Juste Milieu 19–21, 25, 27, 29, 108–9, 111, 153–4, 158, 163–4, 204–5, 207, 236–7, 250, 258, 275–6, 283, 295–6
Mill, John Stuart 288–9
Millot, Abbé de 46–7
Mirabeau, Comte de 38, 42, 183, 247
Mixed (constitution, monarchy, regime) 155, 165, 169–73, 205–6
Moderation 3, 8–9, 14, 30–1, 34–5, 63, 76–7, 76n.53, 77–8, 84–5, 111, 115, 121–3, 129n.160, 134n.183, 135–6, 165–7, 181–2, 221–2, 228, 237–8, 263–5, 277–8, 299, 301
Modernity 31–2, 57n.122, 162, 288–9, 294–5
Mohammed, *see also* Islam 59–60, 84–5
Monarchy
  Monarchy (general) 7–8, 15, 54, 59–60, 144, 149, 155, 169–70, 174–5, 181–2, 200, 209–10, 212, 222, 228
  Austrian (Habsburg) monarchy 149, 282
  British monarchy 61, 116–24, 172–3, 261
  French monarchy 25–6, 54, 56–7, 62–3, 89–91, 93, 96, 99, 217, 220–1, 243, 247, 252, 255, 270–1, 277–8, 286–7, 298
  Prussian monarchy 143, 175–6, 204–5, 212–13
  Restoration monarchy, (*see also* French monarchy) 25–6, 229
  Roman monarchy 169–70, 210
  Universal monarchy 61, 138, 142, 147–8, 159, 170–1, 175–6, 195, 210, 217, 221, 228, 239–40, 262–3, 276, 296, 301
Monarchical Principle 196, 200, 222
Monarchiens 101, 108, 111n.60, 113, 269
Mongolians 182, 267–8
Moniteur, Le 144–5
Monopoly (trade) 176–7, 187–8, 283–4
Monster, monstrous 59–60, 88, 119, 129, 255, 276
Montgaillard, comte de 128, 131
Montlosier, comte de 129, 129n.160, 133, 135
Montoya, Alicia 34
Moors, *see also* Muslims and Islam 63
Morality 3, 29, 89, 95n.155, 117, 160, 162, 192, 243, 251–2, 296, 299
Moreau, Jacob-Nicolas 273
Morgenland, *see also* Asia and Orient 285
Moses, *see also* Law 156
Moser, Johann 205–6, 206n.48
Möser, Justus 27, 144
Mother (concept) 34, 152, 169
Müller, Adam 20, 27, 33, 35, 141, 149–60, 163–6, 181–3, 186, 194, 210, 212, 218, 230, 249, 254–5, 260–2, 267, 269, 295–6

Müller, Jan Werner 27–8
Muller, Jerry 17
Müller, Johannes von 203
Muslims, *see also* Islam and Moors 63, 80, 174, 264–5
Mysticism, mystical, *see also* esoterism 39, 52–3, 59, 65–6, 241, 247–8
Muthu, Sankar 268
Mytilene 208–9

Naples 106–7
Napoleon I (emperor) 7, 34–5, 38–9, 137–41, 147–54, 156–7, 168, 184–92, 195, 198–9, 204n.39, 221–2, 226, 229–33, 235–7, 239–40, 242, 257–8, 274–6, 281
Napoleon III (emperor) 276, 281–2
Napoleonic Empire 3, 7–10, 22–3, 31, 38–9, 137–41, 145–60, 163–6, 183–9, 194–201, 203–4, 206–7, 210, 227–8, 230–2, 238–40, 244–5, 248–50, 281, 284
Napoleonic Wars 16, 22, 35–6, 126–7, 139–40, 164, 222–3, 226, 243, 294
Nation
  Nation (general) 12, 45–7, 62, 158–9, 170–1, 188–9, 210, 282, 292, 299–300
  Dutch Nation 239–40
  English Nation 118, 243, 260–1
  French Nation 106, 108–9, 113, 161–2, 255
  German Nation (modern) 138–40, 161–2, 165–6, 186, 199, 221, 278, 295, 297–8
  Nation State 4, 58–9, 158–9, 282, 292, 297, 299–300
National Assembly (France), *see also* Estates-General, Legislative Assembly and Convention 90, 105–6, 110–11, 154–5
National conservatism 1–2, 4
National Conservatives Conference Rome 1–2
National-Socialism 141, 160–1, 295–9
Nationalism 1, 4, 22, 28–9, 139–40, 145, 163–4, 196, 270–1, 283, 291–3, 293n.143, 294–5, 301–2
Natural History 177–8
Natural Rights, *see also* Law and Rights 50, 58–60
Nature 179, 182, 189–91, 196, 250
Naval power 61, 126–7, 255–6
Near East 97–8, 190, 279
Necker, Jacques 90–1, 103–4
Nero (emperor) 90–1
Netherlands, the
  Netherlands, the (general) *see also* United Kingdom of the Netherlands 43, 231–2, 244–5

Netherlands, the (*cont.*)
  Northern Netherlands, the, *see also* Batavian Republic, Dutch Republic 17, 31, 100, 186, 199–200, 213, 215, 229–30, 268–9, 276, 291, 294–5
  Southern Netherlands, Austrian or Habsburg Netherlands, *see also* Belgium 70–2, 75, 78–9, 81, 91–2, 98, 112, 116–17, 127–8, 219–20, 224, 229–30, 244, 291
New World, The, *see also* America 42–3, 88, 112, 188, 266–9
Nicolai, Friedrich 40
Niebuhr, Barthold 27, 208
Noah, Sons of 82, 250
Nobility, *see also* aristocracy 14, 57–8, 71–2, 89, 105, 107, 121, 155, 157, 188, 197, 213–14, 217, 255, 282
Normandy, Normans 37–9
Novalis 160–2
Novel, *see also* literature 37–8, 46, 50, 73, 293

Obscurantism, obscurantist 37, 58–60, 64, 236–7
Occident 162, 255–6, 267, 296–7
Oikophobia 2
Old Regime, *see* ancien régime
Old World, The 182–3, 228
Orange (dynasty), *see also* stadtholder 85, 115, 215–17, 229–32, 271–2
Orange, William I of (stadtholder) 85, 215–16
Orange, prince Willem Frederik of, *see also* king Willem I 229–30
Orban, Victor 1
Orient, oriental, *see also* Asia and Morgenland 34–5, 60, 77–8, 84–5, 149, 162, 221, 228, 255–6, 265n.15, 267, 301
Organism, organic 92n.141, 149–50, 154–5, 157, 162, 181, 187n.113
Orléans (dynasty) 106–7, 286–7
Orthodoxy, orthodox church (religion) 23, 60, 236–7, 240–1, 248–9, 256, 256n.153, 294, 301
Ottoman Empire, Ottomans, *see also* Sultan and Turks 72, 155–6, 204–5, 211–12, 214, 218–19, 226–7, 232, 236–7, 243, 255–6, 264–5, 270–1
Oubli, *see also* forgetting 237–8, 264

Paine, Thomas 38–9
Palestine, *see also* Israel 174
Palm, Johannes van der 239–40
Palmer, Robert 18n.47, 68n.4, 69
Papacy (Pope) 5, 44, 59–61, 63, 70–1, 78–9, 81, 84, 93, 108, 174–5, 185–6, 204, 218–19, 231, 236–7, 240–1, 244–5, 247–53, 255–7, 262, 266, 278

Paris 19–20, 37, 89–90, 103, 122, 128–30, 161–2, 168, 185–6, 189, 229, 232–5, 286–7
Paris, First Treaty of 232
Paris, Second Treaty of 233–4
Parlements (France) 94, 103–4, 135
Passions 46–7, 121, 178, 199, 252–3, 261, 264
Patriarch 84, 93–4, 190, 200
Patriot Revolution (Dutch) 198–9
Patriotism, *see also* Nationalism 4, 20–1, 62, 72, 88, 92, 153, 158–9, 181, 186, 234, 257–8, 301
Paul, Saint, Pauline 69, 71, 262
Peace, Perpetual 20, 42, 52–3, 65–6, 101–2, 141, 143–5, 156, 163, 187–8, 187n.113, 192, 206–7, 235, 238–40, 243–4, 246, 257–8, 262
Pedagogy 46–9, 96, 169, 209
Peloponnesian Wars 178–9
Perjury 62–3
Persia, Persian Empire 83–5, 199, 209, 254–5, 285
Pessimism, pessimist 7, 41n.21, 94, 97–8, 143, 187–8, 248–9, 276n.58, 282
Pestel, Friedemann 269
Petersburg, Saint 106–7, 112–13, 248, 250
Philip II (king of Spain) 88, 88n.117, 176, 213–16
Philology, philological 197–8, 207–9
Philosophes, *see also* anti-philosophy, anti-philosophes 16–20, 41–2, 67, 115–16, 153–4, 162, 192, 208, 218–19, 242–3, 247, 249, 256–7, 261, 278, 298
Philosophy 7–8, 11, 18–21, 25, 40, 67, 150, 153–4, 158, 161, 167–8, 173–4, 179, 182–3, 192, 198, 242–3, 250, 253–5, 261–3, 270–2, 274–6, 283–6
Phoenicians 190
Physiocrats 177
Piedmont-Sardinia, Kingdom of, *see also* Sardinia 247
Pitt, William 123–7, 188, 273
Pitts, Jennifer 227, 265–6
Plagiarism 49–50, 81
Plato 83, 94–5
Plot, *see also* conspiracy 27, 75, 87, 91, 91n.133, 95, 125, 219, 247–8, 266–7
Pocock, John 17, 289
Poetry, poem, poet 7, 31, 69–70, 73, 160, 197, 298–9
Poland, *see also* Commonwealth 60, 143, 148, 176, 180, 212–13, 218, 232–3
Polish participation 148
Political Economy, *see also* economy 15n.32, 153n.92, 165, 177, 181–2, 200–2, 210
Polybius 169–70, 181, 188–91, 207–8, 279, 285

Popular conservatism 33
Popular Sovereignty 7–8, 57–8, 92–3, 200, 219–20, 222, 270–1, 274
Portugal 223–4, 291–2
Pluralism, *see also* competition, diversity, and fragmentation 13–16, 29, 39–40, 84–5, 137–41, 162, 165–7, 169–74, 176–9, 182–3, 185–6, 188, 193–7, 212, 262–3, 269, 276–89, 293–300
Prades, Jean-Martin de 74–5
Pradt, Abbé de 127–8, 223
Prerogative (royal) 110–11
Prejudice 16, 50–2, 65–6, 79, 88–9, 131–2
Prince-Bishopric, Prince-Bishop 191, 193–4
Primitive, primitives, *see also* savage 171, 174, 178, 182, 190, 267–8, 291
Princely court (in exile), *see also* Coblenz 105–8, 123–4, 128–9
Procopius 55–6
Progress 3–4, 11, 14, 19–20, 23–5, 29, 40–5, 48, 52, 57–66, 73, 94, 97–8, 111, 121, 124, 136–8, 142, 148, 153, 156, 158, 167, 171–6, 178–9, 182–94, 203–4, 206, 215, 224–6, 237, 242–6, 251–2, 256–8, 261, 265, 280–2, 287–8, 291, 301
Property 5, 69–70, 87, 90–1, 110–11, 118n.102, 129, 132–5, 192–3, 213, 237–8, 263–4
Prosperity 1–2, 43–4, 51, 132–4, 177–8, 200, 210, 230, 257–8, 299
Protestantism 26, 88, 158–60, 215–16, 240–1, 243, 254, 256n.153, 273, 280–1, 296–7
Providence 11, 46–7, 53, 80–1, 89–90, 92, 98, 143, 154–5, 165, 181–2, 189–91, 193–4, 229, 247–8, 252, 256–7, 277
Prussia, *see also* monarchy 87, 100–1, 105, 143, 146–9, 175–9, 200n.23, 204–6, 212–13, 218–21, 230–4, 276–9, 284n.103, 285–6, 291–2, 295–7
Public opinion 72–3, 75, 98, 100–1, 114, 118, 126–7, 131, 148–9, 183–4, 217, 219, 222, 234–5, 238–9, 242
Pufendorf, Samuel von 46, 48, 201–2, 213
Pure Royalism, *see* royalism
Pütter, Johann 205–6

Querelle (des anciens et des modernes) 41, 56–7, 178–9
Quadruple alliance 233

Race, Racism 21, 34–5, 44, 223–4, 250
Radical centre 31
Radicalism 28, 31, 102, 111, 134, 203–4, 218–20, 301
Radicalization 62–4, 72, 105, 118, 179–80

Ranke, Leopold von 8, 40–1, 196, 276–83, 286, 289–90, 294–7
Rastatt 100–1
Raynal, Guillaume-Thomas 86, 88–9, 223, 225, 266–7
Reaction 25, 30, 31n.116, 32, 107–9, 134–5, 180, 274–5, 277–8, 286–7
Reason, reasonableness 34–5, 37, 46–7, 51–3, 57–8, 60–3, 65–6, 73–5, 132–3, 137–8, 151, 173–4, 179, 207, 221–2, 240, 252, 285–6
Reason of State 92n.142, 146, 206n.48, 240
Rebellion 84–5, 88, 256
Rechtsstaat, *see also* Law, Rule of 154–5, 155n.101, 157
Reconciliation 73–4, 104n.19, 129, 134, 145–6, 158, 236–7, 240–1, 244–5, 255–6, 262, 264–5
Reform 5, 27–8, 51–2, 91–2, 98–9, 138–9, 146–7, 166–8, 178, 183, 198–9, 215–16, 228, 235–6, 246–7, 284n.103
Reformation, *see also* Counter-Reformation 15, 68, 84–6, 120, 127, 139, 174, 203, 214–16, 224, 240–1, 243, 250, 258–9, 274–6, 280–1, 283–6, 291, 297
Refugees, *see also* exiles and émigrés 5, 71, 112–13, 289–90
Regeneration, *see also* renewal 2–3, 5, 9, 39–40, 51–3, 65–6, 149–50, 158, 160, 162–4, 186–7, 189–91, 193–5, 231, 244–5, 253, 256, 258, 267, 282, 293–4, 300
Regensburg 71
Regicide 119, 126
Rehberg, August 27, 144, 220
Relativism (criticism of), relativist 78
Religion, *see also* Wars of Religion Catholic Church, Orthodoxy, Islam and Jews, Protestantism 5, 43–4, 52–3, 73–80, 86–9, 91–3, 98, 103–4, 117–18, 118n.102, 119, 119, 129, 132–3, 151, 155–6, 155, 157, 157, 158–9, 159, 171, 171, 176–7, 179, 182–3, 182, 192–3, 192, 193–4, 199, 234–5, 240–1, 242, 243, 243, 246, 262, 264–5, 266–7, 267–8, 272–3, 275–6, 277, 279–80, 301,
Renaissance 15, 42–3, 47, 68, 84, 93, 96–7, 142, 185–6, 190, 211, 280–2
Renewal, *see also* Regeneration 3, 5, 9, 35–6, 39, 52–3, 53n.99, 65–6, 97–8, 160–4, 182–3, 188–9, 191–2, 194, 214–16, 236–7, 257–9, 275, 281–2, 301–2
Republic
  American Republic (United States), *see also* America 88, 144–5, 225–6, 266

Republic (cont.)
    Athenian Republic 175, 254
    Batavian Republic 100–1, 115
    Christian Republic (Respublica
        Christiana) 167, 192
    Dutch Republic (United Provinces) 71, 85, 88,
        115, 127–8, 180, 197–8, 205–6, 215–16,
        224–6, 229–30, 291
    European Republic 18, 22–3, 34–5, 56,
        127, 139, 143–8, 156, 165, 213–14,
        264–5, 267–8
    Republic (general) 30, 155, 166–7, 236, 252,
        254, 257
    Republic of Letters 41–2, 73, 167
    Republic of Mainz 168, 179–80
    Revolutionary (French) Republic 11, 31, 37,
        72, 99, 144, 147, 220–1, 255–8, 263–4
    Roman Republic 175, 208–9
Republicanism 22–3, 144–5, 166–7, 215
Restoration,
    Restoration (general) 24n. 77, 30, 51–4, 57,
        59–60, 62, 141–2, 158, 160–1, 163–4, 167,
        185–6, 225–6, 237–40, 248–9, 264
    Restoration (period) 8, 31, 35–6, 229, 264,
        275, 283–4, 295, 299
    Restoration Bourbon Dynasty 38–9, 103–4,
        115, 124–5, 132–3, 229–31, 242, 286–7
    Restoration Habsburg dynasty 71
    Restoration Orange dynasty 244–5
    Restoration of the State system 216–23
Réveil, see also Awakening 273n.41
Revelation 53–4, 65–6, 68–9, 73–4, 96, 158, 182,
    189–90, 273n.40
Rheims 70
Rhine 161–2, 167–8, 221, 232–3, 244
Rhineland, Rhinelander, see also Mainz 12–13,
    144–5, 165–6, 169, 184n.96, 186–7, 191,
    230, 236, 261
Richelieu, Cardinal de 176, 183
Richelieu, Duc de 106–7, 234
Rights, see also Law, natural rights and
        Constitution
    Individual Rights 92–3, 111, 135, 228,
        264–5
    National, state, Rights 85, 109, 146–8, 192–3
    Property Rights, see also property 110–11, 132
    Rights of Man, Human Rights 90–1, 130, 132,
        192–3, 270–1, 299
    Traditional, ancient Rights 91–2, 148–9,
        154–5
Rigoley du Juvigny, Jean-Antoine 69, 93–8, 179
Ritter, Gerhard 296–7
Rivarol, Antoine 120
Rivarol, Claude-François 120

Robertson, William 43–5, 48–9, 56, 138–9,
    171–2, 174–5, 202–3, 211–12, 286
Robespierre, Maximilien de 34–5, 108–9, 184,
    275–6, 294–5
Rootlessness, rootless (criticism of) 1, 20–1, 271
Roman Empire 3–4, 14, 43–4, 55–9, 83–4, 152,
    169–74, 178–9, 186, 193, 199, 210, 213–14,
    254, 274–5, 278–80, 285, 287, 290–1
Roman Law, see Law
Romanticism, Romantics 16, 39–41, 43, 84,
    92n.141, 140–1, 145–6, 158, 160–4, 196,
    242, 256–7, 267, 297–8, 301–2
Rome, see also Roman Empire 1–2, 28, 56–7,
    83–5, 94–6, 131, 152, 169–70, 192, 208–10,
    254, 256, 279, 285
Rothfels, Hans 296–7
Rougemont, Denis de 298–9
Rousseau, Jean-Jacques 37–8, 51, 55, 73–4, 78,
    86, 132, 200, 274–6
Rowe, Michael 169, 184
Royalism, (ultra, pure) royalist 25–6, 111, 115,
    124–5, 128–9, 133–6, 249–51, 261, 283–4,
    289–90
Rule of Law, see Law
Russell, William 37–8, 40–1, 48–50, 54–5, 63–5
Russia 87, 143, 155–6, 171, 176, 187–8, 212–13,
    218–21, 226–7, 229, 231–4, 248–51, 256,
    267–8
Russian Revolution 18–19

Sacrifice 71–2, 106, 131, 156–7, 255
Saint-Martin, Louis-Claude de 247
Saint-Pierre, abbé de 187–8, 192, 239–40
Saint-Simon, comte de 240, 292
Salon, salonnière 28–9, 34, 34n.132, 73,
    112–13, 247
Sardinia, see also Piedmont 105–6, 231, 241,
    247–8, 261
Sartorius, Georg 198–9
Satanic (Revolution) 247–50
Sattelzeit 11–12
Saxe-Weimar, prince of 152
Saxon (early) 58–9
Saxony 152, 161–2, 232–3
Savage, see also primitive 117, 122
Saviour, see also Christ 65–6, 159, 221
Scandinavia 35, 60, 143
Schiller, Friedrich 7, 37–8
Schism, schismatic 84–6, 119, 240–1, 248, 254
Schlegel, August 161–2
Schlegel, Friedrich 22n.68, 144–5, 161–2
Schlözer, August von 45, 198, 203–4, 210
Schmauß, Jan 142
Schönborn, Johann von 187

Schulin, Ernst 276–7
Schweizer Monatsheft 297
Schmitt, Carl 149–50, 288n.119, 296n.158
Schröckh, Johann 46–7
Schroeder, Paul 234
Schulze, Matthias 233–4
Sciences, scientific 52, 60–1, 73–4, 76, 84, 93–4, 97–8, 110, 150–1, 172–4, 181–3, 200–3, 205–6, 206n.48, 211, 217, 277–8, 282, 295
Scotland, Scottish (Enlightenment), *see also* political economy 37, 45, 48–50, 64–5, 103–4, 118, 138–9, 152–3, 171–2, 177, 181–2, 210, 210n.70, 216–17, 247
Scripture, Holy, *see also* Bible, Writ 68–9, 83, 90, 272–3
Secret societies, *see also* conspiracy and plot 7–8, 52, 87, 176, 219
Sects 75, 84–5, 93–4, 171, 247–8
Secularism, secular 2, 5, 18, 22, 41, 52, 67, 69, 83–5, 138, 191, 201, 241, 251–2, 256–7, 272–3, 273n.40, 300
Security, Security System 122, 172–3, 226–7, 231–5, 243, 245–6, 258, 268–9, 283
Seneca 83, 94–5, 95n.155
Serna, Pierre 31
Shakespeare, William 178–9
Siemann, Wolfram 231–4
Sieyès, Abbé de 144–5
Simplicity 58, 177–8, 197
Skinner, Quentin 30
Slavery 54, 58–9, 88–9, 111, 156–7, 232–3, 239–40, 252, 266–7, 274–5
Slavic 277, 284–5
Smith, Adam 152–3, 153n.92, 177, 210n.70
Spector, Céline 41–2, 42n.25, 43, 260
Spittler, Ludwig 157n.113, 197–9, 204–5, 204n.43
Social Contract 37, 51, 53–4
Social Order 82, 86, 88–9, 91, 132–3, 180–2, 234–5, 247
Sociability 28–9, 73, 155, 219, 234–5
Socialism, (early) socialists 192, 240, 282, 288–9, 292, 301–2
Sorcerer, sorcery 69–70, 88
Socrates 95
Sonderweg 149–50
Sovereignty, *see* Popular Sovereignty
Soviet Union 296
Spain, *see also* Iberian peninsula 31, 54, 59–60, 63, 85, 88–9, 100–1, 106–7, 112, 120, 155–6, 177, 188, 221, 224, 231–2, 291–2
Srbik, Heinrich von 295–6

Staatenhistorie, Staatengeschichte 196–7, 200–6, 228
Staatswissenschaften, Science of the State 217
Stability 3, 28n.103, 100–1, 134, 199–200, 215–16, 221–2, 233–4, 237–8, 246, 264, 270–1, 275, 299
Staël, Madame de 28–9, 112–13, 241, 247, 284
Statistics 200–1, 218, 232–3, 290–1
Stoicism, Stoa 21, 71, 83, 156–7, 159–60, 262, 264n.7
Stourdza, Alexandre 236–7, 256, 256n.153
Strasbourg 236
Sully, Duc de 187–8, 239–40, 244
Sultan, Ottoman, *see also* Ottoman Empire 232, 236–7, 270–1
Superstition, superstitious 37, 43–4, 50–3, 56–8, 62, 70, 95n.158, 171–2, 274
Sweden, Swedish 60, 176, 212–13
Switzerland, Swiss (Federation) 35, 64, 139, 154n.98, 170–1, 186, 199–200, 202–3, 212, 247, 279, 284, 298–9

Tacitus 55–6, 58, 58n.129, 169–70, 181
Talleyrand, Charles-Maurice de 232
Taxation, taxes 103–4, 111, 132–3
Temperance, temperate, *see also* Moderation, Climate, Limited government 77, 178, 181–2
Terror
   (French) Revolutionary Terror 2–3, 38–40, 62–3, 69–70, 96–7, 102, 114, 125, 132, 181, 242, 247–8, 286
   Fear of Terror 8–9, 100–1, 124, 200, 220, 233–4, 272, 283–6, 301
Theatre 37–8, 73, 89–90
Theft, thieves 87, 234, 263–4
Theodicy 189–90, 193–4, 300
Theology, Theologians 33–4, 60, 70, 74–5, 90, 150, 192, 197–8, 244, 251–2, 256–7, 272
Thermidor 25–6, 100–1, 108–9, 124, 139, 220–1
Thessaly, king of 110
Thierry, Augustin 240
Thiers, Adolphe 273
Thinker-agent 25, 33, 116, 134–5, 168–9
Thirty Years' War 178–9, 187, 216
Thorbecke, Johan 289–93
Thucydides 208
Tilsit, Peace of 221
Tocqueville, Alexis de 281, 288–9
Toleration, Tolerance, *see also* Intolerance 37, 51, 53–4, 58–60, 92–3, 192–3
Tory 188, 289, 291
Totalitarianism 1–2, 18–19, 296
Trade, *see also* commerce, economy and market

Trade, (cont.)
  Criticism of (free) trade 15, 210, 220, 223–6
  Free trade 15, 176–8, 216–17
  International trade 42, 177, 224, 226–7
  Slave trade 223–6, 268–9
  Trade (general) 43–4, 61, 103–4, 132–3, 176–9, 209
Twiss, Travers 270–1
Truthfulness 51, 68–9
Tsar, see Alexander I
Turin 105–6, 247–51, 261
Turks, see also Ottoman Empire 60, 211–12
Tuscany 100–1
Tyranny, tyrant, see also despotism 50–3, 57–64, 83, 91–2, 109–11, 116–17, 173–4, 255–6, 266–7

Ulloa, Alfonso 43
Ultramontanism 75, 241, 241n.66, 249
Ultraroyalism, see royalism
United Kingdom of the Netherlands 127–8, 229–30, 244, 271–2, 291
United States (of America), see America and American republic
Unity in Diversity, see also Discordia Concors, 1–2, 14n.31, 139, 155, 172, 276–9, 296, 298–9
Universal History 42, 44–7, 54, 69, 80–5, 97–8, 167–9, 181n.75, 201–5, 210–12, 236, 261, 265, 267–8
Universal monarchy, see monarchy
Universalism (criticism of) 29–30, 207, 254–5, 257–8, 297–8
Usefulness, see also utilitarianism 48–9, 242
Usurpation, usurper 109–11, 116–17, 129, 148, 173–4, 180, 221
Utilitarianism (criticism of), utility, see also Usefulness 76, 142, 153–4, 199, 242
Utopia, utopianism, utopian 2n.11, 3n.14, 51–2, 88–9, 142, 149–50, 200, 206–7, 213, 221–2, 239–40, 252, 258, 285–6, 292, 298–9
Utrecht, Peace of 101

Valjavec, Fritz 27, 140–1, 298
Valour, see also chivalry 182, 267–8
Varennes, Flight to 108
Vattel, Emer de 213
Vatican, see also Papacy and Catholic Church 282
Velema, Wyger 17

Vendée 107, 115
Vergennes, Comte de 99–100
Verona, Declaration of 125, 125n.139
Versailles 103–4
Vettori, Francesco 42–3
Vichy (regime) 249
Vick, Brian 28–9, 145–6, 234–5, 282
Vienna
  Congress of Vienna 28–9, 35–6, 143, 195, 206, 229, 260
  Vienna Order 165–8, 193–4, 221–2, 229, 292
  Vienna (other) 148–50
Villers, Charles de 215n.89, 283–4
Virtue, virtuous 58–9, 76n.53, 78–9, 88–9, 91–2, 166–7, 169–71, 174, 181–2, 190n.128, 197, 298–300
Vogt, Niklas 12–13, 15, 20, 22–3, 33–5, 148–9, 164–5, 195, 202, 207–8, 216, 221, 230, 236, 246, 258, 261–5, 267–8, 296
Völkerslag, see Battle of the Nations
Voltaire 43–4, 44n.38, 45–51, 55–6, 65, 78–9, 86, 89, 93–4, 128–9, 171, 202–3, 286
Volcano 129, 133, 237–8

Wales, Welsh 64
Warrior, see also Valour 60, 156, 174, 181–2, 186–7
Wars of Liberation, German 221
Wars of Religion 43–4, 103–4, 240–1
Waterloo, Battle of 233, 244, 255
Weathervanes (political, Girouette) 189n.121, 206n.50, 230
Weber, Max 215, 270n.26
Wellington, Duke of 233–4, 233n.25
Westphalia, Peace of 127–8, 187, 205–6, 216, 240, 243
Whig 28, 116, 118, 120, 289
Wieland, Martin 21, 265n.11
Willem I (king of the Netherlands) 244–5, 262, 271–2, 275
William III, king-stadtholder 217
Woolf, Stuart 13, 37, 265
World War (First), see also World Wars 2–4, 22, 112–13, 149–50, 234, 271, 271n.33, 293
World War (Second), see also World Wars 2–3, 295n.155, 296–7
World Wars (Twentieth-century) 3–4, 31–2, 282, 293
Writ, Holy, see also Bible, Holy Scripture 41, 97–8, 272–3